The Birth of the American Horror Film

For my close friend Robert Singer
– GDR

The Birth of the American Horror Film

Gary D. Rhodes

EDINBURGH
University Press

Edinburgh University Press is one of the leading university presses in the UK. We publish academic books and journals in our selected subject areas across the humanities and social sciences, combining cutting-edge scholarship with high editorial and production values to produce academic works of lasting importance. For more information visit our website: edinburghuniversitypress.com

© Gary D. Rhodes, 2018

Edinburgh University Press Ltd
The Tun—Holyrood Road
12 (2f) Jackson's Entry
Edinburgh EH8 8PJ

Typeset in 11/13 Ehrhardt by
IDSUK (DataConnection) Ltd

A CIP record for this book is available from the British Library

ISBN 978 1 4744 3085 2 (hardback)
ISBN 978 1 4744 3086 9 (paperback)
ISBN 978 1 4744 3087 6 (webready PDF)
ISBN 978 1 4744 3088 3 (epub)

The right of Gary D. Rhodes to be identified as author of this work has been asserted in accordance with the Copyright, Designs and Patents Act 1988 and the Copyright and Related Rights Regulations 2003 (SI No. 2498).

Queen's University Belfast contributed towards the production costs of this volume.

Contents

List of Figures   vi
Acknowledgments   x

    Introduction   1

Section I   The Rise of Horror-themed Cinema
1. Literature   21
2. Theatre   37
3. Visual Culture   63
4. Moving Pictures   94

Section II   Film Genres
5. Devils   125
6. Witches   147
7. Ghosts   163
8. Supernatural Creatures   187
9. Death, Murder, and Execution   215
10. Evolution and Devolution   234
11. The Other(s)   256
12. The Powers of the Mind   281
13. Mad Scientists   309
14. American Literature Onscreen   337

Section III   Exhibition and Reception
15. Exhibition and Reception   367

Index   398

Figures

I.1 and I.2   Two frames from *Execution of Mary, Queen of Scots* (Edison, 1895)   2
I.3   American postcard dated 1910   4
I.4   Charles Ogle as the monster in *Frankenstein* (Edison, 1910)   14
2.1   Published in *The Magic Lantern* in 1874, this illustration reveals how the Pepper's Ghost effect was achieved   45
2.2   An 1894 poster promoting the magician Kellar   48
2.3   Publicity photo of Richard Mansfield as Dr. Jekyll and Mr. Hyde   52
2.4   Publicity photo of Wilton Lackeye as Svengali   53
2.5   Francis Wilson's play *The Spiritualist* (1913)   54
3.1   Published in *Harper's Weekly* in May 1869   64
3.2   Emanuel Leutze's *Ichabod and Brom Bones* (1864)   68
3.3   Published in the 28 December 1867 issue of the *National Police Gazette*   70
3.4   Slide 4 of Joseph Boggs Beale's *The Raven*   74
3.5   An American "movable slip" slide, which could give motion to the skeleton, causing him to remove his skull   75
3.6   Stereo view entitled *There's Death in the Cup* (Keystone, 1898)   79
3.7   Slide 14 of the illustrated song *The Ghost of the Violin* (Scott and Van Altena, 1912)   82
3.8   Slide 14 of *Beautiful Eyes* (Scott and Van Altena, 1909)   83
3.9   Slide 12 of *The Ghost of the Goblin Man* (Scott and Van Altena, 1912)   84
3.10   Slide 4 of *Oh That Boog-a-Boo Man* (DeWitt C. Wheeler, 1910)   84
3.11   The title character of Thanhouser's serial *Zudora* (1914) uncovers the magic lantern that projected a skeletal hand   86
4.1   An illustration of Edison's Black Maria, published in *Frank Leslie's Popular Monthly* (February 1895)   96
4.2   A nobleman shrinks before Mephistopheles in Georges Méliès's *The Devil's Castle / Le manoir du diable* (1896)   99
4.3   *Merlin the Magician* (American Mutoscope, 1898)   101
4.4   A frame from *The Ghost Train* (American Mutoscope and Biograph, 1901)   102
4.5   Lubin's comedy *The House of Terror* (1909) made a notable use of silhouettes   104
4.6   Published in the 5 February 1910 issue of *Moving Picture World*   108
4.7   *The House of Fear* (Imp, 1915) featured advances in night photography   112
4.8   Trade advertisement for Alice Guy Blaché's *The Woman of Mystery* (Solax, 1914)   113
5.1   A frame from *"The Prince of Darkness"* (American Mutoscope & Biograph, 1900)   130

5.2	A frame from *A Terrible Night* (American Mutoscope and Biograph, 1900)	130
5.3	Augustus Carney in *Alkali Ike Plays the Devil* (Essanay, 1912)	132
5.4	*Fantasma* (Edison, 1914)	136
5.5	Still photograph depicts *Dante's Inferno* (Milano, 1911)	137
5.6	From left to right, Edward Connelly, Bessie Barriscale, and Arthur Maude in *The Devil* (New York Motion Picture Company, 1915)	138
5.7	Trade advertisement for Milano's *In the Toils of the Devil* (1913), released in America by Monopol	139
6.1	The original British poster for Kalem's *The Mountain Witch* (1913)	151
6.2	Advertisement for *The Witch Girl* (Victor Film Co., 1914), published in the *Universal Weekly*	154
6.3	*The Myth of Jamasha Pass* (American, 1912)	155
6.4	*The Trials of Faith* (Reliance, 1912)	157
6.5	*The Witch of Salem* (Domino, 1914)	157
6.6	*The Witch* (Eclair American, 1913)	158
7.1	Advertisement for *The Ghost Story* (Vitagraph, 1907), published in *Views and Film Index*	163
7.2	*The Ghost* (Pathé, 1914), as published in *Moving Picture World* on March 14, 1914	166
7.3	"Ham" (Lloyd V. Hamilton) and "Bud" (Bud Duncan) in *Lotta Coin's Ghost* (Kalem, 1915)	168
7.4	Advertisement published in *The Billboard* on February 23, 1907	170
7.5	Trade advertisement for *Colonel Heeza Liar, Ghost Breaker* (Pathé, 1915)	171
7.6	*Courage of Sorts* (American, 1913)	173
7.7	Trade advertisement for *Spiritualism Exposed* (Pan American, 1913), published in *Moving Picture World*	177
7.8	*The Spook Raisers* (Kalem, 1915)	178
7.9	Trade advertisement for *The Circular Staircase* (Selig Polyscope, 1915), published in *Motion Picture News*	180
8.1	Lobby card for *Niobe* (Paramount/Famous Players, 1915)	188
8.2	*His Bachelor Dinner* (Reliance, 1915)	192
8.3	A frame from *The Red Spectre* (Pathé Frères, 1907)	193
8.4	Two frames from *When the Mummy Cried for Help* (Nestor, 1915)	197
8.5	Lithographed advertising card for *The Vengeance of Egypt* (Gaumont, 1912)	199
8.6	*The Legend of the Phantom Tribe* (101 Bison, 1914)	202
8.7 and 8.8	Two frames from the Pathé Frères film *Loïe Fuller*	205
8.9	*The Dust of Egypt* (Vitagraph, 1915)	207
9.1	A frame from *The Finish of Bridget McKeen* (Edison, 1901)	217
9.2	Original movie poster for *Vendetta* (Kleine-Eclipse, 1914)	221
9.3	Images from *Martyrs of the Inquisition* (Pathé Frères, 1906), as published in Lubin's 1907 catalog *Life Motion Pictures*	223
9.4	American Mutoscope and Biograph's *Execution of a Murderess* (1905)	224
9.5	*An Execution by Hanging* (American Mutoscope and Biograph, 1912)	225
10.1	Sidney Bracy in *The Miser's Reversion* (Thanhouser, 1914)	235
10.2	Publicity still for *His Terrible Secret; or The Man Monkey* (c. 1907)	238

10.3	Trade advertisement for *The Human Ape, or Darwin's Triumph* (Great Northern, 1909), published in *Moving Picture World*	239
10.4	*The Primitive Instinct* (Kalem, 1914)	240
10.5	Frame from *The Mischievous Monkey* (American Mutoscope, 1897)	241
10.6	*The Black Box* (Universal, 1915)	243
10.7	*Balaoo, The Demon Baboon* (Eclair, 1913)	244
10.8	Published in *Moving Picture World*	244
10.9	*The Hunchback* (Kalem, 1913)	247
10.10	*The Star of the Side Show* (Thanhouser, 1912)	249
11.1	Publicity still for *The Arrow Maiden* (Reliance, 1915)	260
11.2	*The Indian Massacre* (101 Bison, 1912)	262
11.3	*Voodoo Vengeance* (World's Best Film Company, 1913)	264
11.4	*Stanley Among the Voodoo Worshippers* (Centaur, 1915)	265
11.5	Trade advertisement for *The Mysterious Mr. Wu Chung Foo*, published in *Moving Picture World*	268
11.6	Publicity still for *The Chinatown Mystery* (Broncho, 1915)	268
11.7	*The Reincarnation of Karma* (Vitagraph, 1912)	270
11.8	*The Death Stone of India* (101 Bison, 1913)	272
12.1	*The Haunting Fear* (Kalem, 1915)	284
12.2	Slide 4 of the illustrated song *That Hypnotizing Man* (Scott and Van Altena, 1911)	293
12.3	*In the Power of the Hypnotist* (Warner's Features, 1913)	294
12.4	Trade advertisement for *The Hypnotic Violinist* (Warner's Features, 1914), published in *Moving Picture World*	296
12.5	Margarita Fischer and Charles Clary in a frame from *The Vampire* (Selig Polyscope, 1910)	297
12.6	Alice Hollister in *The Vampire* (Kalem, 1913)	298
12.7	Advertisement promoting Maurice Tourneur's *Trilby* (Equitable, 1915), published in *Motion Picture News*	299
13.1	*The Vivisectionist* (Kalem, 1915)	314
13.2	*From the Beyond* (Eclair American, 1913)	315
13.3	*If I Were Young Again* (Selig Polyscope, 1914)	317
13.4	Double-exposed publicity still of Alwin Neuss as the title characters in *Dr. Jekyll and Mr. Hyde; or, a Strange Case* (Great Northern, 1910)	320
13.5	M. J. McQuarrie in the title roles of *Dr. Jekyll and Mr. Hyde* (Kinemacolor, 1913), as featured on the cover of *Moving Picture News*	321
13.6	The scientist (Alec B. Francis) in *Lola* (World Film Corporation, 1914)	323
13.7 and 13.8	Two different frames depict the creation of the monster in *Frankenstein* (Edison, 1910)	327
13.9	*Life Without Soul* (Ocean Film Corporation, 1915)	329
14.1	Published in *Moving Picture News* on April 22, 1912	338
14.2	Published in *Moving Picture World* on April 19, 1913	340
14.3	*The Phantom Violin* (Universal, 1914)	341
14.4	*The Spectre Bridegroom* (Eclair American, 1913)	343
14.5	A still from *Feathertop* (Eclair American, 1912), featured on the cover of *Moving Picture News*	345

14.6	and 14.7 Two images from *The Lunatics* (Leading Players, 1914)	348
14.8	Alice Guy Blaché's *The Pit and the Pendulum* (Solax, 1913)	351
14.9	A frame from D. W. Griffith's *The Avenging Conscience or "Thou Shalt Not Kill"* (1914)	353
14.10	Eclair American's *The Raven* (1912)	355
15.1	Published in the Washington, D.C. *Evening Star* on 19 October 1895	371
15.2	Sheet music cover of Cora Salisbury's *Ghost Dance* (1911)	378
15.3	The 24-sheet for *Dante's Inferno* (Milano, 1911)	380
15.4	Theatre publicity for a screening of *Dante's Inferno* (Milano, 1911)	381
15.5	Artwork published in *Motography* on 4 January 1913 as an example of an objectionable type of moving picture poster	382
15.6	Postcard featuring Edison character actor Charles Ogle, c. 1911	389

Acknowledgments

I would like to offer my sincere thanks to the various archives, libraries, museums, and universities that kindly offered assistance during the research phase of this project: the American Heritage Center at the University of Wyoming, the Annenberg Rare Book and Manuscript Library at the University of Pennsylvania, the Ardmore Public Library of Oklahoma, the Bancroft Library at the University of California at Berkeley, the Billy Rose Theatre Division of the New York Public Library, the British Film Institute in London, the Charles E. Young Research Library at the University of California/Los Angeles, Cinegraph of Hamburg, the Department of Special Collections at the University of California at Santa Barbara, the EYE Film Institute in Amsterdam, the Free Library of Philadelphia, the Harry Ransom Center at the University of Texas at Austin, the Irish Film Institute of Dublin, the Louis B. Mayer Film and Television Study Center in the Doheny Library at the University of Southern California, the Margaret Herrick Library of the Academy of Motion Picture Arts and Sciences in Beverly Hills, the Marnan Collection, LLC in Minneapolis, Minnesota, the Motion Picture, Broadcasting and Recorded Sound Division/Moving Image Section at the Library of Congress in Washington, D.C., the Museum of the Moving Image in New York, the National Archives of the United States, the Réunion des musées nationaux—Grand palais in France, the Special Collections Department at the University of Iowa, the Special Collections Division at the University of Washington Libraries, the Theatre Historical Society of America, and the Wisconsin Center for Film and Theatre Research.

In addition, I want to express gratitude to the following individuals whose encouragement has helped make this book possible: Forrest J Ackerman, Leonardo D'Aurizio, Marty Baumann, Doug Bentin, Scott Berman, Richard Bojarski, Tom Brannan, Olaf Brill, Bob Burns, Mario Chacon, Richard Daub, Michael J. David, David Durston, Scott Essman, William K. Everson, Fritz Frising, Lawrence Fultz, Jr., Christopher R. Gauthier, Gordon R. Guy, G. D. Hamann, Matt Heffernan, David J. Hogan, Roger Hurlburt, Steve Jochsberger, Steve Kaplan, Anthony Kerr, Nancy Kersey, Eugene Kirschenbaum, Frank Liquori, Peter Michaels, Mark A. Miller, Lynn Naron, John Norris, Jim Nye, Dennis Payne, Victor Pierce, William Pirola, Jeffrey Roberts, Gerald Schnitzer, Bruce Scivally, Richard Sheffield, Samuel M. Sherman, Brian Taves, Mario Toland, John Ulakovic, and Jon Wang.

A number of persons have given so much of their time and support that they deserve my deepest thanks: Rebecca Bannon, Buddy Barnett, Stefano Baschiera, Anne-Catherine Biedermann, Deborah Borton, Terry Borton, Kevin Brownlow, Richard Bush, Larry Cederblom, Bill Chase, George Chastain, Eddie Clark, Ned Comstock, Michael Copner,

Robert Cremer, Kristin Dewey, Jack Dowler, Edward "Eric" Eaton, John Ellis, Thomas Elsaesser, Phillip Fortune, Beau Foutz, Robert Gitt, Robert Guffey, Lee Harris, Bruce Hershenson, Frederique Kartouby, Margaret Kieckhefer, Michael Lee, Tiphaine Leroux, Mark Martucci, D'Arcy More, Charles Musser, Constantine Nasr, Henry Nicolella, Jan Olsson, JoAnn Palmeri, Desmond O'Rawe, Mark Ryan, Sean Sharp, Annette Shulz, Zoran Sinobad, Anthony Slide, John Soister, Billy Stagner, David Stenn, Richard Strachan, George E. Turner, Tom Weaver, David Wentink, Glenn P. White, and Tony Williams.

In conclusion, I want to thank three colleagues whose time and advice are ultimately responsible for this book reaching publication. At Edinburgh University Press, Gillian Leslie was extremely supportive of this monograph from the moment she first heard me describe it. I deeply appreciate her support and kindness, including in the hard work she expended for a book of this extended word count and large number of illustrations.

Robert Singer and I shared many hours talking about this project while it was in the planning stages. His ideas had a major impact on its structure. Once writing began, he read each chapter and provided valuable feedback. His confidence in the project and moral support throughout have meant more than I can properly express.

After I completed the manuscript, Robert J. Kiss carefully scrutinized every sentence. His vast knowledge of this subject area meant that he was able to suggest many additions, including some crucial film examples I had overlooked, as well as a number of corrections that I deeply appreciate. He also kindly shared many illustrations from his own collection, and informed me of other images in various archives.

As with Gillian Leslie and Robert Singer, I cannot thank Robert J. Kiss enough. Indeed, I am deeply indebted to all of the persons who helped on this book.

Gary D. Rhodes
Belfast, Northern Ireland
2017

Introduction

> Darkness there and nothing more.
> —Edgar Allan Poe, *The Raven* (1845)

Walter Herries Pollock's short story *The Phantasmatograph* first appeared in *Longman's Magazine* of London in May 1899. Within a few weeks, the Cleveland *Plain-Dealer* published it in America.[1] The nineteenth century was rife with "graph" inventions, of course, from the telegraph and phonograph to the photograph and cinematograph. Pollock's narrator describes a device similar to motion pictures, but one capable of "photographing or Kodaking thought—human, or, for that matter, animal thought." Once the lights dim in a room "draped heavily with black velvet," moving images materialize during a demonstration. They were "less a ghost than a ghost's spectre," but were still horrifying. Pollock wrote:

> The invisible orchestra responded to every beat, every quiver of passion. And for the acting!—I must not call it acting; the thing was too real, too poignant. And through all the glory and beauty of the music that inexplicable Figure of Dread dominated the whole scene with a nameless sense of terror.[2]

Recounting the event in "tremulous tones," the puzzled narrator explains that, when the devilish Phantasmatograph scene ended, "all was dark."

Pollock's tale came at a relatively early period in the era of American cinema, the first public exhibition of projected moving pictures taking place in New York in April 1896. Within a few years, various U.S. companies were selling trick films produced in France by Georges Méliès. In February 1899, for example, the Edison Manufacturing Company offered such "Mystical Subjects" as Méliès's *Le cabinet de Méphistophélès*, retitling it *The Devil's Laboratory*.[3] Later that same year, New York distributor F. M. Prescott sold *Le cabinet de Méphistophélès* under the guise of *Mephisto in His Laboratory*.[4] Such Méliès films had a profound influence on early American cinema. Here was phantasmata of the type that Pollock illuminated in his short story, although usually more humorous in tone.

Historians generally cite 1915 as concluding the early cinema period, signaled in some measure by D. W. Griffith's epic production *The Birth of a Nation* (1915). Just one year earlier, Griffith had directed *The Avenging Conscience or "Thou Shalt Not Kill"* (1914, aka *The Avenging Conscience*), which adapted elements of Edgar Allan Poe's short story *The Tell-Tale Heart* (1843) and his poem *Annabel Lee* (1849). Critical reaction to *The Avenging Conscience* was largely favorable, and it seems to have had the desired effect on many audience members.

In 1914, *Movie Pictorial* said, "*The Avenging Conscience* reminds us that it is good most men's minds are not projecting machines."[5] Put another way, it was good that a Phantasmatograph did not exist, that no device could "Kodak" the actual thoughts of humans and put them on display for the world to see. For some viewers, it seems, *The Avenging Conscience* had come close enough to that reality, as did a substantial body of moving pictures that preceded it.

Even before the age of American film projection began, the Edison Manufacturing Company manufactured death for the Kinetoscope, a peepshow device on which individual viewers could watch short films. In August 1895, Edison employees Alfred Clark and William Heise created *Execution of Mary, Queen of Scots*, which used "stop-motion substitution" to depict the decapitation of its title character by the blow of an ax, and an executioner holding up her severed head.[6] Without moving the camera, the filmmakers replaced the actor portraying Mary with a dummy immediately prior to shooting the beheading. The two images were spliced together, thus making the execution appear to take place in a single, continuous shot.[7] Here was the first special effect in the history of the cinema, one in which the same cut altered the film and Mary's body.

Figures I.1 and I.2 Two frames from *Execution of Mary, Queen of Scots* (Edison, 1895). (*Courtesy of the Library of Congress, Motion Picture, Broadcasting and Recorded Sound Division/Moving Image Section*)

Though based on the infamous execution of 1587, *Execution of Mary, Queen of Scots*—which was also sold under the titles *Execution* and *Execution Scene*—features no historical context, its narrative consisting solely of a grisly death scene that lasts less than fifteen seconds, but which remains arresting cinema.[8] According to an 1895 newspaper advertisement, *Execution of Mary, Queen of Scots* represented the very first "Chamber of Horrors" moving picture to be "seen on the kinetoscope," adding that it was "blood-curdling in the extreme."[9] The moving picture had embraced horror for the very first time, but certainly not the last. Clark and Heise shot *Joan of Arc* (aka *Burning of Joan of Arc*) on the same day as *Execution of Mary, Queen of Scots*; the film focused exclusively on Joan's capital punishment.[10] Then, in September 1895, the duo filmed *Lynching Scene* and *Scalping Scene* at the Edison facilities, creating as a result the first horror-themed film series.[11]

While horror-themed entertainment existed long before the advent of cinema, the medium proved particularly adept at articulating it, whether as phantasmata or as corporeality. In *The*

Art of the Moving Picture (1915), Vachel Lindsay perceived how quickly and effectively cinema could traverse the "borderline between All Saint's Day and Hallowe'en."[12] When he wrote those words, two decades had passed since Edison decapitated Mary, during which film companies had produced hundreds of other moving pictures that had crossed the same borderline. As Shakespeare wrote in *Othello*, "On horror's head horrors accumulate."

Nevertheless, some years ago, a colleague of mine who specializes in the horror genre expressed great surprise that such an accumulation occurred. Aside from Edison's *Frankenstein* (1910) and a small number of Méliès films, he was unaware that horror-themed entertainment registered in any major way during the first twenty years of American cinema. And understandably so, as no foundational history of this period exists. Here then is the key intervention I hope to make with *The Birth of the American Horror Film*, to illuminate a largely overlooked body of moving pictures released during the era of early cinema, as well as the contexts that informed it.

Spectral Evidence

Horror in the American cinema begins in 1895, but horror as an emotion has gripped American life for centuries, as in the case of the Lost Colony of Roanoke, found mysteriously abandoned in 1587, the same year that Mary, Queen of Scots was beheaded. But no horrifying event from the colonial era looms larger than the Salem Witch Trials of 1692. Twenty persons were executed, fourteen of them women. Over three hundred years later, the events still captivate us, with Danvers, Massachusetts remaining a popular tourist site where visitors attempt to glimpse an inglorious past, one in which—as the *Chicago Tribune* stated in 1892—the "New World aped a few superstitions of the Old."[13]

Defending the witch trials in his book *The Wonders of the Invisible World* (1693), Puritan minister Cotton Mather declared, "It is therefore exceeding necessary that in such a day as this, men be informed what is Evidence and what is not."[14] The judges who condemned witches in Salem took various factors into account, but relied heavily on "spectral evidence" (aka "spectre evidence"), meaning witness testimony that claimed the spectral appearance of the accused had appeared to him or her, even though the accused's physical body was elsewhere. Here was not only a sign of witchcraft, but also of Satan's power.

According to a modern legal definition, "In spectral evidence, the admission of victims' conjectures is governed only by the limits of their fears and imaginations, whether or not objectively proven facts are forthcoming to justify them."[15] Such fears in Salem cost twenty people their lives. Nancy Ruttenburg has determined that the "near exclusive reliance upon spectral evidence, to the degree that it figured prominently in every conviction, appears to be the distinguishing characteristic of the Salem trials."[16] The use of such evidence ended in October 1692, but its legacy remains.

One of colonial America's greatest traumas had resulted in large measure from a willingness to believe unbelievable evidence, a vexing conundrum.[17] Alison Tracy writes:

> Salem continues to fascinate not simply because of its witchcraft, or even because it represents some sort of encounter with the supernatural, but because it offers a glimpse of a society's encounter with meaninglessness, and thereby confronts us with the necessity of our individual participation in the consensual fictions that create and maintain meaning.[18]

A heavy investment in the supernatural took a heavy toll. Defenders like Cotton Mather were few in number, and rightly so, as the tragedies wrought by spectral evidence exposed the dangers of superstition, particularly during the Enlightenment of the eighteenth century.

In 1742, for example, the *American Weekly Mercury* advised readers to be wary of placing credence in the existence of "terrible Ghosts and Spectres."[19] Seven years later, the *New-York Gazette* remarked:

> Some Ghosts and Spectres owe their Existence to a timorous or distempered Imagination, in the Midst of a dark and gloomy Interval; others take their Rise from the reciprocal Pleasure of deluding, and of being deluded: And for the rest, we must impute them to the early Errors of Infancy, and a motley Mixture of the low and vulgar Education: Mothers and Grandmothers, Aunts and Nurses, begin the Cheat, and from little Horrors and hideous Stories . . . they train us up by Degrees to the Belief of a more substantial Ghost and Apparition.[20]

The ignorant beliefs of the past were at odds with the enlightened present, a fact that seemed even more pronounced in America by the end of the eighteenth century. In 1800, for example, a Philadelphia newspaper condemned the "superstition and ignorance" of early colonists as being "unparalleled."[21]

Figure I.3 American postcard dated 1910.

"If the people only become more firmly convinced that such a thing as a real ghost never did appear on earth, and never will," the *Albany Argus* noted in 1829, "a great benefit will be accomplished."[22] "We know of nothing more foolish" than belief in a "haunted house," the *Newburyport Herald* wrote in 1837.[23] Nevertheless, the Enlightenment hardly eradicated the supernatural. "The unfortunate are always superstitious," the *Alexandria Gazette* bemoaned in 1843, using class structures to separate those who believed from those who did not.[24] And an American magazine warned in 1851 that trusting in legends could produce "disastrous effects" in the "human mind."[25]

One needed only to observe the maelstrom of Salem to see such disasters at work, to see how readily people can be deceived.

Humbugged

In 1836, Edgar Allan Poe published an essay on Maelzel's Chess Player, which had been invented in 1769, promoted in London in 1783, and exhibited in New York in 1826.[26] From there it achieved popular success in such cities as Philadelphia and Boston.[27] The automaton engaged challengers in the game of chess, often winning, much to the amazement of onlookers, among them Benjamin Franklin. As Poe indicated, "it has been an object of intense curiosity," one that would later inspire Ambrose Bierce's short story *Moxon's Master* (1909).[28] Was the robotic device sentient, a mechanical form of artificial intelligence, or was it just another fraud? In 1826, the *New York American* dubbed it "the greatest puzzle seen."[29]

After considering various possible explanations, Poe concluded, "We do not believe that any reasonable objections can be urged against the solution of the Automaton Chess Player." For an author who regularly touted his skills at ratiocination and who in large measure invented detective fiction, Maelzel's Chess Player remained an enigma. But Poe did understand that there *was* an answer. The mystery could be unraveled. All conjuring tricks—no matter how well conceived and performed—had logical explanations. One only had to uncover them.

In 1844, Poe was himself responsible for an elaborate fraud. The *New York Sun* published his report that a flying machine had crossed the Atlantic Ocean in three days. "The great problem is at length solved," his story began. After the ruse was disclosed, the tale became known as *The Balloon-Hoax*. Poe's was a clever trick, to be sure, but not the first of its kind. In 1835, the same newspaper had printed a series of six fraudulent stories about the discovery of life on the moon.[30]

Hoaxes in America during the nineteenth century were commonplace. In 1862, Mark Twain published a short newspaper article claiming a petrified man had been discovered in Nevada.[31] Seven years later, the Cardiff Giant—a ten-foot-tall, petrified man—was allegedly unearthed in New York.[32] When its exhibitor learned that New Yorkers were paying to see P. T. Barnum's replica of his giant, he remarked, "There's a sucker born every minute," a quote later attributed to Barnum. After both giants were exposed as fakes, Mark Twain wrote *A Ghost Story* (1888). In it, the Cardiff Giant haunts a museum that purports to own his petrified carcass. As the narrator admonishes him, "You have been haunting a plaster cast of yourself . . . Confound it, don't you know your own remains?"

The setting of Twain's story was an oblique reference to P. T. Barnum's American Museum. Along with founding the Barnum and Bailey Circus, Barnum was arguably the greatest showman of the nineteenth century. In 1841, he opened his museum, unveiling his first major hoax—the Feejee Mermaid—the following year. Barnum did not usually lie, but instead advertised his exhibits as questionable curiosities.[33] Nowhere is this clearer than in his famous exhibit, "What Is It?," which invited audience participation in its identification. The great trickster made little secret of his approach, that of the "humbug."

Barnum tempted and even provoked the public's skepticism, understanding that visitors to his museum enjoyed debating frauds and detecting deception.[34] In turn, audience satisfaction at Barnum's exhibits seemed to justify his exaggerations.[35]

The Age of Barnum became what James W. Cook has called a "marketplace of playful frauds," a broad spectrum of popular culture in the nineteenth century, one that "routinely involved a calculated intermixing of the genuine and fake, enchantment and disenchantment, energetic public exposé and momentary suspension of belief."[36] To suspect or even know one was being deceived could provide pleasure of a type that also allowed celebrity magicians to flourish. For example, Herrmann the Great and Harry Kellar attracted large crowds at postbellum American theaters with conjuring tricks far more complex than those of earlier ages.

The nineteenth century was riven by contradiction. It is not inappropriate to speak of it as a period of science and reason, meaning the detectives of Poe and Conan Doyle, the theories of Chambers and Darwin, and the technological advances of Edison and Tesla. But the century also abounded with new religions like Mormonism, and with pseudo-sciences like phrenology. Despite the Enlightenment, the boundary between religion and science remained porous. In 1839, an American newspaper described a Russian automaton as resembling Satan.[37] In 1893, *The Literary World* referred to hypnotism as the "new witchcraft."[38] The Moon Hoax of 1835 was indeed a hoax; the Martian canals Percival Lowell described in books like *Mars* (1895) were not. They were just mistakes.

Nowhere are the blurred lines between science and religion, as well as truth and deception, more apparent than in the rise of Spiritualism. Beginning in 1848, Kate and Margaret Fox allegedly conversed with spirits at their New York farmhouse by means of a system of raps. Their fame spread rapidly, fuelling a popular sensation.[39] The Fox Sisters inspired not only the religious, but also the scientific. According to Ann Braude, "Spiritualism's claim to be scientific . . . was not unreasonable within the context of popular scientific knowledge at mid-century."[40] Talking with the dead elicited inquiries from experts working in such fields as physics, psychology, and psychiatry.[41] Then-recent technologies like the photograph and the phonograph were employed in efforts to record spectral manifestations, pursuits that might well have inspired Pollock's short story *The Phantasmatograph*.

But in 1888, Kate and Margaret Fox publicly confessed that they had faked everything. Kate denounced it as a "humbug from beginning to end."[42] Margaret called it a "horrible deception."[43] Then, in 1889, Margaret reversed herself, claiming she had given "expression to utterances that had no foundation in fact."[44]

Were the incantations the fraud, or the recantations? Was there a ghost, or just a ghost's spectre? Whichever one believed, the Fox Sisters had at some stage perpetrated a hoax on the American public.

The Sleep of Reason Produces Monsters

"We read ghost stories, presumably, because—to put it grossly—we like to be humbugged and because we like to be scared."[45] So wrote novelist Mary S. Watts in the pages of the *New York Times* in 1908, as part of an effort to explain the appeal of horror-themed entertainment.

While her word choice invoked the Age of Barnum, her subject matter was hardly new. In 1824, the *New Monthly Magazine and Literary Journal* enthused, "It is so soothing to be agitated, so delightful to be shocked, so animating to be frightened to death, and moreover so sweet to have a perpetual excuse for gossiping and shuddering . . ."[46] Fifteen years later, the *New-York Mirror* admitted that the "self-satisfied" person of the modern world could gloat over being superior to ancestors who believed in "barbarism and superstition." But the newspaper added, "knowledge is not all clear gain," with enlightened persons having "robbed themselves" of so many "spirit-stirring legends, and wild, and fanciful, and pleasant illusions, by their impertinent habits of investigation."[47]

It is not the intention of the present volume to explain why people have enjoyed horror-themed entertainment, either in the past or in the present. Many writers have undertaken that mission, from Sigmund Freud to Noël Carroll, from Lafcadio Hearn to Stephen King.[48] Neither is it the goal of this volume to define the horror genre, as attempted elsewhere by the likes of H. P. Lovecraft and Devendra Varma.[49] Suffice it to say, horror manifests in many forms, from phantasmata to corporealia, from the devilish inferno to the grisly execution.

This book does propose that two major trajectories are present in the history of American horror, and they had a profound effect on the types of moving pictures produced in the United States during the early cinema period, as well as on the reactions American viewers gave to contemporaneous films produced in other countries.

The first trajectory is an ongoing desire to rationalize the supernatural. Such an approach regularly involves what Tzvetan Todorov has called the "Fantastic," meaning the duration in which a reader (or, by extension, film viewer) experiences a hesitation, uncertain as to whether the supernatural is really at play. The uncertainty generally leads either to the "Marvellous," meaning the "supernatural accepted," or the "Uncanny," meaning the "supernatural explained."[50] Todorov's "Uncanny" offers an appropriate name for the first trajectory, which extends from Washington Irving to Scooby-Doo.

Why is this the case? I would submit that there is no single cause, but there are sequences of associations, one perhaps being Ann Radcliffe's popularity in America, her English Gothic novels relying heavily on the supernatural explained.[51] However, I would also stress the long shadow cast by spectral evidence, meaning the monumental problems that can result from accepting the supernatural, as well as the humbugged nineteenth century, in which detecting frauds became a cultural enterprise. Instead of illusions producing delusions, the reverse became true in American horror-themed entertainment.

None of this is to suggest that the "Marvellous" is absent from American horror. If Radcliffe debunked the supernatural, Matthew Gregory Lewis confirmed it, and his English Gothic novels and plays were popular in America as well. The same could be said of the works of such authors as Charles Dickens and Bram Stoker. However, the appearance of the "Marvellous" often came in the form of comedy rather than drama, whether in the literature of Mark Twain or in the American embrace of Méliès. Moreover, the larger point is that, in terms of sheer numbers of indigenous entertainment, the "Uncanny" is by far the more dominant.

The second trajectory is to eschew the supernatural in favor of other types of horror: *Execution of Mary, Queen of Scots* instead of *The Devil's Laboratory*; human monsters rather than supernatural creatures; fears of the present and future over the past, meaning science and technology over superstitions and legends. Let us not forget that Cotton Mather's major contribution to America may not have been his ramblings about witchcraft, but instead his support for inoculations to prevent diseases like smallpox, as well as in his experiments with plant hybridization.[52]

Thinking again in terms of sheer numbers, we can see this trajectory unfold in later twentieth-century cinema. While in some ways the supernatural vampire of *Dracula* (1931) was the catalyst of horror in Classical Hollywood, as well as the popularization of the terms "horror film" and "horror movie," the bulk of genre efforts during the thirties and forties feature mad scientists. Science fiction dominates in the fifties, and murderers do the same in the slasher films of the seventies, eighties, and nineties. There are of course exceptions, whether in the form of vampires and ghosts, or in the form of murderers made supernatural as narrative justification for bringing them back to life in sequels.

But the numbers cannot be ignored. American horror onscreen has followed in the tradition of *Execution of Mary, Queen of Scots* far more often than it has *The Devil's Laboratory*.

Cinema, Lost and Found

Writing about early cinema, Ben Brewster notes, "Periodization is a dubious enterprise; everything is always changing into something else."[53] To be sure, evolution is a central component of early cinema, an important consideration for any study of the period. One way to express these shifts is in terms of exhibition, meaning the pre-nickelodeon era, which lasts until roughly 1905, the nickelodeon era, which lasts until roughly 1912, and the post-nickelodeon era that follows.[54]

Another approach is to study changes in film content. For example, Tom Gunning has famously described the earliest moving pictures as constituting a "cinema of attractions," in which the presentation of images was central, with narrative being at best a secondary concern. Here again *Execution of Mary, Queen of Scots* provides a worthwhile example. The shock of the image is more important than the historical tale, which is embedded in the title of the film rather than in the onscreen action. This "cinema of attractions" period lasts until roughly 1903, followed by a transitional phase that lasts until 1908. By 1910 and after, a cinema of narrative integration becomes commonplace.[55]

In tandem with narrative and aesthetic evolutions is the question of national cinemas. During the age of early cinema, the American moving picture was very much an international enterprise. As Richard Abel has detailed, imported French films dominated American exhibition during the early cinema period, particularly before 1910.[56] Italian features then played an important role in encouraging American filmmakers to produce multi-reel movies. In some respects, the period between the 1890s and 1915 is very much one in which films in America (meaning all of those exhibited in the United States) had to be Americanized (meaning the dominant number produced in the United States).

To augment this discussion, we should also contemplate Matthew Solomon's work on Méliès as a "transnational" filmmaker, one who was producing much of his work with an eye toward markets outside of/in addition to France, to the extent that he set up offices and a production company in the United States.[57] The relationship between American cinema and moving pictures produced in other countries was thus more complicated than the binary "American films" and "foreign films." These complexities are also apparent in the Nordisk Film Company of Copenhagen, Denmark—which produced a number of important moving pictures that will be discussed in this book—and its branch office in New York, the Great Northern Film Company. Great Northern not only distributed Danish productions made by its parent company, but also (in the words of Ron Mottram) "played a prominent role among independent film producers and distributors during the period in which the Motion Picture Patents Company was attempting to monopolize the film industry."[58] What all of this means is that, to an extent, early American cinema was an international cinema.

Wherever they were produced, early films have often been dismissed as "primitive," a view that I reject. As Tom Gunning writes:

> The challenge that early cinema offers to film history is a search for a method of understanding the transformations in narrative form in cinema's first decades; a method that maintains an awareness of early film's difference from later practices, without defining it simply as a relation of divergence from a model of continuity (that, in fact, has not yet appeared).[59]

For this book, such a challenge means avoiding the belief that these films represent the output of inexperienced or naive filmmakers stumbling or even groping toward a cinema that would have to be perfected in some later era. Rather, I believe that herein are films worthy of study on their own merits.

Likewise, Gunning's advice also serves as a warning against mounting any teleological argument, including in the area of genre. As Lincoln Geraghty and Mark Jancovich recommend:

> If one wants to know how *Trip to the Moon* [Méliès, 1902] and *The Phantom of the Opera* [Universal, 1925] were understood within the periods of their original release, one needs to be clear about the precise way in which they were generically identified at the time, rather than presuming that one can simply draw upon one's own understanding of generic categories.[60]

Consider Charles Musser's work on Edwin S. Porter's *The Great Train Robbery* (Edison, 1903), a film regularly considered to be the first, or one of the first, westerns. Perceiving this to be a "retrospective reading," one that positions the film within a film genre that did not yet exist, Musser opts to examine *The Great Train Robbery* in relation to moving pictures that *preceded* it, specifically in "its ability to incorporate so many trends, genres and strategies fundamental to the institution of cinema at the time."[61] These included the travel genre (specifically the railway subgenre), the genre of re-enacted news events, and the crime genre. It was not until at least a few years after its debut that critics and audiences primarily interpreted *The Great Train Robbery* as a western.[62]

The same issue is importantly at stake in the present study, to the extent that I do not refer to the films of this period as "horror movies" or, for that matter, as "horror films." To begin, the issue of terminology has long been a matter of concern for horror in entertainment. Ann Radcliffe famously delineated a difference between the words "horror" (which "nearly annihilates" the reader) and "terror" (which is marked by its "obscurity"); Boris Karloff echoed similar distinctions a century later.[63] To these terms we could add various others that were used in the nineteenth and early twentieth centuries, including "weird" (sometimes spelled "wierd") and "gruesome" (sometimes spelled "grewsome"). Likewise, we could consider variations on the word "horror," as in the notable case of Jane Austen's *Northanger Abbey* (1803), in which the character Catherine Morland relies on "horrid" to describe certain Gothic novels.

All that said, journalists occasionally used the adjective "horror" to describe certain moving pictures in the early cinema period, and it is important to employ Altman's methodology of looking "closely at the terms actually used by contemporaries" of given films.[64] Of *The Secret Room* (Kalem, 1915), for example, a reviewer in the *Moving Picture World* wrote:

> It is one that demanded some relief at the close, for it builds up a veritable nightmare and would have been almost insufferable if one couldn't wake up from it—insufferable from sheer horror.... People have thought up situations of terror before this and even put them into pictures ... but in this picture showing is made real. We have only seen three or four other film offerings portraying horror that were as effective. When the spectator sees it he will know whether he has strong nerves or not.[65]

Such descriptions could be easily applied to horror movies of the twenty-first century. Nevertheless, there is an enormous gulf between the application of a word and the naming of a genre that conjures recognizable codes and conventions. These are the reasons why I choose to concentrate, like Musser, on the entertainment that *preceded* the films under review.

To be absolutely clear, the horror movie genre as we know it did not exist in the early cinema period, nor did the generic or marketing term "horror movie." While I do believe the moving pictures under review very much lead to the later "horror movie," I have also avoided terms like "proto-horror" that would imply the inevitability of such a historical result.

How then to rectify this problem? I have opted to refer to the moving pictures herein as "horror-themed," which they are to the extent that they either tried to frighten or shock viewers, or that they invoked tropes associated with prior horror-themed entertainment, like haunted houses or ghosts, even if those tropes were sometimes used for comedic purposes. While perhaps imperfect, given that it privileges a particular word later adopted by Hollywood, I believe "horror-themed" accurately characterizes aspects of given moving pictures in a manner akin to the aforementioned review of *The Secret Room*. It also employs a term that was definitely in contemporaneous usage. And unlike the term "horror movie," it avoids the invocation of generic expectations and exhibition practices that either did not exist or were not yet codified in the early cinema period.

The Birth of the American Horror Film

In researching this topic and constructing this narrative, my methodology has been that of New Film History as defined by such scholars as Thomas Elsaesser.[66] By this I mean that I have attempted to understand films as being unique artifacts that feature distinctive aesthetics and formal properties, and that also bear similarities to earlier traditions in literary, theatrical, and visual cultures. Similarly, I view the moving pictures under review as being involved in a complex relationship with various social contexts, many of them predating cinema. Furthermore, I have tried to make as rigorous and exhaustive use of archives as possible, carefully examining primary sources, ranging from surviving films, photographs, and lantern slides to relevant documents, among them newspapers, magazines, books, film company catalogs, industry trade publications, posters, and various other ephemera. I have also attempted to work from an awareness of and engagement with major secondary sources in relevant areas, including but certainly not limited to Film Studies, Horror Studies, Theatre Studies, Literary Studies, and Cultural Studies.

As much as can be examined, however, much cannot be. Approximately 90 per cent of the moving pictures produced before 1915 are considered lost.[67] Given how forgotten most of the films discussed herein are, as well as the sheer volume that do not survive, I would describe my research as being not dissimilar to Leonard Barkan's discussion of the "autopsy" that must be performed on sculptures unearthed in archeological digs, which are usually recovered as fragments. The same is true of many lost films. Occasionally, individual images exist, whether deposited at the Library of Congress for copyright reasons, or reproduced in early catalogs and trade publications: here is a part of a whole that cannot be seen. "The more ruined," Barkan writes, "the more [the fragment] inscribes; the more it inscribes, the more it invokes the modern imagination."[68]

In many cases, unfortunately, no fragment from a lost moving picture exists, but its content is refracted in synopses and critical reviews that do survive, as well as in other ephemera like publicity materials. Here is the nether region in which so many of the films discussed herein reside. They do not exist, but can be understood through ancillary sources that also invoke the modern imagination. Rather than fragments, here are contours that give shape to a vanished cinema, sometimes with great accuracy and sometimes—given conflicting data in these sources—not. "Less a ghost than a ghost's spectre," as Pollock wrote.

With regard to practical matters, I would note that I have intentionally privileged American release titles, citing them first even when the films under review were produced in other countries, as my goal is specifically to examine the evolution of horror in American cinema. Likewise, I have privileged American years of release, which sometimes came later than in their countries of origin. (I would add that some of the American years of release I give differ from other modern sources, which have often relied on surviving film company catalogs. Digitized newspaper advertisements and articles have assisted in determining that particular moving pictures were screened earlier than previously understood.)

Given the challenges involved in the formation of this history, and the expansive terrain to be covered, I have divided the book into three sections and fifteen chapters.

Section I is entitled *The Rise of Horror-themed Cinema*. Its first three chapters survey what might collectively be called "pre-cinema." André Gaudreault rightly suggests that there are problems with the term "pre-cinema." It implies a teleological argument of its own kind, with prior media working in a predetermined drive toward the arrival of film.[69] It can also confuse chronology. Media that existed prior to the advent of cinema often continued to survive and even flourish parallel to it. However, the concentration of these first three chapters is largely on the proliferation of horror-themed entertainment in America before the advent of cinema, while giving necessary attention to the same in the years 1895 to 1915.

Chapter 1 presents an investigation of Gothic and horror-themed literature in the United States. Some English novels that embraced the supernatural became popular in America, and some American authors wrote tales that accepted the supernatural or relied on fantastical uncertainty. But the majority of indigenous literature either shunned the topic, opting instead to explore non-supernatural horror, as Poe so often did, or invoked the supernatural only to rationalize it away, as can be seen in a tradition that begins with Charles Brockden Brown and continues through Mary Roberts Rinehart and beyond.

Chapter 2 chronicles Gothic and horror-themed American theatre, its coverage extending to variety shows and vaudeville sketches, as well as to public demonstrations of science and pseudo-science. Here the supernatural appears prominently given the American success of such British plays as Matthew Gregory Lewis's *The Castle Spectre* (1797) and James Robinson Planché's *The Vampyre; or, The Bride of the Isles* (1820), as well as in the popularity of Pepper's Ghost during and after the American Civil War. Likewise, public séances became common in the second half of the nineteenth century. That said, lecturers and journalists expended much time explaining the science behind Pepper's Ghost, just as magicians did in exposing the trickery of mediums; together these exemplify a humbugged stage. Moreover, the most popular horror-themed plays in the final years of the nineteenth century featured human monsters rather than ghosts, as is evident in *Dr. Jekyll and Mr. Hyde* (1887) and *Trilby* (1895).[70]

Chapter 3 explores horror-themed visual culture, from paintings and engravings to photography and magic lantern slides. Illustrations in some books and magazines represented the supernatural, but the overwhelming number did not, opting instead to depict murder and death. The same was true of photography, which—when it did purport to capture the supernatural—resulted in such cases as the trial of William H. Mumler. Supernatural imagery in nineteenth-century America appeared most consistently in the form of magic lantern slides, but a majority of these were humorous in tone, projecting images of comical ghosts and skeletons.

Chapter 4 charts the evolution of the moving picture from its origins and early emphases on both trickery and nonfiction through the rise of a fictional cinema of "realism." Here the worlds of directors like Georges Méliès and Segundo de Chomón evolve into those of D. W. Griffith and Alice Guy Blaché. The chapter also addresses the importance of repeated motifs that these filmmakers employed in horror-themed cinema, ranging from night photography to the use of dreams as a narrative framing device.

Section II of this volume, *Film Genres*, explores a collection of different horror-themed genres that were present in early American cinema, both indigenous and imported. Here are genres that were largely borne out of specific contexts, as will be investigated, but that developed particular conventions due to the unique formal properties of the cinema. All of the genres under review contributed meaningfully to the eventual rise of the "horror movie." As Altman explains:

> Before they are fully constituted through the junction of persistent material and consistent use of that material, nascent genres traverse a period when their only unity derives from shared surface characteristics deployed within other generic contexts perceived as dominant.[71]

During the early cinema period, the genres explored in Section II were usually regarded as distinct from one another, hence their separation into numerous chapters. Eventually, however, most of them were subsumed into the Hollywood "horror movie." Genres would become subgenres.

Chapters 5 through 8 examine supernatural beings, meaning Devils and Demons; Witches and Witchcraft; Ghosts; and Supernatural Creatures (among them werewolves, mummies, and reanimated skeletons). In a relatively small number of cases, moving pictures of the era presented dramatic representations of the supernatural. However, two other approaches were far more frequent, meaning the "Uncanny," tales of the supernatural explained, which could be dramatic or comical in tone. Secondly, humorous depictions of the supernatural accepted were common, as famously seen in the films of Méliès, which attained popularity in America in large measure due to their special effects, but also due to the long-standing American tradition of treating horror through comedy.

By contrast, Chapters 9 through 14 investigate natural horrors, beginning with Death, Murder, and Executions before moving onto Evolution and Devolution ("missing links" and physical deformities); the Other (specifically Native Americans, Blacks, Asians, and Indians); Mad Scientists (including but hardly limited to Dr. Jekyll and Dr. Frankenstein); and finally American Literature Onscreen (as in adaptations of Irving, Hawthorne, and Poe). Here is the second of the two aforementioned trajectories in which American horror operated, as exemplified in moving pictures that came out of many contexts, not least of which was *Execution of Mary, Queen of Scots*. Whether or not particular viewers believed in ghosts and goblins, many of them certainly shared an aversion to and fascination with the natural horrors paraded over and over again in early cinema, often with a dread seriousness rarely found in screen treatments of the supernatural.

Section III, *Exhibition and Reception*, concludes this book with a single chapter. Chapter 15 identifies not only the marketing of these films, including the use of terminology and of holidays like Halloween, but also in the presentation of them, meaning how exhibitors programmed them alongside non-horror-themed films and what kinds of live musical accompaniment they provided. This chapter also attempts to recover how particular critics and audience members reacted to the films under review.

Conclusion

On November 1, 1908, the *Sunday Star* of Washington, D.C. happily reported that the "Witches Were All Good" during the previous evening.[72] "A witch is absolutely necessary to the complete success of a Hallowe'en party," *Dennison's 1912 Bogie Book* advised.[73] Naughty or nice, essential or not, these witches might have faced a very different fate had they announced their personifications in colonial America, even if just on the single day of October 31. But all of that had changed after 1692. Vesting too much in the supernatural accepted had led moral persons to commit immoral crimes. The country became far less trusting of the unknown, so much so that Americans took great pleasure participating in and detecting deceptions during the nineteenth century, up to and including the trickery of cinema.

André Bazin once said, "Every new development added to the cinema must, paradoxically, take it nearer and nearer to its origins. In short the cinema has not yet been invented."[74] While these early, horror-themed films are now over a century old and the predominant number of them are lost, I believe they remain important, and not merely because of their relationship to later cinema. To quote Barkan yet again, "The more ruined, the more it inscribes; the more it inscribes, the more it invokes the modern imagination."[75]

In 1931, one unhappy "movie fan" wrote to the *Chicago Tribune* after viewing James Whale's *Frankenstein* (Universal, 1931). He was "outraged at the effrontery of any producer attempting to put over something so obviously crude," something that prevented him from getting "one single thrill out of it."[76] By contrast, he recalled seeing a version of

Figure I.4 Charles Ogle as the monster in *Frankenstein* (Edison, 1910).

Frankenstein produced by the Edison Manufacturing Company in 1910, to the extent he remembered details about it even after the passage of two decades. The early film continued to unreel in his memory.

I first saw a photograph from Edison's *Frankenstein* in about 1977 when I was five years old, staring at a children's book on the subject of Frankenstein in the cinema.[77] The image haunted me. In the mid-1980s, I was enthralled by a CNN report on the film's rediscovery in a collector's personal archive, due in large measure to another fragment, this time a brief film clip that the news station broadcast. Approximately thirteen years later, I purchased a copy of the entire film on VHS. To invert Pollock, the ghost's spectre had at long last become a ghost, still intangible in some respects, but far more visible to my eyes than ever before.

It is my sincere hope with this volume to perform a similar function for film history, to make visible moving pictures that have not remained as famous as Edison's *Frankenstein*, to project them again, if not necessarily with film prints, then with a Phantasmatograph of my own design, illumined by literally thousands of primary sources and flickering on a screen that has remained dark for too long.

Notes

1. Walter Herries Pollock, "The Phantasmatograph," *Longman's Magazine*, May 1899, 58–69. The story also appeared in *The Plain Dealer* (Cleveland, Ohio) on May 21, 1899.
2. Ibid., 68.
3. Advertisement, *New York Clipper*, February 18, 1899, 870.

4. *New Films, Supplement No. 3* (New York, F. M. Prescott: November 20, 1899). Available in *A Guide to Motion Picture Catalogs by American Producers and Distributors, 1894–1908: A Microfilm Edition* (New Brunswick: Rutgers University Press, 1985), Reel 1.
5. "The Split-Reel," *Movie Pictorial*, December 1914, pagination missing. This article appears on the microfilm of *Movie Pictorial* archived at the New York Public Library/Lincoln Center for the Performing Arts in New York City. The original page was a fragment. Along with missing pagination, it is also difficult to determine its date with exactitude. It is most likely from the December 1914 issue, but could instead have been published in January 1915.
6. *Execution of Mary, Queen of Scots* is available on the DVD boxed set *Edison: The Invention of the Movies* (New York: Kino, 2005).
7. Charles Musser, *The Emergence of Cinema: The American Screen to 1907* (Berkeley: University of California Press, 1990), 86–7.
8. *Catalogue: Edison and International Photographic Films* (New York: Maguire & Baucus, April 1897), 7. Available in *A Guide to Motion Picture Catalogs by American Producers and Distributors, 1894–1908: A Microfilm Edition*, Reel 1.
9. Advertisement, *The Evening Star* (Washington, D.C.), October 19, 1895.
10. Charles Musser, *Edison Motion Pictures, 1890–1900* (Washington, D.C.: Smithsonian Institution Press, 1997), 190.
11. Ibid., 193–4.
12. Vachel Lindsay, *The Art of the Moving Picture* (New York: Liveright Publishing Corporation, 1970), 65.
13. "Music and Drama," *Chicago Tribune*, October 10, 1892, 4.
14. Cotton Mather, *The Wonders of the Invisible World, Being an Account of the Tryals of Several Witches Lately Executed in New-England* (London: John Russell Smith, 1862), 222.
15. *State v. Dustin*, 122 N.H. 544, 551 (N.H. 1982).
16. Nancy Ruttenburg, *Democratic Personality: Popular Voice and the Trial of American Authorship* (Stanford: Stanford University Press, 1998), 35.
17. Sarah Rivett, "Our Salem, Our Selves," *The William and Mary Quarterly*, Vol. 65, No. 3 (July 2008), 499.
18. Alison Tracy, "Uncanny Afflictions: Spectral Evidence and the Puritan Crisis of Subjectivity," in *Spectral America: Phantoms and the National Imagination*, edited by Jeffrey Andrew Weinstock (Madison: University of Wisconsin Press, 2004), 35.
19. "Of Superstition," *American Weekly Mercury* (Philadelphia, Pennsylvania), December 16, 1742, 1.
20. "Of Spectres and Apparitions," *New-York Gazette*, August 12, 1751.
21. "Witchcraft," *Constitutional Diary and Philadelphia Evening Advertiser* (Philadelphia, Pennsylvania), January 28, 1800, 4.
22. "The Waltham Ghost," *Albany Argus* (Albany, New York), August 14, 1829.
23. "A Haunted House," *Newburyport Herald* (Newburyport, Massachusetts), September 21, 1837, 2.
24. "The Witch of Endor," *Alexandria Gazette* (Alexandria, Virginia), March 29, 1843, 2.
25. "New England Superstitions," *Sartain's Union Magazine of Literature and Art*, July 1851, 47.
26. James W. Cook, Jr., "From the Age of Reason to the Age of Barnum: The Great Automaton Chess-Player and the Emergence of Victorian Cultural Illusionism," *Winterthur Portfolio*, Vol. 30, No. 4 (Winter 1995), 231–57.
27. Stephen P. Rice, "Making Way for the Machine: Maelzel's Automaton Chess-Player and Antebellum American Culture," *Proceedings of the Massachusetts Historical Society*, Vol. 106 (1994), 1–16.
28. Edgar Allan Poe, "Maelzel's Chess-Player," *Southern Literary Messenger*, April 1836, 318.
29. Quoted in Cook, 252.

30. Matthew Goodman, *The Sun and the Moon: The Remarkable True Account of Hoaxers, Showmen, Dueling Journalists, and Lunar Man-Bats in Nineteenth-Century New York* (New York: Basic Books, 2010).
31. Kerry Driscoll, "The Fluid Identity of 'Petrified Man,'" *American Literary Realism*, Vol. 41, No. 3, 214–31.
32. For more information on this subject, see Michael Pettit, "'The Joy of Believing': The Cardiff Giant, Commercial Deceptions, and Styles of Observation in Gilded Age America," *Isis*, Vol. 97, No. 4 (December 2006), 659–77.
33. James W. Cook, "Introduction: The Architect of the Modern Culture Industry," in *The Colossal P. T. Barnum Reader*, edited by James W. Cook (Urbana, Illinois: University of Illinois Press, 2005), 6.
34. Neil Harris, *Humbug: The Art of P. T. Barnum* (Boston: Little, Brown & Company, 1973), 77.
35. Harris, 79.
36. James W. Cook, *The Arts of Deception: Playing with Fraud in the Age of Barnum* (Cambridge, MA: Harvard University Press, 2001), 5, 12, 17.
37. "Another Frankenstein," *The Times-Picayune* (New Orleans, Louisiana), June 6, 1839, 2.
38. "Hypnotism, Mesmerism, and the New Witchcraft," *The Literary World: A Monthly Review of Current Literature*, July 15, 1893, 225.
39. David Chapin, "The Fox Sisters and the Performance of Mystery," *New York History*, Vol. 81, No. 2 (April 2000), 157–88.
40. Ann Braude, *Radical Spirits: Spiritualism and Women's Rights in Nineteenth-Century America* (Boston: Beacon Press, 1989), 4.
41. Sas Mays and Neil Matheson, "Introduction: Technologies, Spiritualisms, and Modernities," in *The Machine and the Ghost: Technology and Spiritualism in Nineteenth- to Twenty-First-Century Art and Culture*, edited by Sas Mays and Neil Matheson (Manchester: Manchester University Press, 2013), 7.
42. Barbara Weisberg, *Talking to the Dead: Kate and Maggie Fox and the Rise of Spiritualism* (New York: HarperSanFrancisco, 2004), 241.
43. Ibid., 242.
44. Ibid., 256.
45. Mary S. Watts, "Ghost-Story Technique," *New York Times*, October 24, 1908, BR609.
46. "Horrors for November," *The New Monthly Magazine and Literary Journal*, July 1, 1824, 424.
47. "Original Essays: On the Decay of the Supernatural," *The New-York Mirror: A Weekly Gazette of Literature and the Fine Arts*, September 28, 1839, 108.
48. Sigmund Freud, *The Uncanny* (London: Penguin Classics, 2003); Noël Carroll, *The Philosophy of Horror, or Paradoxes of the Heart* (New York: Routledge, 1990); Lafcadio Hearn, "Gothic Horror," in *Shadowings* (Boston: Little, Brown & Company, 1905), 213–22; Stephen King, *Stephen King's Danse Macabre* (New York: Everest House, 1981).
49. Devendra P. Varma, *The Gothic Flame, Being a History of the Gothic Novel in England: Its Origins, Efflorescence, Disintegration, and Residuary Influences* (Metuchen, New Jersey: Scarecrow Press, 1988); Howard Phillips Lovecraft, *Supernatural Horror in Literature* (New York: Dover Publications, Inc., 1973).
50. Tzvetan Todorov, *The Fantastic: A Structural Approach to a Literary Genre* (Ithaca: Cornell University Press, 1975), 41–2.
51. Here I am referring to such novels as *The Mysteries of Udolpho* (1794).
52. Kenneth Silverman, *The Life and Times of Cotton Mather* (New York: HarperCollins, 1984).
53. Ben Brewster, "Periodization of Early Cinema," in *American Cinema's Transitional Era: Audiences, Institutions, Practices*, edited by Charlie Keil and Shelley Stamp (Berkeley: University of California Press, 2004), 74.

54. While I find it necessary to use the term "pre-nickelodeon" to designate the moving pictures produced before late 1905, I realize that it is a term not without its own problems, at least insofar as it implies teleology.
55. Tom Gunning, "'Now You See It, Now You Don't': The Temporality of the Cinema of Attractions," *Velvet Light Trap*, No. 32 (1993), 10–11.
56. Richard Abel, *The Red Rooster Scare: Making Cinema American, 1900–1910* (Berkeley: University of California Press, 1999), xi.
57. Matthew Solomon, "Negotiating the Bounds of Transnational Cinema with Georges Méliès, 1896–1908," *Early Popular Visual Culture*, Vol. 14, No. 2 (May 2016), 155–67.
58. Ron Mottram, "The Great Northern Film Company: Nordisk Film in the American Motion Picture Market," *Film History*, Vol. 2, No. 1 (Winter 1988), 71.
59. Tom Gunning, "Non-Continuity, Continuity, and Discontinuity: A Theory of Genres in Early Films," in *Early Cinema: Space, Frame, Narrative*, edited by Thomas Elsaesser with Adam Barker (London: British Film Institute, 1990), 86.
60. Lincoln Geraghty and Mark Jancovich, "Introduction: Generic Canons," in *The Shifting Definitions of Genre: Essays on Labeling Films, Television Shows and Media*, edited by Lincoln Geraghty and Mark Jancovich (Jefferson: McFarland, 2008), 2.
61. Charles Musser, "The Travel Genre in 1903–1904: Moving Towards Fictional Narrative," in *Early Cinema: Space, Frame, Narrative*, edited by Thomas Elsaesser with Adam Barker (London: British Film Institute, 1990), 130.
62. Ibid., 131.
63. Ann Radcliffe, "On the Supernatural in Poetry," *The New Monthly Magazine*, No. 7 (1826), 145–52.
64. Rick Altman, *Film/Genre* (London: British Film Institute, 2003), 30.
65. Hanford C. Judson, "*The Secret Room*," *Moving Picture World*, February 20, 1915, 1146.
66. Thomas Elsaesser, "The New Film History," *Sight and Sound*, Vol. 55, No. 4 (Autumn 1986), 246–51.
67. Leonard Barkan, *Unearthing the Past: Archaeology and Aesthetics in the Making of Renaissance Culture* (New Haven: Yale University Press, 1999), 120.
68. Ibid., 124.
69. André Gaudreault, *Film and Attraction: From Kinematography to Cinema* (Champaign: University of Illinois Press, 2011), 32–3.
70. The titles and dates I give here are for the stage adaptations, not of the original literary works.
71. Altman, 36.
72. "Ghosts Were Plenty," *The Sunday Star* (Washington, D.C.), November 1, 1908, 2.
73. *Dennison's 1912 Bogie Book* (reprinted by Bramcost Publications in 2010), 22.
74. André Bazin, "The Myth of Total Cinema," in *What Is Cinema?*, Vol. 1, edited by Hugh Gray (Berkeley: University of California Press, 1967), 21.
75. Ibid., 124.
76. "The Voice of the Movie Fan," *Chicago Tribune*, January 10, 1932, 6.
77. Ian Thorne, *Frankenstein* (Mankato: Crestwood House, 1977), 30.

SECTION I

The Rise of Horror-themed Cinema

CHAPTER 1

Literature

> Trembling I write my dream, and recollect
> A fearful vision at the midnight hour;
> So late, Death o'er me spread his sable wings,
> Painted with fancies of malignant power!
>
> —Philip Freneau, *The House of Night* (1779)

Philip Freneau's graveyard poem, published in 1779 and then in revised form in 1786, features the famous verse, "I sing the horrors of the *House of Night*." Subsequent verses include "Of coffins, shrouds, and horrors of a tomb," "Of ghosts that nightly walk the church-yard o'er," and of "Spectres attending, in black weeds array'd." While it is difficult to pinpoint the precise origins of American Gothic literature, *The House of Night* is a likely candidate, predating the myriad novels and short stories that followed. "Born on the vaporous wings of a Stygian dew," the poem informs, with its progeny manifold.

In the American Gothic are the roots of American horror-themed literature, and with it an ongoing desire to explain or disavow the supernatural. "There has always been something in the air of America as fatal to superstition as the soil of Iceland is to snakes," Charles Leonard Moore wrote in 1915. "After Ponce de Leon's [sic] quest, and the witchfires of New England, there is hardly a gleam of the supernatural in our history."[1]

The action in Freneau's poem results from a dream, which became a common approach to invoking and simultaneously explaining the presence of the supernatural. In subsequent literature, enlightened American characters actively challenge the events and superstitions that they encounter. Consider, for example, Herman Melville's novella *Benito Cereno* (1855): "This poor fellow now, thought the pained American, is the victim of that sad superstition which associates goblins with the deserted body of man, as ghosts with an abandoned house. How unlike are we made!" In this case, Melville draws on a tradition of distancing the country from others with more primitive beliefs, a group that could include, depending on the literary work in question, everyone from Africans and Native Americans to the white Europeans who inhabit the "Old World."

More commonly, American writers chose to rationalize the supernatural as being the product of all-too-human trickery. In William Austin's *The Man with the Cloaks: A Vermont Legend* (1836), the narrator announces, "There was nothing supernatural in this; the body is often the plaything of the mind." The mental state of first-person narrators also became a particularly successful mechanism for writing about the supernatural while still explaining it. This approach would even act as a bridge for the transition from the American Gothic to American Realism during the nineteenth century.

That transition helped keep horror-themed literature vibrant, as well as varied, thus creating what Robert A. Wiggins has referred to as a "dark tradition," one that could frighten readers by employing a vast array of possible genres, settings, and characters. Many of these relied not on the supernatural, but instead on such subjects as pseudo-science, otherness, and—perhaps most popular of all—murder. For writers of short stories and dime novels, as well as of newspaper reports and allegedly nonfiction books, the subject of murder became an extremely prominent component of American horror, particularly during the nineteenth century, regardless of whether it appeared in the works of Edgar Allan Poe or in journalistic coverage of Lizzie Borden.[2]

By contrast, as American literature moved into the later nineteenth century, the supernatural increasingly provided the source for as much humor as it did horror, familiar tropes becoming the subject of laughter, even scorn. Mark Twain's *A Curious Dream: Containing a Moral* (1870) parodied the very kind of graveyard fiction that Freneau had treated seriously. The tale—which Vitagraph adapted into a moving picture in 1907—features a skeleton who complains that the living have neglected his cemetery.

Even then, as suggested by the title, Twain's story is nothing more than a "singular dream." It is a "vision," to use the same terminology Freneau had to describe *The House of Night* over 125 years earlier.

Early American Literature

David Punter has argued, "American Gothic is, as it were, a *refraction* of English: where English Gothic has a direct past to deal with, American had a level interposed between present and past, the level represented by a vague historical 'Europe,' an often already mythologized 'Old World.'"[3] William Hughes clarifies, "As a national Gothic literature, American Gothic is simultaneously dependent upon and wholly distinct from the English tradition that influenced so many of its earliest practitioners."[4] Put another way, American writers used the English as a reference point to imitate or, in the more memorable cases, to differentiate their work.

Importantly, it should be said that American readers of the period were familiar with the British Gothic. Horace Walpole's *The Castle of Otranto* (1765) inaugurated the Gothic novel; some Americans knew it quite well. In 1825, for example, an American magazine observed that Walpole's aim in *The Castle of Otranto* was the "art of exciting surprise and horror."[5] Among its various achievements was to initiate a tradition of Americans reading horror-themed literature written in other countries, but distributed in the United States.

In 1797, for example, the *American Universal Magazine* wrote of Matthew Gregory Lewis's Gothic novel *The Monk* (1796): "We have been induced to pay particular attention to this work, from the unusual success which it has experienced."[6] That success came in part because of the ghostly figure of "The Bleeding Nun," a woman who eschewed religion in favor of "unbridled debauchery," at least until she commits murder and is murdered in return. The character would prove enduring in American theatre and visual culture of the nineteenth century, as Chapters 2 and 3 will examine.

In the years that followed, Jane Austen's *Northanger Abbey* (1818) also appeared in America, as did many of the "horrid" novels its narrative describes. Charles Maturin's *Melmoth the Wanderer* (1820) was also published in the United States. Of the latter, the writer of one newspaper article in 1835 confessed, "This was among the first of the forbidden books which we ever read, and its descriptions have clung most fixedly to our minds ever since."[7]

Horror-themed short stories were also imported into the United States, including in the form of anthologies. In 1813, M. Carey of Philadelphia published Matthew Gregory Lewis's *Tales of Terror, with an Introductory Dialogue*.[8] It featured stories of ghosts, goblins, and sprites. Then, in 1833, Charles Gaylord of Boston published Henry St. Clair's collection *Tales of Terror, or the Mysteries of Magic*, a "selection of wonderful and supernatural stories, translated from the Chinese, Turkish, and German," among them *The Gored Huntsman, The Boarwolf, The Cavern of Death, The Mysterious Bell*, and *The Haunted Forest*.[9]

However, Ann Radcliffe's novel *The Mysteries of Udolpho* (1794) seems to have been the most influential on American writers, particularly in its narrative reliance on the explained supernatural.[10] In 1798, the *Farmer's Weekly Museum*, published in New Hampshire, observed:

> . . . a style of writing, claiming close affinity with the rude romance of the twelfth century, has been lately introduced; and great names and debauched Taste have given currency to the marvelous, the terrific and the gloomy. Lord Orford, more generally known perhaps, by the familiar name of Horace Walpole, was among the first of those, who, in the full blaze of the eighteenth century, chose to excite from the shades of gothic superstition the dreary phantoms of the cave & cloister. . . . But the example of Mrs. Radcliffe has seduced a tribe of minor authors, and old castles, sheeted ghosts, gliding light, and dark dungeons, described with intolerable prolixity, nauseate the judicious reader. . . . We have 'Haunted Caverns' and 'Haunted Priories.' We have 'Mysteries Elucidated' and Mysteries not Elucidated, together with Mysteries so mysterious that they can never be elucidated.[11]

The article concludes by remarking that Gothic novels were "not like our world." They were instead so much "moonshine and vapour [sic]."

In 1806, an unattributed American poem saluted Ann Radcliffe, "occasioned by reading in the newspapers an [inaccurate] account of her insanity." Verses include the following:

> —O Radcliffe, this at last thy fate,
> To sink to such a dreadful state!
> See the shudders, starts, and raves
> Of grinning ghosts and gaping graves,
> Of antique arms and haunted halls,
> Of tottering turrets, mouldering walls.[12]

By the time the poem appeared in print, Radcliffe's novels had been popular in the United States for over a decade. As one author noted of American readers in 1797, "the dairymaid and hired hand no longer weep over the ballad of the cruel stepmother, but amuse themselves into an agreeable terror with the haunted houses and hobgoblins of Mrs. Radcliffe."[13]

The two major writers in early American literature repeatedly rationalized the supernatural. In 1820, an article in *Blackwood's Edinburgh Magazine*—famous in part for publishing horror-themed fiction—announced, "[S]o far as we know, there are two American authors only, whose genius has reason to complain of British neglect—and with a very great deal of reason both may unquestionably do so—namely, Charles Brockden Brown and Washington Irving."[14]

Born in Philadelphia in 1771, Charles Brockden Brown became America's first great novelist. Unfortunately, horror studies have at times ignored his importance.[15] Nevertheless, he had a major impact, not only in America, but also on a number of British authors.[16] His canon includes *Ormond; or, The Secret Witness* (1799) and *Arthur Mervyn; or, The Memoirs of the Year 1793* (1799–1800), both of which are Gothic novels in which plagues and epidemics loom large.

For his first novel, *Wieland, or The Transformation* (1798), Brown drew upon a 1781 tragedy in which a New York farmer's religious delusion led him to kill his family.[17] Brown describes a family living in a mansion near Philadelphia. The character Theodore Wieland slaughters his relatives because he believes God has told him to do so. However, the voice he hears is apparently that of the all-too-human Carwin, a "biloquist" (ventriloquist) and an "imp of mischief." The following year, his novel *Edgar Huntly; or, Memoirs of a Sleep-Walker* (1799) features a title character whose somnambulism causes him to commit murder. When he awakens in a dark cavern, Huntly kills a panther before rescuing a white woman held prisoner by a Native American tribe.

Brown went so far as to decry "puerile superstition" in his preface to *Edgar Huntly*.[18] He also suggested that the American wilderness could substitute for the "Gothic castles and chimeras" of British novels.[19] Nature could serve as a haunted house for the new country. Perhaps Jeffrey Andrew Weinstock presents a more adept description when he suggests, "The birth of the American Gothic . . . must be considered as Brown's artistic transmogrification of a confluence of cultural forces in light of available literary templates."[20]

The American writer Washington Irving likewise drew inspiration from the British Gothic tradition, using his keen wit to satirize it. *The Sketch Book of Geoffrey Crayon, Gent.* (1819–20, aka *The Sketch Book*) includes thirty-four stories, among them *Rip Van Winkle*, in which the title character allegedly falls asleep for twenty years after drinking moonshine in the mountains. But as Benjamin Franklin Fisher IV has pointedly asked, "Did Rip really sleep in the mountains for years, or has he invented this weird account merely as a subterfuge for remaining away . . . for so long?"[21]

Two of the other best-known tales in *The Sketch Book* also eschew the supernatural accepted. *The Spectre Bridegroom* features a character pretending to be a ghost in order to win the favor of a woman. More famously, in *The Legend of Sleepy Hollow*, schoolmaster Ichabod Crane disappears from a New England town after being chased by the Headless Horseman. But Irving strongly implies that Crane's rival Brom Bones disguised himself as the mythical horseman, and that nothing supernatural has actually transpired. *The Legend of Sleepy Hollow* was "*fabulous* indeed," one journalist wrote in 1840.[22] Attesting to its popularity, another journalist asked in 1853, "Who has not read [it]?"[23]

Fisher observes that, "Irving's stories generally tie firmly to human psychology rather than to inexplicable phenomena."[24] On the rare occasions he did invoke the unexplained supernatural, Irving relied on humor, as in the case of *The Devil and Tom Walker* (1824). A notable exception was *The Adventure of a German Student* (1824). Its title character goes mad after apparently indulging in a night of lust with a "pallid and ghastly" female corpse. Here is a shocking tale told without any semblance of comedy, and yet it is not devoid of ambiguity, as Irving indicates early in the story that the character had dreamed of the female with whom he would eventually sleep, a dream that "produced an extraordinary effect upon him."

To be sure, some readers in America apparently preferred the kind of approach used in *The Adventure of a German Student*, or, for that matter, *The Monk*. In 1820, one critic condemned the explained supernatural as a:

> ... fault which so unfortunately spoils the longer tales for the second perusal—the excitement of curiosity to the greatest height by a succession of prodigies apparently supernatural and pregnant with terror; and then, the sedulous dissolution of the enchantment, by explaining away everything as produced by merely human and frivolous causes. When the reader looks back, after the catastrophe for which he has ardently panted, the enchantment, so marvellously raised, is gone for ever. He feels that an affront has been offered to his imagination, and that he has been cheated out of his terror by false pretenses.[25]

The same article proceeded to note that the reader is thus inclined to "regard the whole" of the novel or story as an "elaborate hoax."

American readers preferring inexplicable phenomena were able to sate their desire in part thanks to imported literature. In 1819, the American press excitedly spread news of the publication of Lord Byron's short story *The Vampyre, A Tale*.[26] The *Rhode Island American* warned readers in April of that year that, "It is said to be of a most horrifick [sic] nature."[27] Reviewing *The Vampyre* after copies arrived on American soil, the *Ladies' Literary Cabinet* dismissed it as being written:

> ... on the spur of the moment, as a catch-penny production, intended to replenish his Lordship's pocket, who has found travelling and the pleasures of Italy somewhat expensive. *The Vampyre* possesses no merit, unless it be meritorious to frighten young ladies out of their wits, and make them afraid to sleep alone; which, by the way, may produce the good effect of promoting matrimony.[28]

Despite some negative reviews, *The Vampyre* seems to have been an immediate success with American readers. Uriah Derrick D'Arcy quickly published a "burlesque" called *The Black Vampyre* in New York, the stated aim being to "ridicule" Byron's tale.[29] Then, in 1820, the American press divulged the shocking news that Lord Byron was not the author of *The Vampyre, A Tale*; it was actually written by Byron's travelling companion, a physician named John William Polidori.[30] The revelation only served to increase *The Vampyre's* publicity.

But Mary Shelley's novel *Frankenstein; or, the Modern Prometheus* (1818) became even more popular with American readers. A review in 1833 called the novel the "very quintessence of the horrible."[31] That same year, another American critic wrote:

> Frankenstein might well be taken to represent those rash individuals who, from having successfully explored a few of the most mysterious paths of knowledge, would carry their presumptuous ken through that veil which is at last interposed between the Creator and the creature.[32]

The novel depends on science as the source of its horror rather than ghosts or other supernatural creatures, though how much that fact had to do with its widespread and ongoing popularity in America is difficult to determine.

At any rate, "Frankenstein" even became a recognizable term in the American press to speak about ideas that spawned outcomes perceived to be problematic, whether in the politics of slavery and abolition, or in the experiments of pseudo-scientists.[33] In 1875, for example, a man in California bled a woman so that he could "construct from it an exact counterpart of her." The press announced that police had arrested the new "Frankenstein" while he was "boiling blood in a kettle and mixing various chemicals with it."[34]

Antebellum Literature

During the decades immediately prior to the American Civil War, the amount of available literature increased dramatically. Many Americans read the tales written by the Irish immigrant Fitz-James O'Brien and also of the Irish-Greek Lafcadio Hearn, who lived part of his life in Cincinnati and New Orleans. The works of such authors as Charles Dickens, Charlotte Brontë, Emily Brontë, and Edward Bulwer-Lytton appeared in America, as did the works of the French writers Honoré de Balzac, Guy de Maupassant, and Jules Verne. This is to say nothing of German authors like Ludwig Tieck and E. T. A. Hoffmann, whose literature was not only known in America, but also became a major influence on various American writers. The panoply of literature and sources in this area was broad, and would have included folkloric traditions imported from numerous countries.

In terms of indigenous publications, a great deal of sensationalized literature described murders. To be sure, as Daniel A. Cohen has noted, American publications on murder and capital punishment date to the first half of the eighteenth century, when "gallows broadsides" printed the dying words of the condemned, as well as some details of their crimes. Then, in the early decades of the nineteenth century, murder trial reports in newspapers gained in popularity, as did biographies and autobiographies of criminals.[35]

As Karen Halttunen has shown in her landmark study *Murder Most Foul: The Killer and the American Imagination* (1998), the subject of murder in popular fiction and nonfiction literature grew dramatically after the 1820s, the result of many causes, including an escalation in literacy rates.[36] Reading became a cultural practice, with murder helping to lead the charge. According to Halttunen:

> This literature did not simply report "intense excitement"; it actively sought to stimulate it, intentionally sending a "thrill of horror" to readers' hearts. . . . Most important, murder literature after 1800 focused overwhelmingly on images of the body in pain and death. The primary technique of sensationalism was body-horror, the effort to arouse the readers' repugnance (and excitement) in the face of the physiological realities of violent death.[37]

Such popular murder literature, which constituted a "new pornography of pain and violence," represented something of a reaction to the changing views on death in the nineteenth century.[38] Halttunen adds, "Reading horror literature thus helped reinforce the rising levels of repression demanded by the growing humanitarian sanctions against violent impulses and actions."[39]

An emphasis on murder did not mean the era was devoid of supernatural tales. For example, Clarence Day's *Remarkable Apparitions, and Ghost Stories* was published in Philadelphia in 1842.[40] His purpose was to offer "authentic histories of communications" with the "unseen world," which included illustrated stories of "spectral warnings, haunted houses and places, extraordinary prophecies, aerial visions, etc." All that said, Day appropriately qualified matters on the title page by describing the stories as *either* "real or imaginary."

The stories were collected from "authentic sources," in other words, even if their contents were hardly authentic. A similar anthology, Carey and Hart's *Ghost Stories: Collected with a Particular View to Counteract the Vulgar Belief in Ghosts and Apparitions* (1846), ostensibly denied the supernatural while collecting tales about it.

The American Gothic novel continued as well, as is evident in George Lippard's very popular *The Quaker City; or, the Monks of Monk Hall: A Romance of Philadelphia Life, Mystery and Crime* (1844–5), with its dwarfish pimp Devilbug. More notable were the works of Herman Melville, author of *Moby-Dick; or, The Whale* (1851), who also wrote *Typee* (1846), which drew upon autobiography and imagination to explore such issues as cannibalism, and *Pierre; or, The Ambiguities* (1852), a Gothic novel informed by such subjects as magnetism and electricity.

But the leading exponents of the American Gothic were Edgar Allan Poe and Nathaniel Hawthorne. "Besides [James Fenimore] Cooper," a journalist for *Scribner's Monthly* wrote in 1876, "the names oftenest mentioned in allusions to imaginative prose writers of America are those of Poe, Irving, and Hawthorne." The same author proceeded to write, "We often hear Poe and Hawthorne classed together as 'weird' or 'grotesque' . . ."[41] The two writers were also contemporaries (Poe born in 1809, Hawthorne in 1804). Poe's publishing career began in 1827, Hawthorne's in 1828.

"We have heard him compared to Charles Brockden Brown," *Russell's Magazine* said in 1857, attempting to construct a historical lineage, "but the comparison does Poe injustice. Browne has the same direction, some of the same energy, but none of the peculiar power."[42] The *Christian Register* wrote of Poe in 1849, "In portraying the more passionate moods of the mind, especially as they appear when colored by superstition, by remorse, and by those vague sentiments which make men feel the near and mysterious presence of invisible agencies, he was unsurpassed."[43] In 1866, the *Pittsfield Sun* wrote, "His writings, though many of them objectionable from their too morbid tone, were never low nor vulgar, but always adapted to the highest intellects and the most refined tastes."[44] *Lippincott's Monthly Magazine* was more concise in 1912, calling him "The Poet of the Night."[45]

"Horror and fatality have been stalking abroad for all ages," Poe writes in *Metzengerstein* (1832), the short story constituting something of a "parody of the Gothic genre as a whole."[46] He later satirized the kind of horror-themed fiction associated with *Blackwood's Edinburgh Magazine* (published in Scotland) in his *How to Write a Blackwood Article* (1838). However, Poe does not fit neatly into the category of American Gothic. As Punter has suggested, "One of the many things which is remarkable about Poe is that he instantly upsets any such generalizations that one might go on to make about the American Gothic."[47]

What is clear is that Poe repeatedly generated horror without reliance on the supernatural, as can be seen in such short stories as *Berenice* (1835), *The Pit and the Pendulum* (1842), *The Tell-Tale Heart* (1843), *The Premature Burial* (1844), and *The Cask of Amontillado* (1846), as well as in such detective mysteries as *The Murders in the Rue Morgue* (1841), *The Mystery of Marie Rogêt* (1842), and *The Gold-Bug* (1843). Torture, murder, and madness mark many of his greatest works.

Poe did author a number of stories that invoke the supernatural. According to Alan Lloyd-Smith, "Supernatural is *suggested* in many of Poe's tales of terror, but it is rarely their essential point, and is frequently explained away by the protagonist's evident insanity."[48]

Thus the "phantasmagoric influences" in *The Tomb of Ligeia* (1838), in which the dead title character "once again stirred," might be nothing more than insane "visions." "Have I not indeed been living in a dream?," the narrator of *William Wilson* (1839) asks. At a given point in the story, the narrator of *The Fall of the House of Usher* (1839) experiences "what *must* have been a dream."[49] The narrator of *The Black Cat* (1845) "very surely" does not dream, he tells us, but does admit, "some intellect may be found which will reduce my phantasm to the common-place." And the narrator of *The Facts in the Case of M. Valdemar* (1845) begins his tale by speaking of a "garbled or exaggerated account" that "became the source of many unpleasant misrepresentations." He attempts to give the facts, but only so far as he can "comprehend" them, a qualification that makes the reader question their veracity. The unreliable narrator is thus a destabilizing yet controlling presence.

However different they were as authors, the ambiguity that appealed to Poe can also be found in the works of Nathaniel Hawthorne. In 1847, Poe condemned Hawthorne for not being "original in any sense," likening his work to that of Ludwig Tieck.[50] That same year, however, the *New Englander* published a very different opinion: "The works of Nathaniel Hawthorne place him, in our judgment, in the first rank of American authors, in the department of imaginative literature."[51]

Hawthorne—who remains best-known for his Gothic novels *The Scarlet Letter* (1850) and *The House of the Seven Gables* (1851)—changed his name from the original spelling "Hathorne," perhaps to obscure his family relation to John Hathorne, one of the notorious judges at the Salem witch trials of 1692 and 1693. Nevertheless, Hawthorne was repeatedly drawn to the subject of witchcraft, more than probably any other American author of the nineteenth century. The subject informed a number of his short stories, notably *The Hollow of the Three Hills* (1830), *The Haunted Quack* (1831), *Alice Doane's Appeal* (1835), and *Young Goodman Brown* (1835).

At times Hawthorne invoked the unexplained supernatural, though usually for the sake of humor. In *Graves and Goblins* (c. 1834), a ghost narrates the story. In *Feathertop, A Moralized Legend* (1852), a witch turns a scarecrow into a human and then back into a scarecrow. In other more famous cases, however, Hawthorne relied on the supernatural for metaphorical purposes. "We are ghosts!" Clifford Pyncheon says in *The House of the Seven Gables*, "We have no right among human beings,—no right anywhere but in this old house, which has a curse on it, and which, therefore, we are doomed to haunt!"

Hawthorne's work also rationalized the supernatural, including in its newfound guise of nineteenth-century pseudo-science. Consider Howard Kerr's analysis: "Despite his dislike of mesmerism, Hawthorne employed it profitably in *The House of the Seven Gables* (1851) and *The Blithedale Romance* (1852) as a source of the marvelous with both supernatural ambience and potentially rational explanation."[52] Kerr believes Hawthorne's skepticism of Spiritualism "took almost humorous initial form" in *The House of the Seven Gables*, and that he had "grown disgusted with spiritualism and mesmerism alike" by the time he wrote *The Blithedale Romance*.[53]

What E. Miller Budick has called the "paradoxes and ambiguities" of Hawthorne's work is apparent in some of his most fascinating short stories.[54] The "supernatural voice" of the dead man in *Roger Malvin's Burial* (1832) is "only audible" to the lead character, which makes the reader question whether it is actually the product of a disturbed mind. In *A Night Scene* (c. 1834), the narrator sees Irishmen who form a "picture which might have been transferred, almost unaltered, to a tale of the supernatural," but it cannot be, as the Irish only seem eerie due to the darkness. And in *The Hollow of the Three Hills* (1837), Hawthorne describes "those strange old times, when fantastic dreams and madmen's reveries were realized among the actual circumstances of life," an era distinct from the enlightened present.

In one of his most terrifying stories, *Young Goodman Brown* (1835), Hawthorne employs the narrative device of a dream, its usage not dissimilar to Freneau's in *The House of Night*. Goodman Brown ventures into the forest and stumbles upon the "grave and dark-clad company" of some of the most important townspeople at a witches' sabbath; they are the devil's acolytes, "quivering to-and-fro." As the tale concludes, Hawthorne asks, "Had Goodman Brown fallen asleep in the forest, and only dreamed a wild dream of a witch-meeting? Be it so, if you will. But, alas! it was a dream of evil omen for young Goodman Brown."

Post-bellum Literature

Donald A. Ringe has contended that, parallel to the rise of Spiritualism, American Gothic literature went into decline. He identifies the end of its "major phase" with the publication of Hawthorne's *The Marble Faun: or, The Romance of Monte Beni* in 1860.[55] The transition away from the Gothic to American Realism did not end horror-themed literature, however. To be sure, the period after the American Civil War saw a marked increase in the number and type of such publications.

As in previous eras, the horror-themed literature of other countries appeared in America, among them the works of such writers as Wilkie Collins, Oscar Wilde, Rudyard Kipling, Arthur Conan Doyle, Marie Corelli, Algernon Blackwood, and M. R. James (as opposed to, say, J. Sheridan Le Fanu, whose work was little known in America in the late nineteenth century). American readers also purchased the novels of H. G. Wells and Robert Louis Stevenson, both of whom—following on to an extent from Mary Shelley—relied on science fiction as the basis for horror. (As Chapters 2 and 13 will show, Stevenson's popular novella *Strange Case of Dr. Jekyll and Mr. Hyde* [1886] found even greater success in America when adapted for the stage and the cinema.)

An array of American authors also wrote horror-themed literature, which was more varied in subject matter and approach than ever before. In the latter decades of the nineteenth century, readers continued to fall prey to what Michael Ayers Trotti has called the "lure of the sensational murder."[56] Speaking of "The Murder Mania," one magazine claimed in 1874, "The carnival of crime continues, and hardly a day passes in which our ears are not pained with the sickening details of some horrible murder. . . . Not less than a dozen murders or trials for murders have occupied the papers within the past week."[57]

American reportage of Jack the Ripper would be one example, but there was no shortage of indigenous murders, ranging from the famous case involving Lizzie Borden to the Bender Family (who murdered at least ten people in Kansas between 1870 and 1873), the Kelly Family (who killed approximately eleven persons during the last four months of 1887), Belle Gunness (who killed between twenty-five and forty persons during the years 1884 to 1908), and Jane Toppan (who confessed to committing thirty-one murders between 1885 and 1901).[58] All of these received extensive press coverage.

Despite the mania for murder, the ghost story continued in various guises. Gertrude Atherton and Robert W. Chambers often relied on ambiguity in their ghost stories, whereas Mary E. Wilkins (aka Mary Wilkins Freeman) unabashedly used the unexplained supernatural in such dramatic tales as *The Vacant Lot* (1903) and *The Southwest Chamber* (1903). As Susan Oaks has written, "Freeman's ghosts . . . plant seeds of self-doubt in the protagonists because they distort conventional physical experience."[59] J. K. Bangs and Frank R. Stockton wrote about real ghosts as well, but—like Mark Twain before them—did so for the sake of humor.

Edith Wharton also authored several well-received ghost stories. As *Gunton's Magazine* of 1903 observed, "The stranger psychology of humanity has for Mrs. Wharton the fascination it possessed for Hawthorne."[60] A critic in the *New York Times* called her story *The Lady's Maid's Bell* (1904), "A ghost story fit to rank with the best of those recently recalled."[61] Among her other notable tales were *The Eyes* (1910) and *Afterward* (1910). As Janet Beer and Avril Horner have observed, Wharton's stories "shift into a parodic and humorous strain that enables her to engage self-reflexivity with the Gothic tradition."[62]

Of all the American authors who wrote horror-themed literature, however, two became particularly prominent during the late nineteenth century. One of them was Ambrose Bierce, the famous journalist and satirist. "It is not too much to say that within his own chosen field—the grim, uncompromising horror story, whether actual or supernatural—he stands among American writers second only to Edgar Allan Poe."[63] So said *The Bookman* in 1911. That same year, responding to the publication of Bierce's collected works, the *New York Times* wrote, "Mr. Bierce's ingenuity in devising blood-curdling situations is equaled only by his skill in squeezing from them the utmost in grim and sickening detail."[64] Many of these "situations" featured natural and psychological horrors, as exemplified by such Civil War stories as *Chickamauga* (1890) and *An Occurrence at Owl Creek Bridge* (1890).

In 1915, not long after Bierce's mysterious disappearance, one magazine reflected, "He originated a kind of occult cult, and it is in the psychic phenomena that he made some of his most daring and interesting excursions."[65] It is true that supernatural agency surfaces in a number of his tales, most notably perhaps in *The Middle Toe of the Right Foot* (1890) and *The Moonlit Road* (1907). More often Bierce, though, invoked the supernatural ambiguously; *Can Such Things Be?* asks the title of his 1893 short story collection. Ambiguity marks such stories as *The Spook House* (1889), *The Death of Halpin Frayser* (1891), and *The Damned Thing* (1893). *The Night-Doings at "Deadman's"* (1874, aka *The Strange Night-Doings at Deadman's*) features the subtitle *A Story that is Untrue*. And *The Famous Gilson Bequest* (1878) concludes with the narrator groping for explanations: "Perhaps it was a phantasm of a disordered mind in a fevered body. Perhaps it was a solemn farce enacted by pranking existences that throng the shadows lying along the border of another world."

Along with Bierce, the key American writer of horror-themed literature in the late nineteenth century was Henry James, even though Martha Banta has identified only eight James stories "in which apparitions appear or are thought to appear."[66] Among them is *The Ghostly Rental* (1876), in which a female character impersonates a ghost, thus providing yet another important example of the explained supernatural in American literature.

James's most famous work in the area is his novella *The Turn of the Screw*, published in 1898 in the book *The Two Magics*. In 1903, *The Independent* praised it as being "perhaps the most awful ghost story ever written in America," proof that the "power of writing ghost stories was not confined to the romanticists; that the realist, by his arduous training in portraying facts as they are, had a certain advantage when he advanced into the spiritual world."[67] Considering this realist advantage, Peter G. Beidler has written, "It is almost as if Henry James wrote two stories," one being a "thrilling narrative about evil ghosts" and the second "makes the story a thrilling psychological study of a deluded governess."[68] In 1899, the *New York Times* published one reader's letter on this very subject:

> There is not a word or a line in the book to show that the author assumed, or wanted his readers to assume, that the spirits of Peter Quint and Miss Jessel haunted the old house and its grounds. There is not one act performed or word spoken to indicate that the children saw or communed with ghosts. The teacher simply misconstrued the perfectly natural conduct of her charge and forced it into harmony with her own subjective experiences.[69]

How many readers of the era interpreted the novel in the same way is difficult to determine, but the following year a critic for *The Bookman* covered similar ground. He noted that the distinguishing feature of the "horror story of to-day from the horror story of the past" was its ability to use realism to create ambiguity, to make it difficult to comprehend "where the commonplace and the probable ends and the impossible and the supernatural begins."[70]

If ambiguity became the crowning achievement of horror-themed literature in the second half of the nineteenth century, influenced as it was by Poe's earlier usage of the same, the sheer number of publications hardly meant that the explained and unexplained supernatural no longer had their adherents. Consider the supernatural vampire. Bram Stoker's novel *Dracula* (1897) became a success when it was published in America in 1899, despite critics who condemned it. The *Chicago Tribune*, for example, claimed the novel did not possess a single "redeeming trait."[71]

Whether or not one valued Stoker's tale, it was dramatically different than the first American vampire novel. In Hawley Smart's dime novel *The Vampire; Or, Detective Brand's Greatest Case* (1885), murder victims have two punctures on their neck, which leads to the fear that a vampire is on the loose, one "who leads an artificial life—who lives on the blood he extracts from his victims—that he sucks from their very veins, drawing the red life-current directly from the heart."

But the solution to the mystery rationalizes the supernatural. As the murderer confesses, "My particular craze, when the fit came on, was to believe I was a vampire, one of those fabulous creatures who lives on human blood. I slew my victims, and then I pricked them in the neck with the dagger point, just as if the vampire's teeth had bitten them." Here was murder and insanity, much closer in the end to the worlds of Charles Brockden Brown and Edgar Allan Poe than to that explored by Bram Stoker.

Conclusion

Brian Stableford has asserted that, by the 1890s, despite the successes of writers like Bierce and James, the "American weird tale was already earmarked for the pulp ghetto."[72] In many respects, this seems to be true. A literary analysis published in 1899 claimed, "ghosts and spooks walk and crowd the pages of literature now; they squeak and gibber in the uncut magazines."[73] But most of them hardly had the imprimatur of prestigious publishers and important authors.

The popularity of dime novels like Hawley's *The Vampire* continued until roughly 1910.[74] Occasionally one of them used the unexplained supernatural, as in the case of *The Haunted Churchyard; Or, Old King Brady, the Detective, and the Mystery of the Iron Vault* (1890).[75] Most of the time, however, they relied on the natural horrors of mysteries, murders, and massacres. In this respect, they followed in the tradition of such murder literature as Charles Wesley Alexander's *The Five Fiends, Or, The Bender Hotel Horror in Kansas* (1874) and Goldsmith B. West's *The Hawes Horror and Bloody Riot at Birmingham* (1888), as well as of the aforementioned newspaper reportage. "It is a tradition of journalism that nothing sells papers like a murder," *Life* magazine declared in 1910.[76]

Whatever merits the new literature possessed or lacked, some Americans continued to read the horror-themed fiction of earlier years. During the space of over two months in the spring of 1904, the *New York Times* published letters from readers from California, Connecticut, Kentucky, New Hampshire, New York, and Washington, D.C., all attempting to chronicle and debate the best "tales of terror." The titles they listed ranged from Dante's *Inferno* to Stoker's *Dracula*. Collectively, they discussed Brockden Brown and Irving, Poe and Hawthorne, Bierce and James, as well as the writers of other countries, among them Radcliffe, Polidori, Bulwer Lytton, Stevenson, and Conan Doyle.[77]

How representative these readers were is difficult to say, but they do suggest that at least some Americans of the time were familiar with the lengthy and international history of horror-themed literature. To an extent, this also seems apparent in an American newspaper advertisement for Gaston Leroux's novel *The Phantom of the Opera* in 1911. In an effort to describe the novel, the ad mentioned Poe and Maupassant as comparators.[78]

In addition to continued readership for old works, American publishers released new horror-themed literature, some not of the "pulp ghetto" variety. Consider F. Marion Crawford; in 1910, the *New York Times* called his tale *The Upper Berth* (1885) "the best ghost story ever written."[79] In 1911, two years after his death, Crawford's collected short stories appeared in the popular book *Wandering Ghosts*, which included, along with *The Upper Berth*, *The Dead Smile* (1899), *For the Blood Is the Life* (1905), and *The Screaming Skull* (1908).

However, American literature in the early years of the twentieth century culminated more with Mary Roberts Rinehart than it did with Crawford, at least insofar as her influence is concerned. Rinehart's most successful novel was *The Circular Staircase* (1908), in which the "Sunnyside ghost" *seems* to walk in an old home. But as in Radcliffe's *The Mysteries of Udolpho*, the novel relies on the explained supernatural (though by the twentieth century the storyline would be classified as a mystery rather than as a Gothic novel).[80] There is no supernatural creature, just a rather ordinary human murderer. The novel, as well as Rinehart and Avery Hopwood's loose Broadway stage adaptation of it as *The Bat* (1920), helped forge the "Old Dark House" genre, in which a creepy old mansion serves as the setting for the explained supernatural. Murder mania with only the trappings of the spectral.

The rational had largely triumphed, so much so that in 1913 a critic made the following plea:

> Wanted—a ghost story: a romance in which the spectre is a real one. . . . The advertiser thus requests because she is weary of the ghost that ultimately proves to be an escaped maniac, a wandering baboon, or a six-year-old masquerading in her aunt's dress.[81]

Notes

1. Charles Leonard Moore, "The Supernatural in Literature," in *Incense and Iconoclasm* (New York: G. P. Putnam's Sons, 1915), 29. The text does refer specifically to "Iceland," though it is possible this was a typographical error and Moore intended to write "Ireland."
2. Karen Halttunen, *Murder Most Foul: The Killer and the American Gothic Imagination* (Cambridge, MA: Harvard University Press, 1998).
3. David Punter, *The Literature of Terror: A History of Gothic Fictions from 1765 to the Present Day, Volume 1: The Gothic Tradition* (London: Longman Group Limited, 1996), 165. Emphasis in original.
4. William Hughes, *Historical Dictionary of Gothic Literature* (Lanham: Scarecrow Press, 2013), 24.
5. Sir Walter Scott, "Life and Character of Walpole," *The Museum of Foreign Literature, Science, and Art*, April 1, 1825, 1.
6. "The Following is a Critic on a Late Much Admired Novel, by M. G. Lewis, Esq. M.P.," *American Universal Magazine*, December 5, 1797, 53.
7. "*Melmoth the Wanderer*," *Baltimore Gazette and Daily Advertiser*, March 27, 1835, 2.
8. Matthew Gregory Lewis, *Tales of Terror, with an Introductory Prologue* (Philadelphia: M. Carey, 1813).
9. Henry St. Clair, editor, *Tales of Terror, or the Mysteries of Magic* (Boston: Charles Gaylord, 1833).
10. Oral Sumner Coad makes this point in "The Gothic Element in American Literature before 1835," *The Journal of English and Germanic Philology*, Vol. 24, No. 1 (January 1925), 79.
11. Reprinted in "Misceleaneous [sic]," *Impartial Herald* (Suffield, Connecticut), September 18, 1798, 4.
12. "Mrs. Radcliffe: *The Wreck of Reason*," *The Polyanthos*, February 1, 1807, 160. The preface to the poem indicates that it had been first published in 1806.
13. Quoted in Richard Davenport-Hines, 272.
14. "On the Writings of Charles Brockden Brown and Washington Iriving," *Blackwood's Edinburgh Magazine*, February 1820, 554. This article was republished in America as "American Writers," *The Atheneum*, May 1, 1820, 124.
15. For example, Walter Kendrick makes no mention of Brown in *The Thrill of Fear: 250 Years of Scary Entertainment* (New York: Grove Press, 1991), nor does Jason Colavito in *Knowing Fear: Science, Knowledge, and the Development of the Horror Genre* (Jefferson: McFarland, 2008).
16. Punter, 166.
17. Emory Elliott, "Introduction," in *Wieland and Memoirs of Carwin the Biloquist*, by Charles Brockden Brown (Oxford: Oxford University Press, 2009), xvi.
18. Charles Brockden Brown, *Edgar Huntly; or, Memoirs of a Sleep-Walker* (New York: Penguin Books, 1998), 3.
19. Ibid., 3.
20. Jeffrey Andrew Weinstock, "Gothic and the New American Republic, 1770–1800," in *The Gothic World*, edited by Glennis Byron and Dale Townshend (New York: Routledge, 2014), 27.

21. Benjamin Franklin Fisher IV, "Washington Irving," in *Supernatural Fiction Writers: Fantasy and Horror, Volume 2*, edited by E. F. Bleiler (New York: Charles Scribner's Sons, 1985).
22. Untitled, *The Knickerbocker; or New York Monthly Magazine*, August 1840, 185.
23. "The Old Dutch Church of 'Sleepy Hollow,'" *Gleason's Pictorial Drawing-Room Companion*, January 8, 1853, 17.
24. Fisher, 690.
25. "Female Literature of the Present Age," *The Atheneum*, May 15, 1820, 235.
26. This story appeared in the *Philadelphia Union*, and was then reprinted in the *Rhode Island American* (Providence, Rhode Island) on June 25, 1819.
27. Untitled, *Rhode Island American*, April 27, 1819.
28. "Literary," *The Ladies' Literary Cabinet*, Vol. 1, No. 5 (June 12, 1819).
29. Untitled, *The Village Record* (West Chester, Pennsylvania), September 18, 1819.
30. "Lord Byron," *St. Louis Enquirer*, September 4, 1820. Many other American newspapers published this same item.
31. "*Frankenstein, or the Modern Prometheus*," *Charleston Courier* (Charleston, South Carolina), June 1, 1833, 2.
32. "Review of the Week," *New York American*, May 25, 1833, 2.
33. For example, see "Sensation Journalism—The Frankenstein of Abolition," *New York Herald*, November 7, 1859, 6.
34. "Another Frankenstein," *Cincinnati Daily Times* (Cincinnati, Ohio), June 30, 1875, 3.
35. Daniel A. Cohen, "Blood Will Out: Sensationalism, Horror, and the Roots of American Crime Literature," in *Mortal Remains: Death in Early America*, edited by Nancy Isenberg and Andrew Burstein (Philadelphia: University of Pennsylvania Press, 2003), 54.
36. Halttunen, 36, 69.
37. Ibid., 73.
38. Ibid., 83.
39. Ibid., 82.
40. Clarence Day, *Remarkable Apparitions, and Ghost Stories* (Philadelphia: T. B. Peterson, 1848).
41. "Poe, Irving, and Hawthorne," *Scribner's Monthly*, April 1876, 799.
42. "Edgar A. Poe," *Russell's Magazine*, November 1857, 161.
43. "Edgar A. Poe," *Christian Register*, November 3, 1849, 176.
44. Frank Foxcroft, "Edgar Allan Poe: A Critical Sketch," *Pittsfield Sun* (Pittsfield, Massachusetts), November 8, 1866, 1.
45. La Salle Corbell Pickett, "The Poet of the Night," *Lippincott's Monthly Magazine*, September 1912, 326.
46. Alan Brown, "The Gothic Movement," in *Edgar Allan Poe in Context*, edited by Kevin J. Hayes (Cambridge: Cambridge University Press, 2013), 244.
47. Punter, 176.
48. Alan Lloyd-Smith, *American Gothic Fiction: An Introduction* (New York: Continuum, 2004), 47. Emphasis in original.
49. Italics appear in the original.
50. Edgar A. Poe, "Tale-Writing—Nathaniel Hawthorne," *Godey's Magazine and Lady's Book*, November 1847, 252.
51. "Nathaniel Hawthorne," *New Englander*, January 1847, 56.
52. Howard Kerr, "'Ghosts and Ghost-Seeing': Spiritualism in American Occult Fiction," in *Literature of the Occult: A Collection of Critical Essays*, edited by Peter B. Messent (Englewood Cliffs: Prentice-Hall, Inc., 1981), 79.
53. Ibid., 80, 81.

54. E. Miller Budick, "The World as Specter: Hawthorne's Historical Art," *PMLA*, Vol. 101, No. 2 (March 1986), 218.
55. Donald A. Ringe, *American Gothic: Imagination and Reason in Nineteenth-Century Fiction* (Lexington: University Press of Kentucky, 1982), 177, 182.
56. Michael Ayers, "The Lure of the Sensational Murder," *Journal of Social History*, Vol. 35, No. 2 (2001), 429–43.
57. "The Murder Mania," *Maine Farmer*, June 21, 1873, 2.
58. See, for example: Janet L. Langlois, *Belle Gunness: The Lady Bluebeard* (Indiana University Press, 1985); Harold Schechter, *Fatal: The Poisonous Life of a Female Serial Killer* (New York: Pocket Books, 2003); Dick C. Gibson, *Serial Killing for Profit: Multiple Murder for Money* (Westport, Connecticut: Praeger, 2009); Joseph A. Conforti, *Lizzie Borden on Trial: Murder, Ethnicity, and Gender* (Lawrence: University Press of Kansas, 2015).
59. Susan Oaks, *Colby Literary Quarterly*, Vol. 21, No. 4 (December 1985), 212.
60. Anna McClure Sholl, "The Work of Edith Wharton," *Gunton's Magazine*, November 1903, 426.
61. "Topics of the Week," *New York Times*, May 21, 1904, BR337.
62. Janet Beer and Avril Horner, "'This Isn't Exactly a Ghost Story': Edith Wharton and Parodic Gothic," *Journal of American Studies*, Vol. 37, No. 2 (August 2003), 270.
63. Frederic Taber Cooper, "Ambrose Bierce: An Appraisal," *The Bookman: A Review of Books and Life*, July 1911, 471.
64. "The Works of Ambrose Bierce," *New York Times*, February 26, 1911, BR110.
65. H. M. East, Jr., "Bierce—The Warrior Writer," *Overland Monthly and Out West Magazine*, June 1915.
66. Quoted in Edward Wagenknecht, *Seven Masters of Supernatural Fiction* (New York: Greenwood Press, 1991), 25.
67. Review, *The Independent*, May 21, 1903, 1212. The quotation in the main text deserves clarification, as Henry James did not actually write *The Turn of the Screw* in America, but rather in England.
68. Peter G. Beidler, *Ghosts, Demons, and Henry James: The Turn of the Screw at the Turn of the Century* (Columbia: University of Missouri Press, 1989), 1.
69. "Topics of the Times," *New York Times*, January 30, 1889, 6.
70. "Chronicle and Comment," *The Bookman*, November 1900, 216.
71. "Three Faulty Novels," *Chicago Tribune*, November 30, 1899, 17.
72. Brian Stableford, "The Later Gothic Tradition, 1825–96," *Horror Literature: A Reader's Guide*, edited by Neil Barron (New York: Garland Publishing, Inc., 1990), 67.
73. Elizabeth Mc L. Rowland, "The Spook in Current Literature," *Congregationalist*, March 16, 1899, 378.
74. E. F. Bleiler, "Introduction," *Eight Dime Novels*, edited by E. F. Bleiler (New York: Dover Publications, 1974), vii.
75. Ibid., x.
76. "Murder Stories," *Life*, August 18, 1910, 262.
77. "Ghost Stories," *New York Times*, March 26, 1904, BR202; F. C. W., "Henry James's Ghost Story," *New York Times*, April 2, 1904, BR228; Henry Llewellyn Williams, Untitled Letter to the Editor, *New York Times*, April 16, 1904, BR268; Roy M. Grover, Untitled Letter to the Editor, *New York Times*, April 23, 1904, BR282; El Soltero, Julius Chambers, "Tales of Terror," *New York Times*, April 30, 1904, BR300; E. C. Ranck, "Tales of Terror," *New York Times*, April 30, 1904, BR300; N. A. Parker, Untitled Letter to the Editor, *New York Times*, May 7, 1904, BR315; H. H., "Ghost Stories," *New York Times*, May 21, 1904, BR346; "Debates in Progress," *New York Times*, May 28, 1904, BR363.

78. Advertisement, *New York Times*, February 11, 1911, 9.
79. "*The Upper Berth*," *New York Times*, April 8, 1910, 8.
80. Carolyn Wells, *Technique of the Mystery Story* (Springfield: The Home Correspondence School, 1913), 169.
81. M. H. Menaugh, "Bookish Chats, No. IX—The Ghost in Fiction," *Colman's Rural World*, January 16, 1913, 10.

CHAPTER 2

Theatre

> Out—out are the lights—out all!
> And, over each dying form,
> The curtain, a funeral pall,
> Comes down with the rush of a storm,
> And the seraphs, all haggard and wan,
> Uprising, unveiling, affirm
> That the play is the tragedy "Man,"
> Its hero the Conqueror Worm.
> —Edgar Allan Poe, *The Conqueror Worm* (1843)

Poe's poem memorably describes the "motley drama" of life, with "horror" being at the very "soul of the plot." Here is a darker version of Shakespeare's *As You Like It*: "All the world's a stage, and all the men and women merely players." And during the seventeenth, eighteenth, and nineteenth centuries, the spectacle of the world stage was replete with horror. Americans witnessed the theatre of war and murder, death and destruction, poverty and famine. To be alive was to be a spectator and participant at what Poe called the "play of hopes and fears, while the orchestra breathes fitfully the music of the spheres."

Theatricality was very definitely a component of the Salem witch trials. "You seem to *act* witchcraft before us," Judge Hathorne said at court to Bridget Bishop, who became the first woman executed for that crime in 1692. Indeed, the phrase "to act witchcraft" appears in the transcripts on a number of occasions. To be in league with the devil was a performative role, one suggestive of what Robin DeRosa has described as a "blasphemous tendency towards ornamentation, duplicity, and inconstancy."[2]

Long after the witch trials, many Americans continued to bear witness to the supernatural, or at least believed that they did. A great many towns and cities had allegedly haunted houses, some with noticeable activity caused by human pranksters.[3] Other Americans attended the "theatre of trance" as performed by Spiritualists, hoping to view ghostly manifestations. Sometimes they were enraptured; sometimes they were not. In 1892, the *Los Angeles Times* reported:

> The guests of the Argyle are not happy over a spook show that was given in that house night before last by a Mrs. Graham. The spook sharp only charged them 50 cents a head, and she probably gave them their money's worth, but they did not see as many spirits as they expected to see and they are not satisfied.[4]

As Bridget Bennett has written, the Spiritualistic performances were partly "efficacious rituals," but partly "theatrical entertainment" of a type that could elicit various responses from participants.[5]

Audience participation could assume various forms at different kinds of motley dramas. One might have read of a nonfiction event or place, such as the Black Museum-style "cabinet of horrors" housed at the Washington, D.C. police department in the late nineteenth century, and simply had to have *imagined* what it was really like.[6] Or one might have attended a waxworks to see and hear about the figures on display—even touch one of them while no one was looking. Waxwork exhibitions appeared in America at least as early as 1798.[7] During the late nineteenth century, "Chamber of Horrors" waxwork exhibits grew in popularity at dime museums (institutions that will be discussed in Chapters 3 and 10), as well as in touring shows, one of the most notable being "Mrs. Jarley's."[8] In addition to tyrants and murderers and executions, these waxworks sometimes included elaborate exhibits of the "Infernal Regions."[9] As Andrea Stulman Dennett notes, such displays focused not on narrative, expecting as they did visitors to know the "rudiments of the event depicted before them," but instead on the attraction, the moment of horror.[10]

However, most displays of horror-themed entertainment in America occurred at theatres, whether in the form of legitimate plays or in variety shows and, later, in vaudeville sketches. For some, the theatre was inherently evil. In 1794, the President of Yale University suggested that attending plays could be a risk to one's "immortal soul."[11] As the *New York Evangelist* noted in 1845:

> Few who enter [the theatre] dream of the dangers which lurk in their path. Could they beforehand see the hidden snares and pit-falls into which many plunge and are lost forever, they would shrink back with horror as from the mouth of hell. Many who enter this gateway never return as they entered. They cannot. Their minds have received injuries which will never be repaired.[12]

The publication specifically warned parents against subjecting their innocent children to the theatre's "poisonous" influence.

Other Americans not only embraced the theatre, but also the specific horrors it offered. In 1825, one American journalist wrote, "There is nothing which strikes a person of quiet habits, yet strong and easily-excited feelings, as more extraordinary than the desire so many people evince of curdling their blood with horror, by running to see the new opera."[13] Two decades later, another writer described a performance of *The Devil and Dr. Faustus* as follows:

> Serpents spouted fire—grinning hydras spouted back at them, some invisible power suspended Faustus by the heels in the centre of the stage, and showers of flame appeared to circle round him, while over all the fiend in dreadful state presided.

The review added, "Yell after yell from the audience attested to their satisfaction of the horror, as the folds of the vast curtain hid the fiends and their victim from view."[14]

Exactly when the American theatre first presented a horror-themed play is difficult to determine. In 1736, students at William and Mary College in Virginia staged Joseph Addison's *The Drummer, or the Haunted House*.[15] The spoken prologue promised:

> Tho' with a Ghost our Comedy be heighten'd,
> Ladies upon my Word you shan't be frighten'd;
> O, 'tis a Ghost that scorns to be uncivil,

A well-spread, lusty, Jointure-hunting Devil;
An Am'rous Ghost, that' faithful, fond and true,
Made up of Flesh and Blood—as much as you.
Then every Evening comes in Flocks, undaunted;
We never think this House is too much Haunted.

As a Boston newspaper noted, *The Drummer, or The Haunted House* was meant to "ridicule superstition" rather than to endorse it.[16] It was staged on numerous other occasions in America in the eighteenth century, including in Philadelphia in 1759 and New York in 1789.[17]

The drive to invoke the supernatural only to rationalize it away became a particularly common theme in the American theatre of the nineteenth century. For example, James Nelson Barker's play *The Tragedy of Superstition* (aka *Superstition* and *Superstition; or, The Fanatic Father*), first performed in Philadelphia in 1824, features a character who confidently announces, "The powers of darkness are at work among us." However, the supernatural is not at play. Instead, the real dangers are superstition and zealotry. Barker's play was clearly inspired by the Salem witch trials, though it positioned the accuser, rather than the accused, in the role of the villain.

All that said, the horror-themed theatre of America was multi-faceted during the eighteenth and nineteenth centuries, more so perhaps than the country's literature. While many plays either exposed the supernatural as a fake or avoided the subject altogether, opting instead for mad scientists and other types of melodramatic villains, the influx of European plays meant that a few of the most popular stage successes portrayed the supernatural without qualification. Here then is a complicated interplay between different approaches to horror theatre, one that became all the more complex with the rise of venues like vaudeville and new forms of special effects and stage equipment during the nineteenth century.

Gothic Plays

The development of horror-themed plays in the eighteenth century seems to have been relatively slow and fragmented. In 1762, the New-Theatre in New York presented a "pantomime entertainment in Grotesque Characters" entitled *Harlequin Collector: Or, The Miller Deceiv'd*, which "introduc'd the celebrated Skeleton Scene."[18] *Fanny the Fantom, or The Cock Lane Ghost* appeared at the Southwark Theatre in Philadelphia in 1769.[19] Three years later, the theatre in Williamsburg, Virginia advertised that Peter Gardiner's "curious set of [puppets]" would "appear on the stage as if alive" to perform a tragedy entitled *Bateman and His Ghost*.[20] Then, in 1791, a theatre in New Jersey staged a two-act "dramatic piece" entitled *The Morris-Town Ghost; or the Force of Credulity*.[21]

Following from *The Drummer, or the Haunted House*, at least a few of the plays in this era were horror-themed comedies. In 1782, the New Theatre in Baltimore offered a "farce called *The Ghost*."[22] The two-act production—which was sometimes referred to as *The Ghost, or the Dead Alive* and *The Ghost, or the Dead Man Alive*—became "much admired," at least according to an advertisement in Savannah in 1800.[23] It was staged as late as 1833.[24] Then, in 1837, Wallack's Theatre in New York mounted the "popular farce" of *My Husband's Ghost*.[25]

However, more than any other genre, Gothic literature informed the horror-themed play. M. Susan Anthony suggests that Gothic plays first appeared in the United States in approximately 1794, and, having created something of a "Gothic mania," became a movement until roughly 1830.[26] She writes:

> Gothic plays successfully negotiated the contradictions of the age by ostensibly instructing young men and women in appropriate moral behavior, while thrilling audiences with spectacular scenery, supernatural effects, and the opportunity to enjoy, albeit vicariously, serious transgressions of acceptable behavior.[27]

The popularity of these plays, particularly in such cities as New York, Boston, Philadelphia, and Charleston, proved important in establishing early American theatres economically, even though their content also provoked the ire of the clergy.[28]

Some Gothic plays in the United States originated with American authors, as in the case of John B. White's *The Mysteries of the Castle; or, The Victim of Revenge* (1806), but many were adaptations of British novels and plays.[29] In some cases, these adaptations Americanized the original dialogue, and increased references to religion while decreasing their allusions to sexuality.[30] For example, William Dunlap's play *Fontainville Abbey* (1795) contained no spectre, even though its English counterpart *Fontainville Forest* (1794) did. While Dunlap's version tried to feature (in the words of one of its characters) "Horror on horror heap'd," it still managed to rationally explain away all of its supernatural activity.[31] Here is an example of a common trend, as the American Gothic theatre relied on fewer supernatural effects than did the British.[32]

These plays also relied less on narrative suspense than on the spectacle of horror. Lighting was used, but only in simple respects, as theatres during this period relied on candlelight and, incrementally after 1816, gaslight.[33] As a result, delineation of daylight and nighttime scenes came far more from characters holding props like lanterns or torches than it did from stage lighting effects.[34] However, later plays in this cycle—such as Benjamin West's dramatization of Maturin's *Melmoth the Wanderer* (1823) and Richard Brinsley Peake's *Presumption, or the Fate of Frankenstein* (1823)—took advantage of technical advances to create "lurid lighting," including "green mediums or green fire burnt at the sides and back of the stage behind standards to give a supernatural tint to spectres . . ."[35]

Nevertheless, these productions regularly featured three-dimensional sets and carefully designed costumes. Background scenery often depicted potentially horrifying spaces, ranging from dank castles and decaying abbeys to hidden rooms and secret chambers. For example, the third act of Henry Siddons's *A Tale of Terror*, staged in Baltimore and Philadelphia in 1803, showcased "A Gloomy Dungeon among the Rocks—The Fortified Castle of Valdarno."[36] Such Gothic sets could also prompt dialogue that underscored their potential to horrify. "What dreadful place is this?", asks a frightened female character in Matthew Gregory Lewis's *One O'Clock! Or, The Knight and the Wood Daemon* (1811).[37]

Sound effects also became important in Gothic plays, including the repeated usage of thunder, lightning, and wind. Among the first to make use of music to heighten the mood was Thomas Holcroft's *A Tale of Mystery: A Melo-Drame* (1802, aka *A Tale of Mistery*), which was also the first play to be promoted as a melodrama. Its score—which played not only before and after character dialogue, but also under some of it—attempted to be "expressive of horror" and "expressive of terror."[38] Subsequent plays like James Robinson Planché's *The Vampyre; or The Bride of the Isles* (1820, aka *The Vampire; or, The Bride of the Isles*) also relied on music to achieve similar effects.

In terms of the number of times they were performed, George Colman the Younger's *The Iron Chest; or, The Mysterious Murder* (1796), based upon William Godwin's 1794 novel *Things as They Are; or The Adventures of Caleb Williams*, Charles Maturin's *Bertram; or, The Castle of St. Aldobrand* (1816), and Holcroft's *A Tale of Mystery* became a few of the more successful Gothic plays in America.[39] Benjamin West's dramatization of Maturin's *Melmoth the Wanderer*—staged in Baltimore in 1830, and Boston and New York in 1831—was one of the last.[40]

Not all of these plays invoked the supernatural. A study by Oral Sumner Coad estimated, "Approximately four-fifths of the [Gothic] plays written [in America before 1835] are free from actual supernaturalism, but gain their effect through setting and mysterious occurrences that arise from natural causes."[41] British plays of this type were also popular. A key example would be Peake's "Grand Romantic Melo Drama" of *Presumption, or The Fate of Frankenstein*, staged in New York for the first time on New Year's Day, 1825, with Mr. Simpson playing the title character and Mr. Jervis as his creation, the "Daemon."[42] Publicity noted that the play, a loose adaptation of Mary Shelley's novel, had earlier received "unbounded applause" in London.[43] One review praised Jervis for having portrayed the daemon in a "very superior manner."[44] *Presumption* then had a lengthy run in Boston from December 1828 to March 1829, with Mr. Bernard playing the title character and Mr. Andrews playing the "Demon."[45] A critic for *The New-England Galaxy and United States Literary Advertiser* informed readers it was, "with all its horrible ingredients (perhaps the more for them) very striking."[46]

More than any other author, the works of Matthew Gregory Lewis loomed large over the American Gothic theatre. *Raymond and Agnes; or The Bleeding Nun*, adapted from a tale in Lewis's 1796 novel *The Monk*, became one of the most enduring. To marry Raymond in spite of her family's wishes, Agnes dresses as the Bleeding Nun, an infamous ghost, to escape her family's castle. Raymond attempts to meet Agnes, but instead encounters the real Bleeding Nun. Lewis describes the event as follows:

> What a sight presented itself to my startled eyes! I beheld before me an animated Cor[p]se. Her countenance was long and haggard; Her cheeks and lips were bloodless; The paleness of death was spread over her features, and her eyeballs fixed stedfastly [sic] upon me were lustreless and hollow. I gazed upon the Spectre with horror too great to be described. My blood was frozen in my veins. I would have called for aid, but the sound expired ere it could pass my lips. My nerves were bound up in impotence, and I remained in the same attitude inanimate as a Statue.

The play became very popular in America, as well as infamous, given the tragic fires that occurred during performances in Richmond, Virginia in 1811 and in Philadelphia, Pennsylvania in 1854.[47] In 1805, sheet music entitled *The Bleeding Nun* made a song from the play available to the public.[48] A variation of the ghostly figure subsequently appeared in *The Forest of Rosenwald; or, The Bleeding Nun* (1821), staged in Washington, D.C. in 1834.[49]

But Lewis's five-act play *The Castle Spectre*—first performed in London in 1797—became the most popular of all his plays, and the second most often staged of any Gothic play in America.[50] Jeffrey N. Cox has called it the "quintessential Gothic drama."[51] In its narrative, the servants are "fully persuaded" that a ghost dressed in armor "parades the old towers and dreary halls which abound" in a "melancholy mansion" in medieval Wales. An ad for its run in Philadelphia in 1800 offered descriptions of its sets, which included a "superb Gothic Hall," a "Gothic Chamber," a "Gothic State Bed Chamber," a "distant view of Conway [sic] Castle by moon light," and a "Gloomy Subterranean Dungeon and Cavern."[52]

The play's most potentially frightening scene involved the "Ghost of Evelina," though her appearance serves to scare the real villain of the play, the Earl of Osmond, thus giving the much-abused Angela an opportunity to stab him. As a stage direction suggests, "The ghost vanishes in a flash of fire, and a loud clap of thunder is heard." Here was the most notable supernatural ghost in the history of Gothic theatre, one that was not at all explained. At the time, at least a few theatre critics argued ghosts should not be seen onstage; the success of Lewis's play indicates that many audiences disagreed.[53] As late as 1849, the *Southern Literary Messenger* observed that *The Castle Spectre* was "well known to theatregoers of the present day."[54]

If Lewis had provided the most notable stage ghost in Gothic theatre, John William Polidori would indirectly do the same with vampires. In what was likely the first performance of a vampire play in the United States, the Pavilion Theatre in New York staged *The Vampyre*, an apparently unauthorized adaptation of Polidori's 1819 tale.[55] Robert Campbell Maywood portrayed Lord Ruthven, making him the earliest stage vampire in American history. Opening night of the "melo-drama" came in July 1819.

By October 1820, yet another theatrical adaptation of Polidori's story appeared in such cities as New York and Washington, D.C. Titled *The Vampyre; or, The Bride of the Isles* (aka *The Vampire, or the Bride of the Isles*), it had originally been written by James Robinson Planché for the London stage. A review published in Boston reported than an actor named "Mr. Brown was the Vampyre . . . his contortions and distortions of countenance were even more hideous than the author could have conceived of his subject." The critic added, "we believe we do but express the opinion of a majority of the spectators."[56] Another article on the Boston performance claimed that the play was "handsomely attended" and was "well-received."[57]

The play begins with two women chanting for a "vampire-corpse" to rise from his tomb. Later, an aristocrat named Lord Ronald places his friend Lord Ruthven's corpse in the moonlight, which transforms him into a bloodthirsty creature that insists on marrying Ronald's daughter, Lady Margaret. To the vampire, Lord Ronald bemoans:

> No, I will not quit my child an instant; horror overwhelms me! I know not what thou art; but a terrible conviction flashes on my mind, that thou art nothing human. A mist seems clearing from my sight; and I behold the now—Oh, horror! horror!—a monster of the grave—a—a Vam—

Before finishing his sentence, Ronald "falls into his servant's arms." He is no match for Ruthven, whose undead existence finally comes to an end when a "thunder-bolt strikes [him] to the ground," causing him to vanish "immediately." To accomplish this effect, theatres installed "vampire traps," meaning trapdoors through which an actor could quickly and safely fall into a hammock beneath the stage and thus disappear from audience view.[58]

Versions of *The Vampire; or, The Bride of the Isles* were staged for the next several years, making it the key vampire play in America during the nineteenth century.[59] As an article in the *New York Literary Journal* observed in 1821, "Since the appearance of the story of the Vampire, the conversation of private parties has frequently turned to the subject, and the discussion has been prolonged and invigorated by the pieces brought at the theatres . . ."[60]

The subject's popularity also resulted in other vampire productions, most notably Dion Boucicault's two-act play *The Phantom* (originally titled *The Vampire* when it premiered in England). At its debut at Wallack's Theatre in New York in 1856, Boucicault assumed the title role himself, a vampire named Alan Raby, whose family castle is in Wales. According to one character, within the castle "dwells a terrible thing—man or fiend." Immediately after he speaks those words a clap of thunder rocks the theatre. The same character then describes travellers who wander into the ruins after nightfall. Their corpses are later discovered, "each with a wound in his throat in the right side, from which they have evidently bled to death—but no blood is spilt around, the face is white and fixed, as if it had died of horror." Another clap of thunder is heard.

Some critical reviews of *The Phantom* were positive. In 1856, one newspaper called it an "an interesting piece, [which] has created a favorable impression upon the audiences."[61] While *The Phantom* never became as successful as Planché's play, theatres did stage it occasionally after its New York premiere. As late as 1870, for example, a revival appeared in Galveston, Texas.[62] And yet, even with the success of some vampire and ghost plays, Oral Sumner Coad concluded, "the dominant influence in American Gothic drama was the 'explained supernatural' that Mrs. Radcliffe popularized."[63]

Pepper's Ghost

An article about the supernatural onstage published in 1851 announced, "Really we are afraid that ghosts have had their day. . . . The failure of attempts upon the stage to produce effect by ghostly apparitions proves how entirely the belief in spectres has passed away from the minds of the present generation."[64] However accurate this opinion might have seemed at the time, the journalist could not have foreseen that ghosts would walk again in the American theatre, thanks to the ability of optics to create an innovative stage effect.

Building on a process devised by Henry Dircks, "Professor" John Henry Pepper presented a new type of Phantasmagoria show in London in December 1862.[65] In its original form at the Royal Polytechnic, "Pepper's Ghost" provided special effects for a stage adaptation of Charles Dickens' *The Haunted Man and the Ghost's Bargain* (1848, aka *The Haunted Man*).[66] Pepper's trick positioned a magic lantern under the stage to project light onto an actor, which was then bounced onto a transparent, reflective pane of glass positioned onstage at a downward 45-degree angle. The hidden actor's image thus appeared before the eyes of the audience, who could not see the glass.[67] Instead, they saw a ghostly apparition that was not only transparent, but which could move with lifelike precision. As Tom Gunning has noted, 'Pepper's Ghost Illusion achieved an enormous success and became part of the stage machinery of the late Victorian spectacular theatre."[68]

News of Pepper's Ghost appeared in the American press in 1863.[69] "American playwrights should get right away to work to make ready ghostly dramas," the *Times-Picayune* of New Orleans advised, "as Pepper's ghost will surely cross the Atlantic."[70] Thanks to

Harry Watkins, it did, first appearing in a play entitled *True to the Last* at Wallack's Theatre in August of that year. One critic wrote:

> An actor in the character of a murderer is seen asleep on a lounge in the rear of the stage, which is dimly lighted. Presently he rises in his sleep and begins to rave under the tortures of his crime. Instantly there appears at his side a bright image of a skeleton, so luminous that it sheds some light on the obscurity around. Though startlingly distinct, it is seen to be only the image of a skeleton as objects on the stage are visible directly through the bones. The murderer strikes his sword directly through the grisly horror, but it is impalpable as air. After a brief space the apparition vanishes as suddenly as it came. It makes no movement up or down, or to either hand, but simply disappears.[71]

An "old man who had been murdered" also materialized luminously, forming a "gory, pitiable spectacle."[72]

Pepper's Ghost became a "sensation," appearing at Wallack's to "very large business" for six weeks.[73] The New York theatre was "crowded nightly by hundreds of our citizens to witness this strange and startling apparition."[74] When *The Haunted Man* was staged, its tale was secondary to the spectacle of the special effects, so much so that when business fell off it was because—as the *New York Clipper* explained—"people do not care to wade through so much of the drama before they get a sight of the chief attraction."[75]

Imitations of Pepper's Ghost proliferated rapidly, though it is difficult to determine how successful their special effects were.[76] On August 22, 1863, the *New York Clipper* announced, "Every place of amusement now manufacturers its own 'ghost,' without consulting Professor Pepper, or his agents."[77] One week later, the same trade publication observed, "The 'Ghost' family is increasing, and shadowy spectres meet us where'er we go."[78] For example, the New Bowery Theatre staged *The Temple of Death*, and the American Theatre presented *The Spectre of Witchley, or a Night with the Ghost*.[79] The popularity of such plays even meant that a New York business advertised "Fright Wigs for Ghost Scenes."[80]

No one seized upon the ghost illusion with more zeal than George L. Fox, a onetime stage clown who managed the Old Bowery Theatre during part of the 1860s.[81] By the end of August 1863, he promised "The Ghost!" would appear "TILL FURTHER NOTICE."[82] In September, he used the effect in two plays, *The Ghost of Altenberg* and *The Mistletoe Bough; or, The Bride and the Ghost*.[83] "Manager Fox, of the old Bowery, has been so successful with his ghost dramas," the *New York Clipper* wrote on November 7, 1863, "that he will in all probability continue them through the entire season, or as long as a good subject for the introduction of the spectral illusion can be found."[84] In October, Fox gave audiences *Midnight; or The Ghost of the Ferry* and *Susan Hopley; or, The Ghost of the Manor House*.[85] In November, it was *The Ghost of Giles Scroggins* (with Fox in the lead role), and in December, a revival of some of the plays he had staged in earlier months.[86] Then, in January 1864, Fox unveiled a "new Ghost Burlesque" entitled *The Rag Woman and Her Dogs*.[87]

Pepper's Ghost also gained fame elsewhere in America. For one week in September 1863, theatregoers in Washington, D.C. could witness a "Wonderful!" and "Appalling!" ghost at Canterbury Hall, as well as the Parisian "Spectral Illusion" at the Washington Theatre, and the "Original Ghost!" at the Varieties.[88] By November, a touring revival of Lewis's *The Castle Spectre* incorporated the new "ghost business."[89] The major ghost play of the century now featured the major ghost stage effect of the century.

Figure 2.1 Published in *The Magic Lantern* in 1874, this illustration reveals how the Pepper's Ghost effect was achieved.

During the second half of 1863, the press published reports on "how ghosts are made" in the theatre, with such articles continuing to appear throughout the rest of the century.[90] Readers who purchased a particular dime novel in 1880 also received literature that "exposed Pepper's ghost illusion."[91] Pepper himself expounded at length on how his patented illusions worked, sometimes at his performances and sometimes in lectures on the subject of optics.[92] He also authored the book *The True History of the Ghost; and All About Metempsychosis* (London: Cassell & Company, 1890, aka *The True History of Pepper's Ghost*). "One would be very slow to accept a ghost story, without a very discriminating examination, after having seen the professor's experiments," a journalist wrote in 1872.[93]

Three years later, a Wisconsin newspaper confidently announced, "Everyone has heard of Pepper's Ghost."[94] Pepper himself became famous as well, with his death in 1890 covered by newspapers throughout the United States.[95] Nevertheless, by the 1880s, fewer productions used his "ghost." One article claimed it was due to the required "contrivances," which were somewhat prohibitive in an "ordinary theatre." The "great reflecting glass on the stage was deemed a perpetual danger to actors not habituated to its presence"; it also could "err in its work" and inadvertently show audiences near the pit their own reflection.[96] Perhaps these explanations are accurate, but what is certain is that Pepper's Ghost was no longer the only kind of ghostly performance on display.

Spiritualism and Magic

Legitimate stage productions were hardly the only kind of performances available to audiences during the nineteenth century. "Wonder shows" became popular in America in the 1830s and 1840s, offering demonstrations of magic, lectures on science, and sometimes an amalgam of the two, with these categories regularly blurred.[97] The topics varied, ranging from "freaks" of nature (a subject that will be explored in Chapter 10) to Mesmerism and hypnotism (Chapter 12).

Variety shows appeared across America from the 1840s, often invoking the supernatural with a set of tricks different than those used by Pepper's Ghost. Gillian M. Rodger notes, "These miscellaneous amusements known as variety, which are the forebears of what developed into vaudeville by the 1880s and 1890s, featured singing dancing and novelty acts in sequence with no overarching theme or narrative structure . . ."[98] Vaudeville theatres would in fact do much the same, presenting variegated entertainment in the form of balanced programs, with sketches that included drama, comedy, and music. As Robert M. Lewis describes, vaudeville was an "eclectic mix" that "distilled [the] essence of the major entertainments, lowbrow, middlebrow, even highbrow."[99]

Such venues regularly presented Spiritualism during the second half of the nineteenth century. The Fox Sisters gave public demonstrations in Rochester as early as the autumn of 1849, but they did not become major figures on the stage.[100] From 1854 until the 1870s, Ira and William Davenport, usually billed as the Davenport Brothers, became the most famous theatrical Spiritualists.[101] In an effort to convince audiences that their act featured no deception, they had themselves bound with ropes. Various phenomena then occurred thanks to their "spirit cabinet."[102] The sounds of tambourines, horns, and guitars were heard, as were loud raps. At some performances, a "bare hand and arm emerged" from the cabinet and rang a dinner bell.[103]

In 1864, at the height of their American fame, one magazine claimed a "squad of policemen is kept on nightly, and the rush for admittance has been so great that ladies are said to have swooned away under the pressure of passing events."[104] Ten years later, a review of the Davenport Brothers' show labeled them "clever performers in their line of business, but no one of ordinary sense believes they have spiritual aid in accomplishing their tricks."[105] What percentage of their audiences believed in them is unknown, but their notoriety spawned various imitators.

From the 1870s to the early twentieth century, for example, Anna Eva Fay (aka Annie Eva Fay) was extremely popular.[106] Publicity called her the "celebrated *spiritual-physical* test medium."[107] As part of her act, which appeared on a lit stage, Fay offered a variation on the Davenport Brothers' cabinet.[108] In 1906, a journalist reported, "Mysterious pencils scratched messages, nails were driven into boards by unseen hands, bells were rung and thrown half across the stage by undeniable force, [and] stoutly sewn clothes were cut by mysterious knives." Fay also spoke answers to questions written and kept by audience members, her accuracy creating a "creepy sensation which runs up and down the public spine."[109]

It was also possible to appear onstage for the express purpose of exposing Spiritualism as a fraud. As early as 1878, the "anti-spiritualist" W. Irving Bishop produced "manifestations" that he affirmed were "brought about by human agency alone"; he also offered a reward of $500 to anyone who could produce genuine phenomena.[110] Ten years later, in 1888, Margaret Fox Kane of the Fox Sisters exposed her own frauds at the New York Academy of Music.[111] Her subsequent appearance on a vaudeville bill in New Jersey was poorly attended, and her "spiritualistic expose" at a Massachusetts music hall faced "interruptions by the audience."[112]

Popular illusionists had the greatest success in proving that mediums possessed no supernatural powers. In the late nineteenth century, the celebrity magician became a "wizard arrayed against wizardry, an exposer of 'supernatural humbugs,'" as Leigh Eric Schmidt has written.[113] For example, Harry Kellar (originally Keller) became a stage magician after having traveled with the Davenport Brothers. In 1885, he declared, "It is the mediumistic tricks I am bent on exposing."[114] He did so onstage, in the press, and even at court.[115] By 1893, Herrmann the Great, who had first appeared onstage in America in the 1860s, echoed similar views, declaring, "I have never seen a spiritualistic manifestation that I could not reproduce through perfectly natural means."[116] In the early twentieth century, Harry Houdini famously pursued the same cause. In fact, it was to Houdini that Anna Eva Fay would eventually confess her trickery.[117]

Magicians not only exposed Spiritualists, but also performed some of their tricks. As Simone Natale writes, "The audience expected to find in these shows phenomena similar to those observed at a spiritualist séance, but within a different interpretative framework: in contrast to mediums, in fact, magicians openly admitted that their feats were the result of illusion and trickery, rather than of supernatural agency."[118] In 1876, for example, Professor Frank Lozardo offered "laughable and wonderful magical séances."[119] Even earlier, during the 1860s, the "Great Wizard" Robert Heller presented illusions that surpassed any performed by "legitimate conjurors or illegitimate spiritualists."[120] His wife gave "second-sight" performances onstage, but Heller made clear that the duo had no supernatural powers, announcing, "What I do is solely by the aid of sleight of hand and scientific appliances . . . There is no such thing as a real ghost."[121]

Somewhat paradoxically, many illusionists embraced publicity that conjured the supernatural. As Fred Nadis has observed, "Magicians wished to offer 'shows of wonder' that fulfilled the audience's nostalgia while yet assuring audiences that miracles, ultimately, had no place in the modern world."[122] For example, journalists knew that Herrmann the Great was a professional magician, but still compared him to Satan.[123] In the late nineteenth century, Kellar's posters regularly featured devils and ghosts. The same was true of his successor Howard Thurston. A poster for Helman the Great (aka H. Morgan Robinson) c. 1899 depicted him in a graveyard with devils and bats; its tagline dubbed him the "Napoleon of Necromancy."[124] And even with his reputation as "The Handcuff King," Houdini was sometimes called a "necromancer" and "wizard."[125]

As an 1897 article on the "Black Art" of magic explained, it was fortunate for prestidigitators that men were no longer condemned for witchcraft as in the days of Salem.[126]

Science on the Stage

In addition to drawing upon the supernatural, stage magicians occasionally relied on science fiction as an ingredient in their publicity and their tricks. In the early 1870s, for example, Professor T. W. Tobin offered his "Frankenstein Mystery, introducing the great feat of Decapitation."[127] One advertisement referred to his act as "Scientific Magic, or Illusions of Science and Delusions of Sense."[128] Later that decade, Andress, the Magician (aka Professor Charles Andress) offered his own version of the "Frankenstein Mystery," cutting an arm, leg, and head from an "apparently living person." One of his advertisements proclaimed,

Figure 2.2 An 1894 poster promoting the magician Kellar.

"So real did this mutilation appear that several ladies fainted at the sight, and a number of nervous persons left the theatre until the completion of the feat."[129]

Electricity also became a popular topic on the stage, ranging from a two-act play in 1881 entitled *The Electrical Doll* to advertisements in the 1880s for Lulu E. Hurst, the "Electrical Wonder and Queen Mesmerist."[130] Hurst performed feats of great strength by use of various tricks based upon leverage and magnetism, leading her to be dubbed the "Georgia Wonder" and "Georgia Magnet."[131] "It was like a flash of lightning followed by a thunderbolt," actress Lily Langtry said of Hurst's power.[132] Among her imitators was Annie May Abbott, the "electrical girl."[133] As with Hurst, Abbott claimed to possess an electrical power she could not explain, one that allowed her to display much strength onstage.[134] Years later, Hurst purported to reveal the "Great Secret" of the electrical act in her autobiography, hoping that such knowledge would "fortify the minds of people against all superstition."[135]

Science also had appeal onstage in a world apart from illusionists and tricksters. "A pretty fairy-land our popular science has brought us to," an American magazine remarked in 1862. "It is like the 'behind scenes' of a theatre."[136] Among the most notable scientific demonstrations during the nineteenth century were those showcasing electricity. Initially these involved galvanism, the application of an electrical current to the corpse of a human or other animal.

"Much remains to be known on this subject before any perfect theory can be established," one American newspaper wrote in 1793, "but the industrious enquiries of those engaged in the subject will doubtless soon bring to light something of great importance."[137] Elizabeth Stephens notes:

> Experiments in galvanic reanimation were a particularly attention-grabbing instance of the wider cultural transformations produced by mechanization taking place in the early 19th century. They fascinated popular and professional audiences alike because they made so strikingly visible the process of mechanization—of automated movement independent of the agency of the individual subject—that was in the process transforming life and experience in every cultural domain.[138]

"Showmen scientists," as Iwan Rhys Morus has called them, transformed exhibitions of galvanic reanimation into public spectacles that horrified many audiences. In 1819, the American magazine *Philanthropist* described one of these displays as conducted on the corpse of a murderer in Scotland:

> The scene was hideous—several of the spectators left the room, and one gentleman actually fainted, from terror, or sickness!!—In the fourth experiment, the transmitting of the electrical power from the spinal marrow to the ulnar nerve, at the elbow, the fingers were instantly put in motion, and the agitation of the arm was so great, that the corps[e] seemed to point to the different spectators, some of whom thought i[t] had come to life!

According to the press, the doctor present, Andrew Ure, "appears to be of opinion, that had not incisions been made in the blood vessels of the neck, and the spinal marrow been lacerated, *the criminal might have been restored to life!*"[139]

Even more lifelike results occurred in 1843 when doctors in Louisville, Kentucky applied galvanism to criminal John White only minutes after his hanging. One journalist reported it was the "most successful" galvanic experiment ever undertaken.[140] Others gave public demonstrations using animals. In 1825, for example, a professor in New York applied electricity to a dead cat, which threw it into "wild convulsions," its eyes opening and closing shut.[141] Over three decades later, a different professor promised to undertake a "monster experiment on a dead sheep" at his public lecture in San Francisco.[142]

As the century progressed, however, electricity came to be associated more with death than with life.[143] Harold P. Brown infamously used electricity to kill living dogs in 1888. When a group of electricians gathered at Columbia College, Brown electrocuted a dog first with direct current (DC) and then with alternating current (AC), the latter killing it.[144] Soon thereafter, Brown electrocuted three more dogs in front of a crowd of eight hundred at the Bellevue Hospital Medical College, all for the sake of dubiously proving that George Westinghouse's AC was more dangerous than Thomas Edison's DC.[145] By contrast, Nikola Tesla gave public lectures in the 1890s in which he allowed AC to pass through his body without harm, creating a spectacle that must have been greater than any "Georgia Magnet" or "Electrical Girl."[146]

Some demonstrations avoided the subject of death, offering instead an opportunity for the public to witness displays of the practical advantages and "fairy romance" of electricity.[147] The International Electrical Exhibition in Philadelphia in 1884 became the first major event of its kind in America, attracting over 300,000 attendees.[148] Other audiences saw electrical displays on vaudeville bills. In 1887, Professor Juke's "Electrical Exhibition" became a popular act.[149] That same year, Koster & Bial's presented Sandor Rosner's "electrical demonstration" in what became a "long and successful engagement."[150] Then, in 1895, Professor Richard A. Steudell performed "electric experiments" at such venues as Wonderful Theatre and Musée in Detroit, Michigan.[151]

More than anywhere else, electrical exhibits became particularly popular at public fairs.[152] Most famous of all perhaps was Electricity Hall at the World's Columbian Exposition in Chicago in 1893, powered by the AC current that Tesla and Westinghouse promoted. As the *Chicago Tribune* observed in May of that year, "Here the wizard which nightly gives new beauty to the court of honor had still stranger wonders to display."[153] *Current Literature* referred to the exhibit—which attracted large crowds—as an "electrical wonderland."[154]

The proliferation of electric power in America quickly found its way to the theatre. Theatrical lighting became electric beginning c. 1879, allowing for a control not possible with gas or even limelight, the latter having been used the first time extensively in *The Black Crook* (1866).[155] In 1881, the *New York Sun* reported the following on a revival of the play:

> The electric light is now used at the New York Theatres to produce various new and startling effects. It is applied to the incantation scene in the *Black Crook* at Niblo's for instance, with curious results. It flames from the eyeless sockets of the necromancer's skull, crackles along the dead branches of skeleton trees, and floods the whole stage with unearthly brilliancy. In the duel scene, the electric wires run through the handles of the swords of the combatants, and when the blades meet a circuit is completed and flashes of lightning play around the weapons in [the] most diabolical fashion. This is probably the first time that electricity has been so systematically applied to stage purposes.[156]

By the time of this performance, *The Black Crook* used electricity to illuminate its "weird, grewsome, and uncanny" skeleton dance, an updated version of the dancing skeletons that had long been popular in marionette shows and magic acts.[157]

In 1889, a theatre manager in Delaware invented a new "apparatus for making flash lightning."[158] Three years later, "about one hundred members of the New York Electrical Society visited the Garden Theatre to witness a performance of *Sinbad* and study the new method of stage lighting employed in the production of the extravaganza."[159] Reporting on a production of *Faust* in New York in 1893, an industry trade newspaper mentioned the opera was "presented with all its magnificent electrical effects."[160] One year later, The Davises (an African-American act comprised of composer Gussie Lord Davis and his wife Lottie B. Davis) heralded their latest sketch *The Jack O' Lantern* for offering the "greatest electrical effect ever produced on the Vaudeville Stage."[161]

However, perhaps electricity onstage assumed its most morbid form in stage plays and magic acts in which characters sat in the electric chair and "died" in front of live audiences.[162] In 1908, one horrified audience in North Carolina witnessed more than they expected when the villain of a melodrama accidentally received 102 volts of real electricity in his head during his *faux* execution. After the curtain fell and the actor was released from the prop electric chair, he slumped over unconscious, requiring a physician's examination. "The shock from the electricity completely unnerved him," the *New York Clipper* reported.[163]

Post-bellum Theatre

As productions of *Faust* indicate, the supernatural did not disappear from the legitimate theatre once it became powered by electricity. Many of these productions relied on comedy. Milton Nobles and J. M. Martin's three-act farce *Haunted Houses* appeared in 1886, for example.[164] Then, in 1892 and 1893, Thomas E. Murray appeared in the musical comedy *Voodoo, or A Lucky Charm*.[165] Most famous of all was perhaps Gilbert and Sullivan's opera *Ruddigore; or, The Witch's Curse* (aka *Ruddygore; or, The Witch's Curse*), which was performed in New York and several other American cities in 1887.[166] The comic opera parodied the Gothic theatre that had so long been out of fashion.[167]

Other plays relied on a kind of fantastical hesitation, creating worlds in which the supernatural might exist. Herman Knickerbocker Viele set *The House of Silence* (1906) in a "weird, mysterious place" that "takes on a supernatural quality" after its owner is murdered.[168] Its chief villain was a hulking gardener, who—as the *Morning Telegraph* noted—"might have been a creation of old Monk Lewis."[169] Brandishing a scythe, he attempts to kill the two young lovers, but is struck dead by a bolt of lightning. The *New York Dramatic Mirror* compared *The House of Silence* (which closed a little more than a week after it opened) to a "chamber of horrors" exhibit.[170]

But in the late nineteenth century, the most prominent stage presentations usually concentrated on other kinds of horror, including on what Alan L. Ackerman, Jr. has described as a dramatic realism, one that "relocated dramatic interest in interior states of consciousness and processes of individual psychology."[171] In 1883, for example, Henry Irving appeared in New York in *The Bells* (1871), at that time a play "unfamiliar" to Americans.[172] When Irving appeared in Chicago, a critic called it a "weird melodrama" in which the audience "can hear the bells that are supposed to be the wild illusion of a murderer's brain."[173] The murderer also sees the apparition of the man he killed, but it is not a real ghost, merely a vision conjured from guilt. In 1896, years after Irving's famous tour, actor Clay Clement appeared in an American revival of the play.[174]

Stage villainy drew on various sources, ranging from the dominant melodramatic style of the era to the nonfiction press. As early as 1889, Harry Kernell's "New Company" presented a "very funny satire" on the Jack the Ripper case called *The Mystery*.[175] That same year, a serious drama entitled *Jack the Ripper* appeared at Holmes' Standard Theatre in New York, its "strength" coming in part from sets that depicted a "realistic Whitechapel scene."[176] Subsequent versions of *Jack the Ripper* appeared in America over the next several years, at least one of which concluded with the murderer being caught and hanged for his crimes.[177]

Far more popular in America was the stage adaptation of Robert Louis Stevenson's novella *Strange Case of Dr. Jekyll and Mr. Hyde* (1886). Thomas R. Sullivan dramatized Stevenson's story into four acts, changing Jekyll into a younger man and adding a love interest. He also shortened the title to *Dr. Jekyll and Mr. Hyde*. Richard Mansfield portrayed the dual role in 1887 when the play appeared in Boston, with one review observing:

> The transformation [from Jekyll to Hyde] is effected without padding, without wigs or beards, without any conspicuous change of costume; but it is complete and marvellous, as clever as anything that has been seen on the stage for a long time.[178]

Figure 2.3 Publicity photo of Richard Mansfield as Dr. Jekyll and Mr. Hyde.
(*Courtesy of George Chastain*)

The same critic drew attention to the play's conclusion, noting that Jekyll "relapses into Hyde and dies, conquered by his own Frankenstein."

Science formed the basis of psychological horror, becoming even more popular in the late nineteenth century than *The Castle Spectre* had been during the Gothic period. When Mansfield appeared on the New York stage in the autumn of 1887, he received largely favorable reviews.[179] "I believe many people come to see that because it is morbid and horrible," said Mansfield, "and they can go away and say they have seen something that kept them awake all night."[180] As for the audiences, one journalist claimed Jekyll's "remarkable transformation" into Hyde had an "electrical effect" on them.[181]

In the spring of 1888, *Puck* magazine ran a cartoon entitled *The "Jekyll and Hyde" Craze*.[182] The play's success spurred various touring companies featuring actors like Daniel Bandmann, Theodore Hamilton, Dore Davidson, and Marlande Clarke. However, Mansfield remained the most associated with the role, appearing in revivals of the play as late as 1906.[183] In 1888, when he appeared in London, Mansfield's talent even led to unsubstantiated accusations that he might have been responsible for the Jack the Ripper murders.[184]

Figure 2.4 Publicity photo of Wilton Lackeye as Svengali. (*Courtesy of George Chastain*)

Svengali became the other key character of horror on the American stage, his fame at least the equal of Jekyll and Hyde's. Paul M. Potter's four-act stage adaptation of George du Maurier's novel *Trilby* (1894) debuted in America in 1895, with Wilton Lackaye portraying Svengali. A kind of "Trilbymania" resulted, parodied in an 1897 vaudeville sketch entitled *Too Much Trilby*.[185] As a magazine wrote in 1896, "It is a moot point whether *Trilby* the play made *Trilby* the book or *vice versa*; there are those, and many, who consider the play by far to be the better of the two..."[186]

The stage adaptation became so popular that numerous touring companies were formed, including a condensed vaudeville version in 1901.[187] However, Lackaye became as associated with Svengali as had Mansfield with Jekyll and Hyde. *The Critic* called his performance "overwrought but indisputably strong."[188] The *Washington Post* was more enthusiastic, telling readers:

> Mr. Lackaye's Svengali is an artistic triumph that will live in the history of the stage. His characterization paints vividly the curious blend of cringing cowardice, inordinate vanity, and terrible mesmeric power that can mold an independent mind into a vehicle for the materialization of his dominating will. He fills the picture of ghastly grotesqueness that Trilby names 'a great black spider.' ... And he does not depend on make-up and spotlight to secure that indefinable influence that gives the stage story its atmosphere...[189]

He appeared in numerous revivals of the play, including in 1898, 1905, 1907, and 1915.[190] As one journalist bemoaned, "It is a pity that . . . Du Maurier's Svengali will endure by virtue of printer's ink [, but] Lackaye's Svengali . . . must die with each drop of the curtain."[191] The comment was true with regard to Lackaye onstage, though (as Chapter 12 will discuss) he did star in a film version of *Trilby* in 1915.

Lackaye's success as Svengali also led him to assume the title role in Charles Klein's play *Dr. Belgraff* in 1896. A German apothecary, Belgraff murders a man and then hypnotizes a woman who learns of his crime.[192] Writing about the "necromantic and uncanny" doctor, the *New York Times* noted, "We have all of the horror of the Du Maurier hypnotist, and none of the relieving fun."[193] Belgraff became forgotten, while Svengali remained famous.

Conclusion

During the early years of the twentieth century, the American stage featured few ghosts. When the subject was broached in the theatre, it was generally to create humor, just as it had been with *The Drummer, or The Haunted House* in 1736. In 1913, for example, Francis Wilson's play *The Spiritualist* (1913) featured a "burlesque" séance.[194] Set in New York, the comedy did not please critics, though one praised its "ingenious" use of "mechanical" stage effects.[195]

Much more popular was *The Ghost Breaker* with H. B. Warner, which opened in New York in 1913. According to *The Billboard*, the "peculiarly constructed melodrama" was

Figure 2.5 Francis Wilson's play *The Spiritualist* (1913). (*Courtesy of the New York Public Library for the Performing Arts*)

"superabundant in thrills extraordinary," but as the American character proves, there is no ghost in the European castle where it is set.[196] The spirit is merely a ruse, with the supernatural explained away in the tradition of Ann Radcliffe. The key difference was the comedic tone, with the male lead catching the fake ghost while he hides behind a portrait, an incident that recalls Washington Irving's short story *The Adventure of My Aunt* (1824). Critics weren't necessarily impressed, but many audiences were. In 1913, Burns Mantle told readers of the *Chicago Tribune*, "Mr. H. B. Warner ... fights the [fake] spooks of a spooky castle with such ardor and imminent danger to life and limb that each night his hysterical feminine admirers in the audience rise part way out of their seats and shout to him to be careful."[197]

However, American audiences did not have to rely on the theatre for horror. They understood what Poe had called the "motley drama" of everyday life. They were "mere puppets" who "come and go," all "at [the] bidding of vast formless things that shift the scenery to and fro." But they were also active participants, even draping themselves in robes of horror one night a year, October 31, as opposed to the other 364 defined by rationalism.

Halloween celebrations became increasingly popular in the late nineteenth century and even more so in the early years of the twentieth. Americans masqueraded as the very ghosts and goblins that were largely absent from the American theatre.[198] Companies like Dennison's not only sold decorations that could transform the home into a haunted house, but also gave advice on possible costumes. Their *Bogie Book* for 1915 suggested various characters, among them a ghost and a witch.[199] Americans could perform horror. They could "act witchcraft," without fear of mortal condemnation.

Nowhere was the possibility of acting in a horror-themed environment more evident at the dawn of the twentieth century than by entering attractions meant to frighten their visitors by immersing them in an activity rather than anchoring them to a theatre seat. These attractions bore resemblance to the "Chamber of Horrors" waxworks of prior decades, but relied heavily on the use of electricity to heighten their effect. In 1899, for example, one journalist described a "weird and fantastic" midway attraction called *Heaven and Hell*. Those who passed through its front door saw laughing spirits and skeletons before being guided by a "monk" into the "infernal regions," where "his Satanic majesty" and a "score of subordinate demons" materialized. The journalist explained that "Weird panoramas and smoking, talking and dancing skeletons cause a creepy feeling not soon to be forgotten."[200]

An even more immersive attraction appeared at the Lewis and Clark Centennial Exposition in Portland, Oregon in 1905. Designed by J. A. Gorman, the "Haunted Castle" allowed visitors to enter a darkened hall, where:

> skeletons stare and gibber and ghosts flit silently about. Bones sail through the air and suddenly jump together into completed skeletons and dance to weird, ghostly music. Headless forms, bodyless heads, and shadowy forms float about.
> ... In this haunted castle, the monster, often called the 'Devil,' appeared from his dark cave and frightened [one visitor] so badly she has not recovered from the shock. She was not alone in the excitement, for the boat load at the rear were so frightened that the boat could not move and the 'Great Monster' had them hypnotized for a few moments.[201]

Here was a "ghost story without words," a play in which the ticket-buyers became actor and audience.

As Poe wrote, "That motley drama—oh be sure, It shall not be forgot."

Notes

1. Quoted in Robin DeRosa, *The Making of Salem: The Witch Trials in History, Fiction and Tourism* (Jefferson, North Carolina: McFarland & Company, 2009), 36–7. Emphasis is mine.
2. Ibid., 37.
3. See, for example, "The Edgefield Ghost," *Baltimore Patriot*, July 28, 1829.
4. "City Briefs," *Los Angeles Times*, March 19, 1892, 8.
5. Bridget Bennett, *Transatlantic Spiritualism and Nineteenth-Century American Literature* (New York: Palgrave Macmillan, 2007), 16.
6. "A Cabinet of Horrors," *Washington Post*, May 17, 1891, 9.
7. "Wax-Work," *City Gazette* (Charleston, South Carolina), February 13, 1798, 4.
8. "The Chamber of Horrors," *New York Clipper*, September 6, 1862; "New York," *New York Clipper*, April 27, 1889; Advertisement, *New York Clipper*, March 2, 1872; Advertisement, *New York Clipper*, November 21, 1874.
9. "The St. Louis Museum," *New York Clipper*, June 3, 1871.
10. Andrea Stulman Dennett, *Weird and Wonderful: The Dime Museum in America* (New York: New York University, 1997), 115.
11. James Fisher, *Historical Dictionary of American Theatre: Beginnings* (Lanham: Rowman & Littlefield, 2015), xxi.
12. "Pleasures of the Theatre," *New York Evangelist*, November 27, 1845, 190.
13. "The Cabinet," *New York Mirror: A Weekly Gazette of Literature and the Fine Arts*, June 4, 1825, 354.
14. Solitaire, "A Night of Horrors," *Graham's American Monthly Magazine of Literature, Art, and Fashion*, December 1845, 274.
15. Robert Manson Myers, "The Old Dominion Looks to London: A Study of English Literary Influences upon The Virginia Gazette (1736–1766)," *The Virginia Magazine of History and Biography*, Vol. 54, No. 3 (July 1946), 211.
16. Untitled, *Boston Evening Post*, December 17, 1750, 1.
17. Advertisement, *Pennsylvania Journal, or Weekly Advertiser* (Philadelphia, Pennsylvania), August 2, 1759, 1; Advertisement, *Daily Advertiser* (New York), October 8, 1789, 2.
18. Advertisement, *New York Gazette*, March 15, 1762, 3.
19. Advertisement, *Pennsylvania Gazette* (Philadelphia, Pennsylvania), January 5, 1769.
20. Advertisement, *Virginia Gazette* (Williamsburg, Virginia), November 19, 1772.
21. Advertisement, *New-Jersey Journal* (Elizabethtown, New Jersey), October 19, 1791.
22. "Baltimore, July 9," *Maryland Journal* (Baltimore, Maryland), July 9, 1782.
23. Advertisement, *Columbian Museum* (Savannah, Georgia), March 21, 1800, 3. This ad refers to the play as *The Ghost, or the Dead Man Alive*. For an example of an ad that refers to the play as *The Ghost, or the Dead Alive*, see Advertisement, *Columbian Herald* (Charleston, South Carolina), June 18, 1794, 3.
24. "Amusements," *Commercial Advertiser* (New York), February 9, 1833, 3.
25. Advertisement, *The Evening Post* (New York), January 23, 1837, 3.
26. M. Susan Anthony, *Gothic Plays and American Society, 1794–1830* (Jefferson: McFarland, 2008), 5.
27. Ibid.
28. Ibid.
29. Nathalie Wolfram, *Novel Play: Gothic Performance and the Making of Eighteenth-Century Fiction*, Ph.D. Dissertation (Yale University, 2012), 4.
30. Anthony, 127, 138.
31. Ibid., 102.

32. Ibid., 116.
33. Fisher, xxiv, 188.
34. Anthony, 101.
35. Quoted in Anthony, 111.
36. Advertisement, *Telegraphe* [sic] *and Daily Advertiser* (Baltimore, Maryland), November 26, 1803, 3; Advertisement, *Gazette of the United States* (Philadelphia, Pennsylvania), December 22, 1803, 3.
37. Quoted in Anthony, 122.
38. Anthony, 107.
39. Anthony, 28.
40. "Adelphi Theatre," *Baltimore Patriot*, November 18, 1830, 3; Advertisement, *Boston Patriot and Daily Chronicle*, June 17, 1831, 3; Advertisement, *Commercial Advertiser* (New York), July 12, 1831, 3.
41. Oral Sumner Coad, "The Gothic Element in American Literature before 1835," *The Journal of English and German Philology*, Vol. 24, No. 1 (January 1925), 79.
42. The phrase "Grand Romantic Melo Drama" appears in Advertisement, *New York American*, January 11, 1825, 3.
43. Advertisement, *The Evening Post* (New York), December 31, 1824, 2.
44. "Theatre-Park," *New-York Mirror: A Weekly Gazette of Literature and the Fine Arts*, January 8, 1825, 190.
45. "Boston Theatre," *Boston Patriot and Daily Chronicle*, December 26, 1828, 3.
46. "Theatricals," *The New-England Galaxy and United States Literary Advertiser*, January 2, 1829, 3.
47. "Burning of the Richmond, Va. Theatre, Dec. 26, 1811," *New York Clipper*, August 26, 1876, 172; "Last Bill of the National Theatre, Philadelphia," *New York Clipper*, July 20, 1872, 124.
48. Advertisement, *Telegraphe* [sic] *and Daily Advertiser* (Baltimore, Maryland), June 18, 1805, 1.
49. Advertisement, *Boston Morning Post*, March 17, 1834, 3; Advertisement, *Washington National Intelligencer* (Washington, D.C.), November 1, 1834, 3.
50. Anthony, 29.
51. Jeffrey N. Cox, "Introduction," in *Seven Gothic Dramas, 1789–1825*, edited by Jeffrey N. Cox (Athens, Ohio: Ohio University Press, 1992), 40.
52. Advertisement, *Gazette of the United States* (Philadelphia, Pennsylvania), April 7, 1800, 2.
53. For one example of a critic who believed ghosts should be seen onstage, see "Ghosts on the Stage," *The Talisman*, January 1, 1830, 49.
54. "'Monk' Lewis," *Southern Literary Messenger*, April 1849, 230.
55. I suggest that the adaptation was loose in large measure because a period advertisement announces the play's three main characters as Lord Ruthven, Aubrey, and Pedro, the latter being a character that does not exist (at least by that name) in Polidori's tale.
56. "The Vampyre," *New England Galaxy* (Boston, Massachusetts), November 3, 1820.
57. "The Vampire," *Boston Commercial Gazette*, October 19, 1820.
58. "Records of a Stage Veteran—No. 5," *The Albion*, June 27, 1835, 203.
59. See, for example, Advertisement, *Charleston Courier*, January 14, 1825.
60. "On Vampires and Vampirism," *New York Literary Journal*, Vol. 4, No. 3, January 1, 1821.
61. "New York Correspondence," *Manitowoc Tribune*, July 17, 1856.
62. Untitled, *Flake's Bulletin* (Galveston, Texas), January 22, 1870.
63. Coad, 79.
64. "On Ghosts," *Gleason's Pictorial Drawing-Room Companion*, August 23, 1851, 269.
65. Melvyn Heard, *Phantasmagoria: The Secret Life of the Magic Lantern* (Hastings: The Projection Box, 2006), 227–230.

66. Helen Groth, "Reading Victorian Illusions: Dickens' *Haunted Man* and Dr. Pepper's 'Ghost,'" *Victorian Studies*, Vol. 50, No. 1 (Autumn 2007), 43–65.
67. Heard, 229–30.
68. Tom Gunning, "To Scan a Ghost: The Ontology of Mediated Vision," *Grey Room*, No. 26 (Winter 2007), 113.
69. "Foreign Matters," *Boston Herald*, July 19, 1863, 4.
70. "Pepper's Improved Patent Ghost," *The Times-Picayune* (New Orleans, Louisiana), August 8, 1863, 1.
71. "Correct Explanation of the Ghost," *Portland Daily Advertiser* (Portland, Maine), September 12, 1863.
72. "The Drama," *The Knickerbocker Monthly: A National Magazine*, September 1863, 287.
73. "The Globe Theatre," *New York Clipper*, August 15, 1891.
74. "Correct Explanation of the Ghost," *Scientific American*, August 29, 1863, 132.
75. "Theatrical Record," *New York Clipper*, August 22, 1863, 147.
76. Dassia N. Posner, "Spectres on the New York Stage: The (Pepper's) Ghost Craze of 1863," in *Representations of Death in Nineteenth-Century US Writing and Culture*, edited by Lucy E. Frank (Burlington: Ashgate Publishing Company, 2007), 87–204.
77. Ibid.,147.
78. "Theatrical Record," *New York Clipper*, August 29, 1863, 155.
79. "Theatrical Record," *New York Clipper*, August 22, 1863; "Theatrical Record," *New York Clipper*, September 19, 1863.
80. Advertisement, *New York Clipper*, October 10, 1863.
81. Laurence Senelick, *The Age and Stage of George L. Fox, 1825–1877* (Hanover: University Press of New England, 1988), 110–15.
82. Advertisement, *New York Clipper*, August 29, 1863, 158.
83. Advertisement, *New York Clipper*, September 5, 1863, 166; Advertisement, *New York Clipper*, September 19, 1863, 183.
84. "Theatrical Record," *New York Clipper*, November 7, 1863.
85. Advertisement, *New York Clipper*, October 3, 1863; Advertisement, *New York Clipper*, October 10, 1863.
86. Advertisement, *New York Clipper*, November 7, 1863; Advertisement, *New York Clipper*, December 12, 1863; Advertisement, *New York Clipper*, December 19, 1863.
87. Advertisement, *New York Clipper*, January 23, 1864.
88. Advertisements, *Daily National Republican* (Washington, D.C.), September 9, 1863.
89. "Theatrical Record," *New York Clipper*, November 7, 1873.
90. "Correct Explanation of the Ghost," *Scientific American*, August 29, 1863, 132; "How Ghosts Are Made," *American Phrenological Journal*, December 1863, 153. See also "The 'Ghost,'" *Milwaukee Sentinel* (Milwaukee, Wisconsin), September 11, 1863; Untitled, *Scientific American*, December 20, 1873, 395; "Pepper's Ghost," *Chicago Tribune*, December 15, 1884, 9; "Those Puzzling Illusions," *Omaha Daily World-Herald* (Omaha, Nebraska), May 22, 1890, 2.
91. Advertisement, *National Police Gazette*, July 31, 1880, 15.
92. With regard to Pepper's lectures on optics, see "Pepper's Ghost," *Daily Inter Ocean* (Chicago, Illinois), April 2, 1874.
93. "Pepper's Ghost," *The Youth's Companion*, December 26, 1872, 418.
94. "Prof. Pepper," *Oshkosh Daily Northwestern* (Oshkosh, Wisconsin), November 17, 1875, 1.
95. See, for example, "Prof. Pepper Dead," *The Evening Post* (Charleston, South Carolina), March 29, 1900, 1.
96. W. J. Lawrence, "Stage Ghosts," *The Eclectic Magazine of Foreign Literature*, February 1888, 210.

97. Fred Nadis, *Wonder Shows: Performing Science, Magic, and Religion in America* (New Brunswick: Rutgers University Press, 2005).
98. Gillian M. Rodger, *Champagne Charlie and Pretty Jemima: Variety Theater in the Nineteenth Century* (Champaign: University of Illinois Press, 2010), 5.
99. Robert M. Lewis, *From Traveling Show to Vaudeville: Theatrical Spectacle in America, 1830–1910* (Baltimore: Johns Hopkins University Press, 2003), 316.
100. David Chapin, "The Fox Sisters and the Performance of Mystery," *New York History*, Vol. 81, No. 2 (April 2000), 173–4.
101. Fisher, 131.
102. Antonio Melechi, *Servants of the Supernatural: The Night Side of the Victorian Mind* (London: Arrow Books, 2008), 207–10.
103. Henry Ridgely Evans, *Hours with the Ghosts; Or, Nineteenth-Century Witchcraft* (Chicago: Laird & Lee, 1897), 140.
104. "Amusements: Diabolism at Cooper Institute," *The Round Table*, May 7, 1864, 327.
105. "A Davenport 'Seance,'" *Alexandria Gazette* (Alexandria, Virginia), January 19, 1874, 1.
106. Alex Owen, *The Darkened Room: Women, Power, and Spiritualism in Late Victorian England* (Chicago: University of Chicago Press, 1989), 54.
107. Advertisement, *New York Times*, February 6, 1876, 11.
108. Evans, 150–4.
109. "Spiritualistic Seance on Stage," *Duluth News-Tribune* (Duluth, Minnesota), December 21, 1906, 16.
110. "For and Against Spiritism," *Daily Inter Ocean* (Chicago, Illinois), March 11, 1878, 3.
111. Barbara Weisberg, *Talking to the Dead: Kate and Maggie Fox and the Rise of Spiritualism* (New York: HarperSanFrancisco, 2004), 241–3.
112. "New Jersey," *New York Clipper*, December 29, 1888; "Massachusetts," *New York Clipper*, November 10, 1888.
113. Leigh Eric Schmidt, "From Demon Possession to Magic Show: Ventriloquism, Religion, and the Enlightenment," *Church History*, Vol. 67, No. 2 (June 1998), 275.
114. "The Tricks of Mediums," *Chicago Tribune*, April 24, 1885, 10.
115. "Kellar Knew It All," *New York Times*, June 25, 1888, 2; "The Tricks of Mediums," *Chicago Tribune*, April 24, 1885, 10; "Exposing the Medium," *Chicago Tribune*, February 26, 1890, 3.
116. A. Herrmann, "The Tricks of Indian Jugglers and of Spiritualists," *Current Literature*, January–April, 1893, 83.
117. Burton Gates Brown, *Spiritualism in Nineteenth-Century America*, Ph.D. Dissertation (Boston University, 1972), 231.
118. Simone Natale, "Specters of the Mind: Ghosts, Illusion, and Exposure in Paul Leni's *The Cat and the Canary*," in *Cinematic Ghosts: Haunting and Spectrality from Silent Cinema to the Digital Era*, edited by Murray Leeder (New York: Bloomsbury Academic, 2015), 64.
119. Advertisement, *New York Clipper*, March 11, 1876.
120. Advertisement, *New York Clipper*, November 5, 1864. For more information on Robert Heller, see "Our Dramatic Portrait Gallery," *New York Clipper*, October 22, 1864, 220.
121. "Heller and the Devil," *Washington Post*, November 16, 1878, 1.
122. Nadis, 115. For more information on Helman the Great, see *The Daily Republican* (Monongahela, Pennsylvania), April 8, 1896, 1.
123. "The First Night of M. Hermann [sic]," *Chicago Tribune*, April 1, 1862, 4.
124. Noel Daniel, editor, *Magic, 1400s–1950s* (Cologne, Germany: Taschen, 2009), 242.
125. See, for example, "No Sweat-Box in His," *Los Angeles Times*, August 15, 1899, 13.
126. "Black Art Explained," *Washington Post*, January 10, 1897, 21.
127. Advertisement, *New York Clipper*, May 3, 1873.

128. Advertisement, *Cairo Bulletin* (Cairo, Illinois), December 18, 1873, 3.
129. Advertisement, *New York Clipper*, October 19, 1878.
130. "At the Bush-Street Theatre," *New York Clipper*, December 24, 1881; Advertisement, *New York Clipper*, February 26, 1887.
131. "The Electric Girl," *Chicago Tribune*, July 15, 1884, 9.
132. Lulu Hurst, *Lulu Hurst (The Georgia Wonder) Writes Her Autobiography and for the First Time Explains and Demonstrates the Great Secret of Her Marvelous Power*, Fourth Edition (Rome, GA: Psychic Publishing Company, 1897), 106.
133. "Utah," *New York Clipper*, August 11, 1894.
134. For more information on Hurst and Abbott, see Graeme Kent, *The Strongest Men on Earth: When Muscle Men Ruled Show Business* (London: Robson Press, 2012).
135. Hurst, 266.
136. "The Fairy-Land of Science," *Littell's Living Age*, February 8, 1862, 367.
137. "Animal Electricity," *City Gazette* (Charleston, South Carolina), May 30, 1793.
138. Elizabeth Stephens, "'Dead Eyes Open': The Role of Experiments in Galvanic Reanimation in Nineteenth-Century Popular Culture," *Leonardo*, Vol. 48, No. 3 (2015), 277.
139. "Horrible Phenomena! Galvanism," *Philanthropist: A Weekly Journal Containing Essays on Moral and Religious Subjects*, April 10, 1819, 282. Emphasis in original.
140. "Galvanic Experiments on the Human Subject," *The Angle American*, December 16, 1843, 183.
141. "Galvanism," *Christian Secretary*, April 18, 1825, 47.
142. "Mesmerism and Electricity," *San Francisco Bulletin*, November 25, 1861, 3.
143. See Mark Essig, *Edison and the Electric Chair: A Story of Light and Death* (New York: Walker & Company, 2005).
144. Thomas P. Hughes, "Harold P. Brown and the Executioner's Current: An Incident in the AC–DC Controversy," *Business History Review*, No. 32 (Spring 1958), 148–9.
145. Richard Moran, *Executioner's Current: Thomas Edison, George Westinghouse, and the Invention of the Electric Chair* (New York: Vintage Books, 2002), 36–62, 92–118.
146. Nadis, 62–3.
147. Ernest Freeberg, *The Age of Edison: Electric Light and the Invention of Modern America* (New York: Penguin, 2013), 120.
148. "The International Electrical Exhibition," *Scientific American*, April 5, 1884, 210; Ernest Freeberg, *The Age of Edison: Electric Light and the Invention of Modern America* (New York: Penguin, 2013), 136.
149. "Reading," November 26, 1887, 588; "Williamsport," *New York Clipper*, December 24, 1887, 652; "Altoona," *New York Clipper*, January 7, 1888, 688.
150. "New York," *New York Clipper*, January 28, 1888, 735.
151. "Michigan," *New York Clipper*, June 15, 1895.
152. Freeberg, 160–3.
153. "Cold Winds Send People Home," *Chicago Tribune*, May 31, 1893, 3.
154. "An Electrical Wonderland," *Current Literature*, July 1893, 338.
155. John L. Fell, "Dissolves by Gaslight: Antecedents to the Motion Picture in Nineteenth-Century Melodrama," *Film Quarterly*, Vol. 23, No. 3 (Spring 1970), 30; Don B. Wilmeth and Christopher Bigsby, editors, *The Cambridge History of American Theatre, Volume One: Beginnings to 1870* (Cambridge: Cambridge University Press, 1998), 104.
156. Quoted in "Electricity on the Stage," *Washington Post*, March 31, 1881, 2.
157. "*The Skeleton Dance*," *Idaho Falls Times* (Idaho Falls, Idaho), April 6, 1893, 7; "Prof. Andress' Success," *New York Clipper*, August 5, 1882.
158. "Delaware," *New York Clipper*, February 23, 1889.

159. "New York City," *New York Clipper*, July 23, 1892, 311.
160. "Empire," *New York Clipper*, September 2, 1893.
161. Advertisement, *New York Clipper*, October 20, 1894, 533.
162. See, for example, "Michigan," *New York Clipper*, May 5, 1900; "Notes and Roster of Barton Bros.' Illusion Show," *New York Clipper*, September 30, 1905; "Adelaide Herrmann," *New York Clipper*, December 10, 1910.
163. "World of Players," *New York Clipper*, April 11, 1908.
164. "New Jersey," *New York Clipper*, June 12, 1886.
165. "*The Voodoo, or A Lucky Charm at the New National*," *Washington Post*, October 30, 1892, 14.
166. "Gilbert and Sullivan," *New York Times*, February 22, 1887, 1.
167. Roxana Stuart, *Stage Blood: Vampires of the 19th-Century Stage* (Bowling Green: Bowling Green State University Popular Press, 1994), 167–73.
168. "Hackett-Mannering in *The House of Silence*," *New York Times*, January 24, 1906, 9.
169. "Weird Play Gives Hackett a Chance," *The Morning Telegraph* (New York), January 24, 1906, 10.
170. "Savoy—*The House of Silence*," *New York Dramatic Mirror*, February 3, 1906, 3; Walter K. Hill, "Broadway Topics," *The Billboard*, February 3, 1906, 6.
171. Alan L. Ackerman, Jr., *The Portable Theater: American Literature and the Nineteenth-Century Stage* (Baltimore: Johns Hopkins University Press, 1999), xiii.
172. "Amusements," *New York Times*, October 30, 1883, 4.
173. "An Irving Night," *Chicago Tribune*, January 13, 1884, 13.
174. "Amusements," *Chicago Tribune*, October 22, 1896, 7.
175. "Kernan's New Washington Theatre," *Washington Post*, November 17, 1889, 6.
176. "New York," *New York Clipper*, January 12, 1889.
177. See, for example, "Almost Too Realistic," *New York Times*, September 23, 1891, 1; "Minnesota," *New York Clipper*, September 19, 1891; "Washington," *New York Clipper*, June 27, 1896; "Georgia," *New York Clipper*, December 25, 1897.
178. William H. Rideing, "*Dr. Jekyll and Mr. Hyde* on the Stage," *The Critic: A Weekly Review of Literature and the Arts*, May 14, 1887, 244.
179. William Winter, *Life and Art of Richard Mansfield, with Selections from His Letters, Volume Two* (New York: Moffat, Yard & Company, 1910), 43.
180. "Mansfield on His Art," *Washington Post*, December 27, 1891, 12.
181. "Mr. Mansfield's Art," *New York Times*, December 25, 1887, 9.
182. "The 'Jekyll and Hyde' Craze," *Puck*, May 23, 1888, 210.
183. Untitled, *New York Times*, March 18, 1906, X1.
184. Martin A. Danahay and Alex Chisholm, editors, *Jekyll and Hyde Dramatized* (Jefferson: McFarland, 2004).
185. "Trilbymania," *The Open Court, a Quarterly Magazine*, April 18, 1895, 4465; "Variety and Minstrelsy," *New York Clipper*, August 15, 1896.
186. "Our Theatrical Playground," *Outing, an Illustrated Monthly Magazine of Recreation*, January 1896, xxviiic.
187. "Vaudeville and Minstrel," *New York Clipper*, December 7, 1901.
188. "*Trilby* at the Garden Theatre," *The Critic: A Weekly Review of Literature on the Arts*, April 20, 1895, 300.
189. "Lackaye in *Trilby*," *Washington Post*, June 4, 1907, 4.
190. "*Trilby* at Great Northern," *Chicago Tribune*, March 21, 1898, 5; "*Trilby* Revived with the Original Players," *Washington Post*, May 14, 1905, T1; "Lackaye in *Trilby*," 4; Alexander Woollcott, "An All-Star *Trilby*," *New York Times*, April 4, 1915, 5.
191. "Actor-Made Svengali Is Greedier than Author's," *Los Angeles Times*, September 28, 1905, II1.

192. "The Easter Week Plays," *New York Times*, April 20, 1897, 9.
193. "Lackaye as Another Svengali," *New York Times*, November 10, 1896, 5.
194. "*The Spiritualist* Opens," *The Billboard*, March 8, 1913, 7. The mention of "burlesque" appears in "*The Spiritualist* Is Queer," *New York Times*, March 26, 1913, 11.
195. "Francis Wilson's Latest," March 29, 1913. Clipping appears in the file for *The Spiritualist* in the Lincoln Center for the Performing Arts at the New York Public Library.
196. "H. B. Warner in *The Ghost Breaker*," *The Billboard*, March 15, 1913, 4.
197. Burns Mantle, "*The Ghost Breaker*, a Medley of Oo-oo! Hist! Zip! Bang!," *Chicago Tribune*, March 9, 1913, B1.
198. See, for example, "For Halloween Night," *Washington Post*, October 25, 1900, 2; "A 'Witch' Party," *Dallas Morning News*, February 26, 1905, 6; "Halloween Sport," *Evening Times* (Grand Forks, North Dakota), November 15, 1909, 7; "Ghosts Stalk Abroad," *Washington Post*, November 1, 1910, 1; "Halloween 'Witches' Planning to Revel as in Days of Yore," *Washington Post*, October 27, 1912, E9; "In Mystic Rites of Merry Halloween Youth and Dignity Prepare to Join," *Washington Post*, October 26, 1913, ES9.
199. *Dennison's 1915 Bogie Book* (reprinted by Bramcost Publications in 2010), 2, 18–19.
200. "Cream of the Midway," *Omaha World-Herald* (Omaha, Nebraska), June 25, 1899, 21.
201. "Ogden Girls Saw the 'Trail' at Portland," *The Standard* (Ogden, Utah), July 15, 1905, 5.

CHAPTER 3

Visual Culture

> The scene was like enchantment, and I fancied its influence had fallen on us who gazed upon it, wretched and apart, fearing to speak and break the silence that brooded over us like a spell.
> —Leslie Walter, *In a Stereoscope* (1863)[1]

When Mary Todd Lincoln visited the Boston studio of William H. Mumler in the early 1870s, she sat alone while he took her photograph.[2] Her late husband was not only one of the most revered men of the nineteenth century, but also—due to various photographs and engravings—one of the most recognizable. Abraham Lincoln's assassination had been one of the greatest tragedies in the history of the United States, with mourners crowding to see his remains as they were taken from Washington, D.C. to Illinois.[3]

Though Lincoln's widow sat alone in Mumler's studio, her photograph bore the likeness of two persons, herself and the unmistakable image of the sixteenth President of the United States, his vaporous hands holding his late wife's shoulders. Though she cried tears of joy at the picture, she was hardly surprised by Lincoln's ghostly visage.[4] Mumler was the inventor of spirit photography, famous for shooting photographs of living persons in which their departed relatives hovered near them. He later recalled that Mary Todd Lincoln traveled all the way from Springfield, Illinois to Boston specifically to have her portrait taken.[5]

Mumler began his career as a spirit photographer in Boston in 1861, not long after Kate and Margaret Fox had introduced Spiritualism to the American public, and just as the country was thrown into a bloody civil war that heightened popular interest in contacting the dead.[6] To customers, Mumler claimed to be a medium; his wife Hannah professed to be one as well.[7] By 1863, Mumler had become successful as well as controversial: at least one of the ethereal "ghosts" in a Mumler photo bore a strong resemblance to someone who was still very much alive.[8]

Relocating to New York City, Mumler's spirit photography gained greater fame and, eventually, more skeptics. "Two men what ain't relations can't have the same grandmother, can they?", a young man asked the mayor of New York in 1869. After having paid Mumler ten dollars for a photograph of his deceased grandmother, the young man met a stranger whose Mumler photograph featured the identical "grandmother." The young man "found to his astonishment . . . the features in the two portraits were the same."[9] Believing himself swindled, he took his grievance to the authorities.

After being arrested, Mumler was put on trial in New York in the spring of 1869. His defenders were steadfast in believing that their deceased relatives had materialized in his photographs.[10] To the prosecution, the photographers were "pretended" images that had "defrauded" customers.[11] Witnesses against Mumler included Jeremiah Gurney, a photographer who demonstrated how to produce "shadowy forms on pictures

SPIRIT PHOTOGRAPHY.

1. Mr. Dobbs, at the request of his Affianced, sits for his Photograph. Unconsciously happens in at Mumler's. | 2. Result — Portrait of Dobbs, with his Five Deceased Wives in Spirituo!!!

Figure 3.1 Published in *Harper's Weekly* in May 1869.

by mechanical means."[12] P. T. Barnum also appeared, his witty testimony provoking a good deal of laughter in the crowded courtroom. Having corresponded with Mumler and having displayed two of his spirit photographs at the American Museum, Barnum pronounced Mumler to be nothing more than a "humbug."[13] A letter published in the *Philadelphia Photographer* in 1869 was even less kind, decrying Mumler's images as featuring the "most bungling and inartistic style."[14]

According to the *Philadelphia Photographer*, the "so-called spiritual photographic swindle" case created "great excitement through the whole country."[15] After protracted testimony, Mumler was acquitted in May 1869 due to a lack of evidence.[16] Until his death in 1884, he maintained that his spirit photographs were genuine. And in his 1875 autobiography, he proudly recounted his many satisfied customers, most famous among them Mary Todd Lincoln.[17]

"There has never been a time when the manufacture of ghosts excited such widespread interest as at the present," the *Boston Herald* reported in 1899. "New styles of apparitions are constantly being patented, and some of the methods for turning them out are as ingenious as they are elaborate. For in these days phantoms have come to be regarded as natural phenomena, produced by optical and mechanical means; they have lost caste, save with the superstitious few, as manifestations of the supernatural."[18]

Horror in American visual culture appeared in many forms, not least of which were Mumler's ghosts. While American Gothic painters conjured something of the "gloomth" that novels of the same genre described, horrifying imagery transformed into something more visceral. Popular publications and photography offered grisly depictions of murder and death, while slide shows materialized apparitions of a type that Mumler might have appreciated; however, they did so not only with an ever-increasing emphasis on horror, but also a sense of obligation to explain how the special effects were achieved, including for the express purpose of diminishing belief in the supernatural.

Paintings

In the eighteenth century, the visual culture of horror manifested in European paintings whose fame reaching the United States. Some Americans were certainly aware of Henry Fuseli's *The Nightmare* (1781), which *The North American Quarterly* in 1835 claimed had "stamped his reputation, and elicited universal applause."[19] Francisco de Goya's *The Sleep of Reason Produces Monsters/El sueño de la razón produce monstruos* (1797–9), *Witches' Flight/Vuelo de brujas* (1797–8), and *Saturn Devouring His Children/Saturno devorando a un hijo* (1819–32, aka *Saturn Devouring His Son*) were also known in United States, as were such later works as Edvard Munch's *The Scream/Schrei der Natur* (1893–1910, aka *The Scream of Nature*).[20]

Rather than emulating any particular European painter, American artists were initially influenced by the Gothic movement. In her landmark study *Painting the Dark Side*, Sarah Burns analyzes "art and the Gothic imagination" created during the nineteenth century by such American artists as David Gilmour Blythe, William Rimmer, and Elihu Vedder.[21] She writes:

> I define this 'gothic' as the art of haunting, using the term as a container for a constellation of themes and moods: horror, fear, mystery, strangeness, fantasy, perversion, monstrosity, insanity. The art of haunting was an art of darkness, often literally: several of the artists I study shared a dark style, characterized by gloomy tonalities, deep shadows and glaring highlights, grotesque figures, and claustrophobic or chaotic spaces.[22]

For Burns, American Gothic artwork explored many repressed themes, among them "personal demons, social displacement (or misplacement), or the omnipresent spectre of slavery and race."[23] Such themes had earlier appeared in American literature, which would in some cases provide these artists with inspiration.

For example, Charles Deas adapted Washington Irving's *The Devil and Tom Walker* into a painting in 1838.[24] John Quidor, whose paintings received little press during his lifetime, also visualized Irving's stories, in works such as *Devil and Tom Walker* (1856), *Tom Walker's Flight* (c. 1856), and *Headless Horseman Pursuing Ichabod Crane* (1858).[25] Albert Pinkham Ryder adapted literary works as well: *The Flying Dutchman* (1887), *Macbeth and the Witches* (c. 1890s), and—most fascinating of all, perhaps because it did not visualize a specific literary passage—*The Temple of the Mind* (1887). Ryder indicated the painting had been inspired by Edgar Allan Poe's poem *The Haunted Palace*, featured in the short story *The Fall of the House of Usher* (1839).[26] Ryder's style—which, the *New York Times* observed in 1901, "delights some people and repulses others"—also extended to landscapes.[27]

Other American artists were drawn to melancholy and decaying landscapes as well, as can be seen in Thomas Cole's *Lake with Dead Trees (Catskill)* (1825), *The Death of Cora*

(c. 1827), and *The Pilgrim of the World at the End of His Journey* (c. 1847). As Burns writes, "Storms, ruin, entrapment, danger, death, and isolation made up a dominant strain in Cole's landscape iconography," thus creating a "dark vision of the American landscape as a place of mystery and terror."[28] Here was an approach similar to that used in literature by Charles Brockden Brown. In 1849, one critic lauded Cole for being the "originator of a new style," the only American who had attempted to paint landscapes in an "imaginative" manner.[29] Nevertheless, his work did not find a major audience. As Daniel Huntington wrote in 1850, "the effect produced by the works of Thomas Cole, on the minds of the mass, may have been slight—almost nothing."[30]

By contrast, Washington Allston achieved great fame. Among his best-known paintings were *Dead Man Restored to Life by Touching the Bones of the Prophet Elisha* (1811–13) and *Saul and the Witch of Endor* (1820–1).[31] Fascinating too is *Spalatro's Vision of the Bloody Hand* (1831), which depicts a scene from Ann Radcliffe's novel *The Italian* (1797). In it, Allston shows not the bloody hand, but instead Spalatro's frightened face, his reaction to a horrifying event.[32] As Diane Chalmers Johnson observes, "Allston achieved the Symbolist's goal of creating an object whose material existence evokes the universal spiritual reality of the imagination."[33]

As Allston's friend Washington Irving said, "He was an admirable story-teller; for a ghost story, none could surpass him. He acted the story as well as told it."[34] Allston was heavily influenced by his travels in Europe, as well as by such artists as Fuseli and Benjamin West.[35] He once referred to his technique as a "mysterious mingling of hues."[36] A poem published in 1848 described Allston with such lines as "Art thou gone indeed?/ And wilt thou speak no more?/nor raise again/Some dreary phantom as thou didst of yore,/That made our flesh to tingle with chill terror?"[37]

Allston also wrote fiction, including a Gothic novel entitled *Monaldi: A Tale* (1841). In it, the title character mistakenly believes that his beloved Rosalia has returned from beyond the grave to haunt him; his delusion leads him to paint a likeness of Satan "enthroned in the majesty of hell." It becomes his masterpiece. "Though only a picture," Monaldi reveals, "*I* have known the original. What is there, I have *seen*." In this novel, Allston's awareness of Gothic literary traditions is apparent, as is the American predilection for the supernatural explained.

Whether or not they attained fame, all of these Gothic artists were limited by the fact that most Americans did not see their work exhibited and certainly could not afford to purchase the originals. Perhaps that is a major consideration, or perhaps not, given that most Americans did not see major Broadway plays or hear famous operas. But what is apparent is that these American Gothic painters had relatively little influence on the visual culture of horror that followed.

Published Illustrations

In 1774, an advertisement published in the *Essex Gazette* of Salem, Massachusetts announced that a Boston publisher had just released a book entitled *The Wonder of Wonders! Or, the Wonderful Appearance of an Angel, Devil, and Ghost*. The advertisement ended by announcing the publication was "Adorned with 4 Plates," representing "The Devil,"

"An Angel with a sword in one hand, a pair of scales in the other," "Belzebub [sic]," and "A ghost, having on a white gown, with his hair much dishevelled."[38]

Most Americans would have encountered illustrations in books and magazines far more often than at art exhibitions. The rise in literacy rates, the proliferation in the number of American publications, and the increasing affordability of the same created a situation where readers could see horror, again and again, owning it and examining it repeatedly in tandem with the written words it accompanied. Here was a new kind of art, accessible to the masses. And some of it—such as the images used for murder literature in the nineteenth century—could be potentially frightening and at times quite gruesome.[39]

From the 1830s, engravings increasingly appeared in popular American magazines.[40] Cynthia Patterson has referred to America in the 1840s as the "hey-day of the illustrated monthly magazines and annuals."[41] By 1893, the *Century Illustrated Magazine* argued that engravings published in magazines "may justly be called a modern art."[42] Indeed, the title of that magazine and a number of others—including *The New York Illustrated Magazine of Literature and Art* and *Arthur's Illustrated Home Magazine*—drew attention to the importance that images held in their pages.

The first notable artist who created such engravings was Felix O. C. Darley. Born in Philadelphia in 1822, he played a central role in the rise of illustrations in America. "His pictures not only seem to breathe," one critic wrote in 1854, "but they also seem to think, which is the highest commendation."[43] Darley's artwork appears in a large and varied array of books of the era, ranging from George Lippard's 1845 Gothic novel *The Quaker City; or, the Monks of Monk Hall: A Romance of Philadelphia Life, Mystery and Crime* to an 1847 edition of *Aladdin; or, The Wonderful Lamp*. He designed illustrations for dime novels, advertisements, and numerous magazines, including for Poe's *The Gold-Bug*, as published in *The Dollar Newspaper* in 1843.[44]

Darley's artwork also appears in Putnam's 1848 edition of Irving's *The Sketch Book of Geoffrey Crayon, Gent.*, and in the same publisher's 1849 edition of *Tales of a Traveller*. In 1850, Art Union printed a folio edition of *The Legend of Sleepy Hollow* that featured six new Darley illustrations for the tale, including his memorable image of the Headless Horseman chasing Ichabod Crane. Here the horseman seems to be a real phantasm, as opposed to Emanuel Leutze's depiction of the same scene in Putnam's *The Hudson Legends* (1864). Leutze's caption *Ichabod and Brom Bones* eliminates all mystery and firmly declares the horseman to be Bones in disguise.[45]

Despite Darley's importance, the person most famous for illustrating horror-themed literature was French artist Gustave Doré, who created a series of haunting etchings for a self-published edition of Dante's *Inferno* in 1861. His final project became a series of steel-plate engravings for a folio edition of Poe's *The Raven*, published by Harper & Brothers in late 1883 and featuring a cover designed by Dora Wheeler and frontispiece created by Elihu Vedder. *Harper's Bazaar* proclaimed *The Raven* to be Doré's "greatest" work.[46] "They bear all the hallmarks of his strange and extravagant genius," said *The Critic*. Indeed, Doré's work became more associated with Poe than with any other artist, including Albert Edward Sterner, who produced twenty images for *The Works of Edgar Allan Poe*, published by Stone & Kimball in 1895.[47]

Figure 3.2 Emanuel Leutze's *Ichabod and Brom Bones* (1864).

By the end of the nineteenth century, book illustrations had become increasingly common. The cover of the first American edition of *Dracula* (Doubleday & McClure, 1899) features artwork of the winding road to the vampire's castle, the setting sun, and a small number of bats, whereas the second edition (Doubleday, 1902) depicts Dracula, a wolf, and a bat. Other novels included interior illustrations as well, as in the case of George Du Maurier's *Trilby* (1895). The original novel contained over one hundred of Du Maurier's engravings, the eeriest being *An Incubus*, which merges Svengali's head with the body of a spider.[48]

W. J. Hennessy provided numerous illustrations for F. Marion Crawford's *The Witch of Prague* (1891), among them a representation of the sepulchral appearance of Beatrice, as described in this passage:

[The Wanderer] was standing at his full height, his arms stretched up to heaven, his face luminously pale, his deep eyes on fire and fixed upon her face, forcing back her dominating will upon itself. But he was not alone.

'Beatrice!' he cried in long-drawn agony.

Between him and Unorna something passed by, something dark and soft and noiseless, that took shape slowly—a woman in black, a veil thrown back from her forehead, her white hands hanging by her side.

Likewise, M. Leone Bracker's frontispiece for Crawford's *Wandering Ghosts* illustrates a key moment in the short story *The Screaming Skull*. Its caption incorporates dialogue from Crawford's story: "What? . . . It's gone, man, the skull is gone!!"

At times, artists seemingly tried to frighten readers, such as with the image that accompanied George MacDonald's poem *The Haunted House* in *Scribner's Monthly* in 1874, and the artwork *Murdered Mary Seneff's Ghost*, as published in *The National Police Gazette* in 1881.[49] By contrast, many other engravings of ghosts were intended to be humorous, rather than horrifying.[50] Some of them made fun of Spiritualists.[51] Others featured not ghosts, but pranksters using white sheets trying to scare their friends.[52]

The key purveyor of horrifying artwork in America in the nineteenth century was *The National Police Gazette*, but it rarely invoked the supernatural.[53] One illustration in 1879 showed a "weird waif" attempting to suck the breath of life out of her sleeping benefactor.[54] That same year, *A Gallows Ball* exposed "barbaric voodoo incantations."[55] Two years later, *A Night of Horror* depicted a "paralytic" dragging her brother's body out of a fire, after which it was "devoured by cats."[56] In 1882, *The Terrors of Art* found children nearly killing one of their friends by covering him with plaster so as "to make a statue of him."[57] Another illustration that year showed a "frenzied" mother finding dogs exhuming her dead baby in a cemetery.[58] Yet another revealed the "horrors of a reform school" in which two women tortured young girls.[59]

The majority of the magazine's engravings featured scenes of murder and death, ranging from the discovery or disposal of corpses to courtroom scenes and executions.[60] Illustrations of lynchings appeared repeatedly, most depicting the action prior to actual hangings and sometimes efforts to halt them.[61] However, on a few occasions, the magazine published images documenting the moment of execution, as in *A Public Lynching in the South* (1886), *How Wholesale Murder Is Avenged in the Wild West* (1888), and the particularly grisly *Women Hanging Huns* (1889).[62]

Most common were engravings of individuals murdering others. In many instances, shootings were depicted in progress, with smoke lifting from revolvers or rifles as the victim falls.[63] Sometimes artwork displayed action immediately before the murder was committed, just prior to the shooting or stabbing of victims.[64] In other cases, artwork depicted the moments immediately after the murder.[65] Both approaches generally lessened the gruesomeness. For example, *Believed She Was a Witch* (1893) illustrates a man who has just shot his aunt. The caption tells us he proceeded to trample her head "into a jelly," an action which is certainly not shown.[66] That said, this same approach also held the potential to heighten the horror. An 1867 illustration depicted a woman who has just stabbed another woman; the tip of her knife is coated in dripping blood.[67]

Occasionally, the *National Police Gazette* presented illustrations of murder in the form of sequential artwork, an approach similar to what comic strips and film storyboards would do in later years.[68] For example, the first panel of *The Michigan Quadruple Murder* (1883) depicts a man and wife asleep in bed. The next illustrates the exterior of their home, and the third panel shows the same man and wife murdered.[69] The three images chronologically visualize the key points in the narrative. Similarly, *The Chatsworth Horror* (1887) presents—as the captions explain—"Thieves Robbing the Dead," "The Victims in a Village Store," "In the Burning Cars," and—by way of a narrative finale–"To the Rescue."[70] Other illustrations depict murderous scenes in more complicated respects,

Figure 3.3 Published in the December 28, 1867 issue of the *National Police Gazette*.

whether using a diagonally split composition to detail two events in the same image, as in *The Massachusetts Revolver Rampant* (1889), or as large images featuring smaller vignettes that not only sequence the narrative, but also present portraits of key characters, as in *The New Hampshire Horror* (1883).[71] These illustrations rely on composition not unlike that later used in filmmaking.

Published artwork of this type continued concurrent with the rise of the moving picture. In 1912, for example, the *Cleveland Plain Dealer* printed a story on Elizabeth Bathory; it features an illustration of the murderous Countess admiring herself in a mirror while holding a bloody cane over a defenseless maiden.[72] Here was imagery as gruesome as most of the engravings published in *The National Police Gazette*, and it appeared in the pages of a mainstream newspaper.

Phantasmagoria

The visual culture of horror was deeply connected to and intertwined with the rise of screen practice, as is particularly evident in the case of the magic lantern. Historians generally credit Christiaan Huygens with inventing the first projecting lantern in the seventeenth century, with surviving designs for his painted glass slides featuring a skeleton in various poses, such that with proper manipulation it would appear to fall apart into bones: moving pictures, at least of a certain kind.[73] The magic lantern's notoriety for projecting horrific images even appears in an early dictionary definition. In 1696, *The New World of English Words: or, a General Dictionary* defined the "magick lanthorn" as a "small Optical Macheen, that shews by a gloomy Light upon a white Wall, Spectres and Monsters so hideous that he who knows not the Secret, believes it to be perform'd by Magic Art."[74] Lantern shows of this type appeared in America as early as 1743.[75]

At the end of the eighteenth century, a new kind of lantern show appeared for the first time, the "Phantasmagoria." Most famous among its early proponents was Étienne-Gaspard Robert, who incorrectly claimed to have been its inventor.[76] Using the stage name Robertson, his earliest "Fantasmagorie" performances date to Paris in 1798.[77] One nineteenth-century account described the Phantasmagoria as being:

> ... nothing more than a Magic lantern, in which the images are received on a transparent screen, which is fixed in view of the spectator. The Magic lantern mounted upon wheels, is made to recede from, or approach the screen; the consequence of which is, the picture on the screen expands to a gigantic size, or contracts into an invisible object, or mere luminous spot . . .[78]

These shows not only featured spectral images of changing scale, but also relied on spoken commentary, music, sounds, and various special effects.[79] Lynda Nead writes, "The visual effects of the slides were enhanced by smoke, lighting, glass and mirrors, creating a total environment devoted to the representation and experience of haunting."[80]

Thanks to John P. Bologna, phantasmagoria shows appeared in America for the first time in 1803.[81] An advertisement in New York in November of that year promised a:

> ... *wonderful display of Optical Illusions*, Which introduces the Phantoms, of Apparitions of the Dead and Absent, in a way more completely illusive, than has ever yet been witnessed, as the objects freely originate in the air, and unfold themselves under various forms and sizes, such as imagination alone has hitherto painted them, occasionally assuming a figure and most perfect resemblance of the heroes and other distinguished characters of past and present times. This Spectrology professes to expose the practices of artful imposters and exorcists, and to open the eyes of those who will foster an absurd belief in *Ghosts* or *Disembodied spirits*.[82]

As X. Theodore Barber notes, phantasmagoria shows "flourished" in America until c. 1839.[83]

In addition to ghosts, these shows also projected artwork of characters from literature and history, as well as representations of natural disasters. The "real and celebrated Phantasmagoria"—as presented in Savannah, Georgia in 1810—promised a "various number of phantoms and apparitions," among them the "Bleeding Nun [an image adapted from Matthew Gregory Lewis's 1796 novel *The Monk*], Robespierre, a Tomb of Monks, a Skeleton digging its own grave, General Moreau (now in the United States), Mirabeau, &c."[84] Two years later, an advertisement in Baltimore announced a "Phantasmagoria" that would feature a "natural representation of the Eruption of Mount Vesuvius, emiting [sic] fire, smoke, vivid lighting, thunder and &c. and will conclude with the multiplication of Caricatures."[85]

By the 1820s, Phantasmagoria shows became more common in America, some featuring appearances by the famous Robertson. According to an article published in Boston in 1825, Robertson's images were:

> ... not terrifying, and do not require a total absence of light. They excite the curiosity of a man of science, and are calculated to amuse every one. They tend moreover to strengthen weak minds, and to dispel those prejudices and false terrors imbibed in our infancy, and which very often accompany our riper years.[86]

The images Robertson displayed not only included ghosts, but also images of the "nation's heroes" and "scenes belonging to history," all being projected with "agreeable and varied music, in character with the different objects presented."

Reviewing one of Robertson's American shows, a critic wrote in 1825, "We have all seen spectres and strange sights, but it is by the elegance of Mr. Robertson's allegorical delineations, and the perfection of his illusions, that he has succeeded in attracting full houses." The same critic added that audience members would witness "astonishing" optical illusions, and that some would attempt to "discover the manner in which they may sometimes have been deceived or imposed upon."[87] In 1855, a magazine article claimed that Robertson "appealed, in fact, to a coarse taste; established a reign of terror; produced every supernatural horror that a man can fear; and said, 'Why do you fear?' There is nothing here but a certain mechanical contrivance, and the application of a few principles of science."[88]

Many articles appeared in newspapers and magazines to explain how phantasmagoria illusions were produced, including the need for a transparent screen for projection rather than a "white wall of sheet."[89] Nevertheless, such articles also noted that "the effect [of phantasmagoria] on the mind is indescribable."[90] Here is what Terry Castle has called the "ambiguity of the phantasmagoria," given that the shows "mediated oddly between rational and irrational imperatives."[91] Even those who did not believe in ghosts could not necessarily understand or explain the technology of phantasmagoria.

In 1839, Monsieur Adrien presented in America "his splendid new illusions of the *Phantasmagoria, or Nocturnal Apparitions*, painted expressly for him by eminent artists in England, France, and Italy."[92] By 1852, he offered the *Grand Phantasmagoria, or Living Phantoms*, which depicted "how the ancient Sorcerers used to make the people believe in Ghosts, Witches, and the 'Mysterious Knockings.'"[93] By 1865, Adrien called his show—which still attempted to illuminate how "ancient sorcerers made the people believe in ghosts, phantoms, and mysterious knockings"—*Laughable Phantasmagoria, or Living Phantoms*.[94] With scientific explanations of the phenomena came an increasing emphasis on humor.

Photographic Lantern Slides

It was not until 1850, over a century after the magic lantern originally appeared in America, that the Langenheim brothers produced the first photographic glass slide, which revolutionized magic lantern shows.[95] As Charles Musser has noted:

> Photography provided the first key element of standardization in screen practice. With the ability to make multiple copies of a single image, slide producers now had a process of manufacture that was much more efficient than hand painting, and this development was accompanied by corresponding advances in lithography, which was also used to make lantern-slide images. Multiple photographic images could be smaller than painted slides yet provided greater detail and were much cheaper to produce. Lanterns could be scaled down, made more portable, and sold for less. Screen practitioners had begun to adopt methods of industrial manufacture.[96]

Photographic slides experienced gradual growth during the 1850s and 1860s.[97] Their numbers increased greatly during the 1880s and beyond, as did their appearances at various kinds of public events.

In 1885, one journalist recalled, "The first time I saw a magic lantern show I thought it about the grandest thing that science and art could get up."[98] Ten years later, a lecturer in New York used a magic lantern and photographic slides to project "ghosts and spirits that have appeared to mankind in all ages of the world's history." An "entertaining" talk, combined with the music of Chopin's *Sonata No. 2 in B-flat Minor* and wind rattling the windows, caused a "shudder" to run "through the rows of silent listeners."[99]

In addition to public lectures, lantern shows also appeared regularly at pseudo-scientific "dime museums." Beginning in the 1870s, these affordable museums flourished in large cities like New York, Chicago, Philadelphia, and Boston; they reached their height of popularity in the 1880s and 1890s.[100] Andrea Stulman Dennett writes, "The dime museum has been nearly forgotten, but during its heyday in the latter half of the nineteenth century, it was as popular an institution in the United States as the movies are today."[101] Variety shows were the most common lantern-slide presentations at these venues, with the topics of individual slides not necessarily having much in common with one another.[102]

Lantern-slide projections were hardly limited to public performances. Magic lanterns could be purchased or rented for schools or private parties, and a number of toy magic lanterns were manufactured for home use as well.[103] In 1910, the magazine *American Boy* even featured an article that taught youngsters "how to make ghost pictures" and "lantern slide plates."[104] More notably, men's organizations regularly screened slides for their private meetings. These "Secret Society Views" were probably projected more regularly than any other slides, given their repeated usage at meeting after meeting.[105] Such images often featured artwork of wizards, dragons, demons, serpents, bats, and other creatures.

Despite being reproduced and manufactured using photographic processes, the images on most horror-themed slides were artwork. At times, these came from pre-existing images. As early as 1867, for example, T. H. McAllister—whose Philadelphia-based company became America's largest distributor of lantern slides in the nineteenth century—sold seventy-six slides that collectively depicted the story of Dante's *Inferno*, the bulk of them being reproductions of Gustave Doré's engravings. The company continued to sell the same slides until as late as 1899, if not later.[106]

However, in most cases, American artists created new images specifically for lantern slide companies. The most prolific of them was Joseph Boggs Beale, who was born in Philadelphia in 1841 and worked for the C. W. Briggs company from 1881 until 1909. Beale created over two thousand images that resulted in 258 lantern slide sets, the content ranging from the patriotic and historical to the literary and religious.[107] Among his horror-themed slides were *All Hallow Ev'n* (1881), *Witch in Sky* (1900), *Delirium Tremens* (1909), which used demons and serpents to depict alcohol abuse, and *Hell*, which was included in a large religious set entitled *The Photodrama of Creation* (1914).[108]

Beale's biographers, Terry and Deborah Borton, have made a compelling argument that Beale's style of artwork employed techniques similar to those later used in filmmaking: storyboards, lighting techniques, and—given that he painted sequential art to visualize narratives—continuity editing.[109] For example, Beale created thirty-two slides to depict *Gray's Elegy* in 1900, twenty-five to depict Dickens's *A Christmas Carol* in 1908 (sold under the title *Marley's Ghost*), twelve to depict *Bridget's Dream* in 1910 (in which clothes comically turn into ghosts), and six to depict *The Legend of Sleepy Hollow* in 1910.[110] He also created six to depict *The Spectre Pig* c. 1902–3. Based on an 1830 poem by Oliver

Figure 3.4 Slide 4 of Joseph Boggs Beale's *The Raven*. (*Courtesy of Terry and Deborah Borton*)

Wendell Holmes, the grisly tale features a butchered pig that returns to haunt the butcher and eventually butcher him.

Musser has identified cinematic characteristics in Beale's work, writing at length about the twelve images he created in 1890 to adapt Edgar Allan Poe's *The Raven*:

> The perspective shifts, 'moving in' and 'panning' from right to left for the first three slides and 'pulling back' for the fourth. This spatial instability creates a mood of unease and disorientation well suited to the poem. It also sets up the next slides, in which spectres appear. Specifically the progressions from slides four to five and then from seven through ten retain single perspectives and display excellent continuity. By dissolving from one view to the next, the exhibitor could thus create a particularly haunting succession of images.[111]

Musser also notes that a lecturer would have read *The Raven* while Beale's slides were projected, with the edges of each slide indicating when the projectionist needed to "cut" to the next slide.

Effects comparable to those later employed in the cinema were not unique to Beale, however. Many lantern operators used "dissolving views," the appearance of which was similar to later dissolves seen in moving pictures. As an 1890 manual for magic lantern usage explained, "one image die[s] gradually away and the next on the list grow[s] gradually in a weird or 'uncanny' sort of way out of the ghost of the last."[112] To some audiences, the very use of a dissolve might have appeared potentially eerie or strange.

Slide manufacturers even produced particular slides intended for dissolves. In 1888, for example, T. H. McAllister sold such dissolving slides as *Haunted Abbey* (1. *Midnight View of an Old Abbey with Sculptured Tomb*, and, 2. *A Ghost Appears above the Tomb*), and *Faust and Marguerite* (1. *Faust in His Laboratory Tempted by Mephistopheles*, and, 2. *Vision of Marguerite Appears*).[113] A decade later, McAllister expanded his dissolving slides to include *Dance of Death* (1. *A Hall at the Gay French Court*, and, 2. *A Witch's Glen; the Dancers Change to Hideous Skeletons Capering around a Seething Cauldron*), and *Haunted House* (1. *A Bedchamber; the Sleeper Starts from His Slumbers*, and, 2. *And Beholds an Unearthly Visitor at His Bedside.*).[114]

But dissolves represented just one of many ways to create the illusion of movement in slides, a practice that was already quite advanced by the mid-nineteenth century. Benjamin Pike, Jr.'s *Catalogue of Optical Goods* (1848) advised:

> To give motion effect to the images, a variety of movable sliders are made for this purpose, many of which produce very curious appearances, but with the usual sliders the images may be made to travel in a circular, elliptical or other direction by moving the lantern in the corresponding way.[115]

Slide manufacturers developed various types of slide frames and levers on them to create movement that did not require the operator to move the lantern physically, as phantasmagoria shows had. For example, "movable slips" allowed a single change of

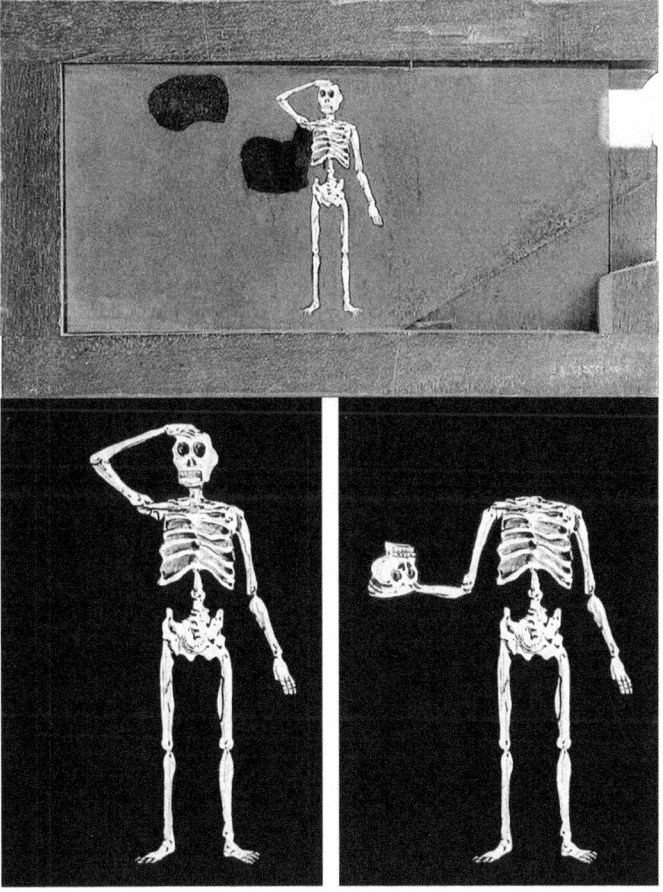

Figure 3.5 An American "movable slip" slide (top), which could give motion to the skeleton, causing him to remove his skull (bottom left and right). (*Courtesy of Larry Cederblom*)

action to a given scene, thus creating what one catalog described as "laughable motion to figures." In 1867, T. H. McAllister sold such movable slips as *Fiend, with Moving Eyes* and *Nightmare Made Visible*.[116] By 1888, McAllister offered many more "Movable Comic Views," with the movement produced by a "portion of the figure being painted on a glass plate, which is quickly drawn to one side." These "highly colored" slides included *A Somnambulist, Beware of the Gorilla, A Bottle Imp, Boy and Demon's Head, Countryman and Dog Changing Heads, Ghost–Donkey in a Churchyard, Ghost Stories, Magician and Ghost, Skeleton Taking Off His Head*, and—in a reworking of Christiaan Huygens' idea—*Skeleton Falling to Pieces*.[117] The company also sold a group of "Humorous Transformations," which worked on the same principle, but were of "finer execution." Among them were *Green Monster (A Dragon), Human Skeleton (Orderly and Disorderly)*, and *Wizard (A Goblin Appears at His Command)*.[118]

Topics that might otherwise inspire fright or revulsion were usually treated comically. One of the most popular, variants of which were sold by numerous companies, was an image of a man sleeping in bed. Movement caused a rat to appear to run inside his open mouth. T. H. McAllister sold such a slide in 1888 under the name *Human Rat Trap (Moral: Don't Sleep with Your Mouth Open)*.[119] In the late 1890s, Montgomery Ward offered a similar slide entitled *The Sleeping Rat Eater*, describing it as follows: "A bearded Russian is sleeping when a rat crawls over the bed and jumps into the sleeper's open mouth."[120]

Some McAllister slides with movement came embedded in larger sets that also included slides that were static, thus allowing for variety in the space of short narratives. As early as 1881, McAllister offered *Haunted Chamber, Berlin* (1. *Throne-room of the Royal Palace*, and 2. *A Spectral Figure with Uplifted Arm Glides across the Floor*) and *Skeleton Dance* (1. *The Ruins of Alloway Kirk, the Moonlight Casting Its Weird Light on the Tombstones in the Foreground*, and 2. *A Skeleton Appears Dancing*).[121] Other examples, which McAllister sold in 1888, included a three-slide set entitled *The Churchyard Revelry*: "1. Represents a Village Church and Churchyard, by day. 2. The same by Moonlight. By a lever movement to the slide a skeleton raises the top of [a] tomb near the Church." The third slide in the set was "Illumination of the Church, the hands of the clock in the tower pointing to the midnight hour—'The witching time of night, when churchyards yawn.' This slide has also a lever movement, by which three skeletons arise from graves in the foreground and dance."[122]

An important device in the development of sequenced images to create an appearance of movement was the Choreutoscope.[123] As one lantern-slide manual described, it depended:

> ... upon the failing of the eye to retain the rapid succession of changes.... There [are] some six to eight designs of figures, in various attitudes, on each slide, which is about ten inches long, but in the Giant Choreutoscope is twenty inches. This long slide is made to pass behind an opening in the frame and during the interval of the change between each figure a shutter covers the opening until the next following design is in its place, when it again opens; the interval between each change is worked *ad lib*. Some of the designs are brought out to their best advantage when shown in conjunction with some set scene, or set of effects, for instance the dancing skeleton indulging in his wild terpsichorean revel in the bedroom scene of the haunted castle, is most weird.[124]

Dancing skeletons became one of the most famous moving images of the lantern-slide era, as well as one of the most humorous.

While the predominant number of lantern slides displaying supernatural imagery were comical, the same was not true of slides depicting real-life tragedies. In these cases, which were relatively rare, serious and sometimes disturbing images were projected. For example, in 1896, an exhibitor presented a "grewsome [sic] entertainment" by projecting "portraits" of "deathbed scenes" accompanied by an Edison phonograph of the "groans and sighs of patients dying in hospital sick wards, or tortured in their surgical amphitheatres."[125] Here was graphic multimedia entertainment, with projected images taken not from paintings, but from photographs.

Photography

In an 1840 essay, Edgar Allan Poe declared that photography was "the most important, and perhaps the most extraordinary triumph of modern science." He also argued that photographs could be regarded as the "absolute truth," a "perfect identity of aspect with the thing represented."[126] Here Poe was commenting upon a particularly recent invention, the origins of the American Daguerreotype dating to 1839.[127] He subsequently wrote that photography would "prove, upon the whole, highly beneficial to the interests of the fine arts."[128] Among those interests were horrors, both natural and supernatural.

Death became a common topic of the nineteenth century, including lynchings photographed by amateurs and local professionals, some of which were turned into postcards.[129] Another key example would be depictions of American Civil War casualties, such as the famous photographs by Matthew Brady and Alexander Gardner. Gardner's *Home of the Rebel Sharpshooter, Gettysburg, Pennsylvania, 1863* became one of the most notable images.[130] As Keith F. Davis has noted, Brady and Gardner sometimes posed their scenes of the war dead to heighten a viewer's emotional response, thus dramatizing the nonfiction they represented.[131] Writing about photographs of Antietam, one journalist observed in 1863:

> These wrecks of manhood thrown together in careless heaps, or [ar]ranged in ghastly rows for burial were alive but yesterday. . . . Many people would not look through this series [of photographs]. Many, having seen it and dreamed of its horrors, would lock it up in some secret drawer, that it might not thrill or revolt those whose soul sickens at such sights.[132]

However much Americans wanted to see the images, many could not until years later. It was not until the 1880s that the half-tone process allowed newspapers and magazines to reproduce photographs. As a result, during the nineteenth century, more Americans likely saw images of the Spanish-American War of 1898 than they did of the U.S. Civil War.[133]

Images of the dead also included the nineteenth-century tradition of post-mortem photography, for some an important type of mourning ephemera.[134] These often involved living relatives sitting or standing alongside the dearly departed, a practice that allowed mourners, in the words of Stanley B. Burns, to "visually embalm" the dead. They were "private expressions of personal loss," which were not usually reproduced for the public.[135] Such photographs became common practice in middle- and apparently some working-class families from the 1860s to the end of the century, more common for a time than wedding photographs.[136] Here was perhaps the culmination of what Poe described, an artistic representation of the truth.

By contrast, other persons saw photography as a means to produce fantastical images, using technology to create that which did not exist. Nancy M. West suggests that an "intense confusion of image and afterlife has always haunted photography, to the extent that the photographic image has persistently occupied an uneasy space between the worlds of science and magic...."[137] Speaking of "magic photographs" and, synonymously, of "photoprestigitation" in 1866, the *Philadelphia Photographer* described printing processes that could yield "amusing entertainment," but added that such trickery was hardly recent, as "the older disciples of Daguerre will remember that the trick is nothing very new after all."[138]

Of these tricks, the most famous tradition became spirit photography of the type inaugurated by Mumler. "Most persons have heard of these 'ghost pictures,'" one magazine wrote in 1874, but views on their veracity varied.[139] As early as 1863, Oliver Wendell Holmes declared that such images were nothing more than wishful thinking on the part of survivors.[140] After visiting Lily Dale, the "summer home of spiritualists," in 1899, a skeptical journalist decried it as being the "acme of fake," thanks to the photographic work of a "Mr. Hearn."[141]

Even those who believed in ghosts raised important questions. As the *Scientific American* observed in 1873, "some persons . . . allege that spirits are invisible; that an invisible thing cannot be photographed; therefore the so-called spirit photographs are base impostures."[142] A photographer who subscribed to Spiritualism denounced one spirit image to be fraudulent in 1879 due to several technical reasons, among them the light and shade on the living person coming from a different position to that on the alleged ghost.[143] In his 1891 book *Hours with the Ghosts, or Nineteenth Century Witchcraft*, Henry Ridgely Evans wrote, "Both Spiritualism and Theosophy contain germs of truth, but both are tinctured with superstition. I purpose, if possible, to sift the wheat from the chaff."[144] For his book, he faked two spirit photographs in an effort to illustrate how easily they could be made.

Others found such images just as compelling as Mary Todd Lincoln apparently did, visual signs of comfort and of the possibility of eventual reunification. In 1890, a woman in Los Angeles became "seriously ill" after seeing a photograph of herself with a spirit unexpectedly lurking in the background, beckoning to her.[145] She was convinced that the photographer was not to blame, which might have been correct, the apparition being due to some kind of mistake or to fraud perpetrated by others. The latter was particularly common at séances in which honest psychic investigators and their cameras were fooled by spirit materializations produced by such mediums as Eusapia Palladino, Florence Cook, and Eva C. (aka Marthe Béraud).[146] While most of the resultant images were obvious fakes, they found sincere believers in many quarters, Arthur Conan Doyle among them.[147]

Potentially horrifying photographs also appeared in the form of stereo views (aka "stereoviews" and "stereographs") sold for home use: two photographs of the same subject on a single card, which—when examined through a viewer—created the illusion of a single, three-dimensional image. "The result is one of the most pleasing as well as one of the [most] wonderful in the science of optics," the *Philadelphia Photographer* wrote in 1871.[148] Though they were sold as early as the 1850s, stereo views reached their peak of popularity in the 1890s, becoming a "parlor entertainment craze," in part due to their affordability.[149] Many of the stereo views were nonfiction, as in the case of photographs of famous persons and locations, whereas others were fictional, featuring models posed for dramatic or comedic purposes.

Some stereo views treated potentially horrifying subjects in a fairly innocuous manner. *Getting Ready for Hallowe'en* (Keystone, 1890s, aka *Fall–Making Hallowe'en Jack-o'-lanterns in the Pumpkin Field*) depicts children carving jack o' lanterns, while *Hallowe'en Party. An Intruder* (Universal Photo Art, 1899) displays a party of young women, one of whom is shocked to see a man entering the room. H. C. White's 1907 *And the Goblins Will Get You If You Don't Watch Out* depicts a grandfather telling a bedtime story to five children, but shows no such creatures. Here were images that were more sentimental than frightening.

The same was true of a number of ghost stereo views. For example, some of the luminous spirits were intended to be guardian angels, among them *Guardian Spirit* (A. P. Sherburne, 1869), *Her Guardian Angels* (Underwood & Underwood, 1893), *Their Guardian Angel* (Universal Photo Art, 1897), and *Her Guardian Angel* (Keystone, 1898).[150] Others visualized dreams, as in *The Dream* (Melander, 1874–5), *Only a Dream* (Keystone, 1894), and *The Little Orphan's Dream* (Keystone, 1897).[151] And then there were nostalgic remembrances of the past, as in *That Old Sweetheart of Mine* (Keystone, 1901), comical warnings, as when a ghost advises a card player in *That's Too Thin* (Melander, 1875), and admonitions against alcohol, as when a skeletal apparition appears before a drinker in *There's Death in the Cup* (Keystone, 1898). Likening alcohol to Satan, Death, or Ghosts proved to be a popular and enduring metaphor.

All that said, images of horrifying demons, devils, and spectres appeared in a large number of stereo views produced in Europe, a number of them imported into the United States, though precisely which and in what quantities is hard to determine. Some were apparently distributed exactly as released in their home countries, while others may have been licensed or even re-created by American companies. For example, in 1869 Holmes sold a stereo view in the United States entitled *A Dream after Seeing Pepper's Ghost*. It is unknown whether or not this was the same image created by the London Stereoscopic Company c. 1865, or if it was a mere appropriation of the earlier title.[152]

Figure 3.6 Stereo view entitled *There's Death in the Cup* (Keystone, 1898).

However, it is certain that American companies produced and distributed a number of potentially horrifying stereo views. At least two feature spectres at the piano.[153] The New York Stereoscopic Company issued *Apparition* (undated), in which a ghost advances on a man while his companions are too shocked to help. *An Unwelcome Visitor* (Keystone, 1895) depicted a female ghost materializing before a man and woman. *The Haunted Lane* (Melander, 1889) features a ghost frightening a man and boy. Years later, *The Haunted Lane* (Littleton, 1906) presented a similar image, with a ghost scaring a man and woman. By that time, Littleton had already released a stereo view with nearly identical composition, an interior scene called *The Haunted Lovers* (1893), in which a female ghost scares a man and woman.

As with photography and published illustrations, however, the most potentially horrifying stereo views were those that depicted real events. At least a few stereo views showed corpses, including *The Dead Left by Receding Flood, 33rd St. and Avenue M* (Underwood & Underwood, 1900) and *Placing Corpse in Coffin for Burial, Messina, Italy* (Keystone, 1909). More grisly were those stereo views that pictured authentic executions and lynchings, as in an untitled lynching of an African-American male in Paris, Texas in front of a large crowd (as sold by James McCusker of Philadelphia in 1893) and in *Execution by the Garrote in the Yard of the City Prison, Havana, Cuba* (Keystone, 1899). Staged photographs of this type could also be grisly, as can be seen in *A Neck-Tie Party, Given by the Vigilants* (T. W. Ingersoll, 1898) and in *And Speedily the 'Punishment Fits the Crime'* (Universal Photo Art, 1901), both depicting cowboy vigilantes hanging criminals.

Illustrated Song Slides

Fictional horror in photography also found a home in the world of the illustrated song. Despite its earlier appearance at other venues, the illustrated song slide found its greatest success at the nickelodeon theatre during the years 1906 to 1913. Nickelodeon exhibitors could rent song slides from film exchanges along with their moving pictures, or they could purchase sets of slides to keep.[154] In some cases, prominent music publishers (rather than slide manufacturers) even gave away song slides or sold them at heavily reduced prices.[155] By hiring a local singer—or "illustrator," as they were sometimes called, the term linking the performer to the onscreen visuals—nickelodeons presented live performances of the newest popular songs to their audiences. In some cases, these singers even achieved local fame.

Demand for song slides grew during the early nickelodeon era, in part because many nickelodeons changed their programs three or more times a week, which meant that individual songs usually had little time to become hits.[156] The use of these songs at nickelodeon theatres had numerous benefits. They increased the duration of the program, while simultaneously giving the film projector a rest; due to the risk of fires, some cities and states required intermittent usage of projectors. Illustrated songs also gave projectionists time to thread up the next reel.[157] Furthermore, they added variety to shows otherwise dominated by moving pictures.

By the autumn of 1906, a number of companies sold song slides to exhibitors and to film exchanges, among them the Boswell Manufacturing Company (which was based in Chicago), Eugene Cline & Company (Chicago), Harstn & Company (New York), the McIntosh Lantern Company (Chicago), and the Selig Polyscope Company (Chicago); the

T. H. McAllister company also distributed song slides during this era.[158] However, due to the number and popularity of their releases, three song slide manufacturers emerged as the most important: Scott & Van Altena and DeWitt C. Wheeler (both located in New York City) and the Chicago Transparency Company (located in Chicago).

With minimum orders of at least fifty sets, these companies prepared relevant illustrations for new songs. Song slide sets were usually comprised of fourteen or, more commonly, sixteen slides per song.[159] The first slide gave the song's title, normally by reproducing the sheet music cover. The next fourteen slides usually presented images of models in costumes and on sets or locations. The models' actions in each slide generally accompanied the song's first verse (four slides), its first chorus (three slides), its second verse (four slides), and its second chorus (three slides). In some cases, the images added narrative information to the lyrics, interacting with them rather than merely providing a visualization of them.[160] The final slide in the set printed the words to the chorus so the audience could join in the singing, something which they did not do during the bulk of the song.[161]

The result was a projected visual narrative with music. In 1917, Charles K. Harris described the song slide as the "little father of photodrama," explaining that their scenes told stories through careful attention to choice of models, costumes, locations, and lighting. He also wrote that the "same methods that were used in making song slides are now being used by the greatest moving picture directors in making their scenarios."[162] Harris was himself a testament to the narrative and aesthetic link between the two media, as he began writing film scenarios after working in the song slide business.[163]

That said, film historians have often overlooked the critical importance of the illustrated song in the nickelodeon era. As Rick Altman writes:

> Even the best histories consider nickel theatres primarily in the context of early cinema, and thus explain their existence and growth primarily through developments specific to the film industry. A more satisfactory approach to the nickelodeon phenomenon would recognize the fundamentally multimedia nature of the storefront theatre program.[164]

Altman also suggests that the illustrated song was important in "setting standards for matching music to the moving picture."[165] Given the comments made by Charles K. Harris, it should be noted that historians have generally discounted the illustrated song's interaction with and possible influence upon the narrative structure and mise-en-scène of early films.

Beyond an ability to augment or even ignore narrative information contained in sheet music lyrics, illustrated songs could feature an array of complicated visuals. Altman has written that song slide visuals at times depicted images of "borrowed arts," such as artwork and cartoons. He also suggests that slide-makers at times created "surreal" images featuring "multiple planes, unexpected matches, and contrasting scales" by means of careful post-production manipulation of the photographs used.[166]

Over ten horror-themed song slide sets were produced in the nickelodeon era, a relatively small number in comparison to the sheer number of sets released, but surviving examples feature complex and varied imagery, and at times they were able to produce potentially horrifying settings more successfully than some moving pictures, specifically in the production of realistic nighttime scenes. Consider *That Mysterious Rag* (Scott & Van Altena, 1911).[167] Slide 1 features an image of two men frightened in the middle of the night, one of them holding a candle; Slide 3 shows one of them scared in his bed, clutching at a sheet. Similar imagery appears in *The Ragtime Dream* (Scott & Van Altena, 1913), with a model holding a candle at night.

Not all of these were intended to be scary. *My Egyptian Mummy* (Scott & Van Altena, 1913) conveyed a romantic song about two lovers. In Slide 2, the male and female leads (who wear Egyptian attire, but not bandages) appear superimposed over sarcophagi in a museum. She appears in front of a pyramid in Slide 4, and the two appear together in an Egyptian structure in Slide 5. Subsequent images feature them together riding on an elephant (Slide 7), together at the Sphinx (Slide 9), and together at what is presumably meant to be the Nile River (Slides 11 and 12). Slide 14 features the two lovers in a flower vignette, with the Sphinx, pyramid, and moon behind them.

By contrast, *The Ghost of the Violin* (Scott & Van Altena, 1912) was likely the most frightening of these illustrated songs. In the dark of night, represented in part by blue tinting, a ghost appears inside an antique store. In Slide 3, he appears in a medium shot; along with his make-up, a vaporous, fog effect makes him appear ethereal. In Slide 5, two scared humans listen to him play eerie violin music. In Slide 7, he appears twice, on screen right and screen left, against a background of dramatic clouds, another visual sign of his discarnate status. In Slide 9, a long shot depicts eight people gathered near a castle turret, a large moon in the background, all of them apparently hearing the strange music. By Slide 12, the ghost appears against a castle wall, playing to his audience. Then, Slide 14 shows the ghost sitting on a wooden frame, continuing to fiddle while two owls and a personified moon appear nearby.

A number of slide sets featured evil hypnotists, the most dramatic being *That Hypnotizing Man* (Scott & Van Altena, 1911). Slide 4 is a particularly menacing and sexualized image: it shows the evil hypnotist looking directly into the camera, bursting through an enormous, sexualized flower, while his victim is asleep. Subsequent images suggest his

Figure 3.7 Slide 14 of the illustrated song *The Ghost of the Violin* (Scott & Van Altena, 1912). (*Courtesy of the Marnan Collection, LLC, of Minneapolis, Minnesota*)

Figure 3.8 Slide 14 of *Beautiful Eyes* (Scott & Van Altena, 1909). (*Courtesy of the Marnan Collection, LLC, of Minneapolis, Minnesota*)

powers are omnipresent in his victim's life. In Slide 5, he appears very small in scale, standing on her arm while she uses a fan to hide her vulnerable eyes. In Slide 7, he bursts through the wall, scaring her. And in Slide 9, she sits frightened at her dressing room table as he emerges through her mirror.

More humorous was *Beautiful Eyes* (Scott & Van Altena, 1909), in which a man wearing a top hat and thick eyebrows hypnotizes a woman in a song that includes the lyric, "He told such beautiful lies/He had me hypnotized, mesmerized." Much the same appears in *Oh, You Spearmint Kiddo with the Wrigley Eyes* (DeWitt C. Wheeler, 1910), which features the lyric "Gee! But you look wise/You mesmerize me, hypnotize me." In this case, however, the hypnotist is the woman. Slide 14 depicts her in a long shot, hypnotizing her lover; lightning bolts shoot out of her hands, the image being an amalgam of artwork and photography.

Comedy was also at work in *The Ragtime Goblin Man* (Scott & Van Altena, 1912), in which the title character wears a fake nose, fake ears, and an elfish hat. The cute creature plays musical instruments in Slide 1 and 4. He also chases two lovers, discovering them at such locations as a huge pumpkin (Slide 5) and a rock fence (Slide 6). As the slides progress, the imagery becomes more fantastical, with the goblin riding an enormous frog and dangling the two lovers off the side of a mountain. A few slides depict the goblin scaring the lovers, including his oversized face matted onto a tree (Slide 12) and the lovers trapped inside an enormous version of his hat (Slide 13). However, Slide 14 concludes the story by showing the three holding hands, the two lovers happy with his non-threatening presence.

Figure 3.9 Slide 12 of *The Ghost of the Goblin Man* (Scott & Van Altena, 1912). (*Courtesy of the Marnan Collection, LLC, of Minneapolis, Minnesota*)

Figure 3.10 Slide 4 of *Oh That Boog-a-Boo Man* (DeWitt C. Wheeler, 1910). (*Courtesy of the Marnan Collection, LLC, of Minneapolis, Minnesota*)

The same type of costume reappeared in two subsequent Scott & Van Altena illustrated songs, one being *The Ghost of the Goblin Man* (1912). Here again the monster scares two lovers, who run directly toward the camera in Slide 5, a fascinating example of deep staging. As with its predecessor, the set alternates between the lovers being frightened, as when he literally cooks them in a frying pan (Slide 12), or being unafraid of him (Slide 8). That same year, *The Boogie Man Rag* featured its title character in a fantastical landscape, sitting atop a trumpet (Slide 7) and on an incline of enormous music notes (Slide 11).

In terms of costumes and sets, the most elaborate of these goblin/bogey song slides was probably *Oh That Boog-a-Boo Man* (DeWitt C. Wheeler, 1910). The title monster is huge, the actor wearing a mask that has horns and wild hair. During the course of the song, he towers over the song's heroine (Slide 3), holds her captive in his cave (Slide 4), and watches her in her bedroom (Slide 8). In two cases (Slides 6 and 16), she is menaced by artwork of his oversized head, contrasting scales being used to accentuate the horror. And yet, at one point, in Slide 12, two boog-a-boo men—who appear similar, save for the fact one is red and the other is green—frolic with her, thus becoming another example of the tendency for these slides to show characters imperiled by monsters in some images, and yet happy with them in others. Together with their humorous lyrics, these illustrated songs were apparently meant to be more comical than they were frightening.

Conclusion

Along with illustrated songs, American visual culture in the early years of the twentieth century was replete with Halloween imagery on holiday decorations and postcards.[168] The proliferation of the latter after 1906 was striking, though normally they did not feature supernatural content. And when the supernatural was depicted, it was usually in the form of comical artwork of anthropomorphized cats and pumpkins.[169] Potentially horrifying imagery appeared only on a small number of postcards. As *Dennison's 1913 Bogie Book* indicated, "Fun is the keynote of Hallowe'en, to-day."[170]

The same could not be said of natural horrors. Americans read of Jack the Ripper's deeds at length in the press, whether in newspapers or in publications like *The National Police Gazette*.[171] There was even a short, "profusely illustrated" book distributed in America called *The History of the Whitechapel Murders*. It promised a "full and accurate account of 'Jack, the Ripper's' fiendish murders."[172] Among the most horrifying images of nineteenth-century culture are the Ripper crime scene photographs, but most Americans did not see them at the time. Nor did they see the crime scene photographs taken at Lizzie Borden's home.

Nevertheless, Americans did view an increasing number of authentic photographs of real-life horrors at the end of the nineteenth century, and not just those of wartime casualties and actual executions. Consider, for example, the photos of Jacob Riis, whose work—some of which appeared in his groundbreaking book *How the Other Half Lives* (1890)—captured the plight of the poor in New York.[173] From opium dens and potter's fields to tenements, Riis's photos exposed the darkness of urban life. Of one tenement he photographed in 1892, Riis described its inhabitants as follows: "[They] looked more like hideous ghosts than living men."[174]

Some of Riis's photographs became lantern slides, as did other photographs depicting natural disasters. In the early twentieth century, Moore, Bond, & Company sold a set of twenty-five slides with lecture notes entitled *The Iroquois Theatre Fire*. Individual slides of the 1904 tragedy included *Loading Bodies into an Ambulance* and *Fire Patrol Loaded with Mangled Dead*.[175] Then, in 1912, A. J. Clapham released a series of lantern slides reproducing photographs of the Rosenthal Murder Case, in which gangsters gunned down bookmaker Herman Rosenthal in New York City, apparently at the behest of a corrupt policeman.[176]

As for the unseen world, it came to light thanks not to spirit photography, but because of Wilhelm Roentgen's discovery of X-rays in 1895. X-rays fascinated the public, as expressed in journalistic accounts, public demonstrations, and even poetry.[177] X-ray photos not only assisted the world of medicine, but also briefly became a fashionable type of "electric" picture; in 1898, the *New York Times* wrote that it was "much more interesting to have one's hand photographed by X rays than to have it molded in plaster."[178] The "Roentgen rays" could also produce "spectral effects," including on the stage, where they could bring a luminous skeleton to life by projecting X-rays at a "living man."[179] As had so often been the case in American visual culture, from phantasmagoria shows to illustrated songs, horror resulted from a scientific advance in optical technology.

In 1914, the intrepid title character of Thanhouser's moving picture serial *Zudora* unravels the mystery of a vaporous skeleton hand image that frightens the natives of a rural village. Its source? An x-ray photograph projected by a magic lantern.[180]

Figure 3.11 The title character of Thanhouser's serial *Zudora* (1914) uncovers the magic lantern that projected a skeletal hand.

Notes

1. Leslie Walter, "In a Stereoscope," *The Knickerbocker Monthly: A National Magazine*, September 1863, 217.
2. Louis Kaplan, *The Strange Case of William Mumler, Spirit Photographer* (Minneapolis: University of Minnesota Press, 2008), 232.
3. James L. Swanson, *Bloody Crimes: The Funeral of Abraham Lincoln and the Chase for Jefferson Davis* (New York: HarperCollins, 2010).
4. William H. Mumler, *The Personal Experiences of William H. Mumler in Spirit-Photography* (Boston: Colby & Rich, 1875), reprinted in Kaplan, 93.
5. Ibid., 93.
6. Martyn Jolly, *Faces of the Living Dead: The Belief in Spirit Photography* (London: The British Library, 2006), 16.
7. Crista Cloutier, "Mumler's Ghosts," in *The Perfect Medium: Photography and the Occult*, edited by Clément Chéroux, Andreas Fischer, Pierre Apraxine, Denis Canguilhem, and Sophie Schmit (New Haven: Yale University Press, 2004), 21.
8. Kaplan, 20.
9. "Spiritual Photography," *Littel's Living Age*, July 31, 1869, 314.
10. "Spiritual Photography," *New York Times*, April 24, 1869, 4.
11. *The Mumler "Spirit" Photograph Case: Argument of Mr. Elbridge T. Gerry, of Counsel for the People, before Justice Dowling, on the Preliminary Examination of Wm. H. Mumler, Charged with Obtaining Money by Pretended "Spirit" Photographs* (New York: Baker, Voorhis, & Co., 1869), 5.
12. "Spiritual Photographs," *New York Times*, April 22, 1869, 8.
13. "Spirit Photographs," *New York Times*, April 29, 1869, 5.
14. "New York Correspondence," *Philadelphia Photographer*, June 1869, 199.
15. "'Spiritual Photographs'—Another Plan," *Philadelphia Photographer*, June 1869, 184.
16. "Spiritual Photographs," *New York Times*, May 4, 1869, 1.
17. William H. Mumler, *The Personal Experiences of William H. Mumler in Spirit-Photography* (Boston: Colby & Rich, 1875), reprinted in Kaplan, 69–139.
18. "The Modern Ghost," *Boston Herald*, April 16, 1899, 44.
19. "Biographies of Artists," *The North American Quarterly Magazine* (October 1835), 335.
20. See, for example, Will H. Low, "A Century of Painting," *McClure's Magazine* (March 1896), 337; James Huneker, "Masters of Hallucination—Kubin, Munch, and Gauguin," *Boston Herald*, May 11, 1913, 33.
21. Sarah Burns, *Painting the Dark Side: Art and the Gothic Imagination in Nineteenth-Century America* (Berkeley: University of California Press, 2004).
22. Ibid., xix.
23. Ibid., xix.
24. Carol Clark, "Haunted Paintings in the World of Print: Charles Deas (1818–1867)," *The Papers of the Bibliographical Society of America*, Vol. 105, No. 4 (December 2011), 421–38.
25. "An Artist of Old New-York," *New York Times*, December 15, 1881, 8.
26. Elizabeth Broun, *Albert Pinkham Ryder* (Washington, D.C.: Smithsonian Institution Press, 1989), 300.
27. "A Handful of Painters," *New York Times*, March 16, 1901, 8.
28. Burns, 5, 9.
29. Charles Lanman, "The Epic Paintings of Thomas Cole," *Southern Literary Messenger* (June 1849), 351.
30. Daniel Huntington, "Character of Thomas Cole, with a Portrait and a Sketch," *Christian Parlor Magazine*, May 1, 1850, 144.

31. "The Fine Arts," *Boston Intelligencer*, May 20, 1820; "Our Artists–No. IV," *Godey's Magazine and Lady's Book* (November 1846), 211; Margaret Fuller Ossoli, "A Record of Impressions: Produced by the Exhibition of Mr. Allston's Pictures in the Summer of 1839," in Margaret Fuller Ossoli, *Art, Literature, and the Drama*, edited by Arthur B. Fuller (Boston: Roberts Brothers, 1889).
32. Kerry Dean Carso, *American Gothic Art and Architecture in the Age of Romantic Literature* (Cardiff: University of Wales Press, 2014), 40–1.
33. Diane Chalmers Johnson, *American Symbolist Art: Nineteenth-Century "Poets in Paint"* (Lewiston: Edwin Mellen Press, 2004), 31.
34. "Washington Allston," *Home Journal*, November 3, 1855, 1.
35. Johnson, 16.
36. Ibid., 27.
37. "Washington Allston," *Home Journal*, November 25, 1848, 3.
38. Advertisement, *Essex Gazette* (Salem, Massachusetts), December 13, 1774.
39. Karen Halttunnen, *Murder Most Foul: The Killer and the American Gothic Imagination* (Cambridge, MA: Harvard University Press, 1998).
40. Frank Luther Mott, *A History of American Magazines, 1741–1850*, Vol. 1 (Cambridge, MA: Belknap Press at Harvard University Press, 1930–68), 519–21.
41. Cynthia Patterson, "'Illustration of a Picture': Nineteenth-Century Writers and the Philadelphia Pictorials," *American Periodicals: A Journal of History & Criticism*, No. 2 (2009), 136–64.
42. August F. Jaccaci, "The Father of Modern Illustration," *Century Illustrated Magazine* (June 1893), 186.
43. E. Anna Lewis, "Art and Artists of America: Felix O. C. Darley," *Graham's American Monthly Magazine of Literature, Art, and Fashion* (July 1854), 70.
44. Theodore Bolton, "The Book Illustrations of Felix Octavius Carr Darley," in *American Antiquarian Society, Worcester, Mass. Proceedings*, Vol. 61 (Worcester, MA: American Antiquarian Society, April 1951), 138.
45. Kayla Haveles, "The Many Faces of the Headless Horseman: Illustrations of *The Legend of Sleepy Hollow*," posted at *Past Is Present: The American Antiquarian Society Blog* on October 29, 2015. Available at http://pastispresent.org/2015/good-sources/the-many-faces-of-the-headless-horseman-illustrations-of-the-legend-of-sleepy-hollow/. Accessed on April 29, 2016.
46. "*The Raven*," *Harper's Bazaar*, November 3, 1883, 699.
47. "The Renascence of Poe," *The Dial*, March 1, 1895, 138.
48. Du Maurier's illustrations earlier accompanied *Trilby's* publication in *Harper's New Monthly Magazine* in 1894.
49. George MacDonald, "*The Haunted House*," *Scribner's Monthly*, January 1874, 272; "Murdered Mary Seneff's Ghost," *National Police Gazette*, April 16, 1881, 4.
50. See, for example, "Our Haunted Boarding-House," *Puck*, July 19, 1882, 318; Untitled, *Life*, August 21, 1902, 154; Untitled, *Life*, October 28, 1909, 577; Untitled, *Life*, October 28, 1909, 582; Untitled, *Life*, October 28, 1909, 589.
51. Examples of illustrations making fun of spiritualists appear in *Life*, January 25, 1912, 220, and in *Life*, September 26, 1912, 1848. An example of an illustration making fun of ghostly suffragettes appears in "The Worst Spook of All," *Puck*, September 10, 1913, 6.
52. See, for example, "A Ghost Story," *Life*, October 13, 1887, 199.
53. In addition to the illustrations described in the main text, the *National Police Gazette* occasionally published artwork of disasters, among them *Boston's Latest Railroad Horror* (1887) and *A Fatal Down-Grade* (1889). See "Boston's Latest Railroad Horror," *National Police Gazette*, March 26, 1887, 16; "A Fatal Down-Grade," *National Police Gazette*, November 2, 1889, 16.
54. "A Weird Waif," *National Police Gazette*, June 14, 1879, 7.
55. "A Gallows Ball," *National Police Gazette*, April 12, 1879, 10.

56. "A Night of Horror," *National Police Gazette*, February 26, 1881, 4.
57. "The Terrors of Art," *National Police Gazette*, September 9, 1882, 8.
58. "A Graveyard Horror," *National Police Gazette*, December 30, 1882, 13.
59. "Horrors of a Reform School," *National Police Gazette*, January 28, 1882, 13.
60. An example of body disposal appears in "They Put Him in a Trunk," *National Police Gazette*, June 15, 1889, 1. Examples of the discovery of corpses appear in "An Invoice of Death," *National Police Gazette*, November 11, 1882, 1; "Mysterious Double Murder," *National Police Gazette*, August 18, 1888, 4; "Suicide or Murder?", *National Police Gazette*, January 12, 1889, 4; "A Mysterious Murder," *National Police Gazette*, May 19, 1894, 9. A courtroom scene appears in "Fainted in the Court Room," *National Police Gazette*, June 1, 1895, 16. An execution scene appears in Untitled, *National Police Gazette*, July 24, 1880, 9.
61. Illustrations depicting the action leading up to lynchings appear in "Lynching a Woman," *National Police Gazette*, January 31, 1880, 8; "A Lynching Puzzle," *National Police Gazette*, September 2, 1882, 9; "Lynching an F. F. V.," *National Police Gazette*, May 30, 1885, 4; "A Wholesale Lynching," *National Police Gazette*, July 4, 1885, 4; "Women Watched Him Strung Up," *National Police Gazette*, February 2, 1889, 5. Efforts to prevent lynchings appear in such illustrations as "Kept the Mob at Bay," *National Police Gazette*, December 12, 1896, 12, and "Two Brothers Stand Off a Thousand Men," *National Police Gazette*, April 15, 1899, 8.
62. "A Public Lynching in the South," *National Police Gazette*, March 13, 1886, 16; "How Wholesale Murder Is Avenged in the Wild West," *National Police Gazette*, January 21, 1888, 8; "Women Hanging Huns," *National Police Gazette*, June 22, 1889, 4.
63. Examples of illustrations depicting murders in progress include "How Many More?", *National Police Gazette*, August 14, 1886, 12; "Was It Murder?", *National Police Gazette*, December 18, 1886, 8; "Double Murder," *National Police Gazette*, March 19, 1887, 5; "She Attempted Murder," *National Police Gazette*, January 25, 1890, 12; "A Cruel Father's Act," *National Police Gazette*, October 4, 1890, 16; "Murder of Detective John Carey," *National Police Gazette*, November 19, 1892, 9; "Shot His Wife and Daughter," *National Police Gazette*, January 27, 1894, 8; "Double Crime of a Lover," *National Police Gazette*, July 7, 1894, 8; "Shot His Stepdaughter," *National Police Gazette*, January 12, 1895, 5.
64. Examples of illustrations depicting the action immediately prior to murderers killing their victims include "Jesse James' Murder," *National Police Gazette*, April 22, 1882, 8; "A Cruel Murder," *National Police Gazette*, March 13, 1886, 5; "A Jockey's Double Murder," *National Police Gazette*, April 27, 1889, 4; "A Colored Fiend's Work," *National Police Gazette*, February 11, 1893, 5; "Jilted, She Wanted Revenge," *National Police Gazette*, September 27, 1902, 8.
65. Examples of illustrations depicting the action immediately after a murder include "Blew His Wife's Brains Out," *National Police Gazette*, April 22, 1893, 5, and "Rejected Lover Shoots Two," *National Police Gazette*, February 25, 1899, 4.
66. "Believed She Was a Witch," *National Police Gazette*, October 7, 1893, 12.
67. Untitled, *National Police Gazette*, December 28, 1867, 4.
68. Examples of sequential art include Untitled, *National Police Gazette*, November 15, 1879, 16; Untitled, *National Police Gazette*, August 21, 1880, 8; "The Boston Murder," *National Police Gazette*, March 25, 1882, 8; "The Stratford Murder Mystery," *National Police Gazette*, September 29, 1883, 9; "The Long Island Tragedy," *National Police Gazette*, December 8, 1883, 9; "Scenes of the Cronin Mystery," *National Police Gazette*, June 8, 1889, 16; *National Police Gazette*, May 17, 1902, 9; "The Murder of Chief Aaron McCord," *National Police Gazette*, April 19, 1890, 9.
69. "The Michigan Quadruple Murder," *National Police Gazette*, December 15, 1883, 8.
70. "The Chatsworth Horror: Awful Scenes Around the Terrible Midnight Accident on the Toledo, Peoria and Western Railroad," *National Police Gazette*, August 27, 1887, 16.

71. "The New Hampshire Horror," *National Police Gazette*, December 15, 1883, 8. Other examples include "The Gallows Get Another Victim," *National Police Gazette*, August 25, 1888, 8; "The Trenton, N.J. Tragedy," *National Police Gazette*, January 25, 1890, 16; "The Murder in the Canada Woods," *National Police Gazette*, March 22, 1890, 16; "Brutal Murder of a Handsome Actress," *National Police Gazette*, April 13, 1895, 9.
72. "The World's Greatest Murderers, XVI–Elizabeth of Transylvania," *The Plain Dealer* (Cleveland, Ohio), August 11, 1912, 3.
73. Paul Clee, *Before Hollywood: From Shadow Play to the Silver Screen* (New York: Clarion Books, 2005), 12–16.
74. Quoted in Hermann Hecht, *Pre-Cinema History: An Encyclopaedia and Annotated Bibliography of the Moving Image Before 1896* (London: Bowker-Saur, 1993).
75. James Delbourgo, *A Most Amazing Scene of Wonders: Electricity and Enlightenment in Early America* (Cambridge, MA: Harvard University Press, 2006), 92–3.
76. Laurent Mannoni, *The Great Art of Light and Shadow: Archaeology of the Cinema* (Exeter: University of Exeter Press, 2000), 137, 141.
77. Melvyn Heard, *Phantasmagoria: The Secret Life of the Magic Lantern* (Hastings: The Projection Box, 2006), 90.
78. *The Art of Projection and Complete Magic Lantern Manual* (London: E. A. Beckett, 1893), 2.
79. X. Theodore Barber, "Phantasmagorical Wonders: The Magic Lantern Ghost Show in Nineteenth-Century America," *Film History*, Vol. 3, No. 2 (1989), 84.
80. Lynda Nead, *The Haunted Gallery: Painting, Photography, Film c. 1900* (New Haven: Yale University Press, 2007), 50.
81. Heard, 179.
82. Advertisement, *The Evening Post* (New York), November 7, 1803, 2.
83. Barber, 78.
84. Advertisement, *Savannah Republican* (Savannah, Georgia), January 13, 1810, 3.
85. Advertisement, *Federal Republican* (Baltimore, Maryland), April 13, 1810, 2.
86. "Circus, Washington Garden," *Boston Commercial Gazette* (Boston, Massachusetts), October 27, 1825, 2.
87. "City Theatre," *Boston Daily American Statesman*, November 3, 1825, 2.
88. "Robertson, Artist in Ghosts," *The Albion, A Journal of News, Politics, and Literature*, February 17, 1855, 74.
89. "A Magic Lantern," *Dwight's American Magazine*, February 1, 1849, 60.
90. "Literary," *The Literary Union*, November 17, 1849, 106.
91. Terry Castle, "Phantasmagoria: Spectral Technology and the Metaphorics of Modern Reverie," *Critical Inquiry*, Vol. 15, No. 1 (Autumn 1988), 30.
92. "The Phantasmagoria," *Philadelphia Inquirer*, August 5, 1839, 2.
93. Advertisement, *Springfield Republican* (Springfield, Massachusetts), December 27, 1852, 3.
94. Advertisement, *Daily Illinois State Journal* (Springfield, Illinois), March 29, 1865, 2.
95. Jens Ruchatz, 'Travelling by Slide: How the Art of Projection Met the World of Travel,' in Richard Crangle, Melvyn Heard, and Ine van Dooren (eds), *Realms of Light: Uses and Perceptions of the Magic Lantern from the 17th to the 21st Century* (London: The Magic Lantern Society, 2005), 35.
96. Charles Musser, *The Emergence of Cinema: The American Screen to 1907* (Berkeley: University of California Press, 1990), 32.
97. David Robinson, Stephen Herbert, and Richard Crangle (eds), *Encyclopaedia of the Magic Lantern* (London: The Magic Lantern Society, 2001), 232.
98. "The Stereopticon," *Dixon Daily Telegraph* (Dixon, Illinois), March 21, 1885, 5.
99. "Wraiths and Gibberers," *New York Times*, November 13, 1895, 3.

100. Robert Bogdan, *Freak Show: Presenting Human Oddities for Amusement and Profit* (Chicago: University of Chicago Press, 1988), 35.
101. Andrea Stulman Dennett, *Weird and Wonderful: The Dime Museum in America* (New York: New York University, 1997), xi.
102. Dennett, 118–20.
103. For example, an advertisement for the rental of magic lanterns for "schools and private parties" appears in the *Boston Post*, December 18, 1879, 3.
104. Advertisement, *The Plain Dealer* (Cleveland, Ohio), March 28, 1910, 5.
105. *Hall's Illustrated Catalogue of Magic Lanterns, Dissolving Lanterns, and Stereopticons for Societies, Parlor Entertainment, Panoramas, and Public Exhibitions*, 56.
106. *Catalogue and Price List of Stereopticons, Dissolving Views, Apparatus, Magic Lanterns, and Artificially Colored Photographic Views* (New York: T. H. McAllister, 1867), 40–1; *Catalogue of Stereopticons, Dissolving Apparatus and Magic Lanterns, with Extensive List of Slides Illustrating All Subjects of Popular Interest* (New York: T. H. McAllister, October 1899), 63.
107. Terry and Deborah Borton, *Before the Movies: American Magic-Lantern Entertainment and the Nation's First Green Screen Artist, Joseph Boggs Beale* (New Barnet: John Libbey, 2014).
108. Borton and Borton, 167, 151, 139.
109. Ibid., 80–3.
110. Ibid., 104, 94, 105, 95, 113–14.
111. Musser, 36.
112. Andrew Pringle, *The Optical Lantern, for Instruction and Amusement* (New York: The Scovill & Adams Company, 1890), 29.
113. *Illustrated Catalogue of Stereopticons, Magic Lanterns, and Dissolving View Apparatus, and of Every Variety of the Best Lantern Views and Lantern Novelties* (Philadelphia: George H. Pierce, December 1888), 63. As the cover of this catalog notes, Pierce was the "sole agent in Philadelphia for the sale of the above goods manufactured by T. H. McAllister."
114. *Catalogue of Stereopticons, Dissolving View Apparatus and Magic Lanterns, with Extensive List of Views for the Illustration of All Subjects of Popular Interest* (New York: T. H. McAllister, April 1898), 85–6.
115. Quoted in Musser, 43.
116. *Catalogue and Price List of Stereopticons, Dissolving Views, Apparatus, Magic Lanterns, and Artificially Colored Photographic Views*, 28.
117. *Catalogue of Stereopticons, Dissolving Apparatus and Magic Lanterns, with Extensive List of Slides Illustrating All Subjects of Popular Interest*, 100. The "movable comic views" *Skeleton Taking Off Head, Skeleton Falling to Pieces*, and *Magician and Ghost* were also offered for sale in *Illustrated Catalogue of Sciopticons, Stereopticons, Magic Lanterns and Views, Mechanical Novelties, Etc.* (Chicago: L. Manasse Company, 1893), 112.
118. *Catalogue of Stereopticons, Dissolving Apparatus and Magic Lanterns, with Extensive List of Slides Illustrating All Subjects of Popular Interest*, 101.
119. *Illustrated Catalogue of Stereopticons, Magic Lanterns, and Dissolving View Apparatus, and of Every Variety of the Best Lantern Views and Lantern Novelties*, 71.
120. *Catalogue of Magic Lanterns, Stereopticons, and Moving Picture Machines* (Chicago: Montgomery Ward & Co., c. 1899), 35. The Magic Lantern Society of the United States and Canada reprinted this catalog in 1996.
121. *Catalogue of Stereopticons, Dissolving-View Apparatus and Magic Lanterns with List of Several Thousand Artistically-Finished Views for the Illustration of all Subjects of Popular Interest* (Philadelphia: T. H. McAllister, 1881), 66.
122. *Illustrated Catalogue of Stereopticons, Magic Lanterns, and Dissolving View Apparatus, and of Every Variety of the Best Lantern Views and Lantern Novelties*, unpaginated.

123. Robinson, Herbert, and Crangle, 65.
124. *The Art of Projection and Complete Magic Lantern Manual*, 157–9.
125. "A Grewsome [sic] Entertainment," *The Patriot* (Harrisburg, Pennsylvania), April 8, 1896, 3.
126. Satwik Dasgupta, "Photography," in *Edgar Allan Poe in Context*, edited by Kevin J. Hayes (Cambridge: Cambridge University Press, 2013), 314.
127. Keith F. Davis and Jane L. Aspenwall, *The Origins of American Photography: From Daguerreotype to Dry-Plate, 1839–1885* (New Haven: Yale University Press, 2007).
128. Dasgupta, 317.
129. See Amy Louise Wood, *Lynching and Spectacle: Witnessing Racial Violence in America, 1890–1940* (University of North Carolina Press, 2009), 77.
130. Jay Ruby, *Secure the Shadow* (Cambridge, MA: The MIT Press, 1995), 13.
131. Keith F. Davis, "'A Terrible Distinctness': Photography of the Civil War Era," in *Photography in Nineteenth-Century America*, edited by Martha A. Sandweiss (New York: Harry N. Abrams, 1991), 171.
132. "Curiosities of Photography," *American Phrenological Journal* (September 1863), 80.
133. Ruby, 16, 17.
134. Nancy M. West, "Camera Fiends: Early Photography, Death, and the Supernatural," *The Centennial Review*, Vol. 40, No. 1 (Winter 1996), 171.
135. Stanley B. Burns, with Elizabeth A. Burns, *Sleeping Beauty II: Grief, Bereavement and the Family in Memorial Photography* (New York: Burns Archive Press, 2002), unpaginated.
136. Cathy Davidson, "Photographs of the Dead: Sherman, Daguerre, Hawthorne," *South Atlantic Quarterly*, No. 89 (1990), 667–701.
137. West, 172.
138. "Magic Photographs," *The Philadelphia Photographer*, July 1866, 218.
139. "Spirit-Photographs," *Every Saturday: A Journal of Choice Reading*, July 4, 1874, 16.
140. Louis Kaplan, "Where Paranoid Meets the Paranormal: Speculations on Spirit Photography," *Art Journal*, Vol. 62, No. 3 (Autumn 2003), 21.
141. E. Lyell Earle, "Lily Dale, the Haunt of Spiritualists," *The Catholic World*, January 1899, 506.
142. "Photography of the Invisible," *Scientific American*, December 6, 1873, 353.
143. Thomas T. Watts, "Spirit Pictures," *The American Socialist*, January 23, 1879, 29.
144. Henry Ridgely Evans, *Hours with the Ghosts, or Nineteenth Century Witchcraft* (Chicago: Laird & Lee, Publishers, 1897), 17.
145. "A Ghost's Photograph," *Michigan Farmer*, December 27, 1890, 7.
146. Pierre Apraxine and Sophie Schmit, "Photography and the Occult," in *The Perfect Medium: Photography and the Occult*, 16.
147. Jen Cadwallader, *Modern Language Studies*, Vol. 37, No. 2 (Winter 2008), 24.
148. Prof. J. Towler, "The Stereograph," *Philadelphia Photographer*, September 1871, 284.
149. John Waldsmith, *Stereo Views: An Illustrated History & Price Guide*, 2nd Edition (Iola: Krause Publications, 2002), 5.
150. Other examples include *Her Guardian Angels* (Littleton, 1893), *Baby's Vision* (Berry, Kelley, & Chadwick, 1897), *The Heavenly Twins* (Keystone, 1899), as well as *Her Guardian Angel* (Keystone, 1894), which features a different image than the similarly titled *Her Guardian Angel* (Keystone, 1898).
151. Melander's *The Dream* stereoview does feature a copyright date that reads "1874–5."
152. Advertisement, *Reading Eagle* (Reading, Pennsylvania), September 24, 1869.
153. Such late nineteenth-century stereoviews include *The Spectre at the Piano* (William H. Rau, undated) and *The Phantom Player Resting* (Montgomery Ward, undated).
154. See, for example, Advertisement, *Moving Picture World*, March 20, 1909, 347; Advertisement, *Moving Picture World*, April 9, 1910, 572.

155. "Good News for Slide Makers," *Views and Film Index*, February 9, 1907, 2; "Destroying the Lantern Slide Business," *Moving Picture World*, October 3, 1908, 253.
156. "Not a Song Hit on the Market," *Moving Picture World*, July 4, 1908, 6.
157. Eileen Bowser, *The Transformation of Cinema, 1907–1915* (Berkeley: University of California Press, 1990), 15.
158. "Our Commercial Index," *Views and Film Index*, September 22, 1906, 7.
159. J. W. Ripley, "All Join in the Chorus," *American Heritage*, Vol. 10, No. 4 (June 1959), p. 51.
160. All that said, some nickelodeon theatre managers tried to save money by reusing slides from previous songs, including in those instances when a slide(s) for another song had been broken ("Destroying the Lantern Slide Business," *Moving Picture World*, October 3, 1908, 253). Moreover, lantern operators occasionally projected the correct slides out of order. For example, one nickelodeon theatre manager in a small town used a noticeably incorrect slide during a performance of *Way Down Upon the Swanee River* ("Things the Audiences Miss," *New York Times*, December 8, 1912, X11).
161. Bowser, 15.
162. Charles K. Harris, "Song Slide the Little Father of Photodrama," March 10, 1917, 1520.
163. As Rick Altman has said, ". . . it is a distortion of history to label these machines film projectors, for they are simply magic lanterns (light source and slide transport) to which moving picture capability had been added." See Rick Altman, *Silent Film Sound* (New York: Columbia University Press, 2004), 183.
164. Altman, 182.
165. Ibid., 192.
166. Altman, unpaginated section entitled "Color Plates."
167. I would like to thank Margaret Bergh and the Marnan Collection, LLC of Minneapolis, Minnesota for allowing me to examine surviving examples of all the illustrated songs discussed in this book.
168. Examples of period Halloween decorations appear in *Dennison's 1912 Bogie Book* (reprinted by Bramcost Publications in 2010), *Dennison's 1913 Bogie Book* (reprinted by Bramcost Publications in 2011), *Dennison's 1914 Bogie Book* (reprinted by Bramcost Publications in 2012), and *Dennison's 1915 Bogie Book* (reprinted by Bramcost Publications in 2010). Other examples appear in Stuart Schneider, *Halloween in America: A Collector's Guide with Prices* (Atglen, Pennsylvania: Schiffer Publishing, Ltd, 1995).
169. For examples of such postcards of the period, see Gabriella Oldham (ed.), *Old-Fashioned Halloween Postcards* (Mineola, New York: Dover Publications, Inc., 1988); Diane C. Arkins (ed.), *Halloween Romantic Art and Customs of Yesteryear: Postcard Book* (Gretna: Pelican Publishing Company, 2000). Other examples appear in Schneider, 58–74.
170. *Dennison's 1913 Bogie Book*, 1.
171. See, for example, "Jack the Ripper's Terrible Work," *National Police Gazette*, December 1, 1888, 16; "Whitechapel's Fiend," *National Police Gazette*, August 17, 1889, 3; "Twelve!", *National Police Gazette*, September 28, 1889, 6.
172. This book was offered for sale in Advertisement, *National Police Gazette*, January 26, 1889, 14.
173. Robinson et al., 255.
174. Bonnie Yochelson and Daniel Czitrom, *Redicovering Jacob Riis: Exposure Journalism and Photography in Turn-of-the-Century New York* (New York: The New Press, 2007), unpaginated plate.
175. *Stereopticons, Lantern Slides, Moving Picture Machines* (Chicago: Moore, Bond & Co., c. 1907), 431.
176. "Rosenthal Murder Slides," *Moving Picture World*, August 17, 1912, 662.
177. See, for example, Mark Meredith, "The X Ray," *New York Clipper*, April 11, 1896, 83.
178. "Her Latest Photograph," *New York Times*, May 29, 1898, 14.
179. "The Modern Ghost," 44.
180. Neil G. Caward, "*The Secret of the Haunted Hills*," *Motography*, December 19, 1914, 845.

CHAPTER 4

Moving Pictures

> The magic shagreen, dwindling fast
> With every wish it gave;
> The magic ring; the magic sword,
> With power to stay or save;
> But greater far than all of these
> Enchanted things, behold!
> The magic film, from the reel
> By skillful hands unrolled.
>
> —Minna Irving, *The Magic Film* (1911)[1]

"Last night I was in the Kingdom of Shadows," Maxim Gorky famously remarked after attending a Lumière film screening in Paris in July 1896. "If you only knew how strange it is to be there," he continued. "It is not life, but life's shadow, it is not motion, but its soundless spectre. . . . It is terrifying to see, but it is the movement of shadows, only of shadows. Curses and ghosts, the evil spirits that have cast entire cities into eternal sleep, come to mind. . . ."[2]

Gorky has not been alone in likening moving pictures to the supernatural. "A ghostly seance this, from first to last," Hunter MacCulloch's 1911 poem *At a Motion Picture Show* describes.[3] One need only consider the question of where cinema resides to see the potency of such metaphors. Film is spooled around a reel, but that is not where the audience sees it. Rather, light passing through the frames pulses temporally and temporarily on a screen. Like a ghost or vampire, the projected moving picture seems to be caught in the twilight between two worlds.

Woodville Latham and his sons might have considered that metaphor while inventing their "Eidoloscope," which Charles Musser has referred to as "the first American machine for projecting motion pictures." Their projector made its public debut in April 1895. It was named after the "eidolon" of Greek literature, meaning a phantom, spectre, or spirit-image of a person.[4] C. Francis Jenkins and Thomas Armat debuted their own invention—America's first commercially viable projector using an intermittent mechanism—in September 1895. They called it the Phantoscope.[5] The Baltimore *Sun* called it "mysterious."[6]

After some mechanical refinements and extensive business negotiations, the Phantoscope became Edison's Vitascope. When it premiered at Koster & Bial's in New York City on April 23, 1896, the Vitascope transformed the American moving picture from being a peepshow experience for one person's eyes (as in the case of Edison's Kinetoscope) into becoming a massive image shared by large audiences. And that invention's new name referred not to seeing the dead, but rather to witnessing life.

Here is where metaphors of the undead cease to be of particular help in understanding early cinema. It was a scientific creation, one unveiled in an era marked by so many other discoveries and inventions. The cinema did not house ghosts and the projector was not a ghostly machine. Rather, as Matthew Solomon has observed, the cinema should be understood as an "anti-spiritualist medium."[7] His research has shed light upon the deep connections between moving pictures and magicians and magic in the nineteenth century.[8] Gunning has spoken to this same issue in even broader terms, writing:

> As so often happens with early cinema, a consideration of its genealogy leads us not so much toward the perspectival schemes of Enlightenment optics as to the ambiguous setting of the fairground: cinema as the product not only of scientists and inventors, but also of conjurors and mountebanks.[9]

Out of these contexts came a variety of moving pictures. "Some of them are horrifying," the *Philadelphia Inquirer* told readers in 1900, "others humorous, still others mystifying."[10]

Many of the cinema's earliest practitioners did attempt to use the medium to capture reality, as in the case of the first Lumière films.[11] Others used it produce special effects, as in the case of Georges Méliès, himself a magician by trade.[12] His "trick" films might have startled some viewers, but the bulk of his output seems to have been intended to inspire humor. In any event, as Gunning has explained, most viewers understood that his films were not real.[13] To this end, Gunning has quoted from Frank Norris's novel *McTeague: A Story of San Francisco* (1899). After viewing a moving picture, Mrs. Sieppe states with conviction, "It's all a drick," before adding, "I ain't no fool; dot's nothun but a drick."[14]

In 1908, *Views and Film Index* broached the same topic, asking, "Who is there that has attended one of these moving picture performances who has not exclaimed, on seeing some apparently impossible scene depicted in flesh and blood verisimilitude before his eyes: 'How in the world did they ever get such a picture as that.'"[15] Four years later, when reviewing *The Electric Laundry/Blanchisserie électrique* (C.G.P.C., 1912, which had been produced by Pathé Frères-Nizza), the *New York Dramatic Mirror* noticed that the audience was left with a familiar question: "How do they do it?"[16] Even when the supernatural accepted appeared in film narratives, American viewers frequently rationalized it with a desire to understand the production process, meaning that effects, however special, were effects nonetheless.

The Kingdom of Shadows was thus the product of scientific invention that relied on a new form of trickery meant to astonish audiences and also provoke them into wondering how such special effects were achieved. New metaphors permanently displaced those of Gorky. As Solomon notes, the "magic of movies is one of the most durable metaphors in all of film culture."[17]

Cinematic trickery provided a key component in what Gunning has called the "cinema of attractions," meaning not only that film exhibitions were themselves attractions (including in terms of the demonstration of projection equipment), but also that during its early years the cinema tended to focus on the presentational and the spectacular to incite "visual curiosity" and supply visual "pleasure."[18] Narrative storylines were minimal. As Gunning notes, "this cinema differs from later narrative cinema through its fascination in the thrill of display rather than its construction of a story."[19]

Gunning originally suggested that the period from 1907 to c. 1911 "represents the true *narrativization* of the cinema."[20] In his later work, he augmented that view by noting the cinema of attractions predominated until c. 1903, followed by a period of transition that lasted until c. 1908.[21] During and after the nickelodeon period, filmmakers like D. W. Griffith had, as David Bordwell notes, "redefined films as psychological narratives and assigned fresh functions to devices earlier exploited as attractions."[22]

The horror-themed film proved ideally suited to early cinema, as durable as it was transmutable, changing with the larger evolutions underway in the same era. Here were moving pictures informed by literature, theatre, and visual culture, but also moving pictures that relied upon a type of magic that only cinematic special effects could create. The ghost resided not in the machine, but only in the illusory images it projected.

The Pre-nickelodeon Era

Comparisons of the difference in cinematic styles between the Lumière Brothers and Méliès are as common as they are valuable, but it is equally important to consider the differences between the Lumières and Edison in 1895, the year before Méliès entered the film business.[23] For such films as *Workers Leaving the Lumière Factory in Lyon/La Sortie de l'Usine Lumière à Lyon* (1895) and *Arrival of a Train at La Ciotat/L'Arrivée d'un Train en Gare de la Ciotat* (1895), the Lumières notably shot nonfiction subjects on location.

By contrast, as early as 1893, the Edison Manufacturing Company filmed indoors at the Black Maria. The building was constructed with a roof that could be opened to supply the sunlight necessary to obtain usable images. Underneath the studio was a revolving platform that allowed the structure to be rotated so as to take advantage of the sun as it moved across the sky. Edison's employee W. K. L. Dickson, who headed the company's motion picture team, once likened the Black Maria to a dungeon, in part because of its "portentous black" background.[24] In February 1895, *Frank Leslie's Popular Monthly* described that background as being one of "Stygian gloom."[25]

Figure 4.1 An illustration of Edison's Black Maria, published in *Frank Leslie's Popular Monthly* (February 1895).

As a result, the early Edison moving pictures appear starkly different than those of the Lumière Brothers.[26] As Musser explains, the black background "eliminated extraneous visual distractions" and "placed its subjects in bold relief."[27] Here is a cinematic world that is, at least to a degree, removed from the real world, an aesthetic approach heightened by the choice of what was filmed: *Edison Kinetoscopic Record of a Sneeze* (1894), *Annabelle Serpentine Dance* (1894), *The Barbershop* (1894), and *The Boxing Cats* (1894). (It was also a world that continued to seem stark, even ominous in the years that followed, with *Views and Film Index* referring to the background of Pathé Frères' 1907 film *Weird Fancies/Fantaisies endiablées* as a "black void."[28])

The Edison films were initially seen on the Kinetoscope, a peepshow device in which an individual viewer watched a single film by peering into the eyepiece of a wooden cabinet. Then, as already noted, Edison projected moving pictures publicly for the first time in April 1896. A notice in the *New York Clipper* announced:

> Koster & Bial's will be the scene of the first public exhibition of Thos. A. Edison's latest invention, the vitascope, as soon as the details, now pending, can be perfected. The new discovery is said to project upon a large area of canvas groups that appear to stand forth from the canvas, and move with great facility and agility, as though actuated by separate impulses. In this way, the bare canvas before the audience becomes instantly a stage upon which living beings move about.[29]

After the event, *The Phonoscope* provided a lengthy description of how the evening unfolded:

> Suddenly all the lights in the theatre are extinguished and an oblong square of light appears in the center of a frame outlined upon the drop curtain of the theatre. Then there is a buzzing sound and instantly a dancing figure, life size, appears in the center of the square of light on the screen. . . . [T]he beholders almost forget that it is but a counterpart of nature and here are many among the audience who express doubt that it is but a figure on a screen, and not the actual dancer in the flesh, shown by some legerdemain or magician's trick.[30]

Here were not the spectres that Gorky perceived, but instead lifelike images resulting from a "magician's trick," one that was not kept entirely secret. Various popular-audience publications of the time described how the invention worked, thus linking print culture with visual culture.[31]

Nonfiction Cinema

American companies soon forged ahead with various kinds of films, including nonfiction. In 1899, for example, *The Phonoscope* reported on the ability of moving pictures to record images of microbes and even solar eclipses.[32] That same year, a newspaper reported on a "kind of mutoscope camera" that could take hourly pictures of a "stalk of corn just sprouting" over a six-month period, the result having "great educational value."[33] Five years later, another newspaper noted that "cinematograph records" were being filmed of medical "operations performed by a certain famous physician and surgeon in Paris."[34]

Scientific footage also held the potential to be horrifying. W. K. L. Dickson once described microscopic "water-goblins" that he filmed:

> A curious feature of the performance is the passing of these creatures in and out of focus, appearing sometimes as huge and distorted shadows, then springing into the reality of their own size and proportions . . . An unseen enemy is usually voted to be peculiarly undesirable, but who would not close their eyes to the unimaginable horrors which micro-photography reveals in connection with the kinetoscope?[35]

To Dickson, the hidden world his camera revealed was "gruesome beyond power of expression."

In many other cases, however, nonfiction cinema in America was faked. Early American cinema is rife with such examples. As Alison Griffiths has written:

> Oppositions between real and faked, authentic and fabricated, and genuine and imitation were . . . subject to flexible interpretation in this period. In addition, the problem of differentiating 'authentic' travel films from reconstructions and re-enactments, which were the bedrock of countless popular films portraying ethnographic subjects as well as coronations, executions, military campaigns, boxing matches, and safaris in the pre-1905 period, blurs the boundaries between fact and fiction.[36]

For example, Edison's "realistic" *Boers Bringing in British Prisoners* (1900) was not shot in Africa, where the Second Boer War took place, but in New Jersey.[37] And one film of the San Francisco earthquake of 1906 was promoted as being a "wonderfully realistic picture of the terrible catastrophe," but in the last scene, "the devil suddenly appears over the wrecked city, gloating over the terrible disaster which has befallen it."[38]

In December 1900, *The Optical Magic Lantern and Photographic Enlarger* reported that it was "being called to task" for an improper use of terminology. The British trade publication, which was read by some industry personnel in America, had used the term "fake" to label fictional moving pictures that relied on special effects, rather than on inauthentic nonfiction films. The trade admitted that those that were openly fictional could more accurately be labeled "trick" pictures.[39]

Trick Pictures

In 1895, as part of an effort to shoot outside of the Black Maria, William Heise and Alfred Clarke filmed *Execution of Mary, Queen of Scots* (Edison, 1895) outdoors. When Mary (played by Robert Thomae) is decapitated, a stop motion substitution occurs. A dummy has taken Thomae's place, though the grisly scene appears to unfold in a single shot. Here was not only the first film edit, but also the first use of special effects in the cinema. Its importance would be difficult to underestimate, as it initiated an approach to filmmaking that continues to the present day.

But while trick films were born in America, they flourished in France, beginning in 1896 thanks to Georges Méliès. In 1901, an American newspaper article described him as an "artist," one of the first times the word was applied to a film director.[40] A 1903 advertisement in the *New York Clipper* declared him to be the "Master Wizard of Motion Photography."[41] Two years later, a "Star" Film catalogue gave Méliès credit for conceiving the "idea of portraying comical, magical, and mystical views," adding "his creations have been imitated without success ever since."[42] His films emerged out of the tradition of *féerie* live theatrical entertainment, which presented fantastical plots, tricks, and music, the product of elaborate stagecraft.[43] As Gunning notes, Méliès's "main claim to fame comes from grafting the nineteenth-century tradition of magic theatre onto the nascent apparatus of motion pictures."[44] Méliès himself once remarked, "My film career has been so tied up with my work at the Robert-Houdin theatre that one can barely tell them apart."[45]

And yet, despite their roots in French popular culture, Méliès's moving pictures resonated strongly with American audiences in the pre-nickelodeon era. As Richard Abel has observed, Méliès films like *A Trip to the Moon/Le voyage dans la lune* (1902) became "almost wholly assimilated into the American cultural landscape," due in part to the fact that American companies like Edison and Lubin sold illegal dupes of them.[46] The grand spectacle of his films and the sophistication of their tricks were other reasons. And then there was the fact that—as chronicled in Chapter 2—America had enjoyed its own tradition of stage magicians during the nineteenth century.

In 1896, Méliès produced *Le manoir du diable* (1896), which would appear in America as early as 1899 under the title *The Devil's Castle*.[47] Edison would release the same film under the title *The Infernal Palace*. It was not Méliès's first film or even his first "trick" film. In it, the devil invades a castle as a bat before transforming into his horned, two-legged self. The home becomes a defamiliarized space, a haunted house.[48] Two noblemen enter the room, with one quickly scared away by a devilish imp. The one who remains sees a skeleton appear. Striking it with his sword, the skeleton becomes a bat that, when grabbed, changes into the devil. His Satanic Majesty scares the nobleman first with a group of white-sheeted ghosts and then a group of broom-carrying witches. The nobleman finally dispatches the devil with a crucifix. In the space of approximately three minutes, *Le manoir du diable* invokes many of the tropes that would become associated with the horror movie, and it did so with a largely serious tone.

Figure 4.2 A nobleman shrinks before Mephistopheles in Georges Méliès's *The Devil's Castle/Le manoir du diable* (1896).

Nevertheless, it is critical to consider Méliès's use of humor. However much his treatment of the supernatural drew upon particular stage conventions in France, his humor elided deftly with the American literary and theatre tradition of treating horror in a comical manner. After all, in the world of Méliès, the supernatural was itself a trick, and that found widespread appeal in America, where various film companies produced their own trick films. As David S. Hulfish wrote in his *Cyclopedia of Motion-Picture Work* (1911), "Trick pictures are usually comedies in that the trick-picture art usually is used to produce laughter."[49]

It should also be said that some of Méliès's trick films represent a reliance on the new possibilities of the cinema in their conception and execution, ranging from production to post-production techniques. For example, in his first trick film, *Escamotage d'une dame chez Robert-Houdin* (1896), he made a woman under a sheet vanish.[50] When the sheet is removed, a skeleton is in her place. To do so, he used substitution splicing. In subsequent films, he would rely on a range of other cinematic devices, including multiple exposures, dissolves, matte shots, replication effects, transparencies, and scale models.[51] Moreover, as Bordwell has pointed out, Méliès edited his films in a sophisticated manner. *A Trip to the Moon* features four shots in the space of only twenty seconds; it constitutes the "most rapidly cut sequence known before 1908."[52]

In many of his moving pictures, Méliès relied on direct address, appearing on a stage set as a magician who acknowledges the audience's presence by looking into the camera and even taking stage bows. Examples include *A Mysterious Portrait/Le portrait mystérieux* (Méliès, 1899), *The Famous Box Trick/Illusions fantasmagoriques* (Méliès, 1903), *The Bewitched Trunk/Le coffre enchanté* (Méliès, 1904), *The Fugitive Apparitions/Les apparitions fugitives* (Méliès, 1904), and *The Living Playing Cards/Les cartes vivantes* (Méliès, 1905).[53] American filmmakers readily copied this type of trick film, as in the case of Selig Polyscope's 1902 film *Legerdemain Up-to-Date* (1902, aka *Legerdemain Up-to-Date, or the Great Herrmann Outdone*). In it, a conjuror appears onstage and reveals, "in an up-to-date manner with which up-to-date tricks can be accomplished," among them "dissolving effects and mysterious changes."[54]

While the major attraction of Méliès's films was trickery, he was also capable of constructing memorable narratives. In *The Cook's Revenge/La vengeance du gâte-sauce* (Méliès, 1900), *How He Missed His Train/Le réveil d'un monsieur pressé* (Méliès, 1900, aka *How He Missed the Train*), and *The Man with the Rubber Head/L'homme à la tête en caoutchouc* (Méliès, 1902), he offered stories of strange events occurring in otherwise natural locations.[55] In other cases, most notably *A Trip to the Moon*, he used scientific innovation and exploration as the basis for his plots. As Solomon has observed, *A Trip to the Moon* joins a "sequence of spatially and temporally distinct scenes to tell a continuous and coherent story."[56]

Méliès also utilized dreams as a narrative framing device to rationalize the tricks his characters encountered, as in *The Astronomer's Dream/La Lune à un mètre* (1899, aka *A Trip to the Moon*) and *The Clock Maker's Dream/Le Rêve de l'horloger* (1904, aka *The Clock-maker's Dream*).[57] American companies also used this approach, as can be seen in *Uncle Josh's Nightmare* (Edison, 1900), *The Horrible Nightmare* (Edison, 1902), *Casey's Nightmare* (Edison, 1903), *Nightmare* (Lubin, 1903), and *Casey's Frightful Dream* (Edison, 1904).[58]

Whatever the narrative excuse for trickery (or lack thereof), many American viewers were curious about how the special effects were created, including in such indigenous productions as *Merlin the Magician* (American Mutoscope, 1898). In an 1899 article, a journalist asked a "cinematograph expert" the question, "How, for example do they get those curious films in which people suddenly appear and disappear, jump out of space and then leap into the air and vanish?" The expert's response began, "It's the simplest thing in the world."[59] Similarly, a 1902 newspaper article quoted a representative from a film manufacturing company as saying, "The whole [trick] thing is so very simple that I'm afraid if we give it away we'll destroy interest."[60] But then the article proceeded to describe exactly how tricks in "mysterious" films were created.

Figure 4.3 *Merlin the Magician* (American Mutoscope, 1898). (*Courtesy of Robert J. Kiss*)

The use of the term "mysterious" in this context is itself important. Extant catalogs published by film manufacturers and distributors seem to have been thoughtful when categorizing moving pictures with potentially horrifying content. "Trick picture" had common currency, but American Mutoscope & Biograph sometimes used the term "fantastic" to describe the same.[61] Selig Polyscope categorized such moving pictures as "Mythical and Mysterious," Vitagraph referred to them as "Mysterious" and, separately, as "Magical," Maguire and Baucus used the terms "Mysterious" and, separately, "Sleight-of-Hand," whereas Edison and the Chicago Projecting Company opted for the single word "Mysterious."[62] (In 1901, a newspaper in Indiana used the phrase "mysterious or 'spook' pictures" to describe the same.[63])

With regard to descriptions of particular films, American film catalogs applied the adjective "weird" to *The Ghost Train* (American Mutoscope & Biograph, 1901), *The*

Figure 4.4 A frame from *The Ghost Train* (American Mutoscope & Biograph, 1901). (*Courtesy of the Library of Congress, Motion Picture, Broadcasting and Recorded Sound Division/Moving Image Section*)

Revolving Table/La table tournante (Pathé Frères, 1904), and *The Inventor Crazybrains and his Wonderful Airship/Le dirigeable fantastique ou le Cauchemar d'un inventeur* (Méliès, 1905).[64] Edison's description of *The Mysterious Urn* (1902) claimed it was "one of the most mystifying of the black art pictures."[65] And, using perhaps the boldest language of all, an American advertisement for Méliès's *The Mysterious Retort/L'alchimiste Parafaragamus ou la cornue infernale* (1906) called it a "terrifying film in its grotesqueness."[66]

The Nickelodeon Era

From late 1905 until 1913, the nickelodeon transformed the American film industry, becoming the major exhibition venue. Musser writes, "The rapid proliferation of specialized storefront moving-picture theatres—commonly known as 'nickelodeons' (a reference to the customary admission charge of five cents), 'electric theatres,' and 'theatoriums'— created a revolution in screen entertainment."[67] Exhibiting and viewing films changed, as did the films themselves, particularly during the period between 1907 and 1913. As Charlie Keil notes, "after 1913, never again would one find such a diverse range of narrational norms within a seven-year period of American filmmaking."[68]

While nonfiction cinema endured, with actualities and travelogue films remaining standard components of moving picture bills during the nickelodeon period, these same bills tended to foreground works with fictional narratives.[69] Special effects continued, as did explanations of the same, not only in the popular press, but also in the moving pictures themselves.[70] In 1912, for example, Edison released the film *How Motion Pictures Are Made and Shown*.[71] At the same time, filmmakers and the press gave attention to innovations in areas like underwater photography, as well as to actors performing "death-defying" stunts for particular film scenes.[72]

By contrast, the Méliès style of trick picture became less popular, a trend that seems to have begun even before the nickelodeon era. When promoting *The Bewitched Traveller/ The Jonah Man; or, The Traveller Bewitched* (Hepworth, 1904), American Mutoscope and Biograph announced, "This is a straight comedy picture, without the magicians, ballet girls and the rest of the familiar characters." As a result, it constituted a "novelty in trick pictures," eschewing some aspects of the "old style trick pictures which were popular so long, and which have only lost their popularity because of a lack of novelties . . ."[73] The new had quickly become the old.

Trickery for the sake of trickery lost much of its allure during the nickelodeon era. In 1911, *Motography* observed: "Tricks popular a few years ago are being abandoned. Sophisticated audiences demand that the ideas be worked out in a logical way."[74] Two years later, *Exhibitors' Times* wrote:

> The palpable trick picture is not nearly so popular as it once was, as the moving-picture patrons no longer wax enthusiastic over the skill of a cinematograph magician. But in spite of this change in popular taste, the trick picture is still employed—although in a fashion that, if successful, will not be detected by the spectator.[75]

During the interim between those two articles, financial problems meant that Georges Méliès had ceased making moving pictures.

If one person became Méliès's immediate heir, it was Segundo de Chomón, a Spanish filmmaker whose expertise in coloring moving pictures led him to work at Pathé Frères in France in 1905. He was "one of the main supervisors (and shortly after, the manager) of the company's trick film section."[76] In many respects, his approach intentionally resembled Méliès's; in 1908, for example, he remade *A Trip to the Moon* as *An Excursion to the Moon/Excursion dans la lune* (Pathé Frères, aka *Excursion to Moon*).[77] But in other respects, Chomón advanced the trick picture, including in his expert use of color and animation.

Of particular importance is the fact that Chomón often used tricks to construct films with serious narratives, most notably in *Legend of a Ghost/La légende du fantôme* (Pathé Frères, 1908).[78] Here is a key link in the evolution of the horror-themed moving picture, with the attraction of cinematic tricks embedded logically into a dramatic narrative in such a way as to seem realistic.

Realism

Eileen Bowser has observed, "American film began to undergo a series of changes in 1908–1909 that would be as radical as those at any time in film history, marking as they did a major shift in the perception of the nature and function of the moving picture."[79] Among these changes were the rise of the star system, an increasing shift toward California as a site for production, and an "uplift movement" that urged producers to make film that would be "morally improving."[80] Most important, though, was the emphasis on the "story film."[81] The pre-D. W. Griffith mode of representation was no longer dominant; the "framework for Hollywood's mode of representation," as Musser calls it, began.[82]

Such moving pictures exhibited an increased running time, often one full reel in length or (as will be examined) even longer.[83] Intertitles (at the time normally called "subtitles") became increasingly common, especially by 1909, as did the use of narrative devices like the flashback, particularly during and after 1911.[84] This is to say nothing of the increased temporal relationship between shots and an emphasis on the psychology of characters, with their motivations made clear, such that they were often responsible for important turning points in film narratives.[85]

These dramatic storylines, as well as an increasing use of film aesthetics such as the close-up and improvements in lighting, meant that a number of potentially horrifying tropes proliferated, some of them appropriated from literature and stage. Shadows of individual characters gained importance; in Lubin's comedy *The House of Terror* (1909), silhouettes in a window appear to show someone being brutalized.[86] Eyes took on ominous characteristics in *Soul to Soul* (Eclair American, 1913) and *The Mysterious Eyes* (American, 1913), with the latter being an early example of a film character peering through holes cut in the eyes of a painting.[87] Mysterious hands—which had appeared as early as *A Dextrous Hand/King of Coins* (Gaumont British, 1903)—became commonplace thanks to films like *The Hand of Mystery* (Rex, 1912), *The Hidden Hand* (Atlas, 1912), and *The Warning Hand* (Essanay, 1912), in which a "mysterious hand" can be seen "reaching through the curtains and lifting items of value, but . . . to whom the hand belongs is not revealed until the last few feet of the picture."[88]

Figure 4.5 Lubin's comedy *The House of Terror* (1909) made a notable use of silhouettes.

Many of the cinematic evolutions described herein were part of an increasing drive toward what industry trade publications referred to as "realism," by which they generally meant verisimilitude. As Keil has said:

> ... the issues of realism that had informed discussions of photography persisted in the criticism of narratives, suggesting that the fundamental question remained one of believability; the oft-repeated phrase 'truthfulness to life' demonstrates the centrality of verisimilitude to the trade press aesthetic. Trade press critics understood that audience comprehension and involvement go hand in hand, always predicated on a film's sustained cultivation of verisimilitude.[89]

In a 1911 issue of *Moving Picture World*, C. H. Claudy spoke of the matter more bluntly, claiming, "we don't thank you, Mr. Producer, we motion picture audiences, for forcing down our throats, the knowledge that this is only a screen and a picture—we want to think it's the real thing."[90]

Realism in many cases meant narrative plausibility. In 1911, Claudy also complained that one in every three moving pictures is:

> ... either built upon an improbability so great it can fairly be termed impossible, or else within it is found an incident, action, happening, so unnatural from what we know—you and I and the rest of the payers of five-cent pieces—that if we do not rise and leave, our gorge does, and only the hope of another and more reasonable film holds us and our gorges to the places![91]

Harrison Dent echoed this view in *Motography* the same year, observing, "Sophisticated audiences demand that the ideas be worked out in a logical way."[92]

Dreams and nightmares continued to be a common framing device, allowing the unrealistic to exist logically in an otherwise realistic film.[93] Some of these moving pictures drew heavily upon earlier films; *A Night Off* (Lubin, 1906) bore narrative similarities to *Casey's Frightful Dream* (Edison, 1904), whereas events in *Dream Spectres/Voleur d'opium* (Gaumont, 1909, aka *The Dream Spectre*) stem from a drug-induced nightmare.[94] Other moving pictures—such as *The Angler's Dream/Le rêve du pêcheur* (Gaumont, 1910) and *An Old-Time Nightmare* (Powers, 1911)—presented the novelty of sleeping characters being tortured by the very animals they attempt to capture.[95]

Most famous of these films was Edwin S. Porter's *The Dream of a Rarebit Fiend* (Edison, 1906), which was inspired by Winsor McCay's newspaper comic strip of the same name.[96] In Porter's film, a drunken man has nightmares in which he is plagued by imps. He then flies through the evening air while still on his bed. Among the tricks Porter employed are double exposures, split-screen, and miniatures. *The Dream of a Rarebit Fiend* presents a narrative that is at once coherent and understandable, but which also conveys something of the incoherent structure of nightmares.[97]

In terms of serious horror-themed cinema, the dream device often became particularly important. *Harlequin's Nightmare/Le cauchemar de Pierrot* (Gaumont, 1909) and *The Nightmare* (Urban-Eclipse, 1910) presented tales in which characters dream they commit murder. *Moving Picture World* described the nightmarish events in both films with the term "horrors."[98] And a character who committed murder dreams about being executed in *The Bells* (Reliance, 1913).[99] These films and others—including notably *Dr. Jekyll and Mr. Hyde; or, a Strange Case/Den skæbnesvangre opfindelse* (Great Northern, 1910)—relied on the dream device in part to explain away horrible or otherwise implausible narrative action.[100]

Realism in the period went beyond narrative concerns, however. Consider the *New York Dramatic Mirror*'s review of *The Inn of Death* (Vitagraph, 1908), which claimed: "Perhaps one point which renders the story so little convincing is the fact that what is supposed to be a ponderous death machine that sinks down over the bed resembles nothing so much as a huge pasteboard box that might have proven insufficient to crush the life out of a cockroach."[101] Here is an example of a viewer wondering not how a trick was performed, but rather asking why it was performed so badly, so unrealistically.

Terminology

Describing horror-themed films was as varied in the nickelodeon era as it had been in earlier years. For example, Herbert Case Hoagland's 1912 book *How to Write a Photoplay* listed the following narrative classifications: "Trick, Farce, Comedy, Dramatic Comedy, Dramatic, Tragic, Scenic, Industrial, Military, Historical, Educational, Biblical, Micro-Cinematographic."[102] Other members of the industry referred to such story types as "melodrama," as well as by more specific categories like "Western," "War," and "Crime".[103] Examining the trade press, as well as the titles of many films, it is apparent that "mystery" became a commonly used term in the late nickelodeon era.[104]

Some film titles in the period might have been suggestive of the emotions they intended to evoke, but still gave little indication of genre specificity. For example, *An Hour of Terror* (American, 1912) was an "Indian tale, replete with those features demanded in good Western stories."[105] By contrast, *Days of Terror* (Vitagraph, 1912) offered a "thrilling plot" set during the French Revolution.[106] Even the usage of a word like "terror" did not necessarily indicate whether a given film was dramatic or comedic. *A Night of Terror* (American Mutoscope and Biograph, 1908) offered the "thrilling" story of a robber attempting to locate some hidden gold, whereas *A Night of Terror* (Edison, 1911) was a "laughable" comedy in which a "tenderfoot" mistakenly believes he is to be murdered.[107]

Many exhibitors seem to have intentionally chosen language for their newspaper ads that avoided drawing attention to potentially horrifying content. Consider the following terminology, all of which appeared in newspaper ads: *Dr. Jekyll and Mr. Hyde* (Thanhouser, 1912) was a "psychological picture;"[108] *The Vengeance of Egypt/L'anneau fatal* (Gaumont, 1912) was "A Story to Bring Back the Thrills of Childhood," as well as a "story that defies description;"[109] *A Bargain with Satan/Der Student von Prag* (Apex, 1913) was a "splendid allegory"[110] *The Werewolf* (101 Bison, 1913) was an "Indian picture;"[111] and *When Soul Meets Soul* (Essanay, 1913) was a "very heavy and impressive drama."[112]

That exhibitors approached the same films differently to one another is also evident. For example, some newspaper ads emphasized the fact that *The Spectre Bridegroom* (Eclair American, 1913) was a literary adaptation.[113] Another referred to it as a "brilliant and glittering comedy."[114] Another described it as "one of the sweetest love stories ever told."[115] Yet another drew attention to the film's duration and special effects, calling it "An illusionary feature extraordinary in two wonderful parts. Introducing the dancing spectre and the great firelight effects."[116]

In those cases when exhibitors believed it necessary to announce potentially horrifying content (likely because the film titles drew upon famous literature), they often chose the term "weird," as if to identify such content without heightening it by way of more extreme words like "terror" or "horror." For example, in one ad, *Frankenstein* (Edison, 1910) was "weird and wonderful."[117] *The Mask of the Red Death/La maschera tragica* (Ambrosio, 1911) was a "weird story."[118] Similar language appeared in an ad for *The Pit and the Pendulum* (Solax, 1913):

> Adapted from Edgar Allen [sic] Poe's blood curdling description of the inquisition. 3 Reels of a hidous [sic], weird spectacle of thrills and sensations. Showing the man tied in the death pit, the razor edge pendulum slowly descending, the rats gnawing the ropes that bind him.[119]

The same description encouraged "all school children" to see the film given that it was a "mysterious story by our American Author, Edgar Allen [sic] Poe."

Americanizing the Cinema

Richard Abel has written at length on the dominance of French cinema in America during the years 1900 to 1910, a trend that began in some measure with Méliès. The desperate need for film product to screen at nickelodeons transformed the United States into the biggest audience the French company Pathé Frères had. "Put simply," Abel writes, "Pathé's presence on the American market provided the single most significant condition of emergence for the nickelodeon."[120] Between 1905 and 1908, French films became the "predominant fare" at American nickelodeons.[121] As the *New York Clipper* wrote in 1907, "Pathé films [were] features on all moving picture programs"; by 1908, Pathé films allegedly constituted 60 per cent of the total number of moving pictures available in America.[122] That said, after 1908, the American industry and trade press "repeatedly stigmatized and/or marginalized" Pathé films for being "foreign or alien to . . . American culture."[123] (This concern is also evident with imported German films during the years 1911 to 1914. For example, Luna-Film productions were released in the United States under the disguised name "Film Releases of America" and Continental-Kunstfilm's bore the emblem of The New York Film Company.)

In terms of the horror-themed moving picture, much of the imported product came from France. Some of the other key films of this type arrived from Denmark, made by the Nordisk Film Company and released by their branch office in New York, the Great Northern Film Company.[124] Subsequent chapters will examine such Great Northern releases as *The Changing of Souls/Sjælebytning* (1908), *The Human Ape, or Darwin's Triumph/Menneskeaben, eller Darwins Triumf* (1909, aka *The Human Ape*), *Dr. Jekyll and Mr. Hyde; or, a Strange Case/Den skæbnesvangre opfindelse* (1910), *Mystery of the Lama Convent/Dr. Nikola III, eller Lamaklostrets hemmeligheder* (1910, aka *Mystery of the Lama Convent; or, Dr. Nicola in Tibet*), *The Somnambulist/Museumsmysteriet, eller Søvngængeren* (1910), and *The Ghost of the Vaults/Spøgelset i gravkælderen* (1911).

In 1909, *Moving Picture World* "put in a plea for the creation of an American moving picture drama," suggesting the adaptation of American literature, citing the likes of Nathaniel Hawthorne and F. Marion Crawford, as well as of American literary genres,

Figure 4.6 Published in the February 5, 1910 issue of *Moving Picture World*.

specifically the western.[125] Abel has also written about the distinctions drawn between American "ethical melodrama" of the period, and the "inappropriately sensational" French Grand Guignol melodrama.[126] Such distinctions between melodramas are apparent in trade press editorials. In 1913, for example, *Moving Picture World* feared the "cheap, melodramatic 'blood curdler'" would "either drive the good features away entirely or lessen their numbers materially."[127]

Some of these concerns involved the treatment of given subjects, with "foreign" films sometimes perceived as containing objectionable content. For the horror-themed film, however, national distinctions at times became muddied due to the narrative material being adapted. For example, *The Necklace of the Dead/Den dødes halsbaand* (1910, aka *Necklace of the Dead*), produced by Nordisk, drew upon such short stories as Poe's *The Fall of the House of Usher* and *The Premature Burial*.

Conversely, D. W. Griffith, the most quintessential American director of the nickelodeon era, drew upon both Poe's *The Cask of Amontillado* and Honoré de Balzac's *La Grande Bretèche* for inspiration when he produced *The Sealed Room* (Biograph, 1909). Shot in America with American actors, Griffith's narrative was set in Europe. To consider again the work of Richard Abel, it could well be said that the horror-themed moving picture in America was "irrevocably enmeshed" in the project of Americanization, not an easy task during an era in which the cinema was in some respects transnational.[128]

The Post-nickelodeon Era

"Is the 'nickel show' on the wane?", *Moving Picture World* asked in 1914.[129] Such a question offers insight into major changes that occurred as the nickelodeon's dominance largely came to an end in 1913. Newly constructed motion picture theatres increasingly became the prime venue for screen entertainment that itself underwent various evolutions.[130] One of the most important and enduring was the emphasis on increased running times for particular films.

Bowser has noted that, during the first few years of the nickelodeon era, a "feature film" was approximately one reel in length, and was in some respect special, whereas after 1909 the "feature" came to mean any multi-reel film. According to James F. Hodges' text *Opening and Operating a Motion Picture Theatre* (1912), the feature "differs from the ordinary film in that it will run from 2,000 to 5,000 feet [meaning two-to-five reels]."[131] It was during the end of the nickelodeon era and shortly thereafter that the term "feature" assumed its modern connotation, though in the early cinema period its status came not merely from length, but also at times from where and how it was advertised and exhibited.[132]

Many persons in the industry, including Carl Laemmle and William N. Selig, attributed the trend of multi-reel features to Europe.[133] During the 1910s, *Dante's Inferno/L'inferno* (Milano, 1911) was often cited as the first to achieve box-office success.[134] But not everyone shared in the enthusiasm. In 1912, the *Moving Picture World* mentioned an exhibitor who believed *Dante's Inferno* was "too long."[135] An editorial in the same publication in March 1915 declared, "The feature is becoming the Frankenstein of the exhibitor and there is as yet no sign of the long wished for clearing of the situation."[136]

While it had many detractors, the feature film also had key supporters, among them film directors D. W. Griffith and Alice Guy Blaché.[137] Griffith was one of those who had during the nickelodeon era best understood the power of editing, including its potential to create suspense. "I have never seen a Griffith picture that did not contain suspense," Louella O. Parsons once enthused. "*The Avenging Conscience* [1914, aka *The Avenging Conscience: or "Thou Shalt Not Kill"*] is full of it."[138] Extended running times also allowed for creative use of narrative structures, ranging from flashbacks to starting films with moments of key narrative action. *The Mystery of the Tapestry Room* (Universal, 1915) began with a murder, the culprit being a "figure in black [who] slides back a panel in the wall and disappears."[139]

These new kinds of features were not the only film releases that took advantage of increased running times. By 1914, movie serials—released over a period of weeks and even months in the form of individual, cliffhanger chapters—became popular, among them *The Perils of Pauline* (Pathé, 1914), *The Exploits of Elaine* (Pathé, 1914–15), and *The Hazards of Helen* (Kalem, 1914). Given their duration, such serials could invoke numerous plot devices and generic conventions. An advertisement for a single chapter of *Lucille Love, The Girl of Mystery* (Universal, 1914) promised it contained: "Excitement—thrills—heart throbs—intrigue—punches—hair-raising situations—wild animals—and hundreds upon hundreds of savages in a terrific battle—all these things are crowded into the fourth installment of *Lucille Love*."[140]

Even as they became subsumed into narratives rather than being the sole attraction, cinematic special effects remained a topic of much discussion.[141] Here the emphasis was not only on technological progress (as in "fade away" attachments that permitted "two pictures to be taken on the same part of the film without doubling the time of the exposure"), but also on artistic uses of the same.[142] The same actor could portray more than one character in the same image.[143] *The Dead Secret* (Monopol, 1913) even featured "quadruple" exposures that allowed characters to see themselves in crystal balls. Its photographic advances became a key component in its publicity.[144]

As the *Literary Digest* wrote in 1914, the "tricks" of motion pictures drew upon "parlor magic" and the "trick photograph," but flourished "like a green bay-tree since the motion of the image on the screen gave it additional opportunities to get in its amazing work."[145] The same article showed an awareness of how the usage of tricks had changed over time. It concluded by declaring that the "film-manufacturer" increasingly valued the "real thing" over "small scale models," because the cinema was becoming "realist in every sense of the word."[146]

But such realism did not necessarily extend to the conclusions of film narratives, meaning what *Moving Picture World* of 1915 referred to as the "always insisted-upon 'happy ending.'"[147] In another article, the trade agreed with the "exhibitors' prevailing opinion that their audiences must have happy endings."[148] For *Motography*, the depiction of screen happiness added to the world's "sum total of happiness."[149] This aspect of American-made film narratives represents a core aspect in the process of "Americanization."

Mise-en-scène

A continued and intensified approach to realism extended noticeably to the mise-en-scène of motion pictures in the 1910s. Everything in the frame—the actors, costumes, props, and lighting of the same—needed to seem authentic and believable, three-dimensional and real, with the painted backdrops of earlier years being eschewed. Trade publications discussed the necessity of appropriate "backgrounds," meaning either carefully chosen locations or well-constructed sets.[150]

Well-constructed could also mean eerie and fantastical. Consider the serial *Zudora* (Thanhouser, 1914), which after episode ten was rechristened *The Twenty Million Dollar Mystery* (aka *The $20,000,000 Mystery*). *Motography* wrote:

> Wonderful photography, elaborate stage settings, an air of orientalism and mysticism, which prevail through the entire production, together with strange sliding panels, revolving doors, an iron room, the walls of which can be slid in upon themselves, make *The Mystery of the Sleeping House*, which is the second adventure of Zudora, one of the most mysterious and interesting pictures that has been thrown on the screen.[151]

A review of the tenth episode praised the "sliding panels, underground passages, [and] unique conveyances for getting from floor to floor" for creating a "general atmosphere of mystery, cunning, and danger."[152]

Thoughtful consideration to mise-en-scène also yielded various changes to film style, some particularly helpful for horror-themed cinema. In 1915, *Wid's Film and Film Folk* stressed the need for shadows, both realistic and artistic.[153] Mise-en-scène needed to evoke an appropriate mood, as in the case of the "swaying treetops" and "banging doors" in *Haunting Winds* (Powers, 1915), or in the "fine lighting effects" in

Zuma, the Gypsy/Zuma (Kleine-Cines, 1913), and in the shadow of a spectral figure in *The Ghost of Seaview Manor* (Dragon, 1913).[154] The years from 1913 to 1915 also saw an increase in the number of moving pictures featuring storm scenes, as in *The Missing Woman/Der Roman einer Verschollenen* (Film Releases of America, 1913), *Fate's Midnight Hour* (Kalem, 1914), and *The Death Mask* (Kay-Bee, 1914).[155] A bolt of lightning even burned a building to the ground in the four-reel *My Boy; or, The Mystery of the Roadhouse Murder* (Lewis Pennant, 1913).[156]

Particularly important advances were made in what the industry referred to as "night photography." As *Moving Picture World* noted in 1915, "There is always something mysterious and unexplained connected with the darkness of night and its strange noises."[157] Efforts at night photography had long been undertaken, but achieved only limited success, as can be seen in Edwin S. Porter's *Panorama of Esplanade by Night* (Edison, 1901) and *Coney Island at Night* (Edison, 1905).[158] As a result, filmmakers often relied on various cinematic approaches to simulate nighttime in their scenes. In 1912, *Moving Picture World* chided the Edison Manufacturing Company for their poor efforts in a film entitled *The Commuter's Wife*:

> The time has gone by, Edison—gone by a long, long time ago—when you can call a scene 'night' and show it in 'daylight' and get away with it. But when you call it 'night' and show half the action in semi-darkness and half in bright and streaming sunlight, then you go so much too far that even the most ignorant of your audiences gives you the laugh.[159]

By contrast, the trade press praised Selig Polyscope for the night photography for its film *The Bridge of Shadows* (1913).[160] *Motography* went so far as to say that the film's "unusual" cinematography "more than atones for one or two minor defects in the plot of the story."[161]

Universal made even greater advances with night photography in *The Brand of His Tribe* (101 Bison, 1914) and *The House of Fear* (Imp, 1915).[162] The studio boasted that *The House of Fear* included images shot "out of doors in the darkness, against the brightly lighted windows of a dwelling—a thing not tried successfully before."[163] Director Stuart Paton achieved appropriately "weird results" for a storyline about a man and his son who tried to scare a wealthy relative to death.[164] As one critic wrote, "It . . . cannot be denied that the atmosphere of the picture stays with one."[165]

What all of this means is that filmmakers could take advantage of an increasing array of possibilities to create potentially horrifying mise-en-scène. Consider, for example, the depiction of Hades in *After the Welsh Rarebit* (Edison, 1913):

> Weird lighting effects, shadows leaping in the smoke and flashing fire, dismal black caverns in the farther recesses of the grotesquely arched Inferno, drinks that scorch the throat, glowing tables that burn things which are placed upon them and yawning pits of fire—all these contribute to an atmosphere that is startlingly realistic.[166]

This is an example of what *Motography* had meant when it once claimed a believable level of detail could in fact be used to "foster illusion."[167] Here was a realistic depiction of the unrealistic.

Reviewing the five-reel "crook melodrama" *The Master Mind* (Jesse L. Lasky Feature Play Company, 1914), the *New York Dramatic Mirror* wrote:

Figure 4.7 *The House of Fear* (Imp, 1915) featured advances in night photography. An example appears in a still at the bottom of this trade advertisement, which was published in *Universal Weekly* on January 9, 1915.

> Every device known to a resourceful director has been utilized if it could be made to contribute to the atmosphere of mystery in which 'The Master Mind' chose to live. Secret doors leading to underground vaults, innocent appearing walls that hide the unexpected, a network of wires to be operated only by the hand of the master—we have them all and used to the best of purposes, for it is an admirably directed picture.[168]

Filmmakers—one of them in this case being Cecil B. DeMille—had once again created an unbelievable world in a believable manner. The illusion of reality and the reality of illusion converged.

The Film Artist

From the early 1910s, discussion of the cinema as an art form became more pronounced.[169] Vachel Lindsay's book *The Art of the Moving Picture* (1915) became a particularly prominent voice in that conversation.[170] The same year as its release, *Moving Picture World* published an editorial entitled "Directors as Artists," which likened directors to alchemists who sometimes had to "transmute base metals into gold." Its author Louis Reeves Harrison announced, "The time may even come when a director will be known by his style, the word including, besides scene setting and lighting, his method of handling actors."[171]

If film was art, then directors were the artists. Chief among them was perhaps D. W. Griffith, who had directed over 450 films at Biograph from 1908 to 1913. His work included a number of horror-themed moving pictures that will be examined in subsequent chapters, including *Edgar Allen* [sic] *Poe* (1909), *The Criminal Hypnotist* (1909), *The Hindoo Dagger* (1909), *The Suicide Club* (1909), *Rose O' Salem Town* (1910), and *Man's Genesis*

(1912). After leaving Biograph, Griffith directed such famous epics as *Judith of Bethulia* (1914) and *The Birth of a Nation* (1915), as well as the aforementioned horror-themed feature, *The Avenging Conscience: or "Thou Shalt Not Kill"* (1914).

While he made so many films of so many types, it would not be incorrect to suggest that Griffith was one of the first major directors of American horror-themed film. Many other important American filmmakers will be chronicled elsewhere in this book, among them Frederick S. Armitage and J. Searle Dawley. But no other American director made as many important horror-themed moving pictures in the nickelodeon era as Griffith.

The year that *The Avenging Conscience* first appeared at theatres, Alice Guy Blaché wrote, "Just as there are thousands of men making a living by playing the piano to every true soloist, there are many men staging photodramas to every director worthy of the name."[172] A pioneer of French cinema, she moved to America with her husband, and by 1913 co-owned her own studio, the Solax Company.[173]

Historians have rightly examined Guy Blaché's important and impressive directorial career. While her work can and should be viewed from many different perspectives, she became just as crucial to the horror-themed film in the years 1913 to 1915 as Griffith had been in the nickelodeon period. Here one can point to many of her Solax films, including *The Wise Witch of Fairyland* (1912), *The Witch's Necklace* (1912), *A Message from Beyond* (1912), *The Eyes of Satan* (1913), *The Case of the Missing Girl* (1913), *The Pit and the*

Figure 4.8 Trade advertisement for Alice Guy-Blaché's *The Woman of Mystery* (Solax, 1914). Published in *Moving Picture World* on May 9, 1914.

Pendulum (1913), *A Drop of Blood* (1913), *Shadows of the Moulin Rouge* (1914), *The Dream Woman* (1914), and *The Woman of Mystery* (1914).

Conclusion

In 1908, *The Film Index* referred to the moving picture form as a "genre."[174] By 1910, *Moving Picture World* described the "genre picture" as being a particular type of film, one that "told a story," one that "stirs the emotions and clings to the memory of the spectator."[175] Bowser describes numerous genres present in films of 1907 to 1915, among them "detective films."[176] A review of *The Solution of the Mystery* (American, 1915) claimed:

> There is a mysterious screen that moves about apparently unaided. There is a mysterious arm which strikes a mysterious blow with a mysterious knife. There is a mysterious disappearance, a mysterious dead man and mysterious events too numerous to mention. In fact the picture reeks with mystery.[177]

At first it might be tempting to suggest that the "mysterious" subject of the first years of early cinema had given way to the "mystery" by the end of the era, that the mystery of the trick was supplanted by the mystery of the narrative. To be sure, the decline of the trick film came parallel to the rise of the story film.[178]

But even if this was the case—and a more complicated situation transpired, one in which the "trick film" might have receded, but tricks did not, being subsumed as they were into film narratives, among them the serial—it would not adequately cover the numerous horror-themed genres that emerged and evolved during the early cinema period, all of which drew on literary, stage, and visual culture traditions of the past. While formative and featuring porous boundaries, these genres—which will be explored in Section II of this book—presented various forms of horror-themed content to film viewers, their focus ranging from the supernatural to the natural, and their tone ranging from dramatic to comedic.

Notes

1. Minna Irving, "*The Magic Film*," *Motion Picture Story Magazine*, July 1911, 50.
2. Quoted in Colin Harding and Simon Popple, *In the Kingdom of Shadows: A Companion to Early Cinema* (London: Cygnus Arts, 1996), 5.
3. Hunter McCulloch, "At a Motion Picture Show," *Motion Picture Story Magazine*, March 1911, 10.
4. Charles Musser, *The Emergence of Cinema: The American Screen to 1907* (Berkeley: University of California Press, 1990), 91.
5. Ibid., 103.
6. "Mr. Edison Outdone," *The Sun* (Baltimore, Maryland), October 3, 1895, 2.
7. Matthew Solomon, *Disappearing Tricks: Silent Film, Houdini, and the New Magic of the Twentieth Century* (Urbana: University of Illinois Press, 2010), 11–27.
8. Ibid., 29.
9. Tom Gunning, "Flickers: On Cinema's Power for Evil," in *Bad: Infamy, Darkness, Evil, and Slime on Screen*, edited by Murray Pomerance (Albany: State University of New York Press, 2004), 31.

10. "Moving Pictures Are All the Rage," *Philadelphia Inquirer*, November 18, 1900, 5.
11. It is important to note that, after Méliès entered the film business, the Lumières frequently produced fictional films in addition to the actualities for which they are best remembered, some of which would be horror-themed. These include Gaston Velle's series of thirteen "phantasmagorical views" in 1902, which included the skeleton-and-haunted-castle short *Le château hanté* (Lumière #2001) and the human automata-themed *Les poupées* (Lumière #2013).
12. Elizabeth Ezra, *Georges Méliès: The Birth of the Auteur* (Manchester: Manchester University Press, 2000), 8–9.
13. Tom Gunning, "An Aesthetic of Astonishment: Early Film and the (In)Credulous Spectator," in *Viewing Positions: Ways of Seeing Film*, edited by Linda Williams (New Brunswick: Rutgers University Press, 1995), 119.
14. Quoted in Tom Gunning, "Primitive Cinema: A Frame-Up? Or the Trick's on Us,' in *Early Cinema: Space, Frame, Narrative*, edited by Thomas Elsaesser with Adam Barker (London: British Film Institute, 1990), 95.
15. "Film Maker's Tricks," *Views and Film Index*, September 12, 1908, 7.
16. "*The Electric Laundry*," *New York Dramatic Mirror*, December 11, 1912, 28.
17. Solomon, 1.
18. Tom Gunning, "The Cinema of Attractions: Early Film, Its Spectator and the Avant-Garde," in *Early Cinema: Space, Frame, Narrative*, edited by Thomas Elsaesser with Adam Barker (London: British Film Institute, 1990), 56.
19. Gunning, "Primitive Cinema: A Frame-Up? Or the Trick's on Us," 100.
20. Gunning, "The Cinema of Attractions," 60.
21. Tom Gunning, "'Now You See It, Now You Don't': The Temporality of the Cinema of Attractions," *Velvet Light Trap*, No. 32 (1993), 10–11.
22. David Bordwell, *On the History of Film Style* (Cambridge, MA: Harvard University Press, 1997), 126–7.
23. Here again I would stress that these comparisons between the Lumière Brothers and Méliès are valuable when examining the films that the Lumières produced *prior* to Méliès's entry into the industry.
24. W. K. L. Dickson and Antonia Dickson, *History of the Kinetograph, Kinetoscope, and Kinetophonograph* (New York: Museum of Modern Art, 2000), 22. Originally published in 1895.
25. "Wonders of the Kinteoscope," *Frank Leslie's Popular Monthly* (February 1895), 245.
26. It is worth noting that there were a small number of exceptions in the Lumières' output, meaning films that did involve the staging of performance-based attractions, perhaps even in response to Edison. These include *Danse sur scène (pas de deux)* (1896) and *Squelette joyeux* (1897).
27. Musser, 78.
28. "Descriptions of New Films," *Views and Film Index*, June 8, 1907. 6.
29. "Koster & Bial's," *New York Clipper*, April 18, 1896, 104.
30. "'Picture Projecting' Devices," *The Phonoscope*, May 1897, 12.
31. See, for example, "The Kinetoscope Stereopticon," *Scientific American*, October 31, 1896, 325; Claxton Wilstach, "Electricity on the Stage," *Godey's Magazine*, November 1896, 518; Henry V. Hopwood, *Living Pictures: Their History, Photo-Production and Practical Working, with a Digest of British Patents and Annotated Bibliography* (London: Optician & Photographic Trades Review, 1899).
32. "Varied Uses of the Kinetoscope," *The Phonoscope*, September 1899; "To Take Moving Pictures of the Sun's Eclipse," *The Phonoscope*, November 1899.
33. "New Style of Camera," *North Adams Evening Transcript* (North Adams, Massachusetts), June 30, 1899.
34. "Show Surgical Operations," *Muskogee Democrat* (Muskogee, Oklahoma), June 23, 1904, 7.

35. Dickson and Dickson, 43.
36. Alison Griffiths, *Wondrous Difference: Cinema, Anthropology, and Turn-of-the-Century Visual Culture* (New York: Columbia University Press, 2002), 216.
37. Charles Musser, *Edison Motion Pictures, 1890–1900* (Washington, D.C.: Smithsonian Institution Press, 1997), 586–7.
38. "Fake and 'Frisco," *Cinematography and Bioscope Magazine* (London: The Warwick Trading Company, June 1906), 41. The film in question was *The San Francisco Disaster* (Sheffield Photo Co., 1906).
39. "Notes," *The Optical Magic Lantern and Photographic Enlarger*, December 1900, 153–4.
40. "Two Governments in Picture Suit," *St. Louis Republic* (St. Louis, Missouri), June 4, 1901, 6.
41. Advertisement, *New York Clipper*, December 12, 1902, 1016.
42. Quoted in Matthew Solomon, "Introduction," in *Fantastic Voyages of the Cinematic Imagination: Georges Méliès's Trip to the Moon*, edited by Matthew Solomon (Albany: State University of New York Press, 2011), 1.
43. Frank Kessler, "*A Trip to the Moon* as *Féerie*," in *Fantastic Voyages of the Cinematic Imagination: Georges Méliès's Trip to the Moon*, edited by Matthew Solomon (Albany: State University of New York Press, 2011), 115.
44. Tom Gunning, "Phantom Images and Modern Manifestations: Spirit Photography, Magic Theater, Trick Films, and Photography's Uncanny," in *Cinematic Ghosts: Haunting and Spectrality from Silent Cinema to the Digital Era*, edited by Murray Leeder (New York: Bloomsbury Academic, 2015), 33.
45. Quoted in André Gaudreault, *Film and Attraction: From Kinematography to Cinema* (Champaign: University of Illinois Press, 2011), 136.
46. Richard Abel, "*A Trip to the Moon* as American Phenomenon," in *Fantastic Voyages of the Cinematic Imagination: Georges Méliès's Trip to the Moon*, edited by Matthew Solomon (Albany: State University of New York Press, 2011), 138–9.
47. Early screenings of *The Devil's Castle* in America will be discussed at length in Chapter 15.
48. A copy of *The Devil's Castle* is available in the DVD boxed set *Georges Méliès: First Wizard of Cinema* (Los Angeles: Flicker Alley, 2008).
49. David S. Hulfish, *Cyclopedia of Motion-Picture Work* (Chicago: American School of Correspondence, 1911), 5.
50. It is difficult to determine whether or not *Escamotage d'une dame chez Robert-Houdin* (1896) was screened in the United States, but it is true that two similar films were produced in America soon thereafter: Edison's *Vanishing Lady* (1897, in which a woman under a sheet vanishes) and American Mutoscope's *The Vanishing Lady* (1898, in which the woman becomes a skeleton). A copy of Edison's *Vanishing Lady* is archived in the Paper Print Collection at the Library of Congress.
51. Ezra, 28–31.
52. Bordwell, 128.
53. *A Mysterious Portrait*, *The Famous Box Trick*, *Bewitched Trunk*, and *The Living Playing Cards* are available on the DVD boxed set *Georges Méliès: First Wizard of Cinema* (Los Angeles: Flicker Alley, 2008). *The Fugitive Apparitions* is available on the DVD *Georges Méliès Encore* (Los Angeles: Flicker Alley, 2010).
54. *Supplement No. 36, July 1st 1902* (Chicago: Selig Polyscope Co., 1902), unpaginated.
55. *The Cook's Revenge*, *How He Missed His Train*, and *The Man with the Rubber Head* are available on the DVD boxed set *Georges Méliès: First Wizard of Cinema* (Los Angeles: Flicker Alley, 2008).
56. Solomon, "Introduction," 6.
57. Méliès also made notable moving pictures in which travellers attempt to sleep but cannot, the tricks resulting from bewitched rooms rather than from their nightmares. Such films include *Going to Bed Under Difficulties/ Le déshabillage impossible* (1900) and *The Inn Where No Man*

Rests/L'auberge du bon repos (1903, aka *He Couldn't Sleep in That Inn*). Copies of both films, as well as of *The Astronomer's Dream* and *The Clock Maker's Dream*, are available in the DVD boxed set *Georges Méliès: First Wizard of Cinema* (Los Angeles: Flicker Alley, 2008).

58. Copies of *Uncle Josh's Nightmare* and *Casey's Frightful Dream* are archived at the Library of Congress.
59. "Trick Pictures," *The Phonoscope*, July 1899; "Making Trick Pictures," *Fort Worth Morning Register* (Fort Worth, Texas), August 20, 1899, 6; "Moving Picture Possibilities," *Daily Northwestern* (Oshkosh, Wisconsin), October 18, 1899, 5.
60. "Latest in Moving Pictures," *The Plain Dealer* (Cleveland, Ohio), July 6, 1902, 31.
61. *Film Catalogue, Supplement No. 1* (New York: American Mutoscope and Biograph Company, April 1903), 27. Available in *A Guide to Motion Picture Catalogs by American Producers and Distributors, 1894–1908*, Reel 2.
62. *The 1903 Complete Catalogue of Films and Moving Picture Machines* (Chicago: Selig Polyscope Company, 1903), 14. Available in *A Guide to Motion Picture Catalogs by American Producers and Distributors, 1894–1908*, Reel 2. *List of New Films, American and Imported* (New York: American Vitagraph Co., 1900). Available in *A Guide to Motion Picture Catalogs by American Producers and Distributors, 1894–1908*, Reel 4. Advertisement, *New York Clipper*, January 6, 1900, 20. *Edison Films for Edison Projecting Machines* (Orange, New Jersey: Edison Manufacturing Company, July 1, 1904), 26. Available in *A Guide to Motion Picture Catalogs by American Producers and Distributors, 1894–1908*, Reel 1. *Catalogue No. 120, Chicago Projecting Co.'s Entertainers Supplies* (Chicago: Chicago Projecting Company, 1907), 233. Available in *A Guide to Motion Picture Catalogs by American Producers and Distributors, 1894–1908*, Reel 6.
63. "It's a Winner," *Fort Wayne Journal-Gazette* (Fort Wayne, Indiana), January 16, 1901.
64. *Picture Catalogue* (New York: American Mutoscope & Biograph, November 1902), 72. Available in *A Guide to Motion Picture Catalogs by American Producers and Distributors, 1894-1908: A Microfilm Edition*, Reel 2. *Complete Catalogue of Genuine and Original "Star" Films* (New York: Star Films, June 1905), 93. Available in *A Guide to Motion Picture Catalogs by American Producers and Distributors, 1894–1908*, Reel 4. It is important to note that this Star Film catalog bears a June 1905 date, but pages from 81 to 148 detail films from the July 1905 to June 1908 period. Either these later pages were appended to the catalog, or the catalog dates to June 1908, with the first eighty pages reprinted and the 1905 date not being revised. *Lubin's Films* (Philadelphia: Lubin, June 1904), 10. Available in *A Guide to Motion Picture Catalogs by American Producers and Distributors, 1894–1908*, Reel 3.
65. *Edison Films, No. 135* (Buffalo: J. F. Adams, September 1902), 96. Available in *A Guide to Motion Picture Catalogs by American Producers and Distributors, 1894–1908*, Reel 1.
66. Advertisement, *New York Clipper*, December 15, 1906, 1151.
67. Musser, *The Emergence of Cinema*, 417.
68. Charlie Keil, *Early American Cinema in Transition* (Madison: University of Wisconsin Press, 2001), 204.
69. A few examples of science-based nonfiction cinema of the nickelodeon era include: *Micro-Cinematography–Sleeping Sickness/La cinématographie ultramicroscopique–Trypanosoma brucei* (Pathé Frères, 1910), *Micro-Cinematography–Recurrent Fever/La cinématographie ultramicroscopique–Fièvre récurrente* (Pathé Frères, 1910), *Examination of the Stomach by X-Ray/Examen de l'estomac par les rayons x* (C.G.P.C., 1911), and *Roentgen's X-Rays/Les rayons invisibles de Rœntgen* (C.G.P.C., 1912). See "*Micro-Cinematography–Sleeping Sickness*," *Moving Picture World*, June 25, 1910, 1101; "*Micro-Cinematography–Sleeping Sickness*," *Moving Picture World*, June 25, 1910, 1178; Advertisement, *Moving Picture World*, October 28, 1911, 267; "*Examination of the Stomach by X-Ray*," *Motography*, December 1911, 267; "*Roetgen's* [sic] *X-Rays*," *Moving Picture World*,

February 3, 1912, 414. For more information on this subject, see Hannah Landecker, "Microcinematography and the History of Science and Film," *Isis*, Vol. 97, No. 1 (March 2006), 121–32.
70. See, for example, "Making a Moving Picture," *Idaho Statesman* (Boise, Idaho), October 21, 1908, 12; "Tricks of the Trade in the Making of Thrilling Moving Pictures," *Baltimore Sun*, May 16, 1909, 24; "Tricks in Moving Pictures," *Washington Post*, August 17, 1910, 6; "Tricks in Moving Pictures," *Literary Digest*, July 1, 1911, 14; "Do Pictures Lie?", *Chicago Tribune*, February 9, 1913, G4.
71. "*How Motion Pictures Are Made and Shown*," *The Kinetogram*, June 1, 1912, 13.
72. "Under Water Pictures," *Moving Picture World*, September 13, 1913, 1158; "Death-Defying Feats of Moving Picture Players," *Moving Picture World*, June 8, 1912, 934.
73. "*The Bewitched Traveller*," *Biograph Bulletin*, No. 29, August 18, 1904, available in *Biograph Bulletins, 1896–1908*, edited by Kemp R. Niver (Los Angeles: Locare Research Group, 1971), 122. A copy of *The Bewitched Traveller* is archived at the British Film Institute.
74. Harrison Dent, "Tricks and Magic in Pictures," *Motography*, April 1911, 32.
75. "Trick Pictures," *Exhibitors' Times*, May 17, 1913, 24.
76. Joan M. Minguet Batllori, "Segundo de Chomón and the Fascination for Colour," *Film History*, Vol. 21, No. 1 (2009), 97.
77. *An Excursion to the Moon* is available on the DVD *Saved from the Flames: 54 Rare and Restored Films, 1896–1944* (Los Angeles: Flicker Alley, 2007).
78. A copy of *Legend of a Ghost* under its British release title *The Black Pearl* is available on the DVD *Fairy Tales: Early Colour Stencil Films from Pathé* (London: British Film Institute, 2012).
79. Eileen Bowser, *The Transformation of Cinema: 1907–1915* (Berkeley: University of California Press, 1990), 53.
80. Ibid., 54.
81. Ibid., 53.
82. Charles Musser, "The Nickelodeon Era Begins: Establishing the Framework for Hollywood's Mode of Representation," in *Early Cinema: Space, Frame, Narrative*, edited by Thomas Elsaesser with Adam Barker (London: British Film Institute, 1990), 256–73.
83. Keil, 45.
84. Ibid, 64–5, 99.
85. Tom Gunning, *D. W. Griffith and the Origins of American Narrative Film: The Early Years at Biograph* (Urbana: University of Illinois Press, 1991), 26, 27.
86. "*The House of Terror*," *Moving Picture World*, May 1, 1909, 564.
87. "*Soul to Soul*," *Moving Picture World*, August 9, 1913, 638; "*The Mysterious Eyes*," *Reel Life*, August 23, 1913, 10.
88. *Edison Films, No. 185* (Orange, New Jersey: Edison Manufacturing Company, October 1903), 23. Available in *A Guide to Motion Picture Catalogs by American Producers and Distributors, 1894–1908: A Microfilm Edition*, Reel 1. "*The Hand of Mystery*," *Moving Picture World*, July 27, 1912, 351; "*The Warning Hand*," *Moving Picture World*, October 19, 1912, 252; Advertisement, *Moving Picture World*, December 21, 1912, 1214; "*The Hand of Mystery*," *Moving Picture World*, July 27, 1912, 351.
89. Ibid., 35.
90. C. H. Claudy, "It 'Went Over,'" *Moving Picture World*, February 4, 1911, 231–2. [The same publication printed various articles on the subject of 'realism' in the cinema. See, for example, W. Stephen Bush, "Dealers and Brokers in Moving Picture Realism," *Moving Picture World*, September 23, 1911, 868; and "Pictures and Stage Realism," *Moving Picture World*, February 1, 1913, 477.]
91. C. H. Claudy, "Impossibilities in the Plot," *Moving Picture World*, July 1, 1911, 1495.
92. Harrison Dent, "Tricks and Magic in Pictures," *Motography*, April 1911, 32.

93. In addition to those examples cited in the main text, film narratives relying on nightmares also included: *A Policeman's Dream* (Vitagraph, 1908), *The Sculptor's Nightmare* (American Mutoscope & Biograph, 1908), *The Night Clerk's Nightmare* (Thanhouser, 1912), *Billy's Nightmare/Le cauchemar de Polycarpe* (Eclipse, 1912), *Betty's Nightmare* (Victor, 1912), *Whiffle's Nightmare/Le cauchemar de Rigadin* (C.G.P.C., 1912), and *Bingles' Nightmare* (Vitagraph, 1913). Examples of similar films from the post-nickelodeon era include: *Cabby's Nightmare/Le rêve du cocher* (Gaston Méliès, 1914), *Josie's Coney Island Nightmare* (Vitagraph, 1914), *Frank's Nightmare* (Thistle, rebadged as Alhambra, 1915), and *Some Nightmare* (Joker, 1915). See "*A Policeman's Dream,*" *New York Dramatic Mirror*, August 8, 1908; "*The Night Clerk's Nightmare,*" *Moving Picture World*, June 8, 1912, 956; "*Billy's Nightmare,*" *Moving Picture World*, July 20, 1912, 268; "*Betty's Nightmare,*" *Moving Picture World*, October 12, 1912, 180; "*Whiffle's Nightmare,*" *Moving Picture World*, November 30, 1912, 877; "*Bingles' Nightmare,*" *Vitagraph Life Portrayals*, August 1913, 23; "*Cabby's Nightmare,*" *Moving Picture World*, April 4, 1914, 104; "*Josie's Coney Island Nightmare,*" *Vitagraph Life Portrayals*, August 1914, 53; "*Frank's Nightmare,*" *Moving Picture World*, February 6, 1915, 894; "*Some Nightmare,*" *Moving Picture World*, March 6, 1915, 1506. *Billy's Nightmare* is archived at the Library of Congress; *Cabby's Nightmare* is available on the DVD set *Gaumont, le cinéma premier (1907–1916)—Volume 2* (Paris: Gaumont, 2009); *The Sculptor's Nightmare* is archived in the Paper Print Collection at the Library of Congress; and *Whiffle's Nightmare* is archived at the Cinémathèque Française and Centre national du cinéma et de l'image animée (CNC).
94. A copy of *A Night Off* is archived at the Library of Congress. Advertisement, *Moving Picture World*, April 24, 1909, 506.
95. "*The Angler's Dream,*" *Moving Picture World*, July 30, 1910, 259; "*An Old-Time Nightmare,*" *Moving Picture World*, September 16, 1911, 778.
96. Charles Musser, *Before the Nickelodeon: Edwin S. Porter and the Edison Manufacturing Company* (Berkeley: University of California Press, 1991), 341.
97. A copy of *The Dream of a Rarebit Fiend* is available in the DVD boxed set *The Movies Begin: A Treasury of Early Cinema, 1894–1913* (New York: Kino Video, 2002).
98. "*Harlequin's Nightmare,*" *Moving Picture World*, November 27, 1909, 759; "*The Nightmare,*" *Moving Picture World*, June 18, 1910, 1049.
99. "*The Bells,*" *Moving Picture World*, March 1, 1913, 889.
100. "*Dr. Jekyll and Mr. Hyde* (Great Northern)," *Moving Picture World*, September 24, 1910, 685.
101. "*The Inn of Death,*" *New York Dramatic Mirror*, November 28, 1908, 8. A copy of *The Inn of Death* is archived at the Library of Congress by way of a paper print deposit.
102. Herbert Case Hoagland, *How to Write a Photoplay* (New York: Magazine Maker Publishing Company, 1912), 11–12.
103. Louis Reeves Harrison, "Melodrama," *Moving Picture World*, May 13, 1911, 1058–9; "What Movies Are the Most Popular?," *Reel Life*, September 13, 1913, 11.
104. "Mystery Stories," *Moving Picture World*, October 17, 1914, 328.
105. "*An Hour of Terror,*" *Moving Picture World*, July 13, 1912, 158.
106. Advertisement, *Moving Picture World*, June 15, 1912, 999.
107. "*A Night of Terror,*" *Biograph Bulletin*, No. 138, May 26, 1908, available in *Biograph Bulletins, 1896–1908*, edited by Kemp R. Niver (Los Angeles: Locare Research Group, 1971), 352–3; "*A Night of Terror,*" *The Kinetogram*, April 15, 1911, 7. A copy of *A Night of Terror* is available in the Paper Print Collection at the Library of Congress.
108. Advertisement, *Idaho Statesman* (Boise, Idaho), February 4, 1912, 8.
109. Advertisement, *Lexington Leader* (Lexington, Kentucky), November 29, 1912, unpaginated; Advertisement, *Xenia Daily Gazette* (Xenia, Ohio), February 21, 1913, 8.

110. Advertisement, *Cleburne Morning Review* (Cleburne, Texas), December 9, 1913, 1. *A Bargain with Satan/Der Student von Prag* is available on the DVD *Der Student von Prag* (Munich: Edition Filmmuseum, 2016).
111. Advertisement, *Adrian Daily Telegram* (Adrian, Michigan), February 6, 1914, 2.
112. Advertisement, *Rockford Republic* (Rockford, Illinois), January 4, 1913, 4.
113. See, for example, Advertisement, *The Evening Tribune* (Albert Lea, Minnesota), February 13, 1913, 3; Advertisement, *Jacksonville Daily Journal* (Jacksonville, Illinois), March 11, 1913, 2.
114. Advertisement, *Elkhart Truth* (Elkhart, Indiana), January 30, 1913, 2.
115. Advertisement, *The Evening Independent* (Massillon, Ohio), March 11, 1913, 7.
116. Advertisement, *The Oil City Derrick* (Oil City, Pennsylvania), February 13, 1913, 3.
117. Advertisement, *Austin Daily Herald* (Austin, Minnesota), June 2, 1910, 3.
118. Advertisement, *Galveston Tribune* (Galveston, Texas), November 20, 1911, 9.
119. Advertisement, *Bonham Daily Favorite* (Bonham, Texas), November 18, 1913, 1.
120. Richard Abel, *The Red Rooster Scare: Making Cinema American, 1900–1910* (Berkeley: University of California Press, 1999), 20.
121. Richard Abel, *Americanizing the Movies and "Movie-Mad" Audiences, 1910–1914* (Berkeley: University of California Press, 2006), 187.
122. Quoted in Abel, *The Red Rooster Scare*, xii; Abel, 48–9.
123. Abel, *The Red Rooster Scare*, xiii.
124. Ron Mottram, "The Great Northern Film Company: Nordisk Film in the American Motion Picture Market," *Film History*, Vol. 2, No. 1 (Winter 1988), 71–86.
125. "An American School of Moving Picture Drama," *Moving Picture World*, November 20, 1909, 712.
126. Richard Abel, *Americanizing the Movies and "Movie-Mad" Audiences, 1910–1914*, 187.
127. "Facts and Comments," *Moving Picture World*, August 30, 1913, 935.
128. Abel, *The Red Rooster Scare*, xv.
129. "Is the 'Nickel Show' on the Wane?", *Moving Picture World*, February 27, 1914, 1065.
130. Bowser, 121–36.
131. James F. Hodges, *Opening and Operating a Motion Picture Theatre* (New York: Scenario Publishing Company, 1912), 16.
132. Michael Quinn, "Distribution, the Transient Audience, and the Transition to the Feature Film," *Cinema Journal*, Vol. 40, No. 2 (Winter 2001), 35–56.
133. Carl Laemmle, "Doom of Long Features Predicted," *Moving Picture World*, July 11, 1914, 185; William N. Selig, "Present Day Trend in Film Lengths," *Moving Picture World*, July 11, 1914, 181.
134. Hugh Hoffman, "The Father of the Feature," *Moving Picture World*, July 11, 1914, 272; Alexander Lichtman, "The Past, Present and Future of the Feature Film," in *The Theatre of Science: A Volume of Progress and Achievement in the Motion Picture Industry* (New York: Broadway Publishing Company, 1914), xxxiii.
135. W. Stephen Bush, "Gauging the Public Taste," *Moving Picture World*, May 11, 1912, 505.
136. "Facts and Comments," *Moving Picture World*, March 27, 1915, 1901.
137. "Feature Production," *Moving Picture World*, May 17, 1913, 711.
138. Louella O. Parsons, *How to Write for the "Movies"* (Chicago: A. C. McLurg, & Co., 1916), 105.
139. Peter Milne, "*The Mystery of the Tapestry Room*," *Motion Picture News*, August 28, 1915, 79.
140. Advertisement, *Universal Weekly*, May 2, 1914, back cover.
141. Ernest A. Dench, *Making the Movies* (New York: The Macmillan Company, 1915), 100–5.
142. "Double Exposures and Ghost Pictures," *Motography*, February 13, 1915, 239. See also "A Double Exposure Camera," *Moving Picture World*, January 23, 1915, 493.
143. "*The Unknown Monster*," *Moving Picture World*, February 27, 1914, 1070.
144. "Amusements," *Greenville Morning Herald* (Greenville, Texas), June 10, 1913.

145. "Tricks in Motion-Pictures," *Literary Digest*, March 21, 1914, 615.
146. Ibid., 616.
147. "*Unfaithful to His Trust*," *Moving Picture World*, April 3, 1915, 64.
148. W. Stephen Bush, "Happy Ending," *Moving Picture World*, November 6, 1915, 1107.
149. "Happy Endings," *Motography*, November 7, 1914, 630.
150. Louis Reeves Harrison, "Backgrounds," *Moving Picture World*, September 11, 1915, 1805.
151. Neil G. Caward, "Zudora's Second Adventure Screened," *Motography*, November 28, 1914, 727. A copy of *The Mystery of the Sleeping House*, Episode 2 of the serial *Zudora*, is archived at the Library of Congress.
152. Neil G. Caward, "*The Twenty Million Dollar Mystery*," *Motography*, January 30, 1915, 155.
153. "Let's Have Some 'Homey' Shadows," *Wid's Film and Film Folk*, December 4, 1915.
154. "*Haunting Winds*," *Motion Picture News*, August 14, 1915, 91; "Latest Purchases," *The Kinetradogram*, April 16, 1913; "*The Ghost of Seaview Manor*," *Moving Picture World*, June 14, 1913, 1137. A copy of *Zuma, the Gypsy* is archived at the Cineteca Nazionale.
155. "*The Missing Woman*," *Moving Picture World*, November 15, 1913, 784; "*Fate's Midnight Hour*," *Moving Picture World*, October 24, 1914, 492; "*The Death Mask*," *Moving Picture World*, September 26, 1914, 1778.
156. "*My Boy; or The Mystery of the Roadhouse Murder*," *Moving Picture World*, November 15, 1913, 790.
157. "*A Voice in the Night*," *Moving Picture World*, February 13, 1915, 1005.
158. *Panorama of Esplanade by Night* is available on the DVD entitled *Films of Edwin S. Porter* (Phoenix, Arizona: Grapevine Video, undated). *Coney Island at Night* is available in the DVD boxed set *Unseen Cinema: Early American Avant-Garde Film, 1894–1941* (Chatsworth: Image Entertainment, 2005).
159. "The Pictures from the Public View," *Moving Picture World*, March 23, 1912, 1051.
160. "Night Photography," *Moving Picture World*, September 6, 1913, 1070; "Night Photography," *Motography*, September 6, 1913, 158.
161. "Some Wonderful Night Photography," *Motography*, September 20, 1913, 197.
162. "Night Photography in 'Bison' Drama," *Universal Weekly*, November 21, 1914, 31; "Night Photography a Great Success," *Universal Weekly*, November 28, 1914, 9.
163. Hanford C. Judson, "In Search of the House of Fear," *Moving Picture World*, December 5, 1914, 1388.
164. "Universal's New Lighting Effect," *Motography*, December 5, 1914, 771.
165. Margaret I. MacDonald, "*The House of Fear*," *Moving Picture World*, January 9, 1915, 200.
166. "Hades," *The Kinetogram*, April 1, 1913, 10.
167. James B. Crippen, "Realism and the Photoplay," *Motography*, April 1911, 15.
168. "*The Master Mind*," *New York Dramatic Mirror*, May 13, 1914. In this instance, the "director" was actually two persons, Cecil B. DeMille and Oscar C. Apfel.
169. Bowser, 255–72.
170. Vachel Lindsay, *The Art of the Moving Picture* (New York: Macmillan, 1915).
171. Louis Reeves Harrison, "Directors as Artists," *Moving Picture World*, December 25, 1915, 2330.
172. Madame Alice Blaché, "The Director—The Present and Future," *Moving Picture World*, April 4, 1914, 49.
173. Alison McMahan, *Alice Guy Blaché, Lost Visionary* (New York: Bloomsbury, 2002), 4.
174. "Films and Realism," *The Film Index*, October 24, 1908, 11.
175. "Genre Pictures and an Example," *Moving Picture World*, May 7, 1910, 725.
176. Bowser, 167, 185.
177. "*The Solution of the Mystery*," *Moving Picture World*, December 11, 1915, 2035.
178. Solomon, *Disappearing Tricks*, 77.

SECTION II

Film Genres

CHAPTER 5

Devils

"A strangely gruesome flight of the imagination." That was how *Moving Picture World* described a three-reel film entitled *The Devil's Darling* (Gaumont-Rialto Star, 1915). The trade publication continued:

> Francine Larrimore as Alice Lane, a girl behind the counter of a department store, who is lured by the older woman as a sacrifice to her devil, plays with ease and grace and lends charm to the atmosphere of darkness that pervades the picture. . . . The closed room whose door opens by means of a hidden spring in which reside the darling's devil and numerous skeletons and skulls, presumably of victims brought into his majesty's clutches through the dark-stained incidents which mark the woman's past, can be enjoyed only when considered as an allegorical representation.[1]

The older woman had sold her soul as part of a Faustian bargain to "retain her beauty." For his part, the devil demanded a virginal woman, as he had so often over the centuries.[2]

In colonial America, Satan stalked his prey, whether on his cloven hooves as he tempted men or on his slithering belly as he incubized women. Evil incarnate was very real to most Americans, including to so many who lived in Salem, Massachusetts or heard about those who pledged allegiance to "His Satanic Majesty." As 1 Peter 5:8 warns in the Holy Bible, "Your adversary the Devil prowls around like a roaring lion, seeking someone to devour."

Medieval literature usually depicted Satan as a trickster, sometimes making him seem almost comical.[3] But the image of the devil transformed during the fourteenth century and in particular during the Reformation. Jeffrey Burton Russell writes that the theology of Luther "encouraged belief in Satan," including in his role as a horrifying interloper in human affairs.[4] Consider the mosaic of Satan on the ceiling of the baptistery of St. John in Florence. Serpents extend from the demon's ears while he literally consumes the flesh of Judas Iscariot. Subsequent artwork commonly gave Satan wings and talons.[5]

Satan's ability to tempt weak men was famously explored in Christopher Marlowe's play *The Tragicall* [sic] *History of the Life and Death of Doctor Faustus* (c. 1592), in which the title character is consigned to Hell after having made a pact with the devil. Here was not comedy, but instead the fear of damnation for evermore. If Dante's *Inferno*, written in the fourteenth century, had become the classic Catholic mythos of Hell, then the Faust legend emerged to perform a similar role for many Protestants, including those who settled in the New World.

Demonic horror was indeed very real in colonial America, manifesting in three key forms, the first two being the belief in satanic worship and the possibility of demonic possession. The third form of demonic horror resulted from the torture of accused witches and demoniacs.[6] While the tragedy of Salem stands as the foremost example of such torture, it represents only one of many that could be cited, as witch-hunts also took place in seventeenth-century Connecticut.

As Brian P. Levack has noted, "In the eighteenth and nineteenth centuries, witchcraft and possession lost much of their capacity to horrify."[7] In terms of literature and theatre, the pendulum swung with regard to the legend of Faust, moving from Marlowe's use of dramatic horror to Goethe's romantic and political two-part retelling of *Faust* (1808/1832), one arguably more suited to the Age of Enlightenment. These evolutions were very much felt in nineteenth-century America, where distinctions between the Old World and New were pronounced.

In the United States, Goethe's *Faust* assumed more than one form. Charles Gounod's operatic adaptation *Faust* (1859) was the first production of the Metropolitan Opera House in New York City when it opened in 1883.[8] And British actor Henry Irving famously appeared onstage in the drama *Faust* in America in 1887.[9] In both texts, elements of subtle comedy emerge and divine intercession saves the title character's soul, a major departure from the Marlovian tradition and one with lasting impact. As the *New York Times* wrote in 1896, "The frequency with which Gounod's *Faust* is repeated at the Metropolitan Opera House suggests the question whether it is destined to immortality."[10]

When it came to the devil, nineteenth-century American literature also employed a degree of humor, most notably in Washington Irving's *The Devil and Tom Walker* (1824), with the miserly Walker striking a deal with "Old Scratch." Poe tackled the subject twice, first in *The Bargain Lost* (1832), revised and retitled *Bon-Bon* in 1835. Then, in *Never Bet the Devil Your Head* (1841), Toby Dammit is decapitated after making a bet with a mysterious old man. While Walker disappears with Old Scratch in a blaze of lightning, Dammit's remains are left on earth and sold for dog meat. Decades later, S. B. Alexander's tale *The Modern Mephistopheles* (1887) featured an American who purchases Faust's castle and calls forth the devil, only to find that he has become old and weak after years of neglect by disbelieving humans.

American readers of the nineteenth century also learned about devilish imps, both metaphorical (as in Poe's 1845 short story *The Imp of the Perverse*) or "real," as in Robert Louis Stevenson's *The Bottle Imp*, which was first published in the *New York Herald* in 1891. Stevenson's imp grants wishes, but lives inside a cursed bottle that condemns the soul of anyone who dies in possession of it.[11] Here was a serious approach to the forfeiture of souls to the inferno, probably the most important since Goethe's *Faust* and, before that, Charles Maturin's *Melmoth the Wanderer* (1820).

Many Americans also read the novels of British author Marie Corelli, whose fiction attempted to reconcile Theosophy and mysticism with Christianity, an effort that would have been unthinkable a century earlier.[12] Among her works was the Faustian novel *The Sorrows of Satan* (1895), in which the devil appears amid the moral decay of a godless England. A stage version appeared on Broadway in 1898. Though it featured "weird" and "blood-curdling effects" to herald the "apotheosis of the release of Lucifer," the play was doomed to box-office failure.[13]

However, theatregoers in the United States had no shortage of opportunities to see Satan onstage, thus making moral condemnations of the theatre as the "workshops of Satan" not entirely incorrect.[14] Of all of these productions, *Faust* remained the most famous in America. In 1910, *Moving Picture World* wrote that "few old theatregoers can see the name [*Faust*] printed without having agreeable recollections both of the play and the opera."[15] Reviewing the 1870 ballet *Uriella, the Demon of the Night*, which featured a tableau of "Beelzebub enthroned on a fiery globe," the *New York Times* wrote:

> The drama of demonology has had what in the slang of the period might be termed a 'good show' among us. Satan and Thespis have been so persistently associated on the metropolitan stage as almost to justify the prejudices of old-fashioned theologians, and to warrant their reiterated assertion that the road to the play-house is the way to the pit indeed. What with [Charles Selby's play *Satan, ou Le diable à Paris/Satan in Paris, or The Mysterious Stranger*; aka *The Mysterious Stranger*] introduced to us by poor Celeste, the unhappy Bertram of Meyerbeer's [1831 opera *Robert le diable/Robert the Devil*], the Mephistopheles of [Gounod's] *Faust*, and the less individualized but equally unequivocal devils of the [1866 musical *The*] *Black Crook*, the [1868 musical *The*] *White Fawn*, and the [1870 musical *The*] *Twelve Temptations*, we have supped so full of demoniacal horrors that even the most sulphurous of fiends fright us no more, and we can gaze unmoved upon all the lurid terrors of the deepest histrionic Tartarus.[16]

For this critic, Satan's ability to frighten had become greatly diminished, even in those stage productions that portrayed him as horrifying rather than comical. As *Scribner's Monthly* remarked in 1872, the "stage-devil" was a "wretched buffoon."[17]

In 1864, Baudelaire famously declared that the devil's "greatest trick is to persuade you that he doesn't exist." But many if not most Christians in America continued to believe in Satan's power on earth, despite the literary and theatrical evolutions of the nineteenth century. At times discussion of the devil was metaphorical, as in 1897, when Jacob A. Riis denounced tenements as the "invention of Satan."[18] In other cases, descriptions of "His Satanic Majesty" were quite sincere, whether in the pulpit or the press. For example, in 1894, the *Chicago Tribune* reported on the "Luciferians," a sect that stole objects from Christian churches to profane in their black masses.[19] Then, in 1897, a woman accused of theft in Washington, D.C. pleaded guilty to the charge, but argued that she committed the crime while possessed by the devil.[20] All the while, many Americans continued to read the Holy Bible, and at least some studied the serious depictions of Satan in Milton's *Paradise Lost* and Dante's *Inferno*.[21]

As a result, it is not at all surprising that Satan and his minions became a major presence in early cinema in America, whether in the form of imported films (particularly from France and, later, from Italy) or in the form of indigenous productions, some quite imitative of their European predecessors. Collectively, these moving pictures paint a complicated portrait of the devil, spanning the comedic to the dramatic, a result that is hardly surprising given the range of adapted source material. And yet, in other respects they show a remarkable consistency, not only in the costumes and make-up design, but also in an emphasis on Faustian bargains, pact rituals, and necromantic magic.

Trick Pictures

Many of the devils and demons that appeared onscreen in the pre-nickelodeon era drew upon the comic traditions of the nineteenth-century literature and stage. The films of Georges Méliès initiated these humorous films. Carl Laemmle, best known as one of the founders of Universal Pictures in 1912, formed his first production company, Independent Moving Pictures, in 1909: IMP, often rendered as "Imp," allowed Laemmle to adorn his ads with Méliès-like devilish imps, an ongoing reminder of their importance to early cinema.[22]

It is difficult to underestimate the importance of Méliès when discussing Satan in early cinema, though it is worth noting that his depiction of the devil and his minions developed in part out of various traditions, including the "diableries" present in French stereo views (aka "stereoviews" and "stereographs") produced from the 1860s to the end of the nineteenth century. These stereo views offered the illusion of three-dimensional artwork of comical devils, sometimes in narrative situations similar to those later seen in Méliès's films. Later "diableries" featured costumed actors on sets that also seem to anticipate Méliès.[23]

On occasion, Méliès represented Satan without the use of overt comedy, as in his groundbreaking moving picture *The Devil's Castle/Le manoir du diable* (1896, which Edison released as *The Infernal Palace*); as Chapter 4 suggested, the film appeared in America as early as 1899.[24] Subsequent Méliès films distributed in America also featured relatively serious devils. For example, in *The Devil and the Statue/Le diable géant ou le miracle de la madonne* (1903, aka *Gigantic Devil*), the title villain appears in a castle and imprisons a maiden. He grows larger and larger until an angel dispels him. Likewise, in *The Infernal Cauldron/Le chaudron infernal* (1903, aka *The Infernal Caldron* [sic] *and the Phantasmal Vapors*), Mephisto dumps three women into a large pot, with flames engulfing their bodies.[25] Their superimposed spirits hover eerily in the air.[26]

The Devil in a Convent/Le diable au couvent (Méliès, 1900), which Selig Polyscope released as *The Sign of the Cross; or the Devil in a Convent*, also features a serious devil, though one can sense an impulse toward a style of humor present in Goethe. In the film, Satan emerges from a fountain and flies in the air before disguising himself as a priest in order to fool a group of nuns. Using his magic, he profanes the convent further by redecorating it with various devilish statues. Then Satan calls forth imps with pitchforks and some lusty female devils. Holy spirits bearing crucifixes dispel all of these evil forces except for Satan. It takes the archangel St. Michael to defeat him, wielding a triumphal spear just as he does in medieval Christian iconography, and in such paintings as Raphael's *St. Michael Vanquishing Satan* (1518).[27]

As with Méliès's other output, his devil films—whether serious or comedic or both—were in some measure created to display his mastery of cinematic tricks. Consider *Le cabinet de Méphistophélès* (1899, which Edison released as *The Devil's Laboratory* and which Lubin released as *Mephisto in His Laboratory*).[28] The Edison catalog promised exhibitors, "Everything is so wierd [sic] and fantastic."[29] And *Beelzebub's Daughter/Les filles du diable* (1903, aka *Belzebub's Daughter*), in which the devil uses his "blazing fingers" to create a fire, represented a "new and novel effect."[30]

The predominant number of Méliès's devil films were intended to be humorous, a point not lost on American distributors. In *The Devil in the School House/L'école infernale* (1902, aka *The Trials of a Schoolmaster*), Satan wreaks havoc on a schoolteacher; a Lubin catalog entry assured exhibitors that it was "very funny."[31] Other examples include *The Treasures of Satan/Les trésors de Satan* (1903), which Edison released under the title *Mephistopheles' School of Magic*.[32] In it, Satan and his female demons capture and then burn a thief, all in a humorous manner. That same year, in *The Cake Walk Infernal/Le cake-walk infernal* (1903, aka *The Infernal Cake Walk*), Méliès had Satan and acrobatic demons dancing in Hell.[33] Then, in 1904, Méliès comically transformed into various personas, Mephistopheles among them, in *The Untamable Whiskers/Le roi du maquillage*.[34]

Méliès's popularity caused other film manufacturing companies to emulate his style, including the French company Pathé Frères. Edison and Lubin released two Pathé comedies featuring Satan, one of them being *Devil's Pot/La marmite diabolique* (1904, aka *Devil's Kettle*). In it, Satan dumps a cook's assistant into a boiling pot. Returning later, the cook dips a ladle into the pot and discovers pieces of his assistant's body, which—except for his head—reassembles on the floor.[35] The two companies also released *Pierrot's Mystification/Pierrot mystifié* (Pathé Frères, 1904), in which a beautiful girl and clown appear in a room, followed by Satan, who proceeds to "bewitch" the place.[36]

Pathé itself distributed *Cave of the Spooks/La grotte des esprits* (aka *Cave of Spooks* and *Wave of Spooks*) in America in 1908; it featured a "bevy of spooks" dancing for "His Satanic Majesty" down in the infernal regions.[37] American companies also distributed other (apparently) foreign-made devil films, though in some cases their origins are difficult to determine.[38] In 1902, for example, Edison released *The Devil's Kitchen*, which later appeared in a 1908 Lubin catalog.[39] An Edison catalog indicated that "pandemonium reigns" once Mephistopheles and some hobgoblins materialize.[40] Also in 1902, Edison released *The Mysterious Urn*, in which Mephistopheles enacts tricks with "several young ladies," and *The Devil's Theatre*, in which hobgoblins perform for Satan's pleasure.[41] (A surviving copy at the Library of Congress does not show Satan, but the print ends abruptly and is likely incomplete.)[42] Then, in 1903, Lubin advertised *The Devil's Amusement*, in which Satan creates magical "antics" with an obese woman.[43]

The first American-made film featuring the devil was apparently *The Cavalier's Dream*, produced by Vitagraph and copyrighted by Edison in December 1898. An Edison synopsis detailed the title character sitting at a "bare" table when a witch enters. She "raps three times," and then the cavalier sees the "table spread for a sumptuous repast." Mephistopheles appears, and the witch transforms into a young girl. The synopsis promised, "The changes and magical appearances are startling and instantaneous."[44] This film predates the earliest known American screenings of Méliès's *The Devil's Castle*.

Particularly important in this cycle of films were American Mutoscope & Biograph's *"The Prince of Darkness"* and *A Terrible Night*, both filmed in America by Frederick S. Armitage c. April 1900.[45] In the first, "His Satanic Majesty" (as a catalog description calls him) frightens a drunken man in his home, resulting in a "weird proceeding."[46] In the second film, Satan disturbs a man sleeping in his bed.[47] Narratively, these two comedies are little different to Méliès's films, though their plotlines are imitative and their special effects arguably more limited. That said, in both moving pictures Satan wears the identical make-up and costume, which features horns, a goatee, and black attire with a black cape.[48] As a result, this particular devil seems to be the first horror-themed character to appear in more than one American film, a type of repetition on which the later horror movie genre would depend.

Whether produced in Europe or America, moving pictures sometimes presented imps even without Satan's presence, ranging from Méliès's *La clownesse fantôme* (1903), which Edison released as *The Magician and the Imp*, to Edison's own *The Imp of the Bottle* (1909), an adaptation of Stevenson's short story.[49] Perhaps the key example of these imp characters appears in Méliès's hilarious film *The Black Imp/Le diable noir*

Figure 5.1 A frame from *"The Prince of Darkness"* (American Mutoscope & Biograph, 1900). (*Courtesy of the Library of Congress, Motion Picture, Broadcasting and Recorded Sound Division/Moving Image Section*)

Figure 5.2 A frame from *A Terrible Night* (American Mutoscope & Biograph, 1900). (*Courtesy of the Library of Congress, Motion Picture, Broadcasting and Recorded Sound Division/Moving Image Section*)

(1905, released in America by Star Films).⁵⁰ A hotel guest makes so much noise trying to stop the mischievous little imp that he is thrown out, thus allowing the imp to sleep soundly in his bed.⁵¹

During the nickelodeon era, comedies about devils varied in plotlines, but some were little more than the aforementioned trick films of the pre-nickelodeon period.⁵² These include *Satan in Prison/Satan en prison* (Méliès, 1907), in which Mephisto makes various objects appear and disappear in his cell before he escapes, and *"Presto" Willie—Magician* (Essanay, 1914), in which Mephisto gives a boy a magic wand.⁵³ *The Flower of Youth/Fleur de jeunesse* (Pathé Frères, 1908) depicts Hell as having "cloaked and veiled figures wandering aimlessly about in a forest of election night red fire and sulphur geysers." Later, when an evil spirit, presumably Satan, visits earth, a fairy routs him back to the inferno.⁵⁴

A number of other comedies focused on Satan leaving the confines of Hell for earth, usually to get away from his wife, to find a new love, or both. Such films include *Satan at Play/Satan s'amuse* (Pathé Frères, 1907), *Mephisto's Affinity* (Lubin, 1908), *Satan on a Rampage/Satan s'ennuie* (Eclipse, 1911), *Satan's Rival/Rival de Satan* (Pathé Frères, 1911), and *The Imp Abroad* (Victor, 1914).⁵⁵ Like *The Flower of Youth*, some of these comedies featured eerie sets. Of *Satan on a Rampage*, for example, *Moving Picture World* praised its "very realistic Hell," adding, "some of the [images] are even startling, of red fire, and in particular, one red scene where smoky but hot-looking torches give just light enough to show the heads and shoulders of the demons who bear them."⁵⁶

Narrative framing devices also provided an excuse for humor. Adapting a comic strip begun in 1904 by Winsor McCay, Edwin S. Porter's *Dream of a Rarebit Fiend* (Edison, 1906) depicts a man who eats and drinks so much he has a hallucinatory nightmare in which a trio of imps disturb his sleep. *After the Welsh Rarebit* (Edison, 1913) also offered a nightmare plotline, with a midnight snack causing its character to dream that he dies and goes to Hell.⁵⁷ In *The Devil's Three Sins/Les trois péchés du diable* (Pathé Frères, 1908), a knight dreams he reneges on his vow not to drink and is menaced by the devil as punishment.⁵⁸ Vitagraph's *Too Much Champagne* (1908) features a drunk who dreams he walks through Hell and sees "devils" and "red fire."⁵⁹ Here such films echo pro-temperance visual culture in which, as Chapter 3 noted, alcohol was often likened to the devil.

The most common comical plotline during the nickelodeon era found human characters costumed as the devil and unintentionally causing mayhem at masquerade balls or on the way to the same. These films include *After the Fancy Dress Ball* (Gaumont, 1907), *The Masqueraders* (Lubin, 1908), *The Doll Maker's Daughter* (Centaur, 1908), *Mephisto at a Masquerade* (Gaumont, 1910), *The Devil* (Powers, 1910), *The Toymaker, the Doll and the Devil* (Edison, 1910), *Alkali Ike Plays the Devil* (Essanay, 1912), *The Devil of a Time* (Punch, 1912, aka *A Devil of a Time*), *The Doll and the Devil* (Pilot, 1913), *The Cabby and the Demon* (Majestic, 1913), *The Devilish Doctor* (Majestic, 1913), and *The Devil and Mrs. Walker* (Kalem, 1914).⁶⁰

Another repeated plot device involved humorous bargains with Satan, which to a greater or lesser degree were parodies of *Faust*. In *Pluto and the Imp* (Edison, 1900), a mortal signs the "Book of Fates" at the "Infernal Palace," but refuses to enter, so an imp tears his body apart, "creating much amusement to an audience."⁶¹ Subsequent examples include *The Devil and the Painter/Il pittore e il diavolo* (Pineschi, 1909) and *Miss*

Figure 5.3 Augustus Carney in *Alkali Ike Plays the Devil* (Essanay, 1912).

Faust/Mademoiselle Faust (Pathé Frères, 1909), which *Moving Picture World* believed would "shock" some viewers because it depicted ballet dancing in Heaven.[62] The following year, George Kleine released Gaumont's *The Beautiful Margaret/Le tout petit Faust*, a "burlesque" on *Faust* that featured stop-motion puppets instead of actors.[63] Then, in 1913, Biograph released *Faust and the Lily*.[64] "This does succeed in making us gasp once or twice and a good laugh follows," *Moving Picture World* wrote.[65]

The most ambitious of these *Faust* parodies was likely Méliès's *The Merry Frolics of Satan/Les 400 farces du diable* (1906, released in America by Star Films).[66] Disguised as an alchemist in a laboratory, Mephistopheles shows an inventor a magic pill. The inventor offers to purchase it, but Mephistopheles instead has him sign a piece of paper without letting him read it. Unwittingly, the inventor has given his soul to Satan. From there, the inventor experiences a wild night. A group of steamer trunks in his home transforms into a train that transports him to an inn. While he's there, Satan, two demons, and two apes prevent him from eating dinner.

Then the inventor gets inside a stagecoach that morphs into a fantastical carriage driven by a skeletal horse. The carriage journeys up the side of Mount Vesuvius until a volcanic explosion gives it the power of flight. A turbulent storm finally causes the carriage's journey through the stars to end. The inventor falls back to earth, whereupon Satan grabs him and drags him to Hell. Various demons spring forth to greet him before roasting him on a spit over a real fire.[67] The culmination of Méliès's screen devils revisited Faust, creating laughs even while returning to the Marlovian tragedy of eternal damnation.

Faust

As Cynthia G. Tucker explains, "The story of the man who sells his soul to the devil in exchange for greater power or possessions is probably as old as humanity itself, and it has certainly been as durable."[68] Tucker's commentary is important, including if applied to America in the nineteenth century, whether in consideration of *The Devil and Tom Walker* or the success of Gounod's opera. However, it is still crucial to question why the story became the most repeated representation of Satan onscreen during the early cinema period in America, a result stemming not only from importation of European films, but also from indigenous productions.

Robert Singer provides the key answer in his essay on silent Faust film productions:

> Magic, for all of Faust's *streben*, is the illusion that sustains the Faustian narrative. Most importantly, magic supplants language; in the silent Faust film, the illusion and intrigue created by the spectacle of magic, like a pre-verbal form of communication, links the audience to the film text.[69]

For Singer, "magic remains at the core of the Faust film text," with these early films providing a recognizable narrative that could be explored and conveyed with the trickery—the "magic"—of cinema.[70] However inadvertently, a 1903 Lubin catalog description for *The Devil's Castle/Le manoir du diable* may well provide a contemporaneous example of this very point. It inaccurately claims the film was "made after the drama of *Faust and Marguerite*."[71] *The Devil's Castle* does not at all draw upon the Faust mythos. But it was a film involving the devil, with its resulting spectacle of tricks allowing Lubin to link the two texts.

By contrast, Méliès did produce a moving picture entitled *Faust and Marguerite/Faust et Marguerite* in 1897, one that appeared on at least some American screens. Over two years later, Edwin S. Porter directed a film with the very same title for the Edison Manufacturing Company. A 1900 catalog description for it claims:

> Marguerite is seated before the fireplace, Faust standing by her side. Mephistopheles enters and offers his sword to Faust, commanding him to behead the fair Marguerite. Faust refuses, whereupon Mephistopheles draws the sword across the throat of the lady, and she suddenly disappears and Faust is seated in her place.[72]

The film proceeds with Marguerite reappearing in the chair. Mephistopheles transforms Faust into a skeleton and makes Marguerite vanish. But the Prince of Darkness flees when a clergyman appears and marries Faust and Marguerite, the Goethe tradition being privileged in this case over the Marlovian.[73]

Méliès's *The Damnation of Faust/La Damnation de Faust* (Méliès, 1903, aka *The Condemnation of Faust*) adapted the 1846 Hector Berlioz song-poem of the same name, its own origins steeped in Goethe. A Star Films advertisement in the *New York Clipper* heralded *The Damnation of Faust* as a "Grand Fantastical Fantasy in 15 Motion Tableaux," one "inspired by Berlioz's Celebrated Song Poem" and "Replete with stupendous situations, bewildering mysteries, and marvelous effects."[74] A Lubin catalog summary promised the film relied on new tricks and effects in order to depict the "Route to the Depths of Perdition," "The Subterranean Cascade," and "The Descent to Satan's Domain."[75] Here again the emphasis was on the magic of the cinema, the descent into Hell created by dangling actors in front of a rolling background.[76]

The Damnation of Faust's plot begins *in media res*, after the death of Marguerite. Real smoke and moving set pieces depict Faust's long descent into the underworld. Out of real flames, dancers who dwell in Satan's inferno emerge and perform a ballet. They soon disappear, replaced by a cascade of water in which a seven-headed hydra and then several demons emerge, some of them wielding torches. Wrapping Faust in his cloak, Mephistopheles descends downward into the pit of Hell. He hurls Faust into a pit of fire, and then spreads his enormous bat wings, with his demons saluting his power.[77] As in the case of the inventor in *The Merry Frolics of Satan*, this particular Faust does not escape cinematic fire and brimstone.[78]

In 1904, Star Films distributed Méliès's new version of *Faust and Marguerite/Faust et Marguerite* in America. A trade advertisement heralded it as:

> A New and Magnificent CINEMATOGRAPHIC OPERA, in 20 Tableaux, inspired from GOETHE'S Masterpiece, with Music from CH. GOUNOD'S celebrated opera, FAUST. It is the first time that a Cinematographic Opera has been produced, and the result is beyond any description, the film being perfect.[79]

In twenty scenes lasting 850 feet, the sprawling narrative begins in "The Laboratory of Dr. Faust" and ends in "The Kingdom of the Elect, Grand Apotheosis."[80] A surviving fragment shows Mephistopheles restoring Faust's youth in exchange for his soul, Faust's burgeoning romance with Marguerite, as well as Faust's condemnation to Hell, and Marguerite's ascension to Heaven.[81]

Five years later, during the nickelodeon era, Faust repopulated the American screen. Between December 1909 and June 1911, four more Faust films were released, though one of them—the Paramount Film Company's *Faust and Marguerite*—may well have been nothing more than a reissue of an earlier film.[82] (These were all in addition to George R. Webb's 1910 "talking pictures" of a *Faust* opera, which were projected at the Fulton Theatre in New York with sound emanating from six phonograph horns.)[83]

Released in December 1909, Edison's *Faust* was the first of these new films.[84] Directed by J. Searle Dawley and shot by Frederick S. Armitage, it inaugurated Edison's prestigious series of "Grand Opera" adaptations.[85] *Moving Picture World* responded:

> When we saw the picture we had no difficulty in recognizing the principal characters of the story, its trend and its development. A sympathetic pianist played snatches of Gounod's music, which helped to place us in sympathy with the picture. . . . *Faust* must be accounted a great Edison success.[86]

The *New York Dramatic Mirror* offered similar praise, drawing attention to the film's "distinguished" acting.[87]

Then, during the summer of 1910, Eclair distributed a different version of *Faust*, one produced by the Società Italiana Cines and directed by Enrico Guazzoni.[88] Drawing directly upon Goethe, rather than as refracted through Gounod, the film received less publicity in America than the Edison version. Nevertheless, *Moving Picture World* enthused, "Rarely has there been a better representation of this wonderful drama," and subsequently praised its "admirable" acting.[89]

"I promise my soul to Satan," Faust declares in an onscreen title in a Pathé Frères version released in 1911. After obtaining his signature, Mephistopheles looks directly into the camera, thus acknowledging the audience as a witness to Faust's imminent doom. This version's portrayal of Hell is particularly dramatic: women writhe in misery on a rocky terrain, and an evil spirit dances around Faust.[90] Emphasizing once again the story's magical elements, *Moving Picture World* praised the special effects, particularly the transformation of Mephistopheles into a dog, a narrative device appropriated from Gounod.[91] On a separate occasion, the same trade wrote:

> A finely colored and beautifully acted art film. . . . The appearance and disappearance of this Demon, who comes and goes in a wink, always takes place in a flash of fiery smoke. It is cleverly accomplished and gives, as far as possible, an uncanny touch to his work.[92]

Writing about this version of *Faust* on a third occasion, *Moving Picture World* promised that its "educational value . . . is very high."[93]

The same may or may not have been true of a number of other dramatic films that were inspired in part or whole by Faust. *The Clockmaker's Secret/Le secret de l'horloger* (Pathé Frères, 1907) has its title character trade his soul in exchange for a clock.[94] In *The Gambler and the Devil* (Vitagraph, 1908), an Irishman signs away his soul for money; a similar story appears in *Satan's Castle/Il castello del diavolo* (Ambrosio, 1913).[95] A music teacher strikes a Faustian bargain in *The Evil Philter/Le philtre maudit* (Pathé Frères, 1909) to win the love of a woman.[96] The friar in *Mephisto and the Maiden* (Selig Polyscope, 1909) pledges his soul to Satan in order to regain lost youth.[97] In *The Devil's Billiard Table/Le billard du diable* (Eclair, 1910), Mephistopheles takes the souls of three men in exchange for challenging a champion pool player that they dislike.[98] (These films are all in addition to Selig Polyscope's 1913 adaptation of *The Devil and Tom Walker*, which will be discussed in Chapter 14).

Among these films, *The Tale of the Fiddle/La légende du premier violon* (Eclipse, 1909) was somewhat unique in that its lead character is a woman who sells her soul for use of a magic violin that will win the love of a young man, thus being a gender inversion of the Faust mythos, one that predates *The Devil's Darling* by more than five years.[99] *Moving Picture World* called *The Tale of the Fiddle* "gloomy."[100] That same description might not have been entirely appropriate for *The Clockmaker's Secret*, *The Gambler and the Devil*, or *Mephisto and the Maiden*, all of which appended happy endings to the story, thus following not only Goethe's romantic tradition, but also the overall trend toward happy endings in nickelodeon-era American melodramas.

Dante's *Inferno*

While the Faust story provided the narrative basis for many dramatic depictions of Satan in the early cinema period, it was not the only mythos adapted to the screen. For example, *Legend of Orpheus/La légende d'Orphée* (Pathé Frères, 1909, aka *A Legend of Orpheus* and *The Legend of Orpheus*) adapted the famous Greek myth, its title character venturing to the underworld to retrieve his lost love, Eurydice, from the "Master of Hades." The film inserted Cupid at the conclusion in order to create a happy ending.[101] Elements of the same story reappeared in *A Mother's Heart/Cuore di mamma* (Ambrosio, 1909), in which a young girl ventures to the

Figure 5.4 *Fantasma* (Edison, 1914).

devil's castle to retrieve her mother, and in *Fantasma* (Edison, 1914), in which Zamaliel, the "monarch of evil and darkness," kidnaps a princess who is later returned to her prince.[102]

Other films presented dramatic versions of plotlines already used in comedies. In *Mephisto's Son/Le fils du diable* (Pathé Frères, 1906), the son of Satan ventures to earth in search of a bride, but must shrink from a priest who carries a cross at the church. His would-be bride commits suicide. The two travel together to Hell, which one newspaper review described as "beautiful, weird, and picturesque in the extreme."[103] Much later, in *The Woman in Black* (Rex, 1914), actor Herbert Rawlinson played a detective who appears as Mephisto at a masquerade ball; the villain he seeks dons the same costume.[104]

More commonly, the devil appeared onscreen in morality tales that—while they did not feature bargains with Satan—warned of his powers. These films include *Satan Defeated/La défaite de Satan* (Pathé Frères, 1911), *The Temptation of Satan* (Warner's Features, 1914) and *The Professor's Nightmare* (Vitagraph, 1915).[105] A key example would be *The Devil, the Servant, and the Man*, which Selig Polyscope produced in 1910 and remade in 1912.[106] In it, a husband becomes jealous of his wife when he mistakenly believes she has not arrived home. Falling asleep, the man dreams that Satan visits him, and then shows him his wife kissing another man. The husband shoots his wife dead and attempts to shoot himself. But Jesus appears and stops him. The husband wakes up and discovers that his faithful wife has been at home asleep all the time.[107]

The Devil, the Servant, and the Man drew inspiration from Ferenc Molnár's play *The Devil/Az ördög* (1907), a tale of suspicioned marital infidelity in the twentieth century, featuring a suave and up-to-date version of Satan. A version of the play became a Broadway hit in 1908; the *New York Times* praised its "brilliant comedy," with George Arliss's performance as the devil being a "creation of exceptional subtlety with a powerfully conveyed impression of dominant intellectuality."[108] *The Devil* was parodied in the film *He Went to See The Devil Play* (Vitagraph, 1909), which introduced yet again the comparison of alcohol and the devil. It was then officially adapted into a five-reel feature in 1915.[109] The New York Motion Picture Company produced *The Devil*, starring not Arliss (who would appear in a subsequent adaptation in 1921), but instead Edward Connelly. *Moving Picture World* praised its acting, as well as its plot, "so constructed that an audience continually wonders what is going to happen next."[110]

Figure 5.5 Still photograph depicts *Dante's Inferno* (Milano, 1911). (*Courtesy of Robert J. Kiss*)

Not surprisingly, a few films adapted aspects of biblical accounts of Satan. *The Demon/Il demone* (Ambrosio, 1911) depicted the "Spirit of Evil" being cast out of heaven.[111] More elaborate was *Satan, or, The Drama of Humanity/Satana, ovvero il dramma dell'umanità* (Ambrosio, 1913, aka *Satan*), a "sumptuous" four-reeler that Ambrosio advertised as the "most expensive production" it had ever made.[112] Relying on a narrative structure not unlike what D. W. Griffith would use in *Intolerance* (1916), the film shows the "Tempter of Mankind" trying to injure humankind in four different time periods, ranging from the pre-Christian era and the life of Christ to the medieval period and the present day.[113]

But the most epic of all the films about Satan produced during the early cinema period was *Dante's Inferno/L'inferno* (Milano, 1911). Running to five reels, it was the first Italian feature film, with its production taking three years to complete. According to John P. Welle, it "set a new standard for production quality and signifies the first serious artistic encounter between the nascent film industry and the Italian literary tradition."[114] In

Figure 5.6 From left to right, Edward Connelly, Bessie Barriscale, and Arthur Maude in *The Devil* (New York Motion Picture Company, 1915). (*Courtesy of Robert J. Kiss*)

the United States, *Dante's Inferno* also became highly prestigious. *Moving Picture World* declared the film was "beyond a doubt . . . the *non plus ultra* of the moving picture art."[115] *Moving Picture News* echoed those sentiments, claiming *Dante's Inferno* "startled the world in its vividness of portrayal."[116] On its original American release, the film allegedly grossed approximately $2 million.[117] It also spawned parodies, among them the 1911 vaudeville sketch *Bud's Inferno*.[118]

But the Milano version of *Dante's Inferno* was not the first film version that Americans saw. *Satan's Smithy/La forge du diable* (Pathé Frères, 1909) was a very loose adaptation of the story, with Satan touring the title character through "all the inside secrets of the infernal regions."[119] Then, in the summer of 1911, *Moving Picture World* noted the availability of a two-reel version of *Dante's Inferno/L'inferno*.[120] Produced by the Italian company Helios, the film appeared on some American screens prior to Milano's feature. In early 1912, critic W. Stephen Bush condemned the Helios film as "base and clumsy" for many reasons, not least of which was the fact he noticed many actors who seemed to laugh while portraying "supposed sufferers."[121]

Even though it was not the first version, it is easy to see why the Milano film had such a profound impact on its original viewers. Restrained acting from a large cast combines with wisely chosen locations and realistic props to result in a powerful film.[122] Its mise-en-scène carefully adapts Gustave Doré's illustrations for *Dante's Inferno* (first published in 1861 and known to at least some Americans, including in the form of lantern slides).[123] The winged demons, the rain of fire, the rivers of filth, the sinners buried upside down, and Lucifer eating one of his victims achieve some of the most arresting and haunting images ever committed to the screen.[124]

The trade press not only commended *Dante's Inferno*, but also implored exhibitors to treat it with a special degree of respect, including in their use of appropriate live music, sound effects, and even live lectures on the subject.[125] W. Stephen Bush wrote such a lecture, which conformed to the film's running time and was delivered while it was screened, rather than as an introduction.[126] Some members of the industry perceived *Dante's Inferno* as a key indication of the "peculiar merits" of the feature film.[127] That said, it is also clear that at least a few viewers believed the film was too long, and that elements of it—particularly its use of nudity—were "vulgar and immoral."[128] Others found their opinion altered after watching it. "Instead of corrupting, I really believe it is uplifting and inspiring," a police captain in New Jersey admitted in 1912.[129]

Conclusion

In the summer of 1913, Monopol promoted its newest feature release, the three-reel Milano production *In the Toils of the Devil/Il patto di Don Giovanni*. One advertisement heralded it as a "Fitting Follower to the Great *Dante's Inferno*."[130] Another promised it was as "Great as Its Predecessor *Dante's Inferno*."[131] They touted the new film's plot as follows: "A pact with the evil one for the sale of a soul is the basis of this beautiful romance, which, under Satan's guidance, clothed in the garb of prosperity and superficial happiness, scatters ruin and misery."[132]

Figure 5.7 Trade advertisement for Milano's *In the Toils of the Devil* (1913), released in America by Monopol. Published in *Moving Picture World* on May 31, 1913.

In other words, the key successor to Dante was not more Dante, but rather another entry in what *Moving Picture World* referred to as the "Faust cycle" of films.[133] The same was true of Nino Oxilia's *Satan's Rhapsody/Rapsodia Satanica* (Cines), which in the summer of 1914 George Kleine announced would be released in the United States.[134] Featuring actress Lyda Borelli, the film's plot was about a "barter made with Satan to restore youth and beauty to an old woman."[135] At roughly the same time, Great Northern distributed the three-reel Danish film *Den mystiske Fremmede*, produced by Nordisk the year before.[136] Retitled *A Deal with the Devil*, the film featured a medical student who dreams that he makes a pact with the devil and receives the ability to look at a patient and know if they will live or die. Eventually he awakens from the nightmare, much relieved that he in not actually in league with Satan.[137]

The key Faust storyline to appear on American screens in the post-nickelodeon era was *The Student of Prague/Der Student von Prag* (Deutsche Bioscop, 1913), a five-reel German feature. Directed by Stellan Rye and written by Hanns Heinz Ewers, the film starred Paul Wegener as the title character, a student who gains all he desires by signing his name to a contract presented by the devilish Scapinelli (John Gottowt). The plot drew upon both Goethe's *Faust* and Edgar Allan Poe's 1839 short story *William Wilson*.

The Apex Film Company distributed *Der Student von Prag* in America from late 1913 under the title *A Bargain with Satan*. One advertisement promoted it as the "Greatest of any double identity feature ever produced—Better than *Faust* and *Dr. Jekyll and Mr. Hyde* put together, though based on neither."[138] As Robert Singer has noted, *Der Student von Prag* became an important link to later Faust films, as well as to the German Expressionist cinema of the 1920s.[139]

As for Satan and his minions, the American cinema would encounter them time and again, but no subsequent period would ever feature the sheer volume of devil films as the era of early cinema. Or the sheer variety, in which religious iconography could be venerated or desecrated, in which earlier beliefs in Satan could be confirmed or challenged, and in which viewers could laugh or shudder at his antics. In the end, the question is not so much what the title character of *The Devil's Darling* provided to His Satanic Majesty, but the many things he offered to us.

Notes

1. Margaret I. MacDonald, "*The Devil's Darling*," *Moving Picture World*, November 6, 1915, 1157.
2. "Mutual Film Corporation Specials," *Moving Picture World*, November 6, 1915, 1140. Similar plot elements appeared in *The Black Fear* (Metro, 1915). See John T. Soister and Henry Nicolella with Steve Joyce and Harry H. Long, *American Silent Horror, Science Fiction and Fantasy Feature Films, 1913–1929* (Jefferson: McFarland 2012), 42–3.
3. Brian P. Levack, "The Horrors of Witchcraft and Demonic Possession," *Social Research: An International Quarterly*, Vol. 81, No. 4 (Winter 2014), 922.
4. Jeffrey Burton Russell, *Mephistopheles: The Devil in the Modern World* (Ithaca: Cornell University Press, 1990), 28.
5. John Leyland, "The 'Evil One' In Art. II," *The Magazine of Art* (January 1896), 305, 306.
6. Levack, 937.
7. Ibid., 927.

8. "Ready to Produce *Faust*," *New York Times*, October 29, 1887, 8; "The Performance," *New York Times*, October 23, 1883, 1.
9. Ibid., 1.
10. "*Faust* at the Opera," *New York Times*, December 24, 1896, 5. Another example of the opera's enduring popularity would be the selections from it released on 78 rpm records. See "Record Bulletins for February, 1913," *Talking Machine World*, January 15, 1913, 52; "Special Window Display," *Talking Machine World*, March 15, 1913, 26; "Teachers Hear the Victor," *Talking Machine World*, November 15, 1913, 19.
11. Other examples include *The Bottle Imp*, an unsigned short story published in *The Knickerbocker; or New York Monthly Magazine* in September 1860, and Grace Duffield Goodwin's *Imp O' Satan*, published in *The Independent* on June 7, 1894.
12. For example, Corelli's work is described in "*The Sorrows of Satan* by Marie Corelli," *Chicago Tribune*, November 10, 1895, 29.
13. "*The Sorrows of Satan*," *New York Times*, December 25, 1898, 6.
14. "Corrupting Amusements," *The Friend: A Religious and Literary Journal*, January 17, 1852, 18.
15. "Faust," *Moving Picture World*, January 15, 1910, 58.
16. "Amusements: Theatrical," *New York Times*, August 30, 1870, 5.
17. "The Demons of the Shadow," *Scribner's Monthly*, December 1872, 233.
18. "Evils of the Tenements," *New York Times*, January 4, 1897, 2.
19. "Worshipers [sic] of Satan," *Chicago Tribune*, June 10, 1894, 30. An earlier account of "supposed worshippers of Satan" appears in "The Devil-Worshippers," *Chicago Tribune*, September 17, 1871, 6.
20. "Shoplifter Blames Satan," *Washington Post*, December 10, 1897, 10.
21. Christopher Kendrick, "Un-American Milton: Milton's Reputation and Reception in the Early United States," *University of Toronto Quarterly*, Vol. 77, No. 3 (Summer 2008), 903–22; "The Two Devils: Or the Satan of Milton and Lucifer of Byron Compared," *The Knickerbocker, or New York Monthly Magazine* (August 1947), 30; "Gustave Doré's Dante," *Saturday Evening Post*, January 17, 1865, 3.
22. Eileen Bowser, *The Transformation of Cinema: 1907–1915* (Berkeley: University of California Press, 1990), 76, 78, 223–4; Advertisement, *The Billboard*, December 11, 1909, 63.
23. Brian May, Denis Pellerin, and Paula Fleming, *Diableries: Stereoscopic Adventures in Hell* (London: London Stereoscopic Company, 2013).
24. With regard to Edison retitling the film as *The Infernal Palace*, see *Edison Films, No. 94* (Orange, NJ: Edison Manufacturing Company, March 1900), 39–40. Available in *A Guide to Motion Picture Catalogs by American Producers and Distributors, 1894–1908: A Microfilm Edition* (New Brunswick: Rutgers University Press, 1985), Reel 1.
25. In a Méliès catalog description, the lead character in *The Infernal Cauldron* is not named Satan, but rather "Belphegor, the executioner of Hell." See *Complete Catalogue of Genuine and Original "Star" Films* (New York: Star Films, June 1905), 32. The Pathé Frères film *Haunted Kitchen/Cuisine hantée* (1907) bears much similarity to *The Infernal Cauldron*, with two of the devil's "emissaries" materializing in a kitchen and dumping a chef in a cauldron. See "*Haunted Kitchen*," *Views and Film Index*, May 4, 1907, 4.
26. Copies of *The Devil and the Statue* and *The Infernal Cauldron* are available in the DVD boxed set *Georges Méliès: First Wizard of Cinema* (Los Angeles: Flicker Alley, 2008).
27. *The 1903 Complete Catalogue of Films and Moving Picture Machines* (Chicago: Selig Polyscope Company, 1903), 19. Available in *A Guide to Motion Picture Catalogs by American Producers and Distributors, 1894–1908: A Microfilm Edition*, Reel 2. A copy of *The Devil in a Convent* is available in the DVD boxed set *Georges Méliès: First Wizard of Cinema*.

28. *Complete Catalogue of Lubin's Films* (Philadelphia: Lubin, January 1903), 22; *Lubin's Films* (Philadelphia: Lubin, 1908), 57. Available in *A Guide to Motion Picture Catalogs by American Producers and Distributors, 1894–1908: A Microfilm Edition*, Reel 3.
29. *Edison Films, No. 94* (Orange, New Jersey: Edison Manufacturing Company, March 1900), 39. Available in *A Guide to Motion Picture Catalogs by American Producers and Distributors, 1894–1908: A Microfilm Edition*, Reel 1.
30. Advertisement, *New York Clipper*, June 13, 1903.
31. *Complete Catalogue of Lubin's Films* (Philadelphia: Lubin, January 1903), 29.
32. *Edison Films, No. 175* (Orange, New Jersey: Edison Manufacturing Company, May 1903), 30. Available in *A Guide to Motion Picture Catalogs by American Producers and Distributors, 1894–1908: A Microfilm Edition*, Reel 1.
33. Copies of *Treasures of Satan* and *The Infernal Cake-walk* are available in the DVD boxed set *Georges Méliès: First Wizard of Cinema* (Los Angeles: Flicker Alley, 2008).
34. A copy of *The Untamable Whiskers* is available in the DVD boxed set *Georges Méliès: First Wizard of Cinema*.
35. *Lubin's Films* (Philadelphia: Lubin, May 1905), 13. Available in *A Guide to Motion Picture Catalogs by American Producers and Distributors, 1894–1908: A Microfilm Edition*, Reel 3.
36. *Lubin's Films* (Philadelphia: Lubin, May 1905), 20.
37. "The Cave of the Spooks," *Moving Picture World*, November 21, 1908, 410; "Wave of Spooks," *Views and Film Index*, November 21, 1908, 10. A copy of this film is archived at the Cinemateca Portuguesa.
38. In addition to the moving pictures described in the main text, Edison released *The Devil's Prison* in 1902. In it, a devil and his imps torture a knight. It was also a foreign-made film with unclear origins. See *Edison Films, Supplement 168* (February 1903), 10, available in *A Guide to Motion Picture Catalogs by American Producers and Distributors, 1894–1908: A Microfilm Edition*, Reel 1.
39. *Lubin's Films* (Philadelphia: Lubin, 1908), 63.
40. Elias Savada, editor, *The American Film Institute Catalog of Motion Pictures Produced in the United States: Film Beginnings, 1893–1910* (Lanham: Scarecrow Press, 1995), 261.
41. Ibid., 711.
42. Ibid., 262.
43. *Complete Catalogue of Lubin's Films* (Philadelphia: Lubin, January 1903), 21; *Lubin's Films* (Philadelphia: Lubin, 1908), 57.
44. Savada, 163. A copy of *The Cavalier's Dream* is archived in the Paper Print Collection at the Library of Congress.
45. Ibid., 865, 1053.
46. *Picture Catalogue* (New York: American Mutoscope & Biograph, November 1902), 68. Available in *A Guide to Motion Picture Catalogs by American Producers and Distributors, 1894–1908: A Microfilm Edition*, Reel 2.
47. *Picture Catalogue*, 68.
48. Copies of *"The Prince of Darkness"* and *A Terrible Night* are available at the Library of Congress.
49. "The Imp of the Bottle," *Moving Picture World*, November 20, 1909, 729; "The Imp of the Bottle," *New York Dramatic Mirror*, November 27, 1909, 13. Another of Méliès's many "imp" films was *The Enchanted Basket/La corbeille enchantée* (1903). See Savada, 307. A copy of *The Magician and the Imp* is available in the DVD boxed set *Georges Méliès: First Wizard of Cinema*.
50. Advertisement, *New York Clipper*, April 22, 1905, 244. An imp also appears in Méliès's *The Mysterious Retort/L'alchimiste Parafaragamus ou la cornue infernale* (1906).
51. A copy of *The Black Imp* is available in the DVD boxed set *Georges Méliès: First Wizard of Cinema* (Los Angeles: Flicker Alley, 2008).

52. In *The Devil's Sale/La vente du diable* (Lux, 1909), the humor results from Satan having to liquidate his property to pay a debt. One plot summary claimed he then "vented his spleen" on the court and on those who purchase his belongings. Whether his rage was represented through cinematographic trickery is difficult to determine. See "The Devil's Sale," *Moving Picture World*, January 2, 1909, 17.
53. "Satan in Prison," *Views and Film Index*, November 23, 1907, 10; "'Presto' Willie," *Moving Picture World*, March 21, 1914, 1524. A copy of *Satan in Prison* is available on the DVD *Georges Méliès Encore* (Los Angeles: Flicker Alley, 2010).
54. "The Flower of Youth," *Variety*, February 15, 1908, 11. A copy of this film is archived at the Swedish Film Institute.
55. "Satan at Play," *Views and Film Index*, October 26, 1907, 9; "Mephisto's Affinity," *Moving Picture World*, June 27, 1908, 547; "Satan on a Rampage," *Moving Picture World*, July 22, 1911, 144; "Satan's Rival," *Moving Picture World*, August 21, 1911, 391; "The Imp Abroad," *Universal Weekly*, January 10, 1914, unpaginated. A copy of *Satan's Rival* is archived at the British Film Institute. Copies of *Satan at Play* are archived at the Deutsche Kinemathek and Filmoteca Española.
56. "Satan on a Rampage," *Moving Picture World*, August 5, 1911, 294.
57. "Hades," *Edison Kinetogram*, April 1, 1913, 10. A copy of *After the Welsh Rarebit* is archived at the Museum of Modern Art, New York City.
58. "The Devil's Three Sins," *Moving Picture World*, March 21, 1908, 243. A copy of *The Devil's Three Sins* is archived at Library and Archives Canada.
59. "Too Much Champagne," *Moving Picture World*, February 22, 1908, 147; "Too Much Champagne," *Variety*, March 14, 1908, 13. Some footage from *Too Much Champagne* is archived at the Library of Congress by way of a paper print deposit.
60. Advertisement, *Moving Picture World*, September 14, 1907, 444; "The Masqueraders," *The Billboard*, October 10, 1908, 8; "The Doll Maker's Daughter," *Moving Picture World*, November 7, 1908, 364; "Mephisto at a Masquerade," *Moving Picture World*, April 23, 1910, 655; "Mephisto at a Masquerade," *Variety*, April 23, 1910, 16; "The Devil," *Moving Picture World*, October 15, 1910, 892; "The Devil," *Moving Picture World*, October 29, 1910, 999; "The Toymaker, the Doll and the Devil," *Edison Kinetogram*, January 2, 1911, 4–5; "Alkali Ike Plays the Devil," *Moving Picture World*, August 24, 1912, 754, 788; "The Devil of a Time," *Moving Picture World*, December 21, 1912, 1230; "The Cabby and the Demon," *Moving Picture World*, January 25, 1913, 398; "The Doll and the Devil," *Moving Picture World*, March 1, 1913, 902; "The Devilish Doctor," *Moving Picture World*, August 23, 1913, 845; "The Devil and Mrs. Walker," *Motography*, December 5, 1914, 790. It is worth noting that Edison sold *The Toymaker, the Doll and the Devil* from November 1910, with an exhibitor reporting a screening of the same c. early December 1910 ("Blunders or Wonders of Cinematography," *Moving Picture World*, December 10, 1910, 1342). However, the *Edison Kinetogram* of January 2, 1911 lists the film's formal release date as January 21, 1911. A copy of *Mephisto at a Masquerade* is preserved at Filmarchiv Austria under the title *Der Teufel ist los*.
61. "Pluto and the Imp," *The Phonoscope*, January 1900, 10.
62. "Miss Faust," *Moving Picture World*, June 5, 1909, 754.
63. "The Beautiful Margaret," *The Billboard*, July 23, 1910, 26. A copy of *The Beautiful Margaret* is available on the DVD set *Gaumont, le cinéma premier (1907-1916) – Volume 2* (Paris: Gaumont, 2009).
64. A copy of *Faust and the Lily* is archived at the Museum of Modern Art in New York City.
65. "Faust and the Lily," *Moving Picture World*, July 19, 1913, 319.
66. "Méliès," *Views and Film Index*, February 9, 1907, 5; see *Complete Catalogue of Genuine and Original "Star" Films* (New York: Star Films, June 1905), 106–12. It is important to note that this Star Film catalog bears a June 1905 date, but pages from 81 to 148 detail films from the July 1905 to June 1908 period. Either these later pages were appended to the catalog, or the

catalog dates to June 1908, with the first eighty pages reprinted and the 1905 date not being revised.
67. A copy of *The Merry Frolics of Satan* is available in the DVD boxed set *Georges Méliès: First Wizard of Cinema* (Los Angeles: Flicker Alley, 2008).
68. Cynthia G. Tucker, "The Faustus Theme," *Interpretations*, Vol. 2, No. 1 (1969), 37.
69. Robert Singer, "Modern Magic: The Pre-War Silent Faust Film," *Harmonias*, edited by Kelly Basilio (Lisbon: Edições Colibri, 2001), 38.
70. Ibid., 60.
71. *Complete Catalogue of Lubin's Films* (Philadelphia: Lubin, January 1903).
72. Quoted in Savada, 340.
73. A copy of *Faust and Marguerite* (1900) is available at the Library of Congress.
74. Advertisement, *New York Clipper*, February 27, 1904, 3.
75. Savada, 243.
76. Elizabeth Ezra, *Georges Méliès: The Birth of the Auteur* (Manchester: Manchester University Press, 2000), 31.
77. The *Damnation of Faust* is available in the DVD boxed set *Georges Méliès: First Wizard of Cinema* (Los Angeles: Flicker Alley, 2008).
78. When *Moving Picture World* reviewed *The Damnation of Faust* in 1909, it told exhibitors that the story was an "evergreen" that should remain "popular on a film." However, the trade also bemoaned the film's "lack of naturalness" due to its painted scenery. The special effects so necessary for the story's success were no longer as magical as it had been when the film was first released in 1904. See "*Damnation of Faust, The*," *Moving Picture World*, April 24, 1909, 530; "*Damnation of Faust*," *Moving Picture World*, May 15, 1909, 636.
79. Advertisement, *New York Clipper*, April 2, 1904, 140.
80. *Geo. Méliès of Paris, Supplement No. 16* (New York: Star Films, 1904), unpaginated. Available in *A Guide to Motion Picture Catalogs by American Producers and Distributors, 1894–1908: A Microfilm Edition*, Reel 4.
81. *Faust and Marguerite* is available in the DVD boxed set *Georges Méliès: First Wizard of Cinema*.
82. The Paramount Film Company's *Faust and Marguerite* is mentioned in "Independent Films Released by [the] Paramount Film Company," *Moving Picture World*, June 4, 1910, 962.
83. "Webb's Talking Pictures," *The Billboard*, May 16, 1910, 73.
84. "*Faust*," *Moving Picture World*, December 25, 1909, 927. A copy of *Faust* (Edison, 1909) is archived at the Library of Congress.
85. "Edison Manufacturing Company Announces Grand Opera Release," *Moving Picture World*, December 11, 1909, 838.
86. "*Faust*," *Moving Picture World*, January 15, 1910, 58.
87. "*Faust*," *New York Dramatic Mirror*, January 1, 1910, 17.
88. Savada, 340. Copies of *Faust* (Eclair, 1910) are archived at the British Film Institute, Cineteca di Bologna, and the EYE Film Institute.
89. "*Faust*," *Moving Picture World*, July 2, 1910, 47; "*Faust*," *Moving Picture World*, July 16, 1910, 144.
90. A copy of *Faust* (Pathé Frères, 1911) exists at the Museum of Modern Art in New York City.
91. "*Faust*," *Moving Picture World*, June 24, 1911, 1439.
92. "*Faust* by Pathe," *Moving Picture World*, June 3, 1911, 1236.
93. "*Faust*," *Moving Picture World*, July 3, 1911, 1520.
94. "Latest Films of All Makers," *Views and Film Index*, November 30, 1907, 8. A copy of *The Clockmaker's Secret* is archived at the Library of Congress.
95. "*The Gambler and the Devil*," *Moving Picture World*, October 3, 1908, 267; "*Satan's Castle* (Two Reels–Ambrosio)," *Moving Picture World*, December 27, 1913, 1522. Some footage

from *The Gambler and the Devil* is archived at the Library of Congress by way of a paper print deposit. A copy of *Satan's Castle* is archived at Ngā Taonga Sound & Vision.
96. "*The Evil Philter*," *Moving Picture World*, December 11, 1909, 851. A copy of *The Evil Philter* is archived at the Centre national du cinéma et de l'image animée (CNC).
97. "*Mephisto and the Maiden*," *New York Dramatic Mirror*, May 8, 1909, 16.
98. "*The Devil's Billiard Table*," *Moving Picture World*, November 12, 1910, 1132.
99. "Urban-Eclipse," *Film Index*, November 6, 1909, 5.
100. "*The Tale of the Fiddle*," *Moving Picture World*, November 20, 1909, 720. A copy of *The Tale of the Fiddle* is archived at Lobster Films.
101. "*Legend of Orpheus*," *Moving Picture World*, December 4, 1909, 811. A copy of *Legend of Orpheus* is archived at the Cinémathèque Française.
102. "New Films Reviewed," *Billboard*, November 20, 1909, 21; Charles R. Condon, "Edison's *Fantasma* a Pleasing Film," *Motography*, December 12, 1914, 809–10. A copy of *A Mother's Heart* is archived at the Fundación Cinemateca Argentina. The opening reel of *Fantasma* is archived at the Library of Congress.
103. "*Mephisto's Son* at Nickelo," *The Daily Democrat* (Shelbyville, Indiana), December 14, 1906, 5. A copy of *Mephisto's Son* is archived at the Cinémathèque Française.
104. "Crook's Female Aid Turns Out Detective," *Universal Weekly*, June 26, 1914, 25.
105. "*Satan Defeated*," *Moving Picture World*, March 4, 1911, 492; "*The Temptation of Satan*," *Moving Picture World*, October 31, 1914, 644; "*The Professor's Nightmare*," *Vitagraph Life Portrayals*, February 1915, 29; "*The Devil*," *Moving Picture World*, April 3, 1915, 144. A copy of *Satan Defeated* is archived at the Gaumont-Pathé Archives.
106. "*The Devil, the Servant, and the Man*," *Moving Picture World*, February 5, 1910, 183; "*The Devil, the Servant, and the Man*," *New York Dramatic Mirror*, April 24, 1912, 28. The cited article in the *New York Dramatic Mirror* indicates that the 1912 version was indeed a remake rather than a reissue of the 1910 version, to the extent that the publication claimed the 1912 version was "more skillfully and artistically presented" than its predecessor and was thus a "great improvement" (28).
107. A copy of the 1912 version of *The Devil, The Servant, and The Man* is available at the Library of Congress. The plot synopsis in the main text is based on my viewing of it.
108. "*The Devil* Appears in Two Theatres," *New York Times*, August 19, 1908, 7.
109. "*He Went to See the Devil Play*," *Film Index*, January 9, 1909, 8. Some footage from *He Went to See the Devil Play* is archived at the Library of Congress by way of a paper print deposit.
110. Lynde Denig, "*The Devil*," *Moving Picture World*, April 3, 1915, 68. A copy of *The Devil* is archived at the Library of Congress.
111. "*The Demon*," *Moving Picture World*, February 25, 1911, 438. A copy of *The Demon* is archived at the Cineteca di Bologna.
112. Advertisement, *Moving Picture World*, January 11, 1913, unpaginated. A recut half-reel of *Satan, or the Drama of Humanity* is archived at the British Film Institute.
113. "Satan," *Moving Picture World*, January 18, 1913, 243.
114. John P. Welle, "Early Cinema, *Dante's Inferno* of 1911, and the Origins of Italian Film Culture," in *Dante, Cinema, and Television*, edited by Amilcare A. Iannucci (Toronto: University of Toronto Press, 2004), 36.
115. "*Dante's Inferno* (Milano Film Company)," *Moving Picture World*, July 22, 1911, 101.
116. "Paradise and Purgatory," *Moving Picture News*, April 20, 1912, 8.
117. Antonella Braida, "Dante's Inferno in the 1900s: From Drama to Film," in *Dante on View: The Reception of Dante in the Visual and Performing Arts*, edited by Antonella Braida and Luisa Calé (Aldershot: Ashgate Publishing, 2007), 47–9.
118. "John W. Dugan and Co.," *Variety*, February 25, 1911, 15.
119. "*Satan's Smithy*," *Moving Picture World*, August 21, 1909, 263.

120. "*Dante's Inferno*," *Moving Picture World*, July 15, 1911, 17.
121. W. Stephen Bush, "*Dante's Inferno* (Helios)," *Moving Picture World*, January 6, 1912, 23. A sizable fragment of the Helios production of *Dante's Inferno* is preserved in the collections of the British Film Institute and the Filmoteca Vaticana.
122. "*Dante's Inferno*," *Billboard*, July 29, 1911, 11.
123. See, for example, "Gustave Doré's Dante," which promised in 1863 that the illustrations were to be distributed in America in an affordable album, thus becoming a "possible purchase to any one." As for the lantern slides, see "Dante's Inferno Stereopticon Lecture," *Moving Picture World*, October 14, 1911, 138.
124. A copy of *L'Inferno* (1911) is available on the DVD *L'Inferno: Music by Tangerine Dream* (London: Snapper, 2006).
125. W. Stephen Bush, "Dante's *L'Inferno*," *Moving Picture World*, July 29, 1911, 188–9; W. Stephen Bush, "Music and Sound Effects for *Dante's Inferno*," *Moving Picture World*, January 27, 1912, 283.
126. "Exhibitors and Lecturers Key to *Dante's Inferno*," *Moving Picture World*, September 23, 1911, 878.
127. "Facts and Comments," *Moving Picture World*, June 8, 1912, 904.
128. W. Stephen Bush, "Gauging the Public Taste," *Moving Picture World*, May 11, 1912, 505; "Selection of Program," *Moving Picture World*, February 24, 1912, 11; "Facts and Comments," *Moving Picture World*, August 31, 1912, 844.
129. "Facts and Comments," *Moving Picture World*, September 7, 1912, 952.
130. Advertisement, *Moving Picture World*, June 14, 1913, 1100.
131. Advertisement, *Moving Picture World*, May 31, 1913, 876.
132. Advertisement, *Moving Picture World*, June 7, 1913, 993.
133. "*The Demon*," 15.
134. "*Satan's Rhapsody*," *Motography*, July 11, 1914, 58. Copies of *Satan's Rhapsody* are archived at the Museum of Modern Art, the EYE Film Institute, and Cineteca di Bologna.
135. "Lyda Borelli in *Satan's Rhapsody* (Kleine)," *Moving Picture World*, July 25, 1914, 588. Despite Kleine's announcement, *Satan's Rhapsody* did not appear on American film screens in 1914. See "On and Off the Screen," *Elkhart Daily Review* (Elkhart, Indiana), September 21, 1914, 2.
136. "Great Northern," *Moving Picture World*, March 6, 1915, 1520.
137. "*A Deal with the Devil*," *Motography*, March 20, 1915, 428. *A Deal with the Devil* is archived at the Danish Film Institute.
138. Advertisement, *Moving Picture World*, November 29, 1913, 1090.
139. Singer, 48–9, 59.

CHAPTER 6

Witches

Reviewing *The New Wizard of Oz* in 1915, *Moving Picture World* described one of its characters as "her Satanic highness, the witch."[1] Here the critic drew an immediate connection between Satan and witchcraft, even in the fanciful world of novelist L. Frank Baum, who had produced the film himself. Such a link is unsurprising, given accounts of witchcraft in the Judeo-Christian tradition (as in the Witch of Endor), in medieval folklore and beliefs (as famously chronicled in Heinrich Kramer's 1487 book *Malleus Maleficarum*), and in superstitions that continued into the era of early cinema. For many persons, witches were real, and they consorted with His Satanic Majesty, who gave them their powers. As Shakespeare wrote in *Macbeth* (1611), "For a charm of powerful trouble, like a hell-broth boil and bubble."

In America, of course, the witch's cauldron boiled over in Salem. As Gretchen A. Adams has observed:

> The specter of Salem witchcraft haunts the American imagination. Few historical events have provided such a wide range of scholars, dramatists, fiction writers, poets, and amateur sleuths with a subject that so stubbornly resists a final resolution.[2]

Grappling with the legacy of Salem provoked a variety of responses, including dark comedy. In 1796, for example, a Vermont newspaper published the following anecdote: "A witch, being at the stake to be burnt, saw her son there, and desired him to give her some drink: No mother, said he, it will do you wrong, for the drier you are the better you'll burn."[3]

Discussion of witchcraft in the eighteenth century shifted blame from the accused to the accuser. In 1731, the *American Weekly Mercury* told of a young girl in Somerset, England who began having inexplicable "fits." The locals believed she was bewitched and planned to execute her. The "Water Ordeal was resolved to be reviv'd," the account reported. But when the suspect did not drown, she was taken to a stable, where she died. The story ended differently than it had in Salem: "The Coroner did his utmost to discover the ringleaders, but in vain. However, the Coroner's Inquest has charged three with murder . . ."[4]

Adams has discussed how Salem moved "from the periphery to the center of cultural memory" in America during the nineteenth century, an era in which the witch trials served a variety of metaphorical purposes, ranging from those who demarcated the line between the "dark colonial past and the bright promise of the national future," to those who used Salem to decry particular regions and/or religions within the United States. It was in this period that the myth of accused witches being burned at the stake arose; however horrible their fate, none of the accused in America had been consigned to the flames.[5] Adams continues, "In its role as a *negative* symbol, Salem witchcraft was as useful as any heroic action, by articulating the inevitable consequences of an ill-advised action."[6]

Owen Davies has augmented this discussion of the nineteenth century by describing the sheer volume of immigrants into America who would have known little or nothing of Salem, but who retained their own cultural beliefs in the supernatural, including in witchcraft.[7] Accusations of witchcraft erupted repeatedly in the eighteenth and nineteenth centuries, including in some Native American communities. Accordingly, he suggests "it would not seem out of place for witchcraft to be central to a late nineteenth-century drama set amongst hillbillies in the Appalachians and Ozarks, or amongst the Pennsylvania Dutch."[8]

"Are there witches among us?" the *Chicago Tribune* pointedly asked in 1877. The newspaper answered its own question by stating that only persons "steeped in a density of ignorance" could "accept witchcraft, or any other exploded humbug of past centuries."[9] Other journalists referred to believers in witchcraft as "foolish people."[10] In these cases, learned writers attempted to school the populace by reminding them that Salem had culminated in a "New England Reign of Terror."[11]

However, such education may well have had little impact. Davies quotes a minister who declared in 1892 that a "majority" of Americans believed in witchcraft.[12] Whatever the exact percentage, press accounts indicate that superstitions continued, including in Wisconsin in 1888, where an "evil eye" had allegedly cast a spell on a family, and in New Jersey in 1893, where a man accused a neighbor of being "possessed of evil charms."[13] In Albany, New York in 1897, a German witch supposedly jinxed a young man.[14] Similarly, the "curse of Salem" was felt in Chicago in 1901, when an Irish woman claimed a Jewish witch had hexed her.[15]

To explain the prevalence of these beliefs, some journalists used geography and ethnicity as excuses, by which they could increase their own sense of superiority. For example, one account suggested in 1885 that these superstitions were relegated to the "farming population in those isolated localities," those who lived some distance from enlightened urbanites.[16] And to be sure, many tales of witchcraft did emerge from rural communities. For example, there was the trial of a Choctaw "witch-killer" who murdered "several innocent persons" in Texas in 1901.[17] Then, in 1907, a Nebraska farmer demanded the arrest of a "witch" who had cast spells on innocent locals.[18]

As for those who disavowed belief in witchcraft, the subject could still provide a degree of fascination and even spectacle. In 1871, for example, a journalist reported on the James Williams family of Fitts Hill, Illinois. Many townspeople believed that witchcraft tormented Williams's two daughters, aged sixteen and eighteen. The elder of the two described how an old woman had unsuccessfully tempted her to become a witch. Refusal meant the old woman caused them to go into spasms and commit bizarre acts. "Hundreds go every night to see the sight," the journalist claimed, adding:

> as their beautiful voices rolled out from the house-top on the still twilight, plaintive, mournful, sweet, their arms waving, bodies turned in this way and that, looking in their light dresses more like fairies, ghosts, or any unearthly apparition than human beings, wave after wave of chill came up my back, and I felt light almost as air. While I did not believe in witches, it seemed the only suitable place I had ever seen for them; and if such things could be, they surely would be there, and *then, right then*.

> ... Now came the most distressing sight I ever witnessed. Two young ladies, rendered wholly unconscious of what they were doing by some unknown cause, running about hunting pins and flies to eat.... There is no mistake about this. I actually saw them with wonderful expertness catch flies off the wall and eat them in spite of the watchfulness of their friends, and then vomit them up. It was horrible to look at, yet there were fiends there laughing at it. During these spells, they would go to a French harp which they own, and are very fond of, and play and sing catches of wild music.[19]

The journalist implored James Williams to seek medical attention for his daughters, as well as to disperse the nightly audience that gathered. But Williams "firmly believed [his daughters] were bewitched and wanted the people to witness it."

The desire to "see" witches could be fulfilled in other respects, including nonfiction texts like Charles Upham's two-volume opus *Salem Witchcraft; with an Account of Salem Village, and a History of Opinions on Witchcraft and Kindred Spirits* (New York: Frederick Ungar, 1867), which included such engravings as *Witch Hill*. Then, in 1892, Henrietta D. Kimball's *Witchcraft Illustrated* examined the subject through text and images that "glance[d] at old and new Salem and its historical resources."[20]

Perceived interest in witchcraft also prompted at least a few writers to invent "authentic" stories. In 1881, for example, *Frank Leslie's Popular Monthly* published an article about accused witch Juliana Cox, who had been executed in Connecticut in 1753. A few years earlier, the same tale appeared in numerous American newspapers.[21] However, as Cynthia Wolfe Boynton has shown, there is no evidence that Juliana Cox ever existed, let alone as a witch.[22] Another spurious tale was that of Colonel Jonathan Buck's monument in Bucksport, Maine. The imprint of a witch's foot allegedly appeared on it, the fulfillment of her curse on the man who condemned her to the stake. At least that is what *New England Magazine* claimed in 1902, with enough credibility that the story resurfaced in newspapers in 1909.[23] While Buck served in the military during the American Revolution, there is absolutely no record of him condemning any witches. In fact, there are no records of any accused witch being executed in Maine. Fiction had simply masqueraded as nonfiction.

During the early decades of the nineteenth century, American literature also drew upon popular notions of witches, as well as the history of Salem. For example, there was Jonathan M. Scott's poem *The Sorceress: or Salem Delivered* (1817) and the unattributed *Salem Witchcraft; or the Adventures of Parson Handy from Punkapog Pond* (published in magazine form in 1820 and then as a book in 1827).[24] Both stories feature what Lisa M. Vetere has described as the "persistent genre figure of the withered hag."[25] According to Diane Purkiss, the witch's ugliness represents a sign of supernatural power, as well as the refusal to be "controlled or managed as a soft or yielding object of desire."[26]

A large number of novels followed, arriving at roughly the same time as the growing demand for "genuine American" literature.[27] These include the anonymously authored *The Witch of New England: A Romance* (1824), *Delusion; or the Witch of New England* (1840), Mary Lyford's *The Salem Belle: A Tale of Love and Witchcraft in 1692* (1842), John W. De Forest's *Witching Times* (1857), Caroline Derby's *Salem* (1874), Pauline B. Mackie's *Ye Lyttle Salem Maide: Story of Witchcraft* (1898), Marvin Dana's *A Puritan Witch* (1903), L. F. Madison's *Maid of Salem Towne* (1906), and Henry Peterson's *Dulcible: A Tale of Old Salem* (1907).[28] Of these, John Neal's *Rachel Dyer* (1828) remains one of the most notable, its pages marked by narrative fiction intermingled with quotations from nonfiction primary sources.

Speaking of these stories and novels, particularly those published prior to the American Civil War, G. Harrison Orians observes:

> Almost all the longer tales were cast in the mould [sic] of the historical romance. . . . But this romantic glow was not easily attained. To anyone not familiar with the wearisome repetition of charges with which the afflicted assailed the accused, it might appear the simplest thing to construct out of the episodes of that time a romance neither harsh nor revolting to refined taste. But the motives of the actors and the sources of enmity were so thoroughly obscured, and the interrelation of accusations so befogged, that it was difficult indeed to weave them into a narrative. Thus beset with confusion, the novelist had to resort to fairly simple patterns of malice or jealousy, patterns which sooner or later suggested other tales, even when the authors were innocent of indebtedness. It was this inherent plot weakness that accounts for the constant recurrence of fair Puritans charged with witchcraft.[29]

Orians also notes the tendency such novelists had to make their "preferred heroines young and beautiful," which "scarcely . . . imparted a correct historical view," but which provided more romance, and—in the years that followed—a template for early cinema.[30]

Gabriele Schwab has calculated that there were "roughly forty works which are direct literary renditions of the Salem events" that "exceed the even more narrow scope of gothic literature." In her reading, this literature reveals the "persistence of the seductive power of the witch as much as the desire for 'displaced' witch-hunts."[31] In other words, the similarity of these novels to melodrama and the Gothic novel "allows one to surmise that they are, in fact, whetting a different reading appetite, which thrives less on the historical interest than on the witch as a feared but seductive object of desire."[32]

The most notable appearance of witches in nineteenth-century American literature came in the works of Nathaniel Hawthorne.[33] Famously, *The Scarlet Letter: A Romance* (1850) presents the minor but important character of Mistress Hibbins, a "witch-lady" based on the historic figure of Ann Hibbins, who was executed in Boston for witchcraft in 1656. As Karl P. Wentersdorf notes, "The element of witchcraft in *The Scarlet Letter* merges subtly with the other elements of literary allegory to constitute an unobtrusive but unmistakable satire on the Puritan aesthetic."[34] Hawthorne returned to the subject briefly in *The House of the Seven Gables* (1851), with character Matthew Maule being named as a martyr in the terrible tragedy of 1692.

Of equal importance in this context are two of Hawthorne's short stories that directly address the issue of Salem witchcraft, one being *Young Goodman Brown* (1835, as discussed in Chapter 1).[35] That same year, in *Alice Doane's Appeal* (1835), the narrator speaks of the "witchcraft delusion," but despite dismissing the supernatural, he still hopes his feet might "sink into the hollow of a witch's grave." In this fragmentary tale, the pilgrimage to Gallows Hill is suggestive of the kind of allure that Salem has had as a tourist destination since the nineteenth century.

In 1891, the *Chicago Tribune* published extended descriptions of surviving buildings and "time-stained" artifacts of note in Salem:

> At the side of the room we leaned upon the roughly-worn pine desk used by Hathorne at the Custom-House, and tried to summon up in imagination the men and women who, on a bleak November Sunday two centuries and a half ago, through the narrow, 'lonely lanes and the unpicturesque prolixity of its main street,' drifted high and deep with snows, bravely and piously plowed their way to the little church of the Salem heretic.[36]

Figure 6.1 The original British poster for Kalem's *The Mountain Witch* (1913), which features the same artwork that appeared on the American poster. (*Courtesy of the EYE Film Institute*)

Subsequent newspapers provided details of other locations, including the homes that belonged to Jonathan Corwin, one of the judges in the Salem witch trials, and of Rebecca Nurse, who had been sentenced to death as a witch in 1692.[37]

But perhaps more common than the spectacle of tourism was the spectacle of drama, the theatricality of witchcraft onstage. The first major American play on witchcraft was James Nelson Barker's *Superstition; or, The Fanatic Father* (1824), as described in Chapter 2. Then, in 1847, the blank verse tragedy *Witchcraft; or, The Martyrs of Salem* appeared in Philadelphia, Boston, and New York. In it, a "melancholy" but innocent woman is executed for being a witch.[38] The *Philadelphia Inquirer* wrote that it exposed how "dangerous" superstition could be, even with "civilized people."[39] The New York *Evening Mirror* called it a "play of the highest order—grand, simple, and tragic."[40]

In 1868, Henry Wadsworth Longfellow published the dramatic poem *Giles Corey of the Salem Farms* in his collection *The New-England Tragedies*.[41] Its title character was a dramatization of the victim pressed to death in Salem. The *New York Times* praised Longfellow's ability to evoke "terror and pity."[42] By contrast, in April 1893, Mary E. Wilkins's play *Giles Corey, Yeoman* (aka *Giles Corey-Yeoman*) opened to poor reviews at New York's Theatre of Arts and Letters.[43]

Far more successful was Marie Hubert Frohman's production of Philip Hamilton's play *The Witch* in 1890. As the *New York Times* wrote:

> It is announced that Marie Hubert Frohman intends to produce in this city a play called *The Witch*, the scene of which is laid at Salem in early colonial days. One of the incidents is the burning of a witch at a stake. Persons convicted of witchcraft were never burned in the New-England colonies. That absurd falsehood has not been heard of for a long term of years. It is hoped Mrs. Frohman will change the stake to the gallows before she produces her play, even at the expense of a vivid pictorial effect.[44]

Contemporaneous reviews indicate that Frohman followed the advice, with the execution method altered to the gallows.[45]

While Marie Madison adapted the play into novel form for publication, *The Witch* toured throughout New England and then throughout much of the rest of the United States.[46] As of August 1892, the Portland *Oregonian* announced the "grim" play was nearing its five hundredth performance.[47] A review in the *Springfield Republican* claimed *The Witch* "animates the most dramatic and weird picture to be found in early colonial history."[48] When it appeared at the Garrick in 1895, the *New York Times* believed that, while it lacked the "poetic instinct" of Wilkins's *Giles Corey*, it was "theatrically" the "more effective piece."[49]

Then, in 1910, a four-act drama entitled *The Witch* opened at the New Theatre in New York.[50] Bertha Kalich starred in this adaptation of H. Wiers-Jenssen's Norwegian play *Anne Pedersdotter*, an "oppressive tragedy of fanaticism, love, and violence."[51] The *New York Times* dubbed it "grim," with its mise-en-scène largely set:

> in shadow, candle-lighted interiors, with groups of figures half in light [and] half in gloom, as befitted the more or less benighted set of people of the story. Picturesqueness the play allows, and so much was attained in the individual and the general performance.[52]

The play's final act—in which a character's dead body appeared in "full view throughout"—was "repelling" enough that it drove "the exclusive audience out."[53]

Where did they go? "About a block away from the New Theatre there is a moving picture establishment that is doing good business on those evenings that [*The Witch* is performed]," one article claimed, adding, "It is a curious sight, the aristocracy of the intellect and wealth rushing away from one of their own productions to mix with [the] hoi polloi of the vaudeville and motion pictures in order to be cheered up."[54]

As was the case with devils, imps, skeletons, and ghosts, Georges Méliès was the first to incorporate witches into moving pictures. Here again we must start with his landmark 1896 moving picture *The Devil's Castle/Le manoir du diable* (aka *The Haunted Castle*) and its depiction of six spectral witches, all ghosts in white sheets carrying large broomsticks.[55] Hag-like witches then appeared in Méliès's *Bachelor's Paradise/Chez la sorcière* (1903) and *The Enchanted Well/Le puits fantastique* (1903).[56] In 1903, Star Films released Méliès's *Le Sorcier* in America under the title *The Witch's Revenge*.[57] In it, a king condemns a male sorcerer to death on the charge of witchcraft. After performing numerous tricks, the sorcerer turns the king's guards into demons and orders the king's execution.[58]

Three years later, Méliès's company released *The Witch/La fée carabosse ou le poignard fatal* (1906).[59] With a pointed hat and flowing gown, its witch rides a broomstick, first through a decrepit cemetery and then through the night sky, all in pursuit of a knight. A "druid priest" (as a Star Films catalog calls him) arrives in time to save the knight and his fair maiden.[60] He uses the witch's own broom to push her off a cliff. Unlike some of Méliès's earlier films, *The Witch* brought to life a character that closely resembled depictions known to American audiences not only through the stage and literature, but also in early twentieth-century Halloween decorations and costumes.

Not surprisingly, given the company's penchant for producing films in the style of Méliès, Pathé Frères also produced a number of trick films about witchcraft. These included Segundo de Chomón's *The Witch's Cave/L'antre de la sorcière* (1906), a "story of love and adventure, showing many gorgeous scenes and startling transformations"; *The Witch Kiss/Le baiser de la sorcière* (1907), a "colored film allowing the power of a witch's kiss"; and *The Witch's Donkey/L'âne de la sorcière* (1909), in which a witch casts a spell on her stolen donkey.[61]

Of the Pathé Frères films directed by Chomón, perhaps the most fascinating was *The Witch's Secret/Le secret de la sorcière* (Pathé Frères, 1908, aka *Witch's Secret*).[62] An old witch leaves her laboratory and flies on a broomstick. In her absence, two thieves enter, their plans becoming upset by a "crowd of white capped figures [that] spring out of the ground, each bearing a bat." The thieves are knocked unconscious, and when they awaken a "gang of weird-looking ogres" gives them another beating. The witch returns to find one of them still in her abode, and "with the vigorous aid of her broom helps him out urgently."[63]

To this group, other film manufacturing companies added even more witch comedies. In 1909, Great Northern released *Cycle Rider and the Witch/Heksen og cyklisten* (aka *The Witch and the Cycle*), in which a witch transforms a bicycle into "all sorts of funny things in the way of wheeled vehicles."[64] The following year, Lux released *Witches' Spectacles* (1910, aka *The Witch's Spectacles*), in which a wealthy woman obtains a special pair of glasses from a witch that allow her to see into the future. A series of "amusing revelations" follows.[65] That same year, George Kleine distributed the Urban-Eclipse film *The Witch of Carabosse/Carabosse vaincue* (1910).[66] Based upon an old legend, a man falls into the clutches of a witch who turns him into a "beast with horns for his temerity."[67] After "many unpleasant experiences" meant to "amuse the audience," he is "released from the spell [to live as] a wiser man."[68]

Witches also appeared in a number of fairy-tale moving pictures, including Edison's 1908 release *The Leprechawn* [sic], in which a "witch-woman" places a curse on an Irish landlord.[69] *Moving Picture World* believed the story "caught the 'witchery of Ireland'"; the *New York Dramatic Mirror* named it "one of the prettiest picture-stories it has been the pleasure of the *Mirror* to review."[70] Other such fanciful films included *Hansel and Gretel* (Edison, 1909), *Moon for Your Love/La lune dans son tablier* (Gaumont, 1909), *The Sleeping Beauty* (Venus, 1913), *The Wonderful Wizard of Oz* (Selig Polyscope, 1910), in which Dorothy (Bebe Daniels) splashes water onto the wicked witch Momba, and the aforementioned *The New Wizard of Oz* (1915, which was itself a retitled version of the 1914 film *His Majesty, the Scarecrow of Oz*).[71]

And then there were dramatic depictions of witches that unfolded outside of fairy-tale narratives. The title character of *The Witch/La sorcière* (Le Lion, 1909) transfers a woman's soul into a female dummy so that her ugly son can have a companion. Once challenged, she "summons all sorts of imps and phantoms to her aid," but the woman's sweetheart finally restores her soul.[72] Five years later, actress Mary Fuller portrayed the title character in *The Witch Girl* (Victor Film Co., 1914), a "strange, likable creature with a touch of the supernatural about her."[73] She "roams the woods without regard to propriety."[74] The male lead (played by Charles Ogle) falls in love with her, and, after the space of a year, she agrees to marry him. *Motography* praised its "pleasing" story.[75]

Figure 6.2 Advertisement for *The Witch Girl* (Victor Film Co., 1914), published in the *Universal Weekly* of October 17, 1914.

Another category of witch films came in the form of tales of the American West, a cinematic reminder of Owen Davies's remark about how unsurprising it would be to see witches depicted in dramas set in rural areas. *The Witch's Cavern* (Selig Polyscope, 1909) was likely the first of these films, telling the "weird" story of a party of campers who "run across a wild man, the half-witted son of a crazy old woman who lives in the mountains" of Yosemite Valley.[76] *Variety* called it a "corker," while the *New York Dramatic Mirror* praised its "poetic touch" of showing the old woman "performing a strange incantation to a magnificent waterfall."[77]

A number of similar moving pictures followed. *The Witch of the Range* (American, 1911) was a "western" in which an "old gypsy with witch-like characteristics" wanders through "picturesque mountain scenery, muttering incantations and casting dark spells over nature" until a group of cowboys unsuccessfully attempts to lynch her.[78] The same year, Kathlyn Williams portrayed the lead role in *The Witch of the Everglades* (Selig Polyscope, 1911).[79] Its title character was a beautiful but "demented" Native American woman with "witchlike characteristics."[80] And *The Wise Witch of Fairyland* (Solax, 1912) was a Native American "hag" who cast spells and mixed love potions.[81] (The subject of Native Americans and Otherness will be covered in Chapter 11.)

The Myth of Jamasha Pass (American, 1912) offered the "allegorical" story of a haunted pass in the "gloomy" Sierras, where "superstitious old men were wont to tell of the mystical maid . . . [who] oft appeared at sundown seeking the souls of men."[82] Two young miners ignore the warning of an elder and camp in the area. One of them awakens to see a "phantom." He reaches out for her, but to his "terror," she vanishes into thin air.[83] Soon the other is awakened as well. Both men end up pursuing "this elusive shadow" off a mountainside, thus falling to their deaths.[84] *Moving Picture World* noted:

> Perhaps she symbolizes the lure of the treasure [of the] mountains—'Death stands above me, whispering low,' she sings. At her first appearance in the picture, being but a mortal maid with whom we are well acquainted, the effect is not very uncanny, but, so well is the locality chosen, and so skilfully [sic] is the action woven to subdue us to the producer's ideas, and also so well is it acted, that soon she takes on not a little dreadfulness.[85]

In another article, *Moving Picture World* claimed the film was "doubtless founded on an Indian legend connected with Jamasha Pass."[86] That may well be true, as it was likely shot on location near the real Jamacha Pass (as it is more commonly spelled). However, the film's plot was not dissimilar to *The Witch's Ballad/La ballata della strega* (Ambrosio, 1910). An Italian-made film released in America, its witch induces a man to "jump into the sea."[87]

The most notable witch films in early cinema were those that visualized witch-hunts and/or trials, thus bringing at least a degree of historical accuracy to the screen, particularly insofar as women who are wrongly accused. In marked contrast to its trick films

Figure 6.3 *The Myth of Jamasha Pass* (American, 1912).

about witches, for example, Pathé Frères released *The Village Witch/La jeteuse de sorts* (1906), which presented a realist tale that exposed the superstitions of old.

The first of these films produced in America was Vitagraph's *The Witch* (1908), which presented the story of a woman charged with witchcraft in the fifteenth century, one that the *New York Dramatic Mirror* called "in some sense instructive."[88] Here was a history lesson and a morality tale on the screen, as well as—to extend Gabriele Schwab's thesis to early cinema—a story that perhaps tried to whet another appetite, meaning "the witch as a feared but seductive object of desire."[89]

In the Days of Witchcraft (Edison, 1909) seems to have become the first moving picture to address the history of witch trials in America, and by extension the first to invoke the erroneous myth that American judges ordered convicted women to be burned at the stake. In this case, however, the accused witch receives a reprieve at the last minute when her lover proves her innocence, thus appending a happy ending to a history that was devoid of the same.[90] The *New York Dramatic Mirror* presumed that the film was set in England, while *Moving Picture World* instead believed that it "faithfully" depicted New England, even to the extent that it had "historic value."[91]

Far more specific to American history was D. W. Griffith's *Rose O' Salem-Town* (Biograph, 1910), set in the year 1692 and reminiscent of Philip Hamilton's play *The Witch* (1892).[92] Here a young woman spurns the advances of a "hypocritical Puritan deacon." In retaliation, he accuses her and her mother of witchcraft. Biograph's publicity drew attention to the fact that "There are many relics of those days still in existence at Salem, and while conditions are such as to prevent our using the actual spots . . . many of the scenes of the picture are closely contiguous to them, our company of players making the trip there for that purpose."[93]

As Charlie Keil observes, *Rose O' Salem-Town* features "relatively 'advanced' storytelling techniques," including a "deft handling of space" and a form of "psychological editing" in which one-quarter of the film's shots unfold in only one-tenth of its running time.[94] Once again, the stake becomes the preferred method of execution, with Rose's mother burned to death. But Rose's sweetheart (along with a group of "friendly Indians") saves her at the last minute, thus resulting in another happy ending, one praised by *Variety*.[95] While *The Nickelodeon* believed the film effectively "revivifies history in commendable style," the trade registered "something of a protest" against the depiction of the Puritan deacon as a "libertine."[96]

Another film of this type appeared in 1912. Reliance's *The Trials of Faith* (aka *Trials of Faith*) was a "very pretty picture of early days in New England." The jealous Priscilla falsely accuses Faith of being a witch. As a trade synopsis noted, "The governor is only too glad to entertain the suspicion against her and she is tried and condemned for witchcraft."[97] She is bound to a tree, and the pyre is set aflame. But Native Americans "break through the crowd" and rescue her, creating what *Moving Picture World* called a "delightful ending to a fine picture."[98]

The following year, 1913, seven films appeared either directly or indirectly covering the topic of Salem witchcraft. In February, Kalem released *The Mountain Witch*, in which a "young minister" arrives in a village, only to protect an accused witch from his parishioners.[99] In May, Selig Polyscope offered *In the Days of Witchcraft*, with Cotton Mather himself sentencing an accused witch to the stake; assisted by her lover, she escapes jail and flees to England.[100] In August, Kay-Bee's *The House of Bondage* told a "drama of Puritan

Figure 6.4 *The Trials of Faith* (Reliance, 1912).

Figure 6.5 *The Witch of Salem* (Domino, 1914).

days" in which an accused witch escapes from prison, but returns to warn those who condemned her about an impending "Indian attack."[101] In September, Eclair American released *A Puritan Episode*, causing *Moving Picture World* to bemoan that an "otherwise excellent" film perverted history by depicting a colonial American being sentenced to the stake.[102] In November, Domino released *The Witch of Salem*, yet another drama about the "atrocious fanaticism" that plagued colonial America.[103] And in December, Domino released *The Curse*, in which a Native American tribe attacks a village shortly after a woman is accused of witchcraft.[104]

Of all the films distributed in 1913, Eclair American's *The Witch* received the most publicity, which extended to a multi-page illustrated synopsis in the August 1913 issue of *Photoplay*.[105] Released in June of that year, this version of *The Witch* reworked *Rose O' Salem-Town*, with character Mary Martin refusing Selectman Marsh's attention. In retaliation, he accuses her mother of witchcraft. Mary relents, marrying Marsh, but her mother's sentence proceeds as planned, at least until Governor Brent intercedes at the last minute. Mary suffers miserably as Marsh's wife until he at long last dies.[106] *Moving Picture World* praised *The Witch* for its historical "fidelity."[107] However, *The Witch* deviated from authentic cases in the same way that the other 1913 witch films did, appending happy endings to stories that in Salem had ended tragically.

As Owen Davies has remarked, "Witches were integral to the cultural fabric of America."[108] To an extent, the same can be said of early cinema in the United States, during which time all manner of witchcraft appeared on the screen. And yet the panoply of witches can be best understood by consideration of three major categories: (mostly

Figure 6.6 *The Witch* (Eclair American, 1913).

imported) trick films in which such characters possessed supernatural powers; American-made films depicting the Native American Other; and the American-made films in which witchcraft was simultaneously present and absent, visible and invisible, films in no witches appeared, but instead victims who were falsely accused of being in league with Satan, their innocence contrasted sharply with the ignorance and sinfulness of their accusers. The cauldron of witchcraft no longer boiled over: it simmered in film after film, the cinema slowly and repeatedly indicting and even attempting to rectify the colonial past.

Notes

1. Hanford C. Judson, "*The New Wizard of Oz*," *Moving Picture World*, March 20, 1915, 1781. L. Frank Baum's Oz Film Manufacturing Company produced and released *His Majesty, the Scarecrow of Oz* in 1914; the company then reissued it in 1915 under the title *The New Wizard of Oz*. Copies of the film are archived at the George Eastman Museum and the Library of Congress.
2. Gretchen A. Adams, *The Specter of Salem: Remembering the Witch Trials in Nineteenth-Century America* (Chicago: University of Chicago Press, 2008), 1.
3. Untitled, *Rutland Herald* (Rutland, Vermont), March 28, 1796, 4.
4. "Extract of a Letter from Somersetshire," *American Weekly Mercury* (Philadelphia, Pennsylvania), June 3, 1731, 3.
5. Adams, 6, 39.
6. Ibid., 5.
7. Owen Davies, *America Bewitched: The Story of Witchcraft after Salem* (Oxford: Oxford University Press, 2013), 3.
8. Ibid., 18.
9. "Are There Witches Among Us?", *Chicago Tribune*, June 1, 1877, 4.
10. The word "foolish" in this context appears in "The Modern Witch," *Colorado Springs Gazette* (Colorado Springs, Colorado), September 17, 1902, 4, as well as in "Jailed as a Witch," *Grand Rapids Press* (Grand Rapids, Michigan), September 15, 1911, 10.
11. "The Witchcraft of 1692; or, The England Reign of Terror," *Anti-Slavery Bugle* (Salem, Oregon), May 25, 1849.
12. Davies, 11.
13. "The Wisconsin Witch," *Chicago Tribune*, July 29, 1888, 9; "Accused of Being a Witch," *New York Herald*, April 18, 1893, 12.
14. "Shriveled by a Witch," *Philadelphia Inquirer*, December 26, 1897, 10.
15. "Chicago Has a Witch," *Washington Bee* (Washington, D.C.), October 12, 1901, 6.
16. "Witches and Witchcraft," *Chicago Tribune*, April 8, 1885, 10.
17. "Witches Shot to Death," *Washington Post*, January 12, 1902, 35.
18. "Witchcraft in West," *Washington Post*, February 11, 1907, 6.
19. "The Witches," *Nashville Union and American* (Nashville, Tennessee), July 9, 1871.
20. Henrietta D. Kimball, *Witchcraft Illustrated* (Boston: George A. Kimball, 1892).
21. See, for example, "An Old Witch," *Nebraska Advertiser* (Brownville, Nebraska), November 29, 1877, 1.
22. Cynthia Wolfe Boynton, *Connecticut Witch Trials: The First Panic in the New World* (Charleston, South Carolina: The History Press, 2014), 98–102.
23. "The Witch's Curse Story Is Revived," *Columbus Daily Enquirer* (Columbus, Ohio), January 24, 1909, 4.
24. When discussing "New England Witchcraft in Fiction," G. Harrison Orians also cataloged "Salem, An Eastern Tale," published in three installments in *The New York Literary Journal*

and Belles-Lettres Repository in the autumn of 1820. See G. Harrison Orians, "New England Witchcraft in Fiction," *American Literature*, Vol. 2, No. 1 (March 1930), 55.
25. Lisa M. Vetere, "The Malefic Unconscious: Gender, Genre, and History in Early Antebellum Witchcraft Narratives," *Journal of Narrative Theory*, Vol. 42, No. 2 (Summer 2012), 119–48.
26. Diane Purkiss, *The Witch in History: Early Modern and Twentieth-Century Representations* (New York: Routledge, 1996), 127.
27. Gabriele Schwab, "Seduced by Witches: Nathaniel Hawthorne's *The Scarlet Letter* in the Context of New England Witchcraft Fictions," in *Seduction and Theory: Readings of Gender, Representation, and Rhetoric*, edited by Dianne Hunter (University of Illinois Press, 1989), 175.
28. *The Witch of New England: A Romance* was subsequently attributed to author John Cadwalader M'Call, just as *Delusion; or the Witch of New England* has been attributed to Buckminster Lee.
29. Orians, 70, 71.
30. Ibid., 71.
31. Schwab, 174.
32. Ibid., 174.
33. Philip McFarland, *Hawthorne in Connecticut* (New York: Grove Press, 2004), 18.
34. Karl P. Wentersdorf, "The Element of Witchcraft in *The Scarlet Letter*," *Folklore*, Vol. 83, No. 2 (Summer 1972), 153.
35. For more information on Nathaniel Hawthorne's relationship with Salem, see *Hawthorne in Salem*, a website created by North Shore Community College and three Salem museums with a grant from the National Endowment for the Humanities: www.hawthorneinsalem.org. Accessed on September 1, 2015.
36. Rena A. Michaels, "The Old Witch Town," *Chicago Tribune*, December 27, 1891, 25.
37. "Salem's Quaint Old Witch House," *Washington Post*, February 19, 1896, 10; "The Days of Witch Hanging," *Kansas City Star*, January 15, 1907, 9.
38. James Fisher, *Historical Dictionary of American Theatre: Beginnings* (Lanham, Maryland: Rowman & Littlefield, 2015), 474.
39. "Local Items," *Philadelphia Inquirer*, July 5, 1847.
40. "Dramatic Criticism," *The Evening Mirror* (New York), June 1, 1847, 1.
41. Henry Wadsworth Longfellow, *The New-England Tragedies* (Boston: Ticknor & Fields, 1868).
42. "New Publications," *New York Times*, October 28, 1868, 2.
43. "The Week at the Theatres," *New York Times*, April 23, 1893, 13; "Miss Wilkins's Witch Play," *New York Times*, April 18, 1893, 4.
44. "Notes of the Stage," *New York Times*, April 20, 1890, 12.
45. "*The Witch* at the Opera House," *Springfield Republican* (Springfield, Missouri), December 9, 1890, 7.
46. Marie Madison, *The Witch: A Novel* (New Haven, Connecticut: New Haven Publishing Company, 1891).
47. "Coming Attractions," *Oregonian* (Portland, Oregon), August 3, 1892, 8.
48. "*The Witch* at the Opera House," 7.
49. "New Theatrical Bills," *New York Times*, December 10, 1895, 5.
50. "New Theatre Gets Mme. Bertha Kalich," *New York Times*, January 17, 1910, 7.
51. "New Plays in Gotham," *Washington Post*, February 20, 1910, S2.
52. "Witchcraft Days at New Theatre," *New York Times*, February 15, 1910, 9.
53. George Henry Payne, "Nickel Show Alone Welcomes New Theatre's Latest Play," *Chicago Tribune*, February 20, 1910, B1.
54. Ibid., B1.
55. A copy of *The Devil's Castle* is available on the DVD *Georges Méliès Encore* (Los Angeles: Flicker Alley, 2010).

56. Copies of *Bachelor's Paradise* and *The Enchanted Well* are available in the DVD boxed set *Georges Méliès: First Wizard of Cinema*.
57. Advertisement, *New York Clipper*, July 25, 1903, 500.
58. A copy of *The Witch's Revenge* is available in the DVD boxed set *Georges Méliès: First Wizard of Cinema* (Los Angeles: Flicker Alley, 2008).
59. A copy of *The Witch* is available in the DVD boxed set *Georges Méliès: First Wizard of Cinema*.
60. *Complete Catalogue of Genuine and Original "Star" Films* (New York: Star Films, June 1905), 116–17. It is important to note that this Star Film catalog bears a June 1905 date, but pages from 81 to 148 detail films from the July 1905 to June 1908 period. Either these later pages were appended to the catalog, or the catalog dates to June 1908, with the first eighty pages reprinted and the 1905 date not being revised.
61. Advertisement, *Anaconda Standard* (Anaconda, Montana), October 27, 1907, 27; Advertisement, *Austin Daily Herald* (Austin, Minnesota), March 20, 1908; "The Witch's Donkey," *New York Dramatic Mirror*, July 17, 1909, 16. A copy of *The Witch's Cave* is available on the DVD *Segundo de Chomón, el cine de la fantasia* (Barcelona: Cameo Media S.L., 2010).
62. A copy of *The Witch Kiss* is archived at the British Film Institute.
63. "Latest Films of All Makers," *Views and Film Index*, January 11, 1908, 8. In addition to the Segundo de Chomón-directed films, Pathé also released *The Black Witch/La sorcière noire* (1907), in which the title character performs magic in a "barbarian" land. A copy of the film is available on the DVD *Fairy Tales: Early Colour Stencil Films from Pathé* (London: British Film Institute, 2012).
64. "The Gray Dame," *Moving Picture World*, September 11, 1909, 344. A copy of *Cycle Rider and the Witch* is archived at the Danish Film Institute.
65. "The Witch's Spectacles," *Moving Picture World*, July 2, 1910, 47.
66. "Urban-Eclipse," *Billboard*, August 6, 1910, 27.
67. "The Witch of Carabosse," *New York Dramatic Mirror*, August 13, 1910, 27.
68. "Witch of Carabosse," *Moving Picture World*, August 6, 1910, 311; "The Witch of Carabosse," *Moving Picture World*, August 27, 1910, 462.
69. "The Leprechawn," *Views and Film Index*, September 26, 1908, 11.
70. "The Leprechawn," *Moving Picture World*, October 10, 1908, 279; "The Leprechawn," *New York Dramatic Mirror*, October 3, 1908, 8.
71. "Hansel and Gretel," *Moving Picture World*, October 9, 1909, 499–500; "Moon for Your Love," *Moving Picture World*, November 20, 1909, 731; "Feature Films Reviewed," *Billboard*, August 9, 1913, 18. A copy of *The Wonderful Wizard of Oz* is available in the DVD boxed set *More Treasures from the American Film Archives* (San Francisco: National Film Preservation Foundation, 2004).
72. "The Witch," *Moving Picture World*, November 6, 1909, 661.
73. "The Witch Girl," *New York Dramatic Mirror*, October 14, 1914, 33.
74. "Mary Fuller in *The Witch Girl* (Victor)," *Moving Picture World*, October 24, 1914, 500.
75. "The Witch Girl," *Motography*, October 31, 1914, 610. It is also worth noting that *The Witch of the Ruins/La folle des ruines* (Pathé Frères, 1910) features a witch character who cares for a lost child. See "The Witch of the Ruins," *Moving Picture World*, May 7, 1910, 751.
76. "The Witch's Cavern," *New York Dramatic Mirror*, November 13, 1909, 15.
77. "*Variety*'s Own Picture Reviews," *Variety*, November 6, 1909, 13; "The Witch's Cavern," 15.
78. "The Witch of the Range," *Motography*, June 1911, 149.
79. A copy of *The Witch of the Everglades* is archived at the EYE Film Institute.
80. "Witch of the Everglades," *Motography*, May 1911, 99.
81. "The Wise Witch of Fairyland," *Moving Picture World*, February 10, 1912, 622.
82. "The Myth of Jamasha Pass," *Moving Picture News*, April 20, 1912, 31.

83. "*The Myth of Jamasha Pass*," *Moving Picture World*, May 11, 1912, 562.
84. Ibid., 562.
85. "*The Myth of Jamasha Pass*," *Moving Picture World*, May 18, 1912, 630.
86. James S. McQuade, "*The Mystical Maid of Jamasha Pass* (American)," *Moving Picture World*, April 27, 1912, 319. It is difficult to determine whether the title of this article (which apparently intended to convey the title of the film) was an error, or whether it reflects a pre-release or alternate title that was changed.
87. "*The Witch's Ballad*," *New York Dramatic Mirror*, March 5, 1910.
88. "*The Witch*," *New York Dramatic Mirror*, October 31, 1908, 8. A small amount of footage from *The Witch* is archived at the Library of Congress. (The German manufacturer Internationale Kinematographen- und Lichteffekt-Gesellschaft [I.K.L.G.] released *Ein Volksgericht im Mittelalter oder Die Zeit des Schreckens und des Grauens*—which would translate as *A People's Court in the Middle Ages, or The Time of Fear and Horror*—in January 1907. Its plot featured a witch-hunt and trial and certainly predates Vitagraph's *The Witch*. However, it was not imported into America.)
89. Schwab, 174.
90. "*In the Days of Witchcraft*," *Moving Picture World*, April 10, 1909, 449.
91. "*In the Days of Witchcraft*," *New York Dramatic Mirror*, April 24, 1909, 14; "*In the Days of Witchcraft*," *Moving Picture World*, April 24, 1909, 517.
92. A copy of *Rose O' Salem-Town* is archived at the Library of Congress.
93. "*Rose O' Salem-Town*," *Moving Picture World*, October 1, 1910, 760.
94. Charlie Keil, *Early American Cinema in Transition* (Madison, Wisconsin: University of Wisconsin Press, 2001), 182–5.
95. "*Variety's* Picture Reviews," *Variety*, October 1, 1910, 18.
96. "*Rose o' Salem Town* [sic]," *The Nickelodeon*, October 1, 1910, 201.
97. "*The Trials of Faith*," *Moving Picture World*, November 16, 1912, 665.
98. Ibid., 665.
99. "*The Mountain Witch*," *Moving Picture World*, February 15, 1913, 704.
100. "*In the Days of Witchcraft*," *Moving Picture World*, August 3, 1913, 505.
101. "*The House of Bondage*," *Moving Picture World*, August 2, 1913, 566.
102. "*A Puritan Episode*," *Moving Picture World*, September 20, 1913, 1285.
103. "Domino: *The Witch of Salem*," *Reel Life*, November 15, 1913, 9.
104. "*The Curse*," *Moving Picture World*, December 20, 1913, 1414.
105. F. Marion Brandon, "*The Witch*: A Sweet Story of Old Salem Days," *Photoplay* (August 1913), 29–33, 98.
106. "Salem Witch Craft [sic] Theme of Photoplay," *Universal Weekly*, June 28, 1913, 15, 25.
107. "*The Witch*," *Moving Picture World*, June 28, 1913, 1360.
108. Davies, 21.

CHAPTER 7

Ghosts

In 1907, Vitagraph released *The Ghost Story*, which was—not unlike later horror movies based on "true" stories—"founded on an actual occurrence that happened some time ago."[1] In it, a "merry party of young people" gathers around a fireside. During a "gruesome and hair-raising ghost story," two of the characters "slip out unobserved." One uses a sheet and skull to costume the other as a "frightful spectre." A synopsis in *Views and Film Index* noted:

> The story-teller is now reaching the climax, describing in sepulchral tones the horrors of the ghostly scene he is portraying. The listeners are held in the thrall of the unearthly narrative, every nerve tense, every heart beating quickly, when suddenly the door opens and the awful apparition glides in and utters a deep groan. The effect is magical—the tightly-sprung nerves stretch tighter and tighter, then . . . shrieks of genuine fear and hysteria burst forth.[2]

A member of the party draws a revolver and fires. The fake ghost "falls bleeding and dead at their feet—the joke has turned into a grim tragedy."

During the eighteenth and nineteenth centuries, American newspapers were rife with stories about ghosts, sometimes in the form of fictional tales and poems, but more commonly as nonfiction accounts decrying belief in the supernatural.[3] In 1825, for example, a

Figure 7.1 Advertisement for *The Ghost Story* (Vitagraph, 1907), published in *Views and Film Index* on September 14, 1907.

newspaper in Vermont wrote, "In all ages persons of weak intellect have believed in apparitions; yet we may confidently affirm that stories of ghosts are mistakes or impositions, and that they may be always detected by a proper exercise of the mental faculties."[4] Some journalists seemed to enjoy writing from a sense of intellectual superiority over those who saw ghosts that didn't exist. "It is strange that any portion of the community should be so stupidly ignorant as to credit for any moment any stories about ghosts, witches, and hobgoblins," a newspaper stated in 1828. "When will such delusions cease?"[5]

Many of these reports ended with logical explanations of their apparitions, which ranged from discussions of England's faked Cock-Lane Ghost to a mentally ill woman wandering nightly in an American cemetery in 1854.[6] In 1846, a reputable citizen of Boston, Massachusetts saw a ghost every time he visited a particular gate in front of a relative's house. "The gentleman is not conscious of having defective vision," one report noted. "It is evident that a morbid action takes place in his brain, through its connection with the optic apparatus, and that the spectre is reproduced by local causes existing at the gate, which cannot yet be explained."[7] In other words, there had to be a logical explanation, even if it was not yet known.

Fictional tales sometimes featured "real" ghosts, whether from indigenous writers like Poe (as in his *Ligeia* of 1838), or in the imported literature of Guy de Maupassant, Wilkie Collins, Richard Middleton, M. R. James, Algernon Blackwood, and others. However, as Chapter 1 noted, most literature in America regularly explained the supernatural, something that could even become a selling point. As early as 1796, the American publicity for Friedrich Schiller's novel *The Ghost-Seer; or, Apparitionist/Der Geisterseher* claimed it was "calculated to expose those miraculous accounts" of ghosts told by the "ignorant."[8] Eight decades later, a newspaper published a poem entitled *The Ghost: A True Story*.[9] In it, the spirit turns out to be not a ghost, but a goat.

Moving pictures proved well suited to creating ghosts, in part due to the trickery that they could employ. In 1901, Frederick S. Armitage shot *The Ghost Train* for American Mutoscope & Biograph. As the company catalog explained, the film was a "mystery picture showing a train running at high speed at night, with only moonlight illumination. The effect is very weird and impressive."[10] The white Ghost Train appears otherworldly, roaring down the tracks, smoke billowing from its stack. It is merely a negative image. Even the "moonlight" is a fake, as what appears to be a night sky was actually daytime.

While such films usually relied on cinematic special effects, they also came to depend on the increasing narrativization of cinema, with story becoming as important as cinematic trickery during and after the nickelodeon era. As *Variety* announced in 1910, "ghosts seem to be all the rage in 'photoplay[s]' nowadays."[11] Three years later, *Reel Life* wrote, "the moving picture lends itself admirably to everything in the ghost line."[12] The reasons were manifold, among them the fact that ghosts—or pranksters pretending to be ghosts—could materialize in various types of stories, including those that featured haunted houses and/or spiritualists.

Apparitions

As Chapter 4 indicated, early trick films often depicted real ghosts (as opposed to human characters in sheets, for example). For instance, in 1899, American Mutoscope & Biograph released *Ballet of the Ghosts*, in which "mysterious figures, draped in white, advance slowly from the gloom." They throw their "drapery" aside and reveal themselves to be "ballet girls."[13] The film footage then reverses, causing them to unnaturally re-drape themselves and return to the gloom. The following year, American Mutoscope & Biograph released *Ghosts in a Chinese Laundry* (1900). A catalog description noted: "Two Chinamen are seen busily ironing. One places an empty clothesbasket on the floor; but as he does so, the ghost of a Chinaman rises from it. The laundrymen are greatly frightened and mystified, and the ghost disappears as mysteriously as it came."[14]

Real ghosts also appeared in numerous comedy films during the nickelodeon era. In 1907, for example, *Views and Film Index* published a critique of the one-reel moving picture *The Ghost Holiday/The Ghosts' Holiday* (Williams, Browne & Earle, 1907):

> It shows a ghost appearing in the church yard [sic] and being joined by a group of other ghosts, skeletons, etc., jumping over tomb stones [sic] and playing about among the graves. Finally they go out into the road and get an automobile, a bicycle, and a horse and visit the village hotel. They see their friends off in the train [and] go boat riding, in which all sorts of things happen. They visit the art galleries and have a good time in general, including attending a ball. At daylight the rooster appears crowing and the ghosts hasten back to the graveyard.[15]

The review also promised that *The Ghost Holiday* was a "novelty of the finest class."

Billboard claimed that "funny things happen" after a "ghostly lord" appears in *Shooting in the Haunted Woods/La chasse au bois hanté* (Gaumont, 1910).[16] Then, in Thanhouser's *When Ghost Meets Ghost* (1913), two spirits (played by Marguerite Snow and James Cruze) decide to make their home with a professor, who moves "ere his house becomes the headquarters of the Ghosts' Union."[17]

In dramatic moving pictures, real ghosts only rarely haunted the living. In *The Tyrant Feudal Lord/Le burgrave, légende du Rhin* (Gaumont, 1908), the spirits of a priest and his parishioners haunt the palace of a cruel aristocrat; according to a plot synopsis, the "shocking experiences are repeated with such frequency and are so intense that they cause the demise of the lord."[18] Quite similar was *The Sword and the King* (Vitagraph, 1909), in which a shepherd's ghost haunts the evil king who "wantonly" murdered him.[19] And in *The Specter/Le spectre* (Pathé Frères, 1908), a cobbler's apprentice murders a man for the money he needs to attract a woman. Thereafter, the ghost of the murdered man follows the apprentice everywhere, eventually causing him to commit suicide.[20]

More often, real ghosts in dramatic narratives attempted to assist the living characters they loved. In *A Timely Apparition/Sacrifice humain* (Urban-Eclipse, 1909), the dead father of a girl returns as an apparition to frighten the villains who pursue her.[21] In *The Ghost's Warning* (Edison, 1911), a ghost implores a woman to marry the man she loves, not the man her father prefers.[22] The antics of a noisy poltergeist in *The Ghost of Granleigh* (Edison, 1913) prevent a wife from committing an "irreparable act of folly" with a man other than her husband.[23] The title ghost of *The Man in the White Cloak/Manden med kappen* (Great Northern, 1913) leads a character to hidden treasure.[24] And in *The Spirit and the Clay* (Vitagraph, 1914), the lead character sculpts a likeness of his wife; after her death, her ghost returns so that he might finish it.[25]

By contrast, many onscreen "ghosts" were merely persons accidentally mistaken for being spirits, a plot device that had earlier been used in Catharine Sedgwick's short story *The Country Cousin* (1830) and in numerous nonfiction press accounts.[26] Examples include

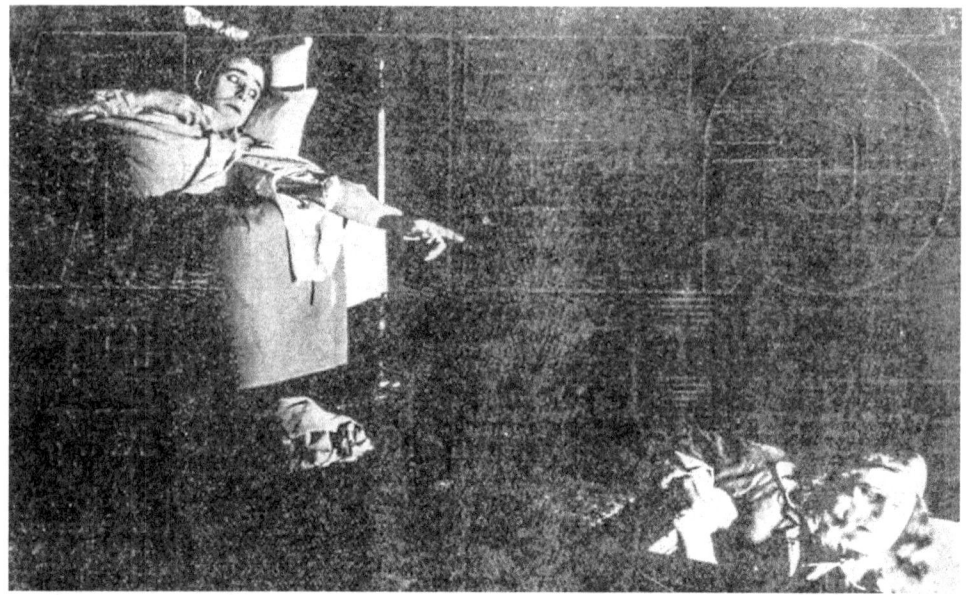

Figure 7.2 *The Ghost* (Pathé, 1914), as published in *Moving Picture World* on March 14, 1914.

the dramas *A Terrible Night/Une nuit d'épouvante* (Eclair, 1912), *The Ghost of Sulphur Mountain* (Gaston Méliès, 1912), *Ghosts* (Essanay, 1912), *The Ghost* (Pathé, 1914), and *The Ghost of Smiling Jim* (Universal-Gold Seal, 1914).[27] The same plot device surfaced in a number of comedies, among them *Bedelia's "At Home"* (Reliance, 1912), *The Skivvy's Ghost/La peur de Monsieur et Madame Denis* (Lux, 1912), *The Haunted Bachelor* (Eclair American, 1912), and *Sweedie's Suicide* (Essanay, 1915), the latter being an entry in the popular 'Sweedie' series of comedies produced during 1914–15 with star Wallace Beery.[28]

Of these films, one of the most fascinating was *The Ghost of the Vaults/Spøgelset i gravkælderen* (Great Northern, 1911), in which a miserly father imprisons his daughter's lover so that she will have to marry his preferred choice of mate. One evening, the father descends into the vaults below his old home, as he hides his gold inside a coffin. His preferred suitor secretly follows and plans to steal the gold, but seeing a ghost causes him to drop the coffin lid.[29] The "white robed apparition" is merely the sleepwalking daughter; she awakens at the noise and falls into the arms of her true love, who has escaped his cell.[30] *Billboard* believed, "The acting, story, scenery, and photography are all good in this film . . ."[31]

Unhealthy minds sometimes produced "ghosts." The title character of the "comedy-drama" *The Haunted Bride* (Rex, 1913) believes herself haunted by a man who committed suicide, even though the man is actually still alive.[32] In the drama *Phantoms* (Selig Polyscope, 1913), an actress falls into a "beatific insanity in which her whole life is phantoms."[33] And in *The Mystery of Carter Breene* (Centaur, 1915), a murderer sees his victim's spirit. While the story is not dissimilar to the aforementioned *The Spectre*, in this case the ghost is merely an image conjured by the murderer's guilty conscience.[34]

Fake cinematic ghosts also resulted from those in search of love.[35] In *Tricked into Giving His Consent/Le consentement forcé* (Pathé Frères, 1908), a father believes he has killed his daughter's lover. To make him feel guilty and thus approve of their union, the lover haunts him by wearing a white sheet.[36] *The Beechwood Ghost* (Powers, 1910) turns out to be nothing more than a young man pretending to be a ghost in order to win a kiss from his sweetheart.[37] And in *The Haunted Rocker* (Vitagraph, 1912), two sweethearts (played by Tom Powers and Clara Kimball Young) frighten the parent who is against their union by making it seem as if his chair is rocking due to—in the language of an onscreen intertitle— "Mystification!"[38] The *New York Dramatic Mirror* praised the film, claiming, "Never has the spirit of farce-comedy been better displayed than in this exceedingly funny and novel picture."[39]

Pranksters dressed themselves as ghosts for other comical reasons as well. The title character of *Bill Taken for a Ghost/Patouillard fantôme* (Lux, 1911), who was well known to American audiences due to the imported "Patouillard" series of films, disguises himself as a spirit among the "dismantled Chateau of Spookeybrook" in order to scare some tourists.[40] In *A Midnight Scare* (Crystal, 1914), Harry puts a sheet over his head in the middle of the night to frighten his cowardly friend Joe.[41] And *Mulligan's Ghost* (Columbus, 1914) is nothing more than a man who pretends to be dead in order to collect on his own life insurance policy.[42]

Dramatic film narratives also featured characters pretending to be ghosts in order to frighten others, as in *The Castle Ghosts/Il fantasma del castello* (Aquila, 1908), *The Haunted Bridge/Il ponte delle streghe* (Raleigh & Robert/Ambrosio, 1909), *Mammy's Ghost* (Vitagraph, 1911), *The White Ghost/Lo spettro bianco a Saint Moritz* (Milano, 1914), *The Ghost of the White Lady/Den hvide dame* (Great Northern, 1914), and *The Spirit of the Bell* (Kay-Bee, 1915).[43] Fake ghosts also tried to frighten the heroines of movie serials, as in the case of *Zudora* (Thanhouser, 1914–15) and *The Exploits of Elaine* (Pathé, 1914–15).[44] Among the most interesting of these plots was *Another's Ghost/Le spectre de l'autre* (Pathé Frères, 1910, aka *Another Ghost*), in which an actor dresses as the ghost of a murdered man to provoke the murderers into a confession.[45]

When mother and father are out, the little girl in *Baby's Ghost/Les malheurs de Cunégonde* (Lux, 1912) scares away two intruders by pretending to be a specter.[46] In *The Ghost in Uniform* (Thanhouser, 1913), the "Thanhouser Kid" masquerades as the spirit of a police officer at a police station.[47] Two tramps get scared out of a farmhouse in *A Narrow Squeak* (Joker, 1914) when they mistake a pig's squeal for a ghost's wail.[48] And in *A Night of Thrills* (Rex, 1914), which included Lon Chaney in its cast, the heroine screams when bumping into her sweetheart at the front door, her shriek warding off thieves elsewhere in the home. (Similar in plot was Vitagraph's *The Skull* of 1913, in which bandits at a jewelry store become frightened at the sight of the "gruesome" title object.[49])

The Ghost of the Hacienda (American, 1913) was yet another of these films. In it, a "notorious highwayman" and his gang attempt to rob a home in Mexico, but the heroine "bethinks of herself a scheme." She dresses as a ghost, "her hair hanging over her shoulders, a candle in her hand, and robed in pure white, glides down the stairs."[50] One synopsis added, "A strange, weird wail came from the lips of the figure and then panic seized the natives. Uttering screams of terror, they fled . . ."[51] *The Exhibitors' Times* praised its "scenic effects" and its "strong" climax.[52]

At least two of these moving pictures survive. In *The Haunted House* (Kalem, 1913), a crook named Spider overhears the "common superstition" that a ghost protects a

Figure 7.3 "Ham" (Lloyd V. Hamilton) and "Bud" (Bud Duncan) in *Lotta Coin's Ghost* (Kalem, 1915)

millionaire's home.[53] Nevertheless, he resolves to steal the family jewels. When he does, the family's little daughter has a tantrum, throwing things and pushing over a wardrobe. Frightened by what seems to be an unearthly spirit, Spider finds himself on the other side of his own gun.[54] Two years later, the popular comedy duo "Ham" (Lloyd V. Hamilton) and "Bud" (Bud Duncan) played "midnight marauders" in *Lotta Coin's Ghost* (Kalem, 1915).[55] While trying to steal Lotta's "billion dollar necklace," they encounter Lotta disguised as a spirit.[56] As the duo flee, Bud gets entangled in a sheet on a clothesline, making Ham believe the ghost is continuing to pursue him.[57]

Haunted Houses

In 1859, a newspaper in Ohio noted, "Almost every country-town or township is possessed of its 'haunted house'—some grim-looking, dilapidated building, which the neighbors firmly believe to be inhabited by ghosts."[58] Two decades later, a Chicago newspaper reported, "Fancy tales of haunted houses have been so often related and so often proven unfounded that the public generally has become incredulous in such matters."[59] Both points of view were accurate. Press accounts of "genuine" haunted houses were common.[60] Likewise, a number of journalists enjoyed exposing the natural causes behind alleged hauntings.[61] These tales included not only private residences, but also hotels and at least one asylum.[62]

In 1792, for example, the *New-Hampshire Spy* printed the story of a servant girl convicted of being pregnant out of wedlock. She blamed the ghosts at her employer's haunted house, as they scared her so much that she confided in a male servant. He "persuaded" her that spirits never appear when "*two people* slept together." In her defense, the girl announced, "I should never have lost my virtue, if it had not been for the fear of the ghosts."[63]

From Pliny the Younger's story *Haunted House* and Plautus's play *Mostellaria* to Horace Walpole's novel *The Castle of Otranto* (1764), haunted houses have provided regular architecture to ghostly narratives. In c. 1843, the British writer Thomas Hood wrote his enduring poem *The Haunted House*. It features the repeated stanza:

> O'er all their hung a shadow and a fear,
> A sense of mystery the spirit daunted,
> And said, as plain as whisper in the ear,
> The place is haunted!

During the second half of the nineteenth century, Hood's poem gained much fame in America, including in the form of an illustrated book published in 1896. To his poem can be added many American works, among them Poe's *The Fall of the House of Usher* (1839) and *The Haunted Palace* poem contained therein, as well as Margaret Verne's overlooked short story *The Haunted House* (1859).[64]

Haunted house films appeared in America as early as the first screenings of *The Devil's Castle/Le manoir du diable* (aka *The Infernal Palace*) in 1899, as well as *Haunted House*, a 150-foot-long obscurity offered for sale in America by F. M. Prescott in 1899.[65] Perhaps it was *The Devil's Castle* under another title, or perhaps it was another Méliès film, such as *Le Château hanté* (1897). More likely, though, it was Lubin's *The Haunted House* (1899), in which a character named Silas Hayseed stays at a hotel. Once he undresses, he sees a "ghost standing in the middle of the room." He implores the ghost not to hurt him. The ghost vanishes, but then "Satan appears from under the sheets and scares him . . ."[66]

Méliès distributed *Le Revenant* (1903) in America in 1903 under the title *The Apparition, or Mr. Jones' Comical Experience with a Ghost*.[67] One of the most charming ghost films of the period, it features a character disturbed by such sights as a candle that changes size and moves without human assistance.[68] That same year, Méliès's *The Inn Where No Man Rests/L'auberge du bon repos* (1903, distributed by Lubin as *He Couldn't Sleep in that Inn*) appeared in America. It also featured tricks involving a candlestick.[69] Then, in 1905, Méliès released *A Roadside Inn/L'hôtel des voyageurs de commerce* (1905, aka *A Road Side Inn*), in which men wearing sheets pretend to be ghosts so as to scare a drunk.

As with other kinds of trick moving pictures, American filmmakers were quick to appropriate Méliès's style. In 1900, American Mutoscope & Biograph released *Tramp in the Haunted House*, in which the title character's dinner at the spooky home goes through a "marvelous transformation."[70] That same year, Edison released *Uncle Josh in a Spooky Hotel*, in which a ghost "appears mysteriously and hits Josh a slap on the cheek." When he realizes he's dealing with the supernatural, Josh "grabs his things and rushes out of the room" in a "great fright."[71]

In 1907, Vitagraph released *The Haunted Hotel* (aka *The Haunted Hotel; or, The Strange Adventures of a Traveler*), which was directed by J. Stuart Blackton, the American filmmaker who, according to Anthony Slide, came closest to rivaling Méliès for special effects.[72]

Figure 7.4 Advertisement published in *The Billboard* on February 23, 1907.

During a storm, a traveler approaches a home, over which witches fly on broomsticks. The front of the house then transforms into the face of a goblin. Once inside, the traveler is "terror stricken at the weird incidents that follow." These include a knife cutting meat and bread of its own accord and a kettle pouring tea without assistance. After dinner, the room begins to rock back and forth, before it "spins round and round, over and over." Then the "huge head of an ogre appears. He gropes around the room and seizing the traveler in one of his huge, claw-like hands, whisks him out of the bed, clothes and all."[73]

The Haunted Hotel became, as Donald Crafton has determined, a "tremendous success."[74] *Billboard* called the film a "genuine 'screamer.'"[75] Years later, Blackton recalled, "What pride I took in carrying out all of the weird happenings in *The Haunted Hotel*! By means of a stop mechanism in the lens-shutter, I endowed heavy pieces of furniture with airy animation."[76] By May 1907, *Views and Film Index* reported that *The Haunted Hotel* was causing "particular comment" in London and Paris.[77]

That might well have been true, as Segundo de Chomón's film *La maison ensorcelée* (Pathé Frères, 1908) was an extremely close remake of Blackton's *The Haunted Hotel*.[78] The key difference is that Blackton's film featured only one traveler; Chomón's had three. The similarities were such that Pathé did not release Chomón's film in America, presumably due to concerns over potential infringement on Vitagraph's copyright. At any rate, Blackton's original remains an amazing accomplishment, ranking among the most entertaining films of the period and one of the most important haunted house films ever produced.

In 1909, Pathé Frères released yet another haunted house film reliant on cinematic tricks. Titled *The Bewitched Manor/Le manoir ensorcelé* (aka *Bewitched Manor House*), its plot had "wierd [sic] spooks" bothering travelers who take refuge in a deserted castle. "Grotesque spook faces" and "fierce looking animals" trouble them until "His Satanic Majesty" materializes. A "good fairy" appears, waving her wand and turning the animals into knights and the castle into a "most hospitable place."[79] Then, three years later, Pathé (under its C.G.P.C. label) released *The Haunted Room/La chambre ensorcelée* (1912), which featured stop motion effects by Emile Cohl. In the film, the occupant stays at a "weird hotel"; when he takes off his shoes, for example, they "dance on the floor in the most exciting manner."[80]

The most original of the later haunted house comedies in this period was *Colonel Heeza Liar, Ghost Breaker* (Pathé, 1915, aka *Colonel Heeza Liar–Ghost Breaker*), which relied on animation rather than live action. The *Pathé Weekly Bulletin* promised the film illustrated a "total disregard for the bounds of fact."[81] As a surviving copy makes clear, the split-reel cartoon is well executed and humorous, with the title character spending the night at Castle Clare.[82] Once the clock strikes midnight, banshees trouble the colonel to the point

Figure 7.5 This trade advertisement for *Colonel Heeza Liar, Ghost Breaker* (Pathé, 1915, aka *Colonel Heeza Liar–Ghost Breaker*) features artwork seen in the film.

he nearly dies of fright. *Moving Picture World* praised J. R. Bray's artwork, as well as the "tremendously amusing" story.[83] Within months, in a sign of the cartoon's success, Pathé released "Part Two" of *Colonel Heeza Liar, Ghost Breaker* (1915).[84]

Real haunted buildings and ruins were rare in dramatic films of the early cinema period. In Segundo de Chomón's *Haunted Castle/Château hanté* (Pathé Frères, 1908, which was advertised without the article *The*), two lost noblemen arrive at a crumbling castle, where they see an old witch. While they enter the ruins, a laughing madman in the dungeon peers at them through a window.[85] Journeying into dark passageways, the noblemen discover "horrible ghosts," and then more of the same when they fall into a dark cavern. At the climax of this 688-foot film, the duo rescue a young woman who is being "insulted" by a "crippled imp."[86]

The following year, in the split-reel film *The Haunted Castle/Les ruines du Château hanté* (Théophile Pathé, 1909), three suitors search for a beautiful woman who serves as the caretaker.[87] Each of them encounters ghosts, with two becoming so scared as to flee. But the third grabs the spirit, whose "unearthly garments fall away and the girl herself falls into [the suitor's] arms."[88] *Moving Picture World* praised the film's cinematography and its "picturesque views" of the castle.[89]

In 1911, Edison released *The Haunted Sentinel Tower* (1911), which the company had shot in Cuba. In it, a guide "trembles" when he gets nearer to the haunted building:

> Laughing at his superstition, [the film's two lovers] start in its direction, when a distant church clock chimes out the midnight hour and clearly upon the walls of the fortification can be seen the ghost of the tragic past. Silently, with fear, they watch these vague figures until they fade away from mortal view, locked in fond embrace. The guide then starts to tell them the story of this ill-fated pair, and here the present fades away into the past . . .[90]

Motography lauded the film's cinematography, its acting, and its "strikingly picturesque scenes."[91] Two years later, Edison released *The Haunted Bedroom* (1913), which starred Augustus Phillips. In it, a ghost guards his sister's treasure, which is hidden at an inn, rather than at a home.[92]

In most cases, haunted houses and other haunted locales turned out to be little more than the products of superstition.[93] For example, in Pathé's one-reel *The Haunted House* (1913), mysterious sounds and lights at the old home result from the friendly but secret meetings of a man and woman whose sons are enemies.[94] In *The Mystery of the Haunted Hotel* (Thanhouser, 1913), the "unmasked" ghost turns out to be the innkeeper's daughter, whose "mind had been unhinged by grief because of the death of the mother she dearly loved."[95]

Not dissimilar was *The Haunted House of Wild Isle* (Kalem, 1915), a two-reel mystery in which an author decides to investigate a spooky old home. The *Kalem Kalender* noted, "As he enters the building a picture falls from the wall. A rifle is shoved through a loophole. Kent drops just in time to escape being shot" by a crazy man who is presumed to be a ghost.[96] With help from his sweetheart, who costumes herself as a ghost, the culprit is finally captured. The *Moving Picture World* and the *New York Dramatic Mirror* praised the film, both drawing attention to its "sustained" use of suspense.[97]

Pranksters in film comedies played on fears of haunted houses to scare their friends and enemies.[98] In 1909, Edison released *'Tis Now the Very Witching Hour of Night* (aka

'Tis Now the Very Witching Time of Night) in which a man accepts a bet to sleep in a haunted house.[99] Led by a magician, the members of a club play tricks on him that would make "regular ghosts" seem "mild and ineffective."[100] The *New York Dramatic Mirror* believed its story was not told as "skillfully as [it] might have been," but its "trick work with the ghosts and visions is handled with good comedy effect."[101] Three years later, Gaston Méliès's *Ghosts at Circle X Camp* (1912) finds a cowboy taunting a "tenderfoot," who in turn dares his bully to sleep in the local haunted house. The tenderfoot dresses as a ghost and scares the bully from the house, after which he reveals his true identity.[102] "It will please and amuse," the *Moving Picture World* promised.[103]

Proving one's bravery to a sweetheart became the plotline of numerous haunted house films.[104] *How the Girls Got Even* (Champion, 1911) finds a trio of young women daring their boyfriends to stay in an old house, complete with ghosts (as played by the young women wearing "white robes").[105] Of *When Spirits Walk* (Frontier, 1913), *Moving Picture World* told readers, "A haunted house film which starts out in the conventional way, the girl agreeing to marry her lover if he will remain over night in the place."[106] And in *Courage of Sorts* (American, 1913), a young doctor agrees to stay in a haunted house after he learns his sweetheart's father intends to scare him with a "sheet and phosphorescent oil."[107] The "tables are turned" on the father "speedily, and in an amusing manner."[108]

Vitagraph's *The Ghost* (1914, aka *The Ghosts*), written by Mary H. O'Connor, became yet another film in this tradition. In it, Jim accepts a dare to sleep in a haunted house. Sleepwalking during the night, he buries his clothes, leaving him to claim the next day

Figure 7.6 *Courage of Sorts* (American, 1913).

that a ghost stole them. His sweetheart won't listen to his proposal of marriage until he explains what really happened.[109] *The Ghost Fakirs* (Starlight, 1915) featured the popular comedy duo "Heinie and Louie" agreeing to sleep in a haunted house in order to prove their bravery to their favorite lady; her preferred beau and his friends scare the duo by pretending to be spooks.[110] That same year, Vitagraph's one-reel *Ghosts and Flypaper* (1915) had a young man rid a house of fake ghosts in order to win his sweetheart's hand.[111] *Moving Picture World* called it a "rattling good" comedy.[112]

Drawing upon the same narrative tradition, as well as some nonfiction press accounts, *The Haunted House* (American, 1913) features a brave suitor uncovering a band of opium smugglers using a deserted home as a hideout.[113] Here the film incorporated what had become another repeated plot line, one that had been reported on a number of occasions in the nineteenth-century press: criminals or fugitives taking advantage of deserted and allegedly haunted homes.[114]

Edison's dramatic one-reeler *The House on the Hill* (1910) finds a "notorious gang" of counterfeiters not only occupying an old home, but attempting to accentuate its local reputation: one of the villains dons a white sheet to scare off potential trespassers.[115] *Beneath the Tower Ruins/Le trésor de Karnak* (Urban-Eclipse, 1911) had two persons wearing ghostly garb to frighten away interlopers while they searched for treasure.[116] Biograph's one-reel comedy *The Ghost* (1911), directed and starring Mack Sennett, offered a more complicated version of the story, with a series of three unrelated thieves pretending to be ghosts at a haunted house and scaring each other off as a result.[117]

In 1913, Warner's Features released *Trapped in the Castle of Mystery*, in which counterfeiters hide in "old Doromy Castle" and dress as ghosts to keep their activities secret.[118] Describing *The Ghost* (Victor Film Co., 1913), *Moving Picture World* called it, "The old, familiar 'haunted house' story," in which the lover (played by James Kirkwood) "makes a bet that he is not afraid to stay in the haunted dwelling over night. Of course, he discovers a den of thieves infesting the place, and there follows an exciting capture of the gang."[119]

In other cases, such as *The Haunted House* (Imp, 1911), characters masqueraded as ghosts in old houses in order to decrease their property value.[120] Here was a story line that had also appeared in several nonfiction press accounts in the nineteenth century.[121] In *The Ghost of a Bargain* (Rex, 1912), a "would-be renter" plays "spook in order to diminish the apparent value of the house." *Moving Picture World* complained that the film was "conducted a bit too farcically to be convincing . . . but it has some good moments."[122] Lubin's *A Deal in Real Estate* (1914) features a home-buyer who disguises himself as a ghost in an empty house in order to get a better price.[123] That same year, Edison released *A Terror of the Night* (1914), with Charles Ogle and Mary Fuller. Its fake ghost is a real-estate agent hoping to purchase a deserted home.[124] Then, in 1915, Lubin's three-reel *The Gray Horror* finds a scoundrel hiring a crook to "nightly haunt" an estate he wishes to buy, all in an effort to scare the owners into selling.[125]

Of all the haunted house films of the early cinema period, however, the most fascinating might have been one without a ghost, real or fake. Based on J. A. Mitchell's 1902 novel of the same name, *The Pines of Lory* (Edison, 1914) has two survivors of a shipwreck (played by Marc McDermott and Miriam Nesbitt) drift through dense fog and land on an island. There they find a "mysterious" home. It is "fully provisioned," but unoccupied save for a dead man "sitting upright on a settee" in the garden.[126] Nearby is a "grave which he had evidently dug for himself."[127] They bury the corpse and build a raft to escape, but one survivor is "carried out to sea" while the other washes back onto the island and suffers from "madness" until both are eventually rescued.[128] *Motography* told readers that there was a "strange magnetism about the picture."[129]

At roughly the same time, there were an increasing number of other onscreen homes that were not haunted, but instead equipped with all manner of mysterious mechanical contrivances.[130] Consider *The House of Mystery/Le mani ignote* (Kleine-Cines, 1913, aka *By Unseen Hands*).[131] The title home in the two-reel detective story is a site where "many strange things happen; the walls drop back, exposing mysterious recesses under the ground, [and] the floors drop out from under them and they are precipitated into a dismal pit . . ."[132] And when reviewing *Count Zarka/Grev Zarkas Bande* (Great Northern, 1914), *Moving Picture World* observed its "trite machinery of hidden doors, unsuspecting holes in the floor, and other fittings of the kind so often seen of late in castles of rich villains."[133]

Spiritualism

By comparison to ghost stories and haunted houses, Spiritualism was a relatively modern phenomenon. As Mary Farrell Bednarowski has noted, Spiritualist circles formed in every American state within several years of initial press coverage of the Fox sisters in 1848.[134] Spiritualism's popularity continued unabated until the early twentieth century.

Nonfiction literature on the subject was abundant, in the form of books and articles that ranged from the skeptical to the supportive. To some, it was a modern form of witchcraft; to others, it was a new kind of science. Indeed, the American Society for Psychical Research was founded in Boston in 1884 before relocating its headquarters to New York in 1905. Elana Gomel writes that Spiritualism's

> converts included Alfred Russel Wallace, the co-discoverer with Darwin of natural selection, Elizabeth Barrett Browning, Harriet Beecher Stowe, Andrew Lang, Cesare Lombroso, John Addington Symonds, and Sir Arthur Conan Doyle, who characterized the atmosphere of the time as 'some psychic cloud descending from on high, and showing itself to those people who were susceptible.'[135]

This is to say nothing of thousands of others. In 1857, a correspondent to the *Chicago Tribune* attended a séance given by one of the Fox sisters. He confidently announced that the manifestations he experienced simply "could not have been made by any person in the room."[136]

By contrast, the sheer volume of articles referring to Spiritualism as a fraud would be hard to catalog. Consider the following story from Boston in 1875:

> Mrs. Seaver, a medium at 33 Eliot Street, held a seance recently, at which several spirits were materialized. Among them was a little infant, whom a woman in the audience immediately recognized as a little one whom she had lost several months before. But, alas for Mrs. S, there was a young man from a rival shop in the company, who 'went for' this materialized baby to discover it to be nothing but a rag baby. Then there was trouble in that circle, the conductor of the show smote the inquisitive young man on the ear, and a general scene of confusion ensued, necessitating the presence of an officer to preserve the peace.[137]

"Latterly the ghost market has been unusually dull," the *New York Times* wrote in 1877, "owing, possibly, to the repeated exposures of materializing mediums."[138] The following year, the *New York Herald* was more blunt, claiming, "Spiritualism in theory is a pretty thing, but in practice it is generally absurd."[139]

Regardless of one's views on the subject, Spiritualism had a major impact on ghost literature of the mid-nineteenth century, as can be seen in such British short stories as Mary Elizabeth Braddon's *The Cold Embrace* (1860) and Vernon Lee's *Oke of Okehurst* (1886, aka *A Phantom Lover*).[140] Its influence can also be felt in the ghost stories of American authors like Annie Trumbull Slosson and Mary E. Wilkins Freeman.[141] And then there were new literary characters, not only mediums, but also Spiritualistic investigators, as in Conan Doyle's short story *Playing with Fire* (1900) and Algernon Blackwood's *John Silence* (1908), as well as in American writer Hamlin Garland's novels *The Tyranny of the Dark* (1905) and *The Shadow World* (1908). In a number of cases, including Richard Harding Davis's novel *Vera, the Medium* (1908), Spiritualists were exposed as frauds.

And so it is hardly surprising that this latter-day and performance-based religion—one that not only influenced literature, but also had a major impact in the theatre—would become the subject of numerous early films. In 1899, the Edison Manufacturing Company distributed the Vitagraph-produced *A Visit to the Spiritualist* (aka *Visit to the Spiritualist*).[142] *The Phonoscope* reported that exhibitors "acknowledged" it as the "funniest of all moving magic films."[143] In the film, a Spiritualist mesmerizes a customer, whose handkerchief grows in size to become a ghost after he drops it on the floor. According to a catalog entry, the "scene closes by numerous ghosts and hobgoblins appearing and disappearing . . ."[144]

That same year, Lubin distributed *Visit to a Spiritualist* (1900), which might have been a different production with a similar plot. Here again a Spiritualist calls forth ghosts for a customer. A handkerchief turns into a ghost, but a catalog synopsis suggests other aspects of the film are different than the Edison release.[145] This was in addition to American Mutoscope & Biograph's comedy *How the Medium Materialized Elder Simpkin's Wife* (1899).[146]

Two Méliès films distributed in America as early as 1903 also addressed the topic of Spiritualism, but less overtly than their predecessors. *The Up-to-Date Spiritualism/Spiritisme abracadabrant* (aka *Up-To-Date Spiritualism*) was nothing more than a man "entering a drawing room inhabited by spirits," in which his hat and coat keep returning to his body and furniture moved of its own accord.[147] *A Spiritualistic Photographer/Le portrait spirite* (aka *Spiritualistic Photographer*), which Lubin distributed as *The Spiritualist in Photography*, features a character who is able to make images appear on a sheet of white paper without the use of a camera.[148]

In 1906, *Views and Film Index* published the following description of Méliès's *A Spiritualist Meeting/Le fantôme d'Alger* (1906), which offered tricks somewhat closer to the subject area:

> The meeting is composed of five women, three men and the conductor of the seance. The members of the company are told to place their hands upon a table and when they have done so, they find they are unable to follow instructions to lift their hands from it, for the table seems to adhere to their hands and rises when they lift them. Mysterious disappearances are also shown and also some curious manipulations of ethereal bodies.[149]

As was so often the case in his devil, witch, and ghost films, Méliès here relied on special effects in an effort to create humor.

Serious depictions of Spiritualism were infrequent. In *Man* (Yankee, 1911), the superintendent of a steel plant attempts to kill a Spiritualist, but stops when an "apparition" of himself from an earlier life appears.[150] Then, in *The Blood-Seedling*, a three-reel film released by Selig Polyscope in 1915, a "spiritual seance" uncovers the identity of a murderer and the location of a victim's corpse.[151] Its plot bears similarities to Anna Hoyt's short story *The Ghost of Little Jacques* (1863) and J. S. King's *A Black Specter* (1892).

Comedies that treated Spiritualism as living up to its claims were equally rare. Based upon a period synopsis, it seems that the medium in *Brown's Seance* (Keystone, 1912) has powers that allow her to know one of the male characters has been unfaithful to his wife.[152] Likewise, synopses suggest that Eddie (Eddie Lyons) might have good reason to be terrified in *When the Spirits Moved* (Nestor, 1915). Not only is he scared during Dr. Bunk's séance, but he is also frightened that night when the two share a bed which "pitches and jerks."[153] More than anything else, though, Eddie becomes afraid of a "ghost" that turns out to be his sleepwalking sweetheart.

Figure 7.7 Trade advertisement for *Spiritualism Exposed* (Pan American, 1913, aka *Spiritualism Exposed!*). Published in *Moving Picture World* on February 15, 1913.

In general, the cinema of the nickelodeon era and beyond focused on the fraudulence in Spiritualism, including in at least two films promoted as being nonfiction. Gaumont's 200-foot-long *The Spirit/Esprit, es-tu là?* (1908) "exposed" the "mysteries" of a Spiritualist meeting, showing how the "entrance of the apparition and the awe of the victims is ludicrous in the extreme."[154] Then, *Spiritualism Exposed* (Pan American, 1913, aka *Spiritualism*

Exposed!) featured famed medium Eva Ray (who had worked as a "trance medium at least as far back as 1906") and "Professor" Fred Curtis in three reels that "laid bare" the "whole bag of tricks" used by mediums.[155] According to *Billboard*, *Spiritualism Exposed* had a "heart-interest story" interwoven into its plot, intermingling fiction with nonfiction.[156]

Fraudulent séances also appeared in numerous comedy films, sometimes resulting from pranksters. In *Spiritualistic Séance/Une expérience de spiritisme* (Pathé Frères, 1908, aka *The Spiritualistic Seance*), a soldier pretends to be a ghost in order to scare away a séance circle so that he can hug his sweetheart.[157] In Mack Sennett's *Won through a Medium* (Biograph, 1911), Nellie's lover hides during a séance in order to frighten the man that her family hopes she will marry.[158] Similarly, *Love and Spirits* (Joker, 1914) has Ernie (Ernie Shields) winning permission to marry Betty (Betty Schade) by scaring her father during and after a bogus séance.[159]

Billy's Seance (Imp, 1911) finds its title character pranked by his friends after he visits a Spiritualist named Madame Ex.[160] Later Billy holds his own fake séance, electrifying the table and making his friends shake wildly. When police arrive on the scene, they also receive shocks from the table.[161] The young title character of *Bobby "Some" Spiritualist/Bébé fait du spiritisme* (Gaston Méliès, 1914) plays a joke by tying strings to some of the furniture before his parents send him to bed and hold their séance. Sneaking into the darkened room, Bobby pulls the strings, making the tables move and vases fall onto his parents' heads.[162]

In other comedies, professional Spiritualists were exposed as swindlers. *The Spirit Hand* (Thanhouser, 1911) featured charlatans who tried to con a widow out of her money by having her "dead husband's hand" materialize during a séance.[163] *Taming the Spooks/Checco e Cocò spiritisti* (Cines, 1913) features the comedy duo "Stout and Thynne" as con men who get arrested after their fakery is revealed.[164] *An Interrupted Seance* (Reliance, 1914, aka *The Interrupted Seance*) featured future film director Tod Browning as a broke actor who decides with his friend to give a fake séance in order to make money. When the

Figure 7.8 *The Spook Raisers* (Kalem, 1915).

ghost rapping causes plaster to fall onto the landlord's head in the apartment below, the landlord disrupts the proceedings and exposes the fraud.[165]

Running away from a police officer at the start of *The Spook Raisers* (Kalem, 1915), the comedy team of "Ham and Bud" find themselves hiding at Madame De Shiver's séance.[166] The duo quickly realizes the medium is a trickster and purloin some of her Spiritualism paraphernalia. An intertitle indicates "Ham and Bud" are "All set for the spirit trade." Their newspaper advertisement announces that Professor Ham, a "mystical medium," will work for five dollars "per spook." But chaos reigns at his first séance, which brings forth a police officer.[167]

Conclusion

As the nickelodeon period ended, the popularity of ghost stories extended to the multi-reel "feature" film. In 1914, H. B. Warner reprised his Broadway role of Warren Jarvis for Lasky's five-reel film adaptation of *The Ghost Breaker*. Before its setting shifts to America, the comedy takes place in part at an allegedly haunted castle in Spain. Together with his African-American servant Rusty (J. W. Burton), who provides comic relief, Jarvis reveals the castle ghosts are fakes, led by a Duke trying to scare away interlopers so that he can search for a hidden treasure.[168] *Moving Picture World* praised the film, noting, "Humor, pathos, thrills, genuine melodrama, novelty place this feature in the first flight of today's American-made pictures."[169]

Drawing upon the popular 1905 novel by Meredith Nicholson, Selig Polyscope produced a five-reel version of *The House of a Thousand Candles* in 1915 with actor Harry Mestayer. Its story tells of a nephew who inherits his uncle's manor house, but only if he follows the dictates of the will, which require him to live alone in the home for one year with only one companion. He must also search for one million dollars in hidden securities. The *Exhibitors Film Exchange* responded to the elaborate feature by claiming "it proves that secret passageways, gloomy vaults, and hidden panels are not exclusively confined to medieval castles!"[170] According to *Motography*, "The odd and bizarre effect given by the arrangement of hundreds and hundreds of tallow candles" on the library set was "indescribable."[171] And *Motion Picture News* believed the film preserved the "eerie atmosphere" of the novel.[172]

Selig Polyscope also produced a five-reel adaptation of Mary Roberts Rinehart's novel *The Circular Staircase* (1908) in 1915. Directed by Edward LeSaint, the film featured Guy Oliver, Eugenie Besserer, and Stella Razeto.[173] *Motion Picture News* described the film as follows: "A shot in the night, three women rushing about to discover the cause, a lifeless body at the foot of the Circular Staircase, the disappearance of two men without apparent reason—and you have all the elements vital to a theme in which Poe would have reveled."[174] At the conclusion, the woman who leased the country home discovers a secret room and a man who is supposed to be dead. He flees through a secret passageway while her screams bring a detective to the scene.[175] *Motography* promised readers that the film featured "much mystery and many grotesque happenings."[176] And *Moving Picture World* expressed admiration for the minimal use of intertitles to convey a complicated story with clarity and still manage to withhold the solution of the mystery to the "very last moment."[177]

When *Variety* mentioned that ghost photoplays were "all the rage" in 1910, it was correct. In many respects, the statement had been true since the beginning of the cinema. However much films produced during and after the nickelodeon period relied

Figure 7.9 Trade advertisement for *The Circular Staircase* (Selig Polyscope, 1915), published in *Motion Picture News* on September 11, 1915.

on increasingly complicated narrative structures, the drive toward the supernatural explained was as strong as it had been in earlier years. In that respect, *The Circular Staircase* was little different than *The Exposed Seance* (American Mutoscope & Biograph, 1900) had been fifteen years earlier. Its brief tale featured a Spiritualist calling forth a ghost in a spirit cabinet. As a catalog synopsis described, a policeman uses a lantern to reveal the ghost to be a fake.[178] It was all just a trick.

Notes

1. A small amount of footage from *The Ghost Story* exists at the Library of Congress by way of a paper print deposit.
2. "The Ghost Story," *Views and Film Index*, September 14, 1907, 6.
3. See, for example, "A Ghost," *Richmond Examiner* (Richmond, Virginia), September 27, 1862; "A Ghost in Jail," *Cincinnati Daily Gazette* (Cincinnati, Ohio), March 13, 1875.
4. "The Ghost," *Spooner's Vermont Journal* (Windsor, Vermont), March 14, 1825.
5. "Ghost Story," *Hampshire Gazette* (Northampton, Massachusetts), June 25, 1828.
6. "The Cock-Lane Ghost," *Boston Intelligencer*, June 12, 1819; "Extraordinary Ghost Story," *Centinel of Freedom* (Newark, New Jersey), September 19, 1854.
7. "Spectral Vision," *Albany Argus* (Albany, New York), February 6, 1846.

8. Advertisement, *The City Gazette* (Charleston, South Carolina), October 15, 1796.
9. "*The Ghost: A True Story*," *The Donaldsonville Chief* (Donaldsonville, Louisiana), May 30, 1874, 1.
10. Elias Savada (ed.), *The American Film Institute Catalog of Motion Pictures Produced in the United States: Film Beginnings, 1893–1910* (Lanham, Maryland: Scarecrow Press, 1995), 407.
11. "*Another Ghost*," *Variety*, October 29, 1910, 14.
12. "Thanhouser: *The Mystery of the Haunted Hotel*," *Reel Life*, October 18, 1913, 9.
13. Savada, 68.
14. *Picture Catalogue* (New York: American Mutoscope & Biograph, November 1902), 70. Available in *A Guide to Motion Picture Catalogs by American Producers and Distributors, 1894–1908: A Microfilm Edition* (New Brunswick: Rutgers University Press, 1985), Reel 2.
15. "Film Reviews," *Views and Film Index*, September 21, 1907, 5.
16. "*Shooting in the Haunted Woods*," *The Billboard*, January 15, 1910, 17.
17. "*When Ghost Meets Ghost*," *The Billboard*, April 12, 1913, 47.
18. "*The Tyrant Feudal Lord*," *Moving Picture World*, July 25, 1908, 69.
19. "*The Sword and the King*," *The Billboard*, July 24, 1909, 43. A small amount of footage from this film is archived at the Library of Congress by way of a paper print deposit.
20. "*The Spectre*," *Views and Film Index*, July 4, 1908, 10. While this synopsis indicates that the cobbler's apprentice commits suicide, a critic in *Moving Picture World* (April 17, 1909) claimed the print he viewed ended with the apprentice on the road, leaving him to complain that the film "doesn't seem to tell the whole story" (478).
21. "*A Timely Apparition*," *New York Dramatic Mirror*, May 22, 1909, 17.
22. "*The Ghost's Warning*," *Edison Kinetogram*, January 15, 1912, 4. An illustrated short story version of this film, written by Louis Reeves Harrison, appeared in *The Motion Picture Story Magazine*, December 1911, 97–105.
23. Louis Reeves Harrison, "*The Ghost of Granleigh*," *Moving Picture World*, August 30, 1913, 943.
24. Louis Reeves Harrison, "*The Man in the White Cloak*," *Moving Picture World*, May 31, 1913, 7. An eight-minute fragment of *The Man in the White Cloak* is archived at the Danish Film Institute.
25. "*The Spirit and the Clay*," *New York Dramatic Mirror*, May 6, 1914, 39.
26. See, for example, "Thrilling Ghost Story," *Centinel of Freedom* (Newark, New Jersey), December 4, 1860. See also Mary Kyle Dallas, "The Haunted House," *Gallipolis Journal* (Gallipolis, Ohio), February 6, 1868, 1.
27. "*A Terrible Night*," *Moving Picture World*, February 12, 1912, 716; "*The Ghost of Sulphur Mountain*," *Moving Picture World*, April 6, 1912, 66; "*Ghosts* (Essanay)," *Moving Picture World*, 53; "*The Ghost*," *Moving Picture World*, May 2, 1914, 673; "*The Ghost of Smiling Jim*," *Motography*, December 19, 1914, 867. An illustrated short story version of *The Ghost of Sulphur Mountain* appeared in *The Motion Picture Story Magazine*, April 1912, 17–23. An illustrated short story version of *The Ghost of Smiling Jim* appeared in *Motion Picture Magazine*, January 1915, 83–8. A copy of *The Ghost* (Pathé, 1914) is archived at the George Eastman Museum.
28. "*Belelia's 'At Home,'*" *The Billboard*, March 2, 1912, 33; "*The Skivvy's Ghost*," *Moving Picture News*, February 17, 1912, 42; "*The Haunted Bachelor*," *Moving Picture World*, September 7, 1912, 1008; "*Sweedie's Suicide*," *Motography*, January 16, 1915, 103.
29. "*The Ghost of the Vaults*," *Moving Picture World*, June 24, 1911, 1462.
30. "*The Ghost of the Vaults*," *Moving Picture News*, June 17, 1911, 23.
31. "*The Ghost of the Vaults*," *Billboard*, June 17, 1911, 50.
32. "Bride Imagines Herself Haunted by Ghost of Suicide," *Universal Weekly*, November 1, 1913, 26.
33. "*Phantoms*," *Moving Picture World*, November 22, 1913, 868.
34. "*The Mystery of Carter Breene*," *Moving Picture World*, December 11, 1915, 2082.
35. Though not an intentional prank, *The Haunted Hat* (Lubin, 1909) featured the title object moving mysteriously down the street. Eventually a kitten emerges from underneath it. See "*The Haunted Hat*," *The Billboard*, August 28, 1909, 14.

36. "*Tricked into Giving His Consent*," *Moving Picture World*, October 10, 1908, 287–8.
37. "*The Beechwood Ghost*," *Moving Picture World*, October 1, 1910, 772.
38. A copy of *The Haunted Rocker* is archived at the British Film Institute. An earlier example of a ghostly rocking chair can be found in the short story *My Grand Mother's Ghost*. Originally published in *Blackwood's Magazine*, it was reprinted in the *Clearfield Republican* (Clearfield, Pennsylvania), January 30, 1861, 1.
39. "*The Haunted Rocker*," *New York Dramatic Mirror*, April 3, 1912, 30. Another example of someone pretending to be a ghost in order to gain approval for the union of young lovers appears in *The Ghost of the White Lady* (Great Northern, 1914). See "Imported Film at Tivoli," *Seattle Times*, April 14, 1914, 12.
40. "*Bill Taken for a Ghost*," *The Billboard*, November 4, 1911, 28.
41. "Guest Shoots Host, Mistaking Him for Ghost," *Universal Weekly*, January 17, 1914, 30.
42. "*Mulligan's Ghost*," *Moving Picture World*, October 24, 1914, 534.
43. "*The Castle Ghosts*," *Moving Picture World*, June 6, 1908, 497; "*The Haunted Bridge*," *Moving Picture World*, May 8, 1909, 608; "*Mammy's Ghost*," *Film Index*, March 4, 1911, 15–16; "Amusements This Week in Augusta," *Augusta Chronicle* (Augusta, Georgia), September 6, 1914; "*The Spirit of the Bell*," *Reel Life*, March 20, 1915, 20. A copy of *The Spirit of the Bell* is archived at the Library of Congress.
44. Clarence J. Caine, "Conspirators Plan to Rob Zudora," *Motography*, February 6, 1915, 303–4; Neil G. Caward, "*The Exploits of Elaine*," *Motography*, April 3, 1915, 526–7.
45. "*Another's Ghost*," *Moving Picture World*, November 5, 1910, 1056.
46. "*Baby's Ghost*," *Moving Picture News*, February 10, 1912, 43.
47. "*The Ghost in Uniform*," *Moving Picture World*, March 8, 1913, 997.
48. "Haunting Spirit Proves to be Sick Pig," *Universal Weekly*, April 11, 1914, 21.
49. "*The Skull*," *Vitagraph Life Portrayals*, February 1913, 11.
50. "*The Ghost of the Hacienda*," *Motography*, September 20, 1913, 211.
51. Beatrice Barton, "*The Ghost of the Hacienda*," *Photoplay Magazine*, October 1913, 81.
52. "*The Ghost of the Hacienda*," *Exhibitors' Times*, September 13, 1913, 18.
53. "*The Haunted House*," *Kalem Kalendar*, April 15, 1913, 11.
54. A copy of *The Haunted House* is archived at the British Film Institute.
55. "*Lotta Coin's Ghost*," *Moving Picture World*, May 8, 1915, 899.
56. "*Lotta Coin's Ghost*," *Kalem Kalendar*, April 1915, 25.
57. A copy of *Lotta Coin's Ghost* is archived at the British Film Institute.
58. George Arnold, "An Hour with a Ghost," *The Weekly Portage Sentinel* (Ravenna, Ohio), October 26, 1859, 1.
59. "A Haunted House," *Daily Inter Ocean* (Chicago, Illinois), June 20, 1877, 3.
60. See, for example, "The Haunted House," *Dutchess Observer* (Poughkeepsie, New York), August 31, 1825, 4; "A Haunted House," *Boston Commercial Gazette*, May 3, 1830, 1; "New-Jersey Dance of Devils," *Commercial Advertiser* (New York, New York), November 8, 1834, 2; "A Haunted House," *Cincinnati Daily Enquirer* (Cincinnati, Ohio), March 9, 1869, 4; "A Very Much Haunted House in Indiana," *Centinel of Freedom* (Newark, New Jersey), July 23, 1872, 3; "That Haunted House," *Portland Daily Press* (Portland, Maine), February 13, 1874, 2; "The County at Large," *Boston Daily Advertiser*, April 8, 1878, 1.
61. "The Haunted House," *Hampshire Gazette* (Northampton, Massachusetts), December 23, 1840, 3; "The Haunted House—The Cat-Astrophe," *The Daily Dispatch* (Richmond, Virginia), August 24, 1852, 1; "The Haunted House in Astoria," *The Evening Post* (New York, New York), November 22, 1858, 3.
62. "A Tale of Terror," *Columbian Register* (New Haven, Connecticut), November 29, 1862; "A Tale of Terror," *The Star of the North* (Bloomsburg, Pennsylvania), October 11, 1865, 1;

"Another Haunted House," *Cincinnati Daily Times* (Cincinnati, Ohio), March 5, 1873, 1; "The Haunted House," *The Commercial Advertiser* (New York, New York), August 18, 1873, 1.
63. "Danger of Haunted Houses," *New-Hampshire Spy* (Portsmouth, New Hampshire), May 5, 1792.
64. Margaret Verne, "*The Haunted House*," *Ballou's Pictorial Drawing-Room Companion*, September 24, 1859, 204. Verne was a pseudonym used by Josephine Slocum Hunt.
65. *Supplement No. 3, New Films* (New York, F. M. Prescott, November 20, 1899), unpaginated. Available in *A Guide to Motion Picture Catalogs by American Producers and Distributors, 1894–1908: A Microfilm Edition*, Reel 1.
66. *Lubin's Films* (Philadelphia: Lubin, 1908), 59. Available in *A Guide to Motion Picture Catalogs by American Producers and Distributors, 1894–1908: A Microfilm Edition*, Reel 3.
67. *Supplement No. 6, Geo. Méliès of Paris* (New York: Star Films, 1903). Available in *A Guide to Motion Picture Catalogs by American Producers and Distributors, 1894–1908: A Microfilm Edition*, Reel 4.
68. A copy of *The Apparition, or Mr. Jones' Comical Experience with a Ghost* appears under the title *Le Revenant* on the DVD boxed set *Georges Méliès: First Wizard of Cinema* (Los Angeles: Flicker Alley, 2008).
69. *The Inn Where No Man Rests* is available on the DVD boxed set *Georges Méliès: First Wizard of Cinema*.
70. *Picture Catalogue* (New York: American Mutoscope & Biograph, November 1902), 69.
71. *Edison Films, No. 105* (Orange, New Jersey: Edison Manufacturing Company, July 1901), 87. Available in *A Guide to Motion Picture Catalogs by American Producers and Distributors, 1894–1908: A Microfilm Edition*, Reel 1. A copy of *Uncle Josh in a Spooky Hotel* is archived in the Paper Print Collection at the Library of Congress.
72. Anthony Slide, *Early American Cinema*, Revised Edition (Metuchen, New Jersey: Scarecrow Press, 1994), 14. *The Haunted Hotel* is archived at the British Film Institute, the George Eastman Museum, and the Library of Congress.
73. "*The Haunted Hotel* (Vitagraph)," *Views and Film Index*, February 23, 1907, 8.
74. Donald Crafton, *Before Mickey: The Animated Film, 1898–1928* (Chicago: University of Chicago Press, 1993), 13.
75. "Greater New York News," *Billboard*, March 2, 1907, 6.
76. "A Glimpse Into the Past," *Moving Picture World*, March 10, 1917, 1527.
77. "Trade Notes," *Views and Film Index*, May 11, 1907, 4. See also Crafton, 16–20.
78. A copy of *La Maison Ensorcelée* is available on the DVD *Segundo de Chomón, el cine de la fantasia* (Barcelona: Cameo Media S.L., 2010).
79. "Bewitched Manor House," *Moving Picture World*, July 17, 1909, 101. A copy of *The Bewitched Manor* (aka *Bewitched Manor House*) is archived at the Centre national du cinéma et de l'image animée (CNC).
80. "*The Haunted Room*," *Moving Picture World*, January 6, 1912, 62. A copy of *The Haunted Room* is archived at the Centre national du cinéma et de l'image animée (CNC).
81. "Colonel Heeza Liar–Ghost Breaker," *Pathé Weekly Bulletin*, October 7, 1915, 6.
82. A copy of *Colonel Heeza Liar, Ghost Breaker* is archived at the British Film Institute.
83. "Colonel Heeza Liar, Ghost Breaker," *Moving Picture World*, February 13, 1915, 986.
84. "Colonel Heeza Liar–Ghost Breaker (Part Two)," *Pathé Weekly Bulletin*, October 14, 1915, 5.
85. "Haunted Castle," *Views and Film Index*, May 9, 1908, 11.
86. "Haunted Castle," *Moving Picture World*, May 9, 1908, 424–5.
87. *The American Film Institute Catalog of Motion Pictures Produced in the United States: Film Beginnings, 1893–1910*, edited by Elias Savada (Lanham, Maryland: Scarecrow Press, 1995), speculates that *Haunted Castle* (1908) and *The Haunted Castle* (1909) might be the same film (p. 448). This is incorrect. A copy of *The Haunted Castle* (Théophile Pathé, 1909) is archived at the Centre national du cinéma et de l'image animée (CNC).

88. "*The Haunted Castle*," *Moving Picture World*, November 27, 1909, 760.
89. Ibid., 760.
90. "*The Haunted Sentinel Tower*," *Edison Kinetogram*, May 1, 1911, 12–13.
91. "*The Haunted Sentinel Tower*," *Motography*, May 1911, 95–6.
92. A copy of *The Haunted Bedroom* is archived at the British Film Institute.
93. Other examples are *The Devil's Signature* (Essanay, 1914), in which one room is said to be haunted, and *The Haunted Attic* (Lubin, 1915). See "Mystery Film Adapted from Munsey Tale," *Motography*, September 5, 1914, 327–8; "*The Haunted Attic*," *Moving Picture World*, April 17, 1915, 443, 446.
94. "*The Haunted House*," *Moving Picture World*, July 26, 1913, 454.
95. "News of Photoplays and Photoplayers," *Burlington Free Press* (Burlington, Vermont), December 29, 1913, 10.
96. "*The Haunted House of Wild Isle*," *Kalem Kalendar*, May 1915, 33.
97. "*The Haunted House of Wild Isle*," *Moving Picture World*, May 15, 1915, 1071; "*The Haunted House of Wild Isle*," *New York Dramatic Mirror*, April 7, 1915, 33. In 101 Bison's two-reel *The Mystery Woman* (1915), an allegedly "crazy girl" lives in the local "haunted house." See "*The Mystery Woman*," *Moving Picture World*, January 23, 1915, 559.
98. See, for example, Harry Graham, "A Ghost Story," *Flag of Our Union*, August 9, 1856, 256.
99. A 22 mm Home Kinetoscope print of *'Tis Now the Very Witching Hour of Night* is archived at the Thomas Edison National Historical Park.
100. "*'Tis Now the [Very] Witching Hour of Night*," *Film Index*, September 25, 1909, 5.
101. "*'Tis Now the Very Wtiching Time of Night*," *New York Dramatic Mirror*, September 25, 1909, 17.
102. "*Ghosts at Circle X Camp*," *Moving Picture World*, June 1, 1912, 856.
103. "*Ghosts at Circle X Camp*," *Moving Picture World*, June 29, 1912, 1226.
104. A similar plot had earlier appeared in the newspaper story "A Ghost Chasing a Ghost," *Washington Reporter* (Washington, Pennsylvania), January 5, 1859. *The Undertaker's Daughter* (Lubin, 1915) echoed the stories told in the films described in the main text, though instead of a haunted house, two young suitors stay in the undertaker's workshop all night, one inside a coffin and the other sitting beside it. See "*The Undertaker's Daughter*," *Moving Picture World*, May 1, 1915, 782.
105. "*How the Girls Got Even*," *Moving Picture News*, August 5, 1911, 22.
106. "*When Spirits Walk*," *Moving Picture World*, November 1, 1913, 497.
107. "American: *Courage of Sorts*," *Reel Life*, October 4, 1913, 16. A copy of *Courage of Sorts* is archived at the Library of Congress.
108. "*Courage of Sorts*," *Moving Picture World*, October 18, 1913, 265.
109. "*The Ghost*," *Vitagraph Life Portrayals*, November 1914, 33.
110. "*The Ghost Fakirs*," *Moving Picture World*, May 22, 1915, 1338. The title of this film is likely a pun on *The Ghost Breaker*.
111. "*Ghosts and Flypaper*," *Vitagraph Bulletin*, November 1915, 45.
112. "*Ghosts and Flypaper*," *Moving Picture World*, December 4, 1915, 1852.
113. "American: *The Haunted House*," *Reel Life*, October 25, 1913, 15.
114. See, for example, "Supposed Haunted House–An Officer Arrests a Ghost," *Providence Evening Press* (Providence, Rhode Island), July 27, 1860, 2; "A Haunted House," *Charleston Daily News* (Charleston, South Carolina), September 16, 1869; "Catching a Ghost: A True Story," *Nashville Union and American* (Nashville, Tennessee), August 2, 1871.
115. "*The House on the Hill*," *Edison Kinetogram*, July 1, 1910, 7–8.
116. "*Beneath the Tower Ruins*," *Moving Picture World*, April 29, 1911, 957.
117. "*The Ghost*," *Moving Picture World*, August 5, 1911, 292. A copy of this film is archived at the Museum of Modern Art, New York City.
118. "*Trapped in the Castle of Mystery*," *Moving Picture World*, December 13, 1913, 1340.

119. "*The Ghost,*" *Moving Picture World*, August 23, 1913, 845.
120. "*The Haunted House* (Imp)," *Moving Picture World*, August 26, 1911, 548.
121. See, for example, "Curious Trial," *The Columbian* (New York, New York), August 26, 1813, 3; "A Haunted House," *The Times-Picayune* (New Orleans, Louisiana), February 21, 1843, 2; "Haunted House," *The National Aegis* (Worcester, Massachusetts), June 24, 1857, 1; "Catching a Ghost Alive," *Salt Lake Tribune* (Salt Lake City, Utah), April 21, 1877.
122. "*The Ghost of a Bargain,*" *Moving Picture World*, September 21, 1912, 1178.
123. "*A Deal in Real Estate,*" *Moving Picture World*, March 28, 1914, 1695.
124. "*A Terror of the Night,*" *New York Dramatic Mirror*, May 27, 1914, 42.
125. "*The Gray Horror,*" *Motography*, May 15, 1915, 801.
126. Advertisement, *New York Dramatic Mirror*, October 28, 1914, 36. A copy of *The Pines of Lory* is archived at the Museum of Modern Art, New York City.
127. "Atmosphere of Mystery Wraps Story," *Motography*, October 24, 1914, 565.
128. "*The Pines of Lory,*" *Moving Picture World*, October 31, 1914, 674.
129. "Atmosphere of Mystery Wraps Story," 565.
130. In addition to the examples given in the main text, mysterious houses also appeared in such films as *The Mystery of Wickham Hall* (Powers, 1914), *The House of Darkness* (Lubin, 1914), *The Mystery of Grayson Hall* (Eclair American, 1914), *The Affair of the Deserted House* (Kalem, 1915), and *The House of Fear* (Pathé, 1915), as well as in the serial *The Black Box* (Universal, 1915). See "*The Mystery of Wickham Hall,*" *Motion Picture News*, July 4, 1914, 47; "*The House of Darkness,*" *New York Dramatic Mirror*, July 15, 1914; "*The Mystery of Grayson Hall,*" *Moving Picture World*, October 24, 1914, 538; "*The House of Fear,*" *Motography*, January 23, 1915, 150–1; "*The Affair of the Deserted House,*" *New York Dramatic Mirror*, January 13, 1915, 34; "Pathé Exchange, Inc.," *Exhibitors Herald*, December 4, 1915, 25; Clarence J. Caine, "Episode Seven, *The Black Box,*" *Moving Picture World*, May 1, 1915, 707. A related example would be *The Mystery of the Seaview Hotel* (Rex, 1914). See "*The Mystery of the Seaview Hotel,*" *Moving Picture World*, December 5, 1914, 1385.
131. "Kleine Release Under New Name," *Moving Picture World*, August 16, 1913, 730.
132. "*The House of Mystery,*" *Motography*, July 26, 1913, 67.
133. "*Count Zarka,*" *Moving Picture World*, March 28, 1914, 59.
134. Mary Farrell Bednarowski, *The Wisconsin Magazine of History*, Vol. 59, No. 1 (Autumn 1975), 5.
135. Elana Gomel, "'Spirits in the Material World': Spiritualism and Identity in the 'Fin De Siécle,'" *Victorian Literature and Culture*, Vol. 35, No. 1 (2007), 194.
136. "Spiritualism: An Evening with the Goblins," *Chicago Daily Tribune*, November 24, 1857, O2.
137. "A Lively Seance," *Lowell Daily Citizen* (Lowell, Massachusetts), July 10, 1875, 1.
138. Quoted in "Smith's Ghost," *Wheeling Register* (Wheeling, West Virginia), March 7, 1877.
139. "Ghost or Log?," *New York Herald*, March 23, 1878.
140. Vernon Lee was a pseudonym used by Violet Paget.
141. Jennifer Bann, "Ghostly Hands and Ghostly Agency: The Changing Figure of the Nineteenth-Century Specter," *Victorian Studies*, Vol. 51, No. 4 (Summer 2009), 663–86.
142. Advertisement, *New York Clipper*, February 3, 1900. Savada (p. 1150) dates *A Visit to the Spiritualist* as 1900, though it is clear Edison offered the film for sale as early as the autumn of 1899. A copy of the film is archived at the UCLA Film & Television Archive.
143. Untitled, *The Phonoscope*, September 1899, 9.
144. *No. 105, Edison Films, Complete Catalogue* (July 1901), 85. Available in *A Guide to Motion Picture Catalogs by American Producers and Distributors, 1894–1908: A Microfilm Edition*, Reel 1.
145. *Complete Catalogue of Lubin's Films* (Philadelphia: Lubin, January 1903), 24. Available in *A Guide to Motion Picture Catalogs by American Producers and Distributors, 1894–1908: A Microfilm Edition*, Reel 3.

146. Savada, 494.
147. Savada, 1139. A copy of *The Up-to-Date Spiritualism* is available in the DVD boxed set *Georges Méliès: First Wizard of Cinema*.
148. *Lubin's Films* (Philadelphia: Lubin, June 1904), 6. Available in *A Guide to Motion Picture Catalogs by American Producers and Distributors, 1894–1908: A Microfilm Edition*, Reel 3. A copy of *The Spiritualistic Photographer* is available in the DVD boxed set *Georges Méliès: First Wizard of Cinema* (Los Angeles: Flicker Alley, 2008).
149. "A Spiritualist Meeting," *Views and Film Index*, September 29, 1906.
150. "Man," *Moving Picture News*, September 16, 1911, 29.
151. "The Blood-Seedling," *Motography*, September 18, 1915, 594.
152. "Brown's Seance," *Moving Picture World*, November 11, 1912, 916.
153. "When the Spirits Moved," *Moving Picture World*, June 26, 1915, 2159.
154. "The Spirit," *Moving Picture World*, April 18, 1908, 354.
155. Advertisement, *Moving Picture World*, February 15, 1913, 705. In some advertisements for this film, Eva Ray is mistakenly identified as Eva Fay, an error that could have been misunderstood as referring to the daughter-in-law of Annie Eva Fay.
156. "Spiritualism Exposed Via the Movies," *Billboard*, February 8, 1913, 15.
157. "*Spiritualistic Seance*," *Moving Picture World*, May 9, 1908, 424. A copy of this film exists at the Gaumont-Pathé Archives.
158. "*Won through a Medium*," *Moving Picture World*, November 11, 1911, 494. A copy of this film is archived at the Museum of Modern Art, New York City.
159. "'Ghost,' on Wires, Breaks Up Seance," *Universal Weekly*, December 19, 1914, 21.
160. "Billy's Seance," *Moving Picture News*, December 9, 1911, 42.
161. A copy of *Billy's Seance* is archived at the EYE Film Institute.
162. "Bobby 'Some' Spiritualist," *Moving Picture World*, April 4, 1914, 104. A copy of this film is archived at the Deutsche Kinemathek.
163. "*The Spirit Hand*," *The Billboard*, March 11, 1911, 29.
164. "Taming the Spooks," *Moving Picture World*, January 25, 1913, 382. A copy of *Taming the Spooks* is archived at the Cineteca dei Friuli.
165. "Reliance: *The Interrupted Seance*," *Reel Life*, February 14, 1914, 15.
166. "The Spook Raisers," *Kalem Kalendar*, July 1915, 23.
167. A copy of *The Spook Raisers* is archived at the Library of Congress.
168. "The Ghost Breaker," *New York Dramatic Mirror*, December 9, 1914, 38.
169. W. Stephen Bush, "The Ghost Breaker," *Moving Picture World*, December 19, 1914, 1692.
170. "The House of a Thousand Candles," *Exhibitors Film Exchange*, August 21, 1915, 16.
171. Neil G. Caward, "The House of a Thousand Candles," August 28, 1915, 415.
172. Harvey F. Thew, "The House of a Thousand Candles," *Motion Picture News*, August 21, 1915, 83.
173. John C. Garrett, "The Circular Staircase," *Motography*, September 25, 1915, 633.
174. Oscar Cooper, "The Circular Staircase," *Motion Picture News*, September 18, 1915, 93.
175. "The Circular Staircase," *Moving Picture World*, October 16, 1915, 522.
176. "The Circular Staircase," *Motography*, October 2, 1915, 633.
177. James S. McQuade, "The Circular Staircase," *Moving Picture World*, September 18, 1915, 2007.
178. Savada, 323.

CHAPTER 8

Supernatural Creatures

In 1908, Georges Méliès distributed *In the Bogie Man's Cave/ La cuisine de l'ogre* (aka *In the Bogieman's Cave*) in America.[1] The film depicts the title character preparing his dinner: he chops a young boy into pieces and tosses the fresh meat into a frying pan. Much to his surprise, however, a fairy emerges out of the pan, as do four gnomes and—as one synopsis noted—the "reincarnated body of the captive boy."[2] The gnomes remove the frying pan from the fire and replace it with the captured bogie man. The burning villain vows he will have revenge, but soon collapses dead.[3]

Here was a fanciful moving picture featuring elements both grisly and humorous, in which supernatural creatures materialize to combat an ogre who was rechristened for English-speaking audiences as the "bogie man," one of the many variant terms and spellings used for that enigmatic monster so often used to scare children into good behavior. At times he has also been the "bogeyman," and the "boogeyman." He will get us if we don't watch out, so the long-standing mythos explains.

In addition to devils, witches, and ghosts, early American cinemagoers witnessed a variety of supernatural creatures on the screen. As with the aforementioned characters, they drew upon traditions of folklore, literature, stage, and lantern slides, making the transition into the cinema thanks to Méliès and Segundo de Chomón, as well as a large number of American directors, Edwin S. Porter among them.

As had been the case with so many ghosts, many of these "supernatural" creatures were not actually supernatural. In *The Animated Scarecrow* (Atlas, 1910), the father of a young lady warns her suitor to stay away from his farm. Defying his orders, the suitor dresses as the farmer's scarecrow. Prodding the "scarecrow" with a pitchfork, the farmer discovers the truth, with the costumed suitor fleeing for his life.[4] The *New York Dramatic Mirror* condemned the film as "clumsily managed" and "defective all through photographically."[5] By contrast, *Moving Picture World* praised its "fun" chase, as well as the "novelty in a scarecrow that runs."[6] Either way, the running scarecrow was in fact nothing more than a running man, a fake.

Inanimate objects actually did come to life in a number of films. Williams, Brown & Earle released *The Professor and His Wax Works* (1908, aka *The Professor's Wax Works*), which displayed the "strange antics of wax figures which come to life."[7] In 1913, Thanhouser's *The Wax Lady* told the story of a man who was unkind to everyone until a fairy-like wax figure comes to life and scares him into being a "benefactor to all mankind."[8] Not dissimilar were *The Hindoo's Ring* (Selig Polyscope, 1908), *The Spirit and the Clay* (Vitagraph, 1914), *The Marble Heart* (Imp, 1915), and *Niobe* (Paramount/Famous Players, 1915), in which statues are imbued with life.[9]

Figure 8.1 Lobby card for *Niobe* (Paramount/Famous Players, 1915). Pictured are actors Hazel Dawn and Charles Smith Abbe. (*Courtesy of Robert J. Kiss*)

In a small number of cases, filmmakers invoked the supernatural with the apparent purpose of telling horrifying stories in order to fascinate and perhaps frighten their audiences. One example came in Oskar Messter's German film *The Specter of the Sea/Der Schatten des Meeres* (1912), released in America in 1913 by the European Feature Film Corporation. Drawing on the legend of "der Gonger," the film starred actress Henny Porten as a woman whom Death incarnate tempts into suicide. A trade advertisement promoted it as the "finest supernatural sensation ever produced."[10] The following year, Kay-Bee produced a two-reel drama entitled *The Banshee* (1913), which depicted the "witchlike creature" of Irish superstition, "whose very name brought terror to the good people."[11] The lead character (played by J. Barney Sherry) refuses to have his baby christened. Passing out after a night of drinking, he has a nightmare in which he commits murder. The appearance of the mythical Banshee causes him to awaken, relieved to find that it was all a dream.[12] One review noted that the Banshee's cry was nothing more than a cat wailing on a window sill.[13]

More than any others, four particular supernatural creatures had long captured the attention of Americans.[14] Two of them—skeletons and mummies—inspired awe and fear even when they represented earthly remains, though at times literature, stage, and filmic representations reanimated them. Two others—werewolves and vampires—were the products of transformations, from human to inhuman. To be sure, all of these characters appeared onscreen infrequently in the period, their presence dwarfed by the sheer number of ghosts and devils, for example.

However, these four creatures did register in early cinema, sometimes with pronounced effect. Whether supernatural incarnate or otherwise, all of them held the parallel and sometimes intersecting potential to induce laughter or fear. As early as American Mutoscope & Biograph's film *The Skeleton at the Feast* (1899), for example, two couples dine together "with much merriment," the wine "flowing freely." A skeleton appears. It advances "slowly through the air" and then "points a warning finger at the quartet."[15] One of them faints, frightened by an image that could also be the source of humor.

Skeletons

One of the most obvious visual signs of death in America has been that of a skeleton, which—as Chapter 3 notes—was commonly the source of comedy in nineteenth-century lantern slides. In tandem was the memento mori of the skull, with or without crossbones. Skulls warned of poison on chemical bottles, and yet they also indicated the ascension to Heaven from this mortal coil, as in the winged skulls present on many of the earliest gravestones in the American colonies.

Skeletons, horrible and sometimes reanimated, appeared repeatedly in literature as well. In *The Story of the Skeleton Hunter* (published in America without attribution in 1836), a knight living "some centuries agone" finds his hair standing "right on end" when he sees a hunter being pursued by a "troop of skeletons mounted on stags of enormous size." After being initially "transfixed with horror," the knight invokes the name of "his own particular saint." As a result, the "whole troop of phantom skeletons and their stags disappeared." The cursed hunter has thus been saved from his purgatorial "nightly punishment."[16]

Most short stories tended toward satirical humor. In 1866, J. T. Trowbridge's *The Skeleton in the House* has a doctor informing a woman about the "frightful skeleton" inside her own body.[17] In 1885, Luke Sharp's *Claiming His Skeleton* presented the "weird story" of a humorous ghost and his own skeleton at a university in Michigan, thus raising the question, "Can a man once dead lay claim to any part of the property he owned while alive?"[18] Then, in 1899, *The Family Specter* featured a walking, talking, and quite bony "family skeleton," one that fades away after a man kisses his wife.[19]

Poetry about skeletons was also frequent in America, the most famous example being Longfellow's *The Skeleton in Armor* (1841), its title referring to an actual skeleton unearthed in Fall River, Massachusetts in 1832. As early as 1784, the *Massachusetts Centinel* published *On Seeing a Human Skeleton*.[20] Six years later, the *Vermont Gazette* printed *Reflections on Viewing a Skeleton*.[21] Both of these poems offered morals about life and death, but they also describe skeletal remains as unpleasant, with the latter notably using the term "ghastly." In the years that followed, "ghastly" became the word (along with "grewsome" and "horror") most commonly used to describe real skeletons, such as those excavated in the wilderness or even inside urban cellars.[22]

The unexpected discovery of skeletons in everyday life held the power to frighten, as newspaper reports attest over and over again in the nineteenth and early twentieth centuries.[23] And on occasion, it seemed as if there was good reason to be scared. In 1900, a man in Alexandria, Indiana took a skeleton to his home, after which there was "almost a nightly visitation of a phenomena [sic], which still remains a mystery." It sounded as if "some person [struck] the side of a house with a board . . . the windows [rattled], and again a loud tapping at the doors and windows [was] heard, and at intervals the entire house [shook] as if a severe windstorm were in progress."[24]

And yet there was also a parallel desire to gaze at skeletons, to inspect and examine them. As early as 1768, the *New-York Gazette and Weekly Mercury* described an anatomical lecture that would display the "construction of every bone in the adult and infant state."[25] Then, in 1790, the *Salem Gazette* described a man who kept his grandfather's skeleton inside his house.[26] Later, skeletons became admitted as evidence in courtroom cases, allowing attorneys to attempt to reconstruct the cause of murders.[27]

Some persons exhibited skeletons for other purposes, including to thrill spectators. In 1893, newspapers reported on a man in Philadelphia who used skulls and bones to decorate his home.[28] During the nineteenth century, the Knights of Pythias often displayed skeletons in their lodge rooms. All of this led to a "skeleton trade" in which market prices became high and in which such items as the skulls of murderers held particular fascination.[29]

One of the most fascinating of these stories came in 1895, when the press described the "bones of the devil" arriving on American soil. Exhumed in Japan, the infernal skeleton was of "gigantic proportions and altogether strange and hideous in appearance, which, according to an inscription found above the tomb, constituted nothing less than the remains of his satanic majesty, as the Japanese understood him."[30] Contemporaneous artwork of the skeleton indicates it was potentially scary, but it was also a fraud in the tradition of the Cardiff giant. As the press wrote at the time, the skeleton had been "manufactured long ago and buried beneath a temple."

Those bones were hardly the first prank to make an impression in America. In 1888, the *Chicago Tribune* wrote about a skeleton being spotted in a cemetery, its skull appearing to "blaze with fire" and its right arm at times ascending "in the air as if to warn mortals of their impending doom." Police quickly investigated what the "horrified" public refused to approach: the moving memento mori wasn't real. It was made of canvas, a string attached to its arm allowing its operation from a "safe distance."[31] Here was a performance of sorts, a type of animation used for a purpose not dissimilar to later moving pictures.

The first example of a skeleton appearing in a film seems to have been Méliès's *Escamotage d'une dame chez Robert-Houdin* (1896). A skeleton also appeared in his *The Devil's Castle/Le manoir du diable* (1896, aka *The Haunted Castle*).[32] One of the various monsters that the knight witnesses appear and then disappear is a skeleton seated on a bench. From that point onward, Méliès used skeletons in a number of his trick films, perhaps most notably in *The Haunted Castle/Le château hanté* (1897), in which another knight is troubled by a ghost, a devil, and a skeleton.[33] In this case, the skeleton stands upright, even after the knight stabs it with his sword. Its resilient stance makes clear that it is no inanimate set of bones, but instead a living being, a monster.

American film companies followed Méliès's lead, with skeletons appearing onscreen to inspire fear in characters and laughter in audiences.[34] Among these indigenous productions were American Mutoscope & Biograph's *The Cremation* (1899) and *The Startled Lover* (1899). In the latter, a man "makes love" to his sweetheart in a parlor. The two quarrel, causing the man to turn away. "As he turns back," one catalog synopsis wrote, "the girl changes like a flash into a skeleton, to her lover's great amazement and terror. While he is still trembling with fear, the skeleton vanishes and the girl reappears, smiling and beckoning to her lover to return to her side."[35] The same company released a similar story soon thereafter with *The Artist's Dream*, but such tricks continued in the years that followed.[36] As late as 1915, Kalem's comedy *Foiled!* featured Reggie (Dave Morris) attempting to hit Rubdub, a troublesome genii (Charles Simpson). In retaliation, Rubdub waves his hand in Reggie's direction, thus transforming him into a skeleton.[37]

In comedy films, the appearance of inanimate skeletons could frighten characters, as was the case in *The Skeleton* (Powers, 1912). In it, children steal a professor's skeleton and use it to frighten a tramp, a romantic couple, an African-American man, and a fisherman. "A laugh will go in any play house where this film is exhibited," *Moving Picture World* promised.[38] Later, in *Curing the Cook* (Edison, 1915), students at a boarding house prank the title character, who tries to "sit all day with a black bottle beside her." To scare her into sobriety, they hang a skeleton in a coat bin. The cook flees from it, to the extent that she falls off the roof and gets run over by a car.[39]

A surviving example of this type of comedy is *The Skeleton* (Vitagraph, 1910).[40] Some young men steal a professor's skeleton, dance around with it jokingly, and then dress it up and leave it on a park bench, causing a policeman to mistake it for a hobo. The film then employs stop-motion effects to make the skeleton come alive; it removes its clothes and dances about. While acknowledging its "laugh provoking" qualities, the *New York Dramatic Mirror* believed that the humor was in fact undercut by some of the "trick" effects.[41] The trade might have found such tricks old-fashioned, but it might also have believed the film was something of a combination of two different approaches to skeleton comedies. Vitagraph's *The Skeleton* marked a somewhat uneven convergence of inanimate skeleton films and those in which the skeleton actually comes to life.

The Skeleton was also the latest in a number of American moving pictures reminiscent of the onstage skeleton dances described in Chapter 2. In the cinema, these began with American Mutoscope's *The Dancing Skeleton* in 1897 (which was likely the first indigenous film to feature a skeleton) and continued with Edison's *Skeleton Dance, Marionettes* in 1898.[42] These films were apparently popular enough that American Mutoscope & Biograph issued *Davy Jones' Locker* in 1900, a "double printing" film that combined negative footage from *Dancing Skeleton* (1897) with footage from *Wreck of the Schooner "Richmond"* (1897), the result making it seem as if the skeleton emerges from below deck to dance for the viewer.[43] A catalog description notes, "During the weird scene, the surf is rushing in from the ocean and pouring over the dismantled wreck."[44]

In 1902, Selig Polyscope released *Dancing Skeleton*, though whether the company produced it themselves is unknown. It is also unknown if this is the same *Dancing Skeleton* distributed by Lubin beginning in 1903, or if the two were different films using the same title.[45] At any rate, in the Selig version, a "large grinning skeleton" stands up, walks to center stage, and then dances until its arm and leg bones leave its body before returning to it. Of its special effects, Selig's catalog attested, "This film was not made from a toy skeleton but from a large life sized one. His jaws can be seen plainly working all the time."[46]

A number of other comedies also featured skeletons moving of their own accord, even if not dancing, among them Méliès's *X Rays/Les rayons* x (1900, aka *A Novice at X-Rays*), Edison's *The Watermelon Patch* (1905), and Pathé's *Cave of the Spooks/La grotte des esprits* (aka *Cave of Spooks* and *Wave of Spooks*).[47] In 1910, Selig Polyscope's *Oh You Skeleton* depicts a woman on a streetcar who discovers a skeleton in the seat next to her. As she runs, the skeleton chases her, the result creating either a "poorly worked out" film (in the words of the *New York Dramatic Mirror*) or one that left audiences laughing "for days to come" (in the words of *Moving Picture World*).[48] A less fanciful storyline, to the extent it occurs in a dream, appeared in *All for a Tooth* (Edison, 1914), in which an "enraged" skeleton bites a man as he journeys through some old catacombs.[49] The following year, *His Bachelor Dinner* (Reliance, 1915) also featured a skeleton in a nightmare sequence, one featuring images suggestive of necrophilia.[50]

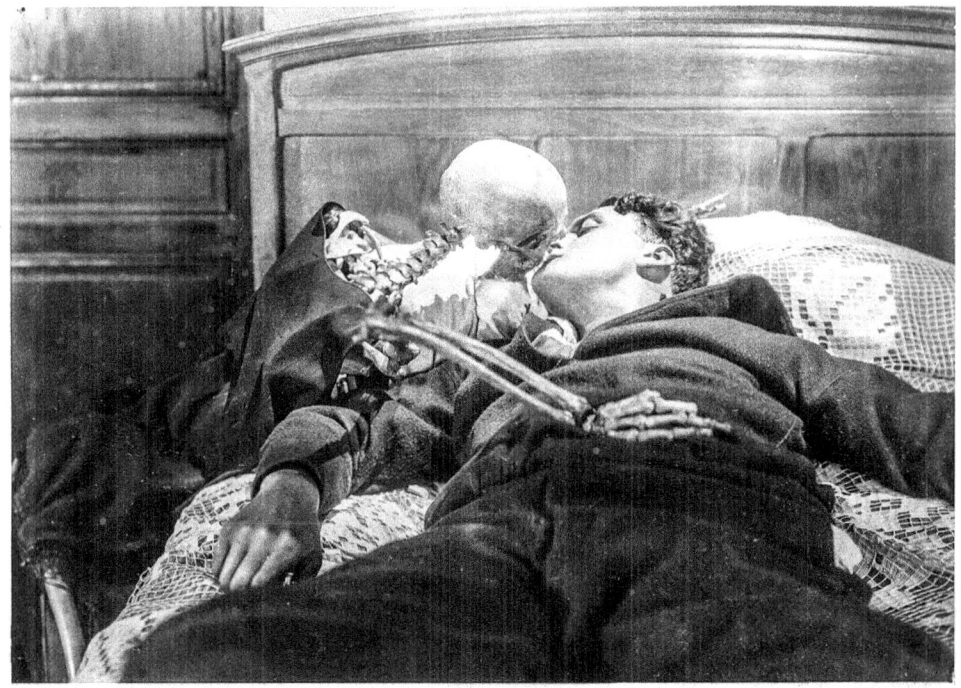

Figure 8.2 *His Bachelor Dinner* (Reliance, 1915). (*Courtesy of the Réunion des musées nationaux–Grand palais*)

Dramatic treatment of skeletons did occur in the cinema, but only rarely. Lifeless but eerie bones appear in the dungeons of films ranging from Louis Feuillade's *The Dungeon of Despair/L'oubliette* (Gaumont, 1913) to *The Phantom Violin* (Universal-Gold Seal, 1914).[51] Medical students throw a skeleton's head at two crooks to delay their advance in *The Skull* (Vitagraph, 1913).[52] And *The Accusing Skeleton* (Warner's Features, 1913) presents a burglar confessing to a crime when he sees the bony remains of his partner-in-crime.[53]

The dramatic portrayal of reanimated skeletons in early cinema was rarer still, though it did occur, as in the cemetery scene of Segundo de Chomón's *Legend of a Ghost/La légende du fantôme* (Pathé Frères, 1908) and in Edison's *The Phantom Signal* (1913).[54] But perhaps the major example came in Chomón's *Le Spectre Rouge* (Pathé Frères, 1907). Releasing it in America in 1908 as *The Red Spectre*, Pathé touted the film as a "magic extravaganza of wondrous magnitude."[55] *Views and Film Index* (likely drawing on a plot synopsis provided by Pathé Frères) described the title character as a "crimson skeleton apparition" who takes part in what promised to be something more than just a trick film: it "combined the art of magic with a story."[56]

The hand-colored spectacle displays the horned and cloaked Red Spectre emerging out of a coffin that stands amid hellish flames.[57] Waving his wand, he materializes five women. They soon disappear, replaced by floating balls of fire. Then the Red Spectre makes two women appear in flaming cauldrons. One at a time, he wraps them in a black tarpaulin, levitates them, and then burns them, thus exhibiting a magic trick of a sort that one might

Figure 8.3 A frame from *The Red Spectre* (Pathé Frères, 1907).

have seen performed onstage by illusionists like Herrmann, Kellar, and Thurston. But then a female devil appears, challenging the Red Spectre's power.

To defeat her, the Red Spectre walks toward the camera and displays a trio of miniature women in three bottles that he fills with a magical liquid. The female devil returns, interrupting the Red Spectre again before he transforms a still image of Pathé's iconic red rooster logo into the projected image of a woman. Eventually the devilish woman spurns the Red Spectre's growing affections. She purloins his magical cloak and pours the magical liquid onto his defeated body, thus transforming him into a lifeless skeleton.

Here was the trickery of a Méliès, as well as some of the humor he perfected. But here is also a drama, one in which the supernatural—and by extension a supernatural skeleton—flourishes without apology, let alone the use of slapstick comedy or even the framing device of a dream. It remains probably the most important skeleton film of the early cinema period.

Mummies

Reportage on mummies in the American press dates to the eighteenth century, but it was during the nineteenth that articles on the subject became commonplace.[58] Journalists regularly levied attention on the history of Egyptian mummies, the embalming process, and the discovery of particular remains.[59] Some stories focused on the arrival of mummies onto American soil, with one newspaper heralding in 1818 what was "perhaps the first ever [mummy] introduced in the United States."[60] Others promoted the local exhibition of mummies.[61] As S. J. Wolfe and Robert Singerman have chronicled, the display of mummies in the United States became very popular in the nineteenth century.[62] As with skeletons, some people wanted to see mummies up close, even to touch them.

In some cases, as in Boston in 1850, these exhibitions culminated with the unwrapping of Egyptian mummies.[63] A "nervous gentleman" wrote about the Boston event as follows:

> For five mortal weeks, the newspapers have bristled with staring advertisements of the exhibition . . . and at every corner of the streets I have been haunted by huge placards embellished with dismal representations in printer's ink, of the exterior of this everlasting specimen of preserved humanity.[64]

Similar mummy "unrollings" occurred in Philadelphia in 1851 and in New York City in 1864.[65]

Equally curious was the practice of "mummy pictures" at the end of the nineteenth century. The "craze" began with Americans posing inside mummy "cases" for photographs while touring such countries as Egypt. The fad's "instant popularity" meant that New York photographers began superimposing customers' faces onto entombed mummies in existing images. "It is whispered that a number of these weird photographs are to circulate on All Hallowe'en, when the ghostly and the ghastly are always in demand," the *New York World* wrote. "Many people think that the idea is too morbid to be encouraged . . . However, this weird fancy is desirable at present . . ."[66]

An even more gruesome fancy came with Americans wanting to own authentic mummies. In 1882, the *New York Times* published an article on the expensive and "grim" hobby.[67] Not surprisingly, this hobby led to the creation of fake mummies in Egypt (and elsewhere) for sale to gullible Westerners.[68] The interest in both viewing and purchasing mummies continued into the early years of the twentieth century. In 1906, the San Jose *Evening News* calculated that "more Egyptian mummies have gone out of Los Angeles than ever were stolen from the tombs of Egypt," their creator representing them as authentic to both individuals and museums. "There are more buyers for curios than there are curios," he said. "If I don't make them, somebody else will."[69]

Connected to the spectacle of the mummy was a horror of the same. In 1867, newspapers quoted a young Philadelphian who had descended into a "mummy pit" while travelling in Egypt:

> . . . down in the very heart of this granite rock, dimly lighted by our two flickering tapers, filled almost to the roof, was a countless, piled-up mass of uncoffined mummies. There they lay in all shapes and postures. Time had burst the twining ligaments of some, and their bony arms and fleshless fingers seemed struggling up from the mass, as if to lay hold of the disturbers of their slumbers. Some were placed upright against the wall, and, in the weird shadows thrown by the candle's light, their features twitched and moved, and their long-sealed lips seemed opening to denounce us.[70]

His account anticipates eventual screen depictions of the same, with reanimated mummies emerging out of the darkness to seek vengeance on the living.

These images conjured horror, as did notions of mummy curses, which were discussed long before Howard Carter's discovery of Tutankhamun's tomb in 1922. In 1904, for example, the American press reported on a "malevolent" mummy case housed at the British Museum. According to the report, a priestess of Amen-Ra had been entombed in it. Its supernatural powers allegedly brought harm to many, ranging from those who discovered it to a man who allegedly went blind after photographing it.[71] Later, in 1914, some claimed the same object was even responsible for the sinking of the *Titanic*.[72]

Fictional literature also addressed the topic of mummies, sometimes without reference to the supernatural. Théophile Gautier's *The Romance of the Mummy/Le roman de la momie* (1857)—a historical novel about ancient Egyptians—was published in America in 1860.[73] And American newspapers serialized Fergus Hume's *The Green Mummy* (1908) in 1909. In that story, a professor purchases an Incan mummy, but upon delivery discovers it has been replaced with the murdered remains of his own assistant.[74]

By contrast, mummies did return to life in Jane C. Louden's 1827 British novel *The Mummy! Or, a Tale of the Twenty-Second Century*, as well as in Louisa May Alcott's 1869 story *Lost in a Pyramid, or The Mummy's Curse*. In the latter, Alcott's character Forsyth relates a "weird story, which will only haunt you if I tell it." He proceeds to recall burning a female mummy in Egypt after stealing a gold box clasped in its not-so-dead hands. A deciphered parchment bequeaths "her curse to whoever should disturb her rest."

Other mummy tales included Sir Arthur Conan Doyle's *Lot No. 249* (1892), in which an Oxford student brings a mummy back to life in order to harm three of his acquaintances, and Bram Stoker's *The Jewel of Seven Stars* (1903), in which an archeologist attempts to reanimate a queen's mummy. There were also a number of now-forgotten short stories published in America, among them *The Mummy's Soul* (1877) by Collins Shackleford. Its character becomes haunted by a mummy he discovered in Egypt, one that follows him home:

> In the chair behind me sat the mummy of the tomb, alive, watching me with its small, cunning eyes, as it tried to free one of its hands from the decaying cerements. It was the mummy I had found, not the one that crumbled to dust before the breath of a pure desert wind. It motioned me with its disengaged hand back to my seat, and strove to stand and oppose my passage, as, with a cry of horror, I rushed from the room.[75]

Also memorable is the short story *He Stole a Princess* (published without attribution in 1891), in which a thief discovers that the mummy he wants to steal is very much alive.[76]

More commonly, however, mummies in American literature and on the American stage became the source of comedy, as can be most famously seen in Edgar Allan Poe's satirical short story *Some Words with a Mummy* (1845).[77] Even earlier, Thomas D. Rice's "Ethiopian" farce entitled *The Virginia Mummy* (1835) became popular in the 1830s and remained so until the 1860s. According to Matthew Rebhorn, the play featured Rice as a character who pretends to be a mummy so that his friend can "infiltrate the laboratory of his lover's ward, Dr. Galen, a mad scientist type who wants to perform various experiments on the mummified body."[78]

Subsequent stage comedies included George D. Day and Allan Reed's *The Mummy*, a British "farce in three acts" presented for the first time in America in 1896. A professor uses electricity and milk to bring the mummy of Ramesses II back to life. Reanimation occurs while the professor is away, with Ramesses II shedding his mummy garb. The professor's houseguest tries on the discarded bandages, with the professor nearly experimenting on him as a result. But everything returns to normal when Ramesses II returns to his case and "disappears in a cloud of dust."[79]

A decade later, Richard Carle's "merry musical melange" *The Maid and the Mummy* (1904) has its scientist hoping to bring a mummy back to life by use of a special elixir. However, the "mummy" is nothing more than someone dressed in a mummy costume, its humor following in the tradition of *The Virginia Mummy*.[80] That same year, *The Mummy Girl*—a musical burlesque in two acts—also appeared at various American theatres. Its "cold, dead mummy" transforms into a "handsome living woman," which creates trouble for the American who stole it in another country, particularly with his jealous wife.[81]

Such plays provided an important narrative template for mummy films produced during the early cinema period, most of which were intended to be humorous. In *The Mummy/La momie* (Pathé Frères, 1908), a woman witnesses a professor dissecting a mummy and mistakenly believes he is cutting up a man.[82] In *The Egyptian Mystery* (Edison, 1909), a charm cursed by Ramesses causes anything its wearer touches to disappear.[83] Then, in *The Mummy* (Thanhouser, 1911), electricity galvanizes a female mummy back to the land of the living.[84] When a young man spurns her attentions, she temporarily turns him into a mummy, thus creating what *Moving Picture World* called a "funny" novelty.[85]

However, the most repeated storyline found characters dressing up as mummies in order to fool others. For example, in *The Mummy and the Cowpunchers* (Kalem, 1912), a con man costumes his daughter such that he can give a fake lecture on the subject of Egyptian mummies, a deception that works well until their partner absconds with the receipts.[86] Then, in *Slim and the Mummy* (Warner's Features, 1914), a "clownish cowboy" guarding a mummy accidentally causes it to turn to dust; to avoid getting the blame, he wraps himself up in the mummy bandages and takes its place.[87]

A print of Kalem's "comedy riot" *The Egyptian Mummy* (1913) survives.[88] In it, Professor Howe (played by John E. Brennan) offers $5,000 for the mummy of Ramesses III. He also shows disdain for Dick (Marshall Neilan), who is in love with his daughter Arvilla (Ruth Roland), to the extent that he strikes him with a cane.[89] As a result, Dick temporarily takes the place of the mummy that arrives in a crate. "Let your daughter marry whom she will," Dick bellows. "Ramses [sic] commands it."[90] And so the "lively" farce ends with Professor Howe acquiescing.[91]

A number of other comedies focused on scientists who believed they could bring mummies back from the dead. For example, *An Egyptian Princess* (Selig Polyscope, 1914) has its professor concocting an elixir of life; he mistakenly believes it works on what is nothing more than a modern woman hiding inside his mummy case.[92] In *Oh, You Mummy!* (Crystal, 1914), actress Pearl White plays a woman who pretends to be a mummy in order to scare old "Professor Diggup."[93] And *When the Mummy Cried for Help*

Figure 8.4 Two frames from *When the Mummy Cried for Help* (Nestor, 1915).

(Nestor, 1915) finds a young man posing as a mummy to make a professor believe his "elixir of life" really works.[94]

Vitagraph's 1914 *The Egyptian Mummy* was another of these comedies, as a surviving copy reveals.[95] Here Dick (Billy Quirk) loves Eva Hicks (Constance Talmadge), but her father Professor Hicks (Lee Beggs) does not approve, believing that she should instead marry a wealthy man. At the time same, the Professor thinks he has perfected his "elixir of life" and plans to spend $5,000 on a mummy to try it out. Dick hires a tramp to pretend to be a mummy in order to fool the Professor; as a result, he can collect the $5,000 and become a man of means. Once again, the antics lead to a happy ending. The *New York Dramatic Mirror* rightly praised Alice Methley's screenplay, which was well-crafted even if largely derivative.[96]

Dramatic portrayals of mummies in films of the period were rare.[97] During the seventh episode of the serial *The Perils of Pauline* (Pathé, 1914), a double exposure depicts a mummy's "spiritual body ... emerging from its swathed figure and whispering its secret" into a character's ear.[98] That same year, in *The Necklace of Rameses* (Edison, 1914), a group of thieves attempts to steal the title jewelry, which has arrived in America around the neck of a mummy.[99] And in *The Clue of the Scarab* (Apex, 1914), a female thief hides inside a museum's mummy case.[100]

Essanay's *When Soul Meets Soul* (1913) finds Professor Delaplace (Francis X. Bushman) coming into possession of the mummified Egyptian priestess Charazel (Dolores Cassinelli).[101] A roll of papyrus in her sarcophagus explains that she must live through the ages until she locates her lost lover. Delaplace falls asleep, at which time a "beautiful dissolving view" shows Charazel approaching him. At that point, the scene flashes back to ancient Egypt, with Francis X. Bushman playing Charazel's lover, Arames. He discovers Charazel at the moment she fatally plunges a knife into her breast. The film returns to the present day, with Delaplace praying for her forgiveness. He is indeed the reincarnation of Arames, and so she may now find peace.[102]

But the most notable mummy film of the era was *The Vengeance of Egypt/L'anneau fatal* (Gaumont, 1912). Its story tells of a scarab ring stolen from a "vindictive mummy," her vengeance falling upon its various subsequent owners, until the ring is finally returned to her "withered hands."[103] Gaumont surprisingly released the film in black-and-white rather than hand-colored form, perhaps in an effort to heighten its stark narrative. According to *Moving Picture World*:

> If some scenes seem loosely connected, others ring right in the center with the impression desired and build up a horror that grips in the strongest way. Also the producer has not depended wholly upon the ring; but, by means of a strange dream of an Egyptian charnel house, in one place, and by using museum scenes of old Egyptian relics, in others, he keeps in the right atmosphere. The story is in the Maupassant school; its object is horror, always a new horror and, in many of its scenes, it is astonishingly effective.[104]

The Vengeance of Egypt became vital to the development of horror-themed American film, depicting a supernatural character for the explicit purpose of terrifying nickelodeon-era audiences.

Figure 8.5 Lithographed advertising card for *The Vengeance of Egypt* (Gaumont, 1912). (Courtesy of Robert J. Kiss)

Werewolves

Mention of werewolves (aka "were-wolves" and "were wolves") appeared in the American press at least as early as 1766.[105] Throughout the 1800s, occasional articles appeared on the subject, particularly during the second half of the century, which—combined with word-of-mouth folklore—meant that many, perhaps even most, Americans were aware of the creatures.[106] As one story published in 1880 indicated:

> We have all had our childish shudderings over stories of the "Gar-Gare, or Were-wolf," that grim ghost of bosky fastnesses of Norway, of Hungary, the Black Forest, and even of the plains of France; that uncanny "thing"—for neither man nor beast was he—that spent half his time as an honest gentleman should, the other half roaming the high woods, and anon assisting, so the common people believed, in a meeting of chosen demons.[107]

Some fifteen years later, another writer explained that "the werewolf story comes down to us from old Roman times."[108]

In terms of nonfiction, Sabine Baring-Gould's *The Book of Werewolves* (Smith, Elder, & Company, 1865) became the most substantial work of the nineteenth century. Published in London and read by at least some Americans, the book was the first to chronicle the history of werewolf folklore.[109] Baring-Gould's text led to other work on the subject, including scholarly papers presented at the Modern Languages of America conference in 1893.[110] More notable perhaps was Elliott O'Donnell's monograph *Werewolves*, published in England in 1912.[111]

Occasionally the werewolf surfaced in fiction. Some Americans might have been aware of Captain Frederick Marryat's *The White Wolf of the Hartz Mountains* (1839), George W. M. Reynolds' *Wagner, the Wehr-Wolf* (1846–7), and Rudyard Kipling's *The Mark of the Beast* (1890), in which a man transforms into a wild animal, walking on all fours and eating raw meat until a mystical spell is removed. American poets also tackled the subject. Graham R. Tomson's *A Ballad of the Were-wolf* appeared in *Macmillan's Magazine* in 1890.[112] Two years later, the *Evening Star* of Washington, D.C. published W. L. Shoemaker's *The Were-Wolf, A Bohemian Gipsy Ballad*. Then, in 1907, Olav Gunstveit's memorable poem *Werewolf* appeared in print.[113]

The Fairy of the Castle, a short story published in America without attribution in 1874, included such descriptions as, "At night she turned into a were-wolf, and ate little children. He claimed to have met her often in the forest, and tried to shoot her, but she seemed bullet-proof."[114] Clarissa Mackie's *The Werewolf* (serialized in 1913) became yet another of these stories, with its character fearfully relaying, "The thing grew larger and took form. Was it a man walking on all fours, or was it a beast walking on two legs?"[115] Julian Hawthorne's *The Werewolf* (1890) remains one of the most compelling of these American short stories, and yet it sadly ranks among the most forgotten. In it, the lead character keeps a grey wolf chained to a tree, causing his lover much concern. Eventually the wolf's spirit enters into his body. The two struggle, with the man killing the wolf only to look down and gaze upon his own corpse, his mind having entered the wolf's body.[116]

By contrast, Eugene Field's short story *The Werewolf* was likely the most widely known. He wrote the tale during the 1880s, but died before it was published. In it, Field describes:

> Out of the forest rushed the werewolf, wood wroth, bellowing hoarsely, gnashing his fangs and tossing hither and thither the yellow form from his snapping jaws. He sought Yseult straight, as if an evil power drew him to the spot where she stood. But Yseult was not afeard; like a marble she stood and saw the werewolf coming.

Field's widow allowed the *Ladies Home Journal* to publish *The Werewolf* in 1896.[117] Famed artist Howard Pyle painted an illustration to accompany it; Pyle himself later wrote *The Salem Wolf* (1909), a story in which one character promises to shoot the "hell-hound" with a silver bullet.[118]

Despite the prevalence of such fiction and nonfiction literature, filmmakers rarely broached the subject of human-to-animal transformations.[119] In 1910, Lux released a comedy entitled *The Snake Man/On demande un homme serpent*, in which a man swallows a number of people before being "seized with indigestion" and disgorging them.[120] *Moving Picture World* praised its "refreshing" novelty.[121] More curious still was *A Florida Enchantment* (Vitagraph, 1914). One of its female characters eats a magic seed and transmutes into a man.[122]

Director Henry MacRae's two-reeler *The Werewolf* (101 Bison, 1913) was very much a supernatural story, one that not only drew upon folkloric traditions, but also upon the popularity of "Indian" films. During the "pioneer days," a Native American maiden named Kee-On-Ee marries a "trail blazer" named Ezra Vance. When their child is only five years old, Ezra's brother forces Kee-On-Ee to return to her tribe. An old enemy murders Ezra, leaving Kee-On-Ee to believe her husband has scorned her. As a result, she "brings up her child, Watuma, to hate all white men."[123]

As an adult, Watuma flirts with a prospector named Clifford, but then makes him jealous by embracing a member of her own tribe. Clifford murders his rival, then flees. Watuma assembles a group of "enraged" Native Americans to attack some white friars. "When one of them raises a cross," a plot summary noted, "Watuma slowly dissolves into a slinking wolf."[124] A hundred years later, Clifford is reincarnated. During a hunting trip, he tries to shoot a wolf, but it "dissolves into the Watuma of old, and there appears before his puzzled eyes the scene where he slew the brave. The wolf woman would caress him, but he throws her off." Watuma later returns in the form of a wolf, but this time she murders Clifford's sweetheart. His punishment is thus "made complete at the death of the one he loved."[125]

Moving Picture World told readers, "For those who care for much shooting and massacre the picture will have appeal. Good photography and interesting backgrounds go far to hold the attention."[126] *Motion Picture News* was less kind, calling the film "absolutely the most asinine affair ever produced. It is an insult to place it in the form seen by the reviewer before any audience.... If this were a fairy story, it would be laughed at."[127]

The Werewolf likely spurred the production of the only other two notable lycanthropy films of the period.[128] In early 1914, 101 Bison released *The Legend of the Phantom Tribe*, written by Ruth Ann Baldwin, directed by Henry MacRae, and starring William Clifford, all three of them having worked together on *The Werewolf*.[129] In it, an entire Native American tribe is slaughtered and then—thanks to double exposure—resurrected. To exact revenge, Wanta, the Witch Woman, "evokes from the corpses the wraiths of the fallen, and they sweep, in a misty cloud, over the village of their slavers."[130] She also transforms one tribal member into a bear, an effect praised by *Moving Picture World* and the *New York Dramatic Mirror*.[131] When screened in Chicago, the police censors required one scene to be excised, that of a woman tied to a tree and being burned alive.[132]

Later that same year, *The White Wolf* (Nestor, 1914) presented another Native American storyline, with the young chief Swift Wind betrothed to Dancing Fawn. Their plans for marriage are upset when a cruel medicine man announces his own affections for Dancing Fawn. Some members of the tribe believe that his spirit is "at times embodied in a wolf."[133] A contemporary plot summary notes:

> Swift Wind is taught a secret by an old trapper. "If a trap is baited with an animal's own hair, the iron jaws will never fail to catch it." The Indian decides how he will overthrow his rival. At his instruction, Dancing Fawn cuts off a lock of hair from the sleeping medicine man. With it, Swift Wind baits the trap. The next day a wolf is caught and as the Indians approach the trap, the beast turns into the medicine man.[134]

The medicine man dies. Swift Wind and Dancing Fawn are thus reunited and resume their plans for marriage. Unlike *The Werewolf* and *The Legend of the Phantom Tribe*, *The White Wolf* gave audiences a happy ending.

Figure 8.6 *The Legend of the Phantom Tribe* (101 Bison, 1914).

Vampires

Discussing vampires in 1844, a Pennsylvania newspaper remarked that "so much has been written" on the subject, a testament to its apparent popularity.[135] Over forty years later, an article in the *Kansas City Times* observed: "Among weird and unnatural horrors of romance and legend, the vampire has always held the foremost place. The casual wraith, the family ghost, the specter in clanking chains, and even the witch's 'familiar' are nowhere in comparison with this graveyard ghoul, said to sustain its loathsome existence by sucking the blood of living persons."[136] Interest in vampires had continued unabated.

It is difficult to determine exactly when the American press first addressed vampirism, but it certainly occurred decades before the Revolutionary War. In 1732, the *American Weekly Mercury* printed a nonfiction account about Hungary that claimed "certain Dead Bodies (called here Vampyres) killed several persons by sucking out all their blood."[137] Six years later, the *New England Weekly Journal* published a story about Eastern European vampires, mentioning one had been discovered in a grave "with his eyes wide open, his countenance fresh and ruddy, with a natural respiration, though dead and utterly motionless."[138]

In the years that followed, American newspapers continued to publish on vampirism, both foreign and domestic. Notably, in 1896, the *Boston Globe* described a community in Rhode Island where the locals still believed in vampires.[139] Another article published that same year reported, "many people [in Rhode Island] have been digging up the dead bodies of relatives for the purpose of burning their hearts."[140] Such commentaries followed from the "Mercy Brown Vampire Incident" of 1892, in which a corpse was exhumed in Rhode Island to end the power of the undead.

In the nineteenth century, rational explanations of this folklore often focused on the vampire bat.[141] "There is a bat in South America which sometimes sucks the blood of animals," the *Saturday Evening Post* explained in 1874, "and if this species once existed in Europe, it may have given rise to the belief that the dead sometimes rise from their graves and nourish themselves on the blood of the living."[142] Vampire bats captured the imagination of many Americans, so much so that in 1893 a store in New York City displayed a living specimen in its window:

> It is confined in a little wire-grated cage, not more than two feet in height and even less in length and breadth. There it hangs from the top bars, day after day, apparently lifeless, except for the slightest movement of the chest. Now and then it moves its head or sips from the little jar of water placed in a corner of the cage.
>
> ... The eyes are small and have an intelligent expression. The tongue is long and sharp and feels as if it were covered with tiny warts. It has six small teeth in the lower jaw and a full row of them in the upper. The little beast is not at all vicious, but rather playful, and seems to know its master well.[143]

In this case, an exhibition of a live vampire bat tried to scientifically explain the roots of supernatural vampires, while simultaneously fuelling the ongoing interest in them.

Given the sheer volume of literature devoted to vampire folklore and vampire bats in the nineteenth century, as well as—as noted in Chapters 1 and 2—the American success of such literature as Polidori's *The Vampyre, A Tale* and Stoker's *Dracula*, and of such stage productions as *The Vampyre, or the Bride of the Isles* and *The Phantom*, it would be logical to assume that these creatures populated many early films. However, this was not the case.

Numerous popular-audience writers have mistakenly referred to Méliès's *The Devil's Castle/Le manoir du diable* (1896) as the first vampire film.[144] This error even appears in the title of John L. Flynn's book *Cinematic Vampires: The Living Dead on Film and Television, from The Devil's Castle (1896) to Bram Stoker's Dracula (1992)*.[145] But however crucial that moving picture was, with all the many horror tropes it introduced to cinema, no vampires appear during its running time. None. To begin, the film's original title and most common English translation in the period indicate that he is in fact a devil. Méliès reiterates this point in the character's appearance: the devil's costume features fabric horns. These points were underscored in film catalog descriptions of the period; in 1903, for example, Lubin describes the climax as follows: "Satan ... vanishes immediately when the Cross [sic] is held before him."[146]

During the era of sound cinema, the use of a cross to dispel vampires became so common as to cloud the fact that the same religious iconography had repeatedly been used in an earlier age to dispel devils. Consider the short story *A Ghost*, published in the *Connecticut Gazette* in August 1797, in which the narrator tells us: "At length I concluded, if it be a demon, he will fly at the sign of the cross."[147] This was also true in the ballet *Uriella, the Demon of the Night*, which was staged in New York in 1870. It was also true in early cinema. In *Mephisto's Son/Le fils du diable* (Pathé Frères, 1906), the son of Satan cowers before a priest carrying a cross.[148] In Vitagraph's *The Gambler and the Devil* (1908), the female lead "holds up a cross before him. The devil covers his eyes with his hands, there is a puff of smoke, and he disappears."[149] Then, in *Satan Defeated/La défaite de Satan* (Pathé Frères, 1911), a character "holds up the crucifix and Satan disappears forever."[150]

With regard to Satan or his minions taking the form of a bat, it is important to recall Ephesians 2:2, which describes Satan as the "prince of the power of the air," as well as the sheer volume of artwork over the centuries that depicts devils and demons as having wings and talons, including Botticelli's and Doré's illustrations for Dante's *Inferno*.[151] Here again, the same can be seen repeatedly in early cinema, ranging from Méliès's *The Devil in a Convent/Le diable au couvent* (Méliès, 1900, aka *The Sign of the Cross; or the Devil in a Convent*), in which Satan flies into the convent, to American trade advertisements for the Italian-made *Satan, or, The Drama of Humanity/Satana, ovvero il dramma dell'umanità* (Ambrosio, 1912), which used artwork of a bat to promote a moving picture about the devil's impact on humankind.[152]

If *The Devil's Castle/Le manoir du diable* is definitely not a vampire film, then it becomes important to question what films of the period might be. The most likely candidate for the first vampire film is *Loïe Fuller*, which Pathé Frères released in the United States in 1905. This French-made moving picture showcased Loïe Fuller, the famous American artist who helped pioneer modern dance. In the film, a bat flies onto the terrace of a country home (or even a castle, perhaps, as we do not see its exterior). A clever transition occurs in which Fuller appears for a moment with the bat on her head and then—the bat having been removed from view—spreads her costume in bat-wing style. With the bat-to-woman transformation complete, Fuller performs a dance and then disappears from view thanks to a dissolve, another cinematic sign of her potential supernaturalism.

Why might this character, in which a bat turns into human form, have been understood as a vampire when the character in *The Devil's Castle* undergoes a similar transformation but was not a vampire? Cultural context provides the answer. For one, vampire dance acts became popular in the 1890s. As early as 1891, a minstrel company offered a "Vampire Dance" as one of the "special features" of its show.[153] Such "vampire dance" acts continued into the early twentieth century, spurred in part by the success of Philip Burne-Jones's painting *The Vampire* (1897) and Rudyard Kipling's poem of the same name.[154] Thus Loïe Fuller—who is in no way garbed as a devil or described as such in the film's title or in catalog synopses—was performing what might well have been understood as one of these vampire dances.

Secondly, and perhaps more importantly in this instance, was the evolving definition of what constituted a vampire at the turn of the twentieth century. Despite the success of Stoker's novel, the foremost understanding of vampirism in America in the early twentieth century was an outgrowth of the Burne-Jones and Kipling representations. Consider this article published in the *Chicago Tribune* in 1903:

> "What is a vampire, anyway?" asked a young woman looking at the Burne-Jones picture now on exhibition.
> "A vampire," [replied] her companion. "A vampire is the rag and a bone and a hank of hair that Kipling talks about."
> They probably had not spent a portion of their youthful lives in a small town visited occasionally by the "greatest show on earth" with its sideshow. If they had they would have known all about the "blood sucking vampire." They would have dreamed about it . . .[155]

Exasperated by cultural confusion over the term, the journalist proceeded to describe vampires in great detail, both in their folkloric roots and in Stoker's novel.

Figures 8.7 and 8.8 Two frames from the Pathé Frères film *Loïe Fuller*, distributed in America in 1905.

The impact of Burne-Jones and Kipling manifested most notably in the stage and film versions of *A Fool There Was* and in the persona of actress Theda Bara (which will be explored in Chapter 12). For the moment, the key issue is that Loïe Fuller, as a bat transforming into a woman and performing a dance, potentially represented the intersection of both supernatural and natural vampires of the era, a point that might been readily understood by some audience members.

At least one viewer saw an onscreen depiction of a supernatural vampire in Segundo de Chomón's aforementioned film *Legend of a Ghost/La légende du fantôme* (Pathé Frères, 1908), in which the heroine and her small "army" descend into the bowels of the earth. According to a plot synopsis in *Moving Picture World*:

> Arriving at the gate of Satan's kingdom, they mount a chariot of fire and, arriving at the devil's palace, give fight to the demons mounting guard over their king, and after having defeated them, rush into the palace. Now Satan, seeing his life in peril, disappears in a cloud of smoke and thunder, and is seen again as he dashes through his vast domains gathering together his people, and while they await the conquering chariot another fight ensues. The devil is beaten again and the bottle of life is stolen by the leader of the victorious army, and they are all about to depart when a terrible explosion takes place and the chariot and its occupants are dashed to the ground. All are killed but the brave woman who undertook the expedition, and she goes forth alone . . .[156]

The synopsis—which was also published in *Views and Film Index*—continues with explicit mention that "dragons and vampires" attempt "to stop her progress towards earth."[157]

With hand-tinted colors and a running time of over twenty minutes, *Variety* praised the film's "curious, mystic light effects," which were "well handled to heighten the weirdness of the scenes."[158] The story—inspired by Dante's *Inferno* and the Greek myth of Orpheus—marks the first known occasion that a period account describes a film as featuring a supernatural vampire. However, viewing a surviving print shows the young lady's difficult journey back to the surface from what appears to be a sea bed; seashells and marine plants present in the sets reinforce the notion that the action takes place in an aquatic environment. The creatures are variously intended to be fish, prawns, seahorses, frogs, newts, and salamanders.

What does this mean? Here is a problem not unlike that *The Devil's Castle* has posed. The American synopsis writer thought a vampire appeared onscreen, but that does not seem to be the case. Rather, it was a misreading of the film's visuals. To be sure, surviving synopses for *Legend of a Ghost* published in other countries do not mention vampires. Nor does the aforementioned review published in *Variety*.

The final occasion in which supernatural vampires were invoked during the early cinema period came in a movie serial. Episode six of the serial *The Exploits of Elaine* (Pathé, 1915) bore the title *The Vampire*. In it, Elaine (Pearl White) shoots an underling of her nemesis, the "Clutching Hand" (played by Sheldon Lewis). In retaliation, he kidnaps Elaine so as to use her blood and "restor[e] life" to his minion.[159] The police rescue Elaine before the dangerous transfusion occurs. The Clutching Hand, something of a medical vampire, escapes from the authorities thanks to a sliding panel in the wall.[160]

Overall, these three examples—*Loïe Fuller*, *Legend of a Ghost*, and *The Vampire* episode from *The Exploits of Elaine*—suggest how elusive the early screen vampire really was. The creature did not appear in *The Devil's Castle*, and it might not have appeared in any of these films either. Many audiences may not have connected *Loïe Fuller*'s dance to vampirism, *Legend of a Ghost*'s "vampire" seems to be nothing more than a synoptic mistake, and while *The Vampire* explicitly invoked vampirism in its title and in a character's need for blood, no supernatural creature materialized during its running time.

Conclusion

As the early cinema period came to an end, American companies continued to produce moving pictures with supernatural creatures. In late 1915, for example, Vitagraph released *The Dust of Egypt*, an elaborate "blue ribbon feature" in which a man named Lascelles (played by Antonio Moreno) allows a friend to store a mummy case in his apartment. That night, Lascelles dreams that he:

> sees the mummy case yield up its body in the form of a beautiful young girl who steps out into the room in all the pomp and splendor of an Egyptian princess of three thousand years ago. Struck dumb with amazement, Lascelles has to put her up for the night. She has great difficulty getting into his pajamas which she wears over her robes.[161]

Vitagraph guaranteed the film was "very amusing," one certain to please discriminating viewers.

As with so many screen ghosts and devils, most representations of skeletons and mummies appeared—like the reanimated princess in *The Dust of Egypt*—for the sake of comedy. Here again, the humor of international filmmakers like Méliès intersected neatly with American traditions that either dismissed the supernatural or treated it comically. What is remarkable, however, is the rarity with which vampires and werewolves appeared

Figure 8.9 *The Dust of Egypt* (Vitagraph, 1915). (*Courtesy of Robert J. Kiss*)

onscreen, the former arguably absent and the latter resulting less from European folklore than from the perceived Otherness of Native Americans.

Nevertheless, these creatures constitute an important presence in early cinema, even if at times it is the result of their absence. And film depictions of them bore similarities to the onscreen treatment of devils, witches, and ghosts. Indeed, the pivotal distinction to be made here is not between these numerous supernatural creatures, but instead the gulf between the genres they constituted and those genres that relied instead on natural horrors.

Notes

1. *In the Bogie Man's Cave* is available in the DVD boxed set *Georges Méliès: First Wizard of Cinema* (Los Angeles: Flicker Alley, 2008).
2. "In the Bogie Man's Cave," *Views and Film Index*, February 1, 1908, 9.
3. In 1909, Pathé Frères released a similar film entitled *The Bogey Woman/Mme. Croquemitaine*. In it, the title character transforms children into vegetables until a fairy instructs a young boy on how to "overcome" her and thus release the others from their "vegetable bondage." See "*The Bogey Woman*," *New York Dramatic Mirror*, July 10, 1909. A copy of the film is archived at the Deutsche Kinemathek.
4. "*The Animated Scarecrow*," *Moving Picture World*, August 13, 1910, 371.
5. "*The Animated Scarecrow*," *Moving Picture World*, August 20, 1910, 27.
6. "*The Animated Scarecrow*," *Moving Picture World*, August 27, 1910, 464.
7. "*The Professor and His Wax Works*," *Views and Film Index*, January 25, 1908, 10.
8. "*The Wax Lady*," *Moving Picture World*, April 5, 1913, 86. A copy of *The Wax Lady* is archived at the Library of Congress.
9. "*The Hindoo's Ring*," *New York Dramatic Mirror*, August 22, 1908, 9; "*The Spirit and the Clay*," *Vitagraph Life Portrayals*, April 1914, 39; Robert C. McElravy, "*The Marble Heart*," *Moving Picture World*, June 26, 1915, 2107; Advertisement, *Motion Picture News*, April 25, 1915, 3. A statue also comes to life in Méliès's *The Statue of William Tell/Guillaume Tell et le clown*, released by Edison in America in 1901. Elias Savada (ed.), *The American Film Institute Catalog of Motion Pictures Produced in the United States: Film Beginnings, 1893–1910* (Lanham, Maryland: Scarecrow Press, 1995), 1015.
10. Advertisement, *Moving Picture World*, March 15, 1913, 1144. Copies of this film are archived at the Bundesarchiv-Filmarchiv, Deutsche Kinemathek, and Deutsches Filminstitut.
11. Advertisement, *Moving Picture World*, July 5, 1913, 12.
12. "*The Banshee*," *Moving Picture World*, July 12, 1913, 205.
13. Louis Reeves Harrison, "*The Banshee*," *Moving Picture World*, July 26, 1913, 408.
14. Along with the other supernatural beings discussed in the main text, fairies appeared onscreen regularly, including in such films as *Fairyland; or The Kingdom of the Fairies/Le royaume des fées* (Méliès, 1903), *The Enchanted Hat/Le chapeau enchanté* (Lux, 1908), *The Magic Rubbers/Lykkens galoscher* (Great Northern, 1908), and *The Enchanted Leg* (Kinemacolor, 1913). Famous fairy tales were also adapted to the screen, including *Beauty and the Beast/La belle et la bête* (Pathé Frères, 1908), *The Sleeping Beauty* (Venus, 1913), and—as the early cinema period ended—a one-reel version of *Cinderella*, released by Pathé Frères in January 1915, presumably a reissue of the company's 1907 *Cinderella/Cendrillon*. Other fairy films of the period include *The Little Easter Fairy* (Lubin, 1908), *The Elixir of Dreams/Le philtre des rêves* (Pathé Frères, 1909), *The Dream Fairy* (Edison, 1913), *The Fairy and the Waif* (World/Frohman, 1915), and *Their Bewitched Elopement* (Joker, 1915). As *Moving Picture World* observed in 1914, "Of good fairy tales for use on the screen there

can never be enough." See Advertisement, *New York Clipper*, September 26, 1903; "*The Enchanted Hat*," *New York Dramatic Mirror*, July 4, 1908, 7; "*The Magic Rubbers*," *Moving Picture World*, September 26, 1908, 241; "*The Enchanted Leg*," *Moving Picture World*, March 15, 1913, 1140; "*Beauty and the Beast*," *Moving Picture World*, November 14, 1908, 384; "*The Sleeping Beauty*," *Motography*, August 9, 1913, 110; "*Cinderella*," *Pathé Weekly Bulletin*, November 26, 1914, 2; "*The Little Easter Fairy*," *Moving Picture World*, April 18, 1908, 351; "*The Elixir of Dreams*," *Moving Picture World*, March 27, 1909, 368; "*The Dream Fairy*," *Moving Picture World*, July 26, 1913, 454; "*The Fairy and the Waif*," *New York Dramatic Mirror*, March 17, 1915; "*Their Bewitched Elopement*," *Motography*, August 7, 1915, 278; W. Stephen Bush, "*The Patchwork Girl of Oz*," *Moving Picture World*, September 26, 1914, 48.
15. Savada, 984.
16. "*The Story of the Skeleton Hunter*," *Hartford Times* (Hartford, Connecticut), March 19, 1836, 4. Though published without attribution in America, the story was taken from Thomas Colley Grattan, *Agnes de Mansfeldt: A Historical Tale* (Brussels: Ad. Wahlen, 1836), 335–7.
17. J. T. Trowbridge, "*The Skeleton in the House*," *The Warren Mail* (Warren, Pennsylvania), April 21, 1866, 1.
18. "*Claiming His Skeleton*," *Greensburg Standard* (Greensburg, Indiana), July 3, 1885. Luke Sharp was a pseudonym of Robert Barr.
19. "*The Family Specter*," *Lima News* (Lima, Ohio), August 10, 1899.
20. "*On Seeing a Human Skeleton*," *Massachusetts Centinel* (Boston, Massachusetts), December 11, 1784, 4.
21. "*Reflections on Viewing a Skeleton*," *Vermont Gazette* (Bennington, Vermont), March 15, 1790, 4.
22. See, for example, "A Suicide's Skeleton: Ghastly Discovery in the Woods Near Sing Sing," *New York Times*, July 22, 1888, 12; "He Kept a Skeleton: A Doctor's Ghastly Relic Visited by the Father of the Dead," *St. Louis Republic* (St. Louis, Missouri), June 8, 1890, II22; "Ghastly Find at the U.S. Brewery," *Oregonian* (Portland, Oregon), May 27, 1891, 8; "Ghastly Discovery," *Knoxville Journal* (Knoxville, Tennessee), April 20, 1894, 4.
23. See, for example, "Frightened by a Skeleton," *New York Times*, July 23, 1876, 10; "A Grinning Skeleton," *Jackson Citizen* (Jackson, Michigan), November 5, 1901, 1.
24. "Strange Phenomena," *Jackson Citizen* (Jackson, Michigan), March 23, 1900, 6.
25. "King's College, Anatomical Theatre," *New York Gazette and Weekly Mercury*, December 26, 1768, 3.
26. "The Philosophical Cobler [sic]," *Salem Gazette* (Salem, Massachusetts), December 28, 1790, 1.
27. "Skeleton Shown in Court Room," *Harrisburg Patriot* (Harrisburg, Pennsylvania), November 23, 1904, 1.
28. "The Trade in Skeletons," *Los Angeles Times*, April 1, 1893, 12.
29. "The Skeleton Business," *Indiana State Sentinel*, August 19, 1875, 2.
30. "The Bones of the Devil," *Jackson Citizen Patriot* (Jackson, Michigan), October 16, 1895, 1.
31. "A Skeleton in a Graveyard," *Chicago Tribune*, December 29, 1888, 1.
32. A copy of *The Devil's Castle* is available in the DVD boxed set *Georges Méliès: First Wizard of Cinema*.
33. A copy of *The Haunted Castle* is available in the DVD boxed set *Georges Méliès: First Wizard of Cinema*.
34. Different from those skeleton comedies discussed in the main text was *Skelley's Skeleton* (Biograph, 1914), in which the title character (played by Charlie Murray) sells his skeleton "while he still walked around in it." See "*Skelley's Skeleton*," *Moving Picture World*, December 27, 1913, 1582. A copy of this film is archived at the Museum of Modern Art, New York City.

35. *Picture Catalogue* (New York: American Mutoscope & Biograph, November 1902), 66. Available in *A Guide to Motion Picture Catalogs by American Producers and Distributors, 1894–1908: A Microfilm Edition* (New Brunswick: Rutgers University Press, 1985), Reel 2. A copy of *The Startled Lover* is archived in the Paper Print Collection at the Library of Congress.
36. Savada, 44. Here I am referring specifically to American Mutoscope & Biograph production number 924, not *The Artist's Dream* (aka *The Artist's Dream and His Rude Awakening*), which the same company released later the same year, being production number 1131. A copy of *The Artist's Dream* is archived in the Paper Print Collection at the Library of Congress.
37. "*Foiled!*", *Kalem Kalendar*, September 1915, 37.
38. "*The Skeleton,*" *Moving Picture World*, November 2, 1912, 451.
39. "*Curing the Cook,*" *The Kinetogram*, January 1915, 14.
40. A copy of *The Skeleton* is archived at the British Film Institute.
41. "*The Skeleton,*" *New York Dramatic Mirror*, February 12, 1910, 16.
42. Savada, 984; Charles Musser, *Edison Motion Pictures, 1890–1900: An Annotated Filmography* (Washington, D.C.: Smithsonian Institution Press, 1997), 471.
43. Savada, 248. *Skeleton Dance*, *Marionettes* and *Davy Jones' Locker* survive in the Paper Print Collection at the Library of Congress.
44. *Picture Catalogue* (New York: American Mutoscope & Biograph, November 1902), 72. Available in *A Guide to Motion Picture Catalogs by American Producers and Distributors, 1894–1908: A Microfilm Edition* (New Brunswick: Rutgers University Press, 1985), Reel 2.
45. Savada, 245.
46. *July Supplement of New Films* (Chicago: Selig Polyscope Co., 1903), unpaginated.
47. Savada, 1211–12, 1165; "*Cave of Spooks,*" *Moving Picture World*, December 5, 1908, 449.
48. "*Variety*'s Picture Reviews," *Variety*, October 29, 1910, 14; "*Oh You Skeleton,*" *Moving Picture World*, November 5, 1910, 1056, 1058. In naming the film, *Variety* called it *Oh, You Skeleton* (with a comma), while in the cited article *Moving Picture World* referred to it as *Oh You Skeleton*. Later, *Moving Picture World* referred to it as both *O! You Skeleton* and *O, You Skeleton*.
49. "*All for a Tooth,*" *Moving Picture World*, August 8, 1914, 857.
50. "*His Bachelor Dinner,*" *Moving Picture World*, April 17, 1915, 462.
51. "*The Dungeon of Despair,*" *Moving Picture World*, January 25, 1913, 400; "*The Phantom Violin,*" *Moving Picture World*, September 26, 1914, 1754. The Gaumont-Pathé Archives have a copy of *The Dungeon of Despair*.
52. "*The Skull,*" *Moving Picture World*, February 22, 1913, 780.
53. "*The Accusing Skeleton,*" *Moving Picture World*, December 6, 1913, 1216.
54. Louis Reeves Harrison, "*The Phantom Signal,*" *Moving Picture World*, November 1, 1913, 474. A copy of *The Phantom Signal* is archived at the Museum of Modern Art, New York City.
55. Advertisement, *Views and Film Index*, August 24, 1907, 2.
56. "Film Review," *Views and Film Index*, August 24, 1907, 6.
57. A copy of the film is available on the DVD *Fairy Tales: Early Colour Stencil Films from Pathé* (London: British Film Institute, 2012).
58. See, for example, "London," *Pennsylvania Chronicle* (Philadelphia, Pennsylvania), April 19, 1773, 13; "Trifles," *Massachusetts Centinel*, April 30, 1788, 4; "Foreign Intelligence," *New York Journal*, June 12, 1788, 2; "The Fragment," *Columbian Gazetteer* (New York), January 6, 1794, 1; "Extract," *Newport Mercury* (Newport, Rhode Island), September 3, 1799, 1.
59. See, for example, "The Mummy Last Night," *Times-Picayune* (New Orleans, Lousiana), February 29, 1852; 8; "Mummy Making," *Philadelphia Inquirer*, August 7, 1877; "Ancient Mode of Embalming the Dead," *Keowee Courier* (Walhalla, South Carolina), August 30, 1877, 1; "The Mummies Identified," *Anderson Herald* (Anderson, Indiana), November 11, 1881; "Rameses the Great," *Aberdeen Daily News* (Aberdeen, South Dakota), January 19, 1883, 3; "That English Mummy," *Sandusky Daily Register* (Sandusky, Ohio), May 5, 1891.

60. "Egyptian Mummy," *Alexandria Gazette* (Alexandria, Virginia), May 29, 1818.
61. "Egyptian Mummy," *New York American*, December 5, 1821; "Egyptian Mummy," *Providence Gazette* (Providence, Rhode Island), July 20, 1822; "The Mummy," *New Hampshire Gazette* (Portsmouth, New Hampshire), April 27, 1824; "Wanted to See the Mummy," *Nashville Union and American* (Nashville, Tennessee), August 18, 1871.
62. S. J. Wolfe with Robert Singerman, *Mummies in Nineteenth Century America: Ancient Egyptians as Artifacts* (Jefferson, North Carolina: McFarland, 2009), 55–95.
63. "A Mummy to be Opened in Boston!," *Salem Observer* (Salem, Massachusetts), May 11, 1850.
64. "The Mummy," *Boston Evening Transcript*, June 6, 1850.
65. "Opening of the Mummies at Philadelphia," *Burlington Weekly Telegraph* (Burlington, Iowa), February 8, 1851, 1; "Unrolling of a Mummy," *Chicago Tribune*, December 22, 1864, 3.
66. Quoted in "Mummy Pictures," *Kalamazoo Gazette* (Kalamazoo, Michigan), October 1, 1898, 7.
67. "Mummies as Bric-a-Brac," *New York Times*, June 25, 1882, 3.
68. "Bogus Mummies," *Chicago Tribune*, June 9, 1888, 6; "Discrediting the Mummy Market," *San Francisco Bulletin*, June 14, 1888, 4.
69. "Mummy Factory Does a Thriving Business in Los Angeles," *Evening News* (San Jose, California), April 24, 1906.
70. "Horrors of a Mummy Pit," *Daily Iowa State Register* (Des Moines, Iowa), May 23, 1867, 3.
71. "Priestess, Dead Centuries Ago, Still Potent to Slay and Afflict," *Atlanta Constitution*, June 19, 1904.
72. "Mummy Causes Loss," *Idaho Statesman* (Boise, Idaho), May 10, 1914, II2.
73. "Literary," *Ohio State Journal* (Columbus, Ohio), April 10, 1860.
74. The *Philadelphia Inquirer* was one of the newspapers that serialized Hume's novel in 1909.
75. Collins Shackleford, "*The Mummy's Soul*," *Canton Advocate* (Canton, South Dakota), November 28, 1877, 2.
76. "*He Stole a Princess*," *Boston Globe*, January 25, 1891, 24.
77. Brian J. Frost has suggested that Poe's story might have been inspired by "Letter from a Revived Mummy," published in the *New York Evening Mirror* on January 21, 1832. See Brian J. Frost, *The Essential Guide to Mummy Literature* (Lanham, Maryland: Scarecrow Press, 2008), 4.
78. Matthew Rebhorn, *Pioneer Performances: Staging the Frontier* (New York: Oxford University Press, 2012), 85.
79. "*The Mummy*," *New York Clipper*, October 24, 1896, 544. This play had already been staged in England in 1895.
80. "Amusements," *The Evening Times* (Grand Forks, North Dakota), September 4, 1906, 4. Elixirs bringing mummies back to life reappeared in the short story *The Mummy and the Panacea* (published in *Gunter's Magazine* in 1910) and in the comedy film *Too Much Elixir of Life* (Thistle/Alhambra, 1915). See "*Too Much Elixir of Life*," *Moving Picture World*, October 9, 1915, 338.
81. "*The Mummy Girl* Presented to Patrons of the Imperial," *Pawtucket Times* (Pawtucket, Rhode Island), December 11, 1906, 3.
82. "Latest Films of All Makers," *Views and Film Index*, March 7, 1908, 8. Copies of *The Mummy* are archived at the British Film Institute and the Cinémathèque Française.
83. "*The Egyptian Mystery*," *New York Dramatic Mirror*, July 24, 1909, 16.
84. "*The Mummy*," *Moving Picture News*, February 25, 1911, 17.
85. "*The Mummy*," *Moving Picture World*, March 18, 1911, 604.
86. "*The Mummy and the Cowpunchers*," *Moving Picture World*, December 7, 1912, 1002.
87. "*Slim and the Mummy*," *Moving Picture World*, November 7, 1914, 789.
88. Advertisement, *Moving Picture World*, May 10, 1913, 570.
89. "*The Egyptian Mummy*," *Kalem Kalendar*, May 15, 1913, 9.
90. A copy of *The Egyptian Mummy* (Kalem, 1913) is archived at the Library of Congress.
91. "*The Egyptian Mummy*," *Moving Picture World*, July 7, 1913, 1031.

92. "*An Egyptian Princess*," *Moving Picture World*, July 18, 1914, 469–70.
93. "*Oh, You Mummy!*," *Motion Picture News*, November 21, 1914, 48. The November 21, 1914 issue of *Moving Picture World* refers to this film by the slightly different title, *O! You Mummy*.
94. "*When the Mummy Cried for Help*," *Motography*, January 16, 1915, 110. Such comedies continued to be produced even as the early cinema period came to a close. See, for example, "*The Live Mummy*," *Pathé Weekly Bulletin*, April 1, 1915, 7; and "*The Missing Mummy*," *Moving Picture World*, December 25, 1915, 2425. The latter film was not released until January 4, 1916.
95. A copy of *The Egyptian Mummy* (Vitagraph, 1914) is archived at the Library of Congress.
96. "*The Egyptian Mummy*," *New York Dramatic Mirror*, December 23, 1914.
97. Here I would note that the rarity of certain supernatural characters onscreen might have enhanced the power of their stories and images on some audience members.
98. "*More Dangers Threaten Pauline*," *Motography*, June 27, 1914, 459.
99. "*The Necklace of Rameses*," *Motion Picture News*, February 14, 1914, 37. Tales of valuables attached to mummies also appeared in *Lord John in New York* (Universal-Gold Seal, 1915) and *The Secret of the Dead* (Domino, 1915), the latter featuring a "party of excavators" who unearth the mummy of a Native American. Affixed to his breast is a treasure map. See John T. Soister and Henry Nicolella with Steve Joyce and Harry H. Long, *American Silent Horror, Science Fiction and Fantasy Feature Films, 1913–1929* (Jefferson, North Carolina: McFarland & Company, 2012), 726–7; "*The Secret of the Dead*," *Motography*, February 20, 1915, 301.
100. "*The Clue of the Scarab*," *Moving Picture World*, September 26, 1914, 1830.
101. "*When Soul Meets Soul* (Essanay)," *Moving Picture World*, December 28, 1912, 1324. A copy of this film is archived at the Library of Congress.
102. McQuade, 1275–6.
103. "*The Vengeance of Egypt*," *Moving Picture World*, October 19, 1912, 251.
104. Ibid., 251.
105. "Quebec, July 14," *Pennsylvania Journal, or the Weekly Advertiser* (Philadelphia, Pennsylvania), August 14, 1766, 2.
106. See, for example, "The Homicide Mania," *Coshocton Democrat* (Coshocton, Ohio), August 15, 1871, 1; "The Awful Were-wolf," *Evansville Courier and Press* (Evansville, Indiana), November 14, 1891, 3; "The Werewolf," *Newport Mercury* (Newport, Rhode Island), October 7, 1905, 6.
107. "Bisclaveret: A Breton Romance," *New York Times*, January 18, 1880, 3. This article was in fact a reprint of a Maurice Kingsley's "Bisclaveret: A Breton Romance," *Macmillan's Magazine* (London and New York: Macmillan & Co.), January 1880, 216–24.
108. "A Somber Canadian Legend," *The Gallup Gleaner* (Gallup, New Mexico), March 21, 1894, 1.
109. Sabine Baring-Gould, *The Book of Were-Wolves* (London: Smith, Elder, & Company, 1865).
110. "Modern Languages," *The Evening Star* (Washington, D.C.), December 27, 1893, 7.
111. Elliott O'Donnell, *Werewolves* (London: Methuen & Company, 1912).
112. Graham R. Tomson, "A Ballad of the Were-wolf," *Macmillan's Magazine* 62 (September 1890), 368.
113. Olav Gunstveit, "*Werewolf*," *Reno Evening Gazette* (Reno, Nevada), June 21, 1907, 4.
114. "*The Fairy of the Castle*," *Yorkville Enquirer* (Yorkville, South Carolina), September 24, 1874, 1.
115. Clarissa Mackie, "The Werewolf," *Batesville Tribune* (Batesville, Indiana), December 31, 1913, 8.
116. Julian Hawthorne, "*The Werewolf*," *Chicago Herald*, June 8, 1890, 27. This story was originally published in the *New York Ledger*.
117. Eugene Field, "*The Werewolf*," *Ladies Home Journal*, March 1896.
118. Howard Pyle, "*The Salem Wolf*," *Harper's Monthly Magazine*, December 1909, 3–12.
119. There were several imported comedies that drew upon the idea of "you-are-what-you-eat," even if their characters only adopted traits of the animals in question while retaining human physical form. To cite three extant examples, all of which were released in the U.S.: *The Result*

of Eating Horse Flesh/Calino a mangé du cheval (Pathé Frères, 1908, aka *The Result of Eating Horse Meat*), *Fricot Drinks a Bottle of Horse Embrocation/Fricot beve la medicina* (Ambrosio, 1910), and *Spiffkins Eats Frogs/Teddy a mangé des grenouilles* (Lux, 1912). There was also *A Strong Diet/Un monsieur qui a mangé du taureau* (Gaumont, 1909), in which a man who has eaten steak from a bull mounts some horns on his head and pretends to have undergone a "you-are-what-you-eat" transformation. A trade review of it suggested, "The destruction which accompanies the action is scarcely to be commended." See "*A Strong Diet,*" *Moving Picture World*, June 19, 1909, 835.

120. "*The Snake Man,*" *Moving Picture World*, April 2, 1910, 533.
121. "*The Snake Man,*" *Moving Picture World*, April 16, 1910, 600.
122. Soister, 204–5. A copy of *A Florida Enchantment* is archived at the Library of Congress.
123. "*The Werewolf,*" *Moving Picture World*, December 6, 1913, 1206.
124. Ibid., 1206.
125. Ibid., 1206.
126. "*The Werewolf,*" *Moving Picture World*, December 6, 1913, 1153.
127. "*The Were Wolf* [sic]," *Motion Picture News*, November 29, 1913, 44.
128. Despite its title, Reliance's *The Wolf Man* (1915, aka *The Wolf-Man*) was not a story of werewolves or the supernatural.
129. "America's Aborigines Visualized Exquisitely in Bison Drama," *Universal Weekly*, February 21, 1914, 16.
130. "The Film of the Week," *The Plain Dealer* (Cleveland, Ohio), March 15, 1914.
131. "*The Legend of the Phantom Tribe,*" *Moving Picture World*, February 27, 1914, 1090; "*The Legend of the Phantom Tribe,*" *New York Dramatic Mirror*, February 25, 1914, 40.
132. "Chicago Police Sensitive," *Variety*, March 6, 1914, 5.
133. "*White Wolf,*" *Motion Picture News*, October 3, 1914, 60.
134. "*The White Wolf,*" *Moving Picture World*, September 26, 1914, 1818.
135. "The Vroucalaca," *The North American* (Philadelphia, Pennsylvania), May 17, 1844, 1.
136. "The Weird, Romantic Vampire," *Kansas City Times*, May 14, 1887, 10.
137. "Medreyga in Hungary," *American Weekly Mercury* (Philadelphia, Pennsylvania), June 15, 1732, 2.
138. Untitled, *New England Weekly Journal* (Boston, Massachusetts), March 14, 1738, 1.
139. "Believe in Vampires," *Boston Globe*, January 27, 1896, 5.
140. "Drinking Human Blood," *Oakland Tribune*, March 27, 1896, 6.
141. See, for example, "The Vampire," *New Hampshire Gazette* (Portsmouth, New Hampshire), February 21, 1826, 4; "The Vampire," *The Times* (Hartford, Connecticut), August 31, 1839, 1; "The Vampire Bat of Brazil," *Daily National Intelligencer* (Washington, D.C.), September 6, 1847, 3; "The Vampire Bat," *The Farmer's Cabinet* (Amherst, New Hampshire), September 18, 1856, 1; "The Vampire Bat," *Kalamazoo Gazette* (Kalamazoo, Michigan), December 27, 1892, 3.
142. "An Old Superstition," *Saturday Evening Post*, Vol. LIII, No. 41, May 9, 1874, 4.
143. "A Blood-Sucking Vampire," *Anaconda Standard* (Anaconda, Montana), August 29, 1893.
144. See, for example, J. Gordon Melton, *The Vampire Book: The Encyclopedia of the Undead* (Canton, Michigan: Visible Ink Press, 2011), 448.
145. John L. Flynn, *Cinematic Vampires: The Living Dead on Film and Television, from The Devil's Castle (1896) to Bram Stoker's Dracula (1992)* (Jefferson, North Carolina: McFarland & Company, 1992).
146. *Complete Catalogue of Lubin's Films* (Philadelphia: Lubin, January 1903), 20. Available in *A Guide to Motion Picture Catalogs by American Producers and Distributors, 1894–1908: A Microfilm Edition* (New Brunswick: Rutgers University Press, 1985), Reel 3.
147. "*A Ghost,*" *Connecticut Gazette* (New London, Connecticut), August 30, 1797, 1.

148. "*Mephisto's Son* at Nickelo," *The Daily Democrat* (Shelbyville, Indiana), December 14, 1906, 5.
149. "*The Gambler and the Devil*," *Moving Picture World*, October 3, 1908, 267.
150. "*Satan Defeated*," *Moving Picture World*, March 18, 1911, 602.
151. Arturo Graf, *Art of the Devil* (New York: Parkstone Press International, 2009).
152. Advertisement, *Moving Picture World*, January 11, 1913, unpaginated.
153. "The Amusement Event of the Season," *Centralia Enterprise and Tribune* (Centralia, Wisconsin), April 11, 1891.
154. See, for example, "Warm Dance Promised," *Variety*, December 27, 1912, 1.
155. "Vampires," *Chicago Tribune*, January 25, 1903, 40.
156. "*Legend of a Ghost*," *Moving Picture World*, May 23, 1908, 463.
157. "Latest Films of All Makers," *Views and Film Index*, May 23, 1908, 10.
158. Rush, "*Legend of a Ghost* (Spectacular)," *Variety*, May 23, 1908, 12.
159. "*The Vampire*," *Motography*, February 13, 1915, 266. Copies of *The Vampire*, Episode 6 of *The Exploits of Elaine*, are archived at the George Eastman Museum and the Museum of Modern Art, New York City.
160. Neil G. Caward, "Dog Actor Displays Wonderful Skill," *Motography*, February 13, 1915, 243.
161. "*The Dust of Egypt*," *Vitagraph Life Portrayals*, October 1915, 42. Some brief clips of *The Dust of Egypt* appear in the short subject *Movie Album* (Vitaphone, 1932), archived at UCLA Film & Television Archive.

CHAPTER 9

Death, Murder, and Execution

As it did for so many new releases, *Moving Picture World* published a lengthy synopsis of Essanay's film *The Devil's Signature* in 1914:

> That night Sanford goes to the room. He is horror-stricken to see a hand emerge from the door of the clothes closet. He summons Huff, and when the hand appears again, he fires four shots at it. They are unable to locate where the bullets struck and the detective gives up in despair. Sanford discovers a push button that opens a door which leads to a dungeon. In this dungeon he finds Craven, a mulatto gardener, who has been killed by the bullets. The murderer has been discovered: they find that his left foot is a cloven hoof, "the devil's signature."[1]

The trade promised viewers would experience "realism, thrills, and shudders, especially in the last reel."[2] According to *Motography*, "It is upon the suspense and mystery element in the story that the success of this film lies . . . those who enjoy weird and bizarre explanations of the mysteries they see presented in photoplay form will fairly revel in this latest offering . . ."[3] *The Devil's Signature* was the latest film to depict violent death, as so many had since *Execution of Mary, Queen of Scots* (Edison, 1895).

To be sure, Americans in the eighteenth and nineteenth centuries were in much closer proximity to death than those living in the twentieth and twenty-first centuries.[4] And yet, for many reasons, attitudes regarding death changed from the time of the American Revolution to the dawn of the twentieth century. These evolutions were an outgrowth of such realities as high infant mortality rates, as well as the somewhat surprising fact that life expectancy actually decreased in America during the period between 1790 and 1860.[5] Casualties in the U.S. Civil War of 1861 to 1865 numbered a staggering 620,000, if not higher.[6] The anonymity of many corpses and the lack of care with which soldiers had to be buried stood in marked contrast to the reverence usually given to the dead.[7] But war was just one of many important factors. As Lucy E. Frank has written:

> Slavery, the unabated genocide of Native Americans, the Civil War, racial violence in the South, and the nation's growing sense of its imperial mission all gave rise to curious, often uneasy dreams of death and haunting within American culture.[8]

To this list we could rightly add differences in ethnic traditions regarding the dead, such as the skepticism some Americans expressed toward Irish wakes.

Burial of the dead exposed other distinctions. Funerals were often a mark of social status, ranging from the elaborate tombs for the wealthy to the unmarked plots of the poor. Those with money could engage in the beautification of death, in part due to the rise of the coffin hardware industry in the nineteenth century.[9] By contrast, during the eighteenth and nineteenth centuries, African-American graves and corpses in potter's fields were the most likely to be disturbed by body snatchers.[10] And yet death was at times viewed as a great equalizer, not only of the dearly departed, but also of the mourning process. Those who were poor might not have been able to afford to purchase physical memorials, but they still experienced emotional pain of a type described in elegiac Graveyard Poetry and in the works of Edgar Allan Poe, who coined the phrase "mournful and never-ending remembrance."

The post-bellum period emphasized an increasing distance from death.[11] Cosmetic decoration and the reconstruction of corpses became commonplace, as did embalming, particularly after its famous usage on the remains of Abraham Lincoln in 1865.[12] A major growth in the funeral home business met these needs, as well as the removal and storage of the dead from the home prior to the funeral. As Gary Laderman has observed, by the twentieth century death had become taboo.[13]

Laderman's remark refers not only to the handling and burial of corpses, but also to the actual process of death. For example, a movement against animal vivisection gained momentum in the late nineteenth century.[14] A more extended debate raged over the issue of public executions. Intellectuals argued against the practice even as many Americans flocked to see them. As late as 1911, the first public hanging in Mississippi in the space of thirty-five years resulted in the following spectacle:

> Thousands of people came to Louisville. They came early by train and private conveyance. Vendors had secured concessions of all kinds and restaurants had been hastily constructed about the scaffold for feeding the throngs with sandwiches, coffee, lemonade, and peanuts. . . . It was more like a gala picnic than the dispatching of a soul to eternity.[15]

Efforts to end these scenes rested largely on the growing belief that, as Elizabeth Barnes has observed, "a civilized society had nothing to gain from such demonstrations and much to lose."[16]

During the 1870s and beyond, the press regularly condemned the use of hanging for its unnecessary cruelty.[17] Electricity was thus promoted as a method to sanitize the death penalty. According to Jürgen Martschukat, the electrocution of four men at Sing Sing in 1891 was heralded as a "great scientific experiment."[18] But in some quarters, this humane reputation was not accepted. As early as 1890, newspaper descriptions of the electric chair relied on such adjectives as "horror."[19] By 1914, the *Washington Post* declared that electrocutions were "grewsome [sic]" and replete with "ghastly details."[20]

The subject of death in this era is not without major contradictions. A growing desire to keep human remains at a distance from daily life coincided with the rise of the new visual culture in America, meaning the increased publication of illustrations in newspapers and magazines, as well as the widespread use of photography. The result was that visual representations of death became increasingly commonplace. As real corpses became hidden from view, artwork and photographs of them were openly displayed.[21]

Press accounts of death were constant, ranging from obituaries to coverage of wars and disasters.[22] In the latter decades of the nineteenth century, many Americans also fell prey to what Michael Ayers Trotti has called the "lure of the sensational murder."[23] American reportage of Jack the Ripper would be one example, but there was no shortage of indigenous murders, ranging from the infamous case involving Lizzie Borden to the Bender Family (who murdered at least ten people in Kansas between 1870 and 1873), the Kelly Family (who killed approximately eleven persons during the last four months of 1887), Belle Gunness (who killed between twenty-five and forty persons between 1884 and 1908), and Jane Toppan (who confessed to thirty-one murders between 1885 and 1901).[24]

Writing on the subject of death in 1913, Louis Reeves Harrison observed in *Moving Picture World*:

> Into the chaos of passion and confusion of thought that intensify human existence at critical moments, nature's solution is often projected. Death clears away difficulties; it settles vexed questions; it reassures seemingly inharmonious elements; it rounds out human destiny; but on this account, the writers and producers of plays, disregarding the relation of commonplace death to commonplace life, use the cessation of life for the sake of a situation that has little else to it, and only create an atmosphere of gloom unillumined by splendid purpose.[25]

Nature's solution was projected, as was the filmmaker's, over and over again, the cessation of life becoming that which so often gave animation to the cinema.

Death

Death onscreen attempted to provoke various emotions, including thrills.[26] In *The Cremation* (American Mutoscope & Biograph, 1899), flames burn a young woman into a skeleton that—thanks to the wave of a magic wand—returns to flesh and blood and life.[27] Using dark comedy, *The Finish of Bridget McKeen* (Edison, 1901) presents the fictional death of an Irish cook who tries to light a stove fire with kerosene.[28] The second of two shots in the film depicts her grave marker, an early example of a fictional cemetery appearing in American

Figure 9.1 A frame from *The Finish of Bridget McKeen* (Edison, 1901). (*Courtesy of the Library of Congress*)

cinema. By contrast, death could be "grewsome [sic]," as in *The Legend of the Lighthouse/La Legénde des phares* (Gaumont, 1909), in which an "old hag" loots corpses that wash ashore.[29] And it could provoke shocks. In *The Statue of Fright/La statue d'épouvante* (Eclipse, 1913), an aggrieved father unveils not a sculpture at a party, but instead his own daughter's corpse.[30]

Filmmakers even treated a subject as socially and religiously taboo as suicide from a variety of perspectives. In *The Suicide* (1903), the fifth entry in American Mutoscope & Biograph's series *The Downward Path*, a man deserts a young woman. Drinking poison becomes her last resort, with the film moralizing against the wicked ways of the big city.[31] A decade later, in *His Suicide* (Lubin, 1914), a man kills himself by swallowing gasoline and then touching a lit match to his mouth; his widow comically bemoans the fact her family didn't have fire insurance.[32] Then, in *Hara-Kari/Harakiri* (Apex, 1914), the lead character commits suicide as part of a solemn act to protect her honor.[33]

As the nickelodeon period ended, the subject of diseases and plagues became a plot device in which fictional films could show widespread loss of life. For example, *In the Line of Duty/Mens Pesten raser* (Sherry/East India Feature Film Co., 1914) and *The Dead Soul* (Lubin, 1915) offered narratives about the Black Death.[34] Of *The Smallpox Scare at Gulch Hollow* (Frontier, 1913), *Moving Picture World* responded, "Three or four scenes in this picture are so hideous and gruesome that they overshadow the good points of the offering."[35] A poster for the film was also intense, illustrating a warning about the epidemic and a victim of the same, with large mosquitos flying over the corpse.

None of this is to say death onscreen always achieved its desired effect. "Death scenes on the films usually afford the actor or actress an opportunity in which to display their ability as contortionists and high divers," *Motography* observed sarcastically in 1912. "So firmly established is the writhing and twisting ceremony of death that no film, nor legitimate play, for that matter, would be complete without the almost superhuman efforts of an active and exceedingly healthy actor."[36] These depictions were at odds with nonfiction films showing funeral processions of President McKinley, Admiral Sampson, and the victims of the Maine disaster.[37]

Natural disasters also captivated many early audiences, even though cameras normally couldn't shoot the events while they were underway. The resulting footage usually formed a corpus of their aftermath.[38] These included films of such tragedies as the Galveston hurricane of 1900 and Great Baltimore Fire of 1904.[39] Advertisements for them often promised horrifying views. Lubin touted its film *Volcanic Eruption of Mt. Pelee at St. Pierre* (1902) for showing the "taking out of the dead," later describing "many" of the corpses as being "so disfigured that they are beyond recognition."[40] Nearly a decade later, Imp heralded the fact it had secured "wonderful moving pictures of the frightful" hurricane and flood in Charleston, South Carolina.[41] And Mutual's *Eastland Horror* of 1915 depicted "the removal of the bodies of the victims of the steamboat disaster in Chicago."[42] A surviving copy of *Dayton Flood Horror* (Dayton Flood Film Co., 1913) reveals just how disturbing these films could be. Grim and apparently nonfiction footage of a dead man and two dead horses appear amid the scenes of disaster.[43]

Collectively, the most prominent of these moving pictures were those taken in San Francisco after the 1906 earthquake. A promotion for one of these films attested it was the "most tensely nerve-tingling moving photograph ever flashed on a screen."[44] Of a pending projection in South Carolina, one journalist excitedly wrote:

No one who reads at all can forget the thrills of horror that he experienced a few weeks ago when the papers teemed with descriptions of the awful catastrophe, and now by means of the faithful eye of the camera an opportunity is presented of seeing these events . . .[45]

In terms of particulars, sales agent William H. Swanson promoted that his footage included such scenes as *Removing the Dead* and *Burying the Dead in Portsmouth Park*, as well as the *Shooting of a Ghoul*, an apparent reference to the onscreen killing of a person looting the corpses.[46] As late as 1908, one film company catalog devoted an entire section to these, treating their numbers as if they constituted a distinct and apparently popular genre.[47]

Nevertheless, not everyone was pleased with the public exhibition of these death films, including some politicians and clergymen. Without realizing it was fake, one minister denounced footage of the aftermath of the Collinwood, Ohio school fire in 1908. "We might as well bring the morgue down to the public square and invite the people to come in and charge an admission," he lamented.[48]

Murder

Early cinema was rife with murder, whether in Edwin S. Porter's *The Great Train Robbery* (Edison, 1903) or D. W. Griffith's *The Musketeers of Pig Alley* (Biograph, 1912). As early as 1899, Frederick S. Armitage filmed *The Demon Barber* for American Mutoscope & Biograph, a visualization of fictitious murderer Sweeney Todd.[49] Two years later, Edison released *Massacre at Constantinople* (1901), which showed the "butcher" of men, women, and children with "long knives."[50] Other examples include *A Career of Crime, No. 3: Robbery & Murder* (American Mutoscope & Biograph, 1900), in which a thief stabs a man to death, and *The Murderer's Vision* (American Mutoscope & Biograph, 1902), in which a murderer witnesses his crime superimposed on the wall of his prison cell.[51]

American Mutoscope & Biograph also distributed the British-made Gaumont film *Revenge!* (1904). In it, a husband strangles the man who has "wronged" his wife. Their catalog description begins with the declarative sentence, "This is a thriller."[52] Two years later, American audiences saw *A Desperate Crime/Les incendiaires* (Méliès, 1906), which began at "nightfall," with hooded bandits binding a husband and wife before stabbing them to death and looting their wealth. After the chief bandit is captured, he is executed and buried in an unmarked grave.[53]

Another type of attraction came in the form of murder scenes adapted from popular plays. Divorced from their narratives, these films concentrated on the cause of death. Examples include *Duel Scene from "Macbeth"* (American Mutoscope & Biograph, 1905) and, even earlier, *A Duel to the Death* (American Mutoscope, 1898).[54] "*To the Death*" (1898), produced by British Mutoscope and released in America, was a counterpart to *A Duel to the Death*. It adapted the "celebrated duel scene from the melodrama *Women and Wine*," but, removed from its original context, the scene became a grisly attraction in which two women fight with butcher knives until one kills the other.[55]

Vitagraph's *The Tiger* (1913) depicted a particularly hideous murder. A "crazy old man" seeks revenge on the animal trainer who "ruined" his daughter. Its tale of "terror and horror" has the old man purchasing a tiger and then luring the animal trainer to his home.[56] Once locked in a "chamber without either door or windows," the trainer notices a secret panel open. He sees the tiger in a cage, its door slowly lifted. Servants later find the trainer's corpse, as well as that of the crazy old man, who "had nothing more to live for" after his revenge was complete.[57] (That same year, discussing the popularity of jungle films, *Moving Picture World* wrote, "We are constantly invited to feast on horrors of the most hair-raising variety in which the wild animals play the leading parts."[58])

As for serial killers, Méliès's *Blue Beard/Barbe-bleue* (1902) seems to have been the first to appear in America. Lubin advertised the film as a "$5,000 production in Twelve Scenes," each of which could be "sold separately if desired."[59] Scene 5 was *The Forbidden Chamber*. A catalog description notes:

> Lady Blue Beard is now in the forbidden chamber, which she finds in complete darkness, but going to the window she unfastens the latch and throws a flood of light upon the scene. Turning around, she is petrified with horror at the sight of seven of Blue Beard's former wives, all dangling neatly from a rope stretched across the room. In her terror she drops the key upon the floor, and upon recovering it finds it smeared with blood, and all her efforts to remove the stain are ineffectual.[60]

As a surviving copy shows, the image of the seven hanging corpses remains eerily effective, as is a shot of Lady Blue Beard in bed, her rest disturbed by their hovering spirits.[61]

Americans next saw George Albert Smith's *Dorothy's Dream* (G.A.S. Films, 1903), which featured a Bluebeard sequence.[62] Pathé Frères produced its own version of the Bluebeard story in 1907, as did Edison in 1909.[63] "The fatal chamber with the wives' heads dangling from hooks looks properly gruesome," the *New York Dramatic Mirror* wrote of the latter.[64] 101 Bison later produced a variation of the story entitled *Monsieur Bluebeard* (1914), its title character being a devotee of the "black art."[65] At roughly the same time, Biograph released *Bluebeard the Second* (1914), an "amusing burlesque" on the famous French folktale.

Humor was hardly limited to that single film. The only known reference to Jack the Ripper on American theatre screens of the era resulted from the distribution of the Italian-made comedy *Berlin Jack the Ripper/Lo sventratore di Berlino* (Comerio, 1909).[66] That same year, Lubin produced *Talked to Death*, in which a woman gabs so much that anyone she encounters drops dead. Eventually she meets another equally verbose woman; the two talk to each other until they expire.[67]

But the greatest number of murders came in mystery films produced during and after the nickelodeon era. Some concentrated on unique methods of killing, as in the poison extracted from *The Deadly Plant/Herbe vénéneuse* (Pathé Frères, 1908).[68] In other cases, these storylines featured wrongly accused men in plot lines not dissimilar to those Alfred Hitchcock explored decades later. Examples include *The Message of the Dead/Jeanne la maudite* (Eclectic, 1913) and *The Mysterious Lodger* (Vitagraph, 1914), the latter written by Rita Humphreys and featuring Maurice Costello in the lead role.[69]

The Red Barn Mystery (Haggar & Sons, 1908, distributed in America by Williams, Brown & Earle) adapted an infamous English murder case of 1828.[70] In it, a young man finds himself at a crossroads. His planned wedding will cause his disinheritance, but cancelling it will provoke the wrath of his fiancée's family. As a result, he lures his fiancée to a barn where he has already dug a grave. Unable to escape his clutches, she dies at his hands. Later the fiancée's grandmother has a dream that "vividly portrays the actual scene of the crime." The authorities investigate, and the murderer is brought to justice. *Moving Picture World* wrote, "The picture is exceedingly fine photographically . . . we consider it one of the finest sensational films of recent times."[71]

After watching *Who Killed George Lambert?/Le départ dans la nuit* (Gaumont, 1913), *Moving Picture World*'s critic calculated it was the third mystery film he had watched in the space of only two days.[72] Not only did the numbers of mysteries accelerate as the nickelodeon period ended, but so too did the numbers of deaths within some individual film plots, perhaps in an effort to outdo the competition. For example, *Terror* (Eclair American, 1915) featured a plague, a murder, and a lynching; *Moving Picture World* believed it "fully lives up to all expectations" of its title.[73] The same trade calculated the contents of *Wormwood* (Fox, 1915), an adaptation of Marie Corelli's 1890 novel:[74]

> One seduction; one death from grief over the seduction; one murder, after which the body is thrown into a lake; two suicides, one by shooting, the other by a leap from a bridge; another death, presumably from sorrow, the remains being exposed after the undertaker has arranged the flowers; a detailed depiction of the mental and physical agonies of a man afflicted with delirium tremens; the death of this man and last of all a maudlin letter to a priest, asking for absolution . . .[75]

According to the review, *Wormwood* was "morbid," being about as "cheerful" as a day spent in a "morgue."

Figure 9.2 Original movie poster for *Vendetta* (Kleine-Eclipse, 1914). (*Courtesy of Bruce Hershenson*)

Two versions of Marie Corelli's 1886 novel *Vendetta* also appeared during the early cinema period, the first being an unofficial adaptation entitled *The Wages of Sin* (Vitagraph, 1908).[76] Then, in 1915, a French-made and feature-length version appeared in America. According to one advertisement, *Vendetta* (Kleine-Eclipse, 1914) told the story of:

> A Man Buried as Dead, returning to consciousness in his coffin, knocking it by his struggles from its niche in the wall; thereby breaking open a casket filled with jewels; smashing his way out [of] the tomb to his castle only to find his wife and dearest friend unfaithful to him; plotting a revenge Hellish in its execution; the killing of his faithless wife in that self-same tomb by earthquake the night of his second marriage to her—these are the essentials of a story we firmly believe unrivaled in the annals of filmed Novels.[77]

Motography explained that the "horrible" aspects of Corelli's tale were preserved, but were "not nearly so repulsive to see on the screen as one might imagine after having read the book."[78]

Executions

The most visceral moving pictures were those that depicted authentic deaths. Among them were nonfiction images of animals dying onscreen. In 1898, Maguire & Baucus sold Edison's *Bull Fight Series*, which included footage of "several horses gored by an enraged bull."[79] Similar films included the "bloodthirsty" *Fight between Tarantula and Scorpion* (American Mutoscope & Biograph, 1900), the view depicted "at close range."[80] Six years later, the same company produced and distributed *Scene in a Rat Pit* (1906), in which a group of men voyeuristically watch a dog chase and kill rats.[81]

In 1903, Selig Polyscope offered a "Stock Yard Series" of films that included such titles as *Koshering Cattle (Hebrew Method of Killing)*, *Sticking Hogs (Front View)*, *Scalding and Scraping Hogs*, [Hogs] *Coming Out of Scraping Machines and Cutting Off Heads*, *Killing Sheep*, *Skinning Sheep*, as well as *Beef, Sheep and Hog Killing*.[82] The most infamous of these films is *Electrocuting an Elephant* (Edison, 1903, aka *Electrocution of an Elephant*), due in part to the fact that it survives.[83] It remains a horrifyingly gruesome record of animal cruelty. Topsy, the elephant, was poisoned, strangled, and electrocuted. Smoke rises from her feet until she topples over dead.

Torture and death onscreen were hardly limited to animals, although those involving humans were usually fictional re-creations. "Gruesome instruments of torture" appeared onscreen in *The Spanish Inquisition/La crémation* (Méliès, 1900, aka *Cremation*), with the executioner forcing a woman into a fire. He attempts to decapitate the skull from her skeleton, but the appearance of the angel of death halts him.[84] Four years later, Méliès produced *A Miracle under the Inquisition/Un miracle sous l'inquisition* (1904), in which an executioner once again consigns a female victim to the flames; however, thanks to the intervention of an angel, the woman reappears in his chair, with the executioner taking her place at the burning pillory.[85] More grisly was the 690-foot-long *Martyrs of the Inquisition/Les martyrs de l'inquisition* (Pathé Frères, 1906).[86] Presenting "realistic and vivid reproductions of this notable torture chamber of the middle ages," the film's five tableaux included "The Prison," the "Torture Chamber," "The Rack," "Torture on the Wheel," and "Burning at the Stake."[87]

While *Execution of Mary, Queen of Scots* became the first execution film, it comprised part of a grim quartet of moving pictures produced by Raff & Gammon at Edison's

Figure 9.3 Images from *Martyrs of the Inquisition* (Pathé Frères, 1906), as published in Lubin's 1907 catalog *Life Motion Pictures*. (*Courtesy of the Margaret Herrick Library*)

facilities in the late summer of 1895. The other three were *Joan of Arc* (aka *Burning of Joan of Arc*), *Lynching Scene*, and *Scalping Scene* (aka *Indian Scalping Scene*).[88] Not only had *Execution of Mary, Queen of Scots* become the first horror-themed film, but it also initiated the first horror-themed film series, a group of death attractions that together formed a cinematic Chamber of Horrors.

Subsequent films presented the executions of historical figures, such as *Joan of Arc/ Jeanne d'Arc* (Méliès, 1900, released in America in 1901, aka *The Burning of Joan of Arc*), and *The Tower of London/La tour de Londres et les dernières moments d'Anne Boleyn* (Méliès, 1905, released in America the same year), which re-enacted the death of Anne Boleyn.[89] Other moving pictures provided re-creations of recent executions. For example, there was *Beheading Chinese Prisoner* (Lubin, 1900), a topical re-enactment of an incident in the Boxer Rebellion. After the fashion of *Execution of Mary, Queen of Scots*, its "executioner displays the head to the spectators to serve as a warning for evil-doers."[90] And American Mutoscope & Biograph's *Execution of a Murderess* (1905, aka *Execution by Hanging*) featured an actress portraying Mary Rogers, who murdered her husband in Vermont in 1902. Similar to *Execution of Mary, Queen of Scots*, the filmmaker used a careful edit to replace the actress with a dummy for the actual hanging.[91]

Film companies sometimes implied that their execution films were authentic, even when they were not, as in the staged but somber and realistic film *Shooting Captured Insurgents* (Edison, 1898).[92] That same year, Lubin offered *Execution of the Spanish Spy*.[93] In 1900, American Mutoscope & Biograph's *Execution of a Spy* showed a firing squad kill

Figure 9.4 American Mutoscope & Biograph's *Execution of a Murderess* (1905). (*Courtesy of Robert J. Kiss*)

the title character.[94] *A Career of Crime, No. 5: The Death Chair* (American Mutoscope & Biograph, 1900) presented an "accurate and thrilling representation" of its topic.[95] The surviving copy depicts an actor adeptly providing anguished expressions and squirming effectively at the time of his "death."[96] Then, in 1902, Ferdinand Zecca's *The History of a Crime/Histoire d'un crime* (Pathé Frères, 1901) appeared in America, its climax being the guillotining of a criminal.[97]

More famously, Edison released Edwin S. Porter's "realistic imitation" of the *Execution of Czolgosz* (1901, aka *Execution of Czolgosz, with Panorama of Auburn Prison*) only two weeks after President McKinley's assassin was put to death.[98] The Superintendent of Auburn State Prison, where Leon Czolgosz was electrocuted, had refused an offer of $2,000 made by the "owner of a kinetoscope" to "take a moving picture" of the assassin "entering the death chamber."[99] In Porter's film, the first two shots are authentic images of the exterior of Auburn State Prison. The third shot initiates the fictional footage, with the warden removing Czolgosz from his cell. The fourth shot shows the electric chair being tested and Czolgosz being put to death in the same.[100] Charles Musser has deemed the film Porter's most ambitious of 1901. The acting is quite restrained; the re-enactment remains disturbing.

But for some early audience members, re-enactments did not go far enough. In 1897, *The Phonoscope* reported that a man in Philadelphia suggested the "grewsome [sic]" proposition that a real execution should be filmed and screened. He argued that such an actuality would become an "enormous hit" with audiences, a possibility that worried the trade publication.[101] Nevertheless, at least two such moving pictures of this type were produced, one less than six months after the Philadelphian's suggestion.

In late 1897, *The Phonoscope* reported at length on Frank Guth's production of *The Hanging of William Carr* (released by Edison), a cinematic record of Carr's execution, his punishment for murdering his three-year-old daughter:

> It was revolting—four hundred persons crying and shrieking and laughing, surging under the very gallows, shunting against the horrible, swinging body. . . . That is how it will look—the hideous, grewsome [sic] views taken by the vitascope man. . . . It is the masterpiece of the vitascope man.[102]

In this instance, *The Phonoscope* blamed the camera's presence for turning the hanging into a travesty, suggesting that the process of filming the event had noticeably affected the manner in which it unfolded, adding that, once Carr was pronounced dead and filming ceased, the crowd "became quiet in an instant." The trade lamented, "The vitascope had all the disgrace and honor and riot [it] wanted. There was no other reason for the frantic conduct of the crowd at the hanging."[103]

A newspaper editorial published in the *Cleveland Leader* pleaded for a state law that would prevent the exhibition of the Carr "vitascope horrors," believing they could have "brutalizing effects" on those who saw them, far more than any of the boxing films that also drew the ire of many citizens.[104] The *Washington Post* directly responded to the *Leader*, asking, "Is a picture of a murderer on his way to the scaffold and waiting for the hangman to do his work a degrading exhibition?" The *Post* proceeded to draw a comparison between authentic death films and "mock murders" committed on the stage, including in the works of Shakespeare. "We have laws enough for the regulation of public executions," the newspaper argued, thus defending the right to screen the Carr film.[105]

Figure 9.5 *An Execution by Hanging* (American Mutoscope & Biograph, 1912).

The following year, in 1898, American Mutoscope produced *An Execution by Hanging* (aka *Execution of Negro at County Jail. Jacksonville, Fla*), which depicted the authentic execution of an African-American male in Florida. Cinematographer Arthur Marvin later recalled that the filming occurred in a somewhat impromptu manner, his party being on their way to cover the Spanish-American War:

> One of our unusual experiences came before the actual beginning of the war, during those weeks of tedious waiting in Tampa. We heard that there was to be an execution by hanging in Jacksonville, and in the interest of science and the camera we decided to obtain views of it if we could. We got permission to set up our machine in the jail yard, and succeeded in photographing the proceeding from the time the death march appeared outside the jail door until the drop was sprung. That is perhaps one of the most unusual subjects ever reproduced in detail by means of photographs.[106]

A catalog description warned the film was "very ghastly," although that seems to be language intended to excite interest rather than dissuade it.[107] Put another way, here was yet another "Chamber of Horrors" subject in the tradition of *Execution of Mary, Queen of Scots*, a film intended to titillate viewers with disgusting imagery.

The subject of capital punishment also became the source of humor in fictional comedies, as in Mack Sennett's *Their First Execution* (Keystone, 1913). In it, the wrong man (played by Ford Sterling) is put in the electric chair and "stubbornly" refuses to die even as the current is increased.[108] *Moving Picture World*'s critic admitted that the film's "ridiculous" approach allowed him to forget the "serious side" of what was essentially "dubious" subject matter.[109]

Related to capital punishment films were several moving pictures that depicted lynchings. In 1904, Mary Church Terrell regretted, "Hanging, shooting, and burning black men, women and children in the United States have become so common that such occurrences create but little sensation and evoke but slight comment now."[110] According to Amy Louise Wood:

> Lynching assumed [a] tremendous symbolic power precisely because it was extraordinary and, by its very nature, public and visually sensational. Those lynchings that hundreds, sometimes thousands, of white spectators gathered and watched as their fellow citizens were tortured, mutilated, and hanged or burned in full view were, for obvious reasons, the most potently haunting.[111]

Wood proceeds to write that the "cultural power of lynching" rested on "spectacle: the crowds, the rituals and performances, and their sensational representations in narratives, photographs, and films."[112]

The national media and entertainment press usually condemned the practice. For example, in 1888, Harry Rouclere, of the "Steen-Rouclere Show," told the *New York Clipper* that his traveling company attended a lynching party near Asheville, North Carolina. In an act of ghoulish commercialism, the victim promised that he would mention their show in his closing speech on the scaffold, though he "weakened at the last moment." The *Clipper* decried Rouclere, telling readers, "For an original advertising scheme this is indeed appalling."[113]

After the aforementioned *Lynching Scene* (Edison, 1895, aka *Frontier Scene*), the next film of this type seems to have been *Lynching Scene at Paris, Texas* (International

Films, 1897, aka *Lynching Scene*). A description published in *The Phonoscope* promised it to be:

> The most thrilling and realistic subject ever offered for sale. This scene shows an angry mob overpowering the sheriff, storming the jail, and dragging their [sic] prisoner to the nearest telephone pole, from which he is immediately swung into eternity, as bullet after bullet is fired into his writhing body. A most impressive and stirring subject.[114]

While it was a staged re-creation of the 1893 lynching of Henry Smith, one catalog description nevertheless touted the moving picture as "genuine." To add credence to the claim, the catalog description went so far as to claim, "By our contract with the authorities, [the] names of party and place cannot be given."[115]

In 1904, Selig Polyscope released *Tracked by Bloodhounds; or, A Lynching at Cripple Creek*. Ads and catalog descriptions for the film claimed that it was "actually" shot in Colorado when the "exciting events occurred," thus implying it was authentic, even though it too was a fictional dramatization.[116] In the film, a tramp murders a woman, whose husband and friends chase him down.[117] The final shot shows the party of men with the culprit. They throw a rope around a tree limb and pull the tramp up, his arms swaying as they do. The climactic moments feature realistic effects and restrained acting.[118] It was, according to an ad in the *New York Clipper*, the "most sensational film ever made."[119]

The other key lynching film of the era was Crescent Films' *Avenging a Crime; or Burned at the Stake* (1904, aka *Lynch Law*).[120] Its plot was similar to *Tracked by Bloodhounds*, with an African-American character (enacted by a Caucasian in blackface) killing a white woman and fleeing, only to be caught by his white pursuers. They tie the murderer to a stake, set him ablaze, and then fire bullets at him.[121] The image is depicted in long shot, which—together with the billowing smoke—makes the death scene lacking in detail. In this case, the audience becomes spectator to the fictional event, but is still kept at some remove from it. As Robert Jackson has noted, films like *Avenging a Crime* "provide a severe but valuable insight into the racial views of mainstream American popular culture in the first years of the cinema."[122] They also impelled Americans to "bear witness, to take moral and social responsibility for the brutal injustice of lynching."[123]

Moving pictures depicting lynchings and executions largely disappeared by the time of the nickelodeon era, which began roughly parallel to the release of *A Reprieve from the Scaffold* (American Mutoscope & Biograph, 1905), a fictional film in which a woman is exonerated just before being hanged.[124] Public debates over capital punishment, the increasing narrative complexity of nickelodeon-era films, and the increased vigilance of local authorities with regard to cinema presentations are all likely reasons.

However, the subject gained renewed discussion in America in 1910, when *Variety* reported that a cinematographer had filmed an actual death by guillotine in France, only to have his footage confiscated after the event.[125] That same year, *Moving Picture World* argued all films of authentic executions should be prohibited, contending, "In this matter, the public have a right to be protected from the inadmissible in the shape of the brutal, the degrading, the gruesome, the repulsive, or the immoral. And certainly, an execution shown on the screen is brutalizing and repulsive." The trade announced it had a "duty" to "denounce" such films.[126]

Moving Picture World editorialized on this issue repeatedly in the years that followed, proclaiming in 1913, "Pictures showing the harrowing details of an execution by hanging ought never to be passed by a board of censorship. It has cost years of agitation to abolish public executions. Are they to be revived by the motion pictures?"[127] The following year, the trade explained, "Morbid instincts and atavistic cravings grow by what they feed upon. Nothing would draw a crowd more quickly than a public execution, but the growth of humanity and modern enlightenment have banished such hideous spectacles within prison walls."[128] Films about them would only project "forbidden themes."[129]

Conclusion

Having largely focused on "authentic" death and executions in the years before 1906, film companies shifted their emphasis during and after the nickelodeon era, producing a much larger body of fictional screen murders, as in the case of such films as D. W. Griffith's *The Birth of the Nation* (1915). Here was an evolution not unlike what American culture had experienced during the eighteenth and nineteenth centuries, with real death being concealed from daily life as much as possible, even as representations of the same surged in visual culture. We wanted to see, but not see the real thing.

This reality seemed even more pronounced as the early cinema period came to a close. In September 1914, an Oklahoma newspaper editorial asserted that emerging First World War footage depicted "mere heaps of slain men and horses, in many cases revealing frightful wounds and disfigurements. The scenes are too shocking for exhibition."[130] The following year, *Moving Picture World* rightly worried about new "pictures exploiting the sensational lynching of a man who had been condemned to death and whose sentence had been commuted."[131] It is difficult to determine whether this footage was authentic, but it seemed real enough to cause the industry to fear the specter of film censorship and its potential to curtail the cinema.

After all, in 1914, *Moving Picture World* reported that an exhibitor in New York "fitted out an imitation of the electric chair in Sing Sing, and placing a man in it he had a 'barker' call attention to the spectacle and urging people to come inside." The gimmick was appalling, the trade believed, but the story had a happy ending, certainly for those who were looking to improve the industry's reputation. The exhibitor in question was arrested for "disorderly conduct."[132] His *faux*-electric chair was quickly dismantled, and removed from public view.

Notes

1. "*The Devil's Signature*," *Moving Picture World*, September 12, 1914, 1548.
2. "*The Devil's Signature*," *Moving Picture World*, September 26, 1914, 1776.
3. "Mystery Film Adapted from Munsey Tale," *Motography*, September 5, 1914, 327.
4. Jay Ruby, *Secure the Shadow: Death and Photography in America* (Cambridge, MA: The MIT Press, 1995), 2.
5. Nancy Isenberg and Andrew Burstein, "Introduction," in *Mortal Remains: Death in Early America*, edited by Nancy Isenberg and Andrew Burstein (Philadelphia: University of Pennsylvania Press, 2003), 1.
6. J. David Hacker, "A Census-Based Count of the Civil War Dead," *Civil War History*, Vol. 57, No. 4 (December 2011), 307–48.

7. Ian Finseth, "The Civil War Dead: Realism and the Problem of Anonymity," *American Literary History*, Vol. 25, No. 3 (Fall 2013), 536.
8. Lucy E. Frank, "Introduction," in *Representations of Death in Nineteenth-Century US Writing and Culture*, edited by Lucy E. Frank (Burlington, Vermont: Ashgate Publishing Group, 2007), 11.
9. Megan E. Springate, *Coffin Hardware in Nineteenth-Century America* (Walnut Creek, California: Left Coast Press, 2015), 57.
10. Michael Sappol, *A Traffic of Dead Bodies: Anatomy and Embodied Social Identity in Nineteenth-Century America* (Princeton: Princeton University Press, 2002).
11. Isenberg and Burstein, 3.
12. James L. Swanson, *Bloody Crimes: The Funeral of Abraham Lincoln and the Chase for Jefferson Davis* (New York: HarperCollins, 2010), 147–8.
13. Gary Laderman, *Habeus Corpus: American Attitudes toward Death, 1799–1883* (New Haven: Yale University Press, 1996).
14. Craig Buettinger, "Women and Antivivisection in Late Nineteenth-Century America," *Journal of Social History*, Vol. 30, No. 4 (Summer 1997), 857–72.
15. "Make Holiday of Hanging," *New York Times*, August 31, 1911, 4.
16. Elizabeth Barnes, "Communicable Violence and the Problem of Capital Punishment in New England, 1830–1890," *Modern Language Studies*, Vol. 30, No. 1 (Spring 2000), 7.
17. Jürgen Martschukat, "The Art of Killing by Electricity: The Sublime and the Electric Chair," *The Journal of American History*, Vol. 89, No. 3 (December 2002), 911.
18. Ibid., 901.
19. Quoted in Martschukat, 918.
20. "Death in Electric Chair as Repulsive as It Is from the Hangman's Noose," *Washington Post*, February 3, 1914, 10.
21. This is not to say that actual corpses and images of the same did not evoke different responses from different persons. Thousands viewed Lincoln's remains in 1865 as they were transported from Washington, D.C. to Springfield, Illinois, but Secretary of War Edwin Stanton forbade photography of the same.
22. Les Sillars, "'Still Another Horror!': Religion and Death in 19th-Century American Newspapers," in *Sensationalism: Murder, Mayhem, Mudslinging, Scandals, and Disasters in 19th-Century Reporting*, edited by David B. Sachsman and David W. Bulla (New Brunswick: Transaction Publishers, 2013), 190.
23. Michael Ayers, "The Lure of the Sensational Murder," *Journal of Social History*, Vol. 35, No. 2 (2001), 429–43.
24. See, for example, Janet L. Langlois, *Belle Gunness: The Lady Bluebeard* (Indiana University Press, 1985); Harold Schechter, *Fatal: The Poisonous Life of a Female Serial Killer* (New York: Pocket Books, 2003); Dick C. Gibson, *Serial Killing for Profit: Multiple Murder for Money* (Westport: Praeger, 2009); Joseph A. Conforti, *Lizzie Borden on Trial: Murder, Ethnicity, and Gender* (Lawrence, Kansas: University Press of Kansas, 2015).
25. Louis Reeves Harrison, "Mysterious Tragedy," *Moving Picture World*, March 8, 1913, 974.
26. For more information on the subject of death in early cinema, see Boaz Hagin, "'If Sensation Is Demanded': Early Cinema's Morbid Scopophilia," in *Mortal Frames: Death and its Meaning in Film* (Ph.D. dissertation, Tel Aviv University, 2007), 25–82.
27. *Picture Catalogue* (New York: American Mutoscope & Biograph, November 1902), 66. Available in *A Guide to Motion Picture Catalogs by American Producers and Distributors, 1894–1908: A Microfilm Edition, Edition* (New Brunswick: Rutgers University Press, 1985), Reel 2.
28. A copy of *The Finish of Bridget McKeen* is available at the Library of Congress. Similar comedies include *The Finish of Michael Casey; or, Blasting Rocks in Harlem* (Edison, 1901) and *Another Job*

for the Undertaker (Edison, 1901), the latter archived in the Paper Print Collection at the Library of Congress. Another example would be the British-made *Mary Jane's Mishap* (G.A.S. Films, 1903), which was screened in the United States.

29. "The Legend of the Lighthouse," *Moving Picture World*, October 9, 1909, 494. A copy of *The Legend of the Lighthouse* is archived at the Centre national du cinéma et de l'image animée (CNC).
30. A copy of *The Statue of Fright* is available at the Library of Congress.
31. A copy of *The Downward Path: The Suicide* is available at the Library of Congress.
32. "His Suicide," *New York Dramatic Mirror*, December 30, 1914, 31.
33. "Hara-Kiri," *Moving Picture World*, January 17, 1914, 346.
34. "During the Plague," *Moving Picture World*, September 20, 1913, 1286; "The Dead Soul," *Motography*, July 31, 1915, 236. *During the Plague* was a pre-release title of *In the Line of Duty*. One reel of *The Dead Soul* is archived at the Museum of Modern Art, New York City.
35. "The Smallpox Scare at Gulch Hollow," *Moving Picture World*, July 26, 1913, 430.
36. "Inaccurate Films," *Motography*, August 31, 1912, 154.
37. Elias Savada (ed.), *The American Film Institute Catalog of Motion Pictures Produced in the United States: Film Beginnings, 1893–1910* (Lanham, Maryland: Scarecrow Press, 1995), 391.
38. Another example would be films about the *Titanic* after it sank, the topic suggesting mass casualties even though they weren't visualized onscreen. See Stephen Bottomore, *The Titanic and Silent Cinema* (Hastings: The Projection Box, 2000).
39. Advertisement, *New York Clipper*, September 22, 1900, 672; Advertisement, *New York Clipper*, February 20, 1904, 1256.
40. Advertisement, *New York Clipper*, May 31, 1902, 324. The description of "many" corpses being "so disfigured that they are beyond recognition" appears in an entry for *Taking Out the Dead and Wounded*, which was a shortened version of *Volcanic Eruption of Mt. Pelee at St. Pierre*. See *Complete Catalogue of Lubin Films* (Philadelphia: Lubin, January 1903), 53. Available in *A Guide to Motion Picture Catalogs by American Producers and Distributors, 1894-1908: A Microfilm Edition*, Reel 3.
41. Advertisement, *The Billboard*, September 16, 1911, 58.
42. "*Eastland Horror*," *Moving Picture World*, August 14, 1915, 1161.
43. A copy of *Dayton Flood Horror* is available at the Library of Congress.
44. Advertisement, *The Billboard*, May 12, 1906, 47.
45. "Fire and Earthquake Scenes," *The News and Courier* (Charleston, South Carolina), May 23, 1906, 10.
46. Advertisement, *The Billboard*, Jun 2, 1906, 22.
47. See, for example, *Amusement for Profit* (Chicago: Amusement Supply Company, 1908), 233. Available in *A Guide to Motion Picture Catalogs by American Producers and Distributors, 1894–1908: A Microfilm Edition*, Reel 6.
48. "Collinwood Fire Pictures Bad Taste," *Moving Picture World*, April 4, 1908, 291.
49. Savada, 255.
50. *Edison Films, No. 105* (Orange, New Jersey: Edison Manufacturing Company, July 1901), 80. Available in *A Guide to Motion Picture Catalogs by American Producers and Distributors, 1894–1908: A Microfilm Edition*, Reel 1.
51. A copy of *A Career of Crime, No. 3: Robbery & Murder* is archived at the Library of Congress; *Picture Catalogue* (New York: American Mutoscope & Biograph, November 1902), 66. Available in *A Guide to Motion Picture Catalogs by American Producers and Distributors, 1894–1908: A Microfilm Edition*, Reel 2.
52. *Bulletin 34* (New York: American Mutoscope & Biograph, October 17, 1904). Reel 2.
53. *Geo. Méliès, Supplement No. 33* (New York: Star Films, 1906).
54. Savada, 291.

55. Savada, 1072. A copy of "*To the Death*" is archived at the British Film Institute.
56. "*The Tiger*," *Moving Picture World*, September 27, 1913, 1391.
57. "*The Tiger*," *Moving Picture World*, September 6, 1913, 1090.
58. W. Stephen Bush, "Punches and Thrills," *Moving Picture World*, March 29, 1913, 1312. Jungle films of the period include *Alone in the Jungle* (Selig Polyscope, 1913), *Beasts of the Jungle* (Solax, 1913), *Face to Face with a Leopard/Face à la panthère* (Lux, 1913), *In the Claws of the Leopard/Sous la griffe* (Gaumont, 1913), *In the Coils of the Python* (Edison, 1913), *In the Midst of the Jungle* (Selig Polyscope, 1913), *In the Wilds of Africa* (101 Bison, 1913), *The Lost Diamond/Le diamant noir* (Eclectic, 1913), *The Terrors of the Jungle* (Selig Polyscope, 1913), *Thor, Lord of the Jungle* (Selig Polyscope, 1913, aka *Thor, Lord of the Jungles*), and *Wamba, a Child of the Jungle* (Selig Polyscope, 1913). See "*Alone in the Jungle*," *Moving Picture World*, June 21, 1913, 1276; "*Beasts of the Jungle*," *Moving Picture News*, January 4, 1913, 16; "*Face to Face with a Leopard*," *Moving Picture World*, January 25, 1913, 400; "*In the Claws of the Leopard*," *Moving Picture World*, February 1, 1913, 475; "*In the Coils of the Python*," *Moving Picture World*, September 20, 1913, 1286; "*In the Wilds of Africa*," *Moving Picture World*, October 11, 1913, 158; "*The Lost Diamond*," *Moving Picture World*, December 20, 1913, 1426; James S. McQuade, "*The Terrors of the Jungle*," *Moving Picture World*, November 8, 1913, 590; James S. McQuade, "*Thor, Lord of the Jungle*," *Moving Picture World*, December 6, 1913, 1126–7; "*Wamba, a Child of the Jungle*," *Moving Picture World*, May 24, 1913, 836.
59. Advertisement, *New York Clipper*, May 3, 1902.
60. *Complete Catalogue of Lubin Films* (Philadelphia: Lubin, January 1903), 10–11. Available in *A Guide to Motion Picture Catalogs by American Producers and Distributors, 1894–1908: A Microfilm Edition*, Reel 3.
61. A copy of *Blue Beard* is available in the DVD boxed set *Georges Méliès: First Wizard of Cinema* (Los Angeles: Flicker Alley, 2008).
62. Advertisement, *New York Clipper*, February 27, 1904, 11.
63. "Latest Films of All Makers," *Views and Film Index*, December 21, 1907, 9.
64. "*Bluebeard*," *New York Dramatic Mirror*, December 4, 1909, 17.
65. "*Monsieur Bluebeard*," *Moving Picture World*, October 10, 1914, 246.
66. "*Berlin Jack the Ripper*," *New York Dramatic Mirror*, October 30, 1909, 15. The title's reference to Berlin stems from the fact that newspapers in early 1909 published stories of attacks upon women in that city, thus "recalling the notorious 'Ripper' cases in other cities." See "*Berlin Jack the Ripper*," *Burlington Evening Gazette* (Burlington, Iowa), February 15, 1909, 1.
67. "*Talked to Death*," *Moving Picture World*, March 6, 1909, 314.
68. "*The Deadly Plant*," *Moving Picture World*, December 26, 1908, 526. A copy of this film is archived at the Cinémathèque Française.
69. "*The Mysterious Lodger*," *Moving Picture World*, September 12, 1914, 1511. A copy of *The Message of the Dead* is archived at the Cinémathèque Française.
70. *The Red Barn Mystery*'s original title in the United Kingdom was *The Red Barn Crime; or, Maria Martin* [sic].
71. "Williams, Brown & Earle," *Moving Picture World*, October 24, 1908, 328.
72. "Film Storiettes," *Universal Weekly*, October 25, 1913, 20; "*Who Killed George Lambert?*," *Moving Picture World*, September 20, 1913, 1286.
73. "*Terror*," *Moving Picture World*, February 6, 1915, 844.
74. The full title of Corelli's novel was *Wormwood: A Drama of Paris*.
75. Lynde Denig, "*Wormwood*," *Moving Picture World*, June 12, 1915, 1788.
76. "*The Wages of Sin*," *Moving Picture World*, September 12, 1908, 204. Some footage from *The Wages of Sin* is archived at the Library of Congress by way of a paper print deposit.

77. Advertisement, *Motography*, August 29, 1914, 5.
78. "Story Grips with Its Awfulness," *Motography*, August 29, 1914, 317.
79. "New Films for 'Screen' Machines," *The Phonoscope*, January 1898, 12.
80. Savada, 346.
81. A copy of *Scene in a Rat Pit* is available at the Library of Congress. In 1894, Edison filmed three *Rats and Terrier* films, as well as one *Rats and Weasel* film; in all of them, the rats were killed onscreen by the dog or weasel. Charles Musser, *Edison Motion Pictures, 1890–1900: An Annotated Filmography* (Washington, D.C.: Smithsonian Institution Press, 1997), 123–4.
82. *The 1903 Complete Catalogue of Films and Moving Picture Machines* (Chicago: Selig Polyscope Co.), 45–6. Selig Polyscope copyrighted the "Stock Yard Series" in 1901, the year they were shot.
83. *Electrocuting an Elephant* is available on the DVD boxed set *Edison: The Invention of the Movies* (New York: Kino, 2005).
84. *Edison Films, No. 105* (Orange, New Jersey: Edison Manufacturing Company, July 1901), 82–3. Available in *A Guide to Motion Picture Catalogs by American Producers and Distributors, 1894–1908: A Microfilm Edition*, Reel 1.
85. *Geo. Méliès of Paris, Supplement No. 15* (New York: Star Films, 1904), unpaginated. Available in *A Guide to Motion Picture Catalogs by American Producers and Distributors, 1894–1908: A Microfilm Edition*, Reel 4. A copy of *A Miracle under the Inquisition* is available on the DVD boxed set *Georges Méliès: First Wizard of Cinema*.
86. Copies of *Martyrs of the Inquisition* are archived at the British Film Institute and the Cinémathèque Française.
87. Savada, 654.
88. Charles Musser, *Edison Motion Pictures, 1890–1900* (Washington, D.C.: Smithsonian Institution Press, 1997), 190, 193–4.
89. Savada, 550, 1081. A copy of *Joan of Arc* is available on the DVD boxed set *Georges Méliès: First Wizard of Cinema*. Here it is worth noting that these films were dramatic in tone, as opposed to the comedy *The Terrible Turkish Executioner/Le bourreau turc* (Méliès, 1904, aka *Decapitation in Turkey*), a copy of which is also available in the DVD boxed set *Georges Méliès: First Wizard of Cinema*.
90. Savada, 86. Copies of *Beheading Chinese Prisoner* are archived at the George Eastman Museum and the Museum of Modern Art, New York City.
91. A copy of *Execution of a Murderess* under the title *Execution by Hanging* is available at the Library of Congress.
92. Kemp R. Niver, *Motion Pictures from the Library of Congress Paper Print Collection, 1894–1912* (Berkeley: University of California Press, 1967), 264, 338. A copy of *Shooting Captured Insurgents* is archived in the Paper Print Collection at the Library of Congress.
93. *Catalogue of New Films for Projection and Other Purposes* (New York, F. M. Prescott: 1899), 24. Available in *A Guide to Motion Picture Catalogs by American Producers and Distributors, 1894–1908: A Microfilm Edition*, Reel 1.
94. A copy of *Execution of a Spy* is archived in the Paper Print Collection at the Library of Congress.
95. *Picture Catalogue* (New York: American Mutoscope & Biograph, November 1902), 244. Available in *A Guide to Motion Picture Catalogs by American Producers and Distributors, 1894–1908: A Microfilm Edition*, Reel 2.
96. A copy of *A Career of Crime, No. 5: The Death Chair* is available at the Library of Congress.
97. A copy of *The History of a Crime/Histoire d'un crime* is available on the DVD boxed set *The Movies Begin* (New York: Kino International, 2002).
98. A copy of *Execution of Czolgosz* (1901) is available at the Library of Congress.

99. "Czolgosz's Body to be Destroyed at Auburn," *New York Times*, October 29, 1901, 1.
100. Exhibitors could purchase the film with or without the two opening shots of Auburn State Prison. Musser, 320.
101. "Our Tattler," *The Phonoscope*, June 1897, 7.
102. "Vitascope Mob at the Hanging," *The Phonoscope*, November–December 1897, 8.
103. Ibid., 8.
104. "Another Picture Horror," *Cleveland Leader* (Cleveland, Ohio), December 21, 1897, 4.
105. "Vitascope Horrors," *Washington Post*, December 25, 1897, 6.
106. "Photography That Is Exceedingly Perilous," *Philadelphia Inquirer*, August 13, 1899, 3.
107. *Picture Catalogue*, 240.
108. "*Their First Execution*," *Moving Picture World*, May 10, 1913, 630.
109. "*Their First Execution*," *Moving Picture World*, May 10, 1913, 598.
110. Mary Church Terrell, "Lynching from a Negro's Point of View," *North American Review*, June 1904, 853.
111. Amy Louise Wood, *Lynching and Spectacle: Witnessing Racial Violence in America, 1890–1940* (University of North Carolina Press, 2009), 1.
112. Ibid., 3.
113. Untitled, *New York Clipper*, July 28, 1888.
114. "New Films for 'Screen' Machines," *The Phonoscope*, November–December 1897, 13.
115. *International Photographic Films for Use on All Projecting Machines Using the Standard Gauge* (New York: International Film Co., Winter 1897–8), 18. Reel 1.
116. Advertisement, *New York Clipper*, March 25, 1905, 134.
117. For an excellent analysis of *Tracked by Bloodhounds; or, A Lynching at Cripple Creek*, see Jan Olsson, "Modernity Stops at Nothing: The American Chase Film and the Specter of Lynching," in *A Companion to Early Cinema*, edited by André Gaudreault, Nicolas Dulac, and Santiago Hidalgo (Chichester: Wiley-Blackwell, 2012), 257–76.
118. A copy of *Tracked by Bloodhounds; or, A Lynching at Cripple Creek* is available at the Library of Congress.
119. Advertisement, *New York Clipper*, September 24, 1904.
120. Savada, 57–8. A copy of *Avenging a Crime; or Burned at the Stake* is archived in the Paper Print Collection at the Library of Congress.
121. Advertisement, *New York Clipper*, December 24, 1904.
122. Robert Jackson, "The Celluloid War before *The Birth of a Nation*: Race and History in Early American Film," in *American Cinema and the Southern Imaginary*, edited by Deborah Barker and Kathryn McKee (Athens, Georgia: University of Georgia Press, 2011), 32.
123. Wood, 5.
124. Niver, 337. A copy of *A Reprieve from the Scaffold* is archived in the Paper Print Collection at the Library of Congress.
125. "Pictures of an Execution," *Variety*, January 22, 1910, 14.
126. "The Inadmissible Subject," *Moving Picture World*, January 22, 1910, 83.
127. "Facts and Comments," *Moving Picture World*, February 1, 1913, 440.
128. "Facts and Comments," *Moving Picture World*, May 9, 1914, 791.
129. W. Stephen Bush, "Forbidden Themes," *Moving Picture World*, November 14, 1914, 902.
130. "Someone Must Be 'Kidding' Muskogee," *Moving Picture World*, October 17, 1914, 350. In this instance, *MPW* was not worried, as no such footage had appeared on American soil.
131. Quoted in "Facts and Comments," *Moving Picture World*, September 18, 1915, 1967.
132. "Facts and Comments," *Moving Picture World*, April 18, 1914, 487.

CHAPTER 10

Evolution and Devolution

The Miser's Reversion (Thanhouser, 1914) told the story of a rich, elderly man who, "like Scrooge, repents of his miserly ways."[1] But unlike *A Christmas Carol* (1843), this moving picture preached morality by invoking Darwin's theory of evolution. Its plot finds the title character partaking of a Hindu's "Elixir of Life."[2] He reverts to a "man of forty, then a man younger, then a baby, then a stone age savage," and finally a "prehistoric man-monkey."[3] Eventually the Miser wakes up, his regressions having been the product of a nightmare. Similar to Scrooge on Christmas morning, he is a changed man.

A newspaper article argued *The Miser's Reversion* was the "oddest drama" ever written, though *Motion Picture News* believed otherwise.[4] Its critic advised that the film could not:

> be called original in the strictest sense of the word. A variation of it has been used in vaudeville, and similar plots have been fictionalized. This does not, however, make it any the less interesting. It is founded on the Darwinian theory of the relationship between man and animal.[5]

In terms not unlike those used to describe Lon Chaney during the silent feature film era, the critic praised Sidney Bracy (aka Sidney Bracey), who played the "Miser," for being a "master of make-up," adding that he "makes up so well for each of [his five roles that depict the Miser's devolution] that it would be hard to recognize the real man underneath. . . . [His appearance as the man-monkey] is a truly remarkable piece of acting."[6] Unlike Chaney, however, Bracy did not achieve lasting fame. After the early cinema period, he played a long succession of bit roles that did not require special make-up, including as a butler in Tod Browning's *Freaks* (MGM, 1932).

Far more than Bracy, monkeys, gorillas, and ape-men attained a prominent place in American popular culture, an achievement based in part on their ability to frighten viewers. In 1861, for example, the *Saturday Evening Post* observed that gorillas were "ugly and monstrous," their geographical origins being Africa, the "land of monsters."[7] Throughout the history of the United States, exhibitions of primates proved highly successful, as in the case of New Orleans in 1856, when a critic ranked the exhibition of a live "Ourang Outang" alongside a production of Shakespeare's *The Merry Wives of Windsor* as being two of the city's top amusements.[8]

As early as 1789, a "Collection of Natural Curiosities" in New York top-billed "A male and female of the surprising species of the Ourang Outang, or the Man of the Woods."[9] The description echoes that of Lord Monboddo, the eighteenth-century Scottish polymath, who notably translated the term "Ourang-Outang" as "Wild Man of the Woods." Monboddo firmly believed that the animal represented a stage in the progress of humankind. He even presumed that the creature could copulate with human females and produce offspring.[10]

Figure 10.1 Sidney Bracy in *The Miser's Reversion* (Thanhouser, 1914). (*Courtesy of Robert J. Kiss*)

Monboddo was not alone in his basic observations. When an "Ourang-Outang" was exhibited in Baltimore in 1799, a newspaper informed readers it was "nearly human."[11] Four decades later, the *Spirit of the Times* wrote about a recently discovered "American Ourang Outang." The indigenous "monster" was a "horrid looking creature" headed for exhibition. Even though it was "disgusting," the publication noted that the "bestial" in question "somewhat resembl[ed] a man."[12]

During the nineteenth century, the relationship between man and ape received continued discussion, including among intellectuals. Published without attribution in 1844, Robert Chambers's book *Vestiges of the Natural History of Creation* offered a "development hypothesis [that] clearly made man an immediate descendant of the apes."[13] But in various respects, ranging from its argumentation and writing style to its impact on the public, the key work on the subject was Charles Darwin's *On the Origin of Species* in 1859, first published in America in 1860, and then retitled *The Origin of Species* in 1872.

Needless to say, Darwin's notions of common descent, natural selection, and the branching pattern of evolution provoked enormous controversy. Among its many implications was that humans are the descendants of earlier animals and, as such, they exist inside of nature, rather than outside of it. More specifically, this once again meant that humans had evolved from ape-like creatures, an issue that became more closely associated in the popular American mind with Darwinism than anything else.

As Ronald L. Numbers observed, "At first Americans reacted coolly to Darwinism."[14] Religious controversy over Darwinism grew over time, reaching an apex in the United

States in the 1870s.[15] An 1872 newspaper article speculated that "The Darwinian theory of 'the origin of species' and 'the descent of man' is now attracting a much greater share of public attention than many people suppose."[16] Discourse in the popular press was not only commonplace, but also achieved, at least on occasion, an impressive level of argumentation.[17] Such debate led to a degree of softened resistance among the American public. According to James R. Moore, a notion of "Christian evolution" gained wide acceptance by 1880.[18] Nevertheless, hostility to Darwinism remained intense in some quarters, particularly among Christian Fundamentalists, including but certainly not limited to those living in the American South.[19]

Various discoveries fueled a level of ongoing public attention and controversy, particularly those that seemed to represent the "Missing Link" between man and ape, even though many intellectuals agreed that a singular missing link made no sense in evolutionary terms.[20] First was the discovery of Neanderthal remains during the first half of the nineteenth century, most famously those uncovered in Germany in 1856. Then, in 1891, Eugène Dubois received an enormous amount of press for finding the "Java Man."[21] In 1912, the "Piltdown Man," allegedly unearthed in a gravel pit in England, made news throughout America. Here was yet another "man-ape" that purported to prove Darwin's theory. In actual fact, the Piltdown Man was a hoax, though its exposure did not occur until decades later.[22]

Though much less notable, the press reported on all manner of other specimens both living and dead. "Darwin Vindicated," declared a journalist who in 1879 described a "young man with the tail of a true baboon type."[23] In 1899, the *Chicago Tribune* claimed a living example of the "forefather of mankind" had been located in the Philippines.[24] A decade later, the *New York Times* reported on the fossils of a "Missing Link" found inside a French cave. "Is it man or Man-Ape?" the newspaper asked.[25]

Darwinism not only remained a viable topic for newspaper journalists, but it also had a profound effect on writers of fiction. In *Darwin's Plots*, Gillian Beer observes that "evolutionary theory had particular implications for narrative and the composition of literature. Because of its preoccupation with time and with change, evolutionary theory has inherent affinities with the problems and processes of narrative."[26] Nineteenth-century fiction explored evolution at length, including in the era before Darwin. For Lawrence Frank, Edgar Allan Poe's *Murders in the Rue Morgue* (1841) is nothing less than an "evolutionary reverie."[27]

Not surprisingly, after the publication of *On the Origin of Species*, the amount of fiction directly or indirectly engaging evolution increased dramatically. For example, Redmond O'Hanlon has discussed Darwin's influence on Joseph Conrad, particularly in his novel *Lord Jim* (1900).[28] Likewise, Mark Twain's essay *What Is Man?* (1906) presents a Socratic dialogue between an Old Man (who is a Darwinist) and a Young Man (who perceives humans as special among God's creations).[29]

In *Literature After Darwin*, Virginia Richter chronicles novels like Edward Bulwer-Lytton's *The Coming Race* (1871) and Stanley Waterloo's *The Story of Ab: A Tale of the Time of the Cave Man* (1897), as well as such well-known tales as H. G. Wells's *The Time Machine* (1895), in which the "Time Traveller" encounters the ape-like Morlocks, and *The Island of Dr. Moreau* (1896), in which the title character experiments on animals to imbue them with human traits.[30] Other key examples include Robert Louis Stevenson's *Strange Case of*

Dr. Jekyll and Mr. Hyde (1886), with Jekyll describing the atavistic Hyde as "ape-like," and Edgar Rice Burroughs's *Tarzan of the Apes* (1912), with Lord Greystoke remarking of an ape, "if it was not a man, it was some huge and grotesque mockery of man."

Darwinian evolution also reverberates in the work of Arthur Conan Doyle, an author born the very year that *On the Origin of Species* was published. In his novel *The Lost World* (1912), prehistoric animals—including a race of "ape-men"—survive in a remote region of South America. His Sherlock Holmes stories also draw upon Darwin. Frank writes at length about *The Hound of the Baskervilles* (1902), drawing particular attention to Holmes as the Man on the Tor, a narrative sequence that echoes the conclusion of Darwin's *The Descent of Man* (1871).[31]

Not surprisingly, the American stage saw the potential currency of the "man-ape," including before Darwin published his research, as in British sketch writer George Herbert Rodwell's *Ourang Outang; or, The Runaway Monkey and His Double* (aka *The Ourang Outang and His Double*), in which a human performer costumed as an orangutan caused lively mayhem with acrobatics both onstage and, if the theatre could accommodate it, in the auditorium too. The sketch was first performed at London's Royal Clarence Theatre in 1833.[32] In 1835, it opened at New York's American Theatre, which coincided with the exhibition of a "living ourang outang" at Peale's Museum.[33] The one-act play proved popular enough that it was revived in the United States during the 1840s and 1850s.[34]

Sketches on the subject of apes and man-apes certainly continued after the publication of *On the Origin of Species* as well. In the 1870s, for example, comedian Bob Hart made a name for himself giving burlesque lectures on the subject of Darwinism, his "pomposity of manner being in grotesque contrast with the illimitable flow of bosh he uttered."[35] And then there was the 1908 vaudeville sketch *The Missing Link*, in which an African-American performer took "the place of a tardy member" of a singing quartet.[36]

After stage adaptations of the *Strange Case of Dr. Jekyll and Mr. Hyde* (as discussed in Chapter 2), the most notable exploration of Darwinian evolution in the American theatre came in Charles E. Blaney's *His Terrible Secret; or The Man Monkey* (1907). William H. Turner starred in the lead role of Melmoth, a man with an ape-like appearance who hears the "call of the wild" while visiting Africa. Though he becomes increasingly animalistic, his love for his employer's daughter allows him to "save her from murderous villainy."[37] According to one plot synopsis, Melmoth's "face has a monkey's features, his head is shaped like a monkey's, and he might be a gigantic monkey dressed like a man for exhibition in a museum. . . . He is a museum freak of nature."[38]

Advertisements for *His Terrible Secret*, which toured America in 1907 and 1908, heralded it as a "Sensational Mysterious Play in 4 Acts."[39] A Boston critic praised the scenes for being "superbly staged, especially in the electrical storm and the scene in which Melmoth takes his terrible revenge on the villain."[40] Responding to a performance in Brooklyn, a correspondent for the *Washington Post* wrote, "it seems to me the most absurdly impressive melodrama, the most ridiculously engrossing, that I ever saw. I have laughed outright in thinking of it, and I have had several nightmares also, in memory of it."[41]

Altogether more common than stage plays were the "Missing Link" freaks exhibited at dime museums, with spectators invited to judge their origins for themselves. Most

Figure 10.2 Publicity still for *His Terrible Secret; or The Man Monkey* (c. 1907).

famously, P. T. Barnum launched a decades-long exhibition of a "man-monkey" only months after the publication of *On the Origin of Species*. Its name: "What Is It?" Costumed to appear like an earlier form of man, some viewers took him to be a "man-ape." In actuality, he was played over the years by a series of African-American performers, the last of whom was William Henry Johnson.[42]

These kinds of exhibits predated both Darwin and Barnum. Robert Bogdan notes that one American newspaper advertised the appearance of a woman who resembled an ape in 1738.[43] Then, c. 1852, a traveling showman named Lyman Warner began exhibiting Hiram and Barney Davis, two mentally disabled brothers born in America. By 1860, Warner claimed that the duo hailed from Borneo, an island already associated in the popular American mind with orangutans. The "Wild Men from Borneo" appeared before the public for over fifty years.[44]

It is hardly surprising, then, that the lengthy history of ape-men and "freaks," of evolution and devolution, became a popular topic for filmmakers during the early cinema period, both in America as well as in Europe. In these cases, the camera focused on perceived missing links and abnormalities, some real, most fictional, but in both cases giving audiences the opportunity to gaze upon what they otherwise had to see at live exhibits. As a result, they were simultaneously close to and removed from the potentially frightening sights they wanted to examine.

Primates

Monkeys, orangutans, and apes appeared onscreen repeatedly during the early cinema period. Some of these films presented nonfiction footage for educational purposes, as in *Monkey Intelligence/Les singes de Bornéo* (Pathé, 1915).[45] *Moving Picture World* referred to the film as a "study of our attributed antecedents."[46] More commonly, these moving pictures focused on humor, including *The Monkey's Feast* (American Mutoscope, 1896), which might well have been the first of its kind.[47] Two years later, the same company's *Joe, the Educated Orangoutang* [sic] (1898) and *Joe, the Educated Orangoutang* [sic], *Undressing* (1898), presented the "trained monkey ... well-known to the circus and vaudeville stage."[48] A number of similar films followed, including *The Educated Chimpanzee* (Edison, 1901) and *Egyptian Fakir with Dancing Monkey* (1903), which the Edison Manufacturing Company promoted as being "very comical."[49]

Some of these comedies cited Darwinian evolution by dressing monkeys and orangutans and placing them in situations akin to the daily life of humans. The aforementioned *Joe, the Educated Orangoutang, Undressing* is one example, but perhaps the most overt was

Figure 10.3 Trade advertisement for *The Human Ape, or Darwin's Triumph* (Great Northern, 1909). Published in *Moving Picture World* on May 22, 1909.

The Human Ape, or Darwin's Triumph/Menneskeaben, eller Darwins Triumf (Great Northern, 1909, aka *The Human Ape*). One advertisement pronounced:

> This is the greatest illustration of animal intelligence ever given in a film. The ape behaves exactly like a man in every way—wears a man's clothes, eats, drinks, and smokes (lighting his own cigarettes), dresses and undresses himself, plays cards, roller skates, rides a cycle with a degree of skill possessed by few human beings, in each case behaving without prompting, exactly as if he were a human being.[50]

A critic for the *New York Dramatic Mirror* wrote that the film was "one of the most interesting it has ever been the good fortune of this writer to witness."[51]

During the nickelodeon era, various comedies featured characters pretending to be primates. For example, a costumed man pretended to be *Aunt Tabitha's Monkey/Le singe de Mlle. Aglaë* (Lux, 1910), thus creating "humorous situations."[52] *Mrs. Casey's Gorilla* (Biograph, 1913) drew upon Darwinian evolution and anti-Irish "Hibernian ape-men" stereotypes, an example of the perversion of science for ideological and social arguments. Its title character throws a "gorilla party," with her husband taking the part of the costumed and caged animal.[53] *Moving Picture World* admitted the film had "some fun in it," but added derisively that Mr. Casey looked "more like a gorilla without his gorilla costume."[54] Then, the following year, the title character of *Universal Ike Makes a Monkey of Himself* (Universal, 1914) uses a "monkey skin" to take the place of a real monkey so as to be closer to its beautiful owner.[55] The ruse works until Ike (Augustus Carney) gives himself away by lighting a cigarette and thus seeming to be all too human.

Along with primates, the subject of early humans also proved to be a popular topic, becoming—as Oliver Gaycken has detailed—"widespread in the early 1910s."[56] Primitive men appeared in such dramatic films as *The Cave Man* (Vitagraph, 1912), *The Virgin*

Figure 10.4 *The Primitive Instinct* (Kalem, 1914).

of the Fire (Reliance, 1912), *The Cave Dwellers* (101 Bison, 1913, aka *The Cave-Dweller's Romance*), *The Cave Men's War* (Kalem, 1913), and *The Primitive Instinct* (Kalem, 1914).[57] Directed by D. W. Griffith and starring Robert Harron and Mae Marsh, *Man's Genesis* (Biograph, 1912) became the most notable of this group.[58] Its allegorical plot finds a boy known as "Weakhands" inventing the stone hammer, defeating "Bruteforce," and winning the affection of "Lilywhite." Biograph openly promoted the film as dealing with "Darwin's argument, as to the evolution of man."[59] In response, one critic observed that *Man's Genesis* "opened up an entirely new field in a powerful way."[60]

Cavemen also became characters in a few comedies, including *The Prehistoric Man* (Urban-Eclipse, 1908, aka *Prehistoric Man*), which positioned its title character in the modern world.[61] More famously, Charlie Chaplin's tramp falls asleep and dreams he is a caveman in *His Prehistoric Past* (Keystone, 1914).[62] In these cases, rather than using make-up to depict Neanderthals or Homo Erectus, filmmakers conveyed primitive man by costume (animal-skin clothing, for example) and technology (stone tools and bows-and-arrows).

As for the missing link, the "man-ape," the earliest film to address the subject was *The Mischievous Monkey* (American Mutoscope, 1897). In it, a hotel guest awakens when a monkey enters his room and "goes through a series of queer antics," according to a 1903 catalog description, which added, "The part of the monkey is taken by a skilled acrobat; and his work in this scene is of a particularly clever sort."[63] For what was likely the first time in film history, a man wearing an ape costume appeared onscreen, and—as a surviving copy reveals—his makeup not only includes fake fur and a tail, but also (for part of his screen time) a man's hat, cape, and trousers.[64]

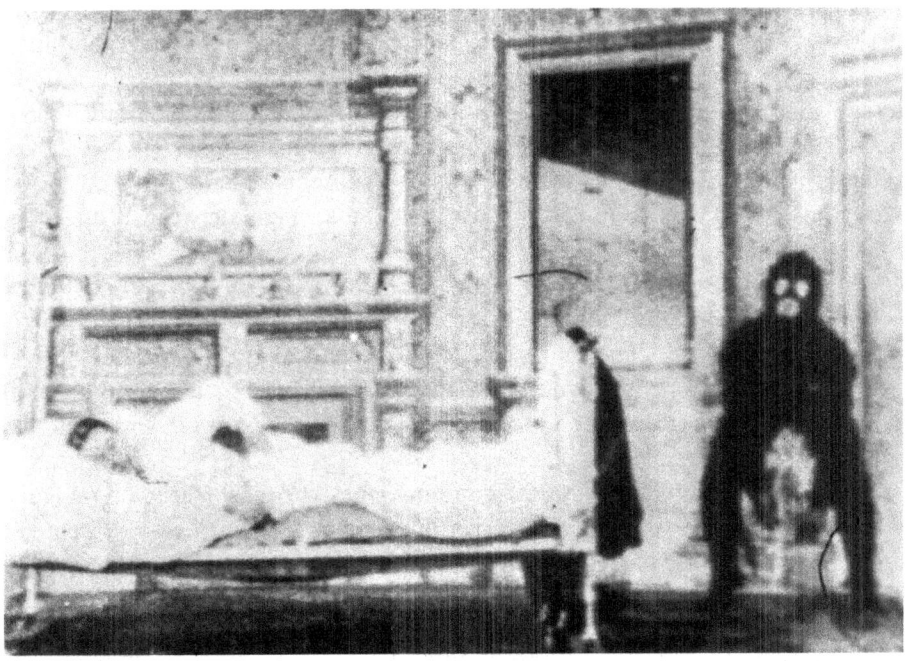

Figure 10.5 Frame from *The Mischievous Monkey* (American Mutoscope, 1897). (*Courtesy of the Library of Congress, Motion Picture, Broadcasting and Recorded Sound Division/Moving Image Section*)

Satirical comedies also featured man-apes, as in the case of *The Professor's Secret/Le sérum de singe* (Gaumont, 1908). A plot summary in the *Moving Picture World* described it as follows:

> Acting on the Darwin Theory that man descended from a monkey, a scientist experiments towards turning man back to the monkey stage. He inoculates a number of persons with the preparation, and after the subjects reach their homes, the reversing process begins, and they become monkified [sic]. Their antics are uproariously funny. The scientist is unable to turn them back to human beings again, so they are collected in a large cage and placed on exhibition. Here they are visited by an ape dressed in human attire.[65]

The following year, in *A Wonderful Remedy/Spécifique merveilleux* (Pathé Frères, 1909), a medieval quack develops a lotion that is supposed to cure ugliness, but instead comically "transforms men into baboons."[66]

Though fewer in number, dramatic depictions of men as ape-like creatures likewise appeared in early cinema. One of the most fascinating was *The Haunted Island* (Powers, 1911), in which two castaways named Gill and Louise wash ashore on an island that seems inhabited. The two ring a bell hanging from a tree, then leave to search the island. Later that night, they hear the bell rung by another hand. Gill and Louise soon discover a trapdoor on the shore, which leads down into a ship buried in the sand.[67] There they discover a pirate flag and a chest of gold.[68] The "mysterious bell ringer" arrives, causing Gill to shoot him. As a plot synopsis noted, "He falls on the shore writhing in agony, and Gill and Louise are horrified to find that he is half man and half monkey."[69] Powers promoted *The Haunted Island* as an "enigma story," one that tried to keep the audience guessing until the end of the film.[70]

In 1914, D. W. Griffith returned to the subject of cavemen in his Biograph film *Brute Force*, which again featured Robert Harron and Mae Marsh.[71] Along with introducing impressive dinosaur special effects, Griffith's moving picture pitted cavemen against a warring Neanderthal tribe, who are more ape-like in their make-up and stance. The cavemen defeat them first by use of clubs, and then, in a subsequent battle, by bow-and-arrow, thus proving—as *Moving Picture World* wrote—"the struggle between brute force and brains has always resulted in a victory for brains."[72]

The following year, episode two of a serial entitled *The Black Box* (Universal, 1915) featured footage of a "strange creature, wild and jibbering" that "keeps company with a leopard and some monkeys."[73] By the end of the serial, viewers learned that the "man-ape" wreaking havoc is actually a professor who "had been bitten by an ape years earlier." Thereafter, he was plagued with "all the cunning and brutality of a wild ape."[74]

Of all the dramatic moving pictures about man-apes, the most fascinating was *Balaoo, The Demon Baboon/Balaoo* (Eclair, 1913, aka *Balaoo, The Demon-Baboon*). Adapted from Gaston Leroux's novel *Balaoo* (1911), the French-made film received American distribution from Union Features.[75] Detailing its plot, the *Eclair Bulletin* noted, "The whole country side was in a state of terror. An unseen monster was roaming the hills and forests lying in wait in dark and secluded spots for the unsuspecting passerby."[76] Villagers argued over what was stalking them, but only one man knew the truth.

Figure 10.6 *The Black Box* (Universal, 1915).

"In order to test his strong belief in the Darwinian Theory that man is descended from monkey," Dr. Coriolis experimented on a baboon and "transformed him into a being that was half human and half ape."[77] But Balaoo, as Coriolis names the creature, escapes and is later caught in an animal trap. A villager named Hubert frees him, with Balaoo becoming Hubert's loyal slave, so much so that he strangles a villager on Hubert's command. Hubert then orders Balaoo to abduct Madeline, Dr. Coriolis's daughter. But Balaoo turns on Hubert when he realizes Madeline might be harmed.[78]

A surviving print reveals a memorable moving picture, one that seems to anticipate Universal horror movies of the 1930s and 1940s.[79] "People everywhere are talking of the mysterious things that are happening," one intertitle explains. Images of Balaoo frightening the townspeople and later being hunted by a search party prefigure similar scenes in James Whale's *Frankenstein* (Universal, 1931). Moreover, the animal trap scene calls to mind George Waggner's *The Wolf Man* (Universal, 1941). As with those later monsters, *Balaoo* conjures as much pathos as he does terror.

Union Features promised *Balaoo* was a "mystery feature sensation" about the "weirdest animal ever created."[80] In *Moving Picture World*, H. C. Judson praised the film, in particular the acting of Lucien Bataille, who portrayed the demon baboon with "astonishment and wonder. He was, at times, so like a baboon that we forgot that he really wasn't one. Wonderful art was needed to make upon us the impression left by this strange being."[81] Though Judson believed some of its "startling" effects were contrived, he added that *Balaoo* held him in "wakeful suspense" for all of its three reels.

Figure 10.7 *Balaoo, The Demon Baboon* (Eclair, 1913).

Figure 10.8 Published in *Moving Picture World* of May 3, 1913.

Freaks

Gaumont's comedy *The Village Scare/L'ornitho lupus* (1909), distributed in America by George Kleine, was set in a "quiet country village . . . thrown into an uproar by the sudden appearance of an animal which has a wolf's body, but is covered with feathers."[82] The creature is not a freak of nature, but instead the product of a childish prank.[83]

By the end of the eighteenth century, the belief that "lusus naturae"—freaks of nature—were the product of evil, or that they were punishments for transgressions, largely fell out of favor. Instead of being nature's mistakes, many persons saw them as, in the words of Bogdan, "a part of God's great order of creatures and subject to scientific study and classification."[84] Such scientific interest served to legitimize the public's "morbid curiosity" in viewing freaks.[85] Rosemarie Garland Thomson writes:

> By challenging the boundaries of the human and the coherence of what seemed to be the natural world, monstrous bodies appeared as sublime, merging the terrible with the wonderful, equalizing repulsion with attraction. . . . From the Jacksonian to the Progressive Eras, Americans flocked to freak shows. With the older narrative of wonder still culturally tenable and the newer narrative of error even more compelling, the mid-nineteenth to early twentieth centuries comprised a heightened, transitional moment for such ceremonial displays.[86]

For Darwin, in *The Descent of Man*, reversion—meaning the re-emergence of traits that had been left behind in the evolutionary process—was possible, as in the case of what he referred to as "microcephalous idiots." Put another way, freaks called "back to life long-lost characters."[87]

By the mid-nineteenth century, terms like "freak" and "curiosity" became applied to two distinct groups of persons, the first being those who were born with particular maladies or deformities that marked them as different and possibly regressive.[88] Another category involved the self-created "gaffed" freak, meaning persons who had intentionally tattooed their bodies or willingly assumed other freakish guises. In many cases, these "gaffes" were founded on fakery and false advertising, making them not altogether dissimilar to the likes of the Piltdown Man.[89]

Initially, freaks in America were exhibited at particular geographical locations, first at Charles Willson Peale's museum in 1786.[90] However, it was P. T. Barnum who "seized on the idea of the museum as an amusement center," launching his famous American Museum in New York in 1841.[91] As the title character of Horatio Alger's novel *Ragged Dick* (1868) says, "I guess I'll go to Barnum's tonight, and see the bearded lady, the eight-foot giant, the two-foot dwarf, and the other curiosities, too numerous to mention."[92]

While some presentations aggrandized the status of the freaks, bestowing upon them titles like "Prince" or "Queen" and touting their unique skills, most of their "managers" promoted them as "inferior."[93] In the 1840s, London's *Punch* magazine coined the term "deformo-mania" to describe popular British society's fascination for freaks.[94] In several cases, the American fascination for freaks spawned celebrities, including Tom Thumb, Jo-Jo the Dog Faced Boy, and Chang and Eng Bunker, on whom Mark Twain based his story *Personal Habits of the Siamese Twins* (1869).[95]

As Jane R. Goodall has observed, Barnum's career—which successfully merged "the fairground and the museum together"—ran parallel to Darwin's, with both men and their associates attempting to discover forgotten species, missing links, and mutations.[96] However different their goals, the two challenged the American public's understanding of what it meant to be human. Not surprisingly, Barnum's success spurred numerous competitors, among them the proprietors of dime museums.[97]

Freaks became attractions at American carnivals that developed in the 1890s, featuring them during their earliest days, but promoting them more prominently from c. 1904.[98] Here was a less prestigious exhibition venue than the circuses and traveling shows of the nineteenth century. Carefully designed advertisements publicized these acts. Writing about freak show posters in 1910, the *Washington Post* remarked, "exaggeration is keynote," with artists taking a "little license" when it comes to depicting "animal freaks" and making all of the curiosities appear "sufficiently grotesque."[99]

All that said, by the twentieth century, America's interest in freak shows had begun to diminish. In 1901, the *Chicago Tribune* informed readers that freaks were "unfashionable."[100] Seven years later, after purchasing the Barnum & Bailey Greatest Show on Earth, the Ringling Brothers decided to eliminate its freak sideshow due to "waning interest."[101] Despite efforts to employ new gimmicks, dime museums also went into a decline in the early years of the twentieth century.[102] The "palmy days of the freaks are over," a dime museum owner bemoaned in 1906. He blamed other entertainment for stealing his customers, particularly burlesque shows and vaudeville theatres.[103] But soon a new amusement seemed responsible. In 1910, a dime museum employee remarked that one of the key competitors was the nickelodeon theatre.[104] "That the moving-picture show has caused the downfall of the freak is conceded by theatrical men generally," the *Washington Post* reported that same year. "The never-ending variety of entertainment offered by the great rolls of films is the reason."[105]

That never-ending variety included freaks in the cinema, which drew upon the traditions of their exhibition in America, as well as on such literature as Victor Hugo's 1831 novel *The Hunchback of Notre-Dame/Notre-Dame de Paris*. As a letter sent to the editor of the *New York Times* pointedly asked in 1905, "What is Quasimodo but a man-ape?"[106] In the age of early cinema, hunchback characters appeared in various types of film for various purposes.[107] For example, they could provide the source of action and adventure, as in the case of *The Hunchback/Le bossu* (Union Features, 1913), in which a "daring cavalier" uses the "disguise of a hunchback" during a "country wide chase where the first false step meant death."[108]

Hunchbacks also became the basis for screen comedy.[109] In *Hunchback Brings Luck/Une veine de bossu* (Pathé Frères, 1908), a pauper named "Mr. Hardup" buys a winning lottery ticket from a hunchback; to thank his "benefactor," he places a notice in a newspaper, which causes a "hundred cripples" to show up at his doorstep.[110] The title character of *Electrified Hunchback/La bosse électrisée* (Lux, 1909, aka *Electrified Humpback*) purchases a machine to "help his deformity, but it creates so much trouble by giving everyone electric shocks" that he "demands his money back."[111] Drawing again upon the "superstition that a hunchback is lucky," *Just for Good Luck/Pour avoir de la veine* (Pathé Frères, 1910) features an accident-prone woman whose troubles end when she marries a hunchback, at least until a cure makes him "straightened."[112] Then, in *Funnicus Marries a Hunchback/Gavroche épouse une bossue* (Eclair, 1913), a man marries a woman to "save a legacy," but then tries to "get rid of [her] deformity by many and strange means." *Moving Picture World* condemned the film for being "quite out of good taste."[113]

Polidor the Hunchback/Polidor gobbo (Picture Playhouse, 1914) offered much the same humor as its predecessors. In it, a beautiful girl scorns Polidor for another man. To rid himself of his "disfigurement," Polidor gives a witch an "immense fortune" in exchange for the secret of "hump" removal. He then rushes to the beautiful girl, just in time to stop her marriage. He uses the secret to put a "hump on her and all the assembled guests. They plead with him to rid them of this sudden visitation, and he does so, but only after gaining the bride's affections."[114]

In a few cases, dramatic portrayals of hunchbacks depicted them as villains. *The Hunchback of Cedar Lodge* (Box Office Attractions/Balboa, 1914) murders his own father.[115] Another key example would be *The Devil's Fiddler/Dødsvarslet eller Memento mori* (Apex, 1914). In a plot reminiscent of George Du Maurier's novel *Trilby* (1894), a "deformed fiddler" named Scaramourse plays for a dancing girl named Juana in order to cast a spell over her.[116] He takes her from her friends to Paris, where she dances in a club. When her friends try to save her, Scaramourse plays music that causes Juana to dance so "wildly" that she dies and collapses onto the floor.[117]

Figure 10.9 *The Hunchback* (Kalem, 1913).

In *The Hunchback* (Kalem, 1913), actor Tom Moore plays "Humpy" Johnson, also known as "The Fiend." A murderer and a thief, he is the "terror of the underworld."[118] *Moving Picture World* observed:

> Tom Moore gives a wonderful portrayal as the hunchback. While this splendid Kalem performer makes the cripple absolutely repulsive, he also contrives to arouse a sense of pity for the unfortunate man. One feels that the hunchback's tigerish nature is due to the constant [allusions] to his deformity. And this feeling of pity remains with the observer even when the cripple is seen committing a murder in a way which shocks to the very core.[119]

Like Balaoo, the Fiend evokes fear and sympathy, a complex combination that had not commonly been seen in the cinema before 1913.

Much more often, moving pictures featured moral and even heroic hunchbacks. Perhaps the most notable was *Notre Dame de Paris* (C.G.P.C., 1911), a direct adaptation of Victor Hugo's novel with Henry Krauss as Quasimodo. Louis Reeves Harrison advised readers of *Moving Picture World* that the film's story was "in some respects a hideous one," but he nevertheless believed it was "so well constructed that it has certain elements of superiority to the novel from which it was adapted." For him, the three-reeler was "handled in a masterly way, and is acted with greater fidelity to the original than any other adaption" he had ever seen.[120] It was popular enough that the General Film Company reissued it in America under the more simple and more Americanized title *Notre Dame* in 1913.[121]

Of *The Hunchback* (Vitagraph, 1909), the *New York Dramatic Mirror* remarked on its similarities to Hugo's novel. The title character is "in the belfry of a church" before he assaults one of his vicious tormentors; he is then taken from the stocks by a "noble lady of authority."[122] He later sacrifices his life to rescue her after two men force her to a "lone building" for evil purposes.[123] The following year, the title character of *Hugo, the Hunchback* (Selig Polyscope, 1910) saves a mistreated woman who tries to commit suicide.[124] The title character of *The Hunchback* (Majestic, 1914) cares for an orphaned girl.[125] And *The Hunchback's Romance* (Imp, 1915) finds its title character—who is "more like a gorilla than a man"—rescuing its female lead from a fire.[126]

While hunchbacks were the most common type of freak to appear in the early cinema period, they were not alone.[127] Similar to comedies that focused on hunchbacked characters being "straightened," *Dr. Skinum* (American Mutoscope & Biograph, 1907) illustrated how science might

> correct any error of nature, be it ever so anomalous. The promulgation of this fact draws to [Dr. Skinum's] office a most startling variety of monstrosities, all anxious to submit to his esoteric powers, whereby they hope to become Utopian as to face and figure.[128]

During the course of the film, a female dwarf is stretched, while an extremely tall woman has her legs literally cut down to size.[129] After hypnotizing a large woman, Dr. Skinum uses his equipment to decrease her weight. Unfortunately, he removes so much fat she is left a baby, and so he places her in a cabinet named—as a surviving print of the film reveals—"I Want to Be a Nice Figure."[130]

Rather than curing deformities, a few films explicitly tried to emulate carnival sideshows and dime museum acts. For example, in 1912, Nestor released *Brides and Bridles*, which offered "intimate glimpses into the unhappy existence of two circus girls," who live among such performers as the "bearded lady," the "living skeleton," and the "snake charmer."[131] Two young cowboys who see their show "punish" the bullying ringmaster and end up marrying the duo.[132] In this case, it is possible that at least some of the actors actually suffered from their onscreen maladies.

By contrast, Thanhouser's 1912 moving picture *The Star of the Side Show* (aka *The Star of the Sideshow*) definitely featured the "Thanhouser players 'doing' freaks" in make-up, which included an "Albino," "The Strong Man," "The Fat Lady,"

Figure 10.10 *The Star of the Side Show* (Thanhouser, 1912).

"The Snake Charmer," "The Bearded Lady," and "The Giant."¹³³ *The Billboard* described the film as follows:

> A peasant couple expected their daughter to grow up into a beautiful woman, but at the age of nineteen she was no bigger than a child of six. They were overjoyed when an offer for the girl's hand was made by another midget, but the girl refused, declaring that her husband must be a man of whom she could be proud. When an American showman [named "P. T. Barum"] made an offer to join his "Congress of Freaks," the girl gladly accepted. In her new life, she fell in love with the loveliest, biggest giant she ever dreamed of, but [his] giantly affections were lavished upon a snake charmer and her romance shattered.¹³⁴

At first the female lead ("Midget Marie") intends to commit suicide after the fashion of Cleopatra, by unleashing one of the snakes. However, as a surviving print indicates, she has a happy ending by marrying the same "little man" who had earlier proposed to her.¹³⁵

Two years later, Kalem released *The Family Skeleton* (1914), which was set in a dime museum. Its plot finds Flo (Ruth Roland) happily married to John (John E. Brennan), who is very large. All is well until she attempts to learn his secret occupation. She follows him into a dime museum, where he disguises himself as the "fat lady."¹³⁶ During the show, John flirts with male customers, who as a result ignore a female sword swallower. In anger, the sword swallower pulls off John's wig, causing Flo to learn the truth. Happy that he hasn't been cheating on her, the two leave the dime museum "in triumph," even though John has been fired. *Moving Picture World* told readers that the "opening introduction of the various freaks was pleasing."¹³⁷

During the early cinema period, these moving pictures culminated in *Freaks* (Joker, 1915). It features an extremely thin pauper named Hamus who adores a "Circassian maid" named Yum Yum, played by Gale Henry, an actress whose screen appeal was rooted in her allegedly "freakish" looks.[138] Here the film draws upon P. T. Barnum, who in the 1860s attempted to procure one of these women from the slave markets of Constantinople. In 1864, Barnum promoted Zalumma Agra as being a "Circassian Beauty." Though conflicting stories exist about her origins, she was likely a woman who was already living in New York.[139] She was among the first of many "Circassians" used as exotic modes of freak performance in the nineteenth century, all believed to have "primal appeal" for spectators.[140]

In the film *Freaks*, the manager gives Hamus a job as a "living skeleton," but Yum Yum ignores his affections because she loves the strong man. In despair, Hamus becomes even thinner, for which his salary is doubled.[141] When Yum Yum learns the strong man secretly has a wife and kids, she finally embraces Hamus.[142] *Motion Picture News* complained that the "leads, made up as freaks, are anything but pleasant to look at."[143] Rather than being comical, they represented "morbid curiosities" on the screen.

Conclusion

In the summer of 1915, *The Photoplayer's Weekly* announced the arrival of a new "cinema star" named Prince Chang:

> He is a gigantic orang-outang [sic], monarch of all he surveys at the Selig Jungle zoo. "Chang" is said to bear the proud distinction of being the first of his kind to play the lead role in motion pictures. He may or he may not become a motion picture matinee idol. One thing is certain, if "Chang" becomes the honored recipient of numerous notes such as are received by other actors, he'll do his very best to try to answer them, for "Chang" will try anything once.[144]

Shortly after appearing in his first and only starring role, *The Orang-Outang* (Selig Polyscope, 1915), Chang died, allegedly made sick by "wounded professional pride."[145] According to *Motion Picture News*, his film was something of an inverse of *Murders in the Rue Morgue*, with the "very human" Chang blamed for a murder committed by a man.[146]

The human qualities of primates or man-apes had not gone unnoticed in so many of the films described in this chapter, nor had those of characters labeled freaks. Much like Hugo's hunchback, audiences could—at least at times—feel sympathy for those who were different. And yet, the difference could also inspire horror, resulting in complicated reactions to the very same film or character.

To look, to stare, to gawk: these were the viewing positions many Americans assumed at displays of primates, man-apes, and freaks, whether exhibited live or in the cinema, whether authentic or gaffed, whether real or humbugged. Gazing at the spectacle became a filmgoing practice, an industrial standard, one that extended not only toward what was perceived as the periphery of humanity, but also at those humans who seemed marginally different.

Indeed, a "mysterious character that seems half man and half ape" appeared in the film *Children of the Jungle* (E. & R. Jungle Film, 1914). The film was set in Africa, and featured a white American woman raised near the country's "natives." A synopsis claimed, "Our sympathy goes at once to the young girl, who has grown to womanhood in this secluded spot," one in which she encountered the simultaneously frightening and fascinating Other.[147]

Notes

1. A. Danson Michell, "*The Miser's Reversion,*" *Motion Picture News*, March 21, 1914, 52. In a curious error, *Moving Picture World* (March 28, 1914) claimed *The Miser's Reversion* was a two-reel film released by Vitagraph.
2. "Feature Drama at Grand," *Rockford Republic* (Rockford, Illinois), March 31, 1914, 4.
3. Michell, 52.
4. "At the Louisiana," *State Times Advocate* (Baton Rouge, Louisiana) April 9, 1914, 6.
5. Michell, 52.
6. Ibid., 52.
7. "The Gorilla," *Saturday Evening Post*, July 13, 1861, 4.
8. "Amusements at New Orleans," *Spirit of the Times*, January 26, 1856, 595.
9. Advertisement, *New-York Daily Gazette*, May 16, 1789.
10. Quoted in Lawrence Frank, *Victorian Detective Fiction and the Nature of Evidence: The Scientific Investigations of Poe, Dickens, and Doyle* (New York: Palgrave Macmillan, 2003), 37–8.
11. Untitled, *New-York Gazette*, February 4, 1799, 3.
12. "A Monster of the First Water," *Spirit of the Times*, April 6, 1839, 49.
13. John Reader, *Missing Links: The Hunt for Earliest Man* (London: Collins, 1981).
14. Ronald L. Numbers, *Darwinism Comes to America* (Cambridge, MA: Harvard University Press, 1998), 1.
15. James R. Moore, *The Post-Darwinian Controversies: A Study of the Protestant Struggle to Come to Terms with Darwin in Great Britain and America, 1870–1900* (Cambridge: Cambridge University Press, 1979), 10.
16. "Darwin," *Quincy Daily Whig* (Quincy, Ilinois), January 24, 1872, 4.
17. See, for example, "Darwinism," *Wheeling Daily Intelligencer*, March 21, 1874.
18. Moore, 10.
19. Numbers, 58–62.
20. Peter C. Kjærgaard, "'Hurrah for the Missing Link!': A History of Apes, Ancestors and a Crucial Piece of Evidence," *Notes and Records of the Royal Society of London*, Vol. 65, No. 1 (March, 20, 2011), 94.
21. Bert Theunissen, *Eugène Dubois and the Ape-Man from Java: The History of the First "Missing Link" and Its Discoverer* (Dordrecht, The Netherlands: Kluwer Academic Publishers Group, 1988).
22. Robert Millar, *The Piltdown Men* (New York: St. Martin's Press, 1972).
23. "Darwin Vindicated," *Daily Commercial* (Vicksburg, Mississippi), April 24, 1879, 4.
24. "Forefather of Mankind," *Chicago Tribune*, March 5, 1899, 42.
25. "Is It Man or Man-Ape?", *New York Times*, January 31, 1909, SM6.
26. Gillian Beer, *Darwin's Plots: Evolutionary Narrative in Darwin, George Eliot, and Nineteenth-Century Fiction* (London: Routledge & Kegan Paul, 1983), 7.
27. Frank, 29–43.
28. Redmond O'Hanlon, *Joseph Conrad and Charles Darwin: The Influence of Scientific Thought on Conrad's Fiction* (Edinburgh: Salamander Press, 1984). *Lord Jim* was published as a novel in 1900; it had earlier been serialized in 1899–1900.
29. Stan Poole, "In Search of the Missing Link: Mark Twain and Darwinism," *Studies in American Fiction*, Vol. 13, No. 2 (Autumn 1985), 201–15.
30. Virginia Richter, *Literature After Darwin: Human Beasts in Western Fiction, 1859–1939* (New York: Palgrave Macmillan, 2011), 4.
31. Frank, 180–1, 194.
32. Allardyce Nicoll, *A History of English Drama 1660–1900* (Cambridge: Cambridge University Press, Second Edition 1955), Vol. 4, 602.

33. "Amusements," *The Evening Post* (New York), May 22, 1835, 3.
34. See, for example, "Amusements &c," *New York Times*, May 22, 1854, 1.
35. "Negro Minstrelsy," *New York Clipper*, August 24, 1872, 167.
36. "The Free Setters Quartette," *New York Clipper*, September 19, 1908.
37. Franklyn Fyles, "The Latest New York Thriller Has a Man-Monkey for Its Hero," *Washington Post*, June 2, 1907, SM2.
38. Ibid., SM2.
39. Advertisement, *Boston Herald*, August 22, 1907, 9.
40. "Grand Opera House," *Boston Post*, August 18, 1908, 4.
41. Fyles, SM2.
42. James W. Cook, Jr., *The Arts of Deception: Playing with Fraud in the Age of Barnum* (Cambridge, MA: Harvard University Press, 2001), 128–9.
43. Robert Bogdan, *Freak Show: Presenting Human Oddities for Amusement and Profit* (Chicago: University of Chicago Press, 1988), 25.
44. Ibid., 121–7.
45. "*Monkey Intelligence*," *Pathé Cinema Bulletin*, April 25, 1914, iii. A copy of this film is archived at the Cineteca Nazionale.
46. "*Monkey Intelligence*," *Moving Picture World*, April 3, 1915, 65.
47. Elias Savada (ed.), *The American Film Institute Catalog of Motion Pictures Produced in the United States: Film Beginnings, 1893–1910* (Lanham, Maryland: Scarecrow Press, 1995), 694. A copy of *The Monkey's Feast* is archived in the Paper Print Collection at the Library of Congress.
48. Ibid., 551. A copy of *Joe, the Educated Orangoutang* is archived in the Paper Print Collection at the Library of Congress.
49. Ibid., 299. Copies of *The Educated Chimpanzee* and *Egyptian Fakir with Dancing Monkey* are archived in the Paper Print Collection at the Library of Congress. Other such films included *The Jealous Monkey* (Edison, 1897), *Acrobatic Monkey* (Edison, 1898), *August, the Monkey/Le singe August* (Pathé Frères, 1904), *The Monkey Bicyclist* (Lubin, 1904), *Monkey, Dog and Pony Circus* (Lubin, 1904), *Monkey Business* (American Mutoscope & Biograph, 1905), and *The Monkey Showmen of Djibal/Les montreurs de singes de Djibah (Égypte)* (Eclair, 1910, aka *The Monkey Showman of Djibah*). See Savada, 6, 54, 544, 693, 694. Copies of *The Jealous Monkey*, *Acrobatic Monkey*, and *Monkey Business* are archived in the Paper Print Collection at the Library of Congress.
50. Advertisement, *Moving Picture World*, May 22, 1909, 695. A copy of *The Human Ape, or Darwin's Triumph* is archived at the Danish Film Institute.
51. "The Human Ape," *New York Dramatic Mirror*, June 5, 1909, 15.
52. "*Aunt Tabitha's Monkey*," *Moving Picture World*, September 17, 1910, 632.
53. "*Mrs. Casey's Gorilla*," *Motion Picture News*, November 29, 1913, 38. A copy of this film is archived at the Museum of Modern Art, New York City.
54. "*Mrs. Casey's Gorilla*," *Moving Picture World*, November 29, 1913, 1007.
55. "Film Storiettes," *Universal Weekly*, April 11, 1914, 10.
56. Oliver Gaycken, "Early Cinema and Evolution," in *Evolution and Victorian Culture*, edited by Bernard Lightman and Bennett Zon (Cambridge: Cambridge University Press, 2014), 102.
57. "*The Cave Man*," *Moving Picture World*, May 4, 1912, 425; "*The Virgin of the Fire*," *Moving Picture News*, November 2, 1912, 26; "*The Cave Dwellers*," *Moving Picture World*, August 2, 1913, 538; "*The Cave Men's War*," *Moving Picture World*, December 20, 1913, 1412; "*The Primitive Instinct*," *Kalem Kalendar*, August 1, 1914, 26.
58. A copy of *Man's Genesis* is archived at the Library of Congress.
59. "*Man's Genesis*," *Moving Picture World*, July 6, 1912, 72.
60. Louis Reeves Harrison, "What Constitutes a Really Great Play?", *Moving Picture World*, August 31, 1912, 845.

61. "*The Prehistoric Man*," *Moving Picture World*, November 14, 1908, 384. Other comedies featured male characters in the modern world attempting to use "cave man" methods to find their mates, as in the case of *A Cave Man Wooing* (Imp, 1912) and *Mating* (Imp, 1913). A copy of *A Cave Man Wooing* is archived at the EYE Film Institute.
62. A copy of *His Prehistoric Past* is available in the DVD boxed set *Chaplin at Keystone* (Los Angeles: Flicker Alley, 2010).
63. *Picture Catalogue* (New York: American Mutoscope & Biograph, November 1902), 14. Available in *A Guide to Motion Picture Catalogs by American Producers and Distributors, 1894–1908: A Microfilm Edition* (New Brunswick: Rutgers University Press, 1985), Reel 2.
64. A copy of *The Mischievous Monkey* is archived at the Library of Congress.
65. "*The Professor's Secret*," *Moving Picture World*, April 11, 1908, 328.
66. "*A Wonderful Remedy*," *Moving Picture World*, October 23, 1909, 569.
67. "*The Haunted Island*," *Moving Picture World*, June 10, 1911, 1328.
68. "*The Haunted Island*," *The Billboard*, June 17, 1911, 30.
69. "*The Haunted Island*," *Moving Picture World*, July 1, 1911, 1532.
70. Advertisement, *Moving Picture World*, June 17, 1911, 30.
71. A copy of *Brute Force* is archived at the Library of Congress. It is worth noting that the film *A Relic of the Olden Days* (Frontier, 1914) seems to have taken its narrative inspiration from Griffith's *Man's Genesis* and *Brute Force*, including in its use of the allegorical character names "Brute Force," "Weak Hands," and "White Flower." See "*A Relic of the Olden Days*," *Moving Picture World*, December 5, 1914, 1425.
72. "*Brute Force*," *Moving Picture World*, May 9, 1914, 821.
73. Neil G. Caward, "*The Black Box* Grows More Interesting," *Motography*, March 27, 1915, 486–7.
74. John C. Garrett, "Universal's *The Black Box*," *Motography*, June 26, 1915, 1058.
75. This novel was serialized in 1911, and then published in an individual volume in 1912.
76. "*Balaoo, the Demon Baboon*," *Eclair Bulletin*, May 1913.
77. Ibid.
78. "*Balaoo, the Demon Baboon*," *Moving Picture World*, May 17, 1913, 744.
79. An incomplete copy of *Balaoo, the Demon Baboon* is archived at the Library of Congress, which features the quoted intertitles. A complete restored print is archived at the Centre national du cinéma et de l'image animée (CNC).
80. Advertisement, *Moving Picture World*, May 3, 1913, 507.
81. H. C. Judson, "*Balaoo* (Union Features)," *Moving Picture World*, May 17, 1913, 686.
82. "*The Village Scare*," *Moving Picture World*, December 11, 1909, 840. A copy of *The Village Scare* is archived at the Cinémathèque Suisse.
83. "*The Village Scare*," *New York Dramatic Mirror*, December 4, 1909, 18.
84. Bogdan, 27.
85. The term "morbid curiosity" appears in "Tragic Retreat of Human Freaks Before Picture Shows," *Washington Post*, February 26, 1911, M6.
86. Rosemarie Garland Thomson, "Introduction," in *Freakery: Cultural Spectacles of the Extraordinary Body*, edited by Rosemarie Garland Thomson (New York: New York University Press, 1996), 3, 4.
87. Quoted in Loren C. Eiseley, "The Reception of the First Missing Links," *Proceedings of the American Philosophical Society*, Vol. 98, No. 6 (December 23, 1954), 458.
88. Thomas Fahy, *Freak Shows and the Modern American Imagination: Constructing the Damaged Body from Willa Cather to Truman Capote* (New York: Palgrave Macmillan, 2011), 6.
89. Tody Hamilton discussed such fakery in "What [the] Public Doesn't Know about Freaks," *Chicago Tribune*, April 28, 1907, 15.
90. Edward L. Schwarzschild, "Death-Defying/Defining Spectacles: Charles Willson Peale as Early American Freak Showman," in *Freakery: Cultural Spectacles of the Extraordinary Body*, edited by Rosemarie Garland Thomson (New York: New York University Press, 1996), 82–96.

91. Bogdan, 32.
92. Quoted in Hildegard Hoeller, "Freaks and the American Dream: Horatio Alger, P. T. Barnum, and the Art of Humbug," *Studies in American Fiction*, Vol. 34, No. 2 (Autumn 2006), 191.
93. Robert Bogdan, "The Social Construction of Freaks," in *Freakery: Cultural Spectacles of the Extraordinary Body*, edited by Rosemarie Garland Thomson (New York: New York University Press, 1996), 29.
94. Lisa A. Kochanek, "Reframing the Freak: From Sideshow to Science," *Victorian Periodicals Review*, Vol. 30, No. 3 (Fall 1997), 228.
95. Mark Twain first published *Personal Habits of the Siamese Twins* in *Packard's Monthly* in August 1869; he later included it in *Mark Twain's Sketches, Old and New* (1875).
96. Jane R. Goodall, *Performance and Evolution in the Age of Darwin: Out of the Natural Order* (New York: Routledge, 2002), 36.
97. Bogdan, 35.
98. Ibid., 58, 60.
99. "Side-Show Canvases," *Washington Post*, July 15, 1910, 3.
100. "Change in Dime Museums," *Chicago Tribune*, June 23, 1901, 54.
101. "No More Freaks with the Circus," *Chicago Tribune*, March 8, 1908, G3.
102. Fahy, 12.
103. "Dime Museums' Glories Dimmed," *Chicago Tribune*, March 18, 1906, I6.
104. "Tragic Retreat of Human Freaks Before Picture Shows," M6.
105. "Passing of the Dime Museum," *Washington Post*, September 4, 1910, M3.
106. Henry Llewellyn Williams, Letter to the Editor, *New York Times*, April 16, 1904, BR268.
107. In addition to those listed in the main text, hunchbacks appeared in such films as *Thor, Lord of the Jungle* (Selig Polyscope, 1913, aka *Thor, Lord of the Jungles*) and *The Fox Woman* (Majestic, 1915). See James S. McQuade, "*Thor, Lord of the Jungle* (Selig)," *Moving Picture World*, December 6, 1913, 1126; "*The Fox Woman*," *Moving Picture World*, July 24, 1915, 726. A copy of *Thor, Lord of the Jungle* is archived at the EYE Film Institute.
108. Advertisement, *Moving Picture World*, January 18, 1913, 283.
109. Another example of these comedy films would be *The Hunchback Fiddler/La légende du violoneux* (Pathé Frères, 1910). See "*The Hunchback Fiddler*," *Moving Picture World*, April 23, 1910, 641.
110. "*Hunchback Brings Luck*," *Moving Picture World*, April 18, 1908, 352.
111. "*Electrified Humpback*," *Moving Picture World*, December 4, 1909, 799.
112. "*Just for Good Luck*," *Moving Picture World*, July 23, 1910, 192–3. A copy of this film is archived at the Cinémathèque Française.
113. "*Funnicus Marries a Hunchback*," *Moving Picture World*, January 25, 1913, 364.
114. "*Polidor the Hunchback*," *Motography*, December 14, 1914, 830.
115. "*The Hunchback of Cedar Lodge*," *Moving Picture World*, August 8, 1914, 838.
116. "*The Devil's Fiddler*," *Motography*, December 12, 1914, 830. Copies of *The Devil's Fiddler* are archived at the Danish Film Institute and at the EYE Film Institute.
117. "*The Devil's Fiddler*," *Moving Picture World*, August 15, 1914, 1016.
118. "*The Hunchback*," *Kalem Kalendar*, December 1, 1913, 11.
119. "*The Hunchback* (Kalem)," *Moving Picture World*, November 29, 1913, 1017.
120. Louis Reeves Harrison, "Notre Dame de Paris," *Moving Picture World*, December 16, 1911, 884. Various copies of *Notre Dame de Paris* survive, including at the Library of Congress, the Museum of Modern Art, the British Film Institute, and the Centre national du cinéma et de l'image animée (CNC).
121. Advertisement, *Motography*, March 15, 1913, 10.
122. A brief amount of footage of this film exists by way of a paper print deposit at the Library of Congress.

123. "*The Hunchback*," *New York Dramatic Mirror*, September 11, 1909, 14.
124. "*Hugo, the Hunchback*," *Moving Picture World*, April 9, 1910, 571.
125. "*The Hunchback*," *Reel Life*, April 11, 1914, 18, 20.
126. "*The Hunchback's Romance*," *Moving Picture World*, July 24, 1915, 720.
127. In 1910, Pathé Frères released a film entitled *A Freak/L'homme mystérieux*, though it does not qualify for the current discussion, given that it showed an "acrobat who seems to be made of rubber, so unusual are his contortions." See "*A Freak*," *Moving Picture World*, December 10, 1910, 1356.
128. "Film Review," *Moving Picture World*, December 14, 1907, 670.
129. A copy of *Dr. Skinum* is archived at the Museum of Modern Art in New York City.
130. Gaumont's comedy *The Lady with the Beard; or, Misfortune to Fortune/La barbe* (1908, distributed in the U.S. by George Kleine) was not dissimilar, though its cure works in reverse. In the film, a man obtains a lotion to remove unwanted hair from his sweetheart, but it instead causes her to grow a beard. See "*The Lady with the Beard; or, Misfortune to Fortune*," *Moving Picture World*, July 18, 1908, 52.
131. "*Brides and Bridles*," *Moving Picture World*, December 14, 1912, 1082.
132. "*Brides and Bridles*," *Moving Picture World*, December 7, 1912, 1012.
133. "The Thanhouser Museum," *Moving Picture World*, March 30, 1912, 1149.
134. "Thanhouser," *The Billboard*, March 30, 1912, 29.
135. A copy of *The Star of the Side Show* is archived at the UCLA Film & Television Archive.
136. "*The Family Skeleton*," *Moving Picture World*, March 14, 1914, 1414.
137. "*The Family Skeleton*," *Moving Picture World*, April 14, 1914, 57.
138. Steve Massa, "The Elongated Comedienne: Gale Henry," in *Lame Brains & Lunatics: The Good, The Bad, and The Forgotten of Silent Comedy* (Albany, Georgia: BearManor Media, 2013), 95–107. *The Star of the Side Show* had earlier featured an actress dressed as a Circassian Beauty.
139. Linda Frost, "The Circassian Beauty and the Circassian Slave: Gender, Imperialism, and American Popular Entertainment," in *Freakery: Cultural Spectacles of the Extraordinary Body*, edited by Rosemarie Garland Thomson (New York: New York University Press, 1996), 249. See also Charles King, "Zalumma Agra, the 'Star of the East' (fl. 1860s)," in *Russia's People of Empire: Life Stories from Eurasia, 1500 to the Present*, edited by Stephen M. Norris and Willard Sunderland (Bloomington, Indiana: Indiana University Press, 2012), 130–7.
140. While Agra was the first to achieve great fame, the Front Street Circus in Baltimore had already exhibited a "Circassian Beauty" as early as 1854. See "Amusements," *The Sun* (Baltimore, Maryland), February 20, 1854, 3.
141. "*Freaks*," *Motography*, July 17, 1915, 138.
142. "*Freaks*," *Motion Picture World*, July 10, 1915, 382.
143. "*Freaks*," *Motion Picture News*, July 17, 1915, 124.
144. "Orang Outang Becomes a Cinema Star," *The Photoplayers' Weekly*, August 19, 1915, 11.
145. "Notes from All Over," *Motography*, September 18, 1915, 586; "Los Angeles Letter," *Moving Picture World*, August 14, 1915, 1114.
146. "*The Orang-Outang*," *Motion Picture News*, August 14, 1915, 92.
147. "*Children of the Jungle*," *Moving Picture World*, November 28, 1914, 1300.

CHAPTER 11

The Other(s)

No actor in the early movie serials was more popular than Pearl White, who retains at least a modicum of fame as a result of *The Perils of Pauline* (Pathé, 1914). Its success led to *The Exploits of Elaine* (Pathé, 1914–15), in which she bested a treacherous villain known as "The Clutching Hand" (Sheldon Lewis). But her troubles mounted in *The New Exploits of Elaine* (Pathé, 1915).

In this follow-up serial, Edwin Arden portrayed the "serpent" Wu Fang, a Chinaman who not only kidnapped Elaine, but also imported rare African ticks in order to poison her friends, condemning them to "certain death."[1] His fiendish inventions included a chair that burns its "occupant to death" and a chemical that "can be timed most accurately to cause spontaneous combustion."[2] At one point, in an effort to blind his plucky adversary, the "yellow devil" even sends Elaine a handkerchief "containing a spark of radium."[3]

The New Exploits of Elaine was hardly the first time a serial portrayed the Chinese as evil; the same had been true of *The Perils of Pauline*, *Lucille Love, the Girl of Mystery* (Universal, 1914), *The Hazards of Helen* (Kalem, 1914–17), and *Zudora* (Thanhouser, 1915), as well as in the original *Exploits of Elaine*.[4] Nevertheless, according to the *New York Dramatic Mirror*, *The New Exploits of Elaine* was somewhat unique:

> Audiences will particularly find none of the crudeness which they have probably become accustomed to associate in films with this race. Both Edwin Arden and W. M. Rale [who played Long Sin, Wu Fang's "inferior"] are not only thorough "Chinks," but the "supers" are for the most part the real, yellow-skinned, furtive-eyed article.[5]

These words obviously constitute an example of the kind of demeaning and offensive racism so common in that era, but also a rather perplexing analysis. Actors Arden and Rale were white: they had to wear "yellowface" make-up in their roles as Chinese villains. The fact that some of the supporting cast and extras might actually have been Chinese hardly seems to be a compelling argument for verisimilitude.

But such were the complexities and contradictions in screen depictions of the "Other," meaning not only the Chinese, but any race or group of people who were different than healthy white Protestants. With notions of difference came those of white superiority. As Linda Frost notes, "The ability to assign primitiveness to other people affirmed the sense of belonging and entitlement that American national membership promised."[6] They are not Us, and so perhaps They should be exhibited for Us to examine.

Along with the Chinese, the "freaks" discussed in Chapter 10 represented a manifestation of the Other, that which was deemed abnormal and thus threatening and even frightening. Carnivals and dime museums existed in part because of this, displaying various practices that were considered unusual. As Robert Bogdan writes of them, "Favorite themes included cannibalism, human sacrifice, head hunting, polygamy, unusual dress, and food preferences that repelled Americans (eating dogs, rodents, and insects)."[7]

From minstrel shows and comic vaudeville sketches invoking ethnic stereotypes to Native American ceremonies performed at Wild West spectacles, the entertainment business was built on notions of difference. The same could be said of the legitimate theatre, where the Other was so often the villain. "We utterly refuse to entertain a white Svengali," the *Chicago Tribune* said of the Jewish hypnotist in 1897.[8] Villainous Others also appeared regularly in American literature, including in Henry Wadsworth Longfellow's *Evangeline* (1847), Herman Melville's *Benito Cereno* (1855), and Stephen Crane's *The Monster* (1898).

Early cinema represents a link in an unbroken chain of American entertainment obsessed with the Other(s) and white superiority over them, including in a number of allegedly nonfiction films. Consider *Motography*'s review of *The Hairy Ainus/Un peuple qui disparaît, les Aïnos* (Pathé, 1913): "An interesting study of the peculiar people who inhabit the islands to the north of Japan and to whom civilization has not yet penetrated."[9] *Moving Picture World*'s description of Gaston Méliès's filming expedition to Bora Bora in 1912 relied on similar language: "The visiting party were awakened from their slumber on shipboard by the rumbling of native drums beating rhythmically to wierd [sic] native chants and grotesque movements of the natives . . ."[10]

In most cases, however, the Other appeared coded as fictional, with connections between pre-cinema and early cinema entertainment being apparent in various contexts, including mainstream America's skepticism of Irish immigrants and their traditions. For example, Dion Boucicault's play *The Shaughraun*, which premiered in New York in 1874, remained extremely popular for the rest of the century. One of its most famous scenes depicts an Irish wake, which became a recurrent feature of American entertainment. Non-Irish audiences became fascinated by what seemed to them a peculiar treatment of death.

Along with popular songs like *Mike McCarthy's Wake* (Frank Harding, 1895), numerous stereo views depicted wakes, illustrating "Irish" actors and actresses drinking, smoking, and/or fighting near the corpse, sometimes even wearing grotesque papier mâché masks that heightened the physical difference between Them and Us.[11] The dearly departed could materialize in spirit form thanks to double exposures, as in Strohmeyer and Wyman's *Be the Howly St. Patrick!—There's Mickie's Ghost* of 1894. In yet another mockery of a sacred tradition, the "corpse" could rise out of the coffin to join in the drinking, as in *McCarthay's Wake, McCarthay Comes to Life* (Universal Photo Art Company, 1897).

Filmmakers in the early cinema period drew on the Irish wake repeatedly, creating comedies in which the "corpse" is only dead drunk, as in *Murphy's Wake* (American Mutoscope & Biograph, 1903), *O'Finnegan's Wake* (Lubin, 1903), *Murphy's Wake* (Walturdaw, 1906, distributed in America by Miles Brothers in 1907), and *Kelly's Ghost* (Crystal, 1914).[12] Similar films featuring allegedly "dead" Irishmen include *The Death of Michael Grady* (Vitagraph, 1910) and *Dan Greegan's Ghost* (Biograph, 1913).[13] Burlesquing the Other was a common approach to dealing with Them.

Another was to portray Them as horrifying. In early cinema, Otherness extended to ancient peoples, including Egyptians, as in *The Human Sacrifice* (Reliance, 1911), or Aztecs, as in *The Altar of the Aztecs* (Selig Polyscope, 1913).[14] Consider also depictions of the itinerant Roma people. In some cases, they issued ominous pronouncements as a result of fortune telling, as in *Gypsy's Revenge* (Lubin, 1907, aka *The Gypsy's Revenge*) and *The Gipsy's Warning* (Gaston Méliès, 1913, aka *The Gypsy's Warning*).[15] They could also be murderers, as in *The Legend of the Lilacs* (Eclair American, 1914).[16] And they committed the offense feared above all else: kidnapping white women or girls, as in films like *Stolen by Gypsies* (Edison, 1905), *The Adventures of Dollie* (Biograph, 1908), and *The Mysterious Double; or, The Two Girls Who Looked Alike* (Kalem, 1909).[17] Here was the peril of physical violation and degradation, as well as miscegenation, all unthinkable crimes, too horrible to consider—except American film audiences did, time and again.

During the pre-nickelodeon era, a number of trick moving pictures relied upon the Other as an excuse for their magical special effects. The perceived preternatural and unnatural allowed for the existence of the supernatural, as in the case of the Chinese. For example, in 1900, Lubin sold *Ching Ling Foo*, which he promoted as being the "only moving picture of the original and great Chinese conjuror."[18] Edison released *Ching Ling Foo's Greatest Feats* in 1902.[19] That same year, Edison also distributed *The Chinese Conjurer and the Devil's Head* and *Extraordinary Chinese Magic/Chinese Magic*.[20]

A related group of moving pictures relied upon "Hindoo" characters. In 1902, Edison distributed *The Hindoo Fakir*, in which an Indian performs magic tricks while directly addressing the camera.[21] The same company's "magic picture series" continued in 1903 with *Extraordinary Black Art*, which presented a "Hindoo conjurer . . . upon the stage."[22] Similarly, the 1903 catalog for Star Films included Méliès's *The Rajah's Dream; or, the Bewitched Wood/Le rêve du radjah ou La forêt enchantée*, *The Brahmin and the Butterfly/La chrysalide et le papillon d'or*, and *The Human Fly/L'homme mouche*, all three presenting Indian characters whose mysticism was responsible for magic onscreen.[23]

Together, these two types of screen magicians show how the plural "Other" could to an extent become the singular. In many film descriptions, the term "Oriental" was vaguely applied to characters originating from Asia, the Middle East, and beyond.[24] As Edward Said has famously written, "'Our' Orient becomes 'ours' to possess and direct."[25] And, as *Moving Picture World* wrote in 1910, "Anything which adequately illustrates any of the features of the mysterious Orient, with its wealth of imagery, appealing directly to the curiosity, is certain to be popular."[26] When discussing *In the Serpent's Power* (Selig Polyscope, 1910), the *New York Dramatic Mirror* referred to the film's "dark featured Orientals or Italians," as if noting the uncertain boundaries of what constituted the "Oriental."[27] Whatever *it* was, though, it was quite possibly dangerous, as it long had been. In 1888, *Current Literature* informed readers that Satan was probably "of Persian origin."[28]

The boundaries between the Others became blurred beyond loosely applied terminology, due in part to the joint results of racism and pseudo-science. Phrenology and ethnology helped cast the Other as less evolved than their distant white cousins. In 1878, the *National Police Gazette* wrote, "The negro, like his kinsman, the monkey, is an imitative animal."[29] Nearly three decades later, American Mutoscope & Biograph released the moving picture *Human Apes from the Orient* (1906). As a surviving copy of the film illustrates, it features two human males.[30] To be ape-like, one either needed to be a dark-skinned Other, or wear make-up that gave the same appearance.

The Others also had "superstitious customs," their paganism being yet another example of the porous boundaries between Them and also the wide gulf between the collective Them and Us.[31] In 1839, Henry Schoolcraft argued that some Native American legends bore noticeable coincidences with "Oriental rites and opinions."[32] And all too often for the comfort of whites, the Others conducted ceremonies with serpents, whether that meant snake dances, snake charming, or even devil worship. Speaking of voodoo in America in

1893, the *New York Times* remarked, "It is curious how this idea of the serpent . . . is a part of the religious belief of about all the East Indian, African, and Central and South American people, to say nothing of some of our Indians."[33] Distinctions existed between these ethnicities, but so did perceived similarities. Heathens were heathens, including in the moving pictures.

In these cases, the camera assumed a position of superiority on behalf of white spectators. As Richard Dyer has argued, the titillating attraction of watching the Other onscreen results (at least in part) from how it divests the shackles of white conformity to act in an unrestrained manner.[34] Complex psychological processes are at work in the construction and reception of the cinematic Other, with the foreign presence constituting a fascinating monstrousness, a representation of those who live outside the barriers that define and confine whiteness.

E. Ann Kaplan has drawn attention to the fact that the "cinema was invented at the height of colonialism at the end of the nineteenth century," a fact that might help explain the sheer numbers of these offensive characters.[35] Drawing on long-standing racial stereotypes in popular culture, early filmmakers created a cinematic ethnoscape that paraded a farrago of Others. However, moving picture narratives most commonly deployed four of them: Native Americans, Blacks, the Chinese, and Indians. Their purpose was to entertain and to frighten white viewers, whose interest in seeing these depictions of them was potentially more sickening and horrifying than the fictional stories in which they appeared.

Native Americans

Immigrants to America generally perceived Native Americans to be savages, whose religions were pagan, if not Satanic, and whose habits were warlike.[36] Not surprisingly, these prevailing views informed American literature. Native American land was haunted, as memorialized in Philip Freneau's poem *The Indian Burying Ground*, first published in 1787, the same year the American Constitution was signed.[37] According to Renée L. Bergland:

> Many of America's most prominent authors seized on the figure of the spectral Native American as central to their attempts to develop a uniquely American national literature: during the first half of the nineteenth century, Charles Brockden Brown, Washington Irving, James Fenimore Cooper, Lydia Maria Child, Edgar Allan Poe, Nathaniel Hawthorne, and Herman Melville all wrote works that relied upon the discourse of the Indian ghost.[38]

As Hawthorne warned Us in *Young Goodman Brown* (1835), "There may be a devilish Indian behind every tree."

And then there was the depiction of the violent Native American, as in Felix O. C. Darley's painting *Emigrants Attacked by Indians on the Prairie* (1860), as well as in such theatre productions as John Augustus Stone's *Metamora; or, The Last of the Wampanoags* (1829).[39] Reproductions of Indian uprisings also commonly appeared in live entertainment during the late nineteenth and early twentieth centuries. In 1871, Wood's Museum presented *The Great Indian Massacre*.[40] In 1896, a venue in Ohio staged *The Custer Massacre*.[41] And in 1909, the 101 Ranch enacted *The Massacre of Pat Hennessey and Party*.[42]

According to Gregory S. Jay, "Few subjects were as popular in the early years of silent film as the Native American."[43] The sheer numbers of "Indian pictures" meant that story lines about them varied greatly, so much so that Eileen Bowser believes they constitute a genre that existed both inside and beyond the western.⁴⁴ Whether viewing them as "noble savages" or just savages, white America found Native Americans and their traditions to be a source of fascination, as well as of the uncanny, as the earliest films on the subject make clear.

For example, early moving pictures presented ghost dances, as in Edison's *Sioux Ghost Dance* (1894, aka *Ghost Dance* and *Ghost*), as well as snake dance ceremonies, including in *Parade of Snake Dancers before the Dance* (Edison, 1901) and *Moki Snake Dance by Walpapi Indians* (Edison, 1901).⁴⁵ Selig Polyscope promoted its 1903 film *Ute Indian Snake Dance* as follows:

> Never before have the Utes permitted a photographer around their teepees when they gave their snake dance. This wierd [sic] rite is performed every fall after the harvest has been good and its meaning is a tribute to the snakes who are supposed to bring plenty of rain [the] next season. . . . Every movement of [the] snakes and Indians can plainly be seen and all the horrible details of the dance are shown in full and wonderful precision. . . . As long as researches are made into Indian lore and customs, this film will stand as an authority on its subject. Its accuracy can never be questioned.⁴⁶

By contrast, 101 Bison openly advertised the fact that *The Snake* (1913) and the "weird serpent dance" seen in it were fictional.⁴⁷

Figure 11.1 Publicity still for *The Arrow Maiden* (Reliance, 1915). (*Courtesy of Robert J. Kiss*)

Native American medicine men appeared in early cinema on many occasions, as in *The Cheyenne Medicine Man* (Bison, 1911), *In the Long Ago* (Selig Polyscope, 1913), and *The Cave Dwellers* (101 Bison, 1913, aka *The Cave-Dweller's Romance*), which the *Universal Weekly* promoted for its "mysticism and wild folk lore [sic]."[48] *Owana, the Devil Woman* (Nestor, 1913) told the story of a medicine woman who transforms a chief's son into a pony.[49] And *The Arrow Maiden* (Reliance, 1915) featured a medicine woman who casts and then removes a spell from a fellow tribal member.[50] Such films were in addition to the comedy *The White Medicine Man* (Selig Polyscope, 1911), which was "based upon the well known ease with which Indians can be hypnotized."[51]

Filmmakers also explored Native American legends and superstitions, including—as detailed in Chapter 8—the shape-shifters of *The Werewolf* (101 Bison, 1913), *The Legend of the Phantom Tribe* (101 Bison, 1914), and *The White Wolf* (Nestor, 1914). Other moving pictures of this type ranged from the one-reel film *The Legend of Scar Face* (Kalem, 1910), in which a disfigured Native American bathes in a certain "mystic spring" that cures his deformities, to the two-reel *The Death Mask* (Kay-Bee, 1914), a "fairy tale" in which a brave Native American attempts to kill three brothers, only to learn that one of them is actually a woman from his own tribe.[52] Then, in 1914, Selig Polyscope released *The Lure of the Windigo*, a two-reeler in which a white man lures a white woman into the forest by imitating the sound of the Native American windigo, a "sighing of the wind through the trees."[53]

Ghosts populated a few Native American dramas of the era. Nestor's 1913 film *A Hopi Legend* depicts the spirits of two dead lovers reuniting in the "Happy Hunting Ground."[54] *Moving Picture World* was not impressed, claiming, "The spirit stuff at the finish is designed to be impressive. In most cases, it is to be feared the 'ascension' will be provocative of ridicule."[55] More unusual was Eclair American's *The Ghost of the Mine* (1914). In it, a man in an old mine sees the "astral form" of a Native American woman.[56] A Mexican murdered her years earlier, but the authorities try to convict the wrong man. To bring the case to its proper conclusion, her ghost helps to expose the real culprit.[57]

When reviewing *The Legend of Lake Desolation* (Pathé, 1911), *Moving Picture World* observed, "The Indian, howling and scalping, killing and burning, is to a normal human mind a horrible and repulsive sight. We have had quite enough of him in moving pictures . . ."[58] This complaint resulted from the sheer volume of films in which Native Americans murdered white settlers, a storyline that had deep roots in American cinema. Consider, for example, *Scalping Scene by Thundercloud* (Edison, 1897).[59] A catalog synopsis heralded the fact that Thundercloud was in fact a "genuine Indian." It also described the film as showing a "tenderfoot" being "spied by Thundercloud, who crawls upon his victim, scalps him on the spot and executes a scalp dance. A thrilling subject."[60] (Thundercloud's appearance made him the first credited actor associated with horror-themed cinema.)[61]

Bloodthirsty Native Americans also became a mainstay of early moving pictures. They could torture their victims without mercy, as in *The Red Man's Revenge* (Urban-Eclipse, 1908, aka *Red Man's Revenge*), or murder them by use of such weapons as poison-tipped arrows, as in *At the White Man's Door* (Vitagraph, 1911).[62] Of *Ogallalah* (Powers, 1911), *Moving Picture World* reported, "it is savage and cruel, as Indians are by nature. It is somewhat disagreeable, but its strength cannot be denied."[63]

Native Americans onscreen could also undertake the most dread of acts: stealing white women, potentially defiling those in their clutches. "The horrible torture inflicted upon white women by Indians of the plains was a matter of common knowledge among frontiersman," *Moving Picture World* claimed in an article on *The Indian Massacre* (101 Bison, 1912).⁶⁴ In *The White Captive of the Sioux* (Kalem, 1910), a tribe kidnaps a white woman and keeps her for fifteen years.⁶⁵ Advertisements claimed it was based on a "well-authenticated historic incident."⁶⁶ Then, in 101 Bison's two-reel *The Heroine of the Plains* (1912), "the Indians steal a white girl," which leads to the necessity of "warfare."⁶⁷

Figure 11.2 *The Indian Massacre* (101 Bison, 1912).

Conflict between whites and Native Americans became the arc of many film narratives in the period, among them *Custer's Last Stand* (Selig Polyscope, 1909), *The Massacre of the Fourth Cavalry* (101 Bison, 1912), *The Cheyenne Massacre* (Kalem, 1913), and *The Big Horn Massacre* (Kalem, 1913).⁶⁸ Civilian massacres appeared onscreen as well, including in *The Pioneers* (American Mutoscope & Biograph, 1903), *The Massacre* (American Mutoscope & Biograph, 1908), *Ononko's Vow* (Edison, 1910), and *The Indian Massacre* (101 Bison, 1912). *Moving Picture World* declared Kalem's 1910 film *In the Dark Valley* was:

> A picture that holds one almost enthralled by the horror it suggests. It purports to be a reproduction of the awful Wyoming Valley massacre, and the scenes are bad enough without the play of imagination. But that helps to make it worse, and the audience lives over again the scenes through which the victims of the massacre passed. One shudders again and again, and even while admitting the fascination of the picture one is glad when it is finished and something else appears, even though it may be an indifferent vaudeville act. This is not a criticism of the picture. It is a tribute.⁶⁹

In conclusion, the puzzled trade confessed, "When a film carries such an influence, one cannot question its strength."

During Native American onslaughts onscreen, individual white victims sometimes survived, as in *Pioneers Crossing the Plains in '49* (Edison, 1908), *The Witch of the Everglades* (Selig Polyscope, 1911), *In the Haunts of Fear* (Pathéplay, 1913, aka *The Haunts of Fear*), and *The Skeleton in the Closet* (Kalem, 1913).⁷⁰ In other cases, as in *An Hour of Terror* (American,

1912), help arrives in the nick of time to save those whites under siege.[71] Perhaps the most famous of these last-minute rescues came in *The Battle of Elderbush Gulch* (Biograph, 1913), a film in which, as John E. O'Connor has noted, director D. W. Griffith depicted the Native Americans as being "absolute savages."[72]

Blacks

Blacks onscreen became the source of terror and repugnant humor, with distinctions between Africans, African-Americans, and Caribbeans often at best imprecise, and all of them commonly portrayed by white actors in "blackface." White America viewed the religions of African slaves as equal to those of Native Americans.[73] Some appalling stereotypes magnified after the American Civil War. As Kathleen B. Casey observes, "In the 1880s racial segregation dramatically expanded, and black men, in particular, were vilified as primal beasts with a penchant for raping white women."[74]

At the same time, Blacks were supposedly superstitious and easily frightened, whether in Poe's short story *The Gold-Bug* (1843) or in the "Ethiopian" vaudeville sketch *Alone in the Morgue* (1897).[75] An illustration depicting an African-American running from an animated skeleton adorns the cover of the dime novel *The Bradys and the Demon Doctor; or, The House of Many Mysteries* (1906).[76] By the time of its publication, Edison had already released *The Watermelon Patch* (1905), a film in which two scarecrows shed their dark clothes, revealing themselves to be skeletons: they frighten and chase several black characters.[77]

Loathsome attempts at humor also attempted to connect Blacks with primitive man or apes. In an early example of programming advice, Lubin suggested that exhibitors project the "funny" film *The Educated Chimpanzee* (1901) with the "darkey" film *Who Said Chicken?* (Lubin, 1901), which offered a close-up of an elderly African-American male, and advertise the dual screening as "The Evolution of Man."[78] Blacks were thus meant to be "laughable" *and* "grotesque," including in *Hallow-e'en in Coon-Town* (American Mutoscope, 1897) and *A Darktown Dance* (Edison, 1900), the grotesqueness apparently resulting from their appearance and behavior.[79] The banjoist in Georges Méliès's *A Nightmare/Le cauchemar* (1903) and the fortune-telling title character in *The Seeress* (American Mutoscope & Biograph, 1904) also serve as examples of Blacks intended to be simultaneously funny and eerie.[80]

Early filmmakers repeatedly positioned Blacks as cannibals in uncivilized countries, some of which were unnamed or even invented. Discourse on cannibalism had often appeared in nineteenth-century press and literature. The most infamous example was the Donner Party tragedy during the winter of 1846–7, in which the cannibals were white Americans.[81] Nevertheless, popular fiction on the subject concentrated on non-whites, as in the case of Herman Melville's *Typee* (1846) and Edgar Rice Burroughs's novel *Tarzan of the Apes* (1912).[82]

A number of early cannibal films were comedies, as in the case of *King of the Cannibal Islands* (American Mutoscope & Biograph, 1908).[83] In it, a Dutch character named Heinie Holtzmeyer charms the "savage beast[s]" by use of his fiddle.[84] As their new leader, he commands the cannibals to cook his nagging wife in their bubbling pot.[85] Dramatic moving pictures also invoked cannibalism in an effort to frighten viewers, as in *Captured by Aboriginals* (Gaston Méliès, 1913) and *The Mystery of the Poison Pool* (Pasquali American, 1914).[86] Advertisements for the latter featured the tag line "Escape from African Cannibal Tribe only to face death in the grip of a 20-foot Python."[87]

Filmmakers of the era also stereotyped the religions of Africans and African-Americans by generating narratives about voodoo, a topic that had been explored at length in the nineteenth-century press and such books as Mary A. Owen's *Voodoo Tales as Told among the Negroes of the Southwest* (1893). Here was the danger, according to some fear-mongering press accounts, of "African superstitions in America."[88] As the *Boston Post* told readers in 1899, voodoo worship was "as dark and as horrid as bestial savagery could make it."[89] A white observer at a voodoo ceremony in South Carolina in 1890 described its participants as "weird and phantom-like, as though a hundred disembodied Druids had returned to mother earth."[90]

Figure 11.3 *Voodoo Vengeance* (World's Best Film Company, 1913).

Voodoo Vengeance (World's Best Film Company, 1913) became the first film to cover the subject. Starring famous animal trainer Captain Jack Bonavita in blackface as the pagan priest, the three-reel moving picture presented the story of:

> ... a religious sect of African fanatics described as Voodoos, whose practices the British government finally stopped. The opening is where a man and woman on the way to the gold district are set upon by savages and killed. Their little girl is taken captive and raised by the tribe ...[91]

Two decades later, the girl, now a beautiful woman, lures the son of a British commissioner into the jungle so that he may "serve as a sacrifice to the moon god." An advertisement in Harrisburg, Pennsylvania in 1913 heralded *Voodoo Vengeance* the "biggest and best and most marvelous picture ever produced."[92] By contrast, The Idle Hour of Aberdeen, South Dakota quickly cancelled a screening of the film, arguing it "failed to come up to the high standard required," language that may suggest it was deemed too daring and/or disturbing.[93]

At any rate, two years later, Centaur produced a similar moving picture, the two-reel *Stanley Among the Voodoo Worshippers* (1915, aka *Stanley Among the Voo Doo Worshippers* and *Stanley and the Voo Doo Worshippers*).[94] In it, travelers in Africa fall prey to a band of "Voo Doos," who throw one of the whites into a pit. The "witch doctor" drops a lion on top of him; when the hero "overcomes the animal bare-handed," the witch doctor carries him off as an "extra fine prize for the heathen god."[95] *Moving Picture World* responded by saying the "atmosphere of the film is very well maintained and the story as it progresses is fairly interesting, although we must admit that the oftener the animal actors make their appearance the more pleasing the picture is."[96]

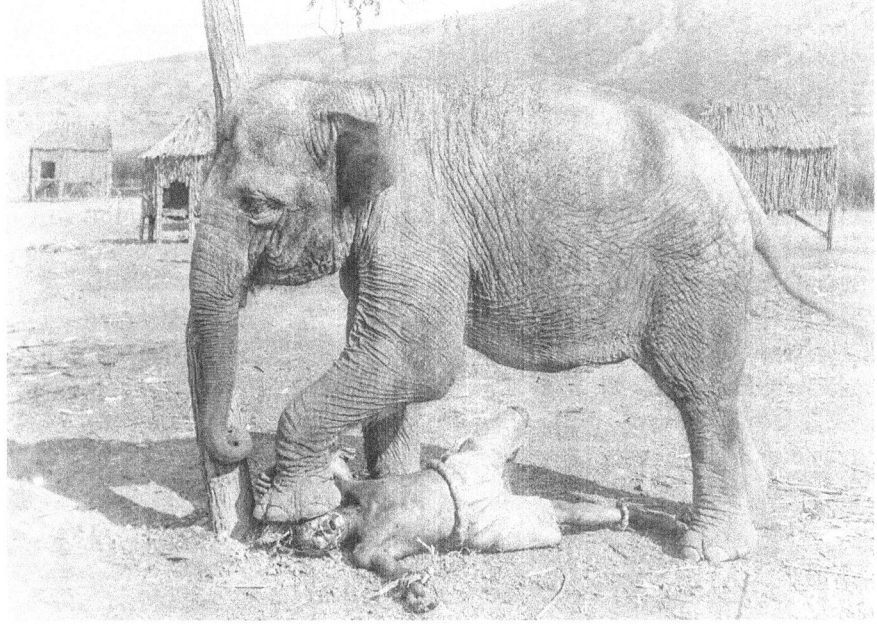

Figure 11.4 *Stanley Among the Voodoo Worshippers* (Centaur, 1915). (*Courtesy of Robert J. Kiss*)

Other film companies chose to set their voodoo stories in the United States. In March 1915, *Moving Picture World* reported on the Coquille Film Company of New Orleans, Louisiana and its plans to produce *Carnival in Black and White*, which was apparently a comedy.[97] In an alleged effort to make the film realistic, the director cast the "most savage childish lot [of African-Americans] obtainable, the type which scarcely if ever is free from fear of voudou [sic], witch magic, that was brought from the Congo." Along with filming some scenes at Congo Square in New Orleans, Coquille utilized a studio set:

> ... wherein the two leads, Edward Faure, who portrayed the voudou [sic] doctor, and Miss Lucy Leveque took the part of a Northern girl strayed away from her fashionable friends and, unknowingly, into the company of the voudou [sic] negroes. She, in fear of her life, had to go through the ceremonies assisting the voudou [sic] doctor. A burning caldron was in the center, from which the celebrants seemed to take live alligators and throw them back into the fire and take them back again. A number of stuffed alligators were strewn about the floor, and grinning monkey heads, real monkey heads, the chief "prop" of the voudou [sic] workers, were disposed in the shadows along the walls.[98]

Moving Picture World's account ended with a suggestion that Coquille would produce more voodoo films, adding, "They should be a hit, for voudouism [sic] for downright black horror can out-do insanity."

As the early cinema period came to a close, one major film about American voodoo did appear at theatres. Sidney Olcott, the famous filmmaker who had earlier worked at Kalem, directed *The Ghost of the Twisted Oaks* for Lubin in 1915. Three reels in length, the moving picture tells the story of Mary Randall (Valentine Grant) and her widowed mother. The two move to Florida after inheriting a plantation. Learning that a voodoo priest holds sway over the African-American workers, Mary has him removed from the property. Then, a ghost

> appears to Mary and [her fiancé Jack], and the action cuts back to disclose the history of the perturbed spirit of "Twisted Oaks," an unfortunate young belle of antebellum days who was killed while trying to save her lover during a duel. After the action shifts back to the present, Mary stumbles upon the Voodoos at worship and the priest determines to use her as a blood sacrifice, but the ghost again appears to Jack and leads him to the rescue.[99]

Unfortunately, only the third reel survives. It displays some of the most impressive images of horror created during the early cinema period, particularly during what one intertitle refers to as the "fanatical dance of the 'Voodoos.'"[100]

Motion Picture News complained that *The Ghost of the Twisted Oaks* relied on "fragmentary" storytelling, but *Motography* praised its scenes of the voodoo worshippers and its use of double exposures.[101] *Moving Picture World* was also impressed, particularly in Arthur Donaldson's portrayal of the voodoo priest and the use of a real rattlesnake during a voodoo ceremony, the result being a scene "startling" in its "realism."[102]

Chinese

From their emigration to California during and after the Gold Rush, the Chinese faced a harsh reception from white America, a regrettable trend that increased during the rest of the nineteenth century, culminating in the Chinese Exclusion Act in 1882.[103] When it came to fictional entertainment, however, the Chinese stereotype is one that transcended geopolitical boundaries.[104] Of the Chinese in American cinema, Michael Richardson explains:

> In the first place, when we use the word "China" here it may also mean at times Japan or Korea as well as China itself. Saying this alerts us to the fact that we are not speaking about a real place or a real people but precisely about a concept that may be utilized to fit certain cultural pre-conceptions, which match an "Orientalism" of the "Far East."[105]

And this expansive notion of "Chinese" represented a threat to white America, a "yellow peril" that filmmakers would transfer from the press to the screen, aided at times by such literature as Sax Rohmer's novel *The Mystery of Dr. Fu-Manchu*, first serialized in 1912 and 1913.[106]

In the cinema, the Chinese could be as mystical as they were menacing. *The Mystery of the Lama Convent/Dr. Nikola III, eller Lamaklostrets hemmeligheder* (Great Northern, 1910, aka *Mystery of the Lama Convent; or, Dr. Nicola in Tibet*) finds Dr. Nicola entering a sacred Chinese temple. The Chinese priests "show him how to be master over life and death, and explain to him their ability to call back to life a dead person."[107] But they soon discover Nicola is actually a white man in disguise and imprison him and his servant. The two eventually escape with "very precious data and curios."[108] Five years later, the thirteenth chapter of *The Exploits of Elaine* (Pathé, 1915) was entitled *The Devil Worshippers*, another reference to pagan religious practices.[109]

At times, Chinese villains were bent on world domination, as in the four-reel *The Fiends of Hell/Guarding Britain's Secrets* (Apex, 1914), in which a Chinese secret society attempts to obtain "all important scientific inventions of the world" by any means necessary.[110] After capturing a detective, they place his head through the aperture of a large clock's face, the "hands of which are swords as keen as razors."[111] The detective has to listen to the clock "ticking the minutes off to his death as the hands creep around toward his throat."[112]

Directed by John H. Collins, *The Mission of Mr. Foo* (Edison, 1915) features a fiendish mandarin who tries to foment a rebellion in the Chinese Republic so that the old Empire can be restored.[113] The *New York Dramatic Mirror* observed, "Orientalism on the screen usually means mysticism and fatalism, and the present [film] is no exception."[114] Operating in a Washington, D.C. hideout concealed behind a secret panel, Foo (portrayed by a white actor in make-up) was clearly influenced by Rohmer's Fu Manchu. Once his plans are discovered, the villain commits suicide by drinking poisoned tea.[115]

Other "yellow devils" pursued less global aims. In *The Mong-Fu Tong/Le mystère de la banque d'Elk-City* (Eclipse, 1913), distributed in America by George Kleine, the insidious Mong-Fu leads a gang of Chinese thieves. Learning Arizona Bill (Joë Hamman) is on their trail, they plant a "giant cobra" in his office.[116] Bill survives, but is later captured and bound by Mong-Fu, who tries to "fondle" Bill's wife right in front of him.[117] But Bill's wife stabs Mong-Fu and cuts her helpless husband loose. The two escape after setting fire to the villain's hideout.[118] Kleine's advertisements promised the film would "stir your blood like old wine—like a tale from Poe!"[119]

The title character of *The Mysterious Mr. Wu Chung Foo* (Feature Photoplay, 1914) operates a secret, subterranean "city," where he works captured slaves to death in his mines. Foo's ape seizes an investigating detective and carries him into the underground dominion. Thankfully, the heroine arrives with soldiers just in time.[120] Once again, perhaps inspired by the female characters in movie serials, it is the woman, not the man, who saves the day.

Chinese villains smuggled opium and operated dens of iniquity for the same. *The Opium Smugglers/Les fraudeurs d'opium* (Gaumont Co., 1914) featured a young woman who saves a detective from "yellow demons" attempting to kill him to protect their drug trade.[121] The *New York Dramatic Mirror* lauded its "marvelous" sets and cinematography.[122] The following year, *The Chinatown Mystery* (Broncho, 1915) presented the tale of an opium-addicted journalist who helps solve a murder.[123]

While Chinese men could be cruel and horrible to Chinese women (as in Selig Polyscope's *Lights and Shadows of Chinatown* in 1908 and Kay-Bee's *The Sign of the Snake* in 1913), they seemed to take a particular interest in white women.[124] A prime example is *The Chinese Death Thorn* (Kalem, 1913), a two-reeler in which Moi Ling (William Herman West), the "head of a Chinese crime syndicate," gets Mildred (Marin Sais) in his clutches. Martin (George Melford, who also produced the film) rescues her, but his brother Dick

Figure 11.5 Trade advertisement for *The Mysterious Mr. Wu Chung Foo* (Feature Photoplay, 1914). Published in *Moving Picture World* on July 11, 1914.

Figure 11.6 Publicity still for *The Chinatown Mystery* (Broncho, 1915). (*Courtesy of Robert J. Kiss*)

later falls prey to the villain. Moi Ling threatens to kill Dick with the title object: a single scratch means "instant death." But the police foil Moi Ling's plans, causing him to use the death thorn on himself.[125] *Moving Picture World* praised *The Chinese Death Thorn* for being a "powerful melodrama," drawing particular attention to the "consummate portrayal" that West gave as the "villainous Oriental, with his 'ways that are dark.'"[126]

Worse still, Chinese villains sold white women into slavery, contaminating their innocent flesh.[127] Five years before *Traffic in Souls* (Imp, 1913), the most famous of the era's "white slave" films (and one in which the villains are not Chinese), D. W. Griffith's *The Fatal Hour* (American Mutoscope & Biograph, 1908) presented the evil doings of the "Mephistophelian" Pong Lee and his "stygian whelp."[128] A female detective uses her "shrewd powers of deduction" to save a white woman from a torture device and put an end to Pong Lee's "atrocious female white slave traffic."[129]

Indians

Whether in the literature of Rudyard Kipling or at the "Oriental Spectacle" at Barnum & Bailey's circus in 1904, the Indian—then usually called the "East Indian," or the "Brahmin," or, most commonly, the "Hindoo"—simultaneously fascinated and frightened many whites in America.[130] On numerous occasions, for example, tales of the murderous "Thugs" [sic] appeared in the nineteenth-century press.[131] As publicity for American Mutoscope & Biograph's 1909 film *The Hindoo Dagger* identified, "The name Hindoo is sure to conjure up in our minds thoughts of mysticism, fetichism [sic], thaumaturgy, and accult [sic] art, and with reason, for Hindustan is, without doubt, the birthplace of all such weird practices."[132]

Coverage of India and its traditions appeared in a large number of moving pictures, ranging from the nonfiction *Palmistry/La chiromancie* (Gaumont, 1913), which explored the origins of palm reading, to such fictional comedies as *The Snake Charmer* (Eclair American, 1914), in which a henpecked husband steals a "strange pipe" from a "Hindoo snake charmer" in order to hypnotize his wife with its "weird" melodies.[133] However different such films were, they bore the similar aim of making India and its inhabitants seem strange, including their religious practices.

A number of films drew upon the Hindu religion for inspiration, particularly beliefs in reincarnation.[134] Among them were the comedy *The Key of Life* (Edison, 1910), and the drama *The Reincarnation of Karma* (Vitagraph, 1912), in which a snake resumes human form every hundred years.[135] The *Los Angeles Times* described the latter as a "weird" tale of the "occult."[136] Then, in 1914, Kalem released the two-reel drama *The Mystery of the Sleeping Death*, in which a white man and woman in the modern world fall into a strange form of unconsciousness.[137] An Indian mystic named Amar unravels the mystery. The man and woman knew each other in an earlier life in India, where a jealous priest cursed them.[138]

Filmmakers sometimes depicted Indian fakirs as con artists, including in *The Society Palmist* (American Mutoscope & Biograph, 1905), *The Yogi* (Imp, 1913), and *In the Grip of a Charlatan* (Kalem, 1913).[139] Similarly, *The Occult* (American, 1913) starred Jack Richardson as the charlatan Raj Singh.[140] Richardson created his own make-up for the role, transforming himself into a character that was "entirely unique and out of the ordinary."[141] Two years later, in *The Strange Case of Princess Khan* (Selig Polyscope, 1915), a Hindu fraudulently

Figure 11.7 *The Reincarnation of Karma* (Vitagraph, 1912).

makes a group see a disembodied spirit. *Motography*'s response: "Seldom is a producer able to get over so much real atmosphere of the weird and mystic as in the case of this picture."[142]

As with screen portrayals of other ethnicities covered in this chapter, the cinematic Hindoo occasionally exhibited proclivities toward white women.[143] Physically kidnapping them was one approach, including in *The Hindoo's Treachery* (American Kinograph, 1910, aka *The Hindoo's Treachery; An Incident in the Afridi Hills*), *The Messenger of Death* (Thanhouser, 1914), *The Mystery of the New York Docks* (Imp, 1914), and *The Rajah's Sacrifice* (Centaur, 1915), as well as in the serial *The Ventures of Marguerite* (Kalem, 1915–16).[144] Worse still was the effort to burn the title character of the serial *The Adventures of Kathlyn* (Selig Polyscope, 1913–14) as a sacrifice on a funeral pyre.[145] Hypnotic control, sometimes exercised from afar, also forced women to go to those Indians who desired them, as can be seen in *The Hindoo Prince* (Solax, 1911) and *The Crystal Globe* (Paragon, 1915).[146] These films represented concerns similar to newspaper accounts in 1912 that white women "all over the United States" were falling prey to the charms of evil Hindu "swamis."[147]

Other Indian characters tried to exact revenge on the white men they hated or feared, as in *The Vengeance of the Fakir* (Eclair American, 1912), *The Poisoned Darts* (Gaston Méliès, 1913), *The Ghost Club/Il treno degli spettri* (Gloria American, 1914), *The Rajah's Vow* (Kalem, 1914), and *The Hindu Nemesis* (Master Producers, 1914).[148] Their storylines are not dissimilar to the revenge plans crafted by Chinese villains in early cinema. Alice Guy Blaché's four-reel *The Woman of Mystery* (Blaché Features, 1914), which starred Vinnie Burns, became the most notable of these tales of vengeance.

A synopsis published in *Motion Picture News* detailed a Hindu priestess who "revenges herself upon a [detective] by means of the uncanny psychic powers she possesses."[149] An advertisement for Blaché's feature heralded it as a "thrilling photo-drama of dual personality and spirit control," in which:

> The mystic power of the soul of a Hindu priestess—driven through dungeon walls by strange forces of the spirit world—compels a detective's other self to commit crimes which he cannot fathom—and plunges him and a beautiful girl into a thrilling warfare with the powers of evil.[150]

Moving Picture World praised *The Woman of Mystery*, claiming its story "holds out to us a cup of strange, elusive wine, harmless yet powerful and exciting. . . . [It] artfully arrests our attentions just as the real event would arrest it, if we should see such a thing."[151]

In terms of sheer numbers, filmmakers produced more variants of Wilkie Collins's novel *The Moonstone* (1868) than any other specific Hindu narrative.[152] In these moving pictures—of which there were approximately twenty between 1909 and 1915—a white person comes into possession of a sacred Hindu object, be it an idol or a gemstone, often by stealing the same from a temple, and suffering dire consequences as a result.[153] Selig Polyscope's version of *The Moonstone* (1909) launched this cycle. *Moving Picture World* praised it for being "very exciting, very mysterious, and very fascinating."[154] Six years later, these films culminated in director Frank Crane's five-reel version of *The Moonstone* (World Film, 1915), which *Variety* claimed did "not look like a winner."[155]

Giving a more positive review of *The Moonstone* of 1915, *Motion Picture News* observed that its "subject matter" had "been greatly favored with the attention of all producers in the past."[156] And their similarities to Collins's novel had been noted on many occasions, as in *Moving Picture World*'s review of *The Idol's Eye* (Imp, 1910).[157] The many other films inspired by *The Moonstone* ranged from *The Hindu Jewel Mystery/La pierre de lune* (Urban-Eclipse, 1911), which was a direct adaptation, to variants like *The Hindoo's Curse* (Vitagraph, 1912), *The Lure of the Sacred Pearl* (Gaston Méliès, 1913), *The Stolen Idol* (Rex, 1913), *The Death Stone of India* (101 Bison, 1913), *The God of Girzah* (101 Bison, 1913), *The Treasure of Buddha/Lotos, die Tempeltänzerin* (Film Releases of America, 1914, aka *The Treasures of Buddha*), *The Mystery of the Hindu Image* (Majestic, 1914), *The Curse of the Scarabee Ruby/Le scarabée rouge* (Gaumont Co., 1914), *The Mystic Jewel* (Majestic, 1915), and—using a story furnished by James Oliver Curwood—*The Vengeance of Rannah* (Selig, 1915).[158]

Despite their derivative content, a number of these moving pictures received positive reviews. For example, *Moving Picture World* wrote that *The Green Eye of the Yellow God* (Edison, 1913) "gives Charles Ogle a splendid opportunity in his role of the 'Mad Carew,' a fearless British officer stationed in India, who defied the gods of the Hindus and paid the penalty of death."[159] Similarly, *Motography* praised *The Brand of Evil* (Essanay, 1913) and its use of double exposures; advertisements promised the film would "make the chills creep up and down your spine."[160]

Perhaps the most unusual variation on *The Moonstone* came in *The Moonstone of Fez* (Vitagraph, 1914), which also incorporated elements from Marie Belloc Lowndes's popular novel *The End of Her Honeymoon* (1913). In it, a woman purchases the title gemstone and soon thereafter has her fortune read. The next morning, the woman has "mysteriously disappeared" from the hotel where she and her daughter are lodging. All of the hotel attendants try to convince her daughter that the woman arrived at the hotel alone, going

Figure 11.8 *The Death Stone of India* (101 Bison, 1913).

so far as to show her a registry that seems to prove their claim. The daughter "begins to fear she has lost her senses."[161] Rather than being attacked by Hindus, the mother in fact died of the Black Plague in the middle of the night, with the hotel management trying to keep the incident quiet. The "Moonstone of Fez" was not responsible for anyone's death.

Conclusion

During the early cinema period, the Other remained simultaneously singular and plural, with the screen depiction of ethnicities featuring as many similarities as differences. Nowhere is this clearer than in the plot of *The Moonstone*, which not only provided the template for the many aforementioned moving pictures about Hindus, but also for those in which cursed objects hailed from Africa, from Asia, and from Native American tribes.[162] In fact, some films even had the dangerous object originating from countries like Mexico and Egypt.[163] The foreign presence was present, and if it was in the form of a pagan religious object, then buyer (and thief) beware.

Indeed, the lines between the cinematic Others were often porous, creating an Us versus Them binary. Early cinema is rife with examples of this blurring, including the fact that Native American actors like Chief Dark Cloud and Eagle Eye portrayed Hindus in the aforementioned *The Mystery of the Hindu Image*, while Asian actors like Sessue Hayakawa and Tsuru Aoki played Native Americans in the aforementioned *The Death Mask*.[164] Here is the perception of shared traits and effective interchangeability. Those who are different to Us are, to an extent at least, similar to each other.

In many respects, of course, the era of early cinema culminates with the release of D. W. Griffith's epic feature *The Birth of a Nation* (1915).[165] The film continued the long-standing practice of white actors using make-up to play other ethnicities. In the words of Michael Taussig, here are "copies that are not copies."[166] Ironically, the Other became more foreign as a result, with blackface, yellowface, and redface make-up resulting in exaggerated, grotesque, and disgusting farces, all presented by the cinema in an era when false rumors in the press (playing on white fears about miscegenation) insisted that one doctor was seeking to do the reverse, experimenting with X-rays in an effort to bleach black skin.[167]

At any rate, not all viewers at the time appreciated the ethnic make-up used in the film industry. Reviewing Vitagraph's *The Wrath of Osaka* in 1913, *Moving Picture World* wrote:

> It is intended to be a tragedy, but, at least in the early scenes, it fails [at] being tragic, because of its players who, as Japanese, are comical. Maurice Costello looks anything but Japanese in his costume, and there was some laughter. The women are passable Japs, but none of the men get by.[168]

In this particular case, the complaint apparently referred not to the racist depictions, but rather the appearance of inauthenticity created by white actors pretending to be the Other.

Most notably, a number of persons and organizations vehemently protested *The Birth of a Nation* for its abhorrent content, which included the Ku Klux Klan lynching a black(face) character. Such a reaction to inaccurate portrayals of particular ethnicities was not new. During the nickelodeon era, for example, many Native Americans decried onscreen depictions of "themselves," with a small number of journalists supporting their cause.[169] Similarly, trade publications warned producers against incorporating ethnic slurs in their films. These sentiments usually stemmed from fears of audience backlash, but in a few cases perhaps came from a more enlightened sentiment. When reviewing *Buried Alive* (Selig Polyscope, 1910), for example, *Moving Picture World* called the film "remarkable because it permits a Chinaman to play a decent role."[170]

Unfortunately, these types of viewer response were not the norm, as most white audiences readily accepted the rampant racial stereotypes they saw in moving pictures. Despite efforts to eradicate racism from the cinema, it continued of course, flourishing for the decades that followed. All too often, as Stephen T. Asma has bemoaned, the Other(s) sadly remained "monstrous."[171]

Notes

1. Neil G. Caward, "Pathé's *Exploits of Elaine*," *Motography*, May 8, 1915, 748.
2. "The New Exploits of Elaine," *Moving Picture World*, May 15, 1915, 1168; Neil G. Caward, "Pathé's *Exploits of Elaine*," *Motography*, May 22, 1915, 837.
3. "The Telltale Heart," *Motography*, June 12, 1915, 991.
4. A. Danson Michell, "*The Perils of Pauline*," *Motion Picture News*, May 30, 1914; "*Lucille Love, the Girl of Mystery*," *Universal Weekly*, May 30, 1914, 9; "*A Deed of Daring*," *Moving Picture World*, July 17, 1915, 537; "Zudora," *Moving Picture World*, January 16, 1915, 434.

5. "*The Watching Eye*," *New York Dramatic Mirror*, April 28, 1915, 34. Actor W. M. Rale was usually billed as either M. W. Rale or Michael Rale.
6. Linda Frost, *Never One Nation: Freaks, Savages, and Whiteness in U.S. Popular Culture, 1850–1877* (Minneapolis, Minnesota: University of Minnesota Press, 2005), 4.
7. Robert Bogdan, "The Social Construction of Freaks," in *Freakery: Cultural Spectacles of the Extraordinary Body*, edited by Rosemarie Garland Thomson (New York: New York University Press, 1996), 29.
8. "To Whitewash Svengali," *Chicago Tribune*, June 19, 1897, 10.
9. "*The Hairy Ainus*," *Motography*, March 1, 1913, 166. A copy of this film is archived at the British Film Institute. A similar example would be *The Ainus of Japan* (Selig Polyscope, 1913), which is also archived at the BFI.
10. Dore Hoffman, "Picture Making in the South Seas," *Moving Picture World*, December 28, 1912, 1281.
11. *Mickie O'Hoolihan's Wake* (Underwood & Underwood, 1894) is an example of a stereo view in which male and female characters are smoking. *Patrick Brannigan's Wake* (Keystone, undated) is an example of a stereo view in which male and female characters are drinking. *McCarthy's Wake: A "Free for All"* (Universal Photo Art Company, 1899) is an example of a stereo view in which the male and female characters are fighting. *McGinty's Wake* (Canvassers, undated) is an example of a stereo view in which the characters wear papier mâché masks.
12. Elias Savada (ed.), *The American Film Institute Catalog of Motion Pictures Produced in the United States: Film Beginnings, 1893–1910* (Lanham, Maryland: Scarecrow Press, 1995), 706, 745. See also Advertisement, *Views and Film Index*, April 20, 1907, 14; "*Kelly's Ghost*," *Moving Picture World*, March 14, 1914, 1385. A copy of *Murphy's Wake* is archived in the Paper Print Collection at the Library of Congress. A similar film would be *A Wake in "Hell's Kitchen"* (American Mutoscope & Biograph, 1900); a copy of that film is also archived in the Paper Print Collection at the Library of Congress.
13. A copy of *Dan Greegan's Ghost* is archived at the Museum of Modern Art, New York City. A dramatic version of the same basic storyline appeared in *The Ghost* (Domino, 1913).
14. "*The Human Sacrifice* (Reliance)," *Moving Picture World*, October 14, 1911, 109–10; "*The Altar of the Aztecs*," *Moving Picture World*, February 15, 1913, 679.
15. *Gypsy's Revenge* (Philadelphia: Lubin, 1907). Available in *A Guide to Motion Picture Catalogs by American Producers and Distributors, 1894–1908: A Microfilm Edition* (New Brunswick: Rutgers University Press, 1985), Reel 3. A copy of *The Gipsy's Warning* is archived at the Library of Congress.
16. "In Mad Jealousy Gypsy Stabs Benefactor," *Universal Weekly*, February 7, 1914, 21.
17. "*The Mysterious Double; or, The Two Girls Who Looked Alike*," *Moving Picture World*, March 20, 1909, 342. A copy of *Stolen by Gypsies* is archived at the Library of Congress.
18. Advertisement, *New York Clipper*, April 7, 1900.
19. Savada, 183.
20. Ibid., 181, 323. *Extraordinary Chinese Magic* was originally released in Britain as *Chinese Magic* (Paul's Animatograph Works, 1900, aka *Chinese Magic Extraordinary* aka *Yellow Peril*). *The Chinese Conjurer and the Devil's Head* was likely an imported picture.
21. A copy of *The Hindoo Fakir* is archived at the Library of Congress.
22. *Edison Films, Supplement 168* (Buffalo, New York: J. F. Adams, February 1903), 11. Available in *A Guide to Motion Picture Catalogs by American Producers and Distributors, 1894–1908: A Microfilm Edition*, Reel 1.
23. *Complete Catalogue of Genuine and Original "Star" Films (Moving Pictures), Manufactured by Geo. Méliès of Paris* (New York: Star Films, 1903), 20, 22, 26. Available in *A Guide to Motion Picture Catalogs by American Producers and Distributors, 1894–1908: A Microfilm Edition*, Reel 4.

24. For example, the title character of *The Oriental Mystic* (Vitagraph, 1909) is Turkish. See "*The Oriental Mystic*," *Moving Picture World*, May 29, 1909, 729. Some footage from this film is archived at the Library of Congress by way of a paper print deposit.
25. Edward Said, *Orientalism* (London: Penguin Books, 2003), xiv.
26. "*Saved from the Sultan's Sentence*," *Moving Picture World*, May 14, 1910, 785.
27. "*In the Serpent's Power*," *New York Dramatic Mirror*, February 19, 1910, 16.
28. "The Devil–Satan Said to be of Persian Origin," *Current Literature*, October 1888, Vol. I, No. 4, 297.
29. "And Satan Also," *National Police Gazette*, June 22, 1878, 2.
30. A copy of *Human Apes from the Orient* is archived at the Library of Congress.
31. "Chinese Superstitions," *Boston Recorder*, April 13, 1843, 57.
32. Quoted in Robert E. Bieder, "The Representations of Indian Bodies in Nineteenth-Century American Anthropology," *American Indian Quarterly*, Vol. 20, No. 2 (Spring 1996), 172.
33. "Worshippers of the Voodoo," *New York Times*, June 25, 1893, 5.
34. Richard Dyer, *White: Essays on Race and Culture* (New York: Routledge, 1997).
35. E. Ann Kaplan, *Looking for the Other: Feminism, Film, and the Imperial Gaze* (New York: Routledge, 1997), 61.
36. Owen Davies, *America Bewitched: The Story of Witchcraft after Salem* (Oxford: Oxford University Press, 2013), 4.
37. Renée L. Bergland, *The National Uncanny: Indian Ghosts and American Subjects* (Hanover: University Press of New England, 2000), 41.
38. Ibid., 1.
39. John C. Ewers, "Not Quite Redmen: The Plains Indians Illustrations of Felix O. C. Darley," *The American Art Journal*, Vol. 3, No. 2 (Autumn 1971), 88–98.
40. Advertisement, *New York Clipper*, April 15, 1871.
41. "Ohio," *New York Clipper*, August 8, 1896, 359.
42. "Miller Bros.' 101 Ranch Notes," *New York Clipper*, May 8, 1909.
43. Gregory S. Jay, "'White Man's Book No Good': D. W. Griffith and the American Indian," *Cinema Journal*, Vol. 39, No. 4 (Summer 2000), 5.
44. Eileen Bowser, *The Transformation of Cinema, 1907–1915* (Berkeley: University of California Press, 1990), 173.
45. Savada, 406, 802, 692. A copy of *Sioux Ghost Dance* is archived at the Library of Congress.
46. *February Supplement of New Films* (Chicago, Illinois: Selig Polyscope Co., 1903), unpaginated. Available in *A Guide to Motion Picture Catalogs by American Producers and Distributors, 1894–1908: A Microfilm Edition*, Reel 2. A copy of *Ute Indian Snake Dance* is archived at the Library of Congress.
47. "Weird Serpent Dance Feature of *The Snake*," *Universal Weekly*, August 2, 1913, 16.
48. "*The Cheyenne Medicine Man*," *Moving Picture World*, May 27, 1911, 1208; James S. McQuade, "*In the Long Ago* (Selig)," *Moving Picture World*, May 10, 1913, 575; "Mysticism and Wild Folk Lore [sic]," *Universal Weekly*, July 26, 1913, 19, 31.
49. "*Owana, the Devil Woman*," *Moving Picture World*, June 7, 1913, 1033.
50. "*The Arrow Maiden*," *Moving Picture World*, July 24, 1915.
51. "*The White Medicine Man*," *Moving Picture World*, July 8, 1911, 1599.
52. "*The Legend of Scar Face*," *Moving Picture World*, August 6, 1910, 311; "*The Death Mask*," *Moving Picture World*, September 26, 1914, 1824.
53. T. S. Mead, "*The Lure of the Windigo*," *Motion Picture News*, December 19, 1914, 62.
54. "*A Hopi Legend*," *Moving Picture World*, December 27, 1913, 1590.
55. "*A Hopi Legend*," *Moving Picture World*, December 27, 1913, 1544.

56. "Shoots Girl for Refusing to Kiss Him," *Universal Weekly*, November 21, 1914, 21.
57. "*The Ghost of the Mine*," *Motography*, November 28, 1914, 761.
58. "*The Legend of Lake Desolation* (Pathe)," *Moving Picture World*, July 29, 1911, 191. A copy of *The Legend of Lake Desolation* is archived at the Cinémathèque Québécoise.
59. Due to its catalog number and description, *Scalping Scene by Thundercloud* seems to have been a different film than *Scalping Scene* (Edison, 1895, aka *Indian Scalping Scene*), as described in Chapter 9.
60. *International Photographic Films for Use on All Projecting Machines Using the Standard Gauge* (New York: The International Film Company, Winter 1897–8), 11. Available in *A Guide to Motion Picture Catalogs by American Producers and Distributors, 1894–1908: A Microfilm Edition*, Reel 1.
61. Ibid.
62. "*At the White Man's Door*," *Moving Picture World*, February 25, 1911, 430; "*Red Man's Revenge*," *Moving Picture World*, June 6, 1908, 496; "*The Red Man's Revenge*," *New York Dramatic Mirror*, June 13, 1908.
63. "*Ogallalah*," *Moving Picture World*, April 8, 1911, 782.
64. "*The Indian Massacre*," *Moving Picture World*, March 9, 1912, 855. A copy of this film, under its reissue title *The Heart of an Indian*, is available on the DVD *Saved from the Flames: 54 Rare and Restored Films, 1896–1944* (Los Angeles: Flicker Alley, 2007).
65. "*The White Captive of the Sioux*," *Moving Picture World*, June 18, 1910, 1059.
66. Advertisement, *Moving Picture World*, June 18, 1910, 1062.
67. "*The Heroine of the Plains*," *Moving Picture World*, January 4, 1913, 52.
68. "*Custer's Last Stand* (Selig Polyscope Co.)," *Moving Picture World*, November 27, 1909, 755; "*The Massacre of the Fourth Cavalry* (Double Reel 101-Bison)," *Moving Picture World*, November 23, 1912, 782; "*The Cheyenne Massacre*," *The Billboard*, May 3, 1913, 30; "*The Big Horn Massacre*," *Moving Picture World*, December 13, 1913, 1261.
69. "*In the Dark Valley*," *Moving Picture World*, May 21, 1910, 633.
70. "*The Witch of the Everglades*," *Moving Picture World*, May 13, 1911, 1081; "*The Haunts of Fear*," *Moving Picture World*, November 1, 1913, 497; "*The Skeleton in the Closet*," *Moving Picture World*, August 9, 1913, 666. A copy of *The Witch of the Everglades* is archived at the EYE Filmmuseum in Amsterdam. Despite its title, the woman named in the title is the mentally disturbed survivor of a Native American massacre, not a supernatural witch.
71. "*An Hour of Terror* (American)," *Moving Picture World*, July 13, 1912, 158.
72. John E. O'Connor, "The White Man's Indian: An Institutional Approach," in *Hollywood's Indian: The Portrayal of the Native American in Film*, edited by Peter C. Rollins and John E. O'Connor (Lexington, Kentucky: The University Press of Kentucky, 1998), 28.
73. Davies, 9.
74. Kathleen B. Casey, "Sex, Savagery, and the Woman Who Made Vaudeville Famous," *Frontiers: A Journal of Women Studies*, Vol. 36, No. 1 (2015), 89.
75. See, for example, Joseph Jones, "Bill Wilson and the Ghost," *Anderson Intelligencer* (Anderson, South Carolina), November 8, 1860, 1; "Laying a Ghost," *Lake Superior News* (Duluth, Minnesota), April 17, 1879. For information on *Alone in the Morgue*, see Advertisement, *New York Clipper*, January 30, 1897, 773.
76. *The Bradys and the Demon Doctor; or, The House of Many Mysteries* appeared in the series *Secret Service: Old and Young King Brady, Detectives*. Though it was in the tradition of dime novels, its cover price was actually five cents.
77. A copy of *The Watermelon Patch* is archived at the Library of Congress.
78. Savada, 298, 1185.
79. "Life on Canvas," *The Phonoscope*, August–September 1897, 6; Savada, 247.
80. A copy of *A Nightmare* is available in the DVD boxed set *Georges Méliès: First Wizard of Cinema* (Los Angeles: Flicker Alley, 2008). A copy of *The Seeress* is archived at the Library of Congress.

81. For more information, see Donald L. Hardesty, *The Archaeology of the Donner Party* (Reno, Nevada: University of Nevada Press, 2005).
82. Geoffrey Sanborn, *The Sign of the Cannibal: Melville and the Making of a Postcolonial Reader* (Durham, North Carolina: Duke University Press, 1998).
83. Examples of comedies about cannibals include *The Missionary and the Maid* (Edison, 1909), *Bill in Love Again/Terrible aventure de Patouillard* (Lux, 1911), *The Hunter's Dream* (Kalem, 1911), *John Tobin's Sweetheart* (Vitagraph, 1913), *Mike and Jake Among the Cannibals* (Joker, 1913), *Josie's Coney Island Nightmare* (Vitagraph, 1914), and *Shorty Among the Cannibals* (Broncho, 1915). See "*The Missionary and the Maid*," *New York Dramatic Mirror*, July 31, 1909, 15; "*Bill in Love Again*," *The Billboard*, March 11, 1911, 29; "*The Hunter's Dream*," *The Billboard*, March 25, 1911, 15; "*John Tobin's Sweetheart*," *Vitagraph Life Portrayals*, September 1, 1913, 37; "Shipwrecked Sailor Taken from Stew Pot and Made King," *Universal Weekly*, November 8, 1913, 24; "*Josie's Coney Island Nightmare*," *Moving Picture World*, August 22, 1914, 1136; "*Shorty Among the Cannibals*," *Reel Life*, March 20, 1915, 14.
84. "*King of the Cannibal Islands*," *Moving Picture World*, April 11, 1908, 325.
85. A copy of *King of the Cannibal Islands* is archived at the Library of Congress.
86. "*Captured by Aboriginals*," *Moving Picture World*, September 13, 1913, 1210; "*The Mystery of the Poison Pool*," *Moving Picture World*, September 26, 1914, 1826, 1828.
87. Advertisement, *Moving Picture World*, September 5, 1914, 1417.
88. "African Superstitions in America," *Daily Albany Argus* (Albany, New York), December 15, 1866, 4.
89. "Terrible Voodoo Dances of the South," *Boston Post*, July 30, 1899, 22.
90. "A Southern Voodoo Dance," *Current Literature*, February 1890, 123.
91. "*Voodoo Vengeance*," *Moving Picture World*, June 21, 1913, 1237.
92. "Victoria Theatre," *The Patriot* (Harrisburg, Pennsylvania), May 13, 1913, 8.
93. Untitled, *Aberdeen Daily News* (Aberdeen, South Dakota), June 18, 1913, 2.
94. "*Stanley Among the Voo Doo* [sic] *Worshippers*," *Motion Picture News*, December 11, 1915, 99.
95. "*Stanley Among the Voo Doo Worshippers*," *Reel Life*, November 27, 1915, 4.
96. "*Stanley and the Voo Doo Worshippers*," *Moving Picture World*, December 4, 1915, 1853.
97. Two trade articles referred to *Carnival in Black and White* as a comedy. See "Coquille Takes Mardi Gras Picture Stories," *Moving Picture World*, March 6, 1915, 1476; "Society in Coquille Film," *Moving Picture World*, March 20, 1915, 1803.
98. "Films Voudou and Hoodoo," *Moving Picture World*, March 27, 1915, 1959.
99. Edward Weitzel, "*The Ghost of the Twisted Oaks*," *Moving Picture World*, November 20, 1915, 1505.
100. A copy of Reel 3 of *The Ghost of Twisted Oaks* is archived at the Library of Congress.
101. "*The Ghost of the Twisted Oaks*," *Motion Picture News*, November 20, 1915, 86; "*The Ghost of the Twisted Oaks*," *Motography*, November 13, 1915, 1035.
102. Weitzel, 1505.
103. William F. Wu, *The Yellow Peril: Chinese Americans in American Fiction, 1850–1940* (Hamden, Connecticut: Archon Books, 1982), 30.
104. At times, films were specific about a villain's country of origin. In 1913, Eclair released *The Spider/L'araignée*, in which a "diabolical" Japanese villain kills the heroine's sweetheart (both of whom are also Japanese) by giving him water infused with a spider's venom. See "*The Spider* (Eclair)," *Moving Picture World*, February 15, 1913, 682.
105. Michael Richardson, *Otherness in Hollywood Cinema* (New York: Continuum, 2010), 51.
106. Ruth Mayer, *Serial Fu Manchu: The Chinese Supervillain and the Spread of Yellow Peril Ideology* (Philadelphia: Temple University Press, 2014).
107. "*Mystery of the Lama Convent; or, Dr. Nicola in Tibet*," *Moving Picture World*, February 5, 1910, 186.

108. Ibid., 186.
109. "*The Exploits of Elaine*," *New York Dramatic Mirror*, March 31, 1915. A copy of *The Devil Worshippers*, Episode 13 of *The Exploits of Elaine*, is archived at the George Eastman Museum.
110. "*The Fiends of Hell*," *Moving Picture World*, October 31, 1914, 706.
111. Ibid., 706.
112. Hanford C. Judson, "*The Fiends of Hell*," *Moving Picture World*, October 31, 1914, 626.
113. A copy of *The Mission of Mr. Foo* is archived at the Museum of Modern Art, New York City.
114. "*The Mission of Mr. Foo*," *New York Dramatic Mirror*, March 3, 1915.
115. "*The Mission of Mr. Foo*," *Motography*, March 13, 1915, 417.
116. "*The Mong-Fu Tong* (George Kleine)," *Moving Picture World*, August 2, 1913, 540.
117. "*The Mong Fu* [sic] *Tong*," *Exhibitors' Times*, July 26, 1913, 18.
118. A copy of *The Mong-Fu Tong* is archived at the Library of Congress.
119. Advertisement, *Moving Picture World*, August 2, 1913, 507.
120. "*The Mysterious Mr. Wu Chung Foo*," *Moving Picture World*, July 18, 1914, 482, 484.
121. "Gaumont Detective Feature," *Motography*, May 16, 1914, 353.
122. "*The Opium Smugglers*," *New York Dramatic Mirror*, May 13, 1914, 50.
123. "*The Chinatown Mystery*," *Motography*, February 13, 1915, 263.
124. "*A Celestial Maiden*," *The Billboard*, October 17, 1908, 8; "Kay-Bee: *The Sign of the Snake*," *Reel Life*, November 22, 1913, 17.
125. "*The Chinese Death Thorn*," *Kalem Kalendar*, December 1, 1913, 5.
126. George Blaisdell, "*The Chinese Death Thorn*," *Moving Picture World*, December 6, 1913, 1134.
127. The Imp "Comedy-Travelogue" entitled *He Solves the Chinese Mystery* (1914) also featured "Chinese white-slavers" who are defeated by Little Matty Roubert, the Universal Boy. See Advertisement, *Universal Weekly*, August 22, 1914, 19.
128. A copy of *The Fatal Hour* is archived at the Library of Congress.
129. "*The Fatal Hour*," *Biograph Bulletin*, No. 162, August 18, 1908. Available in *Biograph Bulletins, 1896–1908*, edited by Kemp R. Niver (Los Angeles: Locare Research Group, 1971), 340.
130. "Show Opens with Durbar," *Washington Post*, May 7, 1904, 9.
131. See, for example, "The Thugs, or Hindoo Murderers," *New York Observer and Chronicle*, February 27, 1841, 36; "A Religion of Murder," *Eclectic Magazine of Foreign Literature*, February 1902, 249.
132. "*The Hindoo Dagger*," *Biograph Bulletin*, No. 215, February 18, 1909. Available in *Biograph Bulletins, 1908–1912*, edited by Eileen Bowser (New York: Farrar, Straus, & Giroux, 1973), 65. A copy of this film is archived in the Paper Print Collection at the Library of Congress.
133. "*Palmistry*," *Moving Picture World*, August 2, 1913, 570; "Weird Melody from Strange Pipe Hypnotizes Listeners," *Universal Weekly*, January 3, 1914, 24.
134. Other reincarnation films of the era did not always apparently refer to Hindus, among them *As It Was in the Beginning* (Thanhouser, 1912), *The Reincarnation of a Soul* (Powers, 1913), *While The Starlight Travels* (Essanay, 1913), and *Reunited* (Eclair American, 1915). See "Hail, the Reincarnation Film!", *Moving Picture World*, January 27, 1912, 309; "*The Reincarnation of a Soul*," *Moving Picture World*, August 30, 1913, 990; "Reincarnation Theme of Essanay Film," *Motography*, September 6, 1913, 165–6; "Parted Lovers Reunited in Reincarnation," *Universal Weekly*, January 9, 1915, 25, 28.
135. "*The Key of Life*," *Edison Kinetogram*, December 15, 1910, 2–3; Louis Reeves Harrison, "*Reincarnation of Komar* [sic] (Vitagraph)," *Moving Picture World*, December 7, 1912, 963–4. The *Edison Kinetogram* suggested that *The Key of Life* would be released in January 1911, but *Moving Picture World* had reviewed it in the November 12, 1910 issue (1118). A copy of *Reincarnation of Karma* is archived at the UCLA Film & Television Archive.
136. "Occult Karma Picture Play," *Los Angeles Times*, January 4, 1913, II7.
137. "*The Mystery of the Sleeping Death*," *Kalem Kalendar*, September 1914, 4.

138. Richard Dale, "[*The*] *Mystery of the Sleeping Death*," *Movie Pictorial*, August 29, 1914. A copy of this film is archived at the EYE Film Institute.
139. "*The Yogi*," *Moving Picture World*, July 19, 1913, 350; "*In the Grip of a Charlatan*," *Moving Picture World*, April 5, 1913, 82. A copy of *The Society Palmist* is archived at the Paper Print Collection of the Library of Congress.
140. Helen Bagg, "*The Occult*," *Photoplay*, December 1913, 38–42.
141. "Photoplay Deals with the Occult," *Motography*, November 15, 1913, 341.
142. Neil G. Caward, "*The Strange Case of Princess Khan*," *Motography*, January 2, 1915, 5.
143. Similar to the films mentioned in the main text was *The Soul of Phyra* (Domino, 1915), though its lead female character is Indian. She moves to London with her British lover, despite the fact she is meant to be sacrificed in India. An intertitle in the surviving copy archived at the British Film Institute explains that "The High Priest, an Adept in Occult Science, Determines to Call the Soul of Phyra to His Presence."
144. "*The Messenger of Death*," *Moving Picture World*, August 8, 1914, 876; "*The Mystery of the New York Docks*," *Motography*, November 7, 1914, 645; "*The Rajah's Sacrifice*," *Motography*, September 18, 1915, 594; "*The Oriental's Plot*," *Kalem Kalendar*, December 1915, 29. A copy of *The Hindoo's Treachery* is archived at the Library of Congress and at the British Film Institute.
145. "Kathlyn Made a Temple Goddess," *Motography*, January 24, 1914, 43.
146. "*The Hindu Prince*," *Moving Picture World*, March 25, 1911, 668; Peter Milne, "*The Crystal Globe*," *Motion Picture News*, December 19, 1914, 64.
147. "American Women Victims of Hindu Mysticism," *Washington Post*, February 18, 1912, SM1.
148. "*The Revenge of the Fakir*," *Moving Picture World*, December 14, 1912, 1087; "The Melies Company in Java," *Moving Picture World*, June 21, 1913, 1235; "*The Ghost Club*," *Variety*, May 29, 1914, 21; Harry W. DeLong, "*The Hindu Nemesis*," *Moving Picture World*, April 11, 1914, 217; "*The Rajah's Vow*," *Kalem Kalendar*, August 1914, 11.
149. "*The Woman of Mystery* (Eclair)," *Motion Picture News*, May 9, 1914, 54.
150. Advertisement, *Moving Picture World*, May 9, 1914, 862.
151. Hanford Chase Judson, "*The Woman of Mystery*," *Moving Picture World*, May 30, 1914, 1264.
152. While it is not stolen, an Indian's "most prized possession" provokes strange occurrences in *The Mystic Ball* (Selig, 1915). See "*The Mystic Ball* Is a Two Reel Selig Special Carrying Unusual Plot," *Paste-Pot and Shears*, August 30, 1915.
153. Though it unfolds with a different plotline than that described in the main text, *A Touching Mystery* (Atlas, 1910) is worth mentioning. In it, a woman dreams that an "East Indian" mysteriously places a necklace on her, locking it with a tiny padlock. During the rest of her nightmare, anything or anyone she touches disappears. Another such moving picture was *The Green Idol* (Reliance, 1915), in which a woman purchases an idol from "Ahmed Akbar," the founder of a new cult. The relic turns out to be a fake. See "*A Touching Mystery*," *Moving Picture World*, October 22, 1910, 950; "*The Green Idol*," *Reel Life*, February 27, 1915, 10.
154. "*The Moonstone* (Selig)," *Moving Picture World*, June 19, 1909, 834.
155. "*The Moonstone*," *Variety*, June 11, 1915, 18. A copy of this film is archived at George Eastman Museum.
156. Peter Milne, "*The Moonstone*," June 26, 1915, 71.
157. "*The Idol's Eye*," *Moving Picture World*, November 12, 1910, 1119.
158. "*The Hindu Jewel Mystery*," *Moving Picture World*, November 11, 1911, 492; "*The Hindoo's Curse*," *Moving Picture World*, September 7, 1912, 998; "*The Lure of the Sacred Pearl*," *Moving Picture World*, June 14, 1913; 1172; "*The Stolen Idol*," *Moving Picture World*, June 14, 1913, 1138; "*The God of Girzah*," *Moving Picture World*, December 13, 1913, 1332; "*The Treasures of Buddha*," *Motion Picture News*, March 14, 1914, 47; "*The Mystery of the Hindu Image*," *New York Dramatic Mirror*, August 5, 1914, 32; "*The Curse of the Scarabee Ruby*,"

Moving Picture World, August 8, 1914, 842; "*The Mystic Jewel*," *Reel Life*, July 17, 1915, 8; "*The Vengeance of Rannah*," *Moving Picture World*, November 27, 1915, 1663.

159. Cine Mato, "Reel Facts and Fancies," *The Billboard*, August 30, 1913, 5.
160. "Hindoo Priests Avenge Theft of God's Eye," *Motography*, November 15, 1913, 347–8. The quotation about "chills up and down your spine" appears in Advertisement, *Moving Picture World*, November 22, 1913, 823.
161. "*The Moonstone of Fez*," *Vitagraph Life Portrayals*, July 1914, 15.
162. The object in *The Kaffir's Skull* (Reliance, 1914) is from Africa, and the object in *The Lure of the Sacred Pearl* (Gaston Méliès, 1913) is from Java. The object in *Celestial Vengeance* (Lubin, 1910) is Chinese. Objects from Native American tribes appeared in *The Witch's Necklace* (Solax, 1912), *The Legend of the Amulet* (Kalem, 1914), and *The Dragon's Claw* (Knickerbocker, 1915). And in *The Mystic Jewel*, the strange gemstone is vaguely coded as "Oriental." See "*The Kafir's Skull*," *Motography*, November 28, 1914, 758; "*The Lure of the Sacred Pearl*," *Moving Picture World*, June 14, 1913, 1172; Advertisement, *Moving Picture World*, February 12, 1910, 229; "*The Witch's Necklace*," *Moving Picture World*, March 13, 1912, 138; "*The Legend of the Amulet*," *Moving Picture World*, October 17, 1914, 336; "*The Dragon's Claw* (Knickerbocker)," *Moving Picture World*, October 2, 1915, 99; "*The Mystic Jewel*," *Motography*, July 24, 1915, 181.
163. The object in *The Mystery of the Laughing Death* (Edison, 1914) is from Mexico. The objects in *The Egyptian Mystery* (Edison, 1909), *The Scimitar of the Prophet* (Kalem, 1913), and *The Stolen Idol* (Rex, 1913) are from Egypt. See "*The Mystery of the Laughing Death*," *Moving Picture World*, March 28, 1914, 1722; "*The Egyptian Mystery*," *Moving Picture World*, July 10, 1909, 61; "*The Scimitar of the Prophet*," *Moving Picture World*, April 5, 1913, 82; "*The Stolen Idol*," *Moving Picture World*, July 14, 1913, 1176.
164. *The Mystery of the Hindu Image* is archived at George Eastman Museum. *The Death Mask* is archived at the Library of Congress under its 1919 reissue title *The Redskin Duel*.
165. Griffith also directed *The Girls and Daddy* (American Mutoscope & Biograph, 1909), which Susan Courtney calls an "obvious prototype" for the depiction of African-Americans in *The Birth of a Nation*. See Susan Courtney, *Hollywood Fantasies of Miscegenation: Spectacular Narratives of Gender and Race, 1903–1967* (Princeton, New Jersey: Princeton University Press, 2005), 31. A copy of *The Birth of a Nation* is available on the DVD *The Birth of a Nation and the Civil War Films of D. W. Griffith* (New York: Kino International, 2002). A copy of *The Girls and Daddy* is archived in the Paper Print Collection at the Library of Congress.
166. Michael Taussig, *Mimesis and Alterity: A Particular History of the Senses* (New York: Routledge, 1993), 115.
167. Carolyn Thomas de la Pena, "'Bleaching the Ethiopians': Desegregating Race and Technology through Early X-Ray Experiments," *Technology and Culture*, Vol. 47, No. 1 (January 2006), 27–55.
168. "*The Wrath of Osaka*," *Moving Picture World*, May 24, 1913, 811.
169. See, for example, "Indians War on Films," *Moving Picture World*, March 18, 1911, 581; "Moving-Picture Classics," *New York Times*, June 4, 1914, 10.
170. "*Buried Alive*," *Moving Picture World*, January 8, 1910, 16. A copy of *Buried Alive* is archived at the British Film Institute.
171. Stephen T. Asma, *On Monsters* (Oxford: Oxford University Press, 2009), 239.

CHAPTER 12

The Powers of the Mind

Philadelphia, 1910: An armed intruder breaks into the home of a bank president named Ruetschlin. Rather than cower in fright, Ruetschlin fixes his powerful eyes on the thief. After he has been jailed, the thief admits, "I never felt so helpless in my life. That man's eyes pierced me through like daggers, and I never for one moment thought of pulling the trigger. Guess he had me mesmerized."

Ruetschlin's wife witnessed everything. She told the press that the "whole thing was like a moving picture show."[1] Her metaphor was apt, especially given the sheer number of films about hypnotism produced during the early cinema period.

Concerns about losing and gaining control over the human mind had deep roots in America, dating at least to Salem, whether in the original belief that the accused were possessed by Satan or, as some later scholars believed, their accusers were delusional. However, these issues found particular resonance during the nineteenth century for several reasons, not least of which were the rise and popularization of pseudo-sciences that were at times linked to the occult. "There is no doubt," one magazine claimed in 1846, "that witchcraft and Mesmerism are synonymous."[2] Decades later, in the 1909 edition of his book *Hypnotism, Including a Study of the Chief Points of Psycho-Therapeutics and Occultism*, Albert Moll observed that occult phenomena, "notwithstanding the absence of all internal affinity, are constantly mentioned in connection with hypnotism."[3]

Much the same was true of mental powers like telepathy and thought transference, which provided the basis for Augustus Thomas's Broadway play *The Witching Hour* (1907), as well as for such films as *A Telepathic Warning* (Vitagraph, 1909), *The Invisible Power* (Kalem, 1914), and *The Cowardly Way* (Equitable, 1915).[4] Similarly, clairvoyance became central to the plots of *Palmistry/L'avenir par les lignes de la main* (Pathé Frères, 1907), *The Crystal Ball* (Centaur, 1909), *Madame Clairo* (Powers, 1910), *What the Cards Foretold* (Edison, 1909), *The Master and the Man* (Imp, 1911), and Franz Hofer's *Mera, the Medium/Ein seltsames Gemälde* (Film Releases of America, 1914).[5]

Moving pictures depicted not only the persons who wielded mental powers, but their victims as well. As but one example of many, Selig Polyscope's moving picture *Hypnotized* (1912) features an entranced newspaper editor who temporarily ends up in an insane asylum, the ultimate destination of those who lose mental control.[6] As embodied by Mesmerists, hypnotists, and female vamps, the powers of the mind could be robust, intense, and formidable—quite a departure from the inverse, meaning those who lost their minds and their will, whether due to insanity or somnambulism.

Mental Illness

The rise of insane asylums during the nineteenth century in the United States followed similar movements in Europe.[7] Such facilities isolated the mentally ill from the rest of society, which led to public speculation and eventual concern about what happened inside them, including the fear that some of these intended sanctuaries had become sites of horror. And yet many persons deemed them necessary. Mental illness received extended discussion at the time, ranging from whispers about Mary Todd Lincoln to the trial of Charles J. Guiteau, who assassinated President Garfield in 1881.[8]

In a small number of cases, nonfiction moving pictures chronicled the subject of mental illness. For example, Theodore H. Weisenburg, a neurology professor in Philadelphia, spent five years filming patients who suffered from "nervous and mental diseases," capturing their medical examinations and even their "gait."[9] Believing his footage could help diagnose patients and train medical students, Weisenburg held a screening at the Medical Society of New York in 1913.[10] Here he was following in a tradition of various nonfiction medical films that depicted topics ranging from epilepsy to all manner of surgeries.[11]

More commonly, fictional films depicted mental illness, including a number of comedies. An early example was American Mutoscope & Biograph's *The Escaped Lunatic* (1904), its plot being very similar to Edison's *Maniac Chase* (1904).[12] In it, a man who believes that he is Napoleon escapes from a mental institute by bending the bars on his cell window. In the form of a substituted dummy, he falls to the ground; in the form of the actor, he runs away, with three guards chasing him. With a crazed expression, he leads his pursuers through an impressive array of locations: over a rooftop, over a hill, and through a stream before fighting them on a bridge. Thanks to trick cinematography, he eventually returns to his cell.[13]

The *Biograph Bulletin* reported, "every audience which has seen the production has gone into paroxysms of laughter imagining it a comedy arranged by actors," as opposed to it being an authentic document of its subject matter, which it was, because "fortunately there were a number of Biograph cameras situated along the country in the vicinity of the asylum."[14] A surviving copy proves Biograph's promotion was false. *The Escaped Lunatic* was a fictional film, despite the company's argument to the contrary.

Another example was *Dr. Dippy's Sanitarium* (American Mutoscope & Biograph, 1906). In it, the inmates put a new attendant through a "course" that "frightens him almost out of his senses."[15] According to a trade advertisement, the film showed:

> what [Dr. Dippy's] patients did to a new attendant. They left him with his life and that's about all. He tries to escape, but they catch him, put him in a huge hogshead, roll him down a steep hill into a barbed wire fence and finally into a pond. Then they tie him up to a wall and use him for a target while a maniac juggler throws knives at him.[16]

As a surviving copy reveals, trick cinematography makes the knives appear to land close to the attendant's head without hitting him.[17]

A number of similar comedies followed, including *Doings of a Maniac/Les exploits d'un fou* (Pathé Frères, 1907), in which an escaped inmate drinks gasoline, eats soap, and disguises himself as a policeman.[18] The following year, *The Mad Musician* (Selig Polyscope, 1908) featured an escaped inmate who wreaks havoc all over town before being returned to his asylum.[19] The title character of *The Maniac* (Lubin, 1911) pretended to be the "long-lost father" of a wealthy young woman.[20] The following year, in *Bill Becomes Mentally Deranged/Patouillard retombe en enfance* (Lux, 1912), the familiar title character (known in France as Patouillard) has "water on the brain" that makes him act childishly until he undergoes a "sensational operation."[21]

In 1914, Florence Lawrence, who had already appeared in Lubin's *The Maniac*, starred in Victor's highly original film *A Mysterious Mystery*. According to *Universal Weekly*, she played herself in the comical story. A "stranger" throws a "rug" over the famous film actress and kidnaps her in his automobile. Once the rug is removed, Florence finds herself disrobed in a sanitarium. As the trade wrote, "She is left a captive in a padded cell, the walls of which are covered with posters of her own self. . . . There appears no means of escape."[22] It is a case of mistaken identity, with Lawrence believed to be an escaped patient with delusions that she is the famous star.

Dramatic portrayals of mental illness appeared onscreen many times during the early cinema period. For example, *The Escape from the Mad House* (Selig Polyscope, 1907) offered a "realistic" story none-too-different than *The Escaped Lunatic*.[23] Similar in story was Albert Capellani's *The Marked Man/Le signalement* (Pathé Frères, 1912), which featured another mental institute escapee. *Moving Picture World* wrote:

> It is a well-acted [and] well-made offering, and, in its big scene we see a maniac who we have been told makes a specialty of infanticide in a house alone with a little girl of about eight and her baby brother. . . . The bread knife is there and he feels at the same time a longing to kill her and a sense of awe and love for her.[24]

The trade also observed that "the audience watched this picture breathlessly." Their response was understandable, as a surviving copy of the film attests to its restrained acting and extremely tense mood.[25]

The title character (played by Francis X. Bushman) of *The Madman* (Essanay, 1912) runs away from prison only to fall to his death from a military balloon.[26] In *The Taint of Madness* (Selig Polyscope, 1914), a woman's insane brother is released from an asylum and accidentally sets fire to the family home.[27] Pathéplay's *The Accusing Eye/Des Meeres Sühne* (1914) features an escaped lunatic who "haunts his destroyer to the very death."[28] Ambrosio's three-reel film *The Magic Note/La romanza di Mignon* (1914) offers a band of robbers hurling a clerk into a sewer, where he spends "terrible nights"; once he escapes, the "unhinged" clerk is registered at a "lunatic asylum."[29] Actress Florence Lawrence portrayed the title role in *The Madman's Ward* (Victor, 1914), an orphan raised by an insane fisherman.[30] And actor Harry Millarde played a "man about town" who "finds himself in the clutches of a madman who intends to torture him" in *The Haunting Fear* (Kalem, 1915).[31]

The topic of mental illness remained controversial, at least to an extent.[32] In 1914, for example, Chicago censors refused to give a permit to any moving picture that featured "repeated scenes of an insane patient and numerous scenes in an insane asylum."[33] Such films could inspire fright, ranging from villains who attempted to drive others insane (as in the case of Essanay's 1914 *The Seventh Prelude*) to those who intentionally locked sane persons in mental institutes (as in Edison's 1915 *Olive in the Madhouse*).[34]

Figure 12.1 *The Haunting Fear* (Kalem, 1915).

In *The Insane Heiress* (Yankee, 1910), Nell solves the mystery of an abducted woman by pretending to be insane. Once incarcerated in an asylum, she chloroforms a nurse in order to change disguises and find more clues.[35] Ambrosio's *The Maniac/Una partita a scacchi* (1912) features an escaped lunatic who forces a man to play chess for his life.[36] And a "deranged maniac" who has strangled his wife escapes from an asylum and attempts to murder another woman in *The Hands/Les mains* (Eclair, 1912).[37]

Alice Guy Blaché's four-reel film *Shadows of the Moulin Rouge* (Solax, 1914) was a "story of the Paris underworld."[38] In it, the "depraved" Dr. Chevrele "takes a fancy to [Dupont's] wife."[39] He remands Dupont to a padded cell in an asylum.[40] Eventually, Dupont escapes and saves his wife, who has faced many "horrifying experiences" of her own in the Parisian underworld.[41] Though it believed the "conventional" conclusion detracted from an otherwise original story, *Motion Picture News* praised the film's acting and photography.[42] *Moving Picture World* lauded its direction, proclaiming *Shadows of the Moulin Rouge* to be the "best feature that ever came out of the Solax studio."[43]

Another important example of insanity onscreen came in *His Phantom Sweetheart* (Vitagraph, 1915), a copy of which survives.[44] Anita Stewart plays the title character, a dancing girl at the Garrick Theatre. An admirer takes her home, where he kisses her in the darkness. She lights a cigarette for him, after which he sees a man's photo. "That— Oh, that's only my husband," she says. "Don't be alarmed—he's in a sanitarium for the insane." But the crazed husband is actually in the house, clenching his fingers as he quietly watches the two. First the husband strangles his wife in a dark room lit only by a single lamp. Then he strangles her new lover. At this point, the lover wakes up—the murderous affair has been nothing more than a nightmare. As directed by Ralph Ince and written by Earle Williams (who also played the male lead), *His Phantom Sweetheart* features powerful, restrained acting, thoughtful cinematography, and atmospheric lighting.[45]

Somnambulism

Losing one's mind was not limited to mental illness. Eric G. Wilson observes, "During the Romantic period, writers on both sides of the Atlantic explored the sleepwalker as a merger of holiness and horror."[46] As Chapter 1 notes, the title character of Charles Brockden Brown's 1799 novel *Edgar Huntly* suffers from sleepwalking. Brown returned to the topic in his 1805 short story *Somnambulism*, in which the narrator believes he may have committed the grisly murder of his lover and her father while in a dreamlike state.

Writing about *Edgar Huntly*, Justine S. Murison observes that "somnambulism has a way of upsetting common beliefs that the mind controlled the body: the waking self could be completely absent or histrionically present in the behavior of the sleepwalker, neither of which attests to the presence of mind."[47] Later tales of this type included Henry Cockton's *Sylvester Sound, the Somnambulist*, serialized in *Magazine for the Millions* in 1844. In it, a phantasmal "spirit" is revealed to be nothing more than a sleepwalker. Esther Serle Kenneth used a similar plot device in her short story *The Haunted Chamber* (1879).[48]

Nineteenth-century newspapers frequently reported on the activities of real somnambulists. One rode a bicycle in her sleep; another awoke in an undertaker's coffin with no knowledge of having gotten inside it.[49] In 1882, a jailed murderer allegedly re-created his "dreadful crime" each night while asleep in his cell.[50] In 1889, a man used somnambulism as his excuse for having "attempted to outrage" a fifteen-year-old girl in her bedroom.[51] Five years later, in an echo of fictional literature, a "ghost" in Evanston, Illinois turned out to be a harmless sleepwalker.[52]

The most famous example in the nineteenth century was that of Jane C. Rider, the "Springfield Somnambulist." In her sleep, she arose from her bed and sewed in the dark. She also prepared dinners and set the table. When others in the household encouraged her to go to bed, she argued—with her eyes still closed—that it was daytime. In other cases, her eyes were wide open even as she remained in a somnambulistic state. And once she awoke, she had no memory of her nightly activities. The press reported on Rider's "paroxysms" at length in 1834, maintaining it was an extraordinary but authentic case.[53]

The earliest moving pictures about somnambulism often drew their story lines from these kinds of nonfiction accounts. For example, both Lubin and American Mutoscope & Biograph distributed the British-made Gaumont film *The Somnambulist* (1904), which Lubin retitled *The Sleepwalker's Dream*. According to the Lubin catalog description, the film depicted a young woman who rises out of her bed and begins walking "as though in a trance." She moves onto the roof, and then over adjacent rooftops until, "missing her footing, she is violently thrown to the ground, fifty feet below." A police officer finds her "extinct" body. But then, an edit returns her to her boudoir, where she is still asleep. Once awake, she realizes the events have only been "a dream, a hideous nightmare."[54] Though it conveniently featured a dream device to avoid an unhappy ending, the film's core story was similar to the many well-publicized deaths and injuries sustained by somnambulists in the nineteenth century.[55]

The Somnambulist (Essanay, 1908) features a bank teller hiding some of his employer's money during a night of sleepwalking. Unable to find it when he awakens, the man is charged with theft and only cleared after he sleepwalks again and leads the other characters to the location where he concealed the money.[56] Similarly, a comedy entitled *The Sleeping Burglar* (Comet, 1912, aka *A Sleeping Burglar*) has an innocent man hiding some of his boss's money while sleepwalking.[57] Here again, the basic plotline was a citation of newspaper stories published in the nineteenth century.[58]

In *The Somnambulist/Museumsmysteriet, eller Søvngængeren* (Great Northern, 1910), a detective discovers that the retired director of an art museum has stolen several items, but did so while he was asleep.[59] In *The Sleep Walker* (Vitagraph, 1911), an innocent female character picks up a jewel box in her slumber and is wrongly accused of theft.[60] In *The Somnambulist/L'obsession du souvenir* (Gaston Méliès, 1914), a husband believes his wife is unfaithful until he learns that she is actually visiting the tomb of her dead son while asleep.[61] And in *The Mystery of Mr. Marks* (Hepworth, 1914, aka *Mystery of Mr. Marks*), a young woman realizes that her father choked a man to death while walking in his sleep, the result of him earlier reading a book about strangulation.[62]

Not surprisingly, sleepwalking also provided ample material for comedy films.[63] A "midnight mix-up farce," *The Somnambulists* (Biograph, 1913) features two sleepwalking husbands who end up in the wrong bedrooms.[64] In *A Sleep Walking Cure* (Selig Polyscope, 1910), a spinster places a tub of cold water at the foot of her staircase to awaken a sleepwalker; it unintentionally helps to catch a burglar.[65] And in *The Somnambulist* (Thanhouser, 1914), the wife of a sleepwalker fits a noose around his neck and ties it to the bed.[66]

In other cases, the sleepwalkers are induced into their state by mesmeric or hypnotic powers. In Edison's drama *The Experiment* (1915), a hypnotist displays his powers by instructing an entranced woman to get out of her bed at midnight, retrieve a knife, and take it to another character.[67] That evening, a burglar in the home causes blood to appear on the blade. As a result, it appears as if the somnambulist has murdered someone with the "blood-spattered knife."[68]

Mesmerism and Hypnotism

In the eighteenth century, Franz Anton Mesmer promoted his belief that an electrically charged "vital fluid" influenced all things, from faraway planets to the human mind. He termed the force "animal magnetism"; others referred to it as Mesmerism. The subject gained widespread fame in America in the 1830s, thanks in large measure to the writings of Dr. Charles Poyen. In 1837, he noted:

> Animal magnetism, I repeat, sprung from observation; Mesmer and all his disciples have claimed for it the title of natural science; they have constantly endeavored to combat superstition, and remove all remaining prejudices concerning the influence of spiritual agents, by contending and showing that the phenomena once attributed to the action of the devil, are the results of a peculiar modification of which the nervous organization of man is susceptible, when placed in certain circumstances.[69]

Some scientists and journalists viewed Mesmerism as a valid intellectual pursuit. A few even used it to explain the "voluntary or involuntary" behavior of the accused witches in Salem.[70]

Another position held that some aspects of Mesmerism were "ordinary" enough to be believed, while the "extraordinary" phenomena associated with it remained questionable.[71] According to Robert C. Fuller, some persons accepted

> mesmeric consciousness could achieve a clairvoyant state. Here the individual has come into direct contact with animal magnetic fluid, and his mind is temporarily imbued with its omnipresent and omniscient properties. At this deepest level of consciousness, subjects feel themselves to be united with the creative principle of the universe (animal magnetism). There is a mystical sense of intimate rapport with the cosmos. Subjects feel that they are in possession of knowledge which transcends that of physical, space-time reality.[72]

In the 1840s, for example, Margaret Fuller coined the term "Ecstatica" to describe her Mesmeric sessions, which acted as a form of pain relief.[73] "I grow more and more what they will call a mystic," she wrote in 1840.[74]

As Emily Ogden has observed, animal magnetism could create "what amounted to religious enthusiasm."[75] And yet many condemned Mesmerism on religious grounds. Hugh M'Neile preached a sermon in 1842 that spoke of Mesmerism as "Satanic Agency."[76] Such occult connections reappeared during the early cinema period. In *The Treasures of Satan/ Les trésors de Satan* (Méliès, 1903), which Edison released under the title *Mephistopheles' School of Magic*, the Devil uses hypnotic powers on the would-be thief of his gold.[77] And the demonic characters of *The Eyes of Satan* (Solax, 1913) and *Alone with the Devil/ Expressens mysterium* (Great Northern, 1914) are humans who use the power of mental suggestion on others.[78]

As Bruce Mills has observed, "Late-eighteenth- and nineteenth-century research on animal magnetism formed one of the central sites of cultural discourse that attracted writers."[79] Not surprisingly, Mesmerism affected many authors, including Europeans whose works were widely read in America. Its influence is apparent in Coleridge's poem *Kubla Khan* (written in 1797 and published in 1816).[80] The same is true of E. T. A. Hoffmann's *The Animal Magnetist/ Der Magnetiseur* (1814), *The Golden Pot: A Fairytale of Modern Times/ Der goldne Topf: Ein Märchen aus der neuen Zeit* (1814), *The Oath/ Das Gelübde* (1817), and *The Uncanny Guest/ Der unheimliche Gast* (1819).[81] Also important in this lineage is Bram Stoker, not only in *Dracula* (1897) and *The Lair of the White Worm* (1911), but also in his nonfiction text *Famous Impostors* (1910), which includes a discussion of Mesmer.[82] (Here Stoker became the latest in a long line of those who viewed Mesmer as a fraud and condemned his adherents for possessing "almost unparalleled gullibility."[83] For example, in his book *Humbugs of New York* [1838], Dr. David Reese pronounced Mesmerism to be "the reigning hum-bug in the United States."[84])

American writers addressed the subject of Mesmerism with some regularity, whether in such notable works as Walt Whitman's poem *I Sing the Body Electric* (1867), or in such forgotten tales as Camilla Willian's *The Magnetic Chain: A Story of Mesmerism* (1867).[85] Edgar Allan Poe famously returned to the subject on a number of occasions, including in *Mesmeric Revelation* (1844), which begins with the sentence, "Whatever doubt may still envelop the *rationale* of mesmerism, its startling *facts* are now almost universally admitted." In both *A Tale of the Ragged Mountains* (1844) and *The Facts in the Case of M. Valdemar* (1845), Poe intermingled Mesmerism with the occult, with the latter tale featuring a Mesmerist who keeps a man in a hypnogogic state even after his death. Some readers of the time actually believed Poe's story was an authentic account.[86]

Mesmerism also features in the works of Nathaniel Hawthorne, particularly in *The House of the Seven Gables* (1851) and *The Blithedale Romance* (1852).[87] In the former, Hawthorne writes, "Modern psychology, it may be, will endeavor to reduce these alleged necromancies within a system, instead of rejecting them as altogether fabulous." In the latter, Hawthorne likens Professor Westervelt—who exercises mind control over a woman—to Satan. In the 1870s, one critic happily noted that Hawthorne "judiciously softened and kept [Mesmerism] in the background" of his work, as opposed to Poe, whose Mesmeric stories represented something of a combination of "Hawthorne and *delirium tremens*."[88]

Given the subject's cultural currency, the American stage readily embraced Mesmerism, with its practitioners indulging in performances that demonstrated their ability to control the minds of others. As Taylor Stoehr has observed, "the mesmerist's power over the will of his somnambulist was what shocked and intrigued the public, more than any of the mysterious feats of clairvoyance, telepathy, and psycho-kinesis."[89] At times, somnambulism even became synonymous with the phrase "mesmeric sleep."[90]

Terry M. Parssinen has analyzed the popularity of these shows in nineteenth-century Britain.[91] As for their presence in America, Mark Twain provided first-person insight in his autobiography. He recounts the arrival of a "mesmerizer" during his youth in Hannibal, Missouri. Volunteering from the audience, Twain pretended to be in a trance, with the Mesmerist confidently telling the onlookers, "I assure you that without a single spoken word to guide him, he has carried out what I mentally commanded him to do, to the minutest detail."[92]

During the second half of the nineteenth century, Mesmerism was hardly alone in its ability to induce a trance-like state in its subjects. In 1860, an American newspaper noted the "French scientific journals are full of accounts of the application of the new discovery, hypnotism."[93] Key to its evolution was James Braid's 1843 book *Neurohypnology or, The Rationale of Nervous Sleep, Considered in Relation with Animal Magnetism*. Braid believed that Mesmeric fluid did not exist, but that instead Mesmerism worked due to the mental power of suggestion over a subject.[94] In many circles internationally, hypnotism became accepted as a legitimate science.[95] Jean-Martin Charcot used hypnotism to treat hysteria during the 1870s, for example. Freud claimed it helped make patients more receptive to his treatment.[96] And a phrenology journal advised that hypnotism could become a "great aid" to parents training their children.[97]

Others viewed hypnotism in mystical terms, just as they had Mesmerism. New Thought proponents in America believed people could use their minds to control matter, including in the healing of the body.[98] For some of them, hypnosis was aligned with these goals. Here was perhaps the "evolution of a sixth sense."[99] As Daniel Pick writes:

> The puzzle of hypnotism stimulated long-standing debate amongst Victorian scientists and doctors; it inspired and troubled novelists; it aroused popular wonderment, even childlike devotion, as well as much alarm from social commentators. It disturbed the boundaries between high and low culture, education and entertainment, fact and fiction, medicine and quackery, waking states, sleep and dreams; it seemed to return its subjects to some long-lost state of being, an irresponsible world, free of the conventions of grown-up "self-mastery."[100]

As a result, Pick continues, hypnotism commanded "both awed and squeamish public attention."[101]

After all, hypnotism was, as *The Cosmopolitan* described in 1890, a "weird art."[102] Critics decried it as another "humbug."[103] Its purported powers were the result of "error, self-delusion, and downright imposture."[104] Even those who believed in hypnosis sometimes condemned it. Theosophists feared that the evil in the mind of the hypnotist might infect the mind of the hypnotized.[105] Others even thought it was the latest incarnation of the "evil eye" superstitions.[106] But whatever else might have been said, the *New York Times* believed that hypnotism had become an American "craze" by 1881.[107]

In 1890, the newspaper remarked, "It is, of course, admitted that [the] facts of hypnotism afford great opportunities for crime."[108] Press reports told of a "young girl" held captive by hypnotism in Wisconsin in 1894, a husband who murdered his wife while hypnotized in Ohio the same year, and a man driven insane by hypnotism in New Jersey in 1897.[109] While some believed hypnotism could help cure somnambulism, many others feared that hypnotists would keep the entranced in their thrall.[110] So great was the concern that in 1899 a bill introduced in the California legislature outlawed the use of hypnotism except by "licensed physicians of the State."[111]

In yet another repeat—even continuation—of Mesmerism, hypnotism became popular in live entertainment. Recalling the early 1890s, dancer Loïe Fuller wrote in her autobiography, "hypnotism at that moment was very much to the fore in New York."[112] For example, in the 1891 show *Quack, M.D.*, Fuller conveyed the subject of hypnosis through dance.[113] Two years later, Patti Rosa starred in the farce *Little Miss Dixie; or, Hypnotism* (1893).[114] Then, in 1904, Victorien Sardou's *The Sorceress/La sorcière* appeared on Broadway.[115] In its story, a woman's knowledge of hypnotism results in accusations of witchcraft.

In addition to travelling Mesmerists, itinerant hypnotists became extremely popular in vaudeville, as well as at dime museums.[116] Some of them employed comedy to lecture on the subject, as "Professor Carpenter" did with much success in the 1880s.[117] Others hypnotized assistants who were "buried alive" and exhumed days later.[118] At the turn of the century, "Professor Leonidas" advertised his act by placing a coffin in pharmacy windows, subtly invoking the occult. At roughly the same time in Great Britain, Walford Bodie (who received a limited amount of press coverage in America) strapped volunteers to an electric chair onstage, hypnotized them for protection against the voltage, and then threw the switch.[119]

Hypnotism also inspired a range of fictional literature, from Guy de Maupassant's short story *The Horla/Le horla* (1887) to F. Marion Crawford's novel *The Witch of Prague* (1891).[120] However, the key literary expression of hypnotism was without a doubt George Du Maurier's *Trilby* (1894). As Chapter 2 noted, the extremely popular novel became an equally popular stage production. In the novel, the Laird tells Trilby:

> I'd sooner have any pain than have it cured in that unnatural way, and by such a man as that! He's a bad fellow, Svengali—I'm sure of it! He mesmerized you; that's what it is—mesmerism! I've often heard of it, but never seen it done before. They get you into their power, and just make you do any blessed thing they please—lie, murder, steal—anything! [A]nd kill yourself into the bargain when they've done with you! It's just too terrible to think of![121]

The Laird's list might also have included sexual contact, which presumably occurs once the entranced Trilby becomes "La Svengali." Here was the culmination of long-standing concerns about the sexual power that Mesmerists and hypnotists could exercise, concerns that had earlier been explored in Charles Dickens's unfinished novel *The Mystery of Edwin Drood* (published in 1870) and Henry James's short story *Professor Fargo* (1874).

As Chapter 2 suggested, *Trilby*'s influence was felt throughout popular culture. In 1895 alone, music publishers promoted such songs as *I Am a Hypnotizier* [sic] *a la Trilby* (J. P. Hart), *Who's Trilby* (Berkeley), *Who Hypnotized O'Leary* (Berkeley), *Like Trilby* (Henry White), *Trilby* (W. N. Sweet), and *Trilby Wasn't Hypnotized by Me* (William J. A. Lieder).[122] And in 1896, Herrmann the Great presented a stage illusion entitled *Trilby*, in which he appeared as Svengali and caused a woman to levitate after making some Mesmeric "passes" over her.[123]

By the age of early cinema, some persons perceived sharp distinctions between Mesmerism and hypnotism. In 1895, a study of "Fortune-Telling in America To-day!" claimed that the "intelligent and cultivated become students of psychology, hypnotism, and psychical phenomena, while the unlettered and credulous dabble in chiromancy, clairvoyance, and astrology."[124] To these persons, hypnosis was scientific and Mesmerism was not.

However, popular culture easily conflated Mesmerism and hypnotism, and *Trilby* and its successors further obscured differences between them. For example, Du Maurier's novel speaks not only of Mesmerism, but also of Svengali's "hypnotic influence." And the chorus of Will Dillon and Harry Von Tilzer's 1910 song *Hip, Hip, Hypnotize Me* goes, "Hip, hip, hip, hip, hypnotize me/Mister Flip, flip, flip, flip, mesmerize me."[125] Put another way, hypnosis could not escape its less credible forebear.

Daniel Pick writes, "Hypnotism itself was on the cusp between tawdry theatre, mysticism and the medical curriculum; between erotic enchantment, spiritual mystery and salubrious scientific pursuit."[126] Such is apparent in Georges Méliès's moving picture *A Mesmerian Experiment/ Le baquet de Mesmer* (1905). In it, the character of Dr. Mesmer (as played by Méliès) appears in a story that unfolds like a magic act.[127] In *The Hypnotist* (Lubin, 1912), the title character is described as a "mesmerist, who appears in a flash of fire and smoke."[128] And the Lyons and Moran comedy *Such a Villain* (Nestor, 1914) illustrates the "evil power of an unscrupulous hypnotist who casts his spell" over a young woman. The hero immerses himself in the study of the same to save her. Rather than being a science, the film's publicity referred to hypnotism as being of the "occult."[129] Likewise, *The Bride of Mystery* (Universal-Gold Seal, 1914) was a story of the "occult" in which a "ghost bell" is heard at night and a young woman becomes hypnotized.[130]

By contrast, in the comedy *The Hypnotic Chair* (Majestic, 1912), a chair "throws its spell over a dozen or more people" only after its electric current is turned on.[131] In *The Invisible Power* (Kalem, 1914), a reputable army surgeon studies hypnotism as a science.[132] And in the "Ham and Bud" comedy *The Hypnotic Monkey* (Kalem, 1915), Ham dreams that a "hypnotist turns Bud into a monkey and then back to his human form."[133] *The Hypnotic Monkey* thus situates itself in the twilight that Pick describes: it draws upon Darwinian evolution (which Du Maurier in fact mentions in the novel *Trilby*), but its hypnotist has powers that stem more from magic than science.

To be sure, hypnotism provided the impetus for a large number of film comedies. An early example was *What Hypnotism Can Do* (American Mutoscope & Biograph, 1899); in it, a hypnotist proves his powers to a "doubting client" by making a ballet girl materialize from nothingness, "poised in the air," before he makes her disappear.[134] That same year, Edison sold the Vitagraph-produced film *[The] Mesmerist and Country Couple*. In it, "Mr. and Mrs. Hayseed" visit a "wonderful Professor" (played by J. Stuart Blackton) who hypnotizes them.

Mr. Hayseed stands on his head, while his wife "begins to disrobe, but she goes behind a screen." Her "bare arm appears over the top, and she drops her clothes on the floor." An Edison catalog description promised "mystical appearances managed with wonderful cleverness."[135] Once again, cinematic hypnotism was depicted as being closer to magic than science, and thus provided a rationale for humorous special effects.[136]

In its publicity for *The Hypnotist's Revenge* (1907), American Mutoscope & Biograph described the context for these moving picture comedies:

> Most of us have at some time attended an entertainment given by some wonderful exponent of the mysterious art of hypnotism and have always noted the presence of some cynical sciolist who would brand the professor a blatant fraud.[137]

As a surviving copy of the film shows, a professor hypnotizes a man who does not believe in his powers. Using contorted hand gestures, the professor orders the man to undertake ridiculous tasks, ranging from jumping on a table to swinging on a chandelier.[138]

Many comical moving pictures took direct inspiration from *Trilby*. *Hypnotizing Mamie* (Kalem, 1913) finds the title character becoming stage assistant to "Professor Svengali" under her new name, "Madam Zaza."[139] In *The Hypnotist/Axel Breidahl som hypnotisør* (Great Northern, 1913), Jim's rival pulls a "Svengali act" that puts him in a trance.[140] A hypnotist named "Professor Swengolly" appeared in *Hypnotism in Hicksville* (Essanay, 1913), and "Professor Smelgarlic" appeared in *Hypno and Trance-Subjects* (Edison, 1915).[141]

Svengali-like hypnotists also featured in *Hypnotized* (Selig Polyscope, 1912) and *Binks Plays Cupid* (Imp, 1913, aka *Binks and the Artist's Models*).[142] At times the "professors" proved their powers were real, as in *Alkali Ike and the Hypnotist* (Essanay, 1913) and *Andy and the Hypnotist* (Edison, 1914).[143] In other cases, including *Secrets of Hypnotism/Les secrets de l'hypnotisme* (Lux, 1908), *Hypnotist's Revenge* (Gaston Méliès, 1909), and *The Hypnotic Subject/Un sujet hypnotique* (Pathé Frères, 1909, aka *Hypnotic Subject*), the hypnotists are exposed as charlatans.[144]

Having heard about hypnotism or seen demonstrations of the same, many characters tried to learn the skill. Reviewing *He Learned the Trick of Mesmerism/Cardebry se venge* (Pathé Frères, 1909, aka *He Learns the Trick of Mesmerism*), the *New York Dramatic Mirror* correctly noted that "ideas similar to this have been frequent in pictures."[145] And they continued long after its release. For example, a woman tries to command her husband in *The Hypnotic Wife/Le magnétisme vengeur* (Pathé Frères, 1909, aka *Hypnotic Wife*).[146] In *The Servant Hypnotist/Le domestique hypnotiseur* (Pathé Frères, 1907), a butler exerts hypnotic control over his employer (played by Max Linder).[147] The title character of *Jones' Hypnotic Eye* (Vitagraph, 1915) even tries to hypnotize his cat, his dog, and his chickens.[148] Most popular of all, at least in the amount of times the plot was repurposed, husbands tried to control their in-laws, as happened in *Ma-In-Law Mesmerized/Gendre et belle-mère* (Gaumont, 1908), *Mother Is Strong on Hypnotism/Belle-maman fait du magnétisme* (Pathé Frères, 1911), *The Hypnotist* (Lubin, 1912), *Jerry's Mother-in-Law* (Vitagraph, 1913), and *Don't Monkey with the Buzz Saw* (Kalem, 1914).[149]

A number of other comedies built their narratives around the kinds of hypnotism manuals commonly sold in magazine and newspaper advertisements of the era.[150] Such was the case in *Hypnotic Nell* (Kalem, 1912), *A Mail Order Hypnotist* (Selig Polyscope, 1912), and *The Hypnotic Collector* (Pilot, 1913).[151] A surviving copy of *Hypnotizing the Hypnotist* (Vitagraph, 1911) is illustrative of these moving pictures. In it, a Svengali-esque hypnotist wears a fake nose and beard. When he visits a woman, her jealous husband hypnotizes her, commanding her to make faces at the hypnotist. Then the husband and hypnotist match wits, using their eyes and hand gestures on each other. The husband wins, making the hypnotist fall in love with a maid who promptly throws him out.[152]

Dramatic depictions of hypnotism and Mesmerism also commonly populated early film screenings. At times, hypnotism helped heroes solve crimes, as in *The Hypnotic Detective* (Selig Polyscope, 1912) and the serial *The Black Box* (Universal, 1915), to rescue those in need, as in *The Invisible Power* (Kalem, 1914), and to reconstruct past events, as in *The Mesmerist/Le magnétiseur* (Pathé Frères, 1908) and *Love and Hypnotism/Amore e ipnotismo* (Cines, 1912).[153] And, in one instance, hypnotism allowed for a form of righteous retribution to occur. *The Weird Nemesis* (Victor, 1915) has a woman commit suicide by drowning after a cruel lover scorns her.[154] The woman's sister gains mental control over the lover, causing him to drown himself.[155]

Following from *Trilby*, most films about hypnotism in the early cinema period posed hypnotists as villains. The earliest film adaptations of Du Maurier's story came in *Trilby Hypnotic Scene* (Edison, 1895, aka *Hypnotic Scene (Burlesque)*), which was advertised as a "burlesque," and *Trilby Death Scene* (Edison, 1895, aka *Death Scene*), a "comic" film in which the images tried to "imitate" the illustrations in Du Maurier's book.[156] The following year, American Mutoscope released *Trilby and Little Billee* (1896), though the adapted scene did not depict Svengali or hypnotism.[157] Indeed, its title may have been as much a reference to Thomas M. Bowers's published song *Trilby and Little Billie* (Thomas Goggan, 1895) as it was to Du Maurier's novel. By contrast, the *New York Clipper* did report on a Vitascope exhibition in Baltimore in July 1896 "showing Svengali and Trilby."[158] Its origins are difficult to determine, unless this is merely a description of *Trilby Hypnotic Scene*.

What is clear is that foreign-made adaptations like *Trilby* (Nordisk, 1908), *Trilby* (Standard Feature Film, 1912), and *Trilby* (London Film Company, 1914) faced a distribution embargo in America.[159] During much of the nickelodeon era, William A. Brady controlled the American film rights to Du Maurier's novel, which he and the Harper Brothers licensed to Adolph Zukor and Famous Players in 1913.[160]

Such legal rights could not keep imitators from the screen, however. Evil hypnotists became a common screen villain in the nickelodeon era. Some of them used somnambulists to do their dirty work.[161] Consider D. W. Griffith's *The Criminal Hypnotist* (American Mutoscope & Biograph, 1909), an early entry in this cycle of films. As a surviving copy illustrates, a bearded hypnotist exhibits his skills at a private home. Upon leaving, he hypnotizes a woman on the street and makes her open the safe in her home. Even though she is under his control, she will not take the money, so he follows her back to the safe and steals it himself.[162] The *New York Dramatic Mirror* wrote, "This is a serious effort to introduce the subject of mental science into motion picture drama, and it must be admitted that the Biograph players have succeeded wonderfully well."[163]

The villains of *Under the Sway/L'influence* (Eclipse, 1912), *Convicted by Hypnotism/Double vie* (Union Features, 1912), *The Strange Story of Sylvia Gray* (Broadway Star Features, 1914, aka *Sylvia Gray*), and *The Fakir* (Domino, 1915) controlled the minds of women who steal for them.[164] Similarly, the "modern Svengali" in the three-reeler *On the*

Verge of War (101 Bison, 1914) entrances a "defenseless girl" and makes her steal secret government documents.[165] Then, in *The Cheval Mystery* (Victor, 1915), a "hypnotist of the Svengali type" wields power over a woman he met "while travelling with a sideshow."[166] She gets accused of murder after he places an incriminating gun in her hand.[167]

The most narratively complex of these films was probably *The Mysteries of Souls/I misteri della psiche* (Itala, 1912, aka *The Mystery of Souls*), in which an uncle named Alberti is guardian to his wealthy niece Lydia. He enlists a gambler named Bernard to murder her, but Bernard secretly uses hypnotic control over Lydia, keeping her in a somnambulistic state so that he might blackmail Alberti.[168] *Moving Picture News* wrote, "Behind the girl we see a vision of Bernard, master of her soul, impelling her to crime."[169] When Bernard is killed, Lydia's mind returns to normalcy, not unlike Trilby after Svengali's death. The *New York Dramatic Mirror* praised *The Mysteries of Souls* for depicting the "most sinister aspects of life" with appropriate "discretion."[170]

Figure 12.2 Slide 4 of the illustrated song *That Hypnotizing Man* (Scott & Van Altena, 1911). (*Courtesy of the Marnan Collection, LLC, of Minneapolis, Minnesota*)

Other hypnotists also focused on controlling women for equally sinister reasons. Such films included *Hypnotized* (Thanhouser, 1910), *An Evil Power* (Selig Polyscope, 1911), *The Evil Power* (Rex, 1913), *The Spell* (Vitagraph, 1913), *The Blood Brotherhood* (Rex, 1913), *Forces of Evil, or The Dominant Will* (Leading Players, 1914), and *The Return of Richard Neal* (Essanay, 1915).[171] Warner's Features offered a curious variation on this storyline with *In the Power of the Hypnotist* (1913), in which Professor Gondorza (Sidney Olcott) exerts an evil mind control over his own daughter (played by Gene Gauntier), rather than over a romantic interest.[172]

Post-nickelodeon cinema like Universal's four-reeler *The Silent Command* (1915) added to these earlier films by using cinematography to accentuate the villain's power. According to *Universal Weekly*, the hypnotist Dr. Sevani (Harry Carter) was "strikingly reminiscent of Wilton Lackaye's work in his famous [stage] role of Svengali in *Trilby*."[173] The "hypnotic mystery" has its hypnotist demand a father turn his daughter over to him. The father refuses, but Sevani's mental powers as conveyed through his eyes are too strong to refuse. *Moving Picture World* remarked, "From the moment [the father] gazes upon the eyes of evil, of truth and paternal love, as pictured in the close-ups, the feeling grows in the observer that something of an almost uncanny psychological nature is going to occur."[174]

Figure 12.3 *In the Power of the Hypnotist* (Warner's Features, 1913).

The Danish-made three-reel moving picture entitled *The Hypnotic Violinist/Zigo* (Warner's Features, 1914) became one of the most faithful to Du Maurier's story. In it, a husband and wife listen to the gypsy violinist Zigo at a restaurant. Zigo decides he wants to "possess" the wife, so he plays his violin at her tableside. As one plot synopsis explained, "With a terror-stricken expression upon her face, she involuntarily threw her arms up before her as if to ward off an unseen foe, then fell back into her chair in fear and trembling."[175] Zigo soon induces the wife to leave her husband. After months of "cruel training" under his hypnotic spell, Zigo teaches her to perform various "death-defying feats."[176] The two score a major success on the stage, but eventually Zigo's spell over her breaks when her husband knocks him senseless. Zigo dies while trying to reassert his control over the woman.[177]

"We hardly need to point out that all these hypnotism pictures have no educational value," *Moving Picture World* advised in 1912.[178] Many persons believed the same of the genre, as well as its close relative, that of the "vampire," which presented similar tales of devilish characters who controlled the mind, body, and souls of their romantic interests.

Vampirism

Arthur Conan Doyle's novella *The Parasite* (1894) features a female Mesmerist named Penclosa who exerts control over a male scientist. She is a "devil woman," a parasite whose grip is loosened only at the time of her death. The tale is, as Pick has observed, a variation of the Svengali story, one that inverts the traditional gender roles of Mesmerist/hypnotist and subject.[179] Appearing the same year as *Trilby*, the novel had little impact by comparison. However, its inversion of gender roles anticipated a new genre related to hypnotism, one that would emerge only a few years later.

In May 1897, the American press announced the "sensational" London exhibition of Philip Burne-Jones's painting *The Vampire*. Some newspapers printed line art drawings of the work, while others described it as well as they could through words. The *Cleveland Plain Dealer* informed readers that *The Vampire* "shows a room flooded with moonlight, in which a dying man, with a wound in his breast, lies sleeping. Over him lies a beautiful woman—who has just drained him of his life blood." The newspaper also indicated that Rudyard Kipling had written a poem of the same name. "Kipling has seen in the female vampire an allegory of the worthless woman," the *Plain Dealer* said, "who loves a man . . . until at last he finds she has stolen all or the better part of his life."[180]

At least a few American newspapers chose to publish Kipling's poem in full at this time.[181] Its famous first verse is as follows:

> A fool there was and he made his prayer
> (Even as you and I!)
> To a rag and a bone and a hank of hair.
> (We called her the woman who did not care)
> But the fool he called her his lady fair
> (Even as you and I!)

As Janet Staiger writes, "The vampire or spider image of sucking away the man's blood was a powerful metaphor for the threat she represented."[182] Here was a dangerous figure, but one that was—unlike the succubus, for example—not actually supernatural.

As noted in Chapter 8, the work of Burne-Jones and Kipling had an immediate impact on the American definition of the term "vampire." In 1899, the *New York Times* remarked:

> People nowadays carelessly use the word "vampire" as a stronger and trifle more loathsome term than "parasite." Burne-Jones once painted a picture called the *Vampire*. It was a very beautiful woman leaning over a man she had just slain. And Kipling wrote some symbolic verses about it.[183]

The journalist added, "Probably few persons know what the real vampire is," the Burne-Jones depiction having so quickly displaced the supernatural creature in popular culture.

In 1909, Porter Emerson Browne adapted the painting and poem into the play (and, soon thereafter, the novel) *A Fool There Was*. It was Browne who helped the new vampire character to come fully into possession of mental powers that matched her sexual prowess.

To be sure, the words "Mesmerism" and "hypnotism" do not appear in his novel. Nevertheless, its vampire has eyes that seem every bit as powerful as Svengali's, as Browne writes in the novelization:

> . . . she made no sound, no movement. The smile still dwelt upon her lips. It was only in the eyes that a difference came—in the black, inscrutable eyes. They gleamed now, heavy-lidded as before. Their gaze was fixed straight into the sunken, hate-lit eyes of the man before her, a man who, but for her, might still have been a boy. She bent forward a little. . . . Her forehead, between the eyes, was now touching the bright muzzle of the weapon. The finger on the trigger trembled— trembled but did not pull.

By contrast, one of her male victims has eyes from which "the light had gone. They were as lamps unlit." He was as much a somnambulist as she a mesmerist.

Opening in New York City in 1909, *A Fool There Was* featured Katharine Kaelred as the "Woman," or—as the *New York Times* called her—the "Vampire Lady."[184] Despite some mediocre reviews, the play became a success, and it had an immediate impact on American cinema. In *American Film Cycles: The Silent Era*, Larry Langman writes, "Between 1914 and 1917, a flood of vampire films was unleashed on American theatres and did not recede until the mid-twenties."[185]

Figure 12.4 Trade advertisement for *The Hypnotic Violinist* (Warner's Features, 1914). Published in *Moving Picture World* on October 24, 1914.

Figure 12.5 Margarita Fischer and Charles Clary in a frame from *The Vampire* (Selig Polyscope, 1910). (*Courtesy of Robert J. Kiss*)

The genre actually appears noticeably earlier than Langman indicates. In 1910, Selig Polyscope produced the moving picture *The Vampire*, which explicitly tried to bring the Burne-Jones painting to life, going so far as to quote Kipling in its intertitles.[186] Publicity for the film described its title character as "Satanic."[187] *The Nickelodeon* told readers, "This is the latest embodiment of Kipling's famous poem, and probably the last, for the vampire's vogue is on the wane. We have had her in poetry, in painting, in drama, in the dance, and now in the photoplay."[188]

But the prediction of the vampire's demise was premature. In 1912, Messter's moving picture *The Vampire/Der Vampyr* appeared at American theatres, with its lead character becoming a "sensible man" again after having a terrible nightmare about a "vampire woman."[189] Kalem produced its own version of *The Vampire* in 1913; *Moving Picture World* called the film—which featured a "vampire dance" performed by Alice Eis and Bert French—"one of the most powerful features" the company had ever released.[190]

Vitagraph touted *The Vampire of the Desert* (1913) as a "dramatic adaptation of Kipling's well-known poem."[191] In 1914, Kalem released the two-reel *The Vampire's Trail* (1914), in which a cabaret singer (Alice Hollister) entices a young married man (Tom Moore) until her "spell is broken."[192] That same year, Universal promoted its comedy *Universal Ike, Jr. and the Vampire* (1914), which starred Bob Fuehrer as a youth who wins a "rivalry" with other cowboys ("fools there was") for the "vampire" (played by Louise Glaum). *Motion Picture News* wrote, "When she has stolen everything he owns, he is sorry he even went into competition."[193]

Other films also used the vampire theme, even if not the term "vampire" in their titles. *As in a Looking Glass* (Monopol, 1913) featured a woman who uses her beauty to attract men to a gambling casino. "To love such a vampire is in itself a sin," *Moving Picture World* claimed in a review, "and all the men who turn to her sell themselves in some way."[194] In *The Burden Bearer* (Lubin, 1913), a young man falls "under the influence" of a "beautiful and notorious vampire."[195] And the male lead in *The Usurer* (Kalem, 1913) is "mercilessly bled into bankruptcy by the human vampire."[196]

Conclusion

The powers of the mind culminated in the early cinema period with two films, one being Maurice Tourneur's five-reel feature adaptation of Du Maurier's *Trilby* (Equitable, 1915).[197] As Kaveh Askari has observed, the film draws heavily upon pictorial representations of the novel and play that had been so common in the 1890s.[198] Its production also spurred other hypnotism features that same year, such as *The Case of Becky* (Jesse L. Lasky, 1915), *The Fool and the Dancer* (Abraham Bloom, 1915), *The Greater Will* (Premo, 1915), and *The Stolen Voice* (William A. Brady, 1915).[199]

For Tourneur's film, Wilton Lackaye reprised his stage role as Svengali, while movie star Clara Kimball Young portrayed the title character. Intertitles explain that Svengali—who hails from the "mysterious East"—possesses an "evil power." He uses the "devil's tricks" to gain control over Trilby's mind and body. Lackaye's performance remains impressive, his hand gestures commanding Trilby to do his will.

Exhibitors Film Exchange called *Trilby* "excellent."[200] *Wid's Films and Film Folk* told readers it was the "greatest combination of artistic presentation, dramatic strength and effective atmosphere ever shown in this country as a film."[201] And *Motography* declared

Figure 12.6 Alice Hollister in *The Vampire* (Kalem, 1913).

that the "filmed work of art" was "impervious to age or period," believing, "years from now, *Trilby* will be the same exquisite piece of workmanship that it is today."²⁰²

Eight months earlier, the six-reeler *A Fool There Was* (1915) appeared on theatre screens. Produced by William Fox, the film featured Theda Bara as "The Vampire" in what onscreen titles refer to as a "psychological drama."²⁰³ Many audiences and critics responded favorably to the film and—given its publicity, storyline, and intertitles—readily drew the connection to Burne-Jones and Kipling. The *New York Dramatic Mirror* wrote:

> During his decline from a strong, self-reliant man of affairs to a spineless weakling, fit only for the alcoholic ward of a hospital, [Edward Jose, as John Shuyler, the "Fool"] undergoes a remarkable change that affects every expression of his personality.²⁰⁴

The vampire, who is called a "devil" at one point in the film, controls the mind and body of the "Fool."²⁰⁵ As with *Trilby*, *A Fool There Was* remains a classic example of nascent feature film.

Figure 12.7 Advertisement promoting Maurice Tourneur's *Trilby* (Equitable, 1915). Published in *Motion Picture News* on September 11, 1915.

And yet, with regard to the larger issue of the powers of the mind onscreen, there are a number of reasons to conclude with Léonce Perret's film *In the Grip of the Vampire/ Le mystère des roches de Kador* (Gaumont,1912), one being that it represents the key cinematic intersection of vampires, hypnotists, and issues of sanity.[206] A terrible male guardian (the "vampire") drugs his female ward and shoots her lover, all in the hope of gaining her fortune. The lover does not die, but the appearance of his "dead body" walking toward the ward drives her "insane." Efforts to restore her mental health fail, until "finally the Cinematograph method is hit upon."[207] An intertitle in the American release print explained:

> The vibrations of cinematographic images transmitted by means of an optic nerve from the retina of the eye to the cells of the brain cause a state of hypnotism which lends itself admirably to suggestion.[208]

In this instance, the cinema had itself become a hypnotist, controlling the mind of the viewer.

Notes

1. "Hypnotic Eyes Foil Thief," *Washington Post*, January 28, 1910, 3.
2. "A Panegyric on Witchcraft, Mesmerism, and Cheap Literature," *The Columbian Lady's and Gentleman's Magazine* (November 1846), 209.
3. Albert, *Hypnotism: Including a Study of the Chief Points of Psycho-Therapeutics and Occultism*, Fourth Enlarged Edition (London: Walter Scott Publishing, 1909), 480.
4. "Telepathy in a Play," *New York Times*, November 19, 1907, 9; "*A Telepathic Warning*," *New York Dramatic Mirror*, January 16, 1909; George Blaisdell, "*The Invisible Power*," *Moving Picture World*, November 7, 1914, 767; John T. Soister and Henry Nicolella with Steve Joyce and Harry H. Long, *American Silent Horror, Science Fiction and Fantasy Feature Films, 1913–1929* (Jefferson, North Carolina: McFarland & Company, 2012), 105–6. Some footage from *A Telepathic Warning* is archived at the Library of Congress by way of a paper print deposit.
5. "*Palmistry*," *Views and Film Index*, June 15, 1907, 6; "*The Crystal Ball*," *The Billboard*, July 3, 1909, 14; "*What the Cards Foretold*," *The Billboard*, December 4, 1909, 21; "*Madame Clairo*," *The Billboard*, August 13, 1910, 27; "*The Master and the Man*," *The Billboard*, May 13, 1911, 34; "*Mera, the Medium*," *Moving Picture World*, July 18, 1914, 482. A copy of *Palmistry* is archived at the Centre national du cinéma et de l'image animée (CNC). A copy of *Mera, the Medium* is archived at the Library of Congress.
6. "*Hypnotized*," *Moving Picture World*, March 2, 1912, 802. A copy of *Hypnotized* is archived at the Museum of Modern Art, New York City.
7. Roy Porter, *Madness: A Brief History* (Oxford: Oxford University Press, 2002), 110.
8. See, for example, "The Great Murder Trial," *New York Times*, December 24, 1881, 1.
9. "Pictures of Mental Diseases Shown," *Motography*, January 18, 1913, 40.
10. Ibid., 40. Weisenburg's films were the result of a technical collaboration with Lubin. For more information, see T. H. Weisenburg, "Moving Picture Illustrations in Medicine," *Journal of the American Medical Association*, December 28, 1912, 2310–13.
11. Nonfiction surgery films are discussed in Chapter 13. As for epilepsy, Walter G. Chase's moving pictures on the subject, filmed in conjunction with American Mutoscope & Biograph, included *Epileptic Seizure* (1905), *Epileptic Seizure, No. 8* (1906), *Epileptic Seizure, No. 9* (1906). See Elias Savada (ed.), *The American Film Institute Catalog of Motion Pictures Produced in the United States: Film Beginnings, 1893–1910* (Lanham, Maryland: Scarecrow Press, 1995), 312. The Library of Congress has prints of Chase's *Epileptic Seizure, No. 1*, *Epileptic Seizure, No. 2*, *Epileptic Seizure, No. 3*, *Epileptic Seizure, No. 4*, *Epileptic Seizure, No. 7*, and *Epileptic Seizure, No. 8*.

12. *No. 288, Edison Films* (Orange, New Jersey: Edison Manufacturing Company, July 1906), 33. Available in *A Guide to Motion Picture Catalogs by American Producers and Distributors, 1894–1908: A Microfilm Edition* (New Brunswick: Rutgers University Press, 1985), Reel 1. A copy of *Maniac Chase* is archived in the Paper Print Collection at the Library of Congress.
13. A copy of *The Escaped Lunatic* is archived at the Library of Congress.
14. *Biograph Bulletin*, No. 33, October 10, 1904, available in *Biograph Bulletins, 1896–1908*, edited by Kemp R. Niver (Los Angeles: Locare Research Group, 1971), 132.
15. *Biograph Bulletin*, No. 86, November 1, 1906, available in *Biograph Bulletins, 1896–1908*, 275.
16. Advertisement, *The Billboard*, November 3, 1906, 31.
17. A copy of *Dr. Dippy's Sanitarium* is archived at the Library of Congress.
18. "Latest Films of All Makers," *Views and Film Index*, December 7, 1907, 8. A copy of *Doings of a Maniac* is archived at the British Film Institute.
19. "*The Mad Musician*," *Moving Picture World*, March 7, 1908, 195.
20. "*The Maniac*," *Moving Picture World*, October 28, 1911, 290.
21. "*Bill Becomes Mentally Deranged*," *Moving Picture World*, April 6, 1912, 74.
22. "Movie Actress Mistaken for Lunatic," *Universal Weekly*, September 5, 1914, 23.
23. *The 1907 Catalogue of the Selig Polyscope and Library of Selig Films* (Selig Polyscope, 1907), 103. Available in *A Guide to Motion Picture Catalogs by American Producers and Distributors, 1894–1908: A Microfilm Edition*, Reel 2.
24. "*A* [sic] *Marked Man*," *Moving Picture World*, December 21, 1912, 1185.
25. A copy of *The Marked Man* is archived at the Danish Film Institute.
26. "*The Madman*," *Moving Picture World*, March 9, 1912, 890. This film was originally scheduled for release on December 5, 1911, but postponed until March 15, 1912.
27. "*The Taint of Madness*," *Moving Picture World*, May 9, 1914, 844.
28. "*The Accusing Eye*," *Moving Picture World*, May 16, 1914, 969.
29. W. Stephen Bush, "*The Magic Note*," *Moving Picture World*, May 16, 1914, 950.
30. "*The Madman's Ward*," *Motion Picture News*, August 22, 1914, 54.
31. "*The Haunting Fear*," *Kalem Kalendar*, June 1915, 17.
32. In addition to the fictional films covered in the main text, some nonfiction films were produced on the subject of mental institutes. In 1912, for example, a 1,000-foot moving picture depicting the "daily routine of life in state hospitals for the insane" played at the state fair in Syracuse, New York. See "Insane Asylum Films," *Motography*, August 31, 1912, 180.
33. "Growing Menace of Chicago Censors," *Motography*, October 3, 1914, 460.
34. "Guardian Plans to Drive Girl Insane," *Motography*, August 1, 1914, 167; "*Olive in the Madhouse*," *Moving Picture World*, February 13, 1915, 984. A copy of *Olive in the Madhouse* is archived at the Library of Congress.
35. "*The Insane Heiress*," *Moving Picture World*, December 24, 1910, 1492.
36. "*The Maniac*," *Universal Weekly*, June 22, 1912, 8. A copy of *The Maniac* is archived at the Museo Nazionale del Cinema.
37. "*The Hands*," *Moving Picture World*, February 3, 1912, 422.
38. It is true that *Shadows of the Moulin Rouge* was officially released on December 26, 1913; however it seems evident that it did not appear on any theatre screens until January 1914, hence the use of that year in the main text.
39. "*Shadows of the Moulin Rouge*," *Moving Picture World*, January 3, 1914, 61.
40. Ibid., 61.
41. "*Shadows of the Moulin Rouge*," *Moving Picture World*, January 17, 1914, 348.
42. "*Shadows of* [*the*] *Moulin Rouge*," *Motion Picture News*, January 24, 1914, 42.
43. W. Stephen Bush, "*The Shadows of the Moulin Rouge*," *Moving Picture World*, January 24, 1914, 417.
44. A copy of *His Phantom Sweetheart* is archived at the British Film Institute.

45. Louis Reeves Harrison, "Two Studies in Life," *Moving Picture World*, April 17, 1915, 397. For another key film about mental illness, see the discussion of *The Lunatics/Le système du docteur Goudron et du professeur Plume* (Leading Players, 1914) in Chapter 14.
46. Eric G. Wilson, "Matter and Spirit in the Age of Animal Magnetism," *Philosophy and Literature*, Vol. 30, No. 2 (October 2006), 329.
47. Justine S. Murison, "The Tyranny of Sleep: Somnambulism, Moral Citizenship, and Charles Brockden Brown's *Edgar Huntly*," *Early American Literature*, Vol. 44, No. 2 (2009), 247.
48. Esther Serle Kenneth, "The Haunted Chamber," *Ballou's Monthly Magazine*, August 1879, 140.
49. "Rode Bicycle in Sleep," *New York Times*, October 22, 1904, 1; "Somnambulist Asleep in Coffin," *New York Times*, November 7, 1905, 6.
50. "Murder Will Out," *National Police Gazette*, November 25, 1882, 3.
51. "A Fiend's Shocking Act," *Washington Post*, August 13, 1889, 1.
52. "Evanston's Ghost Is Identified," *Chicago Tribune*, November 24, 1894, 6.
53. See, for example, "The Springfield Somnambulist," *Spirit of the Age and Journal of Humanity*, March 13, 1834, 1; L. W. Belden, "An Account of Jane C. Rider, the Springfield Somnambulist," *The Boston Medical and Surgical Journal*, September 10, 1834, 1.
54. *Lubin's Films* (Philadelphia: Lubin, May 1905), 10. Available in *A Guide to Motion Picture Catalogs by American Producers and Distributors, 1894–1908: A Microfilm Edition*, Reel 3.
55. See, for example, "Death from Somnambulism," *Gloucester Telegraph* (Gloucester, Massachusetts), October 3, 1838, 2; "Accident from Somnambulism," *The Sun* (Baltimore, Maryland), September 21, 1840, 2; "Fatal Case of Somnambulism," *Wheeling Register* (Wheeling, West Virginia), December 19, 1878, 1; "A Somnambulist's Fall," *New York Times*, July 16, 1883, 12; "A Somnambulist's Fall," *New York Times*, October 31, 1885, 4; "A Somnambulist's Fatal Fall," *New York Times*, October 28, 1889, 9; "A Somnambulist's Fall," *New York Times*, March 17, 1890, 1; "A Somnambulist's Fall from a Roof," *New York Times*, October 24, 1895, 9; "Somnambulist Kills Himself," *New York Times*, July 8, 1896, 5; "Somnambulist's Fall Proves Fatal," *Washington Post*, June 25, 1897, 10; "Fall of Three Stories Wakens a Somnambulist," *Chicago Tribune*, May 13, 1901, 1; "Somnambulist Badly Hurt," *Washington Post*, August 9, 1904.
56. "Essanay Mfg. Co.," *The Film Index*, December 5, 1908, 8.
57. "*The Sleeping Burglar*," *Moving Picture World*, December 7, 1912, 977.
58. See, for example, "Buried Money: A Strange Case of Somnambulism," *The Patriot* (Harrisburg, Pennsylvania), July 29, 1873, 1.
59. "*The Somnambulist*," *Moving Picture World*, May 14, 1910, 804.
60. "*The Sleep Walker*," *Moving Picture World*, July 8, 1911, 1585.
61. "*The Somnambulist*," *Moving Picture World*, January 10, 1914, 210. A copy of this film is archived at the EYE Film Institute.
62. "*Mystery of Mr. Marks*," *Moving Picture World*, October 17, 1914, 408. A copy of this film is archived at the British Film Institute.
63. Other examples include *Sleep Walker/Le sonneur somnambule* (Gaumont, 1908, aka *The Somnambulic Bell Ringer*), which features a man who walks in his sleep and rings the church bell in the middle of the night, with the villagers giving him an "awful beating." By contrast, the title character of *Polidor, the Sleep-Walker/Polidor sonnambulo* (Picture Playhouse, 1914) merely pretends to be a somnambulist to attend a late-night party without his wife's permission. See "*Sleep Walker*," *Moving Picture World*, June 5, 1909, 769; "*Polidor, the Sleep-Walker*," *Moving Picture World*, December 5, 1914, 1436. A copy of this film, albeit with intertitles removed and voices dubbed into the characters' mouths, appears in the compilation *Polidor Ganimede* (Fotovox, 1940), which is archived at the Cineteca dei Friuli.

64. "The Somnambulists," *Moving Picture World*, December 13, 1913, 1279. A copy of this film is archived at the Museum of Modern Art, New York City.
65. "A Sleep Walking Cure," *Moving Picture World*, August 6, 1910, 297. A copy of this film is archived at the Museum of Modern Art, New York City.
66. "The Somnambulist," *New York Dramatic Mirror*, May 20, 1914, 39. A newspaper story in 1903 told of a man chaining himself to a bed to avoid sleepwalking. See "To Chain Himself in Bed," *New York Times*, October 12, 1903, 5.
67. The basic idea of a somnambulist inadvertently attempting murder had appeared in nonfiction press accounts. See "Mysterious Attempt at Murder," *Chicago Tribune*, April 16, 1873, 8.
68. "The Experiment," *Moving Picture World*, February 20, 1915, 1182. A copy of this film is archived at the Museum of Modern Art, New York City.
69. Charles Poyen, *Progress of Animal Magnetism in New England* (Boston: Weeks, Jordan, & Company, 1837), 29.
70. "Mesmerism and Witchcraft," *Berkshire County Whig* (Pittsfield, Massachusetts), March 23, 1843, 1.
71. See, for example, "What Is True and What Is False in Mesmerism," *American Phrenological Journal* (August 1845), 284.
72. Robert C. Fuller, *Mesmerism and the American Cure of Souls* (Philadelphia: University of Pennsylvania Press, 1982), 46.
73. Deborah Manson, "'The Trance of the Ecstatica': Margaret Fuller, Animal Magnetism, and the Transcendent Female Body," *Literature and Medicine*, Vol. 25, No. 2 (Fall 2006), 298–324.
74. Quoted in Manson, 309.
75. Emily Ogden, "Mesmer's Demon: Fiction, Falsehood, and the Mechanical Imagination," *Early American Literature*, Vol. 47, No. 1 (2012), 151.
76. Walter K. Kelly, "A Few Words on Mesmerism," *The Monthly Magazine*, Vol. XCVI (July 1842), 180.
77. *Edison Films, No. 175* (Orange, New Jersey: Edison Manufacturing Company, May 1903), 30. Available in *A Guide to Motion Picture Catalogs by American Producers and Distributors, 1894–1908: A Microfilm Edition* (New Brunswick: Rutgers University Press, 1985), Reel 1.
78. "The Eyes of Satan," *Moving Picture World*, February 8, 1913, 618; "Alone with the Devil," *Moving Picture World*, April 4, 1914, 59. A copy of *Alone with the Devil* is archived at the Danish Film Institute.
79. Bruce Mills, *Poe, Fuller, and the Mesmeric Arts: Transition States in the American Renaissance* (Columbia, Missouri: University of Missouri Press, 2006), 9.
80. Eric G. Wilson, "Matter and Spirit in the Age of Animal Magnetism," *Philosophy and Literature*, Vol. 30, No. 2 (October 2006), 329–45.
81. Maria M. Tatar, "Mesmerism, Madness, and Death in E. T. A. Hoffmann's *Der goldne Topf*," *Studies in Romanticism*, Vol. 14, No. 4 (Fall 1975), 365–89.
82. Catherine Wynne, "Mesmeric Exorcism, Idolatrous Beliefs, and Bloody Rituals: Mesmerism, Catholicism, and Second Sight in Bram Stoker's Fiction," *Victorian Review*, Vol. 26, No. 1 (2000), 43–63.
83. See, for example, "Mesmer and Mesmerism," *The National Magazine: Devoted to Literature, Art, and Religion*, September 1856, 217.
84. David Meredith Reese, *Humbugs of New-York; Being a Remonstrance against Popular Delusion; Whether in Science, Philosophy, or Religion* (New York, 1838), 17.
85. Willian's *The Magnetic Chain* was published as a serial in *Flag of Our Union* in 1867. For more information on Whitman and Mesmerism, see Harold Aspiz, *Walt Whitman and the Body Beautiful* (Urbana, Illinois: University of Illinois Press, 1980).
86. Sidney E. Lind, "Poe and Mesmerism," *PMLA*, Vol. 62, No. 4 (December 1947), 1077–94.

87. Taylor Stoehr, "Hawthorne and Mesmerism," *Huntington Library Quarterly*, Vol. 33, No. 1 (November 1969), 33–60.
88. "Nathaniel Hawthorne," *Littell's Living Age*, January 25, 1873, 195.
89. Stoehr, 52.
90. Francis Gerry Fairfield, "Hypnotism and Mesmerism," *The Phrenological Journal and Science of Health* (August 1874), 86.
91. Terry M. Parssinen, "Mesmeric Performers," *Victorian Studies*, Vol. 21, No. 1 (Autumn 1977), 87–104.
92. *Mark Twain's Own Autobiography: The Chapters from the* North American Review, edited by Michael J. Kiskis (University of Wisconsin Press, Second Edition, 2010), 84.
93. "Hypnotism," *Alexandria Gazette* (Alexandria, Virginia), May 3, 1860, 2.
94. Fred Kaplan, "'The Mesmeric Mania': The Early Victorians and Animal Magnetism," *Journal of the History of Ideas*, Vol. 35, No. 4 (October–December 1974), 702.
95. "Hypnotism," *New York Times*, June 29, 1890, 4.
96. Sigmund Freud, *The Origin and Development of Psychoanalysis* (New York: Henry Regnery, 1965), 65.
97. "Night Terrors," *Phrenological Journal and Science of Health*, June 1899, 189.
98. Beryl Satter, *Each Mind a Kingdom: American Women, Sexual Purity, and the New Thought Movement, 1875–1920* (Berkeley: University of California Press, 1999).
99. "Mysteries of Hypnotism," *New York Times*, February 13, 1889, 9.
100. Daniel Pick, *Svengali's Web: The Alien Encounter in Modern Culture* (New Haven, Connecticut: Yale University Press, 2000), 69.
101. Ibid., 69.
102. Professor Donato, "Hypnotism—The Weird Art," *The Cosmopolitan*, August 1890, 443.
103. "The Humbug of Hypnotism," *Current Literature*, Vol. 8, No. 2 (June 1893), 240.
104. Ernest Hart, "The Eternal Gullible, with Confessions of a Professional 'Hypnotist,'" *Century Illustrated Magazine*, October 1894, 833.
105. "The Theosophists," *Los Angeles Times*, June 13, 1892, 5.
106. "Effects of the Evil Eye," *Chicago Tribune*, August 4, 1889, 15.
107. "Mesmerism in Society," *New York Times*, April 3, 1881, 2.
108. "Dangers of Hypnotism," *New York Times*, December 28, 1890, 4.
109. "Kept Captive by Hypnotism," *Washington Post*, December 9, 1894, 24; "Murderer Hypnotized, Not Insane," *Chicago Tribune*, December 23, 1894, 1; "Hypnotism Made Him Crazy," *New York Times*, March 5, 1897, 6.
110. "Hypnotism as a Cure for Somnambulism," *Times and Register*, January 18, 1890, 62.
111. "Letter to the Times," *Los Angeles Times*, January 25, 1899, 7.
112. Loie Fuller, *Fifteen Years of a Dancer's Life, with Some Account of Her Distinguished Friends* (Boston: Small, Maynard & Company, 1913), 25.
113. Felicia McCarren, "The 'Symptomatic Act' circa 1900: Hysteria, Hypnosis, Electricity, Dance," *Critical Inquiry*, Vol. 21, No. 4 (Summer 1995), 753–4.
114. "Chicago Playhouses," *New York Times*, September 3, 1893, 16.
115. "Playbills," *Chicago Tribune*, March 5, 1905, C1. A feature-length adaptation of Sardou's *The Sorceress* was filmed in 1915 and released in February 1916. Advance press reports in July 1915 drew attention to the film's associations both with vamp dramas like *A Fool There Was* (with which it shared a director, Frank Powell) and *Trilby*, with male lead Alfred Hickman notable as the "creator of Little Billy [sic]" in the original Broadway production. See "Coming Fox Releases Make Noteworthy Quartet," *Motion Picture News*, July 3, 1915, 44; and "Brevities of the Business," *Motography*, July 17, 1915, 125.
116. Fred Nadis, *Wonder Shows: Performing Science, Magic, and Religion in America*: (New Brunswick: Rutgers University Press, 2005), 91–3.

117. "The World of Amusement," *New York Clipper*, October 29, 1881; "Dramatic," *New York Clipper*, January 13, 1883; "Massachusetts," *New York Clipper*, December 15, 1883, 655.
118. "Playing Corpse for His Living," *Trenton Times* (Trenton, New Jersey), July 19, 1906.
119. Nadis, 85.
120. Atia Sattar, "Certain Madness: Guy de Maupassant and Hypnotism," *Configurations*, Vol. 19, No. 2 (Spring 2011), 213–41.
121. George Du Maurier, *Trilby* (New York: Harper & Brothers, 1894), 75.
122. Advertisement, *New York Clipper*, March 16, 1895, 28; Advertisement, *New York Clipper*, March 23, 1895, 44; Advertisement, *New York Clipper*, April 6, 1895, 76; Advertisement, *New York Clipper*, June 1, 1895, 206; Advertisement, *New York Clipper*, July 27, 1895, 334.
123. "The Illusion of Trilby," *Scientific American*, August 8, 1896, 131.
124. Henry Carrington Bolton, "Fortune-Telling in America To-Day: A Study of Advertisements," *Journal of American Folklore*, Vol. 8, No. 31 (October–December 1895), 299.
125. Will Dillon and Harry Von Tilzer, *Hip, Hip, Hypnotize Me* (New York: Harry Von Tilzer Music Publishing Company, 1910).
126. Pick, 19.
127. *Supplement No. 26, Georges Méliès of Paris* (New York: Star Films, 1905), unpaginated. Available in *A Guide to Motion Picture Catalogs by American Producers and Distributors, 1894–1908: A Microfilm Edition*, Reel 4. A copy of *A Mesmerian Experiment* is available on the DVD *Georges Méliès Encore* (Los Angeles: Flicker Alley, 2010).
128. "*The Hypnotist*," *Moving Picture World*, July 6, 1912, 70.
129. "Christie Produces an Occult Burlesque," *Universal Weekly*, February 28, 1914, 17.
130. "Hypnotized Dancer Is Tool of Crook," *Universal Weekly*, February 7, 1914, 12–13.
131. "*The Hypnotic Chair*," *Moving Picture World*, December 7, 1912, 1016; "*The Hypnotic Chair*," *Moving Picture World*, December 14, 1912, 1082.
132. George Blaisdell, "*The Invisible Power*," *Moving Picture World*, November 7, 1914, 767.
133. "*The Hypnotic Monkey*," *Kalem Kalendar*, August 1915, 5.
134. *Picture Catalogue* (New York: American Mutoscope & Biograph, November 1902), 67. Available in *A Guide to Motion Picture Catalogs by American Producers and Distributors, 1894–1908: A Microfilm Edition*, Reel 2.
135. *No. 105, Edison Films, Complete Catalogue* (Orange, New Jersey: Edison Manufacturing Company, July 1901), 84–5. Available in *A Guide to Motion Picture Catalogs by American Producers and Distributors, 1894–1908: A Microfilm Edition*, Reel 1.
136. A copy of *The Mesmerist and Country Couple* is archived in the Paper Print Collection at the Library of Congress.
137. "*The Hypnotist's Revenge*," *Biograph Bulletin*, No. 103, July 20, 1907, available in *Biograph Bulletins, 1896–1908*, 301.
138. A copy of *The Hypnotist's Revenge* is archived at the Library of Congress.
139. "Hypnotizing Mamie," *Kalem Kalendar*, November 1913, 13.
140. "*The Hypnotist* (Great Northern)," *Moving Picture World*, August 30, 1913, 968.
141. "Hypnotism in Hicksville," *Moving Picture World*, January 25, 1913, 386; "*Hypno and Trance–Subjects*," *Moving Picture World*, February 27, 1915, 1333. A copy of *Hypno and Trance–Subjects* is archived at the Museum of Modern Art, New York City.
142. "Hypnotized," *Moving Picture World*, March 23, 1912, 1063; "*Binks Plays Cupid*," *Moving Picture World*, September 27, 1913, 1393.
143. "*Alkali Ike and the Hypnotist*," *Moving Picture World*, June 14, 1913, 1164; "*Andy and the Hypnotist*," *Moving Picture World*, April 4, 1914, 98.
144. "Secrets of Hypnotism," *Moving Picture World*, August 1, 1908, 89; "Hypnotist's Revenge," *New York Dramatic Mirror*, November 13, 1909, 15; "The Hypnotic Subject," *New York*

Dramatic Mirror, March 6, 1909, 12; "Hypnotic Subject," *Moving Picture World*, February 27, 1909, 250.

145. "He Learned the Trick of Mesmerism," *New York Dramatic Mirror*, October 9, 1909, 16.
146. "Hypnotic Wife," *New York Dramatic Mirror*, September 4, 1909, 18.
147. "Film Review," *Views and Film Index*, August 17, 1907, 6. A copy of *The Servant Hypnotist* is archived at the Library of Congress.
148. "Jones' Hypnotic Eye," *Vitagraph Life Portrayals*, June 1915, 11.
149. "Ma-In-Law Mesmerized," *Moving Picture World*, April 11, 1908, 328; "Mother Is Strong on Hypnotism," *Moving Picture World*, November 11, 1911, 470; "The Hypnotist," *Moving Picture World*, July 6, 1912, 70; "Jerry's Mother-in-Law," *New York Dramatic Mirror*, November 26, 1913, 33; "Don't Monkey with the Buzz Saw," *Kalem Kalendar*, August 1, 1914, 7. A copy of *Mother Is Strong on Hypnotism* is archived at the British Film Institute; a copy of *Jerry's Mother-in-Law* is archived at the EYE Film Institute; and a copy of *Don't Monkey with the Buzz Saw* is archived at the UCLA Film & Television Archive.
150. Powers's moving picture *Mental Science* (1910) offered a similar storyline, with its lead character finding a book that instructs him on how to impose his "will-power" on others. See "Mental Science," *Moving Picture World*, November 5, 1910, 1072.
151. "Hypnotic Nell," *Moving Picture World*, May 25, 1912, 728; "Hypnotizing the Hypnotist," *Moving Picture World*, December 16, 1911, 904; "A Mail Order Hypnotist," *Moving Picture World*, July 6, 1912, 72; "The Hypnotic Collector," *Moving Picture World*, May 3, 1913, 520.
152. A copy of *Hypnotizing the Hypnotist* is archived at the British Film Institute.
153. "The Hypnotic Detective," *New York Dramatic Mirror*, February 21, 1912, 30; "First Installment of *The Black Box*," *Universal Weekly*, March 1915, 9; "The Invisible Power," *Motography*, November 14, 1914, 687; "The Mesmerist," *Views and Film Index*, September 12, 1908, 10; "Love and Hypnotism," *Moving Picture World*, March 30, 1912, 1198. A copy of *The Hypnotic Detective* is archived at the UCLA Film & Television Archive; a copy of *The Mesmerist* is archived at the Cinémathèque Française; and *Love and Hypnotism* is archived at the Filmoteca Española.
154. "The Weird Nemesis," *Motography*, July 24, 1915, 184.
155. "The Weird Nemesis," *Moving Picture World*, July 24, 1915, 651.
156. Charles Musser, *Edison Motion Pictures, 1890–1900: An Annotated Filmography* (Washington, D.C.: Smithsonian Institution Press, 1997), 187.
157. *Picture Catalogue* (New York: American Mutoscope & Biograph, November 1902), 9. Available in *A Guide to Motion Picture Catalogs by American Producers and Distributors, 1894–1908: A Microfilm Edition* (New Brunswick: Rutgers University Press, 1985), Reel 2. In 1898, the Edison Manufacturing Company produced *Ella Lola, A La Trilby* [Dance]. Featuring stage star Ella Lola, the film was not an adaptation of George du Maurier's *Trilby*. A copy of that film is archived in the Paper Print Collection at the Library of Congress.
158. "Maryland," *New York Clipper*, July 11, 1896, 292.
159. A copy of the first reel of *Trilby* (London Film Company, 1914) is archived at the British Film Institute.
160. See, for example, "*Trilby* Barred in America," *New York Dramatic Mirror*, May 15, 1912, 25; Advertisement, *Moving Picture World*, April 19, 1913, 244.
161. Another example would be *The Spell of the Hypnotist/Un tesoro* (Helios, 1912). In it, the title character mentally commands a servant to stab an "old miser," thus making it easier to steal his fortune. See "*The Spell of the Hypnotist*," *Moving Picture World*, February 10, 1912, 528.
162. A copy of *The Criminal Hypnotist* is archived at the Library of Congress.
163. "*The Criminal Hypnotist*," *New York Dramatic Mirror*, January 30, 1909, 65. A copy of *Convicted by Hypnotism* is archived at the Centre national du cinéma et de l'image animée (CNC).

164. "*Under the Sway*," *Moving Picture World*, June 1, 1912, 829; G. F. Blaisdell, "*Convicted by Hypnotism*," *Moving Picture World*, November 16, 1912, 641; "*Sylvia Gray*," *Moving Picture World*, December 26, 1914, 1906; "*The Fakir*," *Moving Picture World*, April 3, 1915, 65. A copy of *Convicted by Hypnotism* is archived at the Centre national du cinéma et de l'image animée (CNC).
165. "Under Hypnotic Influence Girl Steals State Documents," *Universal Weekly*, May 30, 1914, 16.
166. Robert C. McElravy, "*The Cheval Mystery*," *Moving Picture World*, June 26, 1915, 2106.
167. "Hypnotist's Victim Accused of Murder," *Universal Weekly*, June 26, 1915, 17.
168. "*The Mysteries of Souls*," *Moving Picture World*, April 6, 1912, 29.
169. "*The Mystery of Souls*," *Moving Picture News*, March 30, 1912, 27.
170. "*The Mysteries of Souls*," *New York Dramatic Mirror*, April 24, 1912.
171. "*Hypnotized*," *Moving Picture World*, December 31, 1910, 1550; "*An Evil Power*," *Moving Picture World*, December 16, 1911, 903; "*The Evil Power*," *Moving Picture World*, August 30, 1913, 994; "*The Spell*," *Vitagraph Life Portrayals*, July 1913, 48; "Black Hander Has Singular Influence Over Girl," *Universal Weekly*, November 8, 1913, 20; Hanford C. Judson, "Shows Power of Hypnotism," *Motography*, July 25, 1914, 123; "*The Return of Richard Neal*," *Moving Picture World*, May 1, 1915, 728.
172. George Blaisdell, "*In the Power of the Hypnotist*," *Moving Picture World*, November 1, 1913, 499. The second reel of the three-reeler *In the Power of the Hypnotist* is archived at the Library of Congress.
173. "*The Silent Command*, a Hypnotic Mystery," *Universal Weekly*, May 29, 1915, 14.
174. Robert C. McElravy, "*The Silent Command*," *Moving Picture World*, May 1, 1915, 743.
175. "*The Hypnotic Violinist*," *Moving Picture World*, October 31, 1914, 706.
176. A brief fragment of *The Hypnotic Violinist* is preserved in the documentary short about leading lady Emilie Sannom, *Filmens vovehals* (Filmfabriken Danmark, 1923), in the collection of the Danish Film Institute.
177. "*The Hypnotic Violinist*," 706.
178. "*The Stronger Mind*," *Moving Picture World*, May 25, 1912, 728.
179. Pick, 169.
180. "The Vampire," *Cleveland Plain Dealer*, May 23, 1897.
181. See, for example, "The Vampire," *Salt Lake Tribune*, May 23, 1897; "The Vampire, Painting and Poem," *Dallas Morning News*, June 13, 1897.
182. Janet Staiger, *Bad Women: Regulating Sexuality in Early American Cinema* (Minneapolis: University of Minnesota Press, 1995), 150.
183. "Without Prejudice," *New York Times*, March 5, 1899, IMS2.
184. "*A Fool There Was*; No Doubt of That," *New York Times*, March 25, 1909, 9.
185. Larry Langman, *American Film Cycles: The Silent Era* (Westport, Connecticut: Greenwood Press, 1998), 345.
186. "*The Vampire*," *Moving Picture World*, November 12, 1910, 1127.
187. Ibid., 1127.
188. "*The Vampire*," *The Nickelodeon*, November 15, 1910, 280.
189. "*The Vampire*," *Moving Picture World*, January 20, 1912, 338.
190. "*The Vampire* (Kalem)," *Moving Picture World*, October 4, 1913, 51. Copies of *The Vampire* are archived at the George Eastman Museum and the Library of Congress.
191. Advertisement, *Moving Picture World*, May 10, 1913, 564.
192. "*The Vampire's Trail*," *New York Dramatic Mirror*, July 29, 1914, 26.
193. "*Universal Ike, Jr. and the Vampire*," *Motion Picture News*, July 11, 1914, 92.
194. H. C. Judson, "*As in a Looking Glass* (Monopole [sic] Film)," *Moving Picture World*, February 2, 1913, 783.
195. "*The Burden Bearer*," *Moving Picture World*, March 29, 1913, 1350.

196. "*The Usurer*," *Moving Picture World*, January 4, 1913, 76.
197. A copy of *Trilby* (1915) is available on a 2009 DVD from Alpha Video of Narberth, Pennsylvania.
198. Kaveh Askari, "Trilby's Community of Sensation," in *Visual Delights—Two: Exhibition and Reception*, edited by Vanessa Toulmin and Simon Popple (Eastleigh: John Libbey Publishing, 2005), 60–72.
199. Soister and Nicolella, 74–7, 241–3, 546–9, 702–3. *The Stolen Voice* was actually released the month prior to *Trilby*; nevertheless, it seems likely that the production of *Trilby* encouraged that of *The Stolen Voice*. Copies of *The Case of Becky* and *The Stolen Voice* are archived at the Library of Congress.
200. "Reviews," *Exhibitors Film Exchange*, September 25, 1915, unpaginated.
201. "Feature Films as Wid Sees Them," *Wid's Films and Film Folk*, September 9, 1915, unpaginated.
202. Charles R. Condon, "*Trilby*," *Motography*, September 25, 1915, 639.
203. A copy of *A Fool There Was* (1915) is available on a 2002 DVD from Kino Video of New York City.
204. "*A Fool There Was*," *New York Dramatic Mirror*, January 20, 1915.
205. Many other screen vamps followed in the wake of Fox's version of *A Fool There Was*, one of the most notable being Olga Petrova in the title role of Metro's 1915 film *The Vampire* (Metro, 1915), who tries to "avenge the wrong done her upon all mankind." Another notable vamp was Valeska Suratt, who starred in *The Soul of Broadway* (Fox, 1915). Other examples released the same year include *Was She a Vampire?* (Powers, 1915), in which an innocent young woman learns her father runs a gambling den, and *Saved from a Vampire* (Biograph, 1915), which inverted genders by unleashing a "He-Vampire" on a young woman. See "*The Vampire* (Metro)," *Moving Picture World*, August 7, 1915; "Fox's Valeska Suratt Film," *Motography*, October 16, 1915, 778; "*Was She a Vampire?*", *Moving Picture World*, July 10, 1915, 384; "*Saved from a Vampire*," *Motography*, March 20, 1915, 459. A copy of *Saved from a Vampire* is archived at the Museum of Modern Art, New York City.
206. A copy of *In the Grip of the Vampire* (under the title *The Mystery of the Rocks of Kador*) is available on the DVD boxed set *Gaumont Treasures, 1897–1913* (New York: Kino International, 2009).
207. "*In the Grip of the Vampire*," *Moving Picture News*, December 21, 1912, 13.
208. "*In the Grip of the Vampire*," *Moving Picture World*, December 28, 1912, 1308.

CHAPTER 13

Mad Scientists

In Victorin-Hippolyte Jasset's three-reel moving picture *Doomed to Die, or the Vial of Wrath/Fragile bonheur* (Union Features, 1913), a man seduces the wife of his friend, a doctor of "bacteriology."[1] In response, the doctor "turns his intimate knowledge of science into an instrument of almost fiendish vengeance."[2] The "Jekyll-Hyde" character, as *Variety* described him, condemns the interloper to "die like a dog."[3] After being exposed to the doctor's "deadly hydrophobia bacillus," the interloper "goes stark mad, and runs about on all fours, gnawing the furniture and barking like a dog." Then the doctor "pushes his wife into the room with the madman, locks the door, and leaves her to her fate."[4] *Moving Picture World* said the film possessed the "feeling as if some stray page from Maupassant or Zola had painted itself on little strips of celluloid, detailing and intensifying those horrors of which the pens of Zola and Maupassant were so fond."[5]

The mad scientist in *Doomed to Die, or the Vial of Wrath* was hardly a new character. The basic notion of a man of science gone wrong had deep roots as a counterpart to the scientist committed to the greater good. In terms of American history, Benjamin Franklin—whose experiments with lightning and the invention of the lightning rod made him internationally famous—exemplifies the latter.[6] His work represented what Immanuel Kant had once referred to as *sapere aude*: daring to know. And Franklin attempted to separate fact from fiction, meaning science from pseudo-science, as when he convened a panel that pronounced Mesmer's theories to be false.[7] According to Philip Dray, Franklin was a "philosopher who banished superstition."[8]

Over a century after Franklin's death, prolific journalist and editor James McCarroll wrote, "Slowly but surely . . . we have been escaping from our bondage [in superstition thanks to] the light of research and more scientific methods."[9] By the early twentieth century, science in the western world had increasingly moved toward professionalization, marked by expert jargon, intrinsic logic, and "esoteric knowledge" not understandable to the masses.[10] Here one can cite the work of Albert Einstein, as in the case of his *Annus Mirabilis* papers of 1905. Such developments are also apparent in H. G. Wells's *The Time Machine* (1895): "'Scientific people,' proceeded the Time Traveller, after the pause required for the proper assimilation of this, 'know very well that Time is only a kind of Space.'"

Historians have debated the role of science in nineteenth-century America. On the one hand, I. Bernard Cohen has bemoaned the "failure of our country to produce a great scientific tradition in the nineteenth century."[11] On the other hand, Nathan Reingold has argued that the century was replete with scientific activity, particularly in the observational sciences.[12] To understand these divergent views, it is worth considering

Paul Lucier's discussion of the two kinds of American scientists that existed in that era, one being the scientist who avoided commercial activity (following in the tradition of Franklin), and the other being a professional who "engaged in commercial relations with private enterprises," the most notable example being Thomas Alva Edison.[13] Whatever else might be said, America had become the leader in many fields of technological invention and innovation.[14]

In July 1896, only a few months after Edison first projected his moving pictures in public, the *Scientific American* heralded the "progress of invention" of the prior fifty years. Cumulatively, it represented a "gigantic tidal wave" of technology and commercial success.[15] Edison, Nikola Tesla, and numerous others contributed to this success, which many Americans believed had improved the quality of human life, including its "moral uplift."[16] To these men, the press applied such terms as "scientist," "genius," "visionary," "inventor," and—more specifically—"electrician."

The press also regularly used "wizard" as a description, the term being more evocative of alchemy or magic than of science. Consider, for example, the following excerpt from the March 1895 issue of *Frank Leslie's Popular Monthly*:

> The public had now begun to regard through a kind of glorified and supernatural mist the "Wizard of Menlo Park" [Edison,] who within the space of a few years gave them from his mysterious Jersey retreat not only the marvelous phonograph and the beautiful incandescent electric lamp, but also a score of other inventions . . .[17]

And of Edison's laboratory, *The Cosmopolitan* in 1889 described objects "reminiscent of the witch's caldron [sic] in *Macbeth*," among them an electrical device emitting "many-colored sparks which fly off at various places with Mephistophelian energy."[18] "A visit to Thomas A. Edison is suggestive of a pilgrimage to the haunts of some mediaeval wizard," the *Los Angeles Times* wrote in 1895. "The Walpurgisnacht in *Faust*, and the summer of the Brocken seem tame in comparison."[19]

To others, these descriptions seemed increasingly inappropriate as the twentieth century approached. In 1894, one journalist wrote:

> At first he appears to have been regarded as something supernatural. He was called the Wizard of Menlo Park. This, in turn, suggested the sleight-of-hand of the "magician" of the stage. Fortunately both these views quickly passed away and he came to be regarded as the master workman in the "art of inventing." This has now given place to a far juster estimate that regards him as a straightforward, enterprising business man who is also a man of science—a combined manufacturer, scholar, scientist, workman, mechanic, electrician, and inventor, a student who means business, a man of business in search of knowledge, a very human man who knows what he wants and gets it. What he wants is the inspiration of this closing century. It is all very modern, intensely American.[20]

Echoing the same sentiment in 1908, *The Dial* observed that Edison was "no longer 'the Wizard of Menlo Park,' as he had first been called in 1878, but rather the Indefatigable Inventor of Orange, where his laboratories are now situated . . ."[21]

To understand this shift, an 1894 article on Tesla provides a possible answer. It explained that the "fairy tales of science" had become realities that were initially regarded as "marvelous," but after a period of time became commonplace. "We have long ceased to wonder at [them] because they are so familiar," the author commented.[22] Similarly, Ernest Freeberg writes in *The Age of Edison: Electric Light and the Invention of Modern America*, "As each new invention arrives we take the old ones for granted."[23]

At the same time, new uses for existing discoveries could be found, including investigations into the unknown, even the occult. The electric chair put many to death, but by 1908, the *New York Times* described a backlash against any scientific experiments that attempted to "revive a man executed in the electric chair."[24] This was during the same time period when many scientists sought to prove the existence of the human soul and the afterlife, whether by studying Spiritualistic mediums or conducting experiments of their own, as in Dr. Duncan MacDougall's efforts to measure the weight loss sustained by a body when the soul departs it at the time of death.[25]

To be sure, the nineteenth century was rife with pseudo-sciences, from Mesmerism to phrenology. Similarly, one could classify medical practice in pre-twentieth-century America as either professional or folk, although the boundary between the two was quite porous.[26] Many persons eschewed Native American and African-American medicines as "witchcraft," but still looked favorably upon spurious pursuits like telepathy.[27] This is to say nothing of tonics, pills, and ointments promulgated by "doctors" who traveled in medicine shows.[28]

By way of another example, there was the "peculiar symbiosis," as Robert Crossley has called it, between astronomy and psychical research in the late nineteenth century, as in the case of the study of Mars. He notes that "popular fervor" for the planet often linked it with the paranormal, as in such novels as Camille Flammarion's *Uranie* (1889, translated into English as *Urania* in 1890) and George Du Maurier's *The Martian* (1897).[29] Here one could also cite popular fascination with comets in the early twentieth century, particularly the return of Halley's comet in 1910. Flammarion's predictions of global disaster led to many outcomes, including a cottage industry of anti-comet defenses that included protective umbrellas and pharmaceuticals.[30]

Not surprisingly, numerous authors incorporated pseudo-sciences into their literature. Sometimes the goal was humor, as in the use of phrenology in Mark Twain's *Adventures of Huckleberry Finn* (1885).[31] In other cases, the intention was more serious. Taylor Stoehr has written about the influence of pseudo-science on the works of Nathaniel Hawthorne, for example.[32] Scientists gone wrong appear in *The Birth-Mark* (1843) and *Rappaccini's Daughter* (1844). Emergent pulp fiction also drew upon the scientific zeitgeist, as in the case of Luis Senarens's short stories about boy inventor Frank Reade, Jr. and his robot, Electric Man.[33]

Good or bad, sane or mad, the scientist in nineteenth-century American literature was usually a modern man, rather than, say, the wizard of fairy tales. His ego held true to the maxim *sapere aude*, even when it led him to hazard in pursuits man was meant to leave alone. "How dangerous is the acquirement of knowledge," Victor Frankenstein ponders in Mary Shelley's 1818 novel, "and how much happier that man is who believes his native town to be the world, than he who aspires to be greater than his nature will allow." Not dissimilar is Jekyll in Robert Louis Stevenson's 1886 *Strange Case of Dr. Jekyll and Mr. Hyde*, who says, "With every day, and from both sides of my intelligence, the moral and the intellectual, I thus drew steadily nearer to the truth, by whose partial discovery I have been doomed to such a dreadful shipwreck: that man is not truly one, but truly two."

While Shelley and Stevenson's mad scientists represent the two key paradigms of the nineteenth century, they were not alone, as the literature of Jules Verne and H. G. Wells attests. Experiments undertaken by the title character of Wells's *The Island of Dr. Moreau* (1896) cross a boundary that "should be unassailable," but was not. Here is a clear instance of what Stephen T. Asma has called the "medicalization of monsters."[34] However, despite such examples, it is important to note that the term "mad scientist" itself had no currency in the nineteenth century.[35] It did not appear in any noticeable way until the publication of Raymond McDonald's novel *The Mad Scientist* in 1908.[36]

According to the *New York Times*, *The Mad Scientist* was "supposed to be a warning against allowing persons promiscuously to invent."[37] Its title character wreaks havoc by creating airborne houses and battleships, by causing a man to grow taller and shorter, by burning up all the water in a lake, and by making all machinery in one city halt for sixty minutes. A civil war ensues, with the mad scientist unleashing his "electro-killers" upon the world. The *Boston Herald* called *The Mad Scientist* a "weird" story written in an effort to "outdo Jules Verne in upsetting the public by predicting [the] astounding destructive possibilities of science."[38] The *Houston Chronicle* believed it explained "what a great scientist like Thomas A. Edison . . . might do if he were to lose his wit."[39]

Rather than the quest for knowledge leading to ennoblement, as in Marlowe's *The Tragicall Historie of Doctor Faustus* (1594), the mad scientist is frequently doomed. Christopher P. Toumey notes:

> The mad scientist stories of fiction and film are homilies on the evil of science. Here are modern-day exercises in the tradition of antirationalism, which argues that rationalist science is dangerous to one's spiritual well-being because it is too clinical, too abstract, and that the scientists who control the mysteries of modern secular knowledge are unaccountable to conventional standards of morality.[40]

Venturing into the unknown could bring about disastrous results. Daring to know was perilous.

During the era of early cinema, mad scientists appeared with regularity, though sharp contrasts between them are apparent, particularly in terms of films made by Georges Méliès and Segundo de Chomón, and those American filmmakers who opted for a different approach. "Méliès's scientists may sometimes work at the cutting edge of technology, but they are really latter-day alchemists or wizards," Christopher Frayling observes.[41] His comment is apt, particularly in consideration of the style of costumes and laboratory props (or painted backgrounds, as the case might be) that Méliès employed in such moving pictures as *The Mysterious Retort/ L'alchimiste Parafaragamus ou la cornue infernale* (1906).[42]

Indeed, one can witness clear distinctions between the men of science in Méliès's *A Trip to the Moon/ Le voyage dans la lune* (1902) and Segundo de Chomón's *A Trip to Jupiter/ Voyage sur Jupiter* (Pathé Frères, 1909), as opposed to those in Edison's *A Trip to Mars* (1910) and Biograph's *A Message from the Moon* (1912).[43] American filmmakers tended to make their inventors and professors appear similar to Edison and Tesla. Images of the two were common in the late nineteenth and early twentieth centuries, whether as engravings or photographs. Edison's likeness even appeared in such moving pictures as *Inventor Edison Sketched by World Artist* (Edison, 1896) and *Mr. Edison at Work in His*

Chemical Laboratory (Edison, 1897).[44] In the latter, Edison wears a white lab coat amid test tubes, his appearance similar to that of the mad scientists in later Hollywood films.

Despite their visual differences, *A Trip to the Moon* and *A Trip to Mars* share a comedic tone, transforming scientists and their obsessive pursuits into a source of humor. Méliès regularly employed such comedy, as in the case of *The Impossible Voyage/ Le voyage á travers l'impossible* (1904), *The Inventor Crazybrains and his Wonderful Airship/ Le dirigeable fantastique ou le Cauchemar d'un inventeur* (1905), and *The Conquest of the Pole/À la conquête du pôle* (1912). American-made films like *How the Professor Fooled the Burglars* (Edison, 1901) and *Inventions of an Idiot* (Lubin, 1909) appropriated the same sense of humor.[45]

Onscreen, the mad scientist of the early cinema period thus transitioned from being alchemist to chemist, from wizard to inventor, in a manner not unlike press descriptions of Edison. So too did his scientific apparatus. In Vitagraph's *Liquid Electricity: or, The Inventor's Galvanic Fluid* (1907), the professor works in his laboratory "amid test tubes, retorts, and complicated electrical appliances."[46] The following year, *Dr. Skinum* (American Mutoscope & Biograph, 1907) toils in what the *Moving Picture World* called a modern "*chambre mysterieux* [sic]."[47]

During and after the nickelodeon era, many American moving pictures eschewed Méliès, preferring instead to offer dramatic depictions of scientists clothed in then-modern apparel and working in then-modern laboratories. Some of these scientists were not at all insane; in fact, a number of nonfiction films showed real doctors performing actual surgeries.[48] And a number of fictional films of the period featured brilliant men whose inventions were at risk of being stolen by evil criminals.[49]

But in other cases, as this chapter will explore, the scientists were themselves crazed or evil or both. They took risks, with their own lives and with the lives of others. When they weren't the source of humor, they held the potential to horrify, particularly in a number of important films adapted from or influenced by the literature of Mary Shelley and Robert Louis Stevenson.

Pseudo-science

Moving picture narratives regularly explored nineteenth-century pseudo-sciences, including—as discussed in Chapter 12—Mesmerism. Phrenology provided the basis for such comedies as *The Phrenologist* (Powers, 1910), *The Sage-brush Phrenologist* (American, 1911), and *With the Aid of Phrenology* (Biograph, 1913).[50] And dramatic films like *Doctor Maxwell's Experiment* (Lubin, 1913, aka *Dr. Maxwell's Experiment*) and *The Surgeon's Experiment* (Majestic, 1914) featured scientists performing fantastical operations on criminals to liberate them of their criminal tendencies.[51]

Mad doctors performed many crazy surgeries in early films, as in the case of *A Quick Recovery* (American Mutoscope & Biograph, 1901), in which a doctor cuts the head off his daughter's lover.[52] When she places it back on the lover's shoulders, he "comes to life and kisses her."[53] Two years later, Méliès released *Up-to-Date Surgery/Une indigestion* (1902, aka *Dr. Lorenz Outdone*). In it, a surgeon saws off a patient's arms and legs before removing various objects from his stomach cavity. Once the operation is over, the doctor puts the man back together, but "in his hurry a leg is placed where an arm should be, and vice versa."[54]

In 1906, Vitagraph released J. Stuart Blackton's film *And the Villain Still Pursued Her* (aka *And the Villain Still Pursued Her; or, The Author's Dream*). Here was yet another comedy, one advertised as a "ton of fun."[55] In particular, it parodies the melodrama genre, structured with the framing story of a writer who falls asleep at his desk. During his dream, the heroine spurns the villain's romantic advances in favor of the writer. The two men duel with pistols, the villain shooting the writer in the head. The heroine performs surgery by first sawing and then screwing into the writer's skull. She removes the bullet and hammers a spike into his head to fill the hole.[56]

In other cases, bizarre operations appeared in dramatic films. In *Sinews of the Dead/ La main de l'autre* (Gaston Méliès, 1914), a doctor "grafts new flesh and muscle" onto a patient who has suffered a hand injury. The man soon learns the doctor obtained the flesh from the "arm of a murderer who died on the scaffold for strangling a woman. This thought preys upon his mind and he goes insane. He spends the rest of his life in an asylum."[57] *Moving Picture World* responded: "A more harrowing conception than the theme of this picture could hardly be dug up. It is illogical, disgusting, and not deserving of further comment, except that it is well-acted, directed, and photographed."[58]

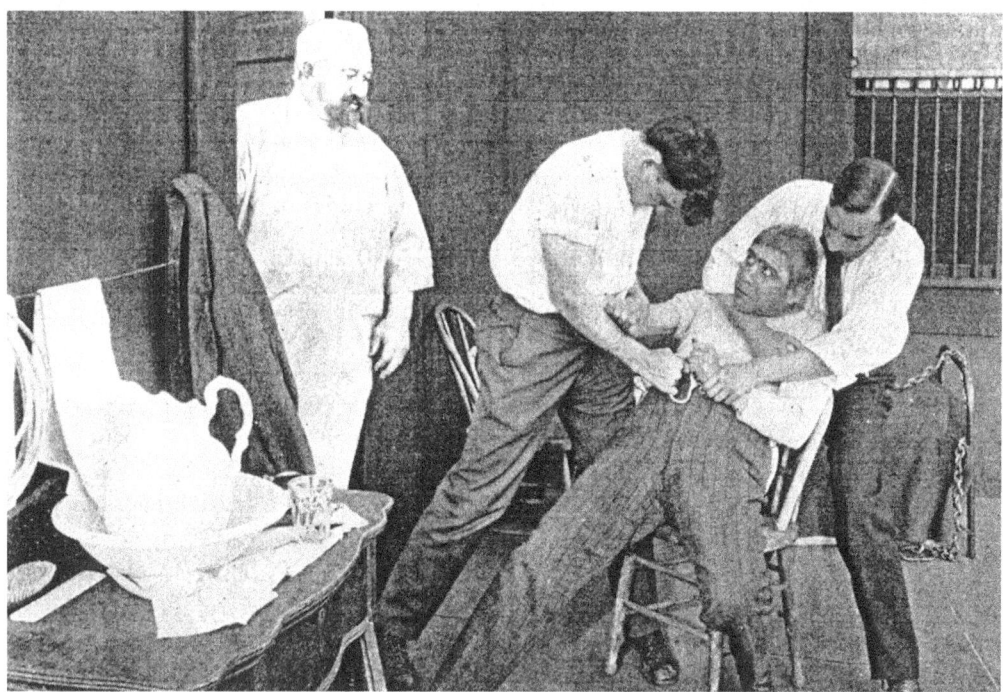

Figure 13.1 *The Vivisectionist* (Kalem, 1915).

Kalem's 1915 film *The Vivisectionist* covered similar narrative ground. In it, screams emanate from Dr. Jardine's house. On his operating table lies a man being held against his own will. Jardine intends to "sever" the man's right arm and "transpose it to the body of his brother, who had lost his arm in an accident."⁵⁹ *Moving Picture World* believed the film achieved an "unusual suspense," and *Motion Picture News* called it a "story out of the ordinary run, with good acting and excellent photography."⁶⁰

These stories culminated in Vitagraph's five-reel feature *Mortmain* (1915), directed by Theodore Marston and starring Robert Edeson in the title role. Marguerite Bertsch's script adapted Arthur Train's 1907 novel of the same name, though *Moving Picture World* and the *New York Clipper* compared the film to the works of Edgar Allan Poe.⁶¹ Lead character Mortmain injures his hand. A surgeon performs an amputation and grafts on a replacement, one that belonged to a murderer. As a result of his new, telltale fingerprints, Mortmain is to be arrested, but then comes out of an anesthetic, the wild tale merely the product of an hallucination.⁶² *Motion Picture News* praised the film as being "uncanny, weird, tremendously startling, and ever increasing in interest with each successive scene."⁶³ *Moving Picture World* added:

> By ghostly light effects in atmospheric settings, and expressive acting that conveys the meaning without spoiling the illusion by disclosing too much, the hidden horror that everyone feels but cannot explain is worked up with consummate skill. And then we are told it was all a dream. This is the one artistic mistake in the picture, due, of course, to the prevalent belief that the public must have a happy ending. It seems, however, as if the concession might have been avoided in a story of this caliber.⁶⁴

As *Variety* observed, the film's "grewsome [sic]" and "repulsive" elements were "wiped out" by a happy ending: the entire story was just a dream.⁶⁵

In other cases, pseudo-science onscreen intersected directly with the occult. Eclair American's three-reel film *From the Beyond* (1913) featured Professor Lodge, who

Figure 13.2 *From the Beyond* (Eclair American, 1913).

hopes to photograph an apparition during one of his daughter's séances.[66] Using his "specially-constructed apparatus," the professor succeeds in capturing an image of Abraham Lincoln's ghost.[67] When a senior professor unethically attacks the veracity of his work, Lodge seeks to improve his reputation with a new experiment: locking himself in a sarcophagus for one month using a "Hindoo" method of suspended animation. After four weeks, during which time his "astral body" has haunted the senior professor, Lodge returns to life with the help of his daughter.[68] "The story is not to be considered seriously," *Moving Picture World* wrote, "though it is well pictured and clearly presented.... Double photography is employed to bring about [Lodge's] ghostly visits."[69]

A related narrative was Frank M. Wiltermood's scenario for *The Human Soul* (Balboa, 1914), which told of an "inventor who has constructed a wondrously powerful photographic camera, the lens and plates of which were of great size and sensitive enough to photograph even the smallest molecules that float in the atmosphere."[70] When the inventor's wife is unfaithful, he injects her with cyanide and photographs her departing soul. *Variety* deemed it a "gruesome subject for a sketch."[71] *Moving Picture World* admitted that aspects of *The Human Soul* were "startling," but still condemned its narrative for being "trashy."[72]

The Changing of Souls/Sjælebytning (Great Northern, 1908) humorously depicted a professor who uses hypnosis to trade his soul into the body of a student and vice versa.[73] In 1914, Victor released *A Dangerous Experiment*, in which a student "interested in the occult ... transfers his soul into the body of an athlete and forces the athlete's soul into his own."[74] The following year, Kalem's two-reel drama *The Secret Room* (1915) found Tom Moore (who also directed) playing a "crystal gazing doctor" who keeps his "imbecile" son locked in a room. He encounters a suicidal man and they make a business contract, in which the doctor will use hypnosis to transfer the man's soul into the body of his own son. The suicidal man breaks their pact, but the mad doctor proceeds until learning his son has died; returning to his senses, the doctor releases the man from his control. The *New York Dramatic Mirror* wrote, "Not only is this a strange story, but it is well presented where the slightest fault would send it to decided obscurity. Its mysticism is its silent hold, while the artistry of Director Moore is the outward evidence of much care and beauty."[75]

Rather than dabbling in surgery or hypnosis, some scientists concocted new serums, medicines, and elixirs in a manner not unlike Dr. Jekyll. Most of these moving pictures were comedies, as in the case of Lubin's 305-foot *Prof. Wise's Brain Serum Injector* (1909, aka *Professor Weise's Brain-Serum Injector*).[76] In *The Dream Pill* (Lubin, 1910), Professor Swank invents a cure for nightmares.[77] Other men of science created *The Elixir of Strength/L'élixir d'énergie* (Pathé Frères, 1907, aka *The Elixir of Life*) and *The Elixir of Bravery/L'élixir de bravoure* (Eclair, 1911).[78] Love drugs appeared in *The Love Microbe* (American Mutoscope & Biograph, 1907), *Professor's Love Tonic* (Essanay, 1909), and *Ham and the Experiment* (Kalem, 1915).[79] And the title chemical in *A Wonderful Fluid/La sève artificielle* (Pathé Frères, 1908, aka *Wonderful Fluid*) humorously causes immediate growth wherever it is applied, restoring leaves to dead bushes and hair to bald men.[80]

The power to become invisible appeared in a number of moving pictures of the period, all of them influenced to some degree by H. G. Wells's novel *The Invisible Man* (1897). A notable example is *The Invisible Men/Les invisibles* (Pathé Frères, 1906). In it, a scientist concocts a solution that makes whomever drinks it disappear from view. Two thieves steal the formula from his laboratory, where they witness a few phantasmagorical events transpire, including a skeleton that flies apart and dances. The duo then use the solution to steal clothes and food before returning to the lab, whereupon the scientist and his assistant are arrested for crimes they didn't commit.[81]

Other examples include *The Invisible Thief/Le voleur invisible* (Pathé Frères, 1909, aka *Invisible Thief*), in which the narrative explicitly references H. G. Wells, as well as *The Invisible Wrestler/Le lutteur invisible* (Lux, 1911).[82] Starring D. W. Griffith, Eddie Dillon, and Mack Sennett, Wallace McCutcheon's 662-foot *The Invisible Fluid* (American Mutoscope & Biograph, 1908) features an "erudite scientist" who creates a "mysterious fluid."[83] A boy has all manner of "fun" with an atomizer of the liquid, which helps him to steal a cash register and evade the police.[84]

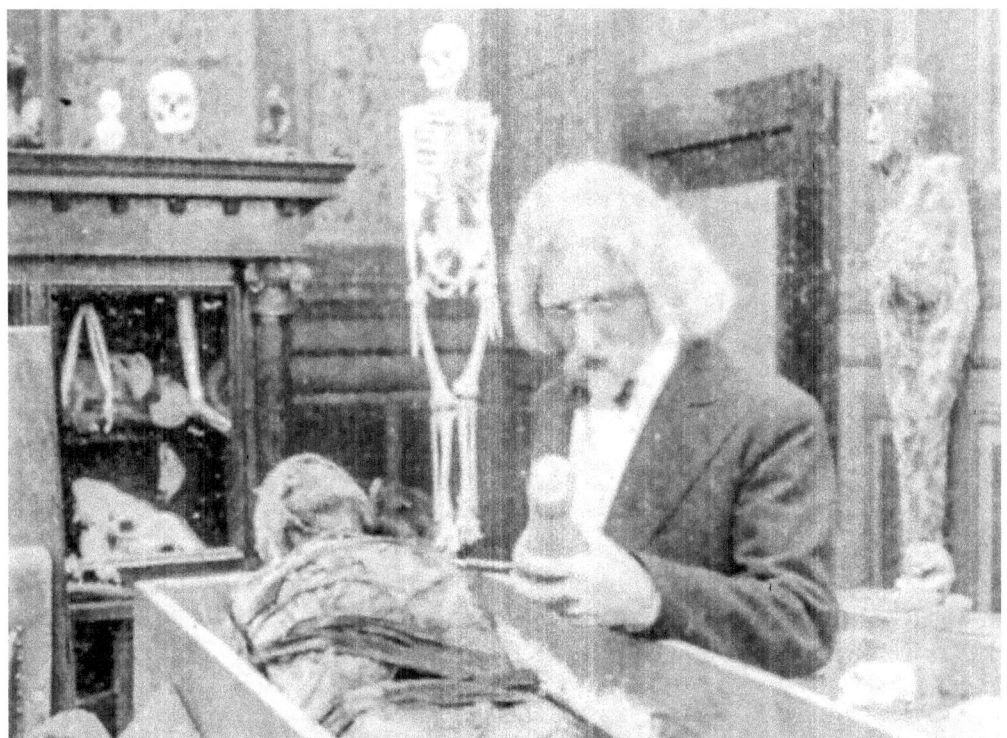

Figure 13.3 *If I Were Young Again* (Selig Polyscope, 1914).

Drawing upon the mythos of the fountain of youth and such literature as Hawthorne's *Dr. Heidegger's Experiment* (1837), various onscreen potions held the power to restore characters to their earlier years, including *The Elixir of Life* (Williamson, 1903), *Dr. Brompton Watts' Age Adjuster* (Edison, 1912), *The Elixir of Youth* (Powers, 1913), and *Professor Oldboy's Rejuvenator* (Kalem, 1914).[85] Selig Polyscope's two-reel drama *If I Were Young Again* (1914) addressed the subject in a different manner, with its scientist discovering a youth-restoring vial inside an Egyptian mummy sarcophagus that arrives at his museum. As opposed to using the potion on the mummy (in the tradition of those mummy films described in Chapter 8), the professor experiments on himself and experiences nothing but trouble. Having learned his lesson, he destroys the elixir and returns to his elder age "at the next moon."[86]

Dr. Jekyll and Mr. Hyde

In 1908, Selig Polyscope announced, "The play [*Dr. Jekyll and Mr. Hyde*] itself is known to every man, woman, and child, while its dramatic supremacy has brought it before the world with universal popularity."[87] Its reach extended not only to literature and stage, but also to the recording industry. In 1908, Columbia Records released a phonograph record of actor Len Spencer performing the *Transformation Scene* from *Dr. Jekyll and Mr. Hyde* with sound effects and orchestral accompaniment.[88]

On a number of occasions, moving picture companies and critics compared characters in dramatic films to Jekyll and Hyde, even when they had dual personalities not caused by scientific experimentation. Examples include *Mystery of the Mountains/Le mystère de la montagne* (Pathé Frères, 1908), *Power of the Cross* (Nestor, 1912), *The Wayward Sister* (Rex, 1913), *The Curious Conduct of Judge Legarde* (Life Photo Film, 1915), and the early Douglas Fairbanks vehicle *Double Trouble* (Fine Arts, 1915).[89] More blatant, at least in terms of its title, was *A Modern Jekyll and Hyde* (Kalem, 1914), during which a respected citizen spends part of his time leading a "desperate gang of criminals."[90]

Vitagraph approached the subject matter in a similar manner, but did so by changing the gender of the lead character. In three reels, the company's "psychic drama" *Miss Jekyll and Madame Hyde* (1915) presented Helen Gardner in the title roles. A company synopsis told readers: "Just imagine a young girl stepping from the quiet seclusion of the convent into her father's luxurious home and the conventional life of the world, and you will have a picture of Madeline Jekyll."[91] To save her father from financial disgrace, Madeline agrees to marry a horrible man named Daggerts, after which she dreams that the way to avert his attentions is to become "hard, sophisticated, and reckless." Once she awakens, Madeline learns that Daggerts has "drop[ped] dead from heart failure," the result of a plot twist in which he learned his partner was actually Satan in disguise.[92] The *New York Dramatic Mirror* believed the film was "very ineffective," being a "hodge podge of conglomerate nothingness."[93]

Stevenson's popular story also provided impetus for a small number of comedies. A character in Selig Polyscope's trick film *A Modern Dr. Jekyll* (1909) obtains a "magic liquid" from an "old recluse scientist" that allows the user to "transform himself instantly into another appearance."[94] *Dr. Jekyll and Mr. Hyde Done to a Frazzle* (Warner's Superba Comedy, 1914) was allegedly a "fun" burlesque because of the "sheer nonsense of it all."[95] And Lubin's *Horrible Hyde* (1915) features an actor who is scared of his landlady; their relationship reverses when she sees him in his Mr. Hyde make-up, which he dons for a local stage adaptation.[96] But when she learns the truth, the tables turn yet again.[97]

The first direct adaptation of Stevenson's tale appeared in March 1908. At 1,035 feet, Selig Polyscope's *Dr. Jekyll and Mr. Hyde* presented the key points of the narrative, the company's publicity claiming it ranked among the "foremost interpretations of moving pictures."[98] However, one theatre manager argued, "The spectators cannot follow the plot, and therefore they lose interest."[99] Worse still, a United States Circuit Court ruled in May 1908 that film adaptations of plays constituted "pantomimes, and, therefore, theatre productions."[100] According to an article in *The Billboard*, moving pictures like Selig's *Dr. Jekyll and Mr. Hyde*—which was specifically named—violated the law unless their manufacturers paid royalties to the copyright holders.[101]

That decision also likely had an impact on a "Broadway theatrical firm" that was "making preparation for the production of a repertoire of modern plays by means of moving pictures and phonograph attachment."[102] Here the reference was perhaps to the moving picture department of Keith & Proctor, whose director claimed in late March or early April 1908 that he had found "success" by presenting a "reduced version of *Dr. Jekyll and Mr. Hyde*" by use of the "cinematograph."[103] His exhibition may well have been nothing more than a screening of the Selig film, which was already in release. In any event, the director intended shortly to "combine the cinematograph with the phonograph."[104]

The "Broadway theatrical firm" in question might instead have been a reference to the American Theatrephone Company (sometimes spelled "Theaterphone"), which was based in New York City. In May 1908, the company purported its "new mechanical device," the Theatrephone, had "finally been perfected."[105] The result meant "moving and talking pictures," thanks to a phonograph hidden behind a stage curtain. Sound was thus synchronized to the onscreen image. To maintain narrative flow, the device was "contrived" such that it automatically shifted from one record player to another. At the end of each act, the "regular curtain of the theatre [was] dropped for intermission exactly as during a regular performance."[106]

An article in *Moving Picture World* claimed Theatrephone demonstrations had successfully occurred in New York City and Boston. The same article listed *Dr. Jekyll and Mr. Hyde* as being among the productions "already prepared," but did not mention if it had been exhibited.[107] A few weeks later, *The Billboard* noted in future tense that *Dr. Jekyll and Mr. Hyde* would be "presented," but—in a subsequent paragraph—repeated *Moving Picture World*'s language that it was "already prepared."[108] In June 1908, *Talking Machine World* also reported the film had been completed.[109] If so, exhibition of it might have been hampered due to the aforementioned judicial edict. At any rate, no evidence of public screenings has surfaced.

By contrast, it is clear that Great Northern released a version of the tale in September 1910. Titled *Dr. Jekyll and Mr. Hyde; or, a Strange Case/Den skæbnesvangre opfindelse*, the film opens with Jekyll in his laboratory showing his potion to a number of friends. When Jekyll falls asleep, the story unfolds as a nightmare from which he later safely awakens. *Moving Picture World* praised the narrative approach for being a "very ingenious way of putting this drama before the young people and the various 'Boards of Censorship.'"[110] The trade also drew attention to the film's acting and "technical" merits, ending with the declaration, "We think it is quite the best representation of *Dr. Jekyll and Mr. Hyde* that we have ever seen, either in moving pictures or on the stage."[111]

Then, in January 1912, Thanhouser released its own version of *Dr. Jekyll and Mr. Hyde*.[112] James Cruze, later a noted film director, portrayed the title roles in what the company touted as a "psychological subject."[113] As a surviving copy shows, the film begins in a unique manner, with a close-up of a book page about the good and evil

Figure 13.4 Double-exposed publicity still of Alwin Neuss as the title characters in *Dr. Jekyll and Mr. Hyde; or, a Strange Case* (Great Northern, 1910). (*Courtesy of Robert J. Kiss*)

present in men, before proceeding to present Jekyll in a laboratory, imbibing his dangerous concoction.[114] After clutching at his throat, an edit allows Jekyll to transform into Hyde. With his hideous teeth, darkened features, and his hunched back, Hyde resembles not only his stage forbears, but also some nineteenth-century depictions of primitive man. While theatrical, the make-up is striking, aided greatly by Cruze's expert performance, which includes a wonderful medium shot of Hyde's hand clasping a bottle of poison during its climactic scene.

Contemporary reviews were largely positive. "Nothing that has been recently released has impressed me any more strongly than this wonderful picture, and . . . I feel that I must speak of it," praised *Moving Picture News*.[115] After calling it a "remarkable portrayal," *Moving Picture World* judged the Thanhouser version to be "more effective" than its cinematic predecessors.[116] And the *New York Dramatic Mirror* observed, "The cleverness with which this weird tale . . . has been adapted . . . is admirable and makes a wonderfully gripping film of dramatic intensity and interest."[117]

Just over one year later, Imp released Herbert Brenon's *Dr. Jekyll and Mr. Hyde* (1913) as a two-reeler, though some advertisements claimed it was three reels.[118] King Baggot portrays the "dual roles," with a dissolve transition conveying his initial transformation. Like Cruze, Baggot dons make-up and a hunched stance similar to that used on the stage, though his make-up is less pronounced (and arguably less horrifying) than Cruze's. Nevertheless, the film's medium shot of Hyde peering through a window and its medium long shot of Jekyll convulsing in a darkened room remain striking images.[119] Given its extended running time, Imp's version also allows more opportunities to depict Hyde's crimes, which include the beating of a young boy and the harassment of women.

Moving Picture World heralded King Baggot's acting as "masterly."[120] *Moving Picture News* told readers the actor had "acquitted himself wonderfully well."[121] The *New York Dramatic Mirror* agreed, but complained the overall film had too many problems to "enthuse over it." For one, the trade believed this version was too long. Its review added: "Some of the photography is not of the best, and some of the studio settings could be improved."[122]

While Imp's version became the most prominent of 1913, it was not alone. The New York-based Kinemacolor Company of America produced *Dr. Jekyll and Mr. Hyde* the same

Figure 13.5 M. J. McQuarrie in the title roles of *Dr. Jekyll and Mr. Hyde* (Kinemacolor, 1913), as featured on the cover of *Moving Picture News*.

year. Frank E. Woods directed and M. J. McQuarrie starred in the dual role.[123] The *New York Clipper* called it a "masterpiece"; the *New York Dramatic Mirror* lauded its acting, the "gruesomeness" of its transformations, and its "realism of color."[124] Though Kinemacolor's was the last new film adaptation of the story to appear on American screens during the early cinema period, Universal did reissue Herbert Brenon's version in 1915.[125]

Creators and Creations

Rather than mixing chemical compounds, many film scientists attempted to create mechanical inventions by modern means, thus following in the tradition of Edison and Tesla. For example, *The Reader of Minds* (Thanhouser, 1914) features an invention that can translate the innermost thoughts of characters and visually illuminate them on a screen.[126] A villain in the serial *Zudora* (Thanhouser, 1914–15) develops a "powerful machine which absorbs and sends out the rays of the sun for his purposes."[127] Even worse was the "Clutching Hand" in *The Exploits of Elaine* (Pathé, 1914–15), who creates a death ray that can "disintegrate anything with which it comes in contact."[128]

These scientists often relied on electricity, including in a number of comedies. The professor in *The Wonderful Electro Magnet* (Edison, 1909) invents a "contrivance" that magnetically draws people to it.[129] In *The House That Went Crazy* (Selig Polyscope, 1914), "Professor Nutt" builds a home in which "everything is mechanical and runs by electricity."[130] Other men of science used electric currents to charge people with renewed energy, as in the aforementioned *Liquid Electricity, or The Inventor's Galvanic Fluid*, in which a chemist creates the "very spirit of life."[131] Then, in that film's "continuation," *Galvanic Fluid: or, More Fun with Liquid Electricity* (Vitagraph, 1908), "Professor Watt" sprays various persons with his high-voltage solution, all for the sake of comedy.[132]

Instead of increasing the pace of living persons, other inventors tried to imbue inanimate matter with life.[133] In *Living Dolls/Les poupées vivantes* (Pathé Frères, 1909, directed by Segundo de Chomón), *Oh! You Unbreakable Doll/L'automate incassable* (Lux, 1913), and *The Scientist's Doll* (Thanhouser, 1914), humans comically take the place of the dolls that inventors are attempting to bring to life.[134] Then, in *The Mechanical Man* (Joker, 1915), Professor Shultz constructs a robot that can sing and dance. He sells it for $20,000, but a janitor accidentally breaks the robot before it is delivered to its new owner. As a result, the janitor pretends to be the mechanical man until Shultz can make the needed repairs.[135]

Tales of life bestowed upon the lifeless also appeared in dramatic moving pictures. In *The Return of Maurice Donnelly* (Vitagraph, 1915), the title character is falsely accused and put to death in the electric chair. While waiting to identify the corpse of her client, Donnelly's attorney Edith

> remembers reading of a scientist's successful resuscitation of dead animals and his desire to try the experiment on the human body. She communicates with him, secures his consent, and by special permission the prison physician delivers the body to the Donnelly home without performing an autopsy. The experiment is performed; it is successful . . .[136]

After having shown "high tension electricity" bringing a rabbit back to life, a "tremendous voltage" restores life to Donnelly. The *New York Dramatic Mirror* claimed the scene was "without doubt the best part of the play, for good lighting effects make the intense spark . . ."[137]

Figure 13.6 The scientist (Alec B. Francis) in *Lola* (World Film Corporation, 1914) stands beside his "machine for restoring animation."

As *Moving Picture World* told readers in 1915, "Everyone is familiar with the weird tale of *Frankenstein*."[138] The novel's popularity led to the production of two films clearly inspired by it. In the autumn of 1914, the World Film Corporation adapted Owen Davis's 1911 Broadway play *Lola* into a five-reel moving picture.[139] Accompanying *Lola* on its release was Davis's novelization, published with photos from the film.[140] In the movie, a scientist uses an electrical apparatus to revivify a corpse.[141] As the *New York Dramatic Mirror* reported:

For his first World Film Corporation production, Director James Young was given, or perhaps selected, an odd story. . . . He stepped into the domain of the supernatural and there found a doctor with a marvelous invention capable of restoring life, provided it was applied in time—the time limit being a few hours after the heart has ceased to beat. But, unfortunately, the restoration of a departed soul did not enter the doctor's calculations. And what, after all, is a body without a soul? No doubt it may be any one of a number of things not nearly so interesting as the soulless Lola as . . . portrayed by Clara Kimball Young. Lola, deprived of her soul, becomes a very wicked woman and to make matters worse she is more than ever beautiful and enticing after the divorce of soul and body. She is a fierce little wolf disguised in the prettiest of sheep's clothing.[142]

At the film's climax, as Lola is dying a second time, the doctor intends to restore her life once again. But knowing the wickedness of her soulless ways, Lola's father convinces the doctor to let her find peace in the afterlife.[143]

The Billboard admired *Lola*'s direction, cinematography, and locations.[144] The *New York Dramatic Mirror* praised Young's "convincing suggestion of sensuous feeling, for women of the erotic type are not often included in the repertoire of this very wholesome actress."[145] "Tragic though the story is," *Motion Picture News* wrote, "it is so unconventional that it is pleasant to see."[146] However, *Variety* may have been the most insightful, comparing the character Lola to Dr. Jekyll and Mr. Hyde while also dubbing her a "Lady Frankenstein."[147]

On December 4, 1914, only days after *Lola* first appeared on theatre screens, Thanhouser released *Naidra, The Dream Woman*. The one-reel film features a scientist who discovers the "secret of artificially creating life" in the pages of an old alchemical book.[148] He makes a "beautiful woman" who is "wholly incapable of giving or receiving love" until she meets a young organist.[149] The scientist is "filled with grief" at the outcome, but then awakens to learn all that has transpired has only been a dream.[150] Naidra (portrayed by Mignon Anderson) never actually existed. "The acting is good," *Moving Picture World* wrote, "and [the film] has many poetical and very pleasing pictures. It may be called an artistic offering."[151]

Imp released *The Eleventh Dimension* in 1915, something of a two-reel variation on *Frankenstein*, featuring an "insane chemist who tries to kill a man and then restore life."[152] As a company synopsis indicated:

> The electric furnace is at white heat. All the test tubes are laid out and retorts cast their reflections around. [The old professor] transfers a few drops of liquor from one tube into another and a pale blue smoke arises—a flash—and to his distorted brain appears the image of a large cat. His hoarse cry of "success at last" is heard by [his daughter], who has crept from her bed and now stands at the open door of the laboratory. The terrible light in his eyes tells her that his brain has at last given way and, frightened, she closes the door.[153]

One of the key scenes in this "startling" drama involved the "crazy old scientist" playing a game of chess for his friend's life.[154]

Frankenstein

Automatons not unlike Frankenstein's monster appeared in numerous early films, including *The Mechanical Doll* (Edison, 1901), *The Mechanical Statue and the Ingenious Servant* (Vitagraph, 1906), and *The Doll's Revenge* (Hepworth, 1907), the latter released in the United States by Williams, Brown & Earle.[155] In it, a boy destroys his sister's mechanical doll. Thanks to stop motion, the "parts come together again and the doll grows in alarming proportions. Another doll appears on the scene and the two pull the little boy to pieces and eat him."[156]

Despite its popularity, however, a direct adaptation of Shelley's novel did not appear onscreen until *Frankenstein* (Edison, 1910). J. Searle Dawley, who had made his first appearance as an actor in a stage version of *Faust*, was director for the Edison Manufacturing Company's production. In 1912, the *Edison Kinetogram* wrote:

It was five years ago that Mr. Dawley first associated himself with the Edison Studio, and he is now the general stage director. During that time he has written no less than one hundred and fifty photoplays, among which are numbered many of the greatest films which the Company has produced. . . . A highly developed artistic sense, an infallible dramatic perception, an eye trained in perspective, and a strong personality, combine to make Mr. Dawley invaluable in producing large spectacular plays . . .[157]

Dawley himself once mentioned that his attraction to the cinema was a form of "picture-lust" that had its roots in the magic lantern shows he saw as a child.[158]

Portraying Dr. Frankenstein was Augustus Phillips, whose successful stage career as a leading man included roles ranging "from Uncle Tom to Othello and Svengali."[159] While at Edison, Phillips appeared in *The Ghost of Granleigh* (1913) and *The Haunted Bedroom* (1913). Mary Fuller—who also appeared in such films as *Bluebeard* (Edison, 1909), *The House of the Seven Gables* (Edison, 1910), *The Ghost's Warning* (Edison, 1911), and *The Witch Girl* (1914)—played Frankenstein's betrothed.

In the pivotal role of the monster was Charles Ogle. As a young man, he had originally planned to be a minister, but, like Phillips and Dawley, Ogle was drawn to the stage, where he established himself as a dependable character actor.[160] With black hair and black eyes, Ogle cut an impressive figure at six feet two inches.[161] After spending approximately two months at Biograph, his career at Edison began in 1908, where he would appear in such films as the aforementioned *Bluebeard*, *The Ghost of Granleigh*, and *The Witch Girl*. In 1914, *Moving Picture World* recounted that Ogle had "done every kind of a role for the camera from the character to the heavy and lead."[162]

Edison's publicity promised the company's "liberal adaptation" of Shelley's novel was "the most absorbing 'silent drama' ever produced."[163] The *Edison Kinetogram* explained that

> . . . we have carefully ommited [sic] anything which might by any possibility shock any portion of an audience. To those who are not familiar with the story we can only say that the film tells an intensely dramatic story by the aid of some of the most remarkable photographic effects that have yet been attempted. The formation of the hideous monster from the blazing chemicals of a huge cauldron in Frankenstein's laboratory is probably the most wierd [sic], mystifying and fascinating scene ever shown on a film.[164]

Running 975 feet in length, *Frankenstein* was released to theatres on March 18, 1910.[165]

Though limited in number, the bulk of the critical response to the landmark film was positive. Consider the following:

> As may well be imagined, this deeply impressive story makes a powerful film subject, and the Edison players have handled it with effective expression and skill. The scene where Frankenstein produces the monster is particularly well done, although a bit too long drawn out. . . . The spirit of the tale is well preserved.—*New York Dramatic Mirror*[166]

> [*Frankenstein* is] vividly and sympathetically acted, holding the interest throughout the film. The formation of the monster in that cauldron of blazing chemicals is a piece of photographic work which will rank with the best of its kind. The entire film is one that will create a new impression of the possibilities of the motion picture as a means of expressing dramatic scenes. —*Moving Picture World*[167]

The Nickelodeon argued that the staging of the monster's creation was "unsatisfactory" and "grotesque."[168] And the trade believed Phillips's acting was "lacking" in the scene after Frankenstein's experiment is successful. However, its review also mentioned that the overall film was "excellently staged" and "vastly more pleasing than the original story."[169]

A surviving copy of Dawley's *Frankenstein* makes clear why the critical response was largely favorable. Though the majority of the films discussed in this book are lost, *Frankenstein* ranks as one of the most impressive of the survivors, particularly of those produced in the United States. Its streamlined narrative positions Frankenstein as a student who leaves his father and sweetheart to pursue his studies, an approach not unlike so many American stories of the nineteenth century in which the young man departs from home in order to achieve success elsewhere.

After two years pass, Frankenstein unlocks the secrets of life and death. He believes his experiment will create the "most perfect human being" who ever lived, but—in a plot point that suggests the influence of such pseudo-sciences as Mesmerism and telepathy—the "evil" in his mind causes the resulting creature to be a monster. In visual composition that recalls Fuseli's *The Nightmare* (1781) and Burne-Jones's *The Vampire* (1897), the monster menaces Frankenstein while he sleeps in his bed. "Love" eventually causes the monster to disappear, with Frankenstein left staring at himself in a mirror. The film suggests the monster is a kind of doppelgänger, the incarnation of Frankenstein's dark side, a theme that borrows from Stevenson's *Strange Case of Dr. Jekyll and Mr. Hyde* and Poe's *William Wilson* (1839).

The creation scene remains the highlight of the film, one that—perhaps ironically, given Thomas Edison's own inventions—eschews electricity in favor of chemistry. Using a cauldron, Frankenstein creates the monster by use of a potion. While Frankenstein watches through an opening in a door in another room, the monster slowly forms in the unholy brew. As its flaming appearance becomes skeletal, the monster's right arm eerily moves. Then, after a cut to Frankenstein in the adjacent room, the horrifying monster appears more fully formed, with both of its arms lurching up and down.

When the locked door opens and the monster's hand and arm appear, Charles Ogle's monster gropes towards his creator. His make-up remains as effective as the creation scene. A notice in the *New York Clipper* described him as a "hideous monster of colossal, unshapely proportions and most frightful mien."[170] Lumbering with a hunched gait, the monster's face is ugly and his hair wild. His frightening appearance is at once distinctive, meaning in terms of prior cinema, and familiar, meaning that the creature looks as if he could have easily been one of P. T. Barnum's exhibits, featuring as he does a familiarly human component—a remnant or an echo of the Self—that had been so key to earlier monsters and freaks.

Five years after the Edison version, the Ocean Film Corporation chose Shelley's *Frankenstein* as the subject matter for its inaugural project. Director Joseph W. Smiley was another who had begun his career as a stage actor, though by 1915 he was best known for his work as a director at Lubin.[171] Jesse J. Goldburg, Ocean's Vice-President and General Manager, adapted Shelley's novel into what became a five-reel feature. In so doing, Goldburg not only altered the title from *Frankenstein* to *Life Without Soul*, but also changed the character names: Victor Frankenstein became "Victor Frawley."

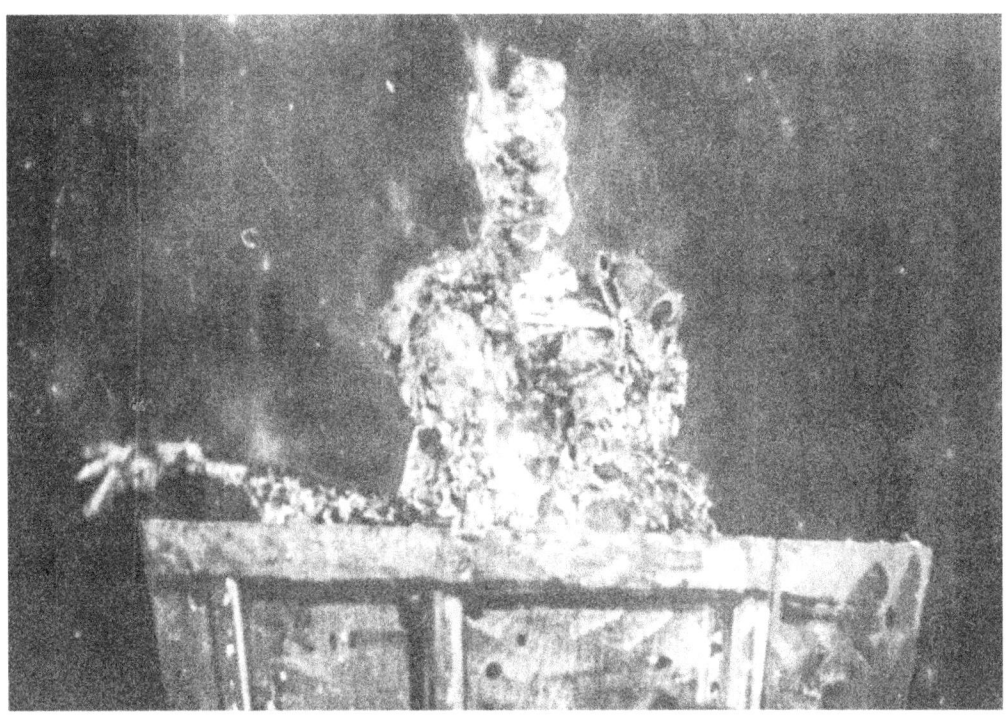

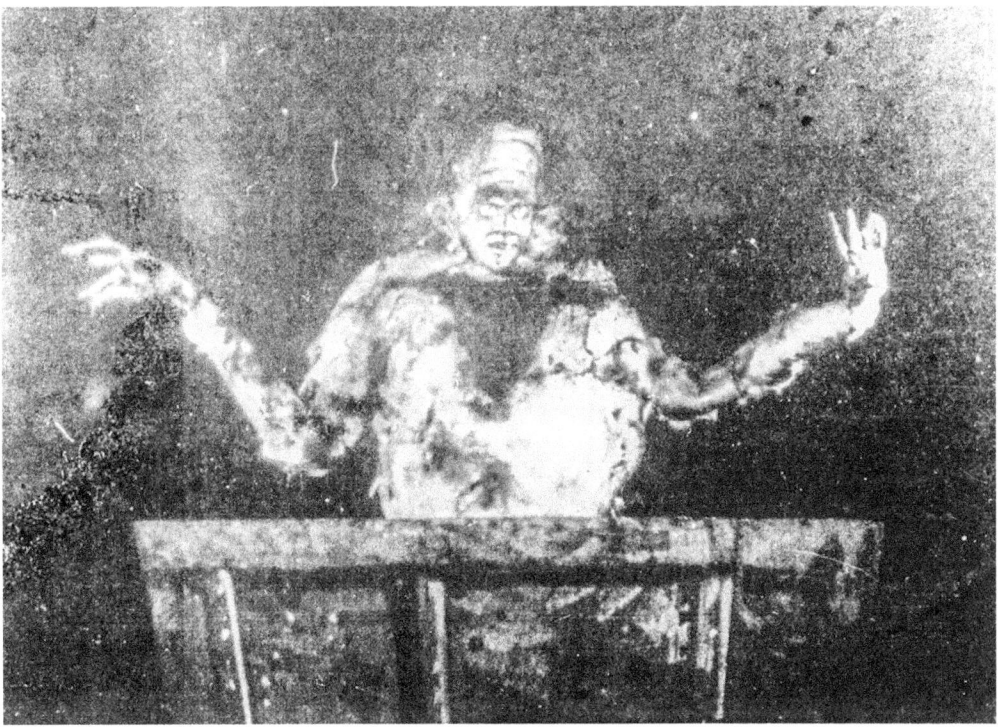

Figures 13.7 and 13.8 Two different frames depict the creation of the monster in *Frankenstein* (Edison, 1910).

Having cast William W. Cohill as Frawley, Percy Standing as "The Creation," and Lucy Cotton as female lead "Elizabeth Lavenza," Smiley shot *Life Without Soul* on location in a number of diverse settings, including Florida, Georgia, New York, and aboard a steamer ship.[172] According to *Motography*:

> Four hundred and sixty-three scenes are incorporated in the script, and the marvelous scenic beauty which the company promises has seldom been equaled in any photoplay, is enhanced and supported by a story unusual in its intensity, dealing with the artificial creature of a being who acts as the nemesis of its creator. In the course of the making of the picture, a fight is staged between the Creation and the crew of the three-masted schooner, in which Percy Standing . . . precipitates the entire crew overboard.
>
> Hazardous exploits were engaged in, one of which called for the blowing up of the side of a mountain, in order to cause a landslide, the huge boulders blocking up a cave in which the Creation has taken refuge.[173]

After completing post-production, Ocean gave a "private showing" of *Life Without Soul* for the "benefit of exchange men, state right buyers, and the trade generally" on November 21, 1915.[174] The company also announced it would be awarding franchises to independent exchanges on December 11, 1915.[175]

Though the film is lost, period synopses note that mad scientist Frawley—whose family warns him not to pursue the "chemistry of life"—falls asleep while reading Shelley's *Frankenstein*. The narrative thus unfolds as a dream in which Frawley does not heed their warnings, its prologue and epilogue not unlike the dream structure of *Dr. Jekyll and Mr. Hyde* (Great Northern, 1910).[176] He imbues his Creation with life not by electricity, but—perhaps drawing upon Dawley's *Frankenstein* and/or Stevenson's *Strange Case of Dr. Jekyll and Mr. Hyde*—a "life-giving fluid."[177] One advertisement has the Creation telling Frawley, "I demand a mate, with whom I can live in the interchange of those relations necessary for my being."[178] Though he does create a woman, Frawley destroys her, inciting the monster to run amok, murdering Frawley's friend, sister, and fianceé.[179] Frawley himself dies of "exhaustion," causing his Creation to commit suicide.[180] Awakening from his nightmare, Frawley abandons his plans and destroys his fluid.[181]

Of the trades, the *New York Dramatic Mirror* responded the most favorably, claiming:

> Seldom has a more intensely absorbing picture been produced. . . . The plot is a radical departure from the conventional motion picture themes. . . . The play is absolutely gruesome, even to the smallest details. There is not the least bit of comedy to relieve the continuous tragedy of the situations. . . . Although gruesome the picture is not in the least objectionable. The cast is exceedingly capable and the beautiful scenes present a strong contrast to the tragic situations which they encompass.[182]

The review ended by noting the story was "well told," but that the "photography could have been better in places."

Some other publications also admired *Life Without Soul*. The film "reflects credit upon the Ocean Film Corporation," *Moving Picture World* wrote.[183] *Motography* commended the settings and acting, drawing particular attention to Standing's "excellent" portrayal.[184] And the *Chicago Tribune* claimed, "The thing is interesting and not very unpleasing, in spite of its grewsomeness [sic]."[185]

Despite such praise, a few critics recorded their concerns. *Variety* wrote, "The Ocean folks have done well with it, despite numerous inconsistencies."[186] *Motion Picture News* responded similarly, claiming, "At times the picture refuses to convince, but its interest is always averagely high because of the theme's unusualness."[187] *The Billboard* believed that a "little more attention might have been paid to piecing and assembling the film; also in the telling of the story, which, in the main part, is complicated and difficult to follow."[188]

Following such criticism, producer Harry Raver "practically re-made" *Life Without Soul* by inserting new footage in early 1916. These were "scientific scenes" that helped to

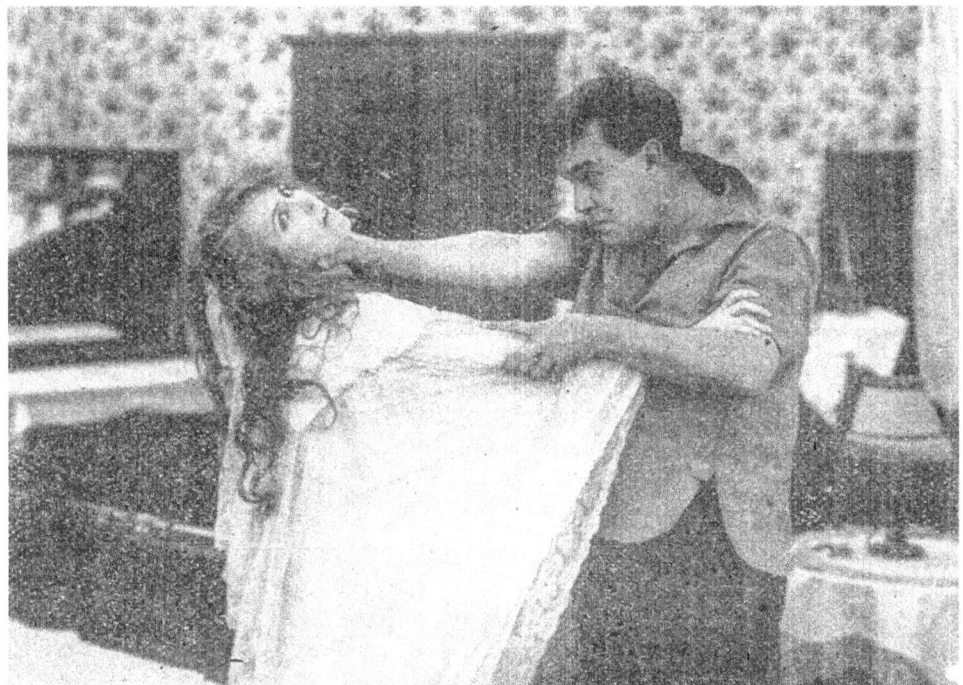

Figure 13.9 *Life Without Soul* (Ocean Film Corporation, 1915).

"clarify the story" and also to infuse the "material" with "still greater interest." Such footage depicted "blood coursing through the veins and arteries, the conjunction of cells and the reproduction of life in the fish world."[189] According to the *New York Dramatic Mirror*, the additions lent a "more convincing atmosphere to the laboratory scenes and cause the final results of the scientist to appear logical."[190] Put another way, these changes echoed the kind of transition that screen depictions of mad doctors underwent during the early cinema period, moving from wizardry to modern science.

Conclusion

The first time that a film company used the phrase "mad scientist" seems to have occurred in 1914. Lafayette McKee played the "Mad Scientist" in Selig Polyscope's *The Fifth Man*, a three-reel jungle film that offered the "thrilling experiences of a man and a girl with a mad scientist and ferocious animals in the Wilds of Central America."[191] In it, the man of science collects animals in cages, among them two humans.[192]

In 1915, a newspaper journalist announced, "a new departure in the field of motion pictures has recently been taken by the Vitagraph Company of America, which has employed a scientist, whose sole duties consist of supervising the work of the actors who may be cast to play surgeons or doctors."[193] Here is another indication of the seriousness with which the screen scientist, and, by extension, the mad scientist, was to be depicted. While absent-minded professors and comical chemists continued to appear in movies during the decades that followed, the American screen largely spurned the approach of Méliès for that of, say, Edison.

Mad scientists and insane chemists onscreen not only came to look like Edison and Tesla, but real-life scientists at times came to sound like their cinematic counterparts. In 1934, the *New York Times* reported that Tesla had created a "death-beam" that was "powerful enough to destroy 10,000 planes 250 miles away."[194] He hoped the invention would make "war impossible," surrounding countries like invisible walls, but he also must have known that any weapon could be misused if it fell into the wrong hands. As J. Robert Oppenheimer, scientific director of the Manhattan Project, famously bemoaned in 1945, quoting from the *Bhagavad-Gita*, "I am become death, the destroyer of worlds."

Notes

1. Victorin-Hippolyte Jasset also directed *Balaoo, The Demon Baboon/Balaoo* (Eclair, 1913, aka *Balaoo, The Demon-Baboon*).
2. W. Stephen Bush, "*Doomed to Die, or The Vial of Wrath*," *Moving Picture World*, September 6, 1913, 1056.
3. "*Doomed to Die*," *Variety*, August 27, 1913, 15.
4. "*Doomed to Die, or The Vial of Wrath*," *Motion Picture News*, August 30, 1913, 8.
5. Bush, 1056.
6. I. Bernard Cohen, *Benjamin Franklin's Science* (Cambridge, MA: Harvard University Press, 1990).
7. Thomas Hardy Leahey and Grace Evans Leahey, *Psychology's Occult Doubles: Psychology and the Problem of Pseudoscience* (Chicago: Nelson-Hall, 1983), 3.
8. Philip Dray, *Stealing God's Thunder: Benjamin Franklin's Lightning Rod and the Invention of America* (New York: Random House, 2005).
9. James McCarroll, "A Familiar Mystery," *Belford's Magazine*, May 1889, 801.
10. Hyman Kuritz, "The Popularization of Science in Nineteenth-Century America," *History of Education Quarterly*, Vol. 21, No. 3 (Autumn 1981), 266.
11. I. Bernard Cohen, "Some Reflections of the State of Science during the Nineteenth Century," *Proceedings of the National Academy of Sciences of the United States of America*, Vol. 45, No. 5 (May 15, 1959), 666.
12. Nathan Reingold (ed.), *Science in Nineteenth-Century America: A Documentary History* (New York: Hill & Wang, 1964).
13. Paul Lucier, "The Professional and the Scientist in Nineteenth-Century America," *Isis*, Vol. 100, No. 4 (December 2009), 699.
14. Ernest Freeberg, *The Age of Edison: Electric Light and the Invention of Modern America* (New York: Penguin, 2013), 144.
15. Edward W. Byrn, "The Progress of Invention during the Past Fifty Years," *Scientific American*, July 25, 1896, 82–3.
16. Charles Barnard, "Thomas Alva Edison," *The Chautauquan: A Weekly Newsmagazine*, March 1894, 677.

17. Henry Tyrrell, "Edison," *Frank Leslie's Popular Monthly*, March 1895, 269.
18. Horace Townsend, "Edison: His Work and His Work-shop," *The Cosmopolitan: A Monthly Illustrated Magazine*, April 1889, 598.
19. "Edison's Latest Marvel," *Los Angeles Times*, April 14, 1895, 17.
20. Barnard, 677.
21. Percy F. Bicknell, "The Wizard of Menlo Park," *The Dial: A Semi-Monthly Journal of Literary Criticism, Discussion, and Information*, March 1, 1908, 126.
22. "Nikola Tesla and His Work," *New York Times*, September 30, 1894, 20.
23. Freeberg, 5.
24. "Electric Chair Ends All," *New York Times*, December 12, 1908, 5; "No Electric Chair Tests," *New York Times*, December 14, 1908, 5.
25. "Soul Has Weight, Physician Thinks," *New York Times*, March 11, 1907, 5.
26. Stephanie P. Browner, *Profound Science and Elegant Literature: Imagining Doctors in Nineteenth-Century America* (Philadelphia: University of Pennsylvania Press, 2005), 1.
27. Kelly Wisecup, *Medical Encounters: Knowledge and Identity in Early American Literatures* (Amherst, Massachusetts: University of Massachusetts Press), 29–31.
28. Ann Anderson, *Snake Oil, Hustlers, and Hambones: The American Medicine Show* (Jefferson, North Carolina: McFarland & Company, 2000).
29. Robert Crossley, "Mars and the Paranormal," *Science Fiction Studies*, Vol. 35, No. 3 (November 2008), 466–84.
30. Roberta Etter and Stuart Schneider, *Halley's Comet: Memories of 1910* (New York: Abbeville Press, 1985).
31. Alan Gribben, "Mark Twain, Phrenology and the 'Temperaments,'" *American Quarterly*, Vol. 24, No. 1 (March 1972), 58–9.
32. Taylor Stoehr, *Hawthorne's Mad Scientists: Pseudoscience and Social Science in Nineteenth-Century Life and Letters* (Hamden, Connecticut: Archon Books, 1978).
33. Freeberg, 227–30.
34. Stephen T. Asma, *On Monsters: An Unnatural History of Our Worst Fears* (Oxford: Oxford University Press, 2009), 141–62.
35. The singular term "scientist" was not coined until c. 1833. See Sydney Ross, "Scientist: The Story of a Word," *Annals of Science*, Vol. 18, No. 2 (1962), 62–85.
36. Raymond McDonald, *The Mad Scientist* (New York: Cochrane Publishing Company, 1908). "Raymond McDonald" was in fact a composite pseudonym used by this novel's two authors, Edward Richard McDonald and Raymond Alfred Leger.
37. "*Uncle Remus*," *New York Times*, July 11, 1908, BR390.
38. "Six New Novels," *Boston Herald*, August 22, 1908, 7.
39. "*The Mad Scientist*," *Houston Chronicle*, July 12, 1908, 34.
40. Christopher P. Toumey, "The Moral Character of Mad Scientists: A Cultural Critique of Science," *Science, Technology, and Human Values*, Vol. 17, No. 4 (Autumn 1992), 411.
41. Christopher Frayling, *Mad, Bad and Dangerous? The Scientist and the Cinema* (London: Reaktion Books, 2005), 53.
42. A copy of *The Mysterious Retort* is available in the DVD boxed set *Georges Méliès: First Wizard of Cinema* (Los Angeles: Flicker Alley, 2008).
43. A copy of *A Trip to Mars* is archived at the Library of Congress, and a copy of *A Message from the Moon* is archived at the Museum of Modern Art, New York City.
44. *Inventor Edison Sketched by World Artist* and *Mr. Edison at Work in His Chemical Laboratory* are available on the DVD boxed set *Edison: The Invention of the Movies* (New York: Kino, 2005).
45. *Edison Films, No. 135* (Buffalo, New York: J. F. Adams, September 1902), 101. Available in *A Guide to Motion Picture Catalogs by American Producers and Distributors, 1894–1908: A Microfilm*

Edition (New Brunswick: Rutgers University Press, 1985), Reel 1. A fragment of *Inventions of an Idiot* is archived at the British Film Institute.

46. "*Liquid Electricity*," *Views and Film Index*, September 7, 1907, 6. A copy of this film is archived at the Museum of Modern Art, New York City.
47. "Film Review," *Moving Picture World*, December 14, 1907, 670. A copy of *Dr. Skinum* is archived at the Museum of Modern Art, New York City.
48. As early as September 1899, *The Phonoscope* reported on moving pictures of "operations being performed by famous surgeons" in Vienna. On October 10, 1908, the *New York Dramatic Mirror* reported, "Moving pictures in connection with surgery [are] coming into general use in the hospitals of this country" (8). While that was an overstatement, subsequent articles did describe how filmed surgeries could benefit doctors and medical students. See, for example, "Films Help Teach Surgery," *Motography*, April 1911, 10; "The Cinematograph in Surgery," *Moving Picture World*, December 21, 1912, 1178; "Films of Surgical Operations," *Motography*, May 2, 1914, 308.
49. Examples include *The Inventor's Secret/Il segreto dell'inventore* (Cines, 1912, released in the U.S. by Kleine), *The Flaming Diagram* (Imp, 1914), *The Inventor's Wife* (Lubin, 1914), *For the Mastery of the World* (Eclair American, 1914), *The Explosion of Fort B 2/L'esplosione del forte B.2* (Picture Playhouse, 1915), *The Mysterious Contragrav* (Universal-Gold Seal, 1915), *The Inventor's Peril* (Lubin, 1915), *The Woman of Mystery* (Biograph, 1915). See Jas. S. McQuade, "*The Inventor's Secret*," *Moving Picture World*, June 29, 1912, 1220; "*The Flaming Diagram*," *Universal Weekly*, March 7, 1914, unpaginated; "*For the Mastery of the World*," *Moving Picture World*, December 5, 1914, 1425; "*The Inventor's Wife*," *New York Dramatic Mirror*, May 6, 1914, 36; "Picture Playhouse Film Co.," *Moving Picture World*, February 6, 1915, 881; "*The Mysterious Contragrao* [sic]," *Moving Picture World*, April 10, 1915, 238; "*The Inventor's Peril*," *Moving Picture World*, May 29, 1915, 1485; Lynde Denig, "*The Woman of Mystery*," *Moving Picture World*, December 18, 1915, 2195.
50. Advertisement, *Moving Picture World*, June 18, 1910, 1028; "*The Sage-brush Phrenologist*," *Moving Picture World*, June 3, 1911, 1267; "*With the Aid of Phrenology*," *New York Dramatic Mirror*, October 22, 1913, 36. A copy of *With the Aid of Phrenology* is archived at the Museum of Modern Art, New York City.
51. "*Doctor Maxwell's Experiment*," *Moving Picture World*, February 22, 1913, 804; "*The Surgeon's Experiment*," *Moving Picture World*, April 5, 1914, 58.
52. A copy of *A Quick Recovery* is archived in the Paper Print Collection at the Library of Congress.
53. Elias Savada (ed.), *The American Film Institute Catalog of Motion Pictures Produced in the United States: Film Beginnings, 1893–1910* (Lanham, Maryland: Scarecrow Press, 1995), 878.
54. *Complete Catalogue of Genuine and Original "Star" Films (Moving Pictures), Manufactured by Geo. Méliès of Paris* (New York: Star Films, 1903), 26. Available in *A Guide to Motion Picture Catalogs by American Producers and Distributors, 1894–1908: A Microfilm Edition* (New Brunswick: Rutgers University Press, 1985), Reel 4.
55. Advertisement, *The Repository* (Canton, Ohio), December 9, 1906, 33.
56. Copies of *And the Villain Still Pursued Her* are available at the British Film Institute and the Library of Congress.
57. "*Sinews of the Dead*," *Moving Picture World*, August 15, 1914, 990.
58. "*Sinews of the Dead*," *Moving Picture World*, August 29, 1914, 1240.
59. "*The Vivisectionist*," *Kalem Kalendar*, June 1915, 29.
60. "*The Vivisectionist*," *Moving Picture World*, June 19, 195, 1956; "*The Vivisectionist*," *Motion Picture News*, June 26, 1915, 81.
61. "*Mortmain* (Vitagraph), Five Reels," *New York Clipper*, September 11, 1915.
62. "*Mortmain*," *Motography*, September 11, 1915, 549–50.
63. Peter Milne, "*Mortmain*," *Motion Picture News*, September 4, 1915, 65.

64. Lynde Denig, "*Mortmain*," September 4, 1915, 1665.
65. "*Mortmain*," *Variety*, September 3, 1915, 21.
66. Arthur Winfield, "*From the Beyond*," *Photoplay*, December 1913, 73–80.
67. "*From the Beyond*," *Eclair Bulletin*, October 1913, 16–20.
68. Ibid., 19–20.
69. "*From the Beyond*," *Moving Picture World*, October 11, 1913, 158.
70. "Here's a New Wrinkle," *Motography*, April 14, 1914, 218.
71. "*The Human Soul*," *Variety*, May 8, 1914, 15.
72. "*The Human Soul*," *Moving Picture World*, August 8, 1914, 838.
73. "*The Changing of Souls*," *Moving Picture World*, December 12, 1908, 484–5.
74. "*A Dangerous Experiment* (Victor)," *Moving Picture World*, January 17, 1914, 297.
75. "*The Secret Room*," *New York Dramatic Mirror*, February 10, 1915, 32.
76. "*Prof. Wise's Brain Serum Injector*," *Moving Picture World*, 19 June 1909, 835. A relatively complete copy of *Prof. Wise's Brain Serum Injector* is archived at the British Film Institute.
77. "*The Dream Pill*," *Moving Picture World*, August 27, 1910, 479. A relatively complete copy of *The Dream Pill* is archived at the British Film Institute.
78. "*The Elixir of Strength*," *Views and Film Index*, November 9, 1907, 8; "*The Elixir of Bravery*," *Moving Picture World*, February 11, 1911, 323. A 28 mm show-at-home print of *The Elixir of Strength* is archived in the collection of the Gaumont-Pathé Archives. A copy of *The Elixir of Bravery* is archived at the Library of Congress.
79. "*Love Microbe*," *Moving Picture World*, October 19, 1907, 526; "A 'Ham Comedy': *Ham and the Experiment*," *Kalem Kalendar*, August 1915, 29. A copy of *The Love Microbe* is archived in the Paper Print Collection at the Library of Congress.
80. "*Wonderful Fluid*," *New York Dramatic Mirror*, August 15, 1908, 7.
81. "*The Invisible Men*," *Moving Picture World*, December 19, 1908, 501. A copy of this film, first seen in America in 1906 and reissued in December 1908, is archived at the Deutsche Kinemathek.
82. "*Invisible Thief*," *Moving Picture World*, July 10, 1909, 65; "*The Invisible Wrestler*," *Moving Picture News*, August 26, 1911, 26. A copy of *The Invisible Thief* is archived at the Centre national du cinéma et de l'image animée (CNC).
83. A copy of *The Invisible Fluid* is archived in the Paper Print Collection at the Library of Congress.
84. "*The Invisible Fluid*," *Moving Picture World*, June 20, 1908, 531.
85. Savada, 61; "*Dr. Brompton Watts' Age Adjuster*," *Moving Picture World*, April 20, 1912, 230; "*The Elixir of Youth*," *Moving Picture World*, April 19, 1913, 281; "*Professor Oldboy's Rejuvenator*," *Motion Picture News*, April 4, 1914, 51. A related film is *A Curious Invention/Plus de progrès* (Pathé Frères, 1910), a comedy in which a scientist invents a device that can restore youth. See "*A Curious Invention*," *Moving Picture World*, June 25, 1910, 1117. A copy of *A Curious Invention* is archived at the Deutsche Kinemathek. A 22 mm Home Kinetoscope-format copy of *Dr. Brompton Watts' Age Adjuster* is archived at the Library of Congress.
86. Neil G. Crawford, "Selig's Story of Restored Youth," *Motography*, November 14, 1914, 659.
87. "*Dr. Jekyll and Mr. Hyde*," *Moving Picture World*, March 7, 1908, 194.
88. The audio of this record appears as a bonus feature on the DVD *Dr. Jekyll and Mr. Hyde* (New York: Kino Video, 2001).
89. "*Mystery of the Mountains*," *Moving Picture World*, July 18, 1908, 51; "*Power of the Cross*," *New York Dramatic Mirror*, December 18, 1912, 34; "*The Wayward Sister*," *Moving Picture World*, May 3, 1913, 490; John T. Soister and Henry Nicolella with Steve Joyce and Harry H. Long, *American Silent Horror, Science Fiction and Fantasy Feature Films, 1913–1929* (Jefferson, North Carolina: McFarland & Company, 2012), 111–12, 158–60. A copy of *Mystery of the Mountains* exists at the Gaumont-Pathé Archives, and a copy of *Double Trouble* is archived at the Library of Congress.

90. "*A Modern Jekyll and Hyde*," *Kalem Kalendar*, December 15, 1913, 11.
91. "*Miss Jekyll and Madame Hyde*," *Vitagraph Life Portrayals*, June 1915, 37.
92. Ibid., 37.
93. "*Miss Jekyll and Madame Hyde*," *New York Dramatic Mirror*, June 30, 1915, 34.
94. "*A Modern Dr. Jekyll*," *New York Dramatic Mirror*, January 1, 1910.
95. "*Dr. Jekyll and Mr. Hyde Done to a Frazzle*," *Moving Picture World*, November 21, 1914, 1077.
96. "*Horrible Hyde*," *Moving Picture World*, August 7, 1915, 1050.
97. "*Horrible Hyde*," *Motion Picture News*, August 14, 1915, 90.
98. "*Dr. Jekyll and Mr. Hyde*," *Moving Picture World*, March 7, 1908, 194.
99. "Whither Are We Drifting?", *Moving Picture World*, October 10, 1908, 276.
100. "Must Pay Royalties on Moving Pictures," *The Billboard*, May 23, 1908, 15.
101. Ibid., 15.
102. Ibid., 15.
103. Louis V. De Foe, "Theatre Sees a Real Danger in the Growth of the Picture Play," *Moving Picture World*, April 4, 1908, 289.
104. Ibid., 289.
105. "Plays on the Stage by Mechanism Alone," *Moving Picture World*, May 23, 1908, 459.
106. Ibid., 459.
107. Ibid., 460.
108. "Plays of the Stage by Mechanism Alone," *The Billboard*, May 30, 1908, 10.
109. "Alas, Poor Yorick!," *Talking Machine World*, June 15, 1908, 68.
110. "*Dr. Jekyll and Mr. Hyde* (Great Northern)," *Moving Picture World*, September 24, 1910, 685.
111. Ibid., 685.
112. "Thanhouser," *The Billboard*, January 13, 1912, 39.
113. Advertisement, *Moving Picture World*, January 13, 1912, 86.
114. A copy of *Dr. Jekyll and Mr. Hyde* (1912) is available on the DVD *Dr. Jekyll and Mr. Hyde* (Los Angeles: Image Entertainment, 1998), as well as on the DVD *Thanhouser: A Study in Film, Volume 1* (Dallas, Texas: Marengo Films, 2002).
115. Margaret I. MacDonald, "A Trip to New Rochelle to the Thanhouser Plant," *Moving Picture News*, January 20, 1912, 30.
116. "*Dr. Jekyll and Mr. Hyde*," *Moving Picture World*, January 27, 1912, 305.
117. "*Dr. Jekyll and Mr. Hyde*," *New York Dramatic Mirror*, January 24, 1912, 40.
118. See, for example, Advertisement, *Moving Picture World*, February 15, 1913, 637.
119. A surviving copy of *Dr. Jekyll and Mr. Hyde* (1913) is available on an undated DVD from Sinister Cinema of Medford, Oregon.
120. "*Dr. Jekyll and Mr. Hyde*," *Moving Picture World*, March 8, 1913, 997.
121. "King Baggott [sic] makes good in *Dr. Jekyll and Mr. Hyde*," *Moving Picture News*, February 22, 1913, 15.
122. "*Dr. Jekyll and Mr. Hyde*," *New York Dramatic Mirror*, March 5, 1913, 32.
123. M. J. McQuarrie was an early form of billing for Murdock [James] MacQuarrie.
124. "*Dr. Jekyll and Mr. Hyde* (Kinemacolor)," *New York Clipper*, June 28, 1913, 14; "Kinemacolor Reviews," *New York Dramatic Mirror*, June 18, 1913, 31.
125. "Universal Program," *Motion Picture News*, August 28, 1915, 81.
126. "*The Reader of Minds*," *New York Dramatic Mirror*, January 6, 1915, 31.
127. Clarence J. Caine, "Zudora's Fifth Adventure Exciting," *Motography*, December 26, 1914, 894.
128. "In the Serial Field," *New York Dramatic Mirror*, March 3, 1915, 35.
129. "*The Wonderful Electro Magnet*," *New York Dramatic Mirror*, December 11, 1909, 16. Similar films include *Prof. Bric-a-Brac's Inventions/L'invention du professeur Brick à Brack* (Pathé

Frères, 1908, aka *L'invention du professeur Bric à Brac*) and *The Electric Girl* (Eclair American, 1914). See "*Prof. Bric-a-Brac's Inventions*," *Moving Picture World*, July 11, 1908, 34; "*The Electric Girl*," *Moving Picture World*, March 14, 1914, 1428. A copy of *Prof. Bric-a-Brac's Inventions* is archived at the Cinémathèque Française.

130. "*The House That Went Crazy*," *Moving Picture World*, September 5, 1914, 1416. Similar films included *Electric Hotel/Electric hôtel* (Pathé Frères, 1908, aka *L'hôtel électrique*) and *The Automatic House* (Empress, 1915). See "*Electric Hotel*," *New York Dramatic Mirror*, December 26, 1908, 8; "*The Automatic House*," *Moving Picture World*, April 17, 1915, 466. A copy of *The House That Went Crazy* is archived at Library and Archives Canada. A copy of *Electric Hotel* is available on the DVD *Segundo de Chomón, el cine de la fantasia* (Barcelona: Cameo Media S.L., 2010).

131. Advertisement, *Views and Film Index*, September 7, 1907, 2; "Moving Picture," *Variety*, November 23, 1907, 11.

132. "*Galvanic Fluid: or, More Liquid Electricity*," *Moving Picture World*, February 8, 1908, 103–4. The term "continuation" to describe *Galvanic Fluid: or, More Liquid Electricity* appears in Advertisement, *Views and Film Index*, February 15, 1908, 2. In the September 5, 1908 issue of *Variety*, a critic reviewed *The Professor's Great Discovery*, a moving picture released by Williamson that was apparently similar to Vitagraph's "liquid electricity" films. Some footage from *Galvanic Fluid: or, More Fun with Liquid Electricity* is archived at the Library of Congress by way of a paper print deposit.

133. Though it comes to life in a child's dream rather than at the hands of an inventor, a rather creepy animated doll appears in *The Spoiled Darling's Doll* (Thanhouser, 1913). A copy of it is archived at the EYE Film Institute.

134. "Living Dolls," *Moving Picture World*, July 17, 1909, 137; "*Oh! You Unbreakable Doll*," *Moving Picture World*, June 28, 1913, 1404; "*The Scientist's Doll*," *Motion Picture News*, March 7, 1914, 48.

135. "*The Mechanical Man*," *Universal Weekly*, June 26, 1915, 30.

136. "*The Return of Maurice Donnelly*," *Vitagraph Life Portrayals*, April 1915, 21.

137. "*The Return of Maurice Donnelly*," *New York Dramatic Mirror*, April 14, 1915, 32.

138. Edward Weitzel, "*Life Without Soul*," *Moving Picture World*, December 4, 1915, 1846.

139. George Blaisdell, "Clara Kimball Young, Artist," *Moving Picture World*, October 3, 1914, 42.

140. Owen Davis, *Lola* (New York: Grosset & Dunlap Publishers, 1915).

141. Hanford C. Judson, "*Lola*," *Moving Picture World*, November 21, 1914, 1091.

142. "*Lola*," *New York Dramatic Mirror*, November 18, 1914, 32.

143. "World," *Motography*, December 5, 1914, 796.

144. "Clara Kimball Young in *Lolo* [sic]," *The Billboard*, November 28, 1914, 54.

145. "*Lola*," *New York Dramatic Mirror*, 32.

146. Peter Milne, "*Lola*," *Motion Picture News*, November 28, 1914, 44.

147. "*Lola*," *Variety*, November 14, 1914, 25.

148. "*Naidra, the Dream Woman*," *Motion Picture News*, December 19, 1914, 85.

149. "*Naidra, the Dream Woman*," *Motography*, December 12, 1914, 825.

150. "*Naidra, the Dream Woman*–Thanhouser," *Reel Life*, November 28, 1914, 12.

151. "*Naidra, the Dream Woman*," *Moving Picture World*, December 13, 1914, 1524.

152. Advertisement, *The Courier-Gazette* (McKinney, Texas), August 14, 1915, 8.

153. "*The Eleventh Dimension*," *Moving Picture World*, July 10, 1915, 382.

154. "Theatrical," *Wilmington Morning Star* (Wilmington, North Carolina), August 3, 1915, 2.

155. Savada, 661; Advertisement, *New York Clipper*, January 19, 1907, 1280. A small amount of footage from *The Mechanical Statue and the Ingenious Servant* is archived in the Paper Print Collection at the Library of Congress.

156. "Williams, Brown & Earle," *Moving Picture World*, April 27, 1907, 124.
157. "J. Searle Dawley," *Edison Kinetogram*, October 1, 1912, 12.
158. "J. Searle Dawley Speaks," *Motion Picture News*, February 28, 1920, 2159.
159. "Augustus Phillips, Pioneer," *Moving Picture World*, February 27, 1915, 1293.
160. "Charles Ogle," *Universal Weekly*, July 11, 1914, 13.
161. "*Motography*'s Gallery of Picture Players," *Motography*, July 4, 1914, 17.
162. "Charles Ogle," *Moving Picture World*, October 17, 1914, 352.
163. Advertisement, *Moving Picture World*, March 19, 1910, 436.
164. "*Frankenstein* (Dramatic)," *Edison Kinetogram*, April 15, 1910, 5.
165. "Edison," *The Billboard*, March 19, 1910, 64.
166. "*Frankenstein*," *New York Dramatic Mirror*, March 26, 1910, 18.
167. "*Frankenstein*," *Moving Picture World*, April 2, 1910, 508.
168. "Some Recent Films Reviewed," *The Nickelodeon*, April 1, 1910, 177.
169. Ibid., 177.
170. "New Films," *New York Clipper*, March 12, 1910, 122.
171. "*Motography*'s Gallery of Picture Players," *Motography*, January 4, 1913, 9.
172. "Ocean Film Corporation Formed," *Moving Picture World*, November 13, 1915, 1316. Smiley and Cohill had already worked together on *The Gray Horror* (Lubin, 1915).
173. "Ocean Company's First Film," *Motography*, November 20, 1915, 1054.
174. "Ocean Film Company Finishes *Life Without a* [sic] *Soul*," *Motion Picture News*, November 27, 1915, 87; "New York to See Ocean's First," *Motography*, November 27, 1915, 1132.
175. "Two 5-Part Features from Novels for Ocean Film," *Motion Picture News*, December 18, 1915, 79.
176. Peter Milne, "*Life Without Soul*," *Motion Picture News*, December 11, 1915, 92.
177. "Ocean Film Completes *Life Without Soul*," *Moving Picture World*, November 20, 1915, 1461.
178. Advertisement, *Motion Picture News*, November 27, 1915, 36.
179. Thomas C. Kennedy, "*Life Without Soul*," *Motography*, December 4, 1915, 1194.
180. "*Life Without Soul*," *The Billboard*, December 4, 1915, 52.
181. Ibid., 52.
182. "*Life Without Soul*," *New York Dramatic Mirror*, November 27, 1915, 36.
183. Weitzel, 1846.
184. Kennedy, 1194.
185. Kitty Kelly, "Flickerings from Film Land," *Chicago Tribune*, December 20, 1915, 18.
186. "*Life Without Soul*," *Variety*, November 26, 1915, 23.
187. Milne, "*Life Without Soul*," 92.
188. "*Life Without Soul*," *The Billboard*, 52.
189. "*Life Without Soul* (Ocean)," *Moving Picture World*, May 6, 1916, 996.
190. "*Life* With Scientific *Soul*," *New York Dramatic Mirror*, May 13, 1916, 33.
191. Advertisement, *Altoona Mirror* (Altoona, Pennsylvania), November 18, 1914, 2.
192. "*The Fifth Man*," *Moving Picture World*, September 26, 1914, 1828.
193. "And the Screen: The Scientist," *Vancouver Daily World* (Vancouver, British Columbia), May 29, 1915, 8.
194. "Tesla, at 78, Bares New Death-Beam," *New York Times*, July 11, 1934, 18.

CHAPTER 14

American Literature Onscreen

In 1912, Gaumont promised its film *The Vengeance of Egypt/L'anneau fatal* possessed the "potency of Poe."[1] In 1915, *Moving Picture World* claimed *The Mystery of the Silent Death* (Essanay, 1915) was "worthy [of] the invention of Edgar Allan Poe."[2] Of *Mortmain* (Vitagraph, 1915), the *New York Clipper* told readers it was "remindful of the morbidly interesting novels of Edgar Allen [sic] Poe."[3] During the era of early cinema, Poe's name proved useful in efforts to describe mysterious and horror-themed moving pictures to exhibitors and the viewing public.[4] Invoking Poe also created a link to a prestigious American literary figure.

Famous literature, whether horrifying or not, became crucial to early film companies.[5] It commanded not only audience attention, but also respectability, whether in the case of Shakespeare, Tolstoy, or (as discussed in Chapter 5) Dante, Marlowe, and Goethe, or (as discussed in Chapter 13) Mary Shelley. As motion picture executive Frank Lewis Dyer observed as early as 1910, "When the works of Dickens and Victor Hugo, the poems of Browning, the plays of Shakespeare and stories from the Bible are used as a basis for moving pictures, no fair-minded man can deny that the art is being developed along the right lines."[6]

The titles and narratives were already well known to many potential viewers, and many of them were in the public domain. To be sure, recent literary works did require the acquisition of rights, but their fan base made the financial investment in them worthwhile. Here one could cite not only Du Maurier's *Trilby*, but also *The Unfaithful Wife* (Fox, 1915), which was based on a Marie Corelli novel, as well as adaptations of H. Rider Haggard's popular novel *She* (by Edison in 1908 and Thanhouser in 1911).[7]

For some, indigenous literature held a particular allure. In 1910, *Moving Picture World* remarked, "much has been said and written the last twelve months on the desirability of providing American film subjects for American moving picture audiences," a reference to the sheer numbers of foreign film imports distributed in the United States.[8] The trade invited readers to propose a definition of what exactly constituted an "American subject." Among the many possible answers was the screen adaptation of American literature, something that had already occurred, including in the case of Vitagraph's 1907 film *A Curious Dream*, which was based on Mark Twain's humorous ghost story *The Curious Dream* (1870).[9]

Consider Eclair American's production schedule of 1912 and 1913, which featured moving picture versions of Longfellow and O. Henry.[10] Among the company's many "Literary Photo Sensations" were adaptations of a trio of authors advertised in 1912: Washington Irving, Nathaniel Hawthorne, and Edgar Allan Poe, who were perceived and

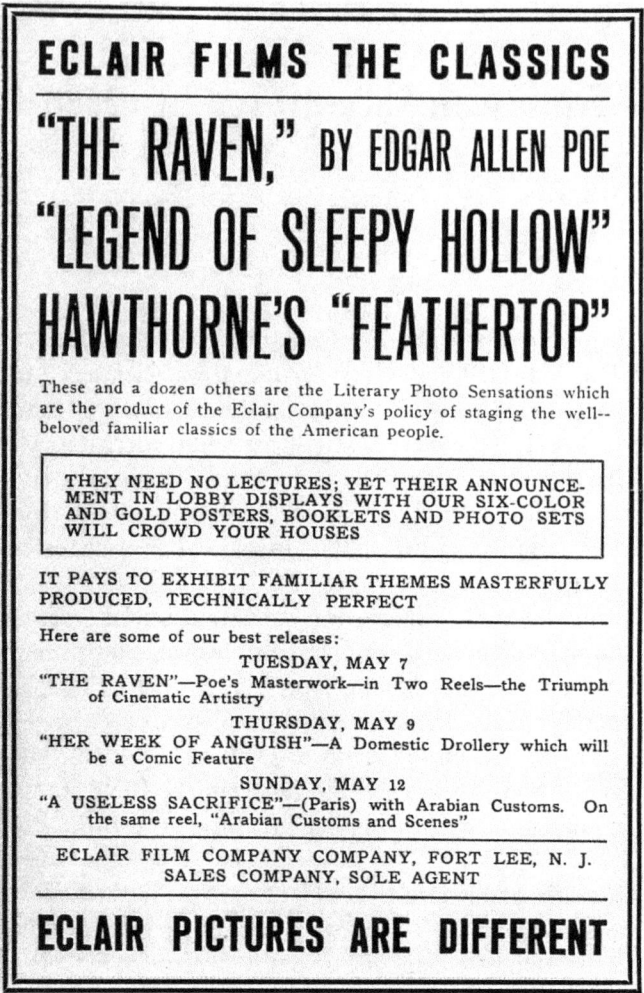

Figure 14.1 Published in *Moving Picture News* on April 22, 1912.

treated at times as a distinct group of authors.[11] The three had a profound impact on the development of literature in the nineteenth century. Film adaptations of their work held the potential to have similar influence on horror-themed American films, including in the further exploration of natural horrors and of the supernatural explained.

After all, a film did not have to be American to conjure Edgar Allan Poe; in 1913, *Moving Picture News* observed that the Italian-made moving picture *The Death Knell/ Sorrisi di un tramonto* (Itala, 1913) resembled the "darkling hours of Poe."[12] Nor was Poe the only benchmark for labeling horror-themed cinema. In 1911, *Moving Picture World* claimed there was "some of the morbid unpleasantness of Poe or De Maupassant" in *Was She Justified?* (Yankee, 1911).[13] And in 1913, in a review of *Doomed to Die, or The Vial of Wrath/Fragile bonheur* (Union Features, 1913), the same trade used Maupassant and Zola as literary points of reference to describe the film's "horrors," foregoing mention of any American writer.[14]

Adapting literature into films proved to be a complex process, one in which some foreign companies produced versions of writers like Poe while American companies repeatedly looked to European authors for inspiration. Consequently, the result meant American horror-themed cinema—following from earlier literary and theatrical traditions in the country—remained international, even while levying particular attention on indigenous writers.

European Literature

American viewers often attended film adaptations of European stories they loved. For example, a few versions of Dickens's *A Christmas Carol* appeared in the United States, all depicting its memorable ghosts. Essanay filmed a version in 1908, while Paramount distributed the British-made London Film Co. version in 1914.[15] Edison produced its own adaptation for Christmas 1910, reissuing the same in December 1911.[16] Directed by J. Searle Dawley, the film features Charles Ogle as Bob Cratchit and Marc McDermott as Scrooge. *Moving Picture World* praised it at length, observing, "The visions and the ghost of Marley are produced in a more visionary way than usual, making them appear much more ethereal."[17] A surviving copy provides evidence of that fact, with Scrooge even grasping his hand into Marley's spectral form.[18]

At least four of Wilkie Collins's tales were adapted in this era.[19] In 1912, G. R. Nichols directed Janet Salsbury in a two-reel adaptation of Collins's 1859 novel *The Woman in White* (Gem, 1912).[20] Prior to viewing the film, *Moving Picture News* expressed its belief and apparent hope that, based upon an advance synopsis, the "picture should conform closely" to the original.[21] After watching it, *Moving Picture World* approved, telling readers, "Full justice has been done the weird quality of the story, and its most thrilling passages lose none of their strength."[22] The trade drew particular attention to the "ghostly appearances" of the title character, and the meeting of two characters in a cemetery, concluding, "The production has feature quality."[23]

The following year, Monopol released a three-reel adaptation of Wilkie Collins's 1857 novel *The Dead Secret* (1913), starring Marion Leonard in a dual role, playing a mother and her own daughter, thanks in part to double, triple, and even quadruple exposures. A review praised this "weird" tale of blackmail, describing the "machinations of the physician-hypnotist and the uncanny manifestations of his occult powers, aided by the Hindu girl and the crystal globe."[24] In this case, the technical virtuosity of the film paralleled its narrative. To an extent, the two had merged.

Turning to an 1855 short story by Collins, Alice Guy Blaché directed Fraunie Franholz and Claire Whitney in a four-reel version of *The Dream Woman* (Blaché Features, 1914).[25] *Moving Picture World* acknowledged the "hair-raising" original had translated into a "startling" film:

> In making the picture, [Blaché] has discarded all except what she needed for her peculiar effect. But the telling quality of the picture comes most from the fact that, by the mysterious alchemy of art, she had changed what material she did use into something her own, fresh, new, life-like, of today. . . . It is a picture in which minute details have been considered. And [Blaché] hasn't given us a chance to say, "Oh, this is only a picture after all." We don't say anything while it is on, we just watch.[26]

Figure 14.2 Published in *Moving Picture World* on April 19, 1913.

The trade was particularly impressed that *The Dream Woman* did not make clear whether the film's plot really occurred or whether one of the characters dreamt it. *Motion Picture News* commented that *The Dream Woman* could have "come from the pen of Edgar Allan Poe, its weirdness and fascination as diabolical as anything he has written."[27]

And then there was (as discussed in Chapter 11) *The Moonstone* (1868), which became a Selig Polyscope film in 1909.[28] Believing that Collins was the "great exemplar for Sir Arthur Conan Doyle" and that he "resemble[d]" Poe, *Moving Picture World* praised the adaptation of his "very weird, very fascinating, [and] very eerie" novel.[29] The trade believed Selig's film was "gorgeously effective and magnificent in spectacle."[30] *Variety*'s response: "Artistically it is an excellent achievement."[31] The *New York Dramatic Mirror* largely agreed, but also drew attention to the fact that the film did not follow the "details" of Collins's novel, resulting in such anachronisms as automobiles in nineteenth-century India.[32]

With literary adaptations came these not-unexpected questions of fidelity to source material, as well as the issue of loose and informal variations of the same. Several adaptations of Charlotte Brontë's 1847 novel *Jane Eyre* appeared: a one-reeler produced by

Thanhouser in 1910, a two-reeler produced by Imp in 1914, a four- (or perhaps five-) reeler produced by Whitman Features in 1914, and a three-reeler produced by Biograph in 1915.[33] These were in addition to *The Mad Lady of Chester/Jane Eyre* (Cines, 1910), a variation in which a squire falls in love with a young woman even though he is "bound forever" to an insane woman "who would tear him to pieces in a fit of madness, were he to approach her."[34]

Formal and informal adaptations also occurred with the literature of Gaston Leroux, the French novelist whom *Moving Picture News* referred to as "well known" in 1913.[35] As Chapter 10 noted, Leroux's 1912 novel *Balaoo* became the 1913 film *Balaoo, The Demon Baboon/Balaoo*. Similarly, his "locked-room" mystery story *Le mystère de la chambre jaune*—first published as a magazine serial in 1907 and then as a novel in 1908—became a three-reel moving picture entitled *The Mystery of the Yellow Room/Le mystère de la chambre jaune* (Union Features, 1913).[36] *Moving Picture News* praised the film's faithfulness to Leroux's original "in all but unessential details."[37]

Figure 14.3 *The Phantom Violin* (Universal, 1914).

In 1914, Grace Cunard wrote and starred in the three-reel Universal film *The Phantom Violin*, with its director Francis Ford (and Cunard's frequent co-star) also portraying the film's "weird" title character.[38] "Perhaps it is more like a work of Edgar Allan Poe's than anything else, as it is gruesome, mystifying from the beginning, [and it ends] in a horrifying manner," *Motion Picture News* commented.[39] *Moving Picture World* thought much the same, mentioning it "reminds one of Poe, of Hoffman's [sic] *Weird Tales*, and of Maupassant."[40]

While a Cunard original story, *The Phantom Violin*—re-released in 1915 as *The Phantom of the Violin*—was apparently inspired by Leroux's *The Phantom of the Opera/Le Fantôme de l'Opéra* (1910).[41] The action "begins in a thunderstorm," with the female lead hearing violin music in the middle of the night. When she investigates the next day, she meets the musician responsible. The two fall in love and marry, with the violinist playing in a French cabaret. But when she later flirts with another man, the violinist goes mad, and discovers a secret passage that leads into a "forgotten" monastery beneath the cabaret, a "region of darkness and goblin horror-dungeons where white bones lie asleep."[42] Eventually he hears his wife playing a parody of one of his compositions in the cabaret above, which causes him to attack her new lover. Then he sets fire to the cabaret and takes his wife "down into the crypt and finally leap[s] with her into the deepest hole of the lower regions of the place." *Moving Picture World* labeled *The Phantom Violin* "decidedly sensational and wierd [sic]."[43]

Nowhere is the diffuse influence of a notable author on early cinema scripts more apparent than in the case of Arthur Conan Doyle. Formal adaptations of his work released in America included *Sherlock Holmes Baffled* (American Mutoscope & Biograph, 1900), *The Adventures of Sherlock Holmes; or, Held for Ransom* (Vitagraph, 1905, aka *Sherlock Holmes or Held for Ransom*), *Sherlock Holmes/Sherlock Holmes i livsfare* (Great Northern, 1908), *Sherlock Holmes II: Raffles Escapes from Prison/Sherlock Holmes II: Raffles flugt fra fængslet* (Great Northern, 1909), and *Sherlock Holmes III: The Detective's Adventure in the Gas Cellar/Sherlock Holmes III: Det hemmelige dokument, eller Opdageren i gaskælderen* (Great Northern, 1909).[44] These were along with the eight two-reel moving pictures produced by the Franco-British Film Company under the "personal supervision of the author" and distributed in America by Union Features in 1912–13.[45]

In May 1914, the *New York Dramatic Mirror* reported that Conan Doyle was planning a trip to America for the purpose of negotiating the exclusive screen rights to the bulk of his canon, including the Sherlock Holmes stories.[46] Subsequent films released in America included *The Hound of the Baskervilles/Der Hund von Baskerville* (Pathé, 1915).[47] Of the German-made production, *Moving Picture World* wrote that it had "evidently been robbed of very little if any of its weirdly thrilling characteristics."[48]

Of equal or even greater importance than the official Conan Doyle adaptations (or even the numerous parodies of the same) were the sheer volume of detective films released in America during the period that owe a large debt to his Sherlock Holmes stories (and arguably, by extension, to Poe's Dupin). In 1911, *Moving Picture World* bemoaned the lack of a person who could put a "thrilling detective play on the screen in Doctor Doyle's finished style."[49] But demands for better quality did not keep American companies from producing dozens of mystery films featuring detectives loosely based on Holmes.[50] This was true to the extent that, by 1915, the same trade observed, "Strange as it may seem, the story of crime mystery is fast degenerating into one of stock properties."[51]

Washington Irving

The literature of Washington Irving provided early filmmakers with much inspiration, particularly his *Rip Van Winkle* (1819), which was adapted for the screen more times than any other American short story in the pre-1915 era.[52] As discussed in Chapter 5, Selig

Polyscope released an adaptation of Irving's 1824 story *The Devil and Tom Walker* in 1913.[53] *Moving Picture World* was distinctly unimpressed with Selig's devil, as portrayed by William Stowell. Nevertheless, the trade believed the "bold and rather bare simplicity" of Edward McWade's script maintained audience interest.[54]

Figure 14.4 *The Spectre Bridegroom* (Eclair American, 1913)

That same year, Eclair American released its version of Irving's *The Spectre Bridegroom* (1913), which had first been published in 1819 and had been dramatized on numerous occasions in nineteenth-century theatre.[55] The two-reel film begins at a "Hallowe'en" party, with young women attempting to divine whom they will marry. A witch (Julia Stuart) suggests that Hilda (Mildred Bright) peer into a mirror at midnight to see the reflection of her husband-to-be. Hilda does, and then meets the man of her dreams in real life. Her "horror-stricken" acquaintances mistake him for a spectre, but eventually learn that he is just a man.[56]

The *Eclair Bulletin* heralded *The Spectre Bridegroom* as a "supremely entertaining adaptation from Washington Irving's masterpiece of magic and mirth."[57] Drawing particular attention to the "interesting scenes in a witch's habitation," *Moving Picture News* praised the film for being "most artistic."[58] The *New York Dramatic Mirror* called it "at once artistic and humorous."[59] *Moving Picture World* also gave a positive review, noting the fact that Eclair had altered the setting from Germany to Revolutionary War-era America. "While this variation does not materially change the effect of the story, neither does it injure the tale in any way; it was perhaps done as a matter of studio convenience."[60] Whether the change was for budgetary reasons or to "Americanize" an American story is difficult to determine.

Two different versions of Irving's *The Legend of Sleepy Hollow* appeared during the early cinema period. Kalem produced the first in 1908.[61] *Views and Film Index* described the final scene of the 825-foot film as follows: "The chase is on, and Ichabod thinks the Headless Horseman is pursuing him. Over the bridge and through the graveyard they go, when suddenly Brom Bones hurls the pumpkin at Ichabod, and the poor school master, falling off his horse, prays for deliverance, and the horseman vanishes."[62] So too does Ichabod, who is never seen again, thus allowing Brom Bones to marry Katrina.

In 1912, Eclair American released its *Legend of Sleepy Hollow*; advertisements, plot summaries, and critical reviews usually printed its title without the article *The*. Publicity promised it was a "worthy representation" of "one of the most famous tales of our literature."[63] Plot summaries indicate that Brom Bones used a sheet and a "pumpkin lantern" to scare Ichabod.[64] *Moving Picture World* admired the moving picture's location shooting and cinematography, but also believed it was not "particularly exciting" and that the Headless Horseman would not fool "even the children."[65] The *New York Dramatic Mirror* was less kind, deeming its conclusion was to be rushed and its narrative suffered from too many unnecessary intertitles.[66]

Drawing on such visual culture as Emanuel Leutze's artwork for an 1864 publication of the tales, both of these adaptations made evident that the mythical horseman was merely a man in disguise, the supernatural explained rather than the fantastical uncertainty present in Irving's original story. Here again the screen seems to have further "Americanized" an American story.

Nathaniel Hawthorne

The literature of Nathaniel Hawthorne became an important, but only occasional, narrative source for early moving pictures. The first of these adaptations came in *The Scarlet Letter*, which Kalem produced as a 900-foot film release of 1908.[67] Imp released a one-reel version of the novel in 1911, followed by Kinemacolor's three-reel version in 1913.[68]

Then, in 1910, the Edison Manufacturing Company produced *The House of the Seven Gables* (1851).[69] The company promoted it as a "Big Feature Film."[70] Thomas Bedding, associate editor of *Moving Picture World*, commented:

> To me, at any rate, these pictures succeed in conveying what I would call a sense of what was in Hawthorne's mind when he wrote his book. I seemed to feel Hawthorne when I was looking at the film, and moreover I wanted the characters to speak, or rather more than on most occasions when I am looking at moving picture films. I felt the picture. I had seized the sentiment of it. It was the refined, scholarly Hawthorne on the screen. I would have known that it was a Hawthorne story if the title had not been printed on the film.[71]

Given the perceived faithfulness to Hawthorne's original, Bedding implored Edison to consider producing a version of *The Blithedale Romance* (1852).

Not everyone agreed with this praise. In the same trade publication, reviewer Louis Reeves Harrison complained that Hawthorne's theme "grew so gloomy [in the Edison film] with excessive [intertitles] that people hitched around in their seats and rubbed their faces wearily, while the man next to me actually went to sleep."[72] And some viewers—particularly in Salem, Massachusetts—decried the "inexcusable blunder of burning at the stake a prisoner accused of witchcraft," as those executed in Salem had (as noted in Chapter 6) been either hanged or pressed.[73]

Figure 14.5 A still from *Feathertop* (Eclair American, 1912), featured on the cover of *Moving Picture News*.

Feathertop (1852) became the third Hawthorne story adapted for the screen. It features an old witch who relies on the devil's assistance to endow a scarecrow with life. Eclair American produced the earliest film of *Feathertop* (aka *Feather Top*) in 1912 as part of the "Literary Photo Sensations" series that also included the company's aforementioned *Legend of Sleepy Hollow*.[74] *Moving Picture World* wrote, "The Eclair people are doing very commendable work in their representations from the masterpieces of American literature," adding that *Feathertop* was a "satirical comedy in the costume of Puritan days," a "worthy release" featuring "good" acting, sets, costumes, and camerawork.[75]

Kinemacolor then produced its own *Feathertop* in 1913 as part of the same group of literary adaptations as its aforementioned *The Scarlet Letter* (1913). The plot summary for Kinemacolor's version notes the witch sends the scarecrow "to woo the daughter of her bitter enemy," but the scarecrow sees his "true self" as reflected in a mirror. As a result, he refuses to "smoke the enchanted pipe" which keeps him alive, preferring instead to fall dead at the witch's feet.[76] Nothing remains of him but sticks, straw, and a pumpkin head. *Moving Picture News* praised *Feathertop*'s "excellent" use of double exposures.[77] In another article, the trade also drew attention to *Feathertop*'s creative use of the Kinemacolor film process: "A beautiful finish to the picture shows a cornfield with the scarecrow silhouetted against a gorgeous sunset sky—this effect being possible only in Kinemacolor."[78]

Edgar Allan Poe

No author had a greater impact on the horror-themed film in America than Edgar Allan Poe. Though largely unappreciated at the time of his death, Poe's literary star was increasingly ascendant during the second half of the nineteenth century, as attested by concerns over the proper marking of his grave and a benefit performance in 1880 to raise money for a memorial statue.[79] In 1899, the *Los Angeles Times* drew attention to a "very decided revival of interest in both the works and the personality of Edgar Allen [sic] Poe."[80] Such memorialization intensified during the early years of the twentieth century, due in no small part to the centennial of Poe's birth in 1909.[81] In 1912, the *New York Times* reported on the "Raven Society" at the University of Virginia, its purpose being the "advancement and perpetuation of Poe's memory."[82] The following year, the Poe cottage in the Bronx became a museum dedicated to the author and his works.[83]

Poe's fame meant that his poems and tales became a source for early film titles, even if not always their narratives. Writing about *The Bells* (Edison, 1912), which starred former *Frankenstein* (Edison, 1910) leading man Augustus Phillips, *Moving Picture World* noted, "The time [setting] is before the war and Poe's famous poem is dragged in (it certainly has nothing to do with the story), perhaps to make it seem poetical."[84] A surviving copy illustrates this very point. Without particular narrative need, the film's intertitles quote such verses as, "tolling, tolling, tolling, in that muffled monotone" and, separately, "On the future! How it tells of the rapture that impels to the swinging and the ringing of the bells, bells, bells."[85]

Presenting Poe's work in public faithfully had proven a difficult task even prior to the rise of cinema, save for public readings of his poetry. Poe himself recited his poetry on many occasions; one listener later described his tone of voice as exemplifying "gloom and almost weird solemnity."[86] To be sure, Poe intended poems like *The Raven* (1845), *Ulalume* (1847), and *The Bells* (1849) to be heard as much as to be read. Not surprisingly, recitals of his poetry continued long after his death.[87]

Dramatizations of Poe's gossamer tales proved far more arduous, though that hardly kept playwrights from trying. For example, in 1891, Webster Edgerly's five-act comedy *The Raven* was performed in Baltimore, with the author portraying Edgar, Agnes Burroughs as Lenore, and the trained bird Dante as the title character.[88] Other examples include *The System of Dr. Tarr* (1905, dramatized by Henry Tyrell and Arthur Hornblow), and *The Tell-Tale Heart* (1909–10, dramatized by Robert B. Kerreis).[89]

In some cases, early filmmakers took inspiration from Poe rather than attempting to adapt him directly. As Chapter 5 notes, the doppelgänger of Poe's *William Wilson* became one of the key influences on *Der Student von Prag* (1913), released in America as *A Bargain with Satan*. Similarly, *Moving Picture World* claimed that Louis Feuillade's *A Plague-Stricken City/Le château de la peur* (Gaumont, 1912) "faintly recalled" *The Masque of the Red Death*.[90] And *The Necklace of the Dead/Den dødes halsbaand* (Great Northern, 1910, aka *Necklace of the Dead*) drew upon such Poe stories as *The Fall of the House of Usher* (1839) and *The Premature Burial* (1844).[91] *Moving Picture World* described it as follows:

> Here is a film which will make a profound impression upon any audience, not so much because of what they see as what is suggested. A girl dies and is buried with a necklace placed on her neck by her lover. The undertaker's assistant, coveting the necklace, goes to the tomb in the night, opens the coffin, and begins to remove the necklace, when he is startled by a movement. Recovering himself, he reasons that possibly the girl has been buried alive, and hastens to her lover. Together they return to the tomb and find that she has got out of the coffin and is waiting inside the closed door, half dead from fright until someone shall release her. The man confesses all, and is given the necklace, but under the circumstances, he believes he should devote it to the church. There isn't much in the story, yet it would be difficult to devise anything which will linger longer in the memory.[92]

In another article, *Moving Picture World* commended *The Necklace of the Dead*'s "gruesome but gripping story" for being brought to life so successfully by the "artists of the Royal Theatre, Copenhagen."[93]

And then there were adaptations of stories that had themselves been based on Poe. *The Lunatics/Le système du docteur Goudron et du professeur Plume* (Leading Players, 1914) was a version of André de Lorde's 1903 Guignol stage play, itself based on Edgar Allan Poe's *The System of Dr. Tarr and Professor Fether*, thus being an outré reworking of American horror-themed literature. The film featured Henri Gouget of the Parisian Théâtre du Grand-Guignol as Dr. Goudron. *Moving Picture World* wrote:

> *The Lunatics* is set in an asylum in which the inmates have got the upper hand and are ruling things while a terrible thunderstorm lasts. . . . The craftiest crazy man of them all has taken [the head doctor's] place. Immaculate in the doctor's frock coat, one of his hands splashed with red, he is now the sententious head doctor and ready to "cure" any others who may need his administrations.[94]

Unsuspecting visitors to the institute meet the new "doctor," who explains his special cure: it involves cutting out a patient's eye and slitting his or her throat. The same trade publication added:

> It is no scientific asylum full of dreary sameness where it happens, but a private sanitarium in an old castle with its grounds and high iron fence. It is weird and awe-inspiring; just the place for a terrible adventure. The photography, in tone and distinctness, in spite of the fact that the storm is heavy overhead, seems alive. Glimpses of the hurrying clouds are shown [as are] long flashes of lightning.[95]

The trade concluded by warning that the "artistic" film was not something "for three-year-olds to see just before going to bed at night."

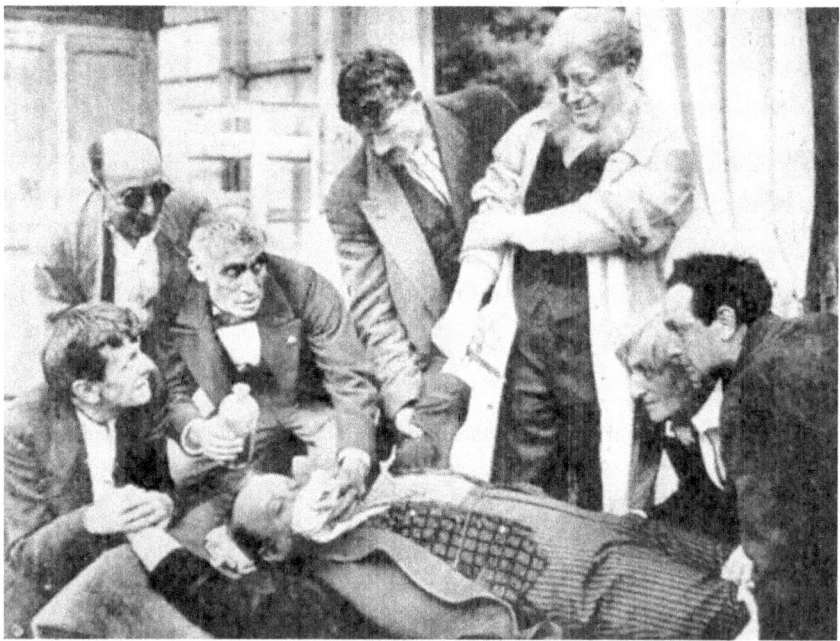

Figures 14.6 and 14.7 Two images from *The Lunatics* (Leading Players, 1914).

Certainly the most common narrative appropriations of Poe's work resulted from *The Cask of Amontillado* (1846), specifically the act of walling up one or more human beings who are still alive. D. W. Griffith's *The Sealed Room* (Biograph, 1909)—a one-reeler that also drew upon Honoré de Balzac's *La grande Bretèche* (1831)—remains the most famous of these moving pictures.[96] When Vitagraph released *Entombed Alive* (1909) later that same year, *Variety* argued it was either a "complete steal" from *The Sealed Room* or a "remarkable coincidence."[97] The *New York Dramatic Mirror* said much the same, believing both moving pictures must have been "adapted from the same interesting legend."[98]

By contrast, when reviewing *Vengeance* (Majestic, 1913), *Moving Picture World* announced it was a "modern version of the plot made familiar by Poe and other writers, in which a human being is walled up in brickwork."[99] Loose variations also appeared in *Entombed Alive/L'emmurée des Balkans* (Gaumont, 1910), *The Nun/Nonnen fra Asminderød* (Great Northern, 1911), *The Golden Hoard, or Buried Alive* (Vitagraph, 1913), and Victorin-Hippolyte Jasset's *Phantom Dungeon/Le trésor des Baux* (Union Features, 1913, aka *The Phantom Dungeon, or The Treasure of Baux*).[100] When discussing Edison's 1911 film version of Verdi's *Aida* (1871), *Moving Picture World* also mentioned Poe, reminded of him presumably because the opera features a character "condemned to be entombed alive."[101]

At least four films of the era borrowed plot elements from *The Murders in the Rue Morgue*, one being *Sherlock Holmes in the Great Mystery* (Crescent, 1908, aka *Sherlock Holmes in the Great Murder Mystery*), in which an escaped gorilla attacks and kills a young lady in her home.[102] In 1914, Eclectic released the three-reel "comedy-drama" *The Phantom Thief/Ténébros* [sic], in which an escaped monkey purloins a pearl necklace.[103] One year earlier, Walter McNamara directed the two-reel *Who Killed Olga Carew?* (Imp, 1913).[104] When its title character is murdered, authorities arrest an innocent "country girl" (played by Jane Gail). During her trial, the judge learns the truth: an ape was the real culprit.[105] The reverse occurred in the plot of *The Orang-Outang* (Selig Polyscope, 1915); in it, the title animal is blamed for his master's homicide until the "real murderer, a third person, confesses."[106]

An official adaptation of the story came in 1914, when Paul Clemons starred in a feature version of *The Murders in the Rue Morgue*. On August 12, 1914, the *New York Dramatic Mirror* wrote:

> Robert Goodman has just completed for the Paragon Photoplays Company a five-reel feature of Edgar Allan Poe's *Murders in the Rue Morgue*. Mr. Goodman, who had many years' experience with the Melies, Majestic, and Universal companies, has been free-lancing and this is the most ambitious picture he has made.[107]

Though copyrighted as *Murders in the Rue Morgue*, an inexplicable title change to *The Mystery of the Rue Morgue* occurred, sometime either before or during November 1914.[108] That same month, a fire started at the building where Paragon Photoplays headquartered, but at least one copy of the film survived.[109] Newspaper advertisements indicate that a theatre in Galveston, Texas screened *The Mystery of the Rue Morgue* in March 1915, as did theatres in Harrisburg, Pennsylvania and Canton, Ohio in September 1915.[110] When the film appeared in Auburn, New York in March 1915, the local newspaper claimed its distributor was the "Exclusive Film Company."[111]

Other film companies also attempted to adapt Poe formally. In 1911, Ambrosio released *The Mask of the Red Death/La maschera tragica* (which used Poe's 1842 spelling of "mask," rather than "masque" as he used in the revised 1845 version) on a split-reel with a comedy entitled *The Hornet/Il moscone*. A plot synopsis in *Moving Picture News* described the Poe film as follows:

> The City of Naples is in the grasp of the plague, and the terrified people are mowed down by the awful disease. The king with his court flees to a distant castle, where death is mockingly defied behind locked doors. Death, a shadowy spectre, carrying his scythe, stalks into the castle, presenting a weird and awe-inspiring sight, and casts the plague upon all except a poor woman and her two little children whose pleadings moved the king to take them along, and who alone, prayed to be spared.[112]

The Ambrosio plot synopsis added that the "exceptional" moving picture featured "wonderful photography."[113]

In 1913, Alice Guy Blaché directed *The Pit and the Pendulum*, a key film not only in the lineage of Poe adaptations, but also in the history of horror-themed cinema, specifically in its unabashed presentation of dramatic horror. Writing about the three-reeler in her autobiography, Blaché recalled:

> We had imagined as a way to deliver [the male lead, played by Darwin Karr] by cutting his ropes . . . while he lies tied to the torture rack, waiting for the fatal sweep of the knife . . . to confide this mission to gutter rats. The cords were copiously smeared with food to attract the rats. They fulfilled their role marvelously, but a few preferred fresh meat, [and] came sniffing at the nose of the actor and even penetrated the legs of his trousers. When at last the ropes broke he was not slow to his feet, swearing there would be no retake.[114]

Unfortunately, the only known surviving copy is incomplete.[115] In it, the "revengeful" Pedro (Fraunie Fraunholz) decides to frame Alonzo (Darwin Karr) for using "sorcery" to steal the church's treasure. The print ends with "unprincipled monks" of the Spanish Inquisition apprehending Alonzo. What survives illustrates effective filmmaking and acting, particularly from Fraunholz, but little of Poe's story and certainly none of the torture scenes that Blaché described.

In language that made clear Blaché's intentions, Solax promoted the "feature" as being "gruesome" and "blood-curdling."[116] *Moving Picture World* explained, "As the ['terrifying but thrilling'] tale itself is really nothing more than a succession of horrors, it was necessary to add a plot and this has been done with considerable skill. Poe undoubtedly appeals to a widespread taste for the classically gruesome and there is no doubt that this taste will be gratified by these pictures."[117] The *Exhibitors' Times* echoed these points, claiming, "It is a very delicate matter to tamper with a story by such a wonderful mind as Poe's, yet this introductory action was so logical and so effective that it undoubtedly enhanced the power of the main situation."[118] And the *New York Dramatic Mirror* commented, "Some liberties have been taken with Edgar Allan Poe's story . . . but altogether it is an excellent production that very well reflects the haunting horror of Poe's tale." The review continues, "There are terrible details in plenty, such as the showing of rats crawling over the body of a man strapped to a plank, that should cause a shudder quite as effectually as even Poe's descriptions."[119]

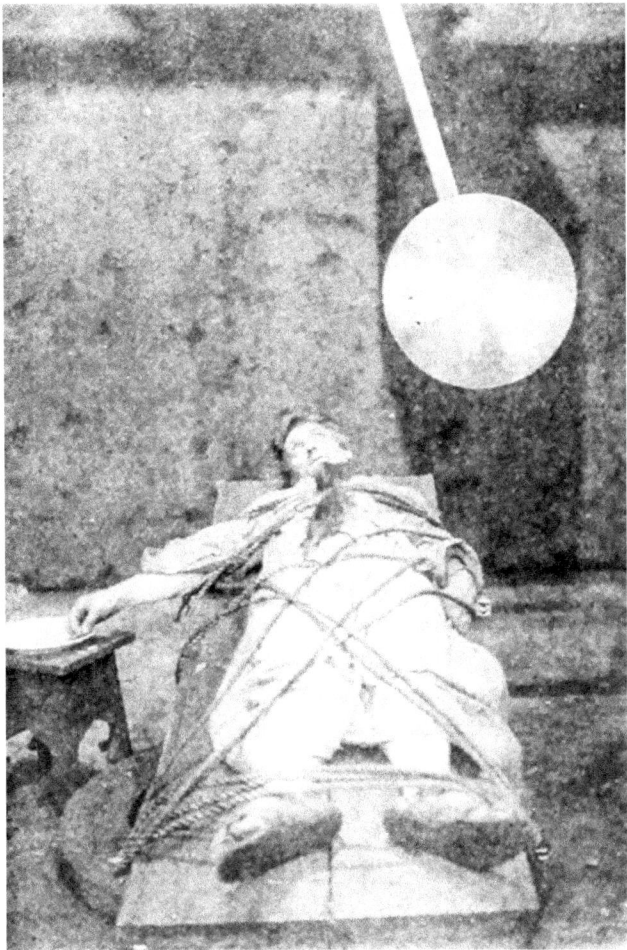

Figure 14.8 Alice Guy Blache's *The Pit and the Pendulum* (Solax, 1913).

Reviewing *The Pit and the Pendulum* in a different issue, *Moving Picture World* informed readers that it dealt:

with terror and horror and creat[ed] an atmosphere around the spectator that is likely to make him shiver. We were indeed astonished at the effectiveness with which the fearful tortures of the story's hero have been illustrated by the Solax producer. The sets are remarkably realistic and this is especially true of the dungeon-filled monastery, into which the luckless hero is dragged and in which, before he is released, he is tortured with fiendish ingenuity. The quiet occupants of many of the dungeons shown are skeletons and all the mechanisms of torture, including the cell with the pit in its floor, down which we see skulls and crawling serpents (this bottom of the pit is not so realistic as it might have been) have been extremely well conceived. The pendulum, massive and sharp, which swings back and forth and ever draws nearer to the bound victim, is also effective, as is the manner of his salvation from it. Rats gnaw the ropes that bind him. Finally, we feel the walls around him growing hot and see them folding in on him.[120]

Critiquing the same scene, the *Exhibitors' Times* declared, "it sweeps the spectator off his feet and deluges him, as it were, in a veritable maelstrom of horror."[121]

The *Exhibitors' Times* also praised the film's aesthetic design, giving further insight into its lost scenes:

> The director . . . intensified the suspense [in the torture scene] by flashing every now and then the rescue party making its way through the subterranean passageways, so that the spectators could not help oscillating between fear and hope. It had the genuine fascination of terror. . . . A clever bit of lighting was accomplished in the dungeon scene when we see the pendulum's shadow swinging to and fro on the wall some time before we see the actual object. Another odd and artistic effect showed the Inquisitors gathered around the upper opening of the cell peering down, the face of each being illumined from below in all its fiendish hideousness.[122]

Despite all of its praise, the trade believed Blaché had gone too far by depicting a "woman on the rack." Audiences might not have agreed, as Blaché remembered the film became an "enormous success."[123]

The difficulties of adapting individual Poe stories faithfully, particularly in the post-nickelodeon period when running times were increasing, led to the most ambitious Poe film of the era, D. W. Griffith's *The Avenging Conscience or "Thou Shalt Not Kill"* (1914). Here was neither a direct adaptation of a specific Poe story nor an unattributed repurposing of his ideas. Griffith's film instead became an amalgam of numerous Poe tales and poems. It is, in effect, Griffith's *The Tell-Tale Heart*, an original narrative adapted from various sources.

Reel Life believed no other director would have "dared to visualize the magic realms, where Poe's weird fancy dwelt," and that in his boldness, Griffith had "surpassed himself." Continuing with its praise, the trade acclaimed *The Avenging Conscience* as the "masterpiece of masterpieces," striking a "new high note in the ascending scale of motion picture production."[124] In a subsequent issue, *Reel Life* declared the film had no "equal on the screen."[125] By contrast, the *New York Clipper*, while impressed, believed that Blanche Sweet was miscast as the female lead, and that the cinematography was inconsistent.[126]

A reviewer for *Movie Pictorial* emphasized the question was not "how faithfully Poe has been dramatized, but whether or not Mr. Griffith has construed something that will entertain the motion-picture public."[127] Speaking to the same issue, the *New York Dramatic Mirror* claimed:

> A great deal of Griffith and a little bit of Poe are encountered in *The Avenging Conscience, or "Thou Shalt Not Kill."* Our most original of directors seems to have been inspired equally by the poet's passion for beauty and the storyteller's genius for conjuring haunting horrors. . . . It seems odd that the output of such diverse moods of genius should be merged in the same picture, yet the resulting effect is not unlike the effect of reading Poe. And that, of course, was Griffith's intention.[128]

Moving Picture News echoed that point, claiming, "It is the spirit and the atmosphere [of Poe] that pervades the entire production. Anyone who is acquainted with Poe will see his somewhat gruesome imagination in every foot of the film; those who are not will realize that the story is the work of a master craftsman."[129]

Viewing *The Avenging Conscience* makes apparent Griffith's sophisticated approach to Poe.[130] In it, the lead character, "The Nephew," played by Henry B. Walthall, reads a book

Figure 14.9 A frame from D. W. Griffith's *The Avenging Conscience or "Thou Shalt Not Kill"* (1914).

of Poe's tales and poems. Griffith presents an onscreen image of Poe and the first page of *The Tell-Tale Heart* (1843). Inspired by what he reads, The Nephew decides to kill his uncle to gain his money and marry Annabel (Blanche Sweet), whom intertitles compare to the title character of Poe's poem *Annabel Lee* (1849). But The Nephew does not kill his uncle at night while he sleeps, nor does he hide the corpse under the floor. Rather, he strangles his uncle in the daytime, and—in a scene reminiscent of both *The Cask of Amontillado* (1846) and *The Black Cat* (1843)—bricks up the corpse in the "wall of the old fireplace."

The Nephew's mental breakdown in front of The Detective (Ralph Lewis) remains a visual tour-de-force, both of Walthall's subtle acting, including his use of eye movements, and of Griffith's aesthetic sensibilities. Close-ups of The Detective's hand tapping a pencil on the table, and The Nephew nervously stopping him, create enormous tension, as do iris shots of The Detective staring intently at The Nephew. As Tom Gunning has written, close-ups in *The Avenging Conscience* play a "determinate psychological role."[131] Here is a key example of Griffith using the apparatus of cinema to adapt the literary atmosphere of Poe in visual terms.

During The Nephew's mental breakdown, Griffith offers a number of haunting images, including double exposures of The Uncle's ethereal body. An intertitle quotes from *The Bells* (1849): "They are neither man nor woman; They are neither brute nor human; They are ghouls!" Such language explains onscreen images of hellish creatures that are part human and part beast. An image of a witch also appears. Other shots depict The Nephew strapped in a chair and being clasped by a skeleton. Later The Nephew sees his beloved Annabel commit suicide by throwing herself off a cliff near waves crashing on the beach.

Griffith provides a happy ending by explaining away the murder as nothing more than a nightmare. The Uncle is alive and well, and so The Nephew is able to enjoy his life with Annabel. The use of dreams allowed Griffith to sidestep a morbid conclusion. At the same time, it is worth considering how Poe's own work engages with dreamscapes, including in his 1849 poem *A Dream within a Dream*, which concludes with imagery not unlike the film, particularly in its presentation of Annabel's suicide: "O God! Can I not save/*One* from the pitiless wave?/Is *all* that we see or seem/But a dream within a dream?"

During the nineteenth century, interest in Poe's life increased as much as, or more than, the interest in his literature. The mythology that grew up around him after his death was compelling, even if often inaccurate, due in no small part to Rufus Griswold's biased 1850 memoir. Though one of Poe's friends decried the essay as a "false" and "perverted, jaundiced vision," it proved influential.[132] Various authors attempted to write accurate biographies during the nineteenth century, though the combined result only seemed to make Poe's life seem more mythical. In 1875, for example, *Scribner's Monthly* described Poe as a "Mad Man of Letters."[133] For many at the time, the man and his literature were inseparable.

The approaching centennial of Poe's birth inspired George Hazelton, author of the Broadway comedy *Mistress Nell* (1900), to write a four-act play about Poe's life.[134] Covering Poe's early life and later tragedies, *The Raven*, as it was titled, featured "considerable comedy," according to one review.[135] Touted as a "new" play, productions started in late 1908 and continued in 1909, with Henry Ludlowe portraying Poe.[136] As part of its publicity, Hazelton claimed to have written *The Raven* with a pen made out of wood from Poe's coffin.

In actual fact, Hazelton had written a version of *The Raven* years earlier. His five-act play *Edgar Allan Poe, or The Raven* was staged in Baltimore in 1895.[137] Moreover, it is possible that Hazelton took inspiration from Henry Tyrell's one-act play *Edgar Poe* (1895), which presented "some suppositious episodes in the life of that poet."[138] Then, under the shortened title *The Raven*, Hazelton's play (or a variation upon it) was staged in Allentown, Pennsylvania in 1904, with Frederick Lewis playing Poe.[139] In other words, Hazelton's "new" play of 1908 was a revision and revival of something he had written at least thirteen years earlier. Then, by 1909, Hazelton adapted his drama into a novel.[140]

Working from a similar desire to honor Poe's centennial and reap financial return from it, D. W. Griffith directed the one-reel *Edgar Allen* [sic] *Poe* for American Mutoscope & Biograph in early 1909. When Kino International released it on DVD, it added modern text that notes "historians" have speculated the misspelling of "Allan" as "Allen" resulted from Biograph's haste to release the film for the centennial.[141] While possible, this speculation is at best incomplete. Various ephemera for Hazelton's play mistakenly give Poe's middle name as "Allen" as well.

At any rate, *Edgar Allen Poe*'s narrative finds the title character unable to support his sickly wife, or even keep her bedridden body warm. A raven appearing in their shabby home inspires Poe to write his famous poem. After being rejected by a few editors, one finally agrees to publish it. Poe purchases a blanket for his wife with his

Figure 14.10 Eclair American's *The Raven* (1912).

payment, but when he gets home he finds her dead. Biograph heralded *Edgar Allen Poe* as "one of the most artistic films ever produced." The company's publicity promoted it as the story of

> undoubtedly the most original poetical genius ever produced by America, and might be regarded the literary lion of the universe, to which fact the public are becoming alive, hence it is most timely that the Biograph should produce a story in commemoration of this season, the centennial anniversary of his birth, showing him to be a man a heart, and not as his enemies have painted him.[142]

The *New York Dramatic Mirror* admired *Edgar Allen Poe*'s "scenic arrangements" and its depiction of Poe's "gentle character," while *Moving Picture World* approved of *Edgar Allen Poe*'s "excellent" action and "heartily commended" the make-up created for its title character.[143]

Similar in approach was Eclair American's 1912 two-reeler *The Raven*, a "photo-poem" directed by Étienne Arnaud and featuring Guy Oliver as Poe. Company publicity drew attention to the film's $10,000 budget and the fact some footage was shot at the "historic Poe cottage at Fordham, New York."[144] Here was yet another entry (with *Legend of Sleepy Hollow* and *Feathertop*) in the company's "Literary Photo Sensations." According to a synopsis, *The Raven* conveyed:

> ... the sad romance of Edgar Allan Poe, his beautiful, dying wife, and their bitter life of struggle for the recognition of genius. The poem is interpreted by the all-seeing eye of the camera, and the success of the poet, in his great inspiration, is shown with beautiful scenic effects and a magnificently staged production exceeding our past successes.[145]

At one point in the film, double-exposure work depicted brief "scenes" from Poe's various stories, including *The Descent into the Maelstrom* (1841), *The Gold-Bug* (1843), *The Black Cat*, *The Murders in the Rue Morgue*, *The Premature Burial*, *The Pit and the Pendulum*, and others.[146] Whether these "scenes" were represented by dramatizations or still images is unknown.

Three-and-a-half years later, audiences saw *The Raven* (Essanay, 1915), director Charles J. Brabin's six-reel adaptation of Hazelton's play. Period publicity described it as follows:

> Edgar Allan Poe, while at college, incurs many debts and is sent home in disgrace. He is ordered from the house by his father. Shortly after, he marries, and tries to make a living by writing, but is a failure financially. His wife dies because he is unable to furnish her with even the bare necessities of life. He is plunged into great grief and despair. All night he sits brooding over his loss. Through his distorted imagination, he sees the ominous raven enter his chamber and croak gloomy forebodings. The spirit of his wife also appears and finally he himself dies, and is wafted to heights supernal, where he is united with his "Lenore."[147]

Henry B. Walthall, who had already starred in *The Avenging Conscience*, portrayed Poe. Columnist "Mae Tinee" (a pseudonym corruption of "matinee") claimed that Walthall spent hours training a raven to say "nevermore" on cue.[148] And Essanay reportedly shot footage on location at the "Poe cottage at Fordham, in the Bronx, and of the bust of Poe now at the Players' Club, New York City."[149]

Motography heralded *The Raven* as a "masterpiece," one in which Poe and Walthall became "synonymous."[150] *Moving Picture World* commended Walthall's acting, as well as the film's narrative structure, which its reviewer believed unfolded continuously, rather than in well-defined "parts" created by reel changes.[151] The *New York Clipper* applauded *The Raven* for being a "first class production" that "should draw as well in five years as it does today."[152] The trade also celebrated Walthall, as did the *Chicago Tribune* and *Movie Pictorial*.[153]

Wid's Films and Film Folk praised Walthall as well, but believed *The Raven*'s use of special effects varied between "well done" and "artificial."[154] *Variety* complained about the film's "papier mache [sic] set pieces" and its length, advising that 2,000 feet should be cut out of what was a "tiresome picture."[155] *The Billboard* thought much the same, warning readers *The Raven* "drags at times, and even the most enthusiastic disciple of Poe is apt to become bored."[156]

A surviving copy of *The Raven* offers evidence in support of these original critiques. The brief exploration of Poe's ancestors seems superfluous, whereas Walthall's performance is restrained and effective within the context of the era. An intertitle explains that "insidious wine" was initially responsible for the "strange fancies" in Poe's mind, with his wife's death providing further creative inspiration and mental deterioration. Images of Poe writing in silhouette and visiting his wife's grave remain effective.[157]

Particularly haunting is *The Raven*'s conclusion. The camera moves inward to depict Poe at home in his chair, then moves outward from his door, the knocker of which raps of its own accord. An eerie shadow of a raven appears on the door. Then a real raven flies in through the window, its famous dialogue "nevermore" artistically depicted in intertitles in a font style made of artistic bones. After a suspenseful and effective visualization of the poem's narrative, Poe dies on the floor.

Conclusion

In late 1915, the *New York Times* noted that actress Virginia Pearson—who would later appear in *The Phantom of the Opera* (Universal, 1925)—was behind a movement to "erect a fitting memorial to Edgar Allan Poe" in New York. One of the reasons: she was set to appear in "some" Poe stories "for the movies."[158] These films were not produced, but the effort indicates once again how prominent Poe had become in early American cinema, particularly with regard to the growth and evolution of horror-themed moving pictures, culminating in the works of Blaché and Griffith.

Nevertheless, Americanizing the American cinema by adapting indigenous literature was not ultimately possible. To be fair, jingoistic efforts of this type might have correctly grouped Poe, Hawthorne, and Irving, presenting them to audiences that in some cases had not read such authors or could not read at all, allowing them access to a literary canon prized by the Other Half, who were educated and moneyed.

But the reliance on world literature for subject matter continued, as in the case of the five-reel version of Dickens's *The Mystery of Edwin Drood* (World Film, 1914), directed by Alice Guy Blaché's husband, Herbert Blaché.[159] Another example would be Thanhouser's two-reel version of Oscar Wilde's *The Picture of Dorian Gray* (1915), with Harris Gordon in the title role.[160] U.S. film companies would continue to adapt world literature, just as other countries would adapt American stories.

Notes

1. Advertisement, *Moving Picture World*, November 2, 1912, 412.
2. "The Mystery of the Silent Death," *Moving Picture World*, May 8, 1915, 899.
3. "*Mortmain* (Vitagraph), Five Reels," *New York Clipper*, September 11, 1915.
4. Reviews of *The Body in the Trunk* (Majestic, 1914) and *His Phantom Sweetheart* (Vitagraph, 1915) in the *New York Dramatic Mirror* also invoked Poe's name. See "*The Body in the Trunk*," *New York Dramatic Mirror*, May 20, 1914; "*His Phantom Sweetheart*," *New York Dramatic Mirror*, April 14, 1915.
5. Eileen Bowser, *The Transformation of Cinema, 1907–1915* (Berkeley: University of California Press, 1990), 256.
6. Frank L. Dyer, "The Moral Development of the Silent Drama," *Moving Picture World*, April 16, 1910, 583.
7. "She," *The Film Index*, November 14, 1908, 11; "She," *Moving Picture News*, December 16, 1911, 42.
8. "What Is an American Subject?", *Moving Picture World*, January 22, 1910, 82.
9. Advertisement, *Views and Film Index*, March 16, 1907, 2. A brief amount of footage of *A Curious Dream* exists at the Library of Congress by way of a paper print deposit.

10. "*The Old Clock on the Stairs*," *Moving Picture World*, September 21, 1912, 1183; "Eclair Co. Gets Exclusive Rights to O. Henry Stories," *Moving Picture News*, January 25, 1913, 15.
11. Advertisement, *Moving Picture News*, April 27, 1912, 33.
12. "*The Death Knell*, Powerful, Keen Inquisition into Soul Stirring Emotion," *Moving Picture News*, June 21, 1913, 8.
13. "*Was She Justified?*", *Moving Picture World*, February 25, 1911, 432.
14. W. Stephen Bush, "*Doomed to Die, or The Vial of Wrath*," *Moving Picture World*, September 6, 1913, 1056.
15. "*A Christmas Carol*," *New York Dramatic Mirror*, December 19, 1908, 7; "*A Christmas Carol*," *Moving Picture World*, December 26, 1914, 1900. A copy of *A Christmas Carol* (1914) is archived at the British Film Institute.
16. "*A Christmas Carol*," *Edison Kinetogram*, November 15, 1911, 7.
17. "*A Christmas Carol*," *Moving Picture World*, January 7, 1911, 32.
18. A copy of *A Christmas Carol* (1910) is available on the DVD *A Christmas Past* (New York: Kino International, 2001).
19. Thanhouser also released a version of *The Woman in White* in 1912. See "*The Woman in White*," *Moving Picture News*, October 19, 1912, 24–5.
20. At times in the trade press, G. R. Nichols was referred to as G. R. Nicholls. A copy of *The Woman in White* is archived at George Eastman Museum.
21. William Lord Wright, "William Lord Wright's Page," *Moving Picture News*, November 9, 1912, 14.
22. "*The Woman in White*," *Moving Picture World*, November 2, 1912, 451.
23. Ibid., 451.
24. George Blaisdell, "*The Dead Secret*," *Moving Picture World*, May 24, 1913, 815.
25. Though first published in 1855, an expanded version of *The Dream Woman* was published in the two-volume collection *The Frozen Deep and Other Stories* (London: Richard Bentley & Son, 1874).
26. Hanford C. Judson, "*The Dream Woman*," *Moving Picture World*, March 21, 1914, 1508.
27. A. Danson Michell, "*The Dream Woman*," *Motion Picture News*, March 21, 1914, 46.
28. "*The Moonstone*," *The Billboard*, June 5, 1909, 8.
29. "*The Moonstone* (Selig)," *Moving Picture World*, June 19, 1909, 834. In the original text, the quoted word "resemble" is plural; for grammatical reasons, I have changed it to singular.
30. Ibid., 834.
31. Frank Wiesberg, "Moving Picture Reviews," *Variety*, June 19, 1909, 11.
32. "*The Moonstone*," *New York Dramatic Mirror*, June 19, 1909, 16.
33. "*Jane Eyre*," *Moving Picture World*, May 7, 1910, 755; "*Jane Eyre*," *Motion Picture News*, February 7, 1914, 38; Lynde Denig, "From the Biograph Studio," *Moving Picture World*, July 24, 1915, 670.
34. "*The Mad Lady of Chester*," *Moving Picture World*, October 15, 1910, 890.
35. "Review of New Features," *Moving Picture News*, September 13, 1913, 11.
36. George Blaisdell, "*The Mystery of the Yellow Room*," *Moving Picture World*, September 20, 1913, 1270.
37. "Review of New Features," 11.
38. "Brevities of the Business," *Motography*, September 26, 1914, 450.
39. Peter Milne, "*The Phantom Violin*," *Motion Picture News*, October 24, 1914, 42.
40. Hanford C. Judson, "*The Phantom Violin*," *Moving Picture World*, September 26, 1914, 1754.

41. Before appearing as a novel in 1910, *The Phantom of the Opera* was published in France in serialized form during 1909 and 1910. With regard to the film's change of title, see "Wife's Treachery Drives Musician Mad," *Universal Weekly*, March 1915, 8.
42. Judson, "*The Phantom Violin*," 1754.
43. Ibid., 1754.
44. A copy of *Sherlock Holmes Baffled* is archived in the Paper Print Collection at the Library of Congress. The Library of Congress also has a brief amount of footage from different scenes from *The Adventures of Sherlock Holmes; or, Held for Ransom*, also by way of a paper print deposit.
45. Advertisement, *Moving Picture World*, September 28, 1912, 1241; Advertisement, *Moving Picture World*, November 12, 1909, 579; "*The Musgrave Ritual*," *Moving Picture World*, March 8, 1913, 1020. The Franco-British Film Company was an Eclair brand, the films having been co-produced by French Eclair and Eclair British.
46. "Film Conan Doyle Stories," *New York Dramatic Mirror*, May 27, 1914.
47. *The Hound of the Baskervilles/Der Hund von Baskerville* has been restored using material from various archives by the Filmmuseum München.
48. M. I. MacDonald, "*The Hound of the Baskervilles*," *Moving Picture World*, February 27, 1915, 1302.
49. Louis Reeves Harrison, "Plots," *Moving Picture World*, July 1, 1911, 1493.
50. The similarities between these screen detectives and Sherlock Holmes did not go unnoticed at the time. Writing about *The Thief* (Essanay, 1910), *The Film Index* noted, "Essanay puts over a 'Sherlock Holmes.'" See "Detective Picture Story," *Film Index*, July 2, 1910, 4.
51. Louis Reeves Harrison, "Detective Stories," *Moving Picture World*, June 12, 1915, 1748.
52. Versions of the tale produced and/or released in America include: *Awakening of Rip* (American Mutoscope, 1896); *Exit of Rip and the Dwarf* (American Mutoscope, 1896); *Rip Leaving Sleepy Hollow* (American Mutoscope, 1896); *Rip Meeting the Dwarf* (American Mutoscope, 1896); *Rip Passing Over the Mountain* (American Mutoscope, 1896); *Rip's Toast* (American Mutoscope, 1896); *Rip's Toast to Hudson* (American Mutoscope, 1896); *Rip's Twenty Years' Sleep* (American Mutoscope, 1896); *Rip Van Winkle* (American Mutoscope & Biograph, 1903, being a compilation of American Mutoscope's 1896 films); *Rip Van Winkle* (Lubin, 1903); *Rip Van Winkle* (Gaumont British, 1903); *Rip's Dream/La légende de Rip Van Winkle* (Méliès, 1905); *Rip Van Winkle* (Selig Polyscope, 1908); *Rip Van Winkle* (Columbia Film Company, 1910); *Rip Van Winkle* (Thanhouser, 1910); *Rip Van Winkle* (Reliance, 1912); *Rip Van Winkle* (Vitagraph, 1912); and *Rip Van Winkle* (Alco-Rolfe, 1914). Related films include *In the Haunts of Rip Van Winkle* (American Mutoscope & Biograph, 1906), *A Modern Rip Van Winkle* (American, 1914), and *Rip Van Winkle Badly Ripped* (Novelty, 1915).
53. "*The Devil and Tom Walker*," *Moving Picture World*, August 9, 1913, 658.
54. "*The Devil and Tom Walker*," *Moving Picture World*, August 16, 1913, 744.
55. See, for example, "General Summary," *New York Clipper*, May 14, 1859; "Amateur," *New York Clipper*, August 7, 1869; "A Boston Amateur Club," *New York Clipper*, April 14, 1877; "The New York Stage," *New York Clipper*, June 8, 1889.
56. "*The Spectre Bridegroom*," *Moving Picture World*, January 18, 1913, 294.
57. "*The Spectre Bridegroom*," *Eclair Bulletin*, January 1913.
58. "*The Spectre Bridegroom*," *Moving Picture News*, January 11, 1913, 9.
59. "*The Spectre Bridegroom*," *New York Dramatic Mirror*, January 29, 1913, 36.
60. Hugh Hoffman, "*The Spectre Bridegroom*," *Moving Picture World*, January 25, 1913, 349.
61. In 1911, Nestor released a moving picture titled *Sleepy Hollow*, but it was not based on the Irving story.

62. "*The Legend of Sleepy Hollow*," *Views and Film Index*, April 25, 1908, 11.
63. "*Legend of Sleepy Hollow*," *Moving Picture News*, April 20, 1912, 40.
64. "*Legend of Sleepy Hollow*," *The Billboard*, April 20, 1912, 52.
65. "*Legend of Sleepy Hollow*," *Moving Picture World*, May 4, 1912, 427.
66. "*The Legend of Sleepy Hollow*," *New York Dramatic Mirror*, May 1, 1912, 31.
67. "*The Scarlet Letter*," *Moving Picture World*, March 28, 1908, 271–2.
68. One reel of the Kinemacolor version is archived at George Eastman Museum.
69. "*The House of the Seven Gables*," *The Film Index*, October 22, 1910, 18.
70. Advertisement, *The Film Index*, October 8, 1910, 21.
71. Thomas Bedding, "The Sentiment of the Picture," *Moving Picture World*, October 15, 1910, 862.
72. Louis Reeves Harrison, "The Picture Drama as a Fine Art," *Moving Picture World*, October 29, 1910, 982.
73. "Blunder in the Moving Pictures," *Moving Picture World*, November 26, 1910, 1242.
74. Advertisement, *Moving Picture News*, April 27, 1912, 33.
75. "*Feathertop*," *Moving Picture World*, June 8, 1912, 946.
76. "Kinemacolor and *Feathertop*," *Moving Picture World*, April 5, 1913, 63.
77. "A Few Words about Film Merits," *Moving Picture News*, April 5, 1913, 18.
78. "*Feathertop* Makes a Fine Film," *Moving Picture News*, March 8, 1913, 33.
79. "The Grave of Poe," *New York Daily Times*, September 7, 1854, 2; "Amusements," *New York Times*, June 29, 1880, 5.
80. "In the Realm of Fresh Literature," *Los Angeles Times*, September 17, 1899, 16.
81. "What Literature Owes to Edgar Allan Poe," *New York Times*, January 10, 1909, SM6.
82. "How Edgar Allan Poe's Memory Is Revered at the University of Virginia," *New York Times*, February 11, 1912, X6.
83. "Poe Cottage Museum," *New York Clipper*, November 22, 1913.
84. "*The Bells*," *Moving Picture World*, August 9, 1913, 637.
85. A copy of *The Bells* (1912) is archived at the British Film Institute.
86. "When Edgar Allan Poe Recited *The Raven*," *New York Clipper*, December 26, 1903.
87. See, for example, "Prof. A Ryan," *New York Clipper*, January 16, 1869; "Dramatic," *New York Clipper*, July 1, 1882.
88. "*The Raven*," *New York Clipper*, May 9, 1891.
89. "New York City," *New York Clipper*, February 18, 1905; "Daly's Theatre," *New York Clipper*, September 25, 1909; "Mornings of Opera and Comedy Begin," *New York Clipper*, November 19, 1910.
90. "*The Plague-Stricken City*," *Moving Picture World*, September 21, 1912, 1178.
91. An advertisement for *The Necklace of the Dead* in *Moving Picture World* (December 24, 1910, 1451) titled the film without the use of the article *The*.
92. "*The Necklace of the Dead*," *Moving Picture World*, January 7, 1911, 35.
93. "A Remarkable Film," *Moving Picture World*, November 26, 1910, 1240. In *Dansk Stumfilm*, Vol. 2 (Copenhagen: Rhodos, 1977, 511–12), Marguerite Engberg publishes worldwide sales figures for Nordisk dramas of 1910, which are based on surviving company ledgers. *The Necklace of the Dead* became the company's biggest success of the year, with 122 prints sold. The average number of prints sold per title for that year was approximately forty-seven. For example, other Nordisk/Great Northern horror-themed films like *Dr. Jekyll and Mr. Hyde; or, a Strange Case* sold forty-four copies and *The Ghost of the Vaults* (produced 1910, but released 1911) sold fifty-two copies.
94. Hanford C. Judson, "*The Lunatics*," *Moving Picture World*, June 20, 1914, 1703.

95. Ibid., 1703.
96. A copy of *The Sealed Room* is available in the two-DVD set *D. W. Griffith: Years of Discovery: 1909–1913* (Chatsworth, California: Image Entertainment, 2002). Two other adaptations of *La grande Bretèche* appeared in America during the autumn/winter season of 1909. The first, released as *The False Oath/Spergiura!* (Ambrosio, 1909), received little coverage in the industry press, but did appear in newspaper listings. A copy is archived at the Museo Nazionale del Cinema. By contrast, the second version—*La grande Bretèche* (Pathé Frères-Film d'Art, 1909, aka *La grande Bretèche (The Great Breach)*)—was released with much publicity and constituted an official adaptation of the story. See "A Coming Headliner," *Moving Picture World*, December 11, 1909, 835. A copy is archived at the Centre national du cinéma et de l'image animée (CNC).
97. "Buried Alive," *Variety*, November 6, 1909, 13.
98. "Entombed Alive," *New York Dramatic Mirror*, November 13, 1909, 15.
99. "Vengeance," *Moving Picture World*, November 1, 1913, 498.
100. "Entombed Alive," *New York Dramatic Mirror*, August 20, 1910, 27; "The Nun," *Moving Picture World*, May 13, 1911, 1089; "The Golden Hoard, or Buried Alive," *Moving Picture World*, March 29, 1913, 1354; "[The] Phantom Dungeon," *Moving Picture World*, November 1, 1913, 534.
101. H. C. Judson, "The Civilizing Value of the Photoplay," *Moving Picture World*, May 27, 1911, 1182.
102. "*Sherlock Holmes in the Great Murder Mystery*," *Moving Picture World*, November 28, 1908, 434–5.
103. "Eclectic's Odd Mystery Film," *Motography*, July 18, 1914, 86.
104. "Film Flashes," *Variety*, October 31, 1913, 14.
105. "*Who Killed Olga Carew?*," *Moving Picture World*, November 22, 1913, 870.
106. "*The Orang-Outang*," *Motion Picture News*, August 14, 1915, 92.
107. "Film Poe Story," *New York Dramatic Mirror*, August 12, 1914, 24.
108. Advertisement, *Moving Picture World*, November 14, 1914, 1006.
109. "Fire in Forty-Fifth Street Exchange Building Cleans Out Three Film Concerns—Apt to Make Regulation More Drastic," *New York Clipper*, November 28, 1914.
110. Advertisement, *Galveston Daily News* (Galveston, Texas) March 25, 1915, 2; Advertisement, *Harrisburg Patriot* (Harrisburg, Pennsylvania), September 17, 1915, 10; Advertisement, *The Evening Repository* (Canton, Ohio), September 3, 1915.
111. "The Cornell," *The Auburn Citizen* (Auburn, New York), March 3, 1915, 12.
112. "*The Mask of the Red Death*," *Moving Picture News*, September 23, 1911, 28.
113. Ibid., 28.
114. Alice Guy Blaché, *The Memoirs of Alice Guy Blaché*, edited by Anthony Slide (Lanham, Maryland: Scarecrow Press, 1996), 72.
115. A copy of *The Pit and the Pendulum* is archived at the Library of Congress.
116. Advertisement, *Moving Picture World*, July 26, 1913, 388.
117. W. Stephen Bush, "*The Pit and the Pendulum*," *Moving Picture World*, August 9, 1913, 644.
118. "*The Pit and the Pendulum: A Study in Suspense*," *Exhibitors' Times*, August 2, 1913, 7.
119. "*The Pit and the Pendulum*," *New York Dramatic Mirror*, July 30, 1913, 28.
120. "*The Pit and the Pendulum*," *Moving Picture World*, August 2, 1913, 537.
121. "*The Pit and the Pendulum: A Study in Suspense*," 7.
122. Ibid., 7.
123. Blaché, 72.
124. "*The Avenging Conscience, Or, Thou Shalt Not Kill*," *Reel Life*, August 1, 1914, 16.

125. "Facts and Figures and Such," *Reel Life*, August 15, 1914, 6.
126. "*Avenging Conscience* (Mutual) Five Reels," *New York Clipper*, August 15, 1914, 7.
127. Vanderheyden Fyles, "*The Avenging Conscience*," *Movie Pictorial*, September 12, 1914, 29.
128. "*The Avenging Conscience*," *New York Dramatic Mirror*, August 12, 1914.
129. Peter Milne, "*The Avenging Conscience*," *Motion Picture News*, August 22, 1914, 48.
130. A copy of *The Avenging Conscience* is available on the DVD *The Avenging Conscience* (New York: Kino International, 2008).
131. Tom Gunning, *D. W. Griffith and the Origins of American Narrative Film* (Urbana, Illinois: University of Illinois Press, 1991), 189.
132. "Edgar Allan Poe," *The International Review*, March 1875, 145.
133. "A Mad Man of Letters," *Scribner's Monthly*, October 1875, 690.
134. "Play Founded on Poe's Life," *Washington Post*, December 6, 1908, SM3.
135. "*The Raven*," *The Billboard*, January 2, 1909, 9.
136. "*The Raven* Staged," *New York Times*, December 24, 1908, 7; "*The Raven* Produced," *New York Clipper*, January 1909.
137. "*Edgar Allan Poe, or The Raven*," *New York Clipper*, November 2, 1895.
138. "New York City," *New York Clipper*, May 25, 1895.
139. "*The Raven* on the Stage," *New York Times*, September 14, 1904, 9.
140. George Hazelton, *The Raven: A Novel* (New York: D. Appleton & Company, 1909).
141. A copy of *Edgar Allen* [sic] *Poe* is available on the DVD *The Avenging Conscience* (New York: Kino International, 2008).
142. "*Edgar Allen Poe*," *Moving Picture World*, February 6, 1909, 152.
143. "*Edgar Allan* [sic] *Poe*," *New York Dramatic Mirror*, February 20, 1909, 16; "*Edgar Allan* [sic] *Poe*," *Moving Picture World*, February 13, 1909.
144. Advertisement, *Moving Picture News*, April 20, 1912, 42; Advertisement, *Moving Picture World*, April 20, 1912, 191.
145. "*The Raven*," *Moving Picture World*, May 4, 1912, 462.
146. This point is made in two different articles: "Poe in Pictures," *Moving Picture World*, April 27, 1912, 313; and "*The Raven*," *Moving Picture News*, May 4, 1912, 33.
147. "*The Raven*," *Exhibitors Film Exchange*, October 23, 1915, 18.
148. Mae Tinee, "Latest News from Movie Land," *Chicago Tribune*, November 28, 1915, E3. At this time, "Mae Tinee" was a byline for Frances Peck (aka Frances Peck Kerner).
149. "Essanay Making Poe's *Raven*," *Moving Picture World*, September 25, 1915, 2160.
150. John C. Garrett, "Some Current Releases Reviewed," *Motography*, November 20, 1915, 1079–80.
151. James S. McQuade, "*The Raven*," *Moving Picture World*, November 20, 1915, 1507.
152. "*The Raven* (Essanay) Six Reels," *New York Clipper*, November 27, 1915, 44.
153. Kitty Kelly, "Henry B. Walthall in *The Raven*," *Chicago Tribune*, December 1, 1915, 19; "The Raven," *Movie Pictorial*, November 1915, unpaginated.
154. "Feature Films as Wid Sees Them," *Wid's Films and Film Folk*, November 25, 1915, unpaginated.
155. "*The Raven*," *Variety*, November 12, 1915, 22.
156. "*The Raven*," *The Billboard*, November 20, 1915, 52.
157. A copy of *The Raven* is available on the DVD *Henry B. Walthall in The Raven—Ghost* (Phoenix, Arizona: Grapevine Video, 2006).
158. "Notes Written on the Screen," *New York Times*, November 28, 1915, X10.
159. "*The Mystery of Edwin Drood*," *Moving Picture World*, October 24, 1914, 501.

160. "*The Picture of Dorian Gray* (Thanhouser)," *Moving Picture World*, July 24, 1915, 675. A copy of *The Picture of Dorian Gray* is archived at the Library of Congress. The New York Film Company sold an earlier film version of the story, titled simply *Dorian Gray*. It was a two-reeler originally released in Denmark in 1910 as *Dorian Gray* (Regia Kunstfilms, aka *Dorian Grays Portræt*). See Advertisement, *Moving Picture World*, April 19, 1913, 297. See also the program for the film in the collection of the Danish Film Institute.

SECTION III

Exhibition and Reception

CHAPTER 15

Exhibition and Reception

[*The Toll of Fear* (Lubin, 1913)] is two reels of unrelieved horror. There were people in the audience who thought it was "great and wonderful"; but some thought it was "too terrible," and one man we noticed turning away from it refused to give us his opinion.
—*Moving Picture World*, 1913[1]

On November 1, 1911, the *Washington Post* reported on the death of Sinclair Chissus, Jr., a five-year-old boy from Redford, Michigan. While in Detroit with his grandmother, Sinclair attended a moving picture show during which "Halloween hobgoblins and witches flitted vividly and weirdly about in a black void." The newspaper explained that the films were "too realistic for little Sinclair." He fainted. And then he died. A physician's diagnosis determined the young filmgoer had been "scared to death."[2] Though reporting on the same event, the *Detroit Free Press* gave a different account. Sinclair had been ill for much of his life, apparently. According to the coroner, "the undue excitement of a day in the city probably affected his weak heart."[3] That he died at a "picture show" was not in dispute, but the full context of his condition and death was.

Could horror-themed moving pictures trigger dramatic responses from their audiences? Only months after Sinclair died, producer William H. Clifford of the Pacific Motion Picture Company announced he was working on a film that would feature the image of a "celebrated Hindoo hypnotist" that would "put under a hypnotic spell all in the audience who are susceptible to hypnotic suggestion."[4] Here was an effort to control the audience, as well as a publicity gimmick not unlike those for which William Castle became famous in the 1950s and 1960s.

Clifford does not seem to have completed the moving picture in question, but his project poses questions of a type not dissimilar to those arising from the fate of Sinclair Chissus, Jr. How were horror-themed films publicized and screened in the early cinema period? Who watched them? How did they react? Understanding exhibition and reception is a crucial pursuit, but one fraught with potential problems and conflicting data.

Early histories of the cinema, such as those written by Terry Ramsaye (1926), Benjamin Hampton (1931), and Lewis Jacobs (1939), argued that the working class constituted the vast majority of nickelodeon viewers.[5] These arguments remained largely unchallenged until the 1970s, when Russell Merritt published an essay on Boston nickelodeons that suggested some exhibitors did not approve of working-class audiences and instead courted the middle class.[6] Then, in 1979, Robert C. Allen published an essay that used primary sources to determine that the majority of nickelodeons in New York City operated in areas associated with the middle class. By contrast, he discovered that relatively few nickelodeons operated in working-class neighborhoods.[7]

The work of Merritt and Allen was not met with widespread acceptance. Robert Sklar challenged their findings in 1988, but it was Ben Singer's 1995 essay "Manhattan Nickelodeons: New Data on Audiences and Exhibitors" that provoked the greatest controversy.[8] By using primary sources that implied New York City had more nickelodeons than Allen had found, Singer disputed the notion that the middle class was the dominant audience. As a result, he concluded that the traditional view of "the immigrant and working-class foundation of early exhibition may not have been as far off the mark as the revisionist historians maintain."[9]

Singer's conclusions were not readily embraced either. The Singer-Allen debate—which William Uricchio and Roberta E. Pearson described as "lively and at times feisty"[10]—became the most notable discussion about early cinema audiences in the history of American film historiography. Melvyn Stokes rightly declared the "controversy has added a good deal to our knowledge of cinema exhibition in New York during the nickelodeon era." However, the debate also triggers as many questions about the persons who attended nickelodeons in New York City as it answers.[11] Stokes concluded, "it is still unclear what, if anything, can be generalized from the New York experience."[12] Indeed, Singer and Allen understood that New York City's nickelodeon audiences were not representative of those that existed in other American cities and towns.

More important than the details of the debate are the larger conclusions that can be drawn from it. Nickelodeons in New York City changed during the period. They went in and out of business, for example. The films they screened evolved, as did their audiences. These complexities emphasize the need for caution, particularly against constructing a singular and monolithic "audience" in which every patron interacted with moving pictures in the same ways. "It is hard to tell how a photoplay will affect different people," *Motography* remarked in 1911. "A film that strikes one man as 'good,' 'bully,' 'a peach,' will strike another as 'punk,' 'rotten,' 'bum.'"[13]

Furthermore, the very same person who might have viewed films in 1895 on a Kinetoscope was likely a different type of viewer when he or she saw films projected at a nickelodeon in 1905, and then again when he or she watched films at a motion picture theatre in 1915. If even the same viewer changed over time (or indeed during the course of a single screening, at which he or she could have experienced a range of reactions), then it becomes advisable to avoid bold, overarching claims made about the audiences of horror-themed films. After all, an audience is by its very definition a fragmentary coalition of persons bounded by the running time of the program: the lights go up, and a new, equally fragmentary group replaces them.

Nevertheless, it is possible to locate in primary sources certain trends and repetitions. For example, many viewers had an interest in seeing films that were authentic, rather than faked, as was the case with some "real" footage of boxing matches and military battles that were staged. But how viewers understood authenticity could vary, however. A 1905 screening in Grand Rapids, Wisconsin featured a program of fiction and non-fiction films. The newspaper noted that some of the fictional films were "so real as to make people feel nervous who sit in the front seats."[14]

While specific responses to particular films survive, they are few in number. Moving picture company catalogs, trade publications, and city newspapers are key resources for understanding early film audiences, as they occasionally recorded viewer reactions to moving picture exhibitions. But such reportage tended to generalize group reactions, rather than detail the differences, subtle or otherwise, that might have existed between patrons at the same performance. Likewise, some writers were no doubt biased, describing responses to support particular points of view, or were simply inaccurate in their reporting.

After all, Sinclair Chissus, Jr. probably did not die of fright after seeing ghosts and goblins projected at a film screening. But that does not diminish the importance of his story, or of all of those Americans who watched horror-themed films during the early cinema period.

The Pre-nickelodeon Era

The problems of reconstructing audiences become evident in examining the history of Edison's Kinetoscope, as well as other peepshow devices like the Mutoscope. Most Kinetoscope viewers were likely male, but some publicity promoted the device to "both ladies and gentlemen."[15] The topics (and scopophilic appeal) of specific films may also have played a role in eliciting interest from women. Charles Musser writes, "The first films had been made by men, primarily for men, and of men, but these conditions were to change soon after [the bodybuilder] Sandow's appearance [in a Kinetoscope moving picture]."[16] Ticket prices might also act as an indicator of who saw these films. In 1894, for example, the Holland Brothers' Kinetoscope parlor charged 25 cents per ticket to view moving pictures, not a particularly affordable price for the working classes.[17]

Details regarding the earliest film audiences are limited. As Musser notes, "ascertaining who watched the early motion-picture shows is a difficult task."[18] For example, little is known about exactly who attended the first public film screening at Koster & Bial's in New York City when the Vitascope made its debut on April 23, 1896. Ticket prices suggest that they were likely from the middle and/or upper classes. However, no breakdown of their ages or gender exists. Period publications speak to their collective, not individual, reactions. The *New York Times* reported that the crowd was "enthusiastic," responding with "vociferous cheering."[19] During the weeks that followed, subsequent audiences at Koster & Bial's—which at times might have included some repeat customers—continued to "applaud" the films, but audience members might well have favored particular moving pictures over others.[20] Indeed, on May 4, 1896, a "surf scene" was "shown twice in response to an encore."[21] At the same time, it is possible that some audience members present that same day preferred other moving pictures.[22]

What is evident is that—even before most Americans viewed any moving pictures at all—at least a small number of viewers in New York City developed preferences for certain kinds of films. Reviewing the bill at Keith's Union Square Theatre in New York in August 1896, the *New York Clipper* announced the Lumière Cinématographe would project new films, as well as "several old favorites."[23] In November 1896, the *Clipper* similarly observed that "audiences seem to take renewed delight in the reflection of many of the old favorite views."[24]

By contrast, repeat viewings were not usually possible for audience members in most American cities and towns. And the kind of viewers who attended Vitascope screenings in Baltimore, Boston, Cleveland, Providence, and Trenton in 1896 might well have been different from those who attended screenings in New York City.[25] For example, who constituted the "small audience" for a moving picture screening on October 12, 1896 at the San Antonio Opera House?[26] What films did they watch, in what order did they see them, and what did they think? And did advertisements promoting "Edison's Vitascope and Refined Concert Co." in Steubenville, Ohio that same year draw an exclusive type of audience member by use of Edison's name, by use of the word "refined," and/or by ticket prices that cost as much as 50 cents?[27]

Similar questions are relevant for much of the itinerant period of exhibition that continued during the late nineteenth and early twentieth centuries.[28] In 1898, for example, film screenings occurred at the German Lutheran Church in Bucyrus, Ohio, the Town Hall in Poughkeepsie, New York, and at a tent meeting in Bartlett, Illinois.[29] By 1900, the American Vitagraph had made appearances at the West End Park in New Orleans and at Kernan's River View Park in Baltimore.[30] Once again, ticket prices indicate that few members of the lower classes attended these performances, but financial cost was not always a prohibitive factor. For one week in 1898, the Vitascope Concert Company presented free concerts at a lake in Wisconsin.[31] Such variances in venue and price suggest that persons of different backgrounds, economic and otherwise, viewed films throughout America. As Musser writes, "from the outset . . . the cinema drew its audiences from across the working, middle, and elite classes."[32]

Images at early film screenings often possessed great verisimilitude. An 1897 article in *Munsey's Magazine* claimed, "These [moving] pictures are always full of life and activity, and form absolutely truthful records of the progress of events."[33] Indeed, Musser suggests that the fact that moving pictures appeared on a large screen had an impact on their believability:

> Projected images were conceived as a novelty in which lifelike movement in conjunction with a life-size photographic image provided a sense of heightened realism and intensified interest in the quotidian. This new level of realism dramatically expanded the screen's importance as a source of commercial amusement.[34]

Some early audience members might have been afraid of the sheer size and realistic movement of what they saw on the screen, just as others might have feared the projection equipment or the dark auditoria necessary for proper illumination.

At the same time, the stereotype that all early viewers were scared of getting hit by cinematic trains or getting wet from onscreen waterfalls is extremely problematic. Indeed, surviving accounts suggest that many audience members of the time were quite adept at understanding what they were watching, including when it came to spotting faked footage of historic events. In June 1897, *The Phonoscope* related an uproar that took place in Little Rock, Arkansas when viewers of a moving picture of the Corbett-Fitzsimmons fight realized it was a fraud. Some of the viewers knew what the two boxers looked like, and realized the persons onscreen were counterfeit: "'Fake!' 'Cheat!' 'Give us our money back!' and various other cries rang out in all parts of the theatre," according to the article.[35]

In terms of horror-themed moving pictures, it is worth repeating that the Columbia Phonograph Co. of Washington, D.C. advertised *Execution of Mary, Queen of Scots*

Figure 15.1 Published in the Washington, D.C. *Evening Star* on October 19, 1895.

(Edison, 1895) as the "first of the Chamber of Horrors series to be seen on the Kinetoscope. The scene is blood-curdling in the extreme."[36] However, an 1897 catalog referred to the film as being merely a "realistic reproduction of an historic scene."[37] Here is a clear example of how differently the same film could be publicized, with the choice of descriptive words having the potential to frame audience expectations and even affect their responses.

In January 1900, the High School Base Ball [sic] Club of Traverse City, Michigan booked "The Edison Moving Picture and Concert Co." as a fundraiser. "Besides realistic battle scenes," the show presented "some comic scenes such as *A Telephone Appointment, Then His Wife Appears* [Edison, 1900, aka *Telephone Appointment*] and *The Infernal Palace*," the latter being Edison's title for *The Devil's Castle/Le manoir du diable* (1896).[38] In this instance, the landmark Méliès film was classified as a comedy, rather than a "Chamber of Horrors"-type subject.

To the extent they survive, specific reactions to the earliest moving pictures are usually refracted through the language of journalists or film companies. A newspaper in 1896 noted that *Execution of Mary, Queen of Scots* was "attracting much attention" at a Kinetoscope parlor in Charleston, South Carolina.[39] That same year, the *Cleveland Plain Dealer* called *Lynching Scene* (Edison, 1895) "ferocious."[40] In 1897, *The Phonoscope* described the "popular favorites" of moving picture audiences, which included the "march of a procession down, apparently, into the very teeth of the audience," a scene that was "almost startling."⁴¹ Then, in 1899, an Edison advertisement claimed that *A Visit to the Spiritualist* (1899, aka *Visit to the Spiritualist*) received "great applause and laughter" at the Eden Musée in New York City.⁴²

By contrast, *The Phonoscope* described an 1898 screening of a lynching film, almost certainly *Lynching Scene at Paris, Texas* (International Films, 1897). An itinerant exhibitor named Will Henderson projected it in Colorado Springs, Colorado, using a "phonograph in connection with the pictures, and the sounds reproduced were said to be the cries of the negro as he was roasting to death."⁴³ The grim aural-visual experience was short-lived. As the trade made clear, the police ordered Henderson out of the city: the entertainment had not proven popular, at least with some patrons.

Film company catalogs often printed predictions of viewer response. For example, in 1899, Lubin promised, "your audience will be thoroughly aroused" by watching Cubans die from gunfire in *Death of Maceo and His Followers* (1899).⁴⁴ And in 1903, Méliès's Star Films reassured exhibitors that the "object" of *The Devil in a Convent/Le diable au couvent* (1900) was to "illustrate the triumph of Christianity over Satan, and while it is quite fantastical and religious, there is not the least action in the film which would be obnoxious or shock the most sensitive audience."⁴⁵

However audience members interpreted particular films, their reactions may have been tempered to a degree by the fact that they were generally watching a series of projected films. In the same way that vaudeville bills offered a balanced program—an aggregation of music and comedy acts, dramatic sketches, and so forth—moving picture programs usually did much the same. In many cases during the pre-nickelodeon era, these "balanced" moving picture programs were then incorporated into a larger vaudeville bill that was itself balanced, the moving picture segment reflective of the variety of the entire show.

At the same time, particular moving pictures did maintain their self-identity. In April 1899, the Ninth and Arch Museum in Philadelphia featured a vaudeville program that ended with Lubin's "cineograph" moving pictures. Foremost among the group were two Méliès films, *A Trip to the Moon/L'homme dans la lune* (the 1899 version, aka *Astronomer's Dream*) and *The Devil's Castle/Le manoir du diable* (1896), the duo being presented as the most important of the bill, "the most striking moving pictures ever taken."⁴⁶ That same month, an advertisement for Huber's Museum promoted the "Historiograph" on a bill with live entertainment made up of: "Royal Japanese Wrestlers and Acrobats, Great Success of Allini's Monkeys, Boxing Bouts, Wire Walking, and Trapeze Performance."⁴⁷ The Historiograph was to present 25 minutes of moving pictures, but *The Devil's Castle*, which would be screened "complete in every detail," was the only one that was named.⁴⁸

Similarly, the specific placement of a moving picture on a particular bill could indicate prestige. In May 1899, the Beach Park of Galveston, Texas presented a "Grand Cinematograph" program of "25 Different Pictures," the films ranging from nonfiction to fiction, from serpentine dances to comedies. *The Devil's Castle* appeared by "special request," according to an advertisement that listed the moving picture as the last to be screened, as if it constituted the pinnacle of the program.⁴⁹ By contrast, the Park Avenue Opera House of Mechanicville, New York screened *The Devil's Castle* in June 1900 in the middle of a Lubin bill that headlined a film of the Jeffries-Corbett boxing match and concluded with *Sapho* (Lubin, 1900). The bill also featured *The Haunted House* (Lubin, 1899), but, according to a newspaper advertisement, a non-trick film separated it from *The Devil's Castle*, presumably to further balance the program.[50]

At least a small number of these films thus developed particular reputations with certain viewers, as seems evident not only in newspaper advertisements, but also in film company catalogs. For instance, in 1905, Star Films expected *A Roadside Inn/L'hotel des voyageurs de commerce* (1905, aka *A Road Side Inn*) to become "as great a success as the celebrated *Inn Where No Man Rests*"/*L'auberge du bon repos* (1903, aka *The Inn Where No Man Rests*).[51] Here Star was attempting to trade on the perceived renown and commercial success of one trick film to promote another of the same type.

With horror-themed films also came questions of why any viewer would want to see them. In 1902, the *Denver Post* described a "gruesomely picturesque scene" in France that depicted "several men" being "executed on the stage" by a guillotine. According to the article, "all Paris" was "enjoying" the "true to life—or death" film version of the same:

> Great crowds attend the show and shudder at its horror. So hideously attractive has it become that the biograph was set to work early in the summer, and now realistic pictures of the bloody executions and are shown everywhere in France, have even reached New York, and, I assume, are joyously on their way to Denver. The pictures are said to be enough to make the stoutest heart shudder . . .[52]

The article concluded by noting how "strange" it was that the "extremely unpleasant, the vicious and the abnormal, should ever find a place on the stage." While it is difficult to determine precisely which film(s) the *Denver Post* was describing, the newspaper might just as well have been talking about *Execution of Mary, Queen of Scots*.

On rare occasion, journalists reported on how different demographic groups might experience particular moving pictures. "To most of us a biograph presentation of a difficult operation would be gruesome, but to a class of medical students it ought to be of great interest and value," one newspaper noted in 1901.[53] Then, discussing a fight film in 1905, a reporter decried an exhibitor in Illinois for holding a "matinee for women and children," as it constituted a "grewsome [sic] misunderstanding of the taste and character of Rockford women," who would have had little interest in seeing footage that was more brutal than "the dying moments of Mr. Hyde in *Dr. Jekyll and Mr. Hyde*."[54] Of course, it is also possible that some women and children did want to see the footage, and this male reporter was acting in a patriarchal capacity, attempting to restrict women's access to boxing pictures, which (*à la* Sandow) constituted a source of scopophilic pleasure by, as Miriam Hansen has written, "affording women the forbidden sight of male bodies in seminudity, engaged in intimate and intense physical action."[55]

Other period journalists concentrated on the impact of cinema on children. The *Boston Herald* of 1904 described how a child might react to *The Fairyland; or The Kingdom of the Fairies/Le royaume des fées* (Méliès, 1903, aka *In the Kingdom of Fairyland*): "Little Tippytoe looks on with wide open eyes that bulge with horror. His tiny fists clinch, and he breathes a succession of gasps. The spectacle has claimed him heart, brain, and soul."[56]

Similarly, the *Dallas Morning News* advised readers that "scary" films depicting "ogres and giants" at a 1905 screening might cause "little children to sit up in bed at night and see things around in the dark corners 'which ain't [there].'"[57]

More commonly, newspapers observed allegedly uniform audience responses. In 1900, the *Philadelphia Inquirer* wrote:

> A real man sets a camera up on a railroad track. As the train approaches, the dummy is deftly substituted. The dummy is, of course, struck by the engine and thrown to one side of the track. A thrill of horror runs through the audience, but the real man takes the place of the dummy, gets up with the greatest unconcern, and leisurely brushes himself off.[58]

Two years later, another newspaper article spoke of a similar situation, with a moving picture of a train running into an onscreen character and provoking an "invariable groan of horror" from viewers.[59]

Such articles in the mainstream press also make clear that some readers had begun to wonder how the moving pictures they watched were made. Consider the following letter to the editor, which was published in the *New York Times* in 1905 and titled "A Suggestion":

> After reading the account of the burning of that "nigger" at Howard, Texas, I am moved to make a suggestion. It was stated that "2,000 persons gathered to see the burning," and that "the roofs of prairie farm houses and farm buildings for miles around were covered with people." With those facts in mind permit me to say that it would be good business to . . . send a [K]inetoscope to the next lynching of the kind in order to secure a complete series of photographs of the event. As every one knows, this photographic material can then be used to portray to people elsewhere just how such work is done.[60]

The author, who lived in Northwood, New York, reveals in his letter an awareness of the brevity of the victims' struggles, noting that they might last only five minutes. As a result, he suggested—for the "interest of public entertainment"—the filmed lynching should use a slow-burning fire, started with limited wood or without kerosene, in order to prolong the killing and thus the running time of the film.

Researching the author of this letter, Jan Olsson has determined that its contents were likely ironic.[61] To this assessment, consideration could also be meaningfully paid to what newspaper readers thought of it, as some of them likely took it to be serious. After all (as Chapter 9 mentioned), *The Phonoscope* had reported in 1897 on one viewer's hopes for an authentic execution film to be produced.[62] And during the early nickelodeon period, *Views and Film Index* recounted that there had in the past been a few "demands for subjects depicting a collision of railroad trains."[63]

The Nickelodeon Era

If the film audience of the period between 1896 and 1905 seems shadowy and hard to reconstruct, the audience of the nickelodeon period has been presented at times as a simple stereotype based on class and gender: most of them were working-class men. Admission prices, usually 5 cents, appealed to members of the lower classes, including to immigrants in locations like New York City.⁶⁴ Writing about film audiences in 1908, W. Stephen Bush—who was active as a film narrator at nickelodeons in New York and Philadelphia—analyzed the stereotype that had already emerged:

> It has been the fashion in certain quarters to look upon the electric theatre as chiefly the poor man's amusement. The undoubted friendship between the moving picture and the poor is a fact on which I love to dwell. Who can tell how much sunshine the pictures have brought into humble homes, where sunshine was unknown before? I have seen the eager faces of the young, chafing perhaps unconsciously under the restraints of poverty, come to the electric theatre as keen in their quest for knowledge as any student of the university. I have seen rough, coarse men, blunted in body and mind by the burden of incessant toil, come out of the theatre with changed expressions and with a plain touch of the spiritual on their faces.⁶⁵

While perceiving the positive influence of the moving picture on the poor, Bush emphasized another key point: the "growing patronage of the moving picture is, let it be plainly understood, by no means confined to what we are pleased to call the 'lower classes.'"⁶⁶

On the issue of age and gender, *Views and Film Index* wrote in 1907 that "whole families" attended nickelodeons; in 1908, the trade added that children constituted the "best patrons."⁶⁷ By contrast, *Moving Picture World* claimed that same year that men made up the majority of the audience.⁶⁸ What is clear is that analyses published during the nickelodeon era often concentrated on urban areas like New York City, and, even then, they were more anecdotal than formal studies. That is all in addition to the fact that trade publications obviously wanted to promote and defend the industry, their reportage being potentially biased as a result. And yet, at the same time, it should be said that their readership consisted largely of exhibitors who dealt with audiences on a daily basis, which could have limited the degree to which the trades felt able to exaggerate or publish false information.

It is evident that nickelodeons in different cities and towns across America attracted different kinds of audiences.⁶⁹ As Kathryn H. Fuller suggests, "outside the largest urban centers, there was a regional flavor to small-town moviegoing."⁷⁰ In 1907, for example, *Moving Picture World* said that women and children initially comprised the largest number of patrons in Dallas, Texas, adding that it was only later that men began "to drop in."⁷¹ That same year, the publication spoke more broadly about the attendance of women and children at nickelodeons, claiming that "mothers do not have to 'dress' to attend them, and they take the children . . ."⁷² In 1913, the *Chicago Tribune* noticed long lines of women and baby carriages in front of nickelodeons in lower-class neighborhoods.⁷³ In some communities, women attended in large enough numbers that the "hat nuisance" became a serious issue. In 1910, Atlanta, Georgia went so far as to pass legislation that prohibited women from wearing hats in theatres.⁷⁴

Along with geographical differences, the passage of time must also be considered. For example, in 1911, *Moving Picture News* announced that the five million Americans who attended film screenings each day represented "every occupation, class, and condition. . . . The physician may frequently find himself next to a laborer, the refined and educated woman next to her own wash lady, the college student in close proximity to what would elsewhere be termed a 'gallery god.'"⁷⁵ As a result, nickelodeons had allegedly become "delightfully democratic."[76] Of course, that was hardly the case for everyone. African-Americans, Hispanic Americans, and other ethnic groups were at times segregated or denied admission. In 1909, for example, two Italians sued a nickelodeon in Chicago for refusing to sell them tickets.[77] But such problems varied from theatre to theatre, from region to region, and from year to year.[78]

These issues are all in addition to the subject of film literacy, including the ongoing and enduring stereotype of the audience member who was so captivated by moving pictures as to believe them real. It is certainly possible to document specific examples of this kind of viewer. In 1908, police arrested a man in Pittsburgh for having fired four shots at the screen, aiming at an onscreen cowboy who was mistreating a female character; a similar incident occurred in Leavenworth, Kansas in 1913.[79] And in 1911, *Moving Picture Story Magazine* published the story of a boy asking his father if he liked the moving pictures. The father replied, "It's a good show, I reckon. But we're sitting so far back I can't hear the actors speak."[80] However, these examples of gullible viewers—which might have been exaggerated—were exceptions, which is why they merited attention in the press at the time.

In 1906, *Views and Film Index* observed a growing "demand" for realism in moving picture shows.[81] Some audience members were acutely aware of minor inconsistencies and errors in films they watched. In 1910, *Moving Picture World* reported, "the number of critical and sharpeyed [sic] fans is increasing every day."[82] The following year, the manager of a theatre in Aberdeen, South Dakota described his patrons, mentioning that they bristled at the actions of onscreen cowboys in western films that seemed at odds with their personal knowledge of real-life cowboys:

> When they see a film representing a trip across the plains in '57 or '49, and showing a prairie schooner, rigged up on iron wheels, they shout in derision; just as they resent the incongruity of a woman, who has been found famishing for lack of food, dressing up in a satin lined cloak and a big fashionable hat, when asked to a Thanksgiving dinner by the man who has discovered her need.[83]

Some viewers had become astute, informal critics who were a far cry from, say, an audience member who was afraid to sit too close to moving pictures of waterfalls for fear of getting wet.

In 1912, *Moving Picture World* examined the factors that constituted the "average patron."[84] The average patron: here is a contradiction in terms. To identify the "average patron," the trade publication pursued an elusive concept. With all that is unknown about nickelodeon-era audiences, it is evident that an array of demographic and psychographic differences marked the millions of persons who attended film screenings in this period. As Eileen Bowser has written, the "nickelodeon audience was neither monolithic nor immutable."[85] Put another way, *Moving Picture World* was unable to find the "average patron," because such a person did not exist.

Exhibition

As opposed to venues that occasionally presented moving pictures in the pre-1905 era, the nickelodeon theatre was a business dedicated to screening films each day, with the exception of Sunday in some areas. While live acts, particularly singers accompanying illustrated slides, were booked at some nickelodeons, their key business was the cinema. The rapid spread of nickelodeons throughout America in 1905 and 1906 meant that many, if not most, were rather meager in terms of their interior design.

However different the nickelodeon was from prior screening practices, the logic of the balanced program remained firmly in place.[86] Horror-themed content was thus embedded into larger shows. For example, at the Aberdeen, South Dakota Bijou in 1909, *In the Days of Witchcraft* (Edison, 1909) appeared on a mixed bill of vaudeville (featuring a comedy duo, banjoists, and a juggler), films (including Lubin's *Which Was the Happiest Time in Your Life?* and *Uncle Reuben's Courtship*, both released in 1909), and an illustrated song.[87] By contrast, the Lyric Grand Theatre in Juneau, Alaska screened *In the Days of Witchcraft* over one year later on a moving picture bill as its first film, projecting it immediately after a musical "overture." Six other films followed, their content ranging from nonfiction "Marine Pictures" to the comedy *Florrie's Birthday/La fête à Berthe* (Pathé Frères, 1909), as well as one illustrated song.[88]

In some cases, horror-themed films appeared as the featured presentation on a bill, as when *The Mask of the Red Death/La maschera tragica* (Ambrosio, 1911) played the Grand in Mansfield, Ohio in 1911.[89] By contrast, other horror-themed films could be screened in the middle of a given moving picture program, as was the case with *The Ghost Holiday/The Ghosts' Holiday* (Williams, Browne & Earle, 1907) in Riverside, California in 1907, where O'Dette's Picture Auditorium scheduled it as the seventh film out of a total of eleven.[90] This programming might well have pleased *Moving Picture World*, which complained about a show in 1913 that concluded not with a comedy to "send them home laughing," but rather with a "most gruesome and terrifying picture called *The Spanish Inquisition*."[91] To the trade, ending the bill with that film represented "very poor judgment."[92]

The duration of a specific moving picture's booking varied from venue to venue as well. Consider *Frankenstein* (Edison, 1910). The Crystal in Shelbyville, Indiana advertised the following bill in April 1910: "*An Interrupted Honeymoon* [Essanay, 1910] and *Frankenstein* & Others."[93] That bill lasted two days. The Elite in Defiance, Ohio advertised two "featured subjects" for its one-day program, *Frankenstein* and *Kitty*, the latter being an illustrated song.[94] By contrast, the Scenic of Hartford, Connecticut headlined *Frankenstein* as its feature for an entire week, even though the theatre normally reserved that status for live acts.[95]

Live music and sound effects accompanying moving pictures also became an important part of the exhibition experience, though different nickelodeons provided very different experiences.[96] According to *Views and Film Index* in 1906, music was "essential to the success" of moving picture exhibitions.[97] Moreover, poor-quality performances—often caused by improper musical selections for a given film scene and/or music noticeably out of sync with the same—were discouraged. In 1913, for example, *Moving Picture News* decried a pianist at a "New York City picture theatre" for playing the song *Every Little Movement Has a Meaning All Its Own* during the dramatic snake transformation scene in *The Reincarnation of Karma* (Vitagraph, 1912).[98]

To assist musicians, trades often published advice on particular musical compositions. In 1910, *Moving Picture World* suggested J. Bodewalt Lampe's *Vision of Salome* (1908) for "demons, magic, etc." For "Fairy Tales," the trade advised "waltzes, intermezzos, graceful numbers generally . . . these pictures vary so much that nothing definite can be suggested."[99] Five years later, *Moving Picture News* described Cora Salisbury's *Ghost Dance* (1911), calling it an

> excellent, as well as pleasing number. Good for the musical portrayal of a ghost, witch or other scenes of mysterious nature, during which there is a suggestion of plotting on the scene. Also good in Arabian or Oriental pictures wherein the plotting action is well defined. . . . Should be played in slow tempo.[100]

This article even went so far as to note that music like *Ghost Dance* worked particularly well with films featuring color tints, thus drawing a link between specific types of music and visual aesthetics.

Film companies occasionally provided specific musical recommendations to accompany their releases. For example, Edison proposed opera music to be played with its version of

Figure 15.2 Sheet music cover of Cora Salisbury's *Ghost Dance* (1911).

Faust (1909).¹⁰¹ The company also gave scene-by-scene advice for *Frankenstein* (1910). The *Eclair Bulletin* published precise directions on which song to play in every scene of *The Spectre Bridegroom* (1913) and *From the Beyond* (1913). Their suggestions included Edward MacDowell's *Witch's Dance* (1884) and Irving Berlin and Ted Snyder's *That Mysterious Rag* (1911) for the former, and Lampe's *Vision of Salome* and Harry Von Tilzer's *The Ghost of the Goblin Man* (1912) for the latter.¹⁰²

Some of these musical choices were composed for particular kinds of cinematic scenes. Consider Volume 1 of *Sam Fox Moving Picture Music*, as composed by John Stepan Zamecnik and published in 1913. Its selections include *Indian Music*, *Chinese Music*, *Oriental Music*, *Funeral March*, *Death Scene*, and *Fairy Music*, each clearly titled and brief in length to fit particular scenes.¹⁰³ But some of these selections may have at times become overused and clichéd. In 1915, *Photoplay* magazine ranked "murder music" as being among the "film horrors," the term "horrors" here meaning that which had become tiresome and disdained.¹⁰⁴

Along with ongoing concerns like music, nickelodeon exhibitors also remained cognizant of particular holidays and booked films relevant to them. These included Halloween, which had become increasingly popular in America during the final decades of the nineteenth century.¹⁰⁵ Indeed, Sinclair Chissus, Jr. was "scared to death" at a Detroit nickelodeon on October 31, 1911. Production of films specifically about Halloween had begun in the pre-nickelodeon era, as evidenced by *Halloween Night at the Seminary* (Edison, 1904), which showed characters bobbing for apples, and *Halloween* (American Mutoscope & Biograph, 1905), in which a man plays a prank on a woman by use of a fake mouse attached to a string.¹⁰⁶ Other examples include the drama *An Ill Wind* (Rex, 1912), in which a woman looks at her mirror at midnight on Halloween in an effort to see the face of the man she will marry, and the comedy *A Bum's Hallowe'en* (Champion, 1913), featuring a tramp who gets admitted into a masquerade under false pretenses.¹⁰⁷

It is also evident that film companies intentionally timed the release of some horror-themed moving pictures for Halloween.¹⁰⁸ Here they followed a practice they also employed for holidays like St. Patrick's Day and Christmas. For example, Thanhouser's industry trade advertisement for *The Fairies' Hallowe'en* (1910) told exhibitors that the "startling" subject could be used with a "lecture round about and during Hallowe'en week."¹⁰⁹ Other timed releases included *Satan at Play/Satan s'amuse* (Pathé Frères, 1907), *The Witch* (Vitagraph, 1908), *The Red Barn Mystery* (Williams, Brown, & Earle, 1908), *Another's Ghost/Le spectre de l'autre* (Pathé Frères, 1910, aka *Another Ghost*), and *The Temptation of Satan* (Warner's Features, 1914).¹¹⁰ The same was true of *Mephisto's Son/Le fils du diable* (1906), for which Pathé Frères offered "colored posters" of 47 x 63 inches in size.¹¹¹

Publicity Materials

Edison's plot synopsis for *'Tis Now the Very Witching Hour of Night* (1909, aka *'Tis Now the Very Witching Time of Night*) spoke directly to the potential audience member:

> Imagine yourself at the midnight hour in an old house that has long had the reputation of being haunted—a house in which several people have attempted to sleep and have failed. You are impelled by a love of the mysterious to see if these reports are true, and have bolstered your courage up to the sticking point for the occasion.

Approaching the building you are impressed by the ominous silence and gloom that envelop it. The hoot of an owl and the sudden apparition of a myriad of bats send cold chills chasing one another up and down your spinal cord.

Entering a large room, your ears are assailed by unearthly noises and discordant sounds. You are about to seat yourself at a table when table and chair disappear as if by magic and you sprawl upon the floor.

You see strange shapes and weird, flitting creatures; you are chased from one room to another by toothless hags and dried-up witches; skeletons grin at you from every nook and cranny of the building, disappearing and reappearing in a most bewildering fashion; a pretty girl comes out of the frame of an old picture, and as you are about to kiss her, you find a donkey's head nestling snugly in your fingers.[112]

It is difficult to determine how many exhibitors used this synopsis in part or whole, but it does raise the broader issue of publicity materials prepared by film manufacturing companies.

During the nickelodeon era, the moving picture poster became ubiquitous, with most of them promoting specific films. In 1911, the Monopol Film Company created the first 24-sheet to advertise a given title, which was for *Dante's Inferno/L'inferno* (Milano, 1911).[113] Thanhouser had one-, three-, and eight-sheet posters for *Dr. Jekyll and Mr. Hyde* (1912).[114] Gaumont offered "heralds" and "1, 3, and 6 Sheet" posters for *The Vengeance of Egypt/ L'anneau fatal* (1912).[115] And Imp supplied "Special 3-Sheet and 6-Sheet Posters" for *Dr. Jekyll and Mr. Hyde* (1913).[116]

While many exhibitors likely used such posters, some relied on informal or even homemade publicity materials. For example, in 1907, *Views and Film Index* observed a poster at one nickelodeon announcing, "See our latest film—*The Devil and the Chemist*." However, after watching the film, the trade's journalist reported that it was "very well known to the trade under a different name."[117] In this case, the exhibitor created his own advertising in order to retitle the film and surreptitiously screen it a second time.

Figure 15.3 The 24-sheet for *Dante's Inferno* (Milano, 1911).

Figure 15.4 Theatre publicity for a screening of *Dante's Inferno* (Milano, 1911).

The control that exhibitors held over publicity materials at their theatres also extended to the use of posters that did not promote any particular film title. In January 1911, a letter published in *Moving Picture World* offered the following account:

> In passing one of the well-known houses, within a block of Broadway, not long ago, I noticed, as I had on several other occasions, quite a string of vividly-colored posters of the four-sheet size strung across the entrance, and leaving just enough head room for one to pass under, depicting murderous Indians in the act of scalping their captors, who were on their knees, seemingly, pleading for mercy; then, on an adjoining sheet, a young hero, in the act of rescuing an unfortunate girl, who had been cast into the waters of a canal by a Desperate Desmond, and in reward for his bravery, received a knife through his heart, the blood stains clearly showing on his shirt. There were, at least, eight or ten more of these posters, each one of a more blood-curdling nature than the other.[118]

Two problems were apparent, one being that the films inside the theatre bore no relation to the posters.

More troubling, though, was the imagery adorning these posters. They depicted "too much horror generally," *Moving Picture World* complained in 1912.[119] Another article in the same publication defined the "horrors" as including "striped convicts, murderous Indians, grinning 'black-handers,' homicidal drunkards, etc."[120] *Motography* condemned such "diabolical posters" in 1913, judging them to be "absolute atrocities."[121] By May

1913, the *Chicago Tribune* argued that moving picture posters needed to be censored.[122] Later that same year, the New York state legislature considered a bill that would have made it a misdemeanor to exhibit posters of "crime, prison horrors, gunplays, and other scenes offensive to common decency."[123]

Along with posters, nickelodeons often relied on newspaper advertisements. On occasion, exhibitors attempted to challenge audience members. An advertisement for J. Stuart Blackton's *The Haunted Hotel* (Vitagraph, 1907, aka *The Haunted Hotel; or, The Strange Adventures of a Traveler*) in Atlantic, Iowa in 1907 represents an early example of this tactic: "If you can explain how some of the situations are produced in this piece, we will gladly return your money and vote you a life membership."[124]

Figure 15.5 Artwork published in *Motography* on January 4, 1913 as an example of an objectionable type of moving picture poster.

Rather than refer to the mysteries of cinematic special effects, exhibitors could also speak to audience members as part of an effort to temper horrifying content that they could not conceal. An advertisement for *Legend of a Ghost/La légende du fantôme* (Pathé Frères, 1908) in Des Moines, Iowa told readers:

> Don't let it "skeer ye," for it's only a moving picture, but it's mighty interesting at that. It portrays a young woman passing through a cemetery at night; [it] shows how she is suddenly startled by a ghost at her side! And—
> But why startle you now—see the picture—get "skeered up" a bit, and then forget about it when you laugh over the vaudeville a few minutes later.[125]

Here the balanced program and placement of *Legend of a Ghost* on it became the solution to allaying audience concerns over horror, either in advance of the screening or during it.

Censorship

In 1907, the *Chicago Tribune* indicted the moving picture, telling readers, "All [nickelodeons] Have Horror Shows," adding:

> In a round of these places on South State street, Milwaukee avenue, and Halsted street, not one show could be found that did not furnish for its patrons, mostly children, a series of horrors such as murder and hanging and madhouse scenes and burglaries.[126]

The article spoke of scenes in which a baby put a loaded revolver in its mouth, and in which a milkman fought with a drunk. It also described Ferdinand Zecca's *From Jealousy to Madness/Jalousie et folie* (Pathé Frères, 1907), in which a wife and her lover drive her husband to madness. After they visit the asylum and deride him in his padded cell, the husband escapes and strangles his wife to death.[127]

In 1910, a letter to the editor of the *New York Times* contended that onscreen murders and suicides constituted "distressing and morbid spectacles" that were "far worse" than the boxing films that had so regularly been decried.[128] "It is complained that scenes of cruelty and horror have been worked into many of the films," the *Oakland Tribune* reported the following year.[129]

According to some journalists, nickelodeons had even become "schools of crime."[130] In 1908, Charles H. Loper of Fresno, California maintained that he murdered his friend after seeing so much violence in moving pictures.[131] Four years later, an arsonist in Cleveland, Ohio was quick to say *Dante's Inferno/L'inferno* (Milano, 1911) gave him the inspiration.[132] At roughly the same time, a man in Baltimore became "deranged" after watching so many "blood and thunder" films; he confessed to murdering someone, even though police could not determine that he had committed any crime.[133]

Those persons concerned about the cinema became particularly worried about its potential effects on children. In 1911, detective William A. Pinkerton feared that moving pictures were "making criminals of young men in this country."[134] By that time, a number of juvenile crimes had been attributed to moving pictures, including more than one murder.[135]

In 1908, *the Washington Post* complained about "blood-curdling scenes" at area nickelodeons, one depicting a husband stabbing a dummy that he believed to be his wife. The newspaper reported, "Several children in the audience began to cry when the debauched husband swung the knife in the air and brought it down on the supposed body of his wife."[136] In 1910, a woman in Duluth, Minnesota wrote to her local newspaper, complaining about films that "cause the children of tender years to fear their own shadows after leaving the theatre, and make youthful cowards of them all."[137] That same year, a doctor in Cedar Rapids, Iowa claimed he had treated twenty children with "night terrors" inflicted by moving pictures:

> One boy of about four years was pursued by a hand that was trying to grasp him, suggested by a scene in which a large artificial hand dropped off every time it was about to be shaken. Another boy of five years was afraid of being shot. Even in the day time [sic] he was afraid if he saw a black coat hanging in a shadow, or a dark corner.[138]

However, concerns over what exactly comprised unsuitable images varied a great deal. "A moving picture exhibit of horrors was gratuitously given at the Temple auditorium Saturday," wrote a newspaper in South Dakota in 1913. "The free show lasted all day and several hundred school children were dragooned into attendance." The content? "Ghastly views of maggots and flies" in a program of "health subjects."[139]

Trade publications also expressed fears about content, believing that violent and immoral moving pictures could damage the industry. "If audiences made up in part or as a whole of sensitive people are to be entertained," *Views and Film Index* wrote in 1907, "slaughter and mangling must be omitted."[140] In 1911, *Moving Picture World* blamed exhibitors who appealed to the "savage instincts of the human race" by screening depraved films.[141] Two years later, the same publication lodged a similar complaint: "Of all the pleas for the cheaply sensational or sensationally cheap film, none is more specious and worthless than this same motto: 'The people want the blood-and-thunder product, and children cry for it.'"[142]

Denunciations of the cinema were not enough to satisfy the moral leaders in many communities. In 1907, Chicago became the first American city to regulate motion pictures.[143] Then, according to Lee Grieveson:

> Censor boards proliferated from 1907, including local boards in cities like Cleveland, Detroit, St. Louis, San Francisco, Seattle, New Orleans, Lexington, Dallas, Kansas City, Nashville, Atlanta; and state boards emerged in Pennsylvania in 1911, Ohio in 1913, Kansas in 1914, and Maryland in 1916.[144]

Here were boards that could define what constituted the immoral and the unacceptable in motion pictures. But their decisions were often contradictory and sometimes problematic.

For example, in 1908, a police censor in Chicago edited a version of *Macbeth* by "chopping out approximately two feet of film that struck him as too realistic." He had a "perfect horror of violence and bloodshed," even if it appeared in Shakespeare.[145] Disparaging these practices and their inconsistencies, the *New York Dramatic Mirror* suggested that censors:

Adopt a fad. Let it be cruelty to animals, ridicule of "constituted authority," down-trodden stenographers or soft collars, anything, so long as you have a fad. Whenever a daring film manufacturer approaches your particular fad pounce on him with both hands and feet. Slash the film recklessly. The more individual fads in a censor board the merrier.[146]

"Never show signs of common sense," the *Dramatic Mirror* concluded, with no small amount of sarcasm. In 1912, *Moving Picture World* had gone even further, denouncing censors as "witch-finders."[147]

All that said, in 1909, members of the film industry voluntarily formed the National Board of Censorship as part of an effort to maintain control rather than cede it to city and state governments. One report claimed that, in 1910, the National Board of Censorship "condemned" 178 moving pictures out of 5,200 examined. It also censored a total of 2,000,000 feet of film that year.[148] Shelley Stamp has written, "By the early 1910s the board was previewing close to 85 percent of the country's film output."[149]

As the nickelodeon era came to an end, censorship seems not only to have had an effect on completed moving pictures, but also on the production of new films. Leona Radnor's book *The Photoplay Writer* (1913) advised would-be screenwriters, "Do not write plays containing acts of violence or crimes."[150] That same year, Essanay's form letter used to reject screenplays included a checklist of seventeen possible reasons for the decision, ranging from "Idea Has Been Done Before" to "Illegible." Also among these was "Robbery, Kidnapping, Murder, Suicide, Harrowing Death-Bed, and All Scenes of an Unpleasant Nature Should Be Eliminated."[151]

Audience Reactions

Describing nickelodeons in Boise, the *Idaho Statesman* wrote in 1909, "The audiences . . . are always interesting features of these shows. Some hysterical woman at a critical moment when the villain is just about to throw the hero over the precipice will shriek out in horror."[152] Here is a significant anecdote, one that speaks clearly to the reception of moving pictures, and yet one that also identifies the problems of understanding the same. Who was this woman? What film did she see? And how common was the kind of response she gave?

In other words, it is important to ask what kind of horror-themed films scared audiences during the nickelodeon era. Consider W. Stephen Bush's comment in 1913:

> We are deluged with "ferocious lions," "man-killing tigers," and a lot of other more or less savage beasts fresh from the press agent's menagerie. We are constantly invited to feast on horrors of the most hair-raising variety in which the wild animals play the leading parts.[153]

Bush's observation is helpful in that—much like the aforementioned "horror" scenes in which a man fought with a drunk and "horror" posters featured "striped convicts"—it speaks to the broad range of images and narratives that could potentially frighten or disturb audience members.

At the same time, it should be noted that the trade press often tried to predict audience response in respects that were so uniform as to be overly simplistic. For example, *Moving*

Picture World wrote that *Dr. Jekyll and Mr. Hyde; or, a Strange Case/Den skæbnesvangre opfindelse* (Great Northern, 1910) "sidestepped all the unpleasantness that might have been expected" in adapting a "morbid and gruesome" tale.[154] Similarly, *Moving Picture News* believed that *Dr. Jekyll and Mr. Hyde* (Thanhouser, 1912) was not "calculated to inspire horror or dread in the spectator."[155]

In some cases, the industry press imposed its own views onto the monolithic "audience." Consider *Moving Picture World*'s review of *The Wages of Sin* (Vitagraph, 1908):

> The story is of foreign conception and repulsive to American ideals. Graves, funerals, coffins and pestilence are no doubt all right in their proper places. The pictures might entertain a convention of undertakers, but not the audience of the ordinary electric theater.[156]

Similarly, in 1909, the same publication predicted that *The Witch/La sorcière* (Le Lion, 1909) would "likely" not be of "much interest to the average audience."[157]

Of films like *Frankenstein*, *Moving Picture World* argued in 1910 that Mary Shelley herself would have "recoiled with disgust from the thought of putting the thing into moving pictures." Such stories, "while delightful literature to coroners, undertakers, grave-diggers and morgue-keepers, fail to please the general public."[158] Three years later, *Moving Picture World* declared:

> People go to moving picture theatres to escape the glooms of life rather than to find them. Gloom in its proper place in the development of a dramatic story is unavoidable, but gloom for gloom's sake is unpardonable. We want the cheerful rather than the cheerless.
> Tombstones and cemeteries do not look a bit more cheerful on the screen than in reality, and few people want to spend more time than is required by attendance at a funeral in places intended for the burial of the dead. The "gloom" film is entitled to a long vacation.[159]

But no vacation came. In 1913, *Variety* grudgingly admitted, "There must be a market in this country for feature films of the sort of *Doomed to Die, or The Vial of Wrath* [*Fragile bonheur*, Union Features, 1913], or importers wouldn't be bringing them in so freely."[160]

Reviewers in trade publications occasionally spoke as if they were part of the audience, rather than outside or above it. Consider *Moving Picture World*'s reactions to *In the Dark Valley* (Kalem, 1910): "One shudders again and again, and even while admitting the fascination of the picture, one is glad when it is finished . . ."[161] "There is a feeling of horror after seeing it, which lingers long," the trade wrote of *The Maze of Fate* (Imp, 1911, aka *The Image of Fate*).[162] And after seeing *The Octopus/Le poulpe* (Eclair, 1913), the trade claimed, "None of us will want to go in bathing where it is likely to be."[163]

Similarly, some trade reviews identified the potential effects of given films in such a way as to make the experience seem acceptable or even positive. "Spectators" of *The Haunted Island* (Powers, 1911) would "feel the creepy, haunted feeling."[164] That same year, *The Ghost of the Vaults/Spøgelset i gravkælderen* (Great Northern, 1911) was "so grewsome [sic] that it makes the audience feel creepy." *The Fear* (Essanay, 1913) was a "creepy one, and will appeal to those who like plenty of chills up the back."[165] And *When Ghost Meets Ghost* (Thanhouser, 1913) was a "specter story that won't scare the youngsters in your audience, for it is a purely comedy plot that is worked up without any 'horrors' or 'terrors.'"[166]

A number of reviews reveal an acknowledgment that different viewers had different tastes. Responding to *The Smallpox Scare at Gulch Hollow* (Frontier, 1913), *Moving Picture World* wrote, "The people who can enjoy such a spectacle are very different from us; it made us itch just to see it."[167] The same trade noted that "People fond of occult subjects" would enjoy *From the Beyond* (Eclair American, 1913), whereas "others will feel that they are going through a series of horrible psychical experiences."[168] And *The Haunted Bedroom* (Edison, 1913) was a "sure enough ghost story and is subject to all the objections some people make to this type of entertainment, but on the other hand many observers will enjoy its thrill."[169]

Varied responses to particular films could also include reactions far different from what the manufacturing companies intended. Instead of being "filled with horror," viewers of *The Hindoo Dagger* (American Mutoscope & Biograph, 1909) at the Fourteenth Street Theatre in New York City actually "laughed at the series of murderous situations."[170] Of *The Haunted House* (Kalem, 1913), *Moving Picture World* noticed, "The audience laughed at what was not intended to be comedy."[171] But perhaps nowhere did an audience's reaction differ more from the intended one than in the case of a 1906 exhibition of one of the many versions of the Passion Play. The "scenes which usually command intense silence were uproariously cheered—the audience actually applauded the crucifixion."[172]

Specific audience responses from the nickelodeon era are few in number, and—as in the case of Sinclair Chissus, Jr.—those that were recorded were not necessarily accurate. For example, in New York City in 1910, a woman attended a screening of *The Forest Ranger* (Essanay, 1910). According to one account, when Native American characters on the screen scalped their victims, the woman shrieked and fell out of her seat, dropping her baby in the process. Throwing up the house lights, the management found the woman convulsing on the theatre floor, her condition apparently induced by the film. Her baby was unharmed, but they rushed the woman to a nearby hospital, where her convulsions continued. Doctors told the *New York Times* that she was near death.[173] But the journalist made at least one error: *The Forest Ranger* did not feature any Native American characters, let alone anyone being scalped. Surveying other press coverage of this incident only amplifies the number of contradictions.[174]

More commonly, press accounts presented generalized responses to specific films, some as self-serving as trade publication articles. For example, a newspaper in Shelbyville, Indiana claimed that the local Nickelo Theatre was "crowded to its utmost capacity at all the performances" of *Mephisto's Son* (Pathé Frères, 1906), so much so that the management had to offer "standing room" admission.[175] Over five thousand viewers watched *Legend of a Ghost* (Pathé Frères, 1908) at the Shubert Theatre on a single evening in New Orleans in 1908.[176] And in 1910, Edison's *Frankenstein* "created no end of amusement and pleasure to all present" at the Dreamland Theatre in Sault Ste. Marie, Michigan.[177]

Post-nickelodeon Era

The transition from nickelodeons to motion picture theatres was one of many important evolutions of the early 1910s, another being the increasing running times of "feature" films. Censorship grew more intense, or at least received greater press coverage, due in no small part to a backlash against "white-slave" and "drug-terror" films.[178] In addition to railing against particular movies and emergent genres, censors carefully examined and cut particular scenes.

Audiences evolved as well, with their tastes and expectations becoming ever more sophisticated. One film magazine said:

> Where, but a few years ago, you were satisfied with imitation automobile wrecks, mid-air adventures of toy aeroplanes, the sinking of miniature battleships, and the staging of exterior scenes against a crudely painted canvas background . . . today you are demanding the actual destruction of the villain's auto, the flight of the heroine in a real aeroplane, the complete wrecking of a real ocean-going steamship, which costs the film manufacturer thousands of dollars, and the use of the identical backgrounds called for by the author's manuscript. In other words, reality has succeeded the make-believe, and film stars today are really risking their lives, where in the past the substitution of a dummy, during a moment when the camera was stopped, saved the leading man any bumps or bruises which might have resulted from his attempting actually to perform the feats called for by the scenario.[179]

Films were not only getting longer, but they were getting more realistic, at least in the eyes of some viewers.

Beginning in October 1914, *Movie Pictorial* hosted a regular column entitled "Realism in the Movies." It published letters from readers across America who identified problems in the films they watched. One wrote that, in *The Witch Girl* (Victor, 1914), Mary Fuller wore an "up-to-date long corset" under her ragged costume; another complained that an ancient Egyptian note in an unnamed film was written in the English language.[180] And a particularly observant viewer noticed that, even though characters in *The House of a Thousand Candles* (Selig Polyscope, 1915) eat a "three or four course dinner after which they danced," a clock visible in the scene showed that only five minutes had passed.[181]

Much of the fan press focused not on viewers, but instead on the stars they admired. In 1910, *Moving Picture World* wrote about "Moving Picture Gods and Goddesses":

> We can understand how a person can "fall in love" with the living and attractive presence of an actor or actress, but it is incomprehensible how men and women will "fall in love" with moving picture actors as seen on the screen, yet it is a fact attested and established by the number of requests and letters we receive from persons inquiring the names of and soliciting introductions to Vitagraph leading men and women.[182]

Names like Henry B. Walthall, King Baggot, and Darwin Karr became well known to many filmgoers, as did—to a lesser extent—character actors such as Charles Ogle. The rise of stars like Florence Lawrence during the nickelodeon era became a business that extended well beyond the moving pictures in which they appeared. *Motion Picture Story Magazine* began publication in 1911, followed by *Photoplay* in 1912.[183] Star memorabilia ranged from banners and buttons to picture postcards.

Trade publications began to notice Lon Chaney—who later became famous as the "Man of a Thousand Faces" as a result of his fantastic make-up in such films as *The Hunchback of Notre Dame* (Universal, 1923) and *The Phantom of the Opera* (Universal,

Figure 15.6 Postcard featuring Edison character actor Charles Ogle, c. 1911. (*Courtesy of George Chastain*)

1925)—due to his work in *The Embezzler* (Universal-Gold Seal, 1914) and *Her Grave Mistake* (Nestor, 1914). The Morgan Lithograph Company even featured Chaney on its posters for *The Grind* (Rex, 1915).[184] However, in 1915, *Photoplay* dubbed Harry Mestayer, who had starred in such films as *The House of a Thousand Candles* (Selig Polyscope, 1915), as the "Actor of a Thousand Roles."[185] That same year, *Movie Pictorial* declared that Edison stock player Marc McDermott—who had appeared in the company's *A Christmas Carol* (1910), *The Ghost's Warning* (1911), *The Necklace of Rameses* (1914), and *The Pines of Lory* (1914)—to be the screen's "Wizard of Makeup."[186]

A few actors even became temporarily associated with horror. In 1914, *The Billboard* reported that Claire Whitney, star of *The Dream Woman* (Blaché Features, 1914), was "interested in spiritualism, and now refuses to sleep in a room without a light burning and spends most of her spare evenings listening to the rappings of a tired spirit on a rickety table."[187] The following year, George Washington Crile, the physician who performed the first successful direct blood transfusion, took photographic portraits of stars like Mary Fuller. He asked them to "recall, if they could, their moment of greatest terror; or to call back their most dreadful experience—and to *express* this emotion facially" for a book entitled *The Origin and Nature of Emotions*.[188]

Conclusion

As the early cinema period came to an end, audiences were not alone in their evolving sophistication. Exhibitors increasingly mounted elaborate advertising gimmicks, including onsite ballyhoo at their movie theatres. At times they relied on assistance from film companies, as when Vitagraph prepared an elaborate press kit for *Mortmain* (1915).[189] In other cases, they developed their own ideas, as when an exhibitor in Pennsylvania distributed stationery with "ghastly" handprints to publicize that same film.[190] A "progressive" exhibitor in Pennsylvania filled his lobby and box office with hundreds of candles in 1915 to promote *The House of a Thousand Candles*.[191]

After seeing "three or four women" becoming "mildly hysterical over the murder scene" in D. W. Griffith's *The Avenging Conscience, or "Thou Shalt Not Kill"* (1914), *Movie Pictorial* wondered if they were in fact "relatives of the management."[192] Exhibitor and viewer had converged.

As for the numerous genres that constituted the horror-themed film in America, they had not yet commingled into becoming the codified "horror movie" of Hollywood. That process would unfold in the decades that followed, particularly from the 1930s onward, resulting from a series of cycles rather than through a simple linear and homogenous evolution. Its complexities can and should take future volumes to explore.

Nevertheless, the years leading to 1915 had produced an array of horror-themed genres on the screen, borne in large measure out of pre-cinema contexts. Even if they do not constitute the "horror movie," they certainly established the narrative, thematic, and aesthetic criteria for it. And regardless of whether audience members fainted, or even died of fright, thousands and thousands of them watched these films.

To revisit Poe, we can agree that there was darkness. But that was not all. There was something more, something ghastly and grim. By horror haunted, it illumined on screens, time and again. Its artifacts, fragments and texts from 1895 to 1915 need be forgotten no more.

> And the silken sad uncertain rustling of each purple curtain
> Thrilled me—filled me with fantastic terrors never felt before.
>
> —Edgar Allan Poe, *The Raven* (1845)

Notes

1. "*The Toll of Fear*," *Moving Picture World*, April 26, 1913, 379.
2. "Films Scare Boy to Death," *Washington Post*, November 1, 1911, 1.
3. "Boy Dies While at Picture Show," *Detroit Free Press*, November 1, 1911, 16.

4. "Doings at Los Angeles," *Moving Picture World*, June 15, 1912, 1014. Clifford later became a staff writer for Thomas Ince. He wrote scenarios for *The Witch of Salem* (Domino, 1913), *The Wrath of the Gods* (New York Motion Picture Company, 1914), and *The Fakir* (Domino, 1915).
5. Terry Ramsaye, *A Million and One Nights: A History of the Motion Picture through 1925* (New York: Simon & Schuster, 1926); Benjamin Hampton, *A History of the Movies* (New York: Covici, Friede Publishers, 1931); Lewis Jacobs, *The Rise of the American Film* (New York: Harcourt, Brace, 1939).
6. Russell Merritt, "Nickelodeon Theatres, 1905–1914: Building an Audience for the Movies," in *The American Film Industry*, edited by Tina Balio (Madison: University of Wisconsin Press, 1976), 59–79.
7. Robert C. Allen, "Motion Picture Exhibition in Manhattan, 1906–1912," *Cinema Journal*, Vol. 18, No. 2 (Spring 1979), 2–15.
8. Robert Sklar, "Oh Althusser! Historiography and the Rise of Cinema Studies," *Radical History Review*, No. 41 (Spring 1988), 10–35; Ben Singer, "Manhattan Nickelodeons: New Data on Audiences and Exhibitors," *Cinema Journal*, Vol. 34, No. 3 (Spring 1995), 5–35.
9. Singer, 28.
10. William Uricchio and Roberta E. Pearson, "Dialogue: Manhattan's Nickelodeons: New York? New York!," *Cinema Journal*, Vol. 36, No. 4 (Summer 1997), 98.
11. Melvyn Stokes, "Introduction: Reconstructing American Cinema's Audiences," in *American Movie Audiences: From the Turn of the Century to the Early Sound Era*, edited by Melvyn Stokes and Richard Maltby (London: British Film Institute, 1999), 1–11.
12. Stokes, 5.
13. James B. Crippen, "Realism and the Photoplay," *Motography*, April 1911, 14.
14. "Twin City Entertainers," *Wisconsin Valley Leader* (Grand Rapids, Wisconsin), May 18, 1905, 1.
15. "A Great Attraction on Our Streets," *The Times-Democrat* (Lima, Ohio), August 3, 1896, unpaginated.
16. Charles Musser, *The Emergence of Cinema: The American Screen to 1907* (Berkeley: University of California Press, 1990), 78.
17. Ibid., 81.
18. Ibid., 118, 183.
19. "Edison's Vitascope Cheered," *New York Times*, April 24, 1896, 5.
20. For example, on May 16, 1896, the *New York Clipper* noted the Vitascope films at Koster & Bial's "all received the approval of the audience," and on May 23, 1896, the publication claimed that the Vitascope films were met with "loud applause." With regard to the changing program, on May 16, 1896, the *New York Clipper* claimed that "several new pictures were shown."
21. "Koster & Bial's," *New York Clipper*, May 9, 1896, 152.
22. It is also possible that a projectionist offered the surf scene in response to a more general call for an encore, rather than a request to see that particular film again.
23. "Keith's Union Square Theatre," *New York Clipper*, August 22, 1896, 392.
24. "Keith's Union Square Theatre," *New York Clipper*, November 7, 1896, 570. These comments were made in relation to a performance of the Lumière Cinématographe.
25. "Maryland," *New York Clipper*, July 11, 1896, 292; "Massachusetts," *New York Clipper*, October 10, 1896, 507; "Rhode Island," *New York Clipper*, June 27, 1896, 279; "Amusements," *Evening Times* (Trenton, New Jersey), September 10, 1896, 2.
26. "The Vitascope," *Daily Light* (San Antonio, Texas), October 13, 1896, 3.
27. Advertisement, *Steubenville Herald* (Steubenville, Ohio), November 30, 1896, 8.
28. For more information on itinerant exhibition, see Calvin Pryluck, "The Itinerant Movie Show and the Development of the Film Industry," in *Hollywood in the Neighborhood: Historical Case*

Studies of Local Moviegoing, edited by Kathryn H. Fuller-Seeley (Berkeley, California: University of California Press, 2008), 37–52.
29. "Where They Were Exhibited Last Month," *The Phonoscope*, October 1898, 16.
30. Advertisement, *New York Clipper*, March 31, 1900.
31. Untitled, *Eau Claire Leader* (Eau Claire, Wisconsin), July 13, 1898, 5.
32. Musser, 183.
33. "The Stage: Footlight Chat," *Munsey's Magazine*, XVI (January 1897), 499.
34. Musser, 118.
35. "Fake Fight Pictures," *The Phonoscope*, June 1897, 12. In this case, *The Phonoscope* reprinted the article, "A Bald Fake: Indignant Uprising by a Duped Audience," *The Arkansas Gazette* (Little Rock, Arkansas), June 10, 1897, 3, but added a final paragraph. The film under discussion was *Reproduction of the Corbett and Fitzsimmons Fight* (Lubin, 1897).
36. Advertisement, *The Evening Star* (Washington, D.C.), October 19, 1895, 8.
37. *Catalogue: Edison and International Photographic Films* (New York: Maguire & Baucus, April 1897), 7. Available in *A Guide to Motion Picture Catalogs by American Producers and Distributors, 1894–1908: A Microfilm Edition* (New Brunswick: Rutgers University Press, 1985), Reel 1.
38. "Amusements," *The Morning Record* (Traverse City, Michigan), January 18, 1900, unpaginated.
39. "Under the Post's Eyes," *The Evening Post* (Charleston, South Carolina), March 14, 1896, 4.
40. "Amusements," *Cleveland Plain Dealer*, July 28, 1896.
41. "'Picture Projecting' Machines," *The Phonoscope*, April 1897, 10.
42. Advertisement, *New York Clipper*, December 9, 1899, 865.
43. Untitled, *The Phonoscope*, June 1898, 8.
44. "New Films for 'Screen' Machines," *The Phonoscope*, April 1899, 17.
45. *Complete Catalogue of Genuine and Original "Star" Films (Moving Pictures), Manufactured by Geo. Méliès of Paris* (New York: Star Films, 1903), 18. Available in *A Guide to Motion Picture Catalogs by American Producers and Distributors, 1894–1908: A Microfilm Edition*, Reel 4.
46. "Ninth and Arch Museum," *Philadelphia Inquirer*, April 30, 1899, 12.
47. Advertisement, *New York Times*, April 2, 1899, 17.
48. Ibid., p. 17.
49. Advertisement, *Galveston Daily News* (Galveston, Texas), May 28, 1899, 1.
50. Advertisement, *Mechanicville Mercury* (Mechanicville, New York), June 16, 1900, unpaginated.
51. *Complete Catalogue of Genuine and Original "Star" Films* (New York: Star Films, June 1905), 106. Available in *A Guide to Motion Picture Catalogs by American Producers and Distributors, 1894–1908*, Reel 4. It is important to note that this Star Film catalog bears a June 1905 date, but pages from 81 to 148 detail films from the July 1905 to June 1908 period. Either these later pages were appended to the catalog, or the catalog dates to June 1908, with the first eighty pages reprinted and the 1905 date not being revised.
52. "Something About Current Theatrical Taste and the New Plays for the Present Season," *Denver Post*, September 14, 1902, unpaginated.
53. Untitled, *Dallas Morning News*, January 30, 1901, 6.
54. "The Theatre," *Rockford Republic* (Rockford, Illinois), December 8, 1905, 12.
55. Miriam Hansen, *Babel & Babylon: Spectatorship in American Silent Film* (Cambridge, MA: Harvard University Press, 1991), 1.
56. "New *Fairyland* within Filene's," *Boston Herald*, December 17, 1904, 2.
57. "Amusements," *Dallas Morning News*, October 27, 1905, 3.
58. "Moving Pictures Are All the Rage," *Philadelphia Inquirer*, November 18, 1900, 5.
59. "By Camera Tricks," *Grand Rapids Press* (Grand Rapids, Michigan), July 12, 1902, 10.
60. John R. Spears, "A Suggestion," Letter to the Editor, *New York Times*, October 8, 1905, 6.

61. Jan Olsson, "Modernity Stops at Nothing: The American Chase Film and the Specter of Lynching," in *A Companion to Early Cinema*, edited by André Gaudreault, Nicolas Dulac, and Santiago Hidalgo (Chichester: Wiley-Blackwell, 2012), 261–5.
62. "Our Tattler," *The Phonoscope*, June 1897, 7.
63. "The Propriety of Some Film Subjects," *Views and Film Index*, May 11, 1907, 3.
64. "The 'Nickel Craze' in New York," *Views and Film Index*, October 5, 1907, 3.
65. Richard L. Stromgren, "The Moving Picture World of W. Stephen Bush," *Film History*, 2:1 (Winter 1988), 13–22.
66. W. Stephen Bush, "Who Goes to the Moving Pictures?," *Moving Picture World*, October 31, 1908, 336.
67. "The Moving Picture Theatre," *Views and Film Index*, August 24, 1907, 2. See also F. J. Haskin, "Nickelodeon History," *Views and Film Index*, February 1, 1908, 5, 14.
68. "The Cult of the Motion Picture Show," *Moving Picture World*, August 8, 1908, 106.
69. For more information on children in the nickelodeon audience, see Roberta E. Pearson and William Uricchio's "'The Formative and Impressionable Stage': Discursive Constructions of the Nickelodeon's Child Audience" in *American Film Audiences: From the Turn of the Century to the Early Sound Era*, edited by Melvyn Stokes and Richard Maltby (London: British Film Institute, 1999). For more information on women as viewers of early cinema, see Lauren Rabinovitz, *For the Love of Pleasure: Women, Movies, and Culture in Turn-of-the-Century Chicago* (New Brunswick: Rutgers University Press, 1998). See also Shelley Stamp, *Movie-Struck Girls: Women and Motion Picture Culture After the Nickelodeon* (Princeton, New Jersey: Princeton University Press, 2000).
70. Kathryn H. Fuller, *At the Picture Show: Small Town Audiences and the Creation of Movie Fan Culture* (Washington, D.C.: Smithsonian Institution Press, 1996), 28.
71. "Moving Pictures at Dallas," *Moving Picture World*, March 23, 1907.
72. "The Nickelodeon," *Moving Picture World*, May 4, 1907, 140.
73. "Taking Baby to a Show," *Chicago Tribune*, April 1, 1913, 8.
74. "Hats Off, Ladies!," *The Nickelodeon*, May 15, 1910, 262. See also "Those Hats Again," *The Nickelodeon*, March 15, 1910, 148; "Arrested for Allowing Women to Wear Hats," *Film Index*, December 3, 1910, 8; "Women Don't Want to Remove Hats," *Film Index*, December 10, 1910, 9.
75. A. L. Barrett, "Moving Pictures and Their Audiences," *Moving Picture News*, September 16, 1911, 8–9.
76. Louis Reeves Harrison, "Why We Go to the Picture Show," *Moving Picture World*, August 17, 1912, 640.
77. "Theatre Shuts Out Odor and Is Sued," *Nickelodeon*, July 1909.
78. For more information on the attendance of different ethnic groups at nickelodeons, see, for example, Judith Thissen's "Jewish Immigrant Audiences in New York, 1905–1914," Giorgio Bertellini's "Italian Imageries, Historical Feature Films, and the Fabrication of Italy's Spectators in Early 1900s New York," and Alison Griffiths and James Latham's "Film and Ethnic Identity in Harlem, 1896–1915," all of which appear in *American Film Audiences: From the Turn of the Century to the Early Sound Era*, edited by Melvyn Stokes and Richard Maltby (London: British Film Institute, 1999), as well as Gary D. Rhodes's *Emerald Illusions: The Irish in Early American Cinema* (Dublin: Irish Academic Press, 2011). In addition, Fuller's *At the Picture Show: Small Town Audiences and the Creation of Movie Fan Culture* offers an examination of the "Regional Diversity of Moviegoing Practices" that offers details on the film attendance of African-Americans, Mexican-Americans, Japanese-Americans, and Chinese-Americans from the nickelodeon era to the 1930s.
79. "Who Says Moving Pictures Are Not As Good as the Real Thing?," *Moving Picture World*, May 23, 1908; "Shot a 'Movie' Villain," *Evening News* (Ada, Oklahoma), May 9, 1913, 1.

80. "Almost a Good Show," *Moving Picture Story Magazine* (October 1911), 47.
81. "The Demand for Realistic Exhibitions," *Views and Film Index*, October 13, 1906, 1.
82. "The Random Shots of a Picture Fan," *Moving Picture World*, October 21, 1910, 198.
83. J. S. McQuade, "Chicago Letter," *Film Index*, January 21, 1911, 8.
84. William H. Kitchell, "The Average Patron," *Moving Picture World*, February 10, 1912, 466.
85. Eileen Bowser, *The Transformation of Cinema: 1907–1915* (Berkeley, California: University of California Press, 1990), 2.
86. See, for example, "Balancing the Program," *Moving Picture World*, June 10, 1911, 1303.
87. Advertisement, *Aberdeen Daily News* (Aberdeen, South Dakota), May 8, 1909, 4.
88. Advertisement, *Daily Record-Miner* (Juneau, Alaska), August 2, 1910, 4.
89. Advertisement, *Mansfield News* (Mansfield, Ohio), November 25, 1911, 16.
90. Advertisement, *Riverside Daily Press* (Riverside, California), December 19, 1907, 1.
91. It is difficult to determine specifics about *The Spanish Inquisition* referred to in this article. Given the time frame, it is possible that the reference here is to *The Pit and the Pendulum* (Solax, 1913), which is set during the Inquisition. It is also possible this article refers to an imported film titled *Horrors of the Spanish Inquisition* (aka *The Chamber of Horrors of the Spanish Inquisition*), which Michael A. Testa made available to theatres in New York and New England in 1912. See Advertisement, *New York Clipper*, August 17, 1912, 12, and Advertisement, *New York Clipper*, August 24, 1912, 12.
92. "Facts and Comments," *Moving Picture World*, August 9, 1913, 611.
93. Advertisement, *The Daily Democrat* (Shelbyville, Indiana), April 8, 1910, 4.
94. Advertisement, *Daily Crescent-News* (Defiance, Ohio), April 7, 1910, 3.
95. "The Scenic," *Hartford Courant* (Hartford, Connecticut), April 19, 1910, 6.
96. For more information on the subject of music at nickelodeon theatres, see Rick Altman, *Silent Film Sound* (New York: Columbia University Press, 2004). For information regarding sound effects, see Stephen Bottomore, "The Story of Percy Peashaker: Debates about Sound Effects in Early Cinema," in *The Sounds of Early Cinema*, edited by Richard Abel and Rick Altman (Bloomington, Indiana: Indiana University Press, 2001), 129–55.
97. "The Demand for Realistic Exhibitions," *Views and Film Index*, October 13, 1906, 1.
98. Ernst Luz, "Picture Music," *Moving Picture News*, March 22, 1913, 18.
99. Clarence E. Sinn, "Music for the Picture," *Moving Picture World*, December 3, 1910, 1285.
100. "Two Excellent Novelettes," *Moving Picture News*, February 15, 1913, 15.
101. Rick Altman, *Silent Film Sound* (New York: Columbia University Press, 2004), 252; "Music Cues for Edison Pictures," *The Kinetogram*, March 15, 1910, 11.
102. Walter C. Simon, "Musical Suggestions for *The Spectre Bridegroom*," *Eclair Bulletin*, January 1913; "Musical Suggestions by 'Rubenstein,'" *Eclair Bulletin*, October 1913, 8.
103. J. S. Zamecnik, *Sam Fox Moving Picture Music Vol. 1* (Cleveland, Ohio: Sam Fox Publishing Company, 1913).
104. "Some Film Horrors," *Photoplay*, April 1915, 131.
105. Lisa Morton, *Trick or Treat: A History of Halloween* (London: Reaktion Books, 2012), 162.
106. Copies of *Halloween Night at the Seminary* and *Halloween* are available at the Library of Congress.
107. "An Ill Wind," *Moving Picture World*, January 4, 1913, 52; "A Bum's Hallowe'en," *Moving Picture World*, March 15, 1913, 1105. A relatively complete copy of *An Ill Wind* is archived at the British Film Institute. Halloween had earlier been the subject of such stereo views as *Hallowe'en Party. An Intruder* (Universal Photo Art Co., 1900), *Getting Ready for Hallowe'en* (Keystone, undated), and *Fall—Making Hallowe'en Jack-o'-Lanterns in the Pumpkin Field* (Keystone, undated).

108. As the nickelodeon era ended, Halloween continued to be a popular time to release horror-themed films, as can be seen in the release dates for *The Hypnotic Violinist/Zigo* (Warner's Features, 1914), *The Fiends of Hell/Guarding Britain's Secrets* (Apex, 1914), *The Witch Girl* (Victor, 1914), and *The Pines of Lory* (Edison, 1914). See "The Temptations of Satan," *Moving Picture World*, October 31, 1914, 644; "The Hypnotic Violinist," *Moving Picture World*, October 31, 1914, 706; "The Fiends of Hell," *Moving Picture World*, October 31, 1914, 706; "The Witch Girl," *Motography*, October 31, 1914, 610; "The Pines of Lory," *Moving Picture World*, October 31, 1914, 674.
109. Advertisement, *Moving Picture World*, October 22, 1910, 906.
110. "Satan at Play," *Views and Film Index*, October 26, 1907, 9; "The Witch," *New York Dramatic Mirror*, October 31, 1908, 8; "Williams, Brown & Earle," *Moving Picture World*, October 24, 1908, 328; "Another Ghost," *Variety*, October 29, 1910, 14; Hanford C. Judson, "The Temptations of Satan," *Moving Picture World*, October 31, 1914, 644.
111. Advertisement, *Billboard*, October 27, 1906, 22.
112. "'Tis Now the Very Witching Time of Night," *Moving Picture World*, September 18, 1909, 385.
113. "First 24-Sheet Picture Poster," *Moving Picture World*, July 29, 1911, 232.
114. "Thanhouser Films *Dr. Jekyll and Mr. Hyde*," *Moving Picture World*, January 13, 1912, 128.
115. Advertisement, *Moving Picture World*, November 16, 1912, 620.
116. Advertisement, *Moving Picture World*, February 15, 1913, 637.
117. "Editorial Comments," *Views and Film Index*, February 9, 1907, unpaginated.
118. "Fake Outside Advertising," *Moving Picture World*, January 28, 1911, 182.
119. "Facts and Comments," *Moving Picture World*, March 16, 1912, 940.
120. W. Stephen Bush, "Arms and the Film," *Moving Picture World*, July 26, 1913, 404.
121. Harry Furniss, "The Poster—A Poser," *Motography*, January 4, 1913, 7.
122. "Gaudy Posters Lure to 'Movies,'" *Chicago Tribune*, May 4, 1913, B4.
123. "Facts and Comments," *Moving Picture World*, October 4, 1913, 23.
124. Advertisement, *Atlantic Daily Telegraph* (Atlantic, Iowa), May 6, 1907, unpaginated.
125. Advertisement, *Des Moines Daily News* (Des Moines, Iowa), June 1, 1908, unpaginated.
126. "Film Shows Busy; Panic Stops One," *Chicago Tribune*, April 15, 1907, 1.
127. Ibid., 4. A copy of *From Jealousy to Madness* is archived at the Cinémathèque de Toulouse.
128. "Moving-Picture Subjects," *New York Times*, July 17, 1910, 8.
129. "Moving Picture Men Too Busy," *Oakland Tribune* (Oakland, California), March 11, 1911, 2.
130. "Five-Cent Theatres Schools of Crime," *Los Angeles Times*, December 21, 1906, II1.
131. "Impelled to Slay by Picture Show," *Moving Picture World*, August 15, 1908, 122. See also "Criminal Pictures," *Los Angeles Herald*, August 6, 1908, 4.
132. "The Poor Movie Again," *Moving Picture News*, August 10, 1912, 25.
133. "Weird Tale of a Murder," *Washington Post*, April 14, 1912, 13.
134. "A School for Vice and Crime," *Moving Picture World*, August 19, 1911, 452.
135. See, for example, "Plays 'Bandit'; Kills Girl," *Chicago Tribune*, July 19, 1909, 2; "Moving-Picture Shows," *Washington Post*, June 6, 1911, 6.
136. "Picture Shows Thrill," *Washington Post*, October 4, 1908, 13.
137. "Opinions of Others," *Duluth News-Tribune* (Duluth, Minnesota), March 19, 1910, 8.
138. "Children Terrorized by Moving Pictures," *Cedar Rapids Daily Republican* (Cedar Rapids, Iowa), November 17, 1910, 7.
139. "Ghastly Vermin Horrors Shown Mere 'Babes,'" *Aberdeen Daily News* (Aberdeen, South Dakota), January 11, 1913, 2.
140. "The Propriety of Some Film Subjects," *Views and Film Index*, May 11, 1907, 3.
141. Cornelius O'Shea, "An Appeal to the Savage," *Moving Picture World*, July 8, 1911, 1570.

142. W. Stephen Bush, "What the People Want," *Moving Picture World*, January 25, 1913, 341.
143. Laura Rabinovitz, *For the Love of Pleasure: Women, Movies, and Culture in Turn-of-the-Century Chicago* (New Brunswick: Rutgers University Press, 1998), 106.
144. Lee Grieveson, *Policing Cinema: Movies and Censorship in Early-Twentieth-Century America* (Berkeley: University of California Press, 2004), 23.
145. "Macbeth Pictures Are Too Realistic," *Grand Forks Daily Herald* (Grand Forks, North Dakota), June 5, 1908, 5. The film discussed in this article was almost certainly *Macbeth, Shakespeare's Sublime Tragedy* (Vitagraph, 1908), which is archived at the Library of Congress by way of a paper print deposit.
146. "How to Be a Censor," *New York Dramatic Mirror*, December 30, 1914, 21.
147. "Facts and Comments," *Moving Picture World*, July 13, 1912, 120.
148. "Problems of Censorship Are Complex," *Salt Lake Telegram* (Salt Lake City, Utah), October 17, 1911, 1.
149. Shelley Stamp, *Movie-Struck Girls: Women and Motion Picture Culture after the Nickelodeon* (Princeton, New Jersey: Princeton University Press, 2000), 6.
150. Leona Radnor, *The Photoplay Writer: How to Write Scenarios that Sell and Where to Sell Them* (New York: The Quaker Press, 1913).
151. Mabel Condon, "What Happens to the Scenario," *Motography*, March 1, 1913, 147.
152. "Boise Has Moving Picture Craze and Managers of Electric Theatres Are Giving People What They Want," *Idaho Statesman* (Boise, Idaho), February 28, 1909.
153. W. Stephen Bush, "Punches and Thrills," *Moving Picture World*, March 29, 1913, 1312.
154. "*Dr. Jekyll and Mr. Hyde*," *Moving Picture World*, September 24, 1910, 685.
155. "Thanhouser Films *Dr. Jekyll and Mr. Hyde*," *Moving Picture News*, January 6, 1912, 22.
156. "*The Wages of Sin*," *Moving Picture World*, October 3, 1908, 253.
157. "*The Witch*," *Moving Picture World*, November 20, 1909, 721.
158. W. Stephen Bush, "Comments of the Fleeting Hour," *Moving Picture World*, April 9, 1910, 552.
159. "Facts and Comments," *Moving Picture World*, October 18, 1913, 241.
160. "*Doomed to Die*," *Variety*, August 29, 1913, 15.
161. "*In the Dark Valley*," *Moving Picture World*, May 21, 1910, 833.
162. "*The Maze of Fear*," *Moving Picture World*, April 22, 1911, 901.
163. "*The Octopus*," *Moving Picture World*, April 19, 1913, 281.
164. "*The Haunted Island*," *Moving Picture World*, July 22, 1911, 127.
165. "*The Fear*," *Moving Picture World*, July 5, 1913, 47.
166. "See 'Em as Ghosts," *Moving Picture World*, April 12, 1913, 150.
167. "*The Smallpox Scare at Gulch Hollow*," *Moving Picture World*, July 26, 1913, 430.
168. "*From the Beyond*," *Moving Picture World*, October 11, 1913, 158.
169. "*The Haunted Bedroom*," *Moving Picture World*, January 3, 1914, 48.
170. "*The Hindoo Dagger*," *New York Dramatic Mirror*, February 27, 1909, 13.
171. "*The Haunted House*," *Moving Picture World*, May 10, 1913, 596.
172. "The Demand for Realistic Exhibitions," *Views and Film Index*, October 13, 1906, 1.
173. "Panic at a Picture Show," *New York Times*, June 27, 1910, 1.
174. See, for example, "Scared by Indian at Picture Show; Dying," *Chanute Daily Tribune* (Chanute, Kansas), July 1, 1910, 3; "Realism at Nickelodeon Sends Woman in Spasm," *Oakland Tribune*, July 4, 1910, 11.
175. "*Mephisto's Son* at Nickelo," *The Daily Democrat* (Shelbyville, Indiana), December 14, 1908, 5.
176. "Shubert Theatre," *New Orleans Item* (New Orleans, Louisiana), June 23, 1908, 10.
177. "Dreamland Theatre," *The Evening News* (Sault Ste. Marie, Michigan), April 22, 1910, 3.
178. "Facts and Comments," *Moving Picture World*, July 18, 1914, 403.
179. Neil G. Caward, "The Day of Realism in the Movies," *Movie Pictorial*, July 1914, 14.

180. "Realism in the Movies," *Movie Pictorial*, February 1915, 21; "Realism in the Movies," *Movie Pictorial*, March 1915, 23.
181. "Realism in the Movies," *Movie Pictorial*, October 1915, 23.
182. "Moving Picture Gods and Goddesses," *Moving Picture Wlorld*, March 26, 1910, 468.
183. Stamp, 6.
184. "*The Embezzler*," *Moving Picture World*, March 28, 1914, 59; "*Her Grave Mistake*," *Moving Picture World*, July 18, 1914, 434; "*The Oubliette*," *Moving Picture World*, August 15, 1914, 962; Advertisement, *Moving Picture World*, *Universal Weekly*, April 17, 1915.
185. "Actor of a Thousand Roles," *Photoplay* (April 1915), 28–9.
186. Edna Francis, "Marc McDermott," *Movie Pictorial* (February 1915), 12–13.
187. Untitled, *Billboard*, March 21, 1914, 162.
188. "What Is the Demon in Mary's Eyes," *Photoplay* (April 1915), 57. Emphasis in original.
189. "Vitagraph's Publicity Helps," *Motography*, September 25, 1915, 628.
190. "Novel Advertising Ideas," *Motography*, October 23, 1915, 838.
191. Ibid., 838.
192. Vanderheyden Fyles, "*The Avenging Conscience*," *Movie Pictorial*, September 12, 1914, 29.

Index

Page numbers in *italics* refer to illustrations, and those followed by n refer to notes.
Titles followed by a date are films, titles of other forms of media are followed by a description.

Abbott, Annie May, 48
Abel, Richard, 8, 99, 107, 108–9
Aberdeen, South Dakota Bijou, 377
The Accusing Eye (1914), 283
Ackerman, Alan L., Jr., 51
"Actor of a Thousand Roles," 389
Adams, Gretchen A., 147–8
Addison, Joseph, 38–9
Adrien, Monsieur, 72
The Adventure of a German Student [story], 24–5
The Adventure of My Aunt [story], 55
Adventures of Huckleberry Finn [story], 311
The Adventures of Kathlyn (1913–14), 270
After the Welsh Rarebit (1913), 111, 131
Afterward [story], 30
age and gender of audience, 375
Age of Barnum, 5–6, *6*
The Age of Edison: Electric Light and the Invention of Modern America [book], 311
Agra, Zalumma, 250
Aida [opera], 349
Albany Argus, 4
Alcott, Louisa May, 195
Alexander, S. B., 126
Alexandria Gazette, 4–5
Alger, Horatio, 245
Alice Doane's Appeal [story], 150
Alkali Ike Plays the Devil (1912), *132*
All for a Tooth (1914), 192
All Hallow Ev'n [lantern slide], 73
Allen, Robert C., 367–8
Allston, Washington, 66
Alone with the Devil (1914), 287
Altman, Rick, 12, 81, 93n
Altman's methodology, 10
Ambrosio, 137, 283, 284, 350
American Boy [magazine], 73
American Civil War, 12, 26, 29, 30, 77, 215, 263
  antebellum literature, 26–9
  post-bellum literature, 29–31
  post-bellum theatre, 51–4
American Daguerreotype, 77
American Film Cycles: The Silent Era [book], 296
American Gothic
  artwork, 65
  literature, 21, 29
  paintings, 64–5
American literature
  adaptations, 13, 107–8, 337–65
  early, 22–6
  and ghosts, 164
  and skeletons, 189
  and witches, 149–50
American Museum, 64, 245
American Mutoscope & Biograph
  apparitions, 164–5
  Blacks, 258
  Bluebeard the Second (1914), 220

Brute Force (1914), 242
The Criminal Hypnotist (1909), 292
D. W. Griffith, 112
Edgar Allen Poe (1909), 354
executions, 223–4, *224*, 226
Faust and the Lily (1913), 132
The Ghost (1911), 174
ghosts, 164
haunted houses, 169
"Hindoos," 269
hypnotism, 291, 292
Jane Eyre (1915), 341
mental illness, 282
murder, 219
Satan, 129
skeletons, 189, 190–1
somnambulism, 285
Spiritualism, 176
suicide, 218
trick pictures, 101, 103
Trilby and Little Billee (1896), 292
American Realism, 21–2, 29; *see also* realism
American Revolution, 215
American Society for Psychical Research, 175
American Theatrephone Company, 319
American Universal Magazine, 22
American Weekly Mercury, 4, 147, 202
American West and witchcraft, 154–5
Americanizing the cinema, 107–9
And The Goblins Will Get You If You Don't Watch Out [stereo view], 79
And the Villain Still Pursued Her (1906), 314
Andress, the Magician (Professor Charles Andress), 47–8
"animal magnetism," 286–7, 288
The Animated Scarecrow (1910), 187
animation, 103
Annabel Lee [poem], 1, 353
Annabelle Serpentine Dance (1894), 97
Anne Pedersdotter [play], 152
Another's Ghost (1910), 167
Anthony, M. Susan, 40
"anti-spiritualism," 46, 95
Apex Film Company, 140
The Apparition, or Mr. Jones' Comical Experience with a Ghost (1903), 169
Apparition [stereo view], 80
apparitions, 164–8
Arden, Edwin, 256
Arliss, George, 137
Armat, Thomas, 94
Armitage, Frederick S., 129, 134, 164, 219
Arnaud, Étienne, 355
Arrival of a Train at La Ciotat (1895), 96
The Arrow Maiden (1915), *260*, 261
The Art of the Moving Picture [book], 3, 112
Art Union, 67
Arthur Mervyn; or, The Memoirs of the Year 1793 [story], 24
Arthur's Illustrated Home Magazine, 67

Artist's Dream, The (1899), 191
As in a Looking Glass (1913), 297–8
Asians, 272–3
Askari, Kaveh, 298
Asma, Stephen T., 273, 312
astronomy, 311
asylum films, 301n
At a Motion Picture Show [poem], 94
Atherton, Gertrude, 30
Auburn State Prison, 224
audience participation, 38
audience reactions, 385–7
audience reception, 366–97
Aunt Tabitha's Monkey (1910), 240
Austen, Jane, 9, 22
Austin, William, 21
"authentic sources," 27
"autopsy," 11
Avenging a Crime; or Burned at the Stake (1904), 227
Avenging Conscience or "Thou Shalt Not Kill" (1914), 1–2, 109, 113, 352–3, 390

Baby's Ghost (1912), 167
Bachelor's Paradise (1903), 152
Baggot, King, 320–1, 388
"balanced," 372, 377
Balaoo, The Demon Baboon (1913), 242–4, *244*, 341
Balaoo [story], 242–4, 341
Baldwin, Ruth Ann, 201
A Ballad of the Were-wolf [poem], 200
ballet, 127, 203
Ballet of the Ghosts (1899), 164–5
The Balloon-Hoax, 5
Baltimore Sun, 94
Balzac, Honoré de, 108, 349
Bangs, J. K., 30
The Banshee (1913), 188
Banta, Martha, 30
Bara, Theda, 206, 299
Barber, X. Theodore, 71
The Barbershop (1894), 97
The Bargain Lost [story], 126
A Bargain with Satan (1913), 140, 347
bargains with Satan, 131–3
Baring-Gould, Sabine, 200
Barkan, Leonard, 11, 13
Barker, James Nelson, 39, 151
Barnes, Elizabeth, 216
Barnum, P. T., 5–6, 64, 238, 245–6, 250
Barnum & Bailey Greatest Show on Earth, 246
Barriscale, Bessie, *138*
The Bat (play), 32
Bataille, Lucien, 243
Bateman and His Ghost [play], 39
Bathory, Elizabeth, 70
The Battle of Elderbush Gulch (1913), 263
Baudelaire, Charles, 127
Baum, L. Frank, 147
Bazin, André, 13
Be the Howly St. Patrick! - There's Mickie's Ghost (1894), 257
Beach Park of Galveston, Texas, 372
Beale, Joseph Boggs, 73–4, *74*
Beautiful Eyes (1909), 83, *83*
The Beautiful Margaret (1910), 132
Bedding, Thomas, 344
Bednarowski, Mary Farrell, 175
The Beechwood Ghost (1910), 167
Beelzebub's Daughter (1903), 128
Beer, Gillian, 236
Beer, Janet, 30
Beery, Wallace, 166
Beheading Chinese Prisoner (1900), 223

Beidler, Peter G., 31
Believed She Was a Witch [engraving], 69
The Bells [play], 51, 353
The Bells (1912), 346
The Bells (1913), 105
Bender Family, 216
Beneath the Tower Ruins (1911), 174
Benito Cereno [story], 21
Bennett, Bridget, 37
Bergland, Renée L., 259
Berlin, Irving, 379
Berlin Jack the Ripper (1909), 220
Berlioz, Hector, 133
Bertsch, Marguerite, 315
Besserer, Eugenie, 179
The Bewitched Manor (1909), 171
The Bewitched Traveller/The Jonah Man (1904), 103
Bible, 127, 137
Bierce, Ambrose, 5, 30
   Can Such Things Be? 30
   Chickamauga, 30
   The Famous Gilson Bequest, 30
   The Middle Toe of the Right Foot, 30
   The Moonlit Road, 30
   An Occurrence at Owl Creek Bridge, 30
"Big Feature Film," 344
Bill Becomes Mentally Deranged (1912), 283
Bill Taken for a Ghost (1911), 167
The Billboard
   Claire Whitney, 389–90
   Dr. Jekyll and Mr. Hyde (1908), 319
   The Ghost Breaker, 54–5
   The Ghost of the Vaults (1911), 166
   The Haunted Hotel (1907), 170, *170*
   Life Without Soul (1915), 329
   Lola (1914), 324
   The Raven (1915), 356
   Shooting in the Haunted Woods (1910), 165
   Spiritualism Exposed (1913), 178
   The Star of the Side Show (1912), 249
Billy's Seance (1911), 178
Biograph Bulletin, 282
The Birth of a Nation (1915), 1, 228, 273, 280n
Bishop, Bridget, 37
Bishop, W. Irving, 46
bizarre operations, 314–15
Blaché, Alice Guy, 12, 109, 113–14, *113*, 270–1, 284, 339, 350–2, *351*, 357
Blaché, Herbert, 357
The Black Box (1915), 242, *243*
The Black Cat [story], 28
The Black Crook [play], 50
The Black Imp (1905), 129–31
Black Maria, 96–7, *96*, 98
A Black Specter [story], 177
The Black Vampyre [burlesque], 25
The Black Witch (1907), 161n
"blackface," 263, 264
Blacks, 263–6
Blackton, J. Stuart, 169–71, 314, 382
Blackwood's Edinburgh Magazine, 23, 27
Blaney, Charles E., 237
The Blithedale Romance [story], 28, 288, 344
The Blood-Seedling (1915), 177
Blue Beard (1902), 220
Bluebeard the Second (1914), 220
Bobby "Some" Spiritualist (1914), 178
Bodie, Walford, 289
body snatchers, 215
Boers Bringing in British Prisoners (1900), 98
Bogdan, Robert, 238, 245, 256–7
The Bogey Woman (1909), 208n

Bologna, John P., 71
Bonavita, Captain Jack, 264
Bon-Bon [story], 126
The Boogie Man Rag [illustrated song], 85
The Book of Werewolves [book], 200
booking films, duration of, 377
The Bookman, 30, 31
Bora Bora, 257
Borden, Lizzie, 22, 85, 216
Bordwell, David, 96, 100
Borelli, Lyda, 140
Borton, Terry and Deborah, 73–4
Boston Globe, 202
Boston Herald, 64, 312, 373
Boston Post, 264
Botticelli, 204
The Bottle Imp [story], 126
Boucicault, Dion, 43, 257
Bowers, Thomas M., 292
Bowser, Eileen, 103, 109, 114, 259–60, 376
The Boxing Cats (1894), 97
Boynton, Cynthia Wolfe, 149
Brabin, Charles J., 356
Bracker, M. Leone, 69
Bracy, Sidney, 234, *235*
Braddon, Elizabeth, 176
Brady, Matthew, 77
Brady, William A., 292
The Bradys and the Demon Doctor; or, The House of Many Mysteries [book], 263, 276n
Braid, James, 288
The Brand of Evil (1913), 271
The Brand of His Tribe (1914), 111
Braude, Ann, 6
Bray, J. R., 172
Brenon, Herbert, 320–1, 322
Brewster, Ben, 8
The Bride of Mystery (1914), 290
Brides and Bridles (1912), 248
The Bridge of Shadows (1913), 111
Bridget's Dream [lantern slides], 73
British Gothic, 22–3
British Museum, 195
British plays in America, 40
Brontë, Charlotte, 340–1
Brown, Charles Brockden, 11, 23–4, 27, 31, 66, 285
   Arthur Mervyn; or, The Memoirs of the Year 1793, 24
   Edgar Huntly; or, Memoirs of a Sleep-Walker, 24, 285
   Ormond; or, The Secret Witness, 24
   Wieland, or The Transformation, 24
Brown, Harold P., 49
Browne, Porter Emerson, 295–6
Brown's Seance (1912), 177
Brute Force (1914), 242, 253n
Buck, Colonel Jonathan, 149
Budick, E. Miller, 28
Bud's Inferno [vaudeville], 138
Bull Fight Series (1898), 222
A Bum's Hallowe'en (1913), 379
The Burden Bearer (1913), 298
burial, 215–16
Buried Alive (1910), 273
burlesque
   The Black Vampyre, 25
   The Mummy Girl, 196
   The Rag Woman and Her Dogs, 44
Burne-Jones, Philip, 204–6, 295, 297, 326
Burns, Sarah, 65–6
Burns, Stanley B., 77
Burns, Vinnie, 270–1
Burroughs, Edgar Rice, 237, 263
Bush, W. Stephen, 138–9, 375, 385
Byron, Lord, 25

C. W. Briggs company, 73
Le cabinet de Méphistophélès (1899), 1, 128
"cabinet of horrors," Washington, D.C., police department, 38
The Cake Walk Infernal (1903), 128
Can Such Things Be? [story], 30
cannibalism, 27, 263
Capellani, Albert, 283
Cardiff Giant, 5
A Career of Crime, No.3: Robbery and Murder (1900), 219
A Career of Crime, No.5: The Death Chair (1900), 224
Carey, M., 23
Carey and Hart, 27
Carle, Richard, 196
Carney, Augustus, *132*
Carnival in Black and White [planned film], 265–6
carnivals, 246
Carr, William, 225
Casey, Kathleen B., 263
The Cask of Amontillade [story], 108, 349
Castle, Terry, 72
Castle, William, 367
The Castle of Otranto [story], 22
The Castle Spectre [story], 12, 41–2, 44, 51
Catalogue of Optical Goods, 75
The Cavalier's Dream (1898), 129
Cave of the Spooks (1908), 129
censorship, 383–5, 387–8
Centaur, 265
Century Illustrated Magazine, 67
"Chamber of Horrors," 38, 51, 55, 223, 226, 371
Chambers, Robert W., 30, 235
Chaney, Lon, 234, 388–9
Chang, Prince, 241
The Changing of Souls (1908), 241
Chaplin, Charlie, 241
Charcot, Jean-Martin, 288
The Chatsworth Horror [illustration], 69
The Cheval Mystery (1915), 293
Chicago Projecting Company, 101
Chicago Transparency Company, 81
Chicago Tribune
   censorship, 383
   Dracula (book), 31
   electricity, 50
   Frankenstein (1931), 13–14
   freak shows, 246
   The Ghost Breaker, 55
   Life Without Soul (1915), 328
   "Missing Link," 236
   posters, 382
   prank skeletons, 190
   The Raven (1915), 356
   Salem Witch Trials, 3, 150
   Satan, 127
   Spiritualism, 175
   Svengali, 257
   vampires, 204
   witches, 148
   women audiences, 375
Chickamauga [story], 30
children, 373–4, 383–4, 386
Children of the Jungle (1914), 250
The Chinatown Mystery (1915), 267, *268*
Chinese, 256, 258, 266–9
The Chinese Death Thorn (1913), 267–9
Chinese Exclusion Act, 266
Ching Ling Foo (1900), 258
Chissus, Sinclair Jr., 367, 369, 379, 387
Chomón, Segundo de, 103, 153, 170, 172, 187, 192–3, 206, 312
Choreutoscope, 76
"Christian evolution," 236
Christian Register, 27

A Christmas Carol [story], 73, 339
A Christmas Carol (1908), 339
A Christmas Carol (1910), 339
A Christmas Carol (1914), 339
The Churchyard Revelry [lantern slides], 76
"cinema of attractions," 8, 95
Cinematic Vampires: The Living Dead on Film and Television, from The Devil's Castle (1896) to Bram Stoker's Dracula (1992) [book], 203
"cineograph," 372
"Circassians," 250
The Circular Staircase [story], 32
The Circular Staircase (1915), 179–80, *180*
Claiming His Skeleton [story], 189
clairvoyance, 281
Clapham, A. J., 86
Clark, Alfred, 2, 98
Clary, Charles, 297
Claudy, C. H., 105, 118n
Clement, Clay, 51
Clemons, Paul, 349
Cleveland Leader, 225
Cleveland Plain Dealer, 70, 295, 371
cliffhangers, 109
Clifford, William H., 201, 367, 391n
The Clockmaker's Secret (1907), 135
close-ups, 104
The Clue of the Scarab (1914), 198
Coad, Oral Sumner, 33n, 41, 43
Cockton, Henry, 285
Cohen, Daniel A., 26
Cohen, I. Bernard, 309
Cohill, William W., 328
Cohl, Emile, 171
The Cold Embrace [story], 176
Cole, Thomas, 65–6
"Collection of Natural Curiosities," 234
Collins, John H., 267
Collins, Wilkie, 271, 339–40
  The Dead Secret, 339
  The Moonstone, 271, 272, 279n, 340
  The Woman in White, 339
Colman, George, the Younger, 41
Colonel Heeza Liar, Ghost Breaker (1915), 171–2, *171*
Columbia Phonograph Co., Washington DC, 370–1
Columbia Records, 318
comedy
  Blacks, 263
  devils, 131
  The Devil's Sale (1909), 143n
  Dr. Jekyll and Mr. Hyde, 318
  electricity, 322
  executions, 226
  freaks, 245–7
  ghosts, 165–6
  Halloween, 379
  haunted houses, 171–3
  Hawthorne, 28
  "Hindoo," 269
  hypnotism, 289–92
  Irving, 24, 126
  mad scientists, 316
  Méliès, 100, 127–8
  mental illness, 282–3
  mummies, 195–8
  Native Americans, 261
  Poe stories, 349
  primates, 239–41
  pseudo-science, 313–14, 316
  science fiction, 313
  skeletons, 189, 190–1, 191, 209n
  slides, 76, 83–4
  somnambulism, 286
  Spiritualism, 176–7
  stage, 196
  supernatural creatures, 207–8
  theatre, 51, 54–5
  Twain, 22, 311
  voodoo, 265–6
  werewolves, 200
  witches, 153
  you-are-what-you-eat, 212–13n
The Commuter's Wife (1912), 111
Conan Doyle, Arthur *see* Doyle, Arthur Conan
Coney Island at Night (1905), 111
Connecticut Gazette, 203
Connelly, Edward, 137, *138*
The Conqueror Worm [poem], 37
Conrad, Joseph, 236
Continental-Kunstfilm, 107
Cook, James W., 6
Coquille Film Company, New Orleans, 265–6
Corelli, Marie, 126, 221–2, 337
corpses, 80
The Cosmopolitan, 289, 310
Cotton, Elizabeth, 328
Count Zarka (1914), 175
The Country Cousin (1830), 165
Courage of Sorts (1913), 173, *173*
Courtney, Susan, 280n
Cox, Jeffrey N., 42
Cox, Juliana, 149
Crafton, Donald, 170
Crawford, F. Marion, 32, 68–9, 107–8
creators and creations, 322–4
The Cremation (1899), 190, 217
Crescent Films, 227
Crile, George Washington, 390
crime scene photographs, 85
The Criminal Hypnotist (1909), 292
The Critic, 53, 67
Crossley, Robert, 311
Cruze, James, 319–21
Cunard, Grace, 341–2
Curing the Cook (1915), 191
A Curious Dream: Containing a Moral [story], 22
The Curious Dream [story], 337
The Curious Dream (1907), 337
A Curious Invention (1910), 333n
Current Literature, 50, 258
The Curse, The (1913), 158
Curtis, "Professor" Fred, 178
Cycle Rider and the Witch (1909), 153
Cyclopedia of Motion-Picture Work [book], 100
Czolgosz, Leon, 224

Daguerre, 78
Dale, Lily, 78
Dallas Morning News, 374
The Damnation of Faust (1903), 133–4, 144n
Dance of Death [lantern slides], 75
Dancing Skeleton (1902), 191
Dancing Skeleton (1903), 191
The Dancing Skeleton (1897), 191
dancing skeletons, 76
A Dangerous Experiment (1914), 316
Danish film, 107
Dante's Inferno [book], 67, 73, 125, 127, 135–9, 139–40, 145n, 204, 206
Dante's Inferno (1911), 109, 137–9, *137*, 380, *380*, *381*, 383
D'Arcy, Uriah Derrick, 25
"dark tradition," 21–2
Darley, Felix O. C., 67, 259
Darwin, Charles, 235, 237, 245–6
  The Descent of Man, 237, 245
  On the Origin of Species, 235, 236, 237

INDEX

Darwinism, 234–55, 290
Darwin's Plots [book], 236
Davenport Brothers (Ira and William), 46, 47
Davies, Owen, 148, 154, 158, 323–4
Davis, Hiram and Barney, 50, 238
Davis, Keith F., 77
Davy Jones' Locker (1900), 191
Dawley, J. Searle, 134, 324–6, 339
Day, Clarence, 26–7
Day, George D., 196
Days of Terror (1912), 106
Dayton Flood Horror (1913), 218
Dead Man Restored to Life by Touching the Bones of the Prophet Elisha [painting], 66
The Dead Secret [story], 339
The Dead Secret (1913), 110, 339
The Dead Soul (1915), 218
The Deadly Plant (1908), 220
A Deal in Real Estate (1914), 174
The Deal with the Devil (1914), 140
Deas, Charles, 65
death, 77, 215–33, 257
The Death Knell (1913), 338
The Death Mask (1914), 111, 261, 273
The Death of Cora [painting], 65–6
Death of Maceo and His Followers (1899), 372
The Death Stone of India (1913), 272
Delirium Tremens [lantern slides], 73
DeMille, Cecil B., 112
The Demon (1911), 137
The Demon Barber (1899), 219
Dennett, Andrea Stulman, 38, 73
Dennison's Bogie Book, 13, 55, 85
Dent, Harrison, 105
Denver Post, 373
DeRosa, Robin, 37
The Descent of Man [book], 237, 245
A Desperate Crime (1906), 219
"detective films," 114, 342
Detroit Free Press, 367
The Devil [play], 136–7
The Devil (1915), *138*
The Devil, the Servant, and the Man (1910), 136–7, 145n
The Devil and Dr. Faustus [play], 38
The Devil and the Chemist (1907), 380
The Devil and the Painter (1909), 131
The Devil and the Statue (1903), 128
The Devil and Tom Walker [story], 24, 65, 126, 342–3
The Devil and Tom Walker (1913), 343
The Devil in a Convent (1900), 128, 204, 372
The Devil in the School House (1902), 128
devils, 125–46
The Devil's Amusement (1903), 129
The Devil's Billiard Table (1910), 135
The Devil's Castle (Le manoir du diable) (1896)
  "Chamber of Horrors," 371
  exhibition, 372–3
  Faust, 133
  haunted houses, 169
  Satan and comedy, 128
  skeletons, 190
  trick pictures, 99, *99*
  vampires, 203–4, 206–7
  witches, 152
The Devil's Darling (1915), 125, 135
The Devil's Fiddler (1914), 247
The Devil's Kitchen (1902), 129
The Devil's Laboratorty (1899), 1, 7–8
Devil's Pot (1904), 129
The Devil's Prison (1902), 142n
The Devil's Sale (1909), 143n
The Devil's Signature (1914), 215
The Devil's Theatre (1902), 129

The Devil's Three Sins (1908), 131
DeWitt C. Wheeler, 81
A Dextrous Hand (1903), 104
"diableries," 128
The Dial, 310
Dickens, Charles, 7, 43, 73, 339, 357
  A Christmas Carol, 73, 339
  The Haunted Man and the Ghost's Bargain, 43
Dickson, W. K. L., 96, 97–8
Dillon, Eddie, 317
Dillon, Will, 290
dime museums, 289
dime novels, 32, 67
Dircks, Henry, 43
"Directors as Artists," 112
disease, 218
"dissolving views," 74–5
Doings of a Maniac (1907), 282
The Dollar Newspaper, 67
The Doll's Revenge (1907), 324
Domino, 158
Donaldson, Arthur, 266
Donner Party tragedy, 263
Doomed to Die, or the Vial of Wrath (1913), 309, 338, 386
Doré, Gustave, 67, 73, 138, 145n, 204
Dorian Gray (1910), 363n
Dorothy's Dream (1903), 220
"double printing" film, 191
double-exposure, 198, 257, 316, *320*
The Downward Path (series), 218
Doyle, Arthur Conan, 78, 195, 237, 295, 340, 342
  The Hound of the Baskervilles, 237
  The Hound of the Baskervilles (1915), 342
  The Lost World, 237
  Lot No. 249, 195
  The Parasite, 295
Dr. Belgraff [play], 54
Dr. Dippy's Sanitarium (1906), 282
Dr. Jekyll and Mr. Hyde, 318–22; see also *[The] Strange Case of Dr. Jekyll and Mr. Hyde*
Dr. Jekyll and Mr. Hyde (1887), 12, *52*
Dr. Jekyll and Mr. Hyde (1908), 318–19
Dr. Jekyll and Mr. Hyde (1912), 319–20, 380, 386
Dr. Jekyll and Mr. Hyde (1913), 51–3, 320–1, 321–2, *321*, 380
Dr. Jekyll and Mr. Hyde Done to a Frazzle (1914), 318
Dr. Jekyll and Mr. Hyde; or, a Strange Case (1910), 105–6, 319, 320, 328, 386
Dr. Skinum (1907), 248, 313
Dracula (1931), 8
Dracula [story], 31, 68, 287
Dray, Philip, 309
A Dream After Seeing Pepper's Ghost [stereo view], 79
The Dream of a Rarebit Fiend (1906), 105, 131
A Dream within a Dream [poem], 354
The Dream Woman (1914), 339–40, 389–90
Dreamland Theatre, Sault Ste. Marie, Michigan, 387
dreams, 100, 105–6
"drug-terrror" films, 388
The Drummer, or the Haunted House [play], 38–9, 54
du Maurier, George, 53–4, 68, 247, 311, 337
  The Martian, 311
  Trilby, 53, 68, 247, 289–95, 298, 308n, 337
Dubois, Eugène, 236
Duel Scene from "Macbeth" (1905), 219
A Duel to the Death (1898), 219
Duncan, Bud, *166*, 168
Dunlap, William, 40
The Dust of Egypt (1915), 207, *207*
Dyer, Frank Lewis, 337
Dyer, Richard, 259

Eastland Horror (1915), 218
Eclair American
   From the Beyond (1913), 315–16
   Faust (1910), 134
   The Ghost of the Mine (1914), 261
   Legend of Sleepy Hollow (1912), 344–5
   "Literary Photo Sensations," 337–8
   A Puritan Episode, A (1913), 158
   The Raven (1912), 355–6, *355*
   The Spectre Bridegroom (1913), 343–4
   The Spider (1913), 277n
   The Witch (1913), 158
Eclair Bulletin, 242, 343, 379
Eclectic, 349
"Ecstatica," 287
Eden Musée, 372
Edeson, Robert, 315
Edgar Allan Poe, or The Raven [play], 354
Edgar Allen Poe (1909), 354
Edgar Huntly; or, Memoirs of a Sleep-Walker [story], 24, 285
Edgar Poe [play], 354
Edgerly, Webster, 346
Edison, Thomas Alva, 310–13, 322, 326, 330, 369
Edison Kinetogram, 324–5
Edison Kinetoscopic Record of a Sneeze (1894), 97
Edison Manufacturing Company
   Aida (1911), 349
   Black Maria, 96–7, *96*, 98
   Bluebeard (1909), 220
   Bull Fight Series (1898), 222
   Chinese films, 258
   A Christmas Carol (1910), 339
   The Commuter's Wife (1912), 111
   Egyptian Fakir with Dancing Monkey (1903), 239
   Execution of Czolgosz (1901), 224
   Execution of Mary, Queen of Scots (1895), 2–3, 222–3
   The Experiment (1915), 286
   Faust (1909), 134
   Faust and Marguerite (1900), 133
   Frankenstein (1910), 14, 324–5, 387
   haunted houses, 169, 172–4
   The House of the Seven Gables (1910), 344–5
   How Motion Pictures Are Made and Shown (1912), 103
   indoor filming, 96–8
   The Leprechawn (1908), 153
   Maniac Chase (1904), 282
   Massacre at Constantinople (1901), 219
   Mephistopheles' School of Magic (1903), 287
   [The] Mesmerist and Country Couple (1899), 290–1
   music, 378–9
   "mysterious," 101–2
   Rats and Terrier films (1894), 232n
   Satan, 128–9, 142n
   Skeleton Dance, Marionettes (1898), 191
   'Tis Now the Very Witching Hour of Night (1909), 379–80
   The Toymaker, the Doll and the Devil (1910), 143n
   Vanishing Lady (1897), 116n
   A Visit to the Spiritualist (1899), 176, 185n, 372
   The Watermelon Patch (1905), 263
"The Edison Moving Picture and Concert Co.," 371
Edison phonograph, 77
Edison's Vitascope and Refined Concert Co., 370
The Educated Chimpanzee (1901), 239, 263
Egyptian Fakir with Dancing Monkey (1903), 239
The Egyptian Mummy (1913), 196
The Egyptian Mummy (1914), 198
The Egyptian Mystery (1909), 196
An Egyptian Princess (1914), 196
Eidoloscope, 94
Einstein, Albert, 309
electric chair, 216, 228, 289, 311, 322
The Electric Laundry (1912), 95
The Electrical Doll [play], 48

electricity, 27, 48–50, 55, 216, 322
Electricity Hall, World's Columbian Exposition, Chicago 1893, 50
Electrified Hunchback (1909), 246
Electrocuting and Elephant (1903), 222
electrocution, 49, 216
The Eleventh Dimension (1915), 324
elixirs, 196, 198, 211n, 234, 316–18
Elsaesser, Thomas, 10
embalming, 216
Emigrants Attacked by Indians on the Prairie [painting], 259
The Enchanted Well (1903), 152
The End of Her Honeymoon [story], 271–2
Engberg, Marguerite, 360n
English Gothic novels, 7
engravings, 67–70
   How Wholesale Murder is Avenged in the Wild West, 69
   The Hudson Legends, 67
   Ichabod and Brom Bones, 67, *68*
   An Incubus, 68
   Tales of a Traveller, 67
   Women Hanging Huns, 69
Enlightenment, 4, 6, 126
Entombed Alive (1909), 349
epilepsy, 300n
Escamotage d'une dame chez Robert-Houdin (1896), 100, 116n, 190
The Escape from the Mad House (1907), 283
The Escaped Lunatic (1904), 282, 283
Essanay, 198, 215, 339, 356, 385
Essex Gazette, Salem, Massachusetts, 66–7
"ethical melodrama," 108
ethnic audiences, 393n
ethnic segregation, 376
ethnology, 258
European Feature Film Corporation, 188
European literature, 339–42
Evans, Henry Ridgely, 78
Evening Mirror, New York, 151
Evening Star, Washington DC, 200, *371*
Every Little Movement Has a Meaning All Its Own [song], 377
The Evil Philter (1909), 135
evolution, 234–55, 290
Ewers, Hanns Heinz, 140
"Exclusive Film Company," 349
An Excursion to the Moon (1908), 103
An Execution by Hanging (1898), 226
An Execution by Hanging (1912), *225*
Execution of a Murderess (1905), 223, *224*
Execution of a Spy (1900), 223–4
Execution of Czolgosz (1901), 224
Execution of Mary, Queen of Scots (1895), 2, *2*, 7–8, 13, 98, 215, 222–3, 226, 370–1, 373
Execution of the Spanish Spy (1898), 223
executions, 69, 80, 215–33
exhibition of films, 366–97
exhibition of mummies, 194
Exhibitors Film Exchange, 179, 298
Exhibitors' Times, 103, 167, 350–2
The Experiment (1915), 286
"explained supernatural," 43
The Exploits of Elaine (1914–15), 109, 167, 206–7, 256, 267, 322
The Exposed Seance (1900), 180
Extraordinary Black Art (1903), 258
The Eyes [story], 30
The Eyes of Satan (1913), 287

The Facts in the Case of M. Valdmar [story], 28, 287
fairies, 208–9n
The Fairies' Hallowe'en (1910), 379
fairs, 50
The Fairy of the Castle [story], 200
The Fairyland; or The Kingdom of the Fairies (1903), 373
fakery, 98, 245
fakirs, 269–70

The Fall of the House of Usher [story], 28, 65, 169, 347
The False Oath (1909), 361n
The Family Skeleton (1914), 249
The Family Specter [story], 189
The Famous Gilson Bequest [story], 30
Famous Imposters [book], 287
Fanny the Fantom, or The Cock Lane Ghost [play], 39
Fantasma (1914), 136, *136*
farce, 39, 51, 196, 289
Farmer's Weekly Museum, 23
The Fatal Hour (1908), 269
Fate's Midnight Hour (1914), 111
Faust, 125–6, 133
Faust (1909), 134, 379
Faust (1910), 134
Faust (1911), 135
Faust [opera], 141n
Faust [play], 50, 51, 126, 126–7, 131, 140
Faust and Marguerite (1897), 133
Faust and Marguerite (1904), 134
Faust and the Lily (1913), 132
"Faust cycle," 140
Fay, Annie Eva, 46, 47
The Fear (1913), 386
Feathertop (1912), 345
Feathertop (1913), *345*, 346
Feathertop, A Moralized Legend [story], 28, 345–6
"feature film," 109, 387–8
féerie live theatrical entertainment, 98
Feuilade, Louis, 347
fidelity to source, 158, 258, 340–1
Field, Eugene, 200
Fiend, with Moving Eyes [moveable slip], 76
The Fiends of Hell (1914), 267
The Fifth Man (1914), 329
Fight between Tarantula and Scorpion (1900), 222
film artist, 112–14
The Film Index, 114
"Film Releases of America," 107
The Finish of Bridget McKeen (1901), 217–18, *217*
First World War, 228
first-person narrators, 21
Fischer, Margarita, *297*
Fisher, Benjamin Franklin IV, 24
Flammarion, Camille, 311
flashback, 104
A Florida Enchantment (1914), 200
The Flower of Youth (1908), 131
The Flying Dutchman [painting], 65
Flynn, John L., 203
Foiled! (1915), 191
Fontainville Abbey [play], 40
Fontainville Forest [play], 40
A Fool There Was [play], 206, 295–6
A Fool There Was (1915), 299, 304n
Ford, Francis, 341–2
"foreign" films, 108, 292
The Forest of Rosenwald; or, The Bleeding Nun [play], 41
The Forest Ranger (1910), 387
fountain of youth, 317–18, 333n
Fox, George L., 44
Fox, William, 299
Fox Kane, Margaret, 46
Fox Sisters (Kate and Margaret), 6, 46, 63, 175
Francis, Alec B., *323*
Franco-British Film Company, 342
Franholz, Fraunie, 339
Frank, Lawrence, 236, 237
Frank, Lucy E., 215
Frank Leslie's Popular Monthly, 96, *96*, 149, 310
"Frankenstein," 25–6, 109, 324–9
Frankenstein (1910), 3, 14, *14*, 107, 324–6, *327*, 377, 379, 386, 387

Frankenstein (1931), 13–14, 243
"Frankenstein Mystery," 47–8
Frankenstein; or, the Modern Prometheus [story], 25–6, 311–12, 323–4, 324–9
Franklin, Benjamin, 309
Frayling, Christopher, 312
A Freak (1910), 255n
freak shows, 237–8
"freaks," 46, 245–50, 256–7
Freaks (1915), 250
Freeberg, Ernest, 311
French films, 8, 107, 204
French Grand Guignol melodrama, 108
Freneau, Philip, 21, 22, 29, 259
Freud, Sigmund, 288
Frohman, Marie Hubert, 152
From Jealousy to Madness (1907), 383
From the Beyond (1913), 315–16, *315*, 379, 387
Frost, Brian J., 211n
Frost, Linda, 256
Fuehrer, Bob, 297
Fuller, Kathryn H., 375
Fuller, Loïe, 289
Fuller, Margaret, 287
Fuller, Mary, 154, 174, 325, 388, 390
Fuller, Robert C., 287
funerals, 215–16
Funnicus Marries a Hunchback (1913), 246
Fuseli, Henry, 65, 66, 326

A Gallows Ball [illustrations], 69
"gallows broadsides," 26
Galvanic Fluid: or, More Fun with Liquid Electricity (1908), 322
galvanism, 48–9
Galveston hurricane, 218
The Gambler and the Devil (1908), 135, 203
Garden Theatre, New York, 50
Gardener, Alexander, 77
Gardiner, Peter, 39
Gardner, Helen, 318
Garfield, President James A., 282
Gaudreault, André, 11
Gaumont
    The Beautiful Margaret (1910), 132
    The Lady with the Beard; or, Misfortune to Fortune (1908), 255n
    Revenge! (1904), 219
    The Somnambulist (1904), 285
    The Spirit (1908), 177
    The Vengeance of Egypt (1912), 198, 337, 380
    The Village Scare (1909), 245
Gautier, Théophile, 195
Gaycken, Oliver, 240
Gaylord, Charles, 23
General Film Company, 248
Geraghty, Lincoln, 9
German Expressionist cinema, 140
Getting Ready for Hallowe'en [stereo view], 79
A Ghost [story], 203
The Ghost, or the Dead Alive [play], 39
The Ghost, or the Dead Man Alive [play], 39
The Ghost (1911), 174
The Ghost (1914), *168*, 173–4
The Ghost: A True Story [poem], 164
The Ghost Breaker [play], 54–5, 179
"A Ghost Chasing a Ghost" [newspaper story], 184n
Ghost Dance (1911), 378, *378*
ghost dances, 260
The Ghost Fakirs (1915), 174
The Ghost Holiday (1907), 165, 377
The Ghost in Uniform (1913), 167
The Ghost of a Bargain (1912), 174

The Ghost of Altenberg [play], 44
The Ghost of Giles Scroggins [play], 44
The Ghost of Granleigh (1913), 165
The Ghost of Little Jacques [story], 177
Ghost of Seaview Manor (1913), 111
The Ghost of the Goblin Man [illustrated song], *84*, 85, 379
The Ghost of the Hacienda (1913), 167
The Ghost of the Mine (1914), 261
The Ghost of the Twisted Oaks (1915), 266
The Ghost of the Vaults (1911), 166, 386
The Ghost of the Violin [illustrated song], 82, *82*
The Ghost of the White Lady (1914), 182n
Ghost Stories: Collected with a Particular View to Counteract the Vulgar Belief in Ghosts and Apparitions [book], 27
A Ghost Story [story], 5
The Ghost Story (1907), 163, *163*
The Ghost Train (1901), *102*, 164
The Ghostly Rental [story], 30
ghosts, 30, 163–86
   stage, 42
Ghosts and Flypaper (1915), 174
Ghosts at Circle X Camp (1912), 173
Ghosts in a Chinese Laundry (1900), 165
"The Ghost's Warning" [story], 181n
The Ghost's Warning (1911), 165
The Ghost-Seer; or, Apparitionist [story], 164
Gilbert and Sullivan, 51
Giles Corey of the Salem Farms [poem], 151
Giles Corey, Yeoman [play], 151–2
The Girls and Daddy (1909), 280n
Godwin, William, 41
Goethe, Johann Wolfgang von, 126, 128, 133, 134, 135, 140
The Gold-Bug [story], 67
Goldburg, Jesse J., 326–9
Gomel, Elana, 175
Goodall, Jane R., 245–6
Gordon, Harris, 357
Gorky, Maxim, 94, 95, 97
Gorman, J. A., 55
Gothic literature, 9, 11, 66; *see also* American Gothic literature
"Gothic mania," 40
Gothic theatre, 12, 39–43; *see also* American Gothic theatre
Gouget, Henri, 347
Gounod, Charles, 126, 134–5
Goya, Francisco da, 65
"Grand Cinematograph," 372
"Grand Opera" adaptations, 134
Grand Phantasmagoria, or Living Phantoms [painting], 72
"Grand Romantic Melo Drama," 41
La Grande Bretèche [story], 108, 349, 361n
La grande Bretèche (1909), 361n
Graves and Goblins [story], 28
Graveyard Poetry, 216
The Gray Horror (1915), 174
Gray's Elegy [poem], 73
Great Baltimore Fire, 218
Great Northern Film Company, 8–9, 107, 140, 153, 319
The Great Train Robbery (1903), 9, 219
"Great Wizard," 47
The Green Eye of the Yellow God (1913), 271
The Green Idol (1915), 279n
The Green Mummy [story], 195
Grieveson, Lee, 384
Griffith, D. W.
   Avenging Conscience or "Thou Shalt Not Kill" (1914), 1–2, 352–3, 390
   The Birth of a Nation (1915), 228, 273
   Brute Force (1914), 242, 253n
   The Criminal Hypnotist (1909), 292
   Edgar Allen Poe (1909), 354
   The Fatal Hour (1908), 269
   feature films, 109
   as film artist, 112–13
   The Girls and Daddy (1909), 280n
   Intolerance (1916), 137
   The Invisible Fluid (1908), 317
   Man's Genesis (1912), 241, 253n
   The Musketeers of Pig Alley (1912), 219
   Native Americans, 263
   and Poe, 357
   psychological narratives, 96
   realism, 12
   Rose O' Salem-Town (1910), 156
   The Sealed Room (1909), 108, 349
Griffiths, Alison, 98
The Grind (1915), 389
Griswold, Rupert, 354
"gruesome," 9
Guazzoni, Enrico, 134
Guiteau, Charles J., 282
Gunness, Belle, 216
Gunning, Tom, 8, 9, 43, 95–6, 98–9, 353
Gunstveit, Olav, 200
Gunton's Magazine, 30
Gurney, Jeremiah, 63–4
Guth, Frank, 225

Haggard, H. Rider, 337
The Hairy Ainus (1913), 257
Halley's comet, 311
Halloween, 55, 379, 394n, 395n
Halloween (1905), 379
Halloween Night at the Seminary (1904), 379
Hallowe'en Party. An Intruder [stereo view], 79
Halloween postcards, 85
Halttunen, Karen, 26
"Ham" and "Bud," *166*, 168, 179, 290
Hamilton, Lloyd V., *166*, 168
Hamilton, Philip, 152, 156
Hampton, Benjamin, 367
The Hands (1912), 284
hanging, 216
The Hanging of William Carr (1897), 225
Hansen, Miriam, 373
Hara-Kari (1914), 218
Harlequin Collector: Or, The Miller Deceiv'd pantomime], 39
Harlequin's Nightmare (1909), 105
Harper & Brothers, 67
Harper's Bazaar, 67
Harper's Weekly, 64
Harris, Charles K., 81
Harrison, Louis Reeves, 112, 181n, 217, 248, 302n, 345
Harron, Robert, 241, 242
Hart, Bob, 237
Hathorne, Judge, 37
Haunted Abbey [lantern slides], 74–5
The Haunted Bedroom (1913), 172, 387
The Haunted Bride (1913), 166
"Haunted Castle," 55
Haunted Castle (1908), 172
The Haunted Castle (1897), 190
The Haunted Castle (1909), 172
Haunted Chamber, Berlin [lantern slides], 76
The Haunted Chamber [story], 285
The Haunted Hat (1909), 181n
The Haunted Hotel (1907), 169–71, 382
Haunted House [lantern slides], 75
The Haunted House of Wild Isle (1915), 172
The Haunted House [poem], 69, 169
The Haunted House (1899), 169, 373
The Haunted House (1911), 174
The Haunted House (1913), 167–8, 172, 174, 387
haunted houses, 55, 168–75
Haunted Houses [farce], 51

The Haunted Island (1911), 242, 386
Haunted Kitchen (1907), 141n
The Haunted Lane [stereo view], 80
The Haunted Lovers [stereo view], 80
The Haunted Man and the Ghost's Bargain [story], 43
The Haunted Man [play], 44
The Haunted Palace [poem], 65
The Haunted Rocker (1912), 167, 182n
The Haunted Room (1912), 171
The Haunted Sentinel Tower (1911), 172
The Haunting Fear (1915), 283–4, *284*
Haunting Winds (1915), 110
Hawthorne, Julian, 200
Hawthorne, Nathaniel
   Alice Doane's Appeal, 150
   American Gothic literature, 27, 28–9, 107–8, 344–6, 357
   The Blithedale Romance, 28, 288, 344
   Feathertop, A Moralized Legend, 28, 345–6
   Graves and Goblins, 28
   The Hollow of the Three Hills, 29
   The House of the Seven Gables, 28, 150, 288, 344–5
   "Literary Photo Sensations," 337–8
   The Marble Faun: or, The Romance of Monte Beni, 29
   Mesmerism, 288
   A Night Scene, 28–9
   pseudo-science, 311
   Roger Malvin's Burial, 28
   The Scarlet Letter: A Romance, 150, 344
   witches, 150, 160n
   Young Goodman Brown, 29, 150, 259
The Hazards of Helen (1914), 109
Hazelton, George, 354, 355, 356
He Learned the Trick of Mesmerism (1909), 291
He Stole a Princess [story], 195
He Went to See The Devil Play (1909), 137
Headless Horseman Pursuing Ichabod Crane [painting], 65
Hearn, Lafcadio, 26
Heaven and Hell, "Chamber of Horrors," 55
Heise, William, 2, 98
Helios, 138
Hell [lantern slides], 73
Heller, Robert, 47
Henderson, Will, 372
Hennessy, W. J., 68
Henry, O., 337
The Heroine of the Plains (1912), 262
Herrmann the Great (H. Morgan Robinson), 47, 290
Hibbins, Ann, 150
The Hindoo Dagger (1909), 269, 387
The Hindoo Fakir (1902), 258
"Hindoos," 258, 269–72, 316, 339, 367
Hip, Hip, Hypnotize Me [song], 290
His Bachelor Dinner (1915), 192, *192*
His Phantom Sweetheart (1915), 284–5
His Prehistoric Past (1914), 241
His Suicide (1914), 218
His Terrible Secret; or The Man Monkey (1907), 237, *238*
"Historiograph," 372
The History of a Crime (1902), 224
The History of the Whitechapel Murders [book], 85
Hoagland, Herbert Case, 106
hoaxes, 5–6
Hodges, James F., 109
Holcroft, Thomas, 40–1, 41
Holland Brothers, 369
Hollister, Alice, *298*
The Hollow of the Three Hills [story], 29
Holmes, Oliver Wendell, 73–4, 78, 79
Holmes' Standard Theatre, New York, 51
Home of the Rebel Sharpshooter, Gettysburg, Pennsylvania, 1863 [photography], 77
Hood, Thomas, 169
A Hopi Legend (1913), 261

Hopwood, Avery, 32
Horner, Avril, 30
Horrible Hyde (1915), 318
"horrid" novels, 22
"horror movie," 8, 9–10, 12, 390
Horrors of the Spanish Inquisition (1912), 394n
Houdini, Harry, 47
The Hound of the Baskervilles [story], 237, 342
An Hour of Terror (1912), 106
Hours with the Ghosts, or Nineteenth Century Witchcraft [story], 78
The House of a Thousand Candles (1915), 179, 388, 389, 390
The House of Bondage (1913), 156–8
The House of Fear (1915), 111, *112*
The House of Mystery (1913), 175
The House of Night [poem], 21, 22, 29
The House of Silence [play], 51
The House of Terror (1909), 104, *104*
The House of the Seven Gables [story], 28, 150, 288, 344–5
The House of the Seven Gables (1910), 344–5
The House on the Hill (1910), 174
The House That Went Crazy (1914), 322
Houston Chronicle, 312
How Motion Pictures Are Made and Shown (1912), 103
How the Girls Got Even (1911), 173
How the Medium Materialized Elder Simpkin's Wife (1899), 176
How the Other Half Lives [story], 85
How to Write a Blackwood Article [essay], 27
How to Write a Photoplay [book], 106
How Wholesale Murder is Avenged in the Wild West [engravings], 69
Hoyt, Anna, 177
Huber's Museum, 372
The Hudson Legends [engravings], 67
Hughes, William, 22
Hugo, Victor, 246, 248
Hulfish, David S., 100
The Human Ape, Darwin's Triumph (1909), *239*, 240
Human Apes from the Orient (1906), 258
Human Rat Trap (Moral: Don't Sleep with Your Mouth Open) [lantern slides], 76
The Human Soul (1914), 316
humbugged, 5–6
Humbugs of New York [book], 287
Hume, Fergus, 195
"Humourous Transformations," 76
The Hunchback (1909), 248
The Hunchback (1913), 246, 247–8, *247*
Hunchback Brings Luck (1908), 246
The Hunchback of Cedar Lodge (1914), 247
The Hunchback of Notre-Dame [story], 246
hunchbacks, 246–8, 254n
Huntington, Daniel, 66
Hurst, Lulu E., 48
Huygens, Christiaan, 70, 76
Hypno and Trance-Subjects (1913), 291
The Hypnotic Chair (1912), 290
The Hypnotic Monkey (1915), 290
The Hypnotic Violinist (1914), 294, *296*
The Hypnotic Wife (1909), 291
hypnotism, 6, 46, 82–3, 270, 281, 286–95, 298, 316, 367; *see also* Mesmerism
Hypnotism, Including a Study of the Chief Points of Psycho-Therapeutics and Occultism [book], 281
Hypnotism in Hicksville (1913), 291
The Hypnotist (1912), 290
The Hypnotist (1913), 291
The Hypnotist's Revenge (1907), 291
Hypnotized (1912), 281
Hypnotizing Mamie (1913), 291
Hypnotizing the Hypnotist (1911), 292

Ichabod and Brom Bones [engravings], 67, *68*
Idaho Statesman, 385
The Idle Hour of Aberdeen, South Dakota, 264
The Idol's Eye (1910), 271
If I Were Young Again (1914), 317–18, *317*
An Ill Wind (1912), 379, 394n
illustrated songs, 80–5, *82*, 93n, *293*, 377
    The Boogie Man Rag, 85
    The Ghost of the Goblin Man, *84*, 85, 379
    The Ghost of the Violin, 82, *82*
    Oh That Boog-a-Boo Man, *84*, 85
    That Hypnotizing Man, 82–3, *293*
    That Mysterious Rag, 81–2, 379
illustrations, 66–70
    A Gallows Ball, 69
    The Massachusetts Revolver Rampart, 70
    The Michigan Quadruple Murder, 69
    Murdered Mary Seneff's Ghost, 69
    The New Hampshire Horror, 70
    A Night of Horror, 69
    A Public Lynching in the South, 69
    The Terrors of Art, 69
    The Witch of Prague, 68
    The Works of Edgar Allan Poe, 67
Imp (Independent Moving Pictures), 127, 218, 320–1, 324, 341, 344, 380
The Imp of the Bottle (1909), 129
imps, 126, 129–30
In a Stereoscope [book], 63
In the Bogie Man's Cave (1908), 187
In the Dark Valley (1910), 262, 386
In the Days of Witchcraft (1909), 156, 377
In the Days of Witchcraft (1913), 156
In the Grip of the Vampire (1912), 300
In the Line of Duty (1914), 218
In the Power of the Hypnotist (1913), 294, *294*
In the Serpent's Power (1910), 258
In the Toils of the Devil (1913), 139, *139*
inanimate objects come to life, 187
Ince, Ralph, 285
Ince, Thomas, 391n
An Incubus [engravings], 68
The Independent, 31
Independent Moving Pictures (Imp), 127, 218, 320–1, 324, 341, 344, 380
The Indian Burying Ground [poem], 259
The Indian Massacre (1912), 261–2, *262*
"Indian pictures," 201, 259–60
Indians, 269–72, 279n
infant mortality rates, 215
The Infernal Cauldron (1903), 128, 141n
The Infernal Palace (1899), 99, 371
"Infernal Regions," 38
The Inn of Death (1908), 106
The Inn Where No Man Rests (1903), 169, 373
The Insane Heiress (1910), 284
International Electrical Exhibition, Philadelphia 1884, 49
An Interrupted Seance (1914), 178–9
Intolerance (1916), 137
invisibility, 316–17
The Invisible Fluid (1908), 317
The Invisible Man [story], 316–17
The Invisible Men (1906), 316–17
The Invisible Power (1914), 290
The Invisible Thief (1909), 317
The Invisible Wrestler (1911), 317
Irish immigrants, 26, 28–9, 240, 257, 274n
The Iron Chest; or, The Mysterious Murder [play], 41
The Iroquois Theatre Fire [lantern slides], 86
Irving, Henry, 51, 126
Irving, Minna, 94
Irving, Washington, 23–4, 55, 65–7, 126, 337–8, 342–4, 357
    The Adventure of a German Student, 24–5
    The Adventure of My Aunt, 55
    The Devil and Tom Walker, 24, 65, 126, 342–3
    The Legend of Sleepy Hollow, 24, 67, 73, 344
    Rip Van Winkle, 24, 342
    The Sketch Book of Geoffrey Crayon, Gent., 24, 67
    The Spectre Bridegroom, 24, 343–4
The Island of Dr. Moreau [story], 312
The Italian [story], 66
Italian films, 8, 338

The Jack O'Lantern [vaudeville], 50
Jack the Ripper, 29, 51, 85, 216, 220
Jack the Ripper [play], 51
Jackson, Robert, 227
Jacobs, Lewis, 367
James, Henry, 30–1
Jancovich, Mark, 9
Jane Eyre [story], 340–1
Jane Eyre (1910), 341
Jane Eyre (1914), 341
Jane Eyre (1915), 341
Japan, 273, 277n
Jasset, Victorin-Hippolyte, 309
"Java Man," 236
Jay, Gregory S., 259
The "Jekyll and Hyde" Craze [cartoon], 52
"Jekyll-Hyde" character, 309
Jenkins, C. Francis, 94
The Jewel of Seven Stars [story], 195
Jews, 257
Joan of Arc (1900), 223, 232n
Joan of Arc (aka *Burning of Joan of Arc*) (1895), 2
Joe the Educated Orangoutang (1898), 239
Joe the Educated Orangoutang, Undressing (1898), 239
Johnson, Diane Chalmers, 66
Johnson, William Henry, 238
Jones' Hypnotic Eye (1915), 291
Judson, H. C., 243
Just for Good Luck (1910), 246

Kaelred, Katharine, 296
Kalem
    In the Dark Valley (1910), 262
    The Egyptian Mummy (1914), 196
    The Family Skeleton (1914), 249
    Foiled! (1915), 191
    The Ghost of the Twisted Oaks (1915), 266
    The Haunting Fear (1915), 284
    The Legend of Sleepy Hollow (1908), 344
    The Mountain Witch (1913), *151*, 156
    The Mystery of the Sleeping Death (1914), 269
    The Secret Room (1915), 316
    The Vampire (1913), 297
    The Vivisectionist (1915), 314–15
Kalem Kalender, 172
Kalich, Bertha, 152
Kansas City Times, 202
Kant, Immanuel, 309
Kaplan, E. Ann, 259
Karloff, Boris, 9
Karr, Darwin, 388
Kay-Bee, 156–8, 188
Keil, Charlie, 102, 105, 156
Keith & Proctor, 319
Keith's Union Square Theatre, New York, 369
Kellar, Harry, 47, *48*
Kelly Family, 216
Kenneth, Esther Serle, 285
Kernell, Harry, 51
Kerr, Howard, 28
The Key of Life (1910), 269
Kimball, Henrietta D., 149

Kinemacolor Company of America, 321–2, 344, 346
Kinetoscope, 2, 97, 368, 369, 371
King, J. S., 177
King of the Cannibal Islands (1908), 263
Kino International, 354
Kipling, Rudyard, 200, 204–6, 295, 297
Klein, Charles, 54
Kleine, George, 132, 140, 146n, 153, 245, 267
Koster & Bial's, 50, 94, 97, 369, 391n
Krauss, Henry, 248

laboratories, 312–13
Lackaye, Wilton, 53–4, *53*, 298
Laderman, Gary, 216
Ladies Home Journal, 200
Ladies' Literary Cabinet, 25
The Lady with the Beard; or, Misfortune to Fortune (1908), 255n
The Lady's Maid's Bell [story], 30
Laemmle, Carl, 109, 127
The Lair of the White Worm [story], 287
Lake with Dead Trees (Catskill) [painting], 65
Lampe, J. Bodewalt, 377, 379
Langenheim brothers, 72
Langman, Larry, 296–7
Langtry, Lily, 48
lantern slides
 All Hallow Ev'n, 73
 Bridget's Dream, 73
 The Churchyard Revelry, 76
 Dance of Death, 75
 Delirium Tremens, 73
 Haunted Abbey, 74–5
 Haunted Chamber, Berlin, 76
 Haunted House, 75
 Hell, 73
 Human Rat Trap (Moral: Don't Sleep with Your Mouth Open), 76
 The Iroquois Theatre Fire, 86
 movement in, 74–6
 My Egyptian Mummy, 82
 Oh, You Spearmint Kiddo with the Wrigley Eyes, 83
 The Photodrama of Creation, 73
 The Ragtime Dream, 82
 The Ragtime Goblin Man, 83–4
 The Raven, 74
 Skeleton Dance, 76
 Skeleton Falling to Pieces, 76
 The Sleeping Rat Eater, 76
 The Spectre Pig, 73–4
 Witch in Sky, 73
Latham, Woodville, 94
Laughable Phantasmagoria, or Living Phantoms [show], 72
Lawrence, Florence, 283, 388
Lee, Vernon, 176
Legedermain Up-to-Date (1902), 100
Legend of a Ghost (1908), 103, 206–7, 382, 387
The Legend of Lake Desolation (1911), 261
Legend of Orpheus (1909), 135
The Legend of Scar Face (1910), 261
The Legend of Sleepy Hollow [story], 24, 67, 73, 344
The Legend of Sleepy Hollow (1908), 344
The Legend of the Lighthouse (1909), 218
Legend of Sleepy Hollow (1912), 344, 345
The Legend of the Phantom Tribe (1914), 201, *202*
Leonard, Marion, 339
The Leprechawn (1908), 153
Leroux, Gaston, 32, 242–4, 341–2
 Balaoo, 242–4, 341
 The Phantom of the Opera, 32, 342, 359n
LeSaint, Edward, 179
Leutze, Emanuel, 67, *68*, 344
Levack, Brian P., 126
Lewis, Frederick, 354

Lewis, Matthew Gregory, 7, 12, 22–3, 40, 41–2, 44
 The Castle Spectre, 12, 41–2, 44, 51
 The Monk, 22, 25, 41
 Raymond and Agnes; or, The Bleeding Nun, 41
Lewis, Robert M., 46
Lewis and Clark Centennial Exposition, Portland, Oregon 1905, 55
Life magazine, 32, 88n
Life Motion Pictures (1907), *223*
Life Without Soul (1915), 326–9, *329*
lighting effects, 104
 electric, 50
 in the theatre, 40
lightning, 309
Lincoln, Abraham, 63, 216, 229n, 316
Lincoln, Mary Todd, 63–4, 78, 282
Lindsay, Vachel, 3, 112
Lippard, George, 27
Lippincott's Monthly Magazine, 27
Liquid Electricity: or, The Inventor's Galvanic Fluid (1907), 313, 322
Literary Digest, 110
"Literary Photo Sensations," 337–8, 345, 355
The Literary World, 6
literature
 and evolution, 237
 and hypnotism, 289–90
 and Mesmerism, 287–8
 and mummies, 195
 and Native Americans, 259
 and the other, 257
 and science, 311–12
 and somnambulism, 285
 and vampires, 203
 and werewolves, 200
Literature After Darwin [book], 236–7
lithographed advertising card, *199*
Little Miss Dixie; or, Hypnotism [farce], 289
Lloyd-Smith, Alan, 27
lobby card, *188*
Loïe Fuller (1905), 204–7, *205*
Lola (1914), 323–4, *323*
Lola [play], 323–4
London Stereoscopic Company, 79
Longfellow, Henry Wadsworth, 151, 189, 337
Longman's Magazine, 1
Loper, Charles H., 383
Lord Jim [story], 236
Lorde, André de, 347
Los Angeles Times, 37, 269, 310, 346
Lost Colony of Roanoke, 3
Lost in a Pyramid, of The Mummy's Curse [story], 195
The Lost World [story], 237
Lot No. 249 [story], 195
Lotta Coin's Ghost (1915), *166*, 168
Louden, Jane C., 195
Love and Spirits (1914), 178
Lowell, Percival, 6
Lowndes, Marie Belloc, 271–2
Lozardo, Professor Frank, 47
Lubin
 Blacks, 263
 Blue Beard (1902), 220
 Ching Ling Foo (1900), 258
 The Dancing Skeleton (1903), 191
 A Deal in Real Estate (1914), 174
 Death of Maceo and His Followers (1899), 372–3
 Execution of the Spanish Spy (1898), 223
 Faust, 133
 The Haunted House (1899), 169
 Horrible Hyde (1915), 318
 The House of Terror (1909), 104, *104*

The Maniac (1912), 283
Martyrs of the Inquisition (1906), *223*
Satan, 129
The Sleepwalker's Dream (1904), 285
vampires, 203
A Visit to the Spiritualist (1900), 176
Volcanic Eruption of Mt. Pelee at St. Pierre (1902), 218
Lucier, Paul, 310
Lucille Love, The Girl of Mystery (1914), 109
Ludlowe, Henry, 354
Lumière Brothers, 96–7
Lumière Cinematographe, 369
Lumière film, 94, 95, 115n, 129
Luna-Film, 107
The Lunatics (1914), 347, *348*
"lure of the sensational murder," 29, 216
The Lure of the Windigo (1914), 261
Lux, 153, 200
Lynching Scene (1895), 2, 226, 371
Lynching Scene at Paris, Texas (1897), 226–7, 372
lynchings, 69, 77, 80, 226–7
Lyons and Moran, 290
Lyric Grand Theatre, Juneau, Alaska, 377

Macbeth [play], 147
Macbeth and the Witches [painting], 65
MacCulloch, Hunter, 94
MacDonald, George, 69
MacDougall, Dr. Duncan, 311
MacDowell, Edward, 379
Mackie, Clarissa, 200
Macmillan's Magazine, 200
MacRae, Henry, 201
The Mad Lady of Chester (1910), 341
The Mad Musician (1908), 282–3
The Mad Scientist [story], 312
mad scientists, 309–36, *323*
Madison, Marie, 152
The Madman (1912), 283
The Madman's Ward (1914), 283
"Mae Tinee," 356
Maelzel's Chess Player, 5
Magazine for the Millions, 285
magazines, 67–70
The Magic Film [poem], 94
magic lantern, 70–2, *86*; see also lantern slides
The Magic Lantern (1874), *45*
The Magic Note (1914), 283
"magic photographs," 78
"magic picture series," 258
The Magician and the Imp (1903), 129
magicians, 47, *48*, 100, 193, 258
magnetism, 27, 48
Maguire and Baucus, 101, 222
The Maid and the Mummy [play], 196
La maison ensorcelée (1908), 170
make-up, 234, 269, 320–1, 326, 388–9
Man (1911), 176–7
The Man in the White Cloak (1913), 165
"Man of a Thousand Faces," 388–9
The Man with the Cloaks: A Vermont Legend [story], 21
man-apes, 236–8, 241–2, 250
"Manhattan Nickelodeons: New Data on Audiences and Exhibitors" [essay], 368
The Maniac (1911), 283
The Maniac (1912), 284
Maniac Chase (1904), 282
"manifestations," 46
Le manoir du diable (1896), 99
Man's Genesis (1912), 241, 253n
Mansfield, Richard, 51, 51–2, *52*
Mantle, Burns, 55
The Marble Faun: or, The Romance of Monte Beni [story], 29

The Mark of the Beast [story], 200
The Marked Man (1912), 283
Marlowe, Christopher, 125–6
Marryat, Captain Frederick, 200
Mars [story], 6
Marsh, Mae, 241, 242
Marston, Theodore, 315
The Martian [story], 311
Martin, J. M., 51
Martschukat, Jürgen, 216
Martyrs of the Inquisition (1906), 222, *223*
Marvin, Arthur, 226
The Mask of the Red Death (1911), 107, 350, 377
The Masque of the Red Death [story], 347
Massachusetts Centinel, 189
The Massachusetts Revolver Rampart [illustrations], 70
Massacre at Constantinople (1901), 219
massacres, 262–3
The Master Mind (1914), 111–12
Mather, Cotton, 3–4, 7, 156
Maturin, Charles, 22, 40, 41, 126
Maude, Arthur, *138*
Maupassant, Guy de, 32, 338
Maywood, Robert Campbell, 42
The Maze of Fate (1911), 386
McAllister, T. H., 73, 74–6
McCarroll, James, 309
McCarthy's Wake: A "Free for All" (1899), 274n
McCarthy's Wake, McCarthy Comes to Life (1897), 257
McCay, Winsor, 105, 131
McCutcheon, Wallace, 317
McDermott, Marc, 339, 389
McDonald, Raymond, 312
McGinty's Wake (undated), 274n
McKee, Lafayette, 329
McKinley, President William, 218, 224
McNamara, Walter, 349
McQuade, James S., 162n
McQuarrie, M. J., *321*, 322
McTeague: A Story of San Francisco [story], 95
McWade, Edward, 343
mechanical inventions, 322
The Mechanical Man (1915), 322
Medical Society of New York, 282
medicine men, 261
melancholy, 65–6
Méliès, Georges
  audience reactions, 372–3
  Blue Beard (1902), 220
  In the Bogie Man's Cave (1908), 187
  Bora Bora, 257
  comedy, 13, 207, 232n
  The Devil's Castle (Le manoir du diable) (1896), 99
  Faust and Marguerite (1897), 133–4
  Ghosts at Circle X Camp (1912), 173
  haunted houses, 169
  The Infernal Cauldron (1903), 141n
  and Lumière, 96, 115n
  mad scientists, 312–13
  A Mesmerian Experiment (1905), 290
  A Miracle under the Inquisition (1904), 222
  The Mysterious Retort (1906), 102
  pseudo-science, 313
  Satan, 204
  skeletons, 190
  Spiritualism, 176
  "transnational" filmmaker, 8
  trick pictures, 1, 95, 98–100, 103, 116–17n, 127–32
  vampires, 203
  witches, 152–3

Melmoth the Wanderer [story], 22, 40, 41, 126
Melville, Herman, 21, 27, 263
   Benito Cereno, 21
   Pierre; or, The Ambiguities, 27
   Typee, 27, 263
mental illness, 282–5, 301n, 302n
Mental Science (1910), 306n
Mephisto and the Maiden (1909), 135
Mephisto in His Laboratory (1899), 1
Mephistopheles, 99
Mephistopheles' School of Magic (1903), 128, 287
Mephisto's Son (1906), 136, 203, 379, 387
"Mercy Brown Vampire Incident," 203
Merlin the Magician (1898), 101, *101*
Merritt, Russell, 367–8
The Merry Frolics of Satan (1906), 132, 134
Mesmer, Franz Anton, 286, 287, 309
A Mesmerian Experiment (1905), 290
Mesmeric Revelation [story], 287
Mesmerism, 28, 46, 281, 286–95; *see also* hypnotism
[The] Mesmerist and Country Couple (1899), 290–1
A Message from the Moon (1912), 312
The Message of the Dead (1913), 220
Messter, Oskar, 188, 297
Mestayer, Harry, 179, 389
Metamora; or, The Last of the Wampanoags [play], 259
Methley, Alic, 198
Metro, 308n
Metropolitan Opera House, New York City, 126
Metzengerstein [story], 27
The Michigan Quadruple Murder [illustrations], 69
Mickie O'Hoolihan's Wake (1894), 274n
The Middle Toe of the Right Foot [story], 30
Midnight; or The Ghost of the Ferry [play], 44
A Midnight Scare (1914), 167
Mike McCarthy's Wake [song], 257
Milano, 138–9, *139*
Millarde, Harry, 283
Mills, Bruce, 287
Milton, John, 127
A Miracle under the Inquisition (1904), 222
The Mischievous Monkey (1897), 241, *241*
mise-en-scène, 110–12, 138
The Miser's Reversion (1914), 234, *235*
Miss Faust (1909), 131–2
Miss Jekyll and Madame Hyde (1915), 318
"Missing Link," 236–8, 241–2
The Missing Link [vaudeville], 237
The Missing Woman (1913), 111
The Mission of Mr. Foo (1915), 267
The Mistletoe Bough; or, The Bribe and the Ghost [play], 44
Mitchell, J. A., 174–5
M'Neile, Hugh, 287
A Modern Dr. Jekyll (1909), 318
A Modern Jekyll and Hyde (1914), 318
Modern Languages of America conference, 200
The Modern Mephistopheles [story], 126
Moll, Albert, 281
Molnár, Ferenc, 136–7
Monaldi: A Tale [story], 66
Monboddo, Lord, 234–5
The Mong-Fu Tong (1913), 267
The Monk [story], 22, 25, 41
Monkey Intelligence (1915), 239
monkeys, gorillas, ape-men, 234–5
The Monkey's Feast (1896), 239
Monopol Film Company, 139, 339, 380
Monsieur Bluebeard (1914), 220
The Moon Hoax, 6
The Moonlit Road [story], 30
The Moonstone [story], 271, 272, 279n, 340
The Moonstone (1909), 271, 340

The Moonstone (1915), 271
The Moonstone of Fez (1914), 271–2
Moore, Bond, & Company, 86
Moore, Charles Leonard, 21, 33n
Moore, James R., 236
Moore, Tom, 247–8, 316
morality tales, 136–7
Morgan Lithograph Company, 389
Morning Telegraph, 51
The Morris-Town Ghost; or the Force of Credulity [play], 39
Mortmain (1915), 315, 337, 390
Morus, Iwan Rhys, 49
A Mother's Heart (1909), 135–6
Motion Picture News
   The Circular Staircase (1915), 179, *180*
   The Dream Woman (1914), 340
   Freaks (1915), 250
   The Ghost of the Twisted Oaks (1915), 266
   Life Without Soul (1915), 328–9
   Lola (1914), 324
   The Miser's Reversion (1914), 234
   Mortmain (1915), 315
   Shadows of the Moulin Rouge (1914), 284
   Trilby (1915), *299*
   Universal Ike, Jr. and the Vampire (1914), 297
   The Vivisectionist (1915), 315
   The Werewolf (1913), 201
   The Woman of Mystery (1914), 271
Motion Picture Patents Company, 9
Motion Picture Story Magazine, 181n, 388
"motley drama," 37–8, 55
Motography
   The Brand of Evil (1913), 271
   Corelli, 222
   The Devil's Signature (1914), 215
   The Ghost of the Twisted Oaks (1915), 266
   The Hairy Ainus (1913), 257
   The Haunted Sentinel Tower (1911), 172
   The House of a Thousand Candles (1915), 179
   Life Without Soul (1915), 328
   photography, 110, 111, 368
   The Pines of Lory (1914), 175
   posters, 381, *382*
   The Raven (1915), 356
   realism, 105, 110
   The Smallpox Scare at Gulch Hollow (1913), 218
   The Strange Case of Princess Khan (1915), 270
   trick pictures, 103
   Trilby (1915), 298–9
   The Witch Girl (1914), 154
Mottram, Ron, 8–9
The Mountain Witch (1913), *151*, 156
"Movable Comic Views," 76
moveable slip slides, 75–6, *75*
   Fiend, with Moving Eyes, 76
   Nightmare Made Visible, 76
Movie Pictorial, 2, 15n, 352, 356, 388, 389, 390
movie serials, 109, 110
"Moving Picture Gods and Goddesses," 388
Moving Picture News
   audience class, 375
   Dr. Jekyll and Mr. Hyde (1912), 320–1, 386
   Dr. Jekyll and Mr. Hyde (1913), *321*
   Eclair films, *338*
   Feathertop (1913), *345*, 346
   Ghost Dance (1911), 378
   The House of a Thousand Candles (1915), 179
   Leroux, 341
   The Mask of the Red Death (1911), 350
   music, 377
   The Spectre Bridegroom (1913), 343–4
   The Woman in White (1912), 339

Moving Picture Story Magazine, 376
Moving Picture World
    American movies, 107–8
    The Animated Scarecrow (1910), 187
    audience reactions, 367, 376, 377, 385–7
    Balaoo, The Demon Baboon (1913), 243, *244*
    From the Beyond (1913), 316
    Brute Force (1914), 242
    censorship, 384–5
    Charles Ogle, 325
    children, 375
    The Chinese Death Thorn (1913), 269
    The Damnation of Faust (1903), 144n
    Dante's Inferno (1911), 109, 138
    In the Days of Witchcraft (1909), 156
    The Dead Secret (1913), *340*
    death, 217
    The Devil and Tom Walker (1913), 343
    The Devil's Darling (1915), 125
    The Devil's Signature (1914), 215
    "Directors as Artists," 112
    Doomed to Die, or the Vial of Wrath (1913), 309
    Dr. Jekyll and Mr. Hyde (1912), 320–1
    Dr. Skinum (1907), 313
    dreams, 105
    executions, 227–8, 228
    The Family Skeleton (1914), 249
    Faust, 126–7, 132, 134–5, 140
    Frankenstein; or, the Modern Prometheus, 323
    Funnicus Marries a Hunchback (1913), 246
    "genre picture," 114
    The Ghost (1914), *168*
    The Ghost Breaker (1914), 179
    haunted houses, 172–5
    Hawthorne, 344–6
    He Went to See The Devil Play (1909), 137
    A Hopi Legend (1913), 261
    The Hound of the Baskervilles (1915), 342
    The Human Ape, Darwin's Triumph (1909), *239*
    The Hunchback (1913), 247–8
    The Hypnotic Violinist (1914), *296*
    hypnotism, 294–5
    Legend of a Ghost (1908), 206
    Life Without Soul (1915), 328
    As in a Looking Glass (1913), 298
    The Marked Man (1912), 283
    massacres, 201
    Méliès, 257
    melodrama, 108
    Monkey Intelligence (1915), 239
    The Moonstone (1868), 340
    Mortmain (1915), 315
    "Moving Picture Gods and Goddesses," 388
    Mrs. Casey's Gorilla (1913), 240
    The Mummy (1911), 196
    music, 377–8
    The Mysteries of Souls (1912), 293
    The Mysterious Mr. Wu Chung Foo (1914), *268*
    The Mystery of the Lama Convent (1910), *108*
    "The *Mystical Maid of Jamasha Pass (American)*," 162n
    The Myth of Jamasha Pass (1912), 155
    Naidra, The Dream Woman (1914), 324
    Ogallalah (1911), 261–2
    "Oriental," 258
    The Phantom Violin (1914), 341–2
    photography, 111
    Poe, 337, 338, 347–51, 355, 356
    The Professor's Secret (1908), 242
    publicity, 381
    A Puritan Episode (1913), 158
    realism, 105, 110, 118n
    The Red Barn Mystery (1908), 220
    Satan, 147

    The Secret Room (1915), 10
    Shadows of the Moulin Rouge (1914), 284
    Sinews of the Dead (1914), 314–15
    The Skeleton (1912), 191
    The Smallpox Scare at Gulch Hollow (1913), 218
    The Snake Man (1910), 200
    The Spectre Bridegroom (1913), 344
    Spiritualism Exposed (1913), *177*
    suicide, 181n
    The Tale of the Fiddle (1909), 135
    Terror (1915), 221
    Theatrephone, 319
    Their First Execution (1913), 226
    The Vengeance of Egypt (1912), 198
    voodoo, 265–6
    wild animals, 220
    witches, 153
    The Woman in White (1912), 339
    The Woman of Mystery (1914), 271
    The Wrath of Osaka (1913), 273
Moxon's Master, 5
Mr. Edison at Work in His Chemical Laboratory (1897), 312–13
Mrs. Casey's Gorilla (1913), 240
"Mrs. Jarley's," 38
Mulligan's Ghost (1914), 167
Mumler, William H., 12, 63–5, 78
mummies, 194–9
The Mummy [farce], 196
The Mummy (1908), 196
The Mummy (1911), 196
The Mummy and the Cowpunchers (1912), 196
mummy curses, 195
The Mummy Girl [burlesque], 196
The Mummy! Or, a Tale of the Twenty-Second Century [story], 195
The Mummy's Soul [story], 195
Munch, Edvard, 65
Munsey's Magazine, 370
murder, 22, 26, 69–70, 215–33
murder literature, 32
"The Murder Mania," 29
Murder Most Foul: The Killer and the American Imagination [book], 26
Murdered Mary Seneff's Ghost [illustrations], 69
The Murderer's Vision (1902), 219
Murders in the Rue Morgue [story], 236, 250, 349
The Murders in the Rue Morgue (1914), 349
Murison, Justine S., 285
Murray, Thomas E., 51
music, 40–1, 377–9, *378*
    Sam Fox Moving Picture Man, 379
The Musketeers of Pig Alley (1912), 219
Musser, Charles, 10
    audiences, 369
    "Eidoloscope," 94
    Execution of Czolgosz (1901), 224
    The Great Train Robbery (1903), 9
    nickelodeons, 102
    photographic lantern slides, 72, 74
    realism, 370
    "story film," 104
Mutoscope, 369
Mutual, 218
My Boy; or, The Mystery of the Roadhouse Murder (1913), 111
My Egyptian Mummy [lantern slides], 82
My Grand Mother's Ghost [story], 182n
My Husband's Ghost [play], 39
The Mysteries of Souls (1912), 293
Mysteries of the Castle; or, The Victim of Revenge [play], 40
The Mysteries of Udolpho [story], 23, 32
The Mysterious Eyes (1913), 104
The Mysterious Lodger (1914), 220

The Mysterious Mr. Wu Chung Foo (1914), 267, *268*
A Mysterious Mystery (1914), 283
The Mysterious Retort (1906), 102, 312
The Mysterious Urn (1902), 102, 129
The Mystery [play], 51
The Mystery of Carter Breene (1915), 166
Mystery of Dr. Fu-Manchu [story], 266, 267
The Mystery of Edwin Drood (1914), 357
The Mystery of Mr. Marks (1914), 286
The Mystery of the Haunted Hotel (1913), 172
The Mystery of the Hindu Image (1914), 273
The Mystery of the Lama Convent (1910), 266–7
The Mystery of the Rue Morgue (1914), 349
Mystery of the Silent Death (1915), 337
The Mystery of the Sleeping Death (1914), 269
The Mystery of the Tapestry Room (1915), 109
The Mystery of the Yellow Room (1913), 341
The Mystic Ball (1915), 279n
"*The Mystical Maid of Jamasha Pass (American)*" [article], 162n
The Myth of Jamasha Pass (1912), 155, *155*

Nadis, Fred, 47
Naidra, The Dream Woman (1914), 324
A Narrow Squeak (1914), 167
Natale, Simone, 47
National Board of Censorship, 385
national cinemas, 8–9
National Police Gazette, 69–70, *70*, 85, 258
Native American stories, 201, 208, 212n, 261
Native Americans, 257, 258, 259–63, 272–3, 276n, 387
natural causes, death from, 41
natural disasters, 218–19
natural horrors, 13
Nead, Lynda, 71
Neal, John, 149
The Necklace of Rameses (1914), 198
The Necklace of the Dead (1910), 108, 347, 360n
Nestor, 248, 261
Neurohypnology or, The Rationale of Nervous Sleep, Considered in Relation with Animal Magnetism [book], 288
Neuss, Alwin, *320*
Never Bet the Devil Your Head [story], 126
New Bowery Theatre, 44
"New Company," 51
The New England Galaxy and United States Literary Advertiser, 41
New England Magazine, 149
"New England Reign of Terror," 148
New England Weekly Journal, 202
New Englander, 28
The New Exploits of Elaine (1915), 256
New Film History, 10
The New Hampshire Horror [illustrations], 70
New Monthly Magazine and Literary Journal, 6–7
New Thought, 288
The New Wizard of Oz (1915), 147
New World of English Words: or, a General Dictionary, The [book], 70–1
New York American, 5
New York Clipper
  audience reactions, 369, 391n
  Avenging Conscience or "Thou Shalt Not Kill" (1914), 352
  Charles Ogle, 326
  The Damnation of Faust (1903), 133
  Dr. Jekyll and Mr. Hyde (1913), 322
  electricity, 50
  lynchings, 226, 227
  Méliès, 98
  Mortmain (1915) and Poe, 315, 337
  Pathé films, 107
  Pepper's Ghost, 44
  The Raven (1915), 356
  Svengali, 292
Vitascope, 97
Volcanic Eruption of Mt. Pelee at St. Pierre (1902), 230n
New York Dramatic Mirror
  The Animated Scarecrow (1910), 187
  censorship, 384–5
  The Devil, the Servant, and the Man (1910), 145n
  Dorothy's Dream (1903), 220
  Doyle, 342
  Dr. Jekyll and Mr. Hyde, 320–2
  The Egyptian Mummy (1914), 198
  electricity, 322
  Faust (1909), 134
  A Fool There Was (1915), 299
  La grande Breteche, 349
  The Haunted House of Wild Isle (1915), 172
  The Haunted Rocker (1912), 167
  The House of Silence, 51
  The Human Ape, Darwin's Triumph (1909), 240
  The Hunchback (1909), 248
  hypnotism, 291, 292
  The Inn of Death (1908), 106
  The Legend of the Phantom Tribe (1914), 201
  The Leprechawn (1908), 153
  Life Without Soul (1915), 328–9
  Lola (1914), 323–4
  The Master Mind (1914), 111–12
  Miss Jekyll and Madame Hyde (1915), 318
  The Moonstone, 340
  The Mysteries of Souls (1912), 293
  The New Exploits of Elaine (1915), 256
  "Oriental," 258, 267
  Poe, 349, 350, 352, 355
  The Secret Room (1915), 316
  The Skeleton (1910), 191
  special effects, 95
  The Spectre Bridegroom (1913), 344
  'Tis Now the Very Witching Hour of Night (1909), 173
  The Witch (1908), 156, 162n
  The Witch's Cavern (1909), 154
New York Electrical Society, 50
New York Evangelist, 38
New York Film Company, The, 107
New York Herald, 126, 176
New York Illustrated Magazine of Literature and Art, 67
New York Literary Journal, 43
New York Motion Picture Company, 137
New York Stereoscopic Company, 80
New York Sun, 5, 50
New York Times
  Albert Pinkham Ryder, 65
  audience reactions, 369, 374, 387
  censorship, 383
  The Devil, 137
  electric chair, 311
  Faust (opera), 126
  ghosts, 6
  The Hunchback of Notre-Dame, 246
  hypnotism, 289
  The Lady's Maid's Bell, 30
  Longfellow, 151
  The Mad Scientist, 312
  "Missing Link," 236
  mummies, 194
  Poe, 346, 357
  snake dances, 259
  Spiritualism, 175
  Svengali, 54
  "tales of terror," 32
  Tesla, 330
  The Turn of the Screw, 31
  Uriella, the Demon of the Night, 127
  vampires, 295
  The Witch, 152
  X-rays, 86

New York World, 194
Newburyport Herald, 4
The New-England Tragedies, 151
New-Hampshire Spy, 168–9
newspapers
  advertisements, 373, 382–3
  and ghosts, 163–4, 184n
  and hypnotism, 288, 289
  and mummies, 194
  and somnambulism, 285
  and vampires, 202–3
  and werewolves, 199
New-York Gazette, 4
New-York Gazette and Weekly Mercury, 190
New-York Mirror, 7
Nichols, G. R., 339
Nicholson, Meredith, 179
Nickelo Theatre, Shelbyville, Indiana, 387
The Nickelodeon, 156, 297, 326
nickelodeon era, 102–9, 131, 165, 177–8, 374–87
nickelodeon theatre, 80–5, 93n, 96, 376–7
A Night of Horror [illustrations], 69
A Night of Terror (1908), 106
A Night of Thrills (1914), 167
night photography, 111, *112*
A Night Scene [story], 28–9
The Nightmare [painting], 65, 326
The Nightmare (1910), 105
Nightmare Made Visible [moveable slip], 76
nightmares, 105–6
Ninth and Arch Museum, Philadelphia, 372
Niobe (1915), *188*
Nobles, Milton, 51
nonfiction cinema, 97–8
Nordisk Film Company, 8–9, 107, 140, 360n
Norris, Frank, 95
The North American Quarterly, 65
Northanger Abbey [story], 9, 22
Notre Dame de Paris (1911), 248
Numbers, Ronald L., 235

Oakland Tribune, 383
Oaks, Susan, 30
O'Brien, Fitz-James, 26
The Occult (1913), 269
An Occurrence at Owl Creek Bridge [story], 30
Ocean Film Corporation, 326–9
O'Connor, John E,, 263
O'Connor, Mary H., 173–4
The Octopus (1913), 386
O'Dette's Picture Auditorium, 377
O'Donnell, Elliott, 200
Ogallalah (1911), 261–2
Ogden, Emily, 287
Ogle, Charles, *14*, 174, 271, 325, 339, 388, *389*
Oh, You Mummy! (1914), 196
Oh, You Spearmint Kiddo with the Wrigley Eyes [lantern slides], 83
Oh That Boog-a-Boo Man [illustrated song], *84*, 85
Oh You Skeleton (1910), 191–2
O'Hanlon, Redmond, 236
Oke of Okehurst [story], 176
Olcott, Sidney, 266
Old Bowery Theatre, 44
"Old Dark House" genre, 32
Oliver, Guy, 179, 355
Olsson, Jan, 374
on location, 96–7, 328
On Seeing a Human Skeleton [poem], 189
On the Origin of Species, 235, 236, 237
On the Verge of War (1914), 292–3
101 Bison, 201, 220, 260, 262
One O'Clock! Or, The Knight and the Wood Daemon [play], 40
Opening and Operating a Motion Picture Theatre [book], 109
opium, 267

The Opium Smugglers (1914), 267
Oppenheimer, J. Robert, 330
The Optical Magic Lantern and Photographic Enlarger (1900), 98
orang utans, 234–5
The Orang-Outang (1915), 349
Oreginian, Portland, 152
Orians, G. Harrison, 150
"Oriental," 258
The Origin and Nature of Emotions [book], 390
Ormond; or, The Secret Witness [story], 24
Orpheus, 135–6, 206
other(s), the, 250, 256–80, *257*
Ourang Outang; or, The Runaway Monkey and His Double [theatrical sketch], 237
"Ourang-Outang," 234–5
The Ourang-Outang (1915), 250
outdoor filming, 98
Owana, the Devil Woman (1913), 261
Owen, Mary A., 264
Oxilia, Nino, 140

Pacific Motion Picture Company, 367
paganism, 258–9
Painting the Dark Side [book], 65
paintings, 65–6, 259, 295
  Dead Man Restored to Life by Touching the Bones of the Prophet Elisha, 66
  The Death of Cora, 65–6
  Emigrants Attacked by Indians on the Prairie, 259
  The Flying Dutchman, 65
  Grand Phantasmagoria, or Living Phantoms, 72
  Headless Horseman Pursuing Ichabod Crane, 65
  Lake with Dead Trees (Catskill), 65
  Macbeth and the Witches, 65
  The Nightmare, 65, 326
  Pilgrim of the World at the End of His Journey, 66
  Saturn Devouring His Children, 65
  Saul and the Witch of Endor, 66
  The Scream, 65
  The Sleep of Reason Produces Monsters, 65
  Spalato's Vision of the Bloody Hand, 66
  The Temple of the Mind, 65
  Tom Walker's Flight, 65
  The Vampire, 204–6, 295, 326
  Witches' Flight, 65
Palmistry (1913), 269
Panorama of Esplanade by Night (1901), 111
Paradise Lost [story], 127
Paramount Film Company, 134
The Parasite [story], 295
Park Avenue Opera House of Mechanicville, New York, 372–3
Parsons, Louella O., 109
Parssinen, Terry M., 288
Pathé Frères
  American market, 107
  Bluebeard, 220
  The Bogey Woman (1909), 208n
  Chomon, Segundo de, 103
  Faust, 135
  A Freak (1910), 255n
  ghosts, 171
  haunted houses, 172
  Loïe Fuller (1905), 204, *205*
  and Méliès, 129, 141n
  posters, 379
  witches, 153, 156, 161n
Pathé Weekly Bulletin, 171–2
Pathéplay, 283
Paton, Stuart, 111
"Patouillard" series, 167
Patrick Brannigan's Wake (undated), 274n
Patterson, Cynthia, 67
Peake, Richard Brinsley, 40, 41
Peale, Charles Willson, 245

Peale's museum, 237, 245
Pearson, Roberta E., 368
Pearson, Virginia, 357
Pepper, "Professor" John Henry, 43, 45
Pepper's Ghost, 12, 43–5, *45*
The Perils of Pauline (1914), 109, 198, 256
Perret, Léonce, 300
Petrova, Olga, 308n
Phantasmagoria, 70–2
Phantasmagoria, or Nocturnal Apparitions [show], 72
The Phantasmatograph [story], 1, 6
The Phantom [play], 43
The Phantom of the Opera [story], 32, 342, 359n
The Phantom of the Opera (1925), 357
The Phantom of the Violin (1915), 342
The Phantom Thief (1914), 349
The Phantom Violin (1914), 341–2, *341*
Phantoms (1913), 166
Phantoscope, 94
Philadelphia Inquirer, 95, 151, 374
Philadelphia Photographer, 64, 78
Philanthropist, 49
Phillips, Augustus, 172, 325–6, 346
The Phonoscope, 97, 176, 224–5, 227, 370, 371–2, 374
The Photodrama of Creation [lantern slides], 73
photographic lantern slides, 72–7
photography, 63–5, 77–80, 316, 390
  crime scene, 85
  Home of the Rebel Sharpshooter, Gettysburg, Pennsylvania, 1863, 77
  night, 111, *112*
  spirit, 63–4
Photoplay, 158, 379, 388, 389
The Photoplay Writer, 385
The Photoplayer's Weekly, 250
"photo-poem," 355
"photoprestigitation," 78
phrenology, 258, 288, 311, 313
Pick, Daniel, 288, 290, 295
The Picture of Dorian Gray (1915), 357, 363n
Pierre; or, The Ambiguities [story], 27
Pierrot's Mystification (1904), 129
Pike, Benjamin, Jr., 75
Pilgrim of the World at the End of His Journey [painting], 66
"Piltdown Man," 236, 245
The Pines of Lory (1914), 174–5
Pinkerton, William A., 383
The Pit and the Pendulum [story], 350–2
The Pit and the Pendulum (1913), 107, 350–2, *351*, 394n
Pittsfield Sun, 27
plagues, 218
A Plague-Stricken City (1912), 347
Plain-Dealer, 1
Planché, James Robinson, 12, 41, 42–3
Pluto and the Imp (1900), 131
Poe, Edgar Allan
  American Gothic literature, 27, 27–32
  American literature onscreen, 337–2, 346–57
  Annabel Lee, 1, 353
  The Bargain Lost, 126
  bargains with Satan, 126
  The Black Cat, 28
  Bon-Bon, 126
  The Cask of Amontillado, 108, 349
  The Conqueror Worm, 37
  death, 216
  A Dream within a Dream, 354
  engravings, 67
  evolution, 236
  The Facts in the Case of M. Valdmar, 28, 287
  The Fall of the House of Usher, 28, 65, 169, 347
  The Gold-Bug, 67
  D. W. Griffith and, 108

haunted houses, 169
The Haunted Palace, 65
How to Write a Blackwood Article, 27
illustrations, 67
Maelzel's Chess Player, 5
The Masque of the Red Death, 347
Mesmeric Revelation, 287
Mesmerism, 287
Metzengerstein, 27
Mortmain (1915) compared to, 315
"motley drama," 37, 55
mummies, 195, 211n
murder, 22
Murders in the Rue Morgue, 236, 250, 349
non-supernatural horror, 11
paintings, 65
photography, 77
The Pit and the Pendulum, 350–2
poetry, 346
The Premature Burial, 347
Raven, 1, 67, 74, 346, 354–5, 390
slides, 74
Some Words with a Mummy, 195
supernatural, 27–8
The System of Dr. Tarr and Professor Fether, 347
A Tale of the Ragged Mountains, 287
The Tell-Tale Heart, 1, 352–3
The Tomb of Ligeia, 28
"weird," 107
William Wilson, 28, 140, 326, 347
Polidor, the Sleep-Walker (1914), 302n
Polidor the Hunchback (1914), 247
Polidori, John William, 25, 42–3, 57n
Pollock, Walter Herries, 1, 6, 11, 14
Porten, Henry, 188
Porter, Edwin S., 9, 105, 111, 131, 133, 187, 219, 224
posters, *221*, 379–82, *382*, 385
post-nickelodeon era, 109–14, 387–90
Potter, Paul M., 53
Powers, 242, 306n
Poyen, Dr. Charles, 286
prank skeletons, 190
"pre-cinema," 11–12
The Prehistoric Man (1908), 241
The Premature Burial [story], 347
pre-nickelodeon era, 16n, 96–102, 369–74
Prescott, F. M., 1, 169
Presto Willie (1913), 131
Presumption, or the Fate of Frankenstein [play], 40, *41*
primates, 239–44, 250
The Primitive Instinct (1914), *240*
primitive man, 236, 240–2, 253n, 263
"The Prince of Darkness" (1900 cycle of films), 129, *130*
The Professor and His Wax Works (1908), 187
"Professor Carpenter," 289
Professor Juke's "Electrical Exhibition," 50
"Professor Leonidas," 289
The Professor's Great Discovery (1908), 335n
The Professor's Secret (1908), 242
pschological horror, 51–2
pseudo-science, 6, 12, 25–6, 28, 73, 258, 281, 309–18
"psychic drama," 318
A Public Lynching in the South [illustrations], 69
publicity materials, 379–83
Puck magazine, 51
Punch magazine, 245
Punter, David, 22, 27
A Puritan Episode (1913), 158
Purkiss, Diane, 149
Pyle, Howard, 200

Quack, M. D. [show], 289
The Quaker City, The; or, the Monks of Monk Hall: A Romance of Philadelphia Life, Mystery and Crime [story], 27
A Quick Recovery, A (1901), 313
Quidor, John, 65

Rachel Dyer [story], 149
Radcliffe, Ann, 7, 9, 23, 32, 43, 55, 66
  The Italian, 66
  The Mysteries of Udolpho, 23, 32
Radnor, Leona, 385
Raff & Gammon, 222–3
The Rag Woman and Her Dogs [burlesque], 44
Ragged Dick [story], 245
The Ragtime Dream [lantern slides], 82
The Ragtime Goblin Man [lantern slides], 83–4
Ramsaye, Terry, 367
The Raven [lantern slide], *74*
The Raven [poem], 67, 74, 346, 354–5, 390
The Raven (1912), 355–6
The Raven (1915), 356–7
Raver, Harry, 329
Rawlinson, Herbert, 136
Ray, Eva, 178, 186n
Raymond and Agnes; or, The Bleeding Nun [play], 41
Razeto, Stella, 179
The Reader of Minds (1914), 322
"real ghosts," 164–5
realism, 12, 51, 103–6, 110, 118n, 376; *see also* American Realism
"Realism in the Movies," magazine column, 388
real-life horrors
  lantern slides, 86
  photographs, 85–6
real-life tragedies on slides, 77
reanimated mummies, 194–5, 196
Rebhorn, Matthew, 195
The Red Barn Mystery (1908), 220
The Red Spectre (1908), 192–3, *193*
Reed, Allan, 196
Reel Life, 164, 352
Reese, Dr. David, 287
Reflections on Viewing a Skeleton [poem], 189
reincarnation, 269
The Reincarnation of Karma (1912), 269, *270*, 377
Reingold, Nathan, 309
Reliance, 156, 213n
A Relic of the Olden Days (1914), 253n
religion
  and Darwinism, 235–6
  and science, 6
Remarkable Apparitions, and Ghost Stories [book], 26–7
repeat viewings of films, 369
A Reprieve from the Scaffold (1905), 227
reputation of films, 373
"retrospective reading," 9
The Return of Maurice Donnelly (1915), 322
revenge, 270–1
Revenge! (1904), 219
Reynolds, George W., 200
Rhode Island American, 25
Rice, Thomas D., 195
Richardson, Jack, 269
Richardson, Michael, 266
Richter, Virginia, 236–7
Rider, Jane C., 285
Riis, Jacob A., 85–6, 127
Rinehart, Mary Roberts, 11, 32, 179
Ringe, Donald A., 29
Ringling Brothers, 246
Rip Van Winkle [story], 24, 342
A Roadside Inn (1905), 169, 373
Robert, Étienne-Gaspard, 71–2
Robert-Houdin theatre, 99

Robertson, 71–2
Rodger, Gillian M., 46
Rodwell, George Herbert, 237
Roentgen, Wilhelm, 86
Roger Malvin's Burial [story], 28
Rogers, Mary, 223
Rohmer, Sax, 266, 267
Roma people, 257–8
The Romance of the Mummy [story], 195
Rose O' Salem-Town (1910), 156, 158
Rosenthal, Herman, 86
Rosenthal Murder Case, 86
Rosner, Sandor, 50
Rossa, Patti, 289
Rouclere, Harry, 226
Ruddigore; or, The Witch's Curse [operetta], 51
Russell, Jeffrey Burton, 125
Russell's Magazine, 27
Ruttenburg, Nancy, 3
Ryder, Albert Pinkham, 65
Rye, Stellan, 140

sacrifice, 270
Said, Edward, 258
Salem Gazette, 190
Salem Witch Trials
  devils, 125–6
  Hawthorne and, 28
  The House of the Seven Gables (1910), 345
  mesmerism, 286
  possession, 281
  superstition, 3–5, 21
  theatricality, 37
  The Tragedy of Superstition, 39
  witches, 147–8, 150–1, 156–8, 160n
Salem Witchcraft; or the Adventures of Parson Handy from Punkapog Pond [poem], 149
Salem Witchcraft; with an Account of Salem Village, and a History of Opinions on Witchcraft and Kindred Spirits [book], 149
The Salem Wolf [story], 200
Salisbury, Cora, 378, *378*
Salsbury, Janet, 339
Sam Fox Moving Picture Man [music], 379
San Francisco earthquake, 218–19
Sandow, 369
Sapho (1900), 373
Sardou, Victorien, 289, 304n
Satan, bargains with, 131–3
Satan and vampires, 203–4
Satan, or, The Drama of Humanity (1912), 204
Satan, or, The Drama of Humanity (1913), 137
Satan Defeated (1911), 203
Satan in Prison (1907), 131
Satan's Castle (1913), 135
Satan's Rhapsody (1914), 140, 146n
Satan's Smithy (1909), 138
Saturday Evening Post, 203, 234
Saturn Devouring His Children [painting], 65
Saul and the Witch of Endor [painting], 66
Saved from a Vampire (1915), 308n
Scalping Scene (1895), 2
Scalping Scene by Thundercloud (1897), 261
"scared to death," 367, 379
The Scarlet Letter: A Romance [story], 150, 344
The Scarlet Letter (1908), 344
The Scarlet Letter (1911), 344
The Scarlet Letter (1913), 344, 346
Scene in a Rat Pit (1906), 222, 232n
Schiller, Friedrich, 164
Schoolcraft, Henry, 258
"schools of crime," 383–4
Schwab, Gabriele, 150, 156

science
    and literature, 311–12
    and religion, 6
    and theatre, 47–50
science fiction, 8, 47–8
Scientific American, 78, 310
scientific footage, 97–8
Scott, Jonathan M., 149
Scott & Van Altena, 81, 85
The Scream [painting], 65
The Screaming Skull [story], 69
Scribner's Monthly, 27, 69, 127, 354
The Sealed Room (1909), 108, 349, 361n
séances, 12, 316
The Secret of the Dead (1915), 212n
The Secret Room (1915), 10, 316
"Secret Society Views" [lantern slides], 73
Sedgwick, Catharine, 165
Selig, William N., 109
Selig Polyscope
    In the Days of Witchcraft (1909), 156
    The Devil, the Servant, and the Man (1910), 136
    The Devil and Tom Walker (1913), 342–3
    devils, 128
    Dr. Jekyll and Mr. Hyde (1908), 318–19
    The Fifth Man (1914), 329
    The House of a Thousand Candles (1915), 179
    hypnotism, 281
    If I Were Young Again (1914), 317–18
    The Lure of the Windigo (1914), 261
    lynchings, 227
    The Moonstone (1909), 271, 340
    "mysterious," 101
    night photography, 111
    skeletons, 191–2
    snake dances, 260
    Spiritualism, 177
    "Stock Yard Series," 222, 232n
    trick pictures, 100
    The Vampire (1910), 297
Senarens, Luis, 311
Sennett, Mack, 174, 178, 226, 317
serial killers, 220
The Servant Hypnotist (1907), 291
Shackleford, Colin, 195
shadows, 104
Shadows of the Moulin Rouge (1914), 284, 301n
Shakespeare, 147
Sharp, Luke, 189
The Shaughraun [play], 257
She (1908), 337
She (1911), 337
She [story], 337
Shelley, Mary, 25–6, 41, 311–12, 324–9, 386
Sherlock Holmes, 342
Sherlock Holmes in the Great Mystery (1908), 349
Shoemaker, W. L., 200
Shooting Captured Insurgents (1898), 223
Shooting in the Haunted Woods (1910), 165
"showman scientists," 49
Shubert Theatre, New Orleans, 387
Siddons, Henry, 40
The Sign of the Cross; or the Devil in a Convent (1900), 128
The Silent Command (1915), 294
silhouettes, *104*
Sinbad [play], 50
Sinews of the Dead (1914), 314
Singer, Ben, 368
Singer, Robert, 133, 140
Singer-Allen debate, 368
Singerman, Robert, 194
skeletal hand, *86*
The Skeleton (1910), 191
The Skeleton (1912), 191

The Skeleton at the Feast (1899), 189
Skeleton Dance [lantern slides], 76
Skeleton Dance, Marionettes (1898), 191
skeleton dances, 191
Skeleton Falling to Pieces [lantern slides], 76
The Skeleton in Armor [poem], 189
The Skeleton in the House [story], 189
"skeleton trade," 190
skeletons, 75, 189–93, 209n
    prank, 190
Skelley's Skeleton (1914), 209n
The Sketch Book of Geoffrey Crayon, Gent. [stories], 24, 67
Sklar, Robert, 368
sleep, 6–8, 116–17n
The Sleep of Reason Produces Monsters [painting], 65
Sleep Walker (1908), 302n
The Sleep Walker (1911), 286
A Sleep Walking Cure (1910), 286
The Sleeping Burglar (1912), 286
The Sleeping Rat Eater [lantern slides], 76
The Sleepwalker's Dream (1904), 285
sleepwalking, 173–4
Slide, Anthony, 169
Slim and the Mummy (1914), 196
The Smallpox Scare at Gulch Hollow (1913), 218, 387
Smart, Hawley, 31
Smiley, Joseph W., 326–9
Smith, George Albert, 220
Smith, Henry, 227
The Snake (1913), 260
The Snake Charmer (1914), 269
snake dances, 260
The Snake Man (1910), 200
Snyder, Ted, 379
social class, 367–70, 374–5
Società Italiana Cines, 134
Solax Company, 113, 284, 350
Solomon, Matthew, 8, 95, 100
A Solution of the Mystery (1915), 114
Some Words with a Mummy [story], 195
somnambulism, 24, 285–6, 288, 289, 302n, 303n
Somnambulism [story], 285
The Somnambulist (1904), 285
The Somnambulist (1908), 286
The Somnambulist (1910), 286
The Somnambulist (1913), 286
The Somnambulist (1914), 286
songs, 41, 257, 290
    Every Little Movement Has a Meaning All Its Own, 377
    Hip, Hip, Hypnotize Me, 290
    Mike McCarthy's Wake, 257
    Witch's Dance, 379
The Sorceress [show], 289, 304n
The Sorceress: or Salem Delivered [poem], 149
The Sorrows of Satan [story], 126
The Soul of Broadway (1915), 308n
The Soul of Phyra (1915), 279n
Soul to Soul (1913), 104
sound, 319
sound effects, 40–1, 377
Southern Literary Messenger, 42
The Southwest Chamber [story], 30
Spalatro's Vision of the Bloody Hand [painting], 66
The Spanish Inquisition (1900), 222
The Spanish Inquisition (1913), 377, 394n
Spanish-American War, 226
special effects, 98–103, 110, 164, 169–70, 176, 191, 242, 258, 356
The Specter (1908), 165
The Specter of the Sea (1912), 188
The Spectre (1908), 166, 181n
The Spectre Bridegroom [story], 24, 343–4
The Spectre Bridegroom (1913), 106, 343–4, *343*, 379
The Spectre of Witchley, or a Night with the Ghost [play], 44
The Spectre Pig [lantern slides], 73–4

Spencer, Len, 318
The Spider (1913), 277n
The Spirit (1908), 177
The Spirit and the Clay (1914), 165
"spirit cabinet," 46
The Spirit Hand (1911), 178
Spirit of the Times, 235
spirit photography, 63–4
Spiritualism, 6, 29, 37, 63, 69, 78, 175–9, 389–90
   fraudulent, 177–9
   and magic, 45–7
Spiritualism Exposed (1913), 177–8, *177*
The Spiritualist [play], 54
The Spiritualist (1913), *54*
A Spiritualist Meeting (1906), 176
A Spiritualistic Photographer (1903), 176
Spiritualistic Séance (1908), 178
"The Split-Reel" [article], 15n
split-reel film, 172
The Spoiled Darling's Doll (1913), 335n
The Spook Raisers (1915), *178*, 179
Springfield Republican, 152
"Springfield Somnambulist," 285
St. Clair, Henry, 23
Stableford, Brian, 31
Staiger, Janet, 295
Stamp, Shelley, 385
Standing, Percy, 328
Stanley Among the Voodoo Worshippers (1915), 265, *265*
Star Films, 133–4, 143n, 152, 161n, 372, 373, 392n
star memorabilia, 388
The Star of the Side Show (1912), 248–9, *249*
The Startled Lover (1899), 190
The Statue of Fright (1913), 218
"Steen-Rouclere Show," 226
Stephens, Elizabeth, 49
stereo views, 78–80, 128
   Apparition, 80
   A Dream After Seeing Pepper's Ghost, 79
   Getting Ready for Hallowe'en, 79
   And The Goblins Will Get You If You Don't Watch Out, 79
   Hallowe'en Party. An Intruder, 79
   The Haunted Lane, 80
   The Haunted Lovers, 80
   An Unwelcome Visitor, 80
"stereographs," 78–80
Sterner, Albert Edward, 67
Steudell, Professor Richard A., 50
Stevenson, Robert Louis, 51, 129
   The Bottle Imp, 126
   [The] Strange Case of Dr. Jekyll and Mr. Hyde, 51–3, 236–7, 311–12, 318–22, 326, 328
Stewart, Anita, 284–5
"Stock Yard Series," 222, 232n
Stockton, Frank R., 30
Stoehr, Taylor, 288, 311
Stoker, Bram, 7, 31, 195, 287
   Dracula, 31, 68, 287
   Famous Imposters, 287
   The Jewel of Seven Stars, 195
   The Lair of the White Worm, 287
Stokes, Melvyn, 368
The Stolen Voice [play], 308n
Stone, John Augustus, 259
Stone & Kimball, 67
stop motion, 2, 98, 132, 171, 324
storms, 111
The Story of the Skeleton Hunter [story], 189
Stowell, William, 343
[The] Strange Case of Dr. Jekyll and Mr. Hyde [story], 51–3, 236–7, 311–12, 318–22, 326, 328
The Strange Case of Princess' Khan (1915), 269–70
Strohmeyer and Wyman, 257

A Strong Diet (1909), 213n
The Student of Prague (1913), 140
substitution splicing, 100
Such a Villain (1914), 290
suicide, 218
The Suicide (1903), 218
Sullivan, Thomas R., 51–3
Sunday Star, Washington DC, 13
supernatural beings, 12–13
supernatural creatures, 187–214
Superstition; or, The Fanatic Father [play], 39, 151
Suratt, Valeska, 308n
surgery films, 300n, 313–14, 314–15
Susan Hopley; or, The Ghost of the Manor House [play], 44
Svengali, 53–4, *53*, 257, 289–96, 298
Swanson, William H., 219
'Sweedie' series of comedies, 166
Sweedie's Suicide (1915), 166
Sweet, Blanche, 352–3
The Sword and the King (1909), 165
Sylvester Sound, the Somnambulist [story], 285
The System of Dr. Tarr and Professor Fether [story], 347

The Taint of Madness (1914), 283
A Tale of Mystery: A Melo-Drame [play], 40–1
A Tale of Terror [play], 40
The Tale of the Fiddle (1909), 135
A Tale of the Ragged Mountains [story], 287
Tales of a Traveller [engravings], 67
Tales of Terror, or the Mysteries of Magic [stories], 23
Tales of Terror, with and Introductory Dialogue [stories], 23
Talked to Death (1909), 220
Talking Machine World, 319
Taming the Spooks (1913), 178
Tarzan of the Apes [story], 237, 263
Taussig, Michael, 273
telepathy, 281
Telephone Appointment, Then His Wife Appears, A (1900), 371
The Tell-Tale Heart [story], 1, 352–3
The Temple of Death [play], 44
The Temple of the Mind [painting], 65
terminology, 9–10, 106–7
Terrell, Mary Church, 226
A Terrible Night (1900), 129, *130*
Terror (1915), 221
A Terror of the Night (1914), 174
The Terrors of Art [illustrations], 69
Tesla, Nikola, 49, 310–11, 312, 322, 330
Thanhouser
   Dr. Jekyll and Mr. Hyde (1912), 319–20
   Halloween, 379
   Jane Eyre (1910), 341
   Lola (1914), 324
   The Picture of Dorian Gray (1915), 357
   posters, 380
   The Star of the Side Show (1912), 248–9
   The Wax Lady (1913), 187
   When Ghost Meets Ghost (1913), 165
   Zudora (1914), 86, *86*
That Hypnotizing Man [illustrated song], 82–3, *293*
That Mysterious Rag [illustrated song], 81–2, 379
theatre, 37–62
   and evolution, 237
   and mesmerism, 288
   and Native Americans, 259
   and Poe, 346, 354–5
   and vampirism, 295–6
   and witchcraft, 151–2
"theatre of trance," 37
theatre publicity, *381*
Theatrephone, 319
Their First Execution (1913), 226

There's Death in the Cup (1908), 79
Things as They Are; or The Adventures of Caleb Williams [play], 41
Thomas, Augustus, 281
Thomson, Rosemarie Garland, 245
thought transference, 281
Thurston, Howard, 47
ticket prices, 369–70, 374–5
Tieck, Ludwig, 28
The Tiger (1913), 219–20
Tilzer, Harry Von, 379
The Time Machine [story], 309
A Timely Apparition (1909), 165
Times-Picayune, New Orleans, 43
'Tis Now the Very Witching Hour of Night (1909), 172–3, 379–80
Titanic, 230n
Tobin, Professor T. W., 47
Todorov, Tzvetan, 7
The Toll of Fear (1913), 367
Tom Walker's Flight [painting], 65
The Tomb of Ligeia [story], 28
Tomson, Graham R., 200
Too Much Champagne (1908), 131
Too Much Trilby [vaudeville], 53
Toppan, Jane, 216
torture, 222, 261–2
A Touching Mystery (1910), 279n
Toumey, Christopher P., 312
Tourneur, Maurice, 298, *299*
The Tower of London (1905), 223
The Toymaker, the Doll and the Devil (1910), 143n
Tracked by Bloodhounds; or, A Lynching at Cripple Creek (1904), 227
Tracy, Alison, 3
Traffic in Souls (1913), 269
The Tragedy of Superstition [play], 39
The Tragicall History of the Life and Death of Doctor Faustus [play], 125–6
Train, Arthur, 315
Tramp in the Haunted House (1900), 169
Trapped in the Castle of Mystery (1913), 174
The Treasures of Satan (1903), 128, 287
The Trials of Faith (1912), 156, *157*
trick photography, 110
trick pictures, 94–103, 114, 127–32, 153, 164–5, 169–71, 258, 282
Tricked into Giving His Consent (1908), 166–7
Trilby (1895), 12, 54
Trilby (1915), 298–9, *299*
Trilby [story], 53, 68, 247, 289–95, 298, 308n, 337
Trilby and Little Billee (1896), 292
Trilby Death Scene (1895), 292
Trilby Hypnotic Scene (1895), 292
"Trilbymania," 53
A Trip to Jupiter (1909), 312
A Trip to Mars (1910), 312–13
A Trip to the Moon (1899), 372
A Trip to the Moon (1902), 99, 100, 103, 312–13
Trotti, Michael Ayers, 29, 216
Trowbridge, J. T., 189
The True History of the Ghost; and All About Metempsychosis [book], 45
True to the Last [play], 44
Tucker, Cynthia G., 133
The Turn of the Screw [story], 31
Turner, William H., 237
Twain, Mark, 5, 7, 22, 236, 288, 311, 337
    Adventures of Huckleberry Finn, 311
    A Curious Dream: Containing a Moral, 22
    The Curious Dream, 337
    A Ghost Story, 5
    What Is Man? 236
Two Magics [story], 31
Typee [story], 27, 263

The Tyrant Feudal Lord (1908), 165
Tyrell, Henry, 354

"uncanny," 7, 13
Uncle Josh in a Spooky Hotel (1900), 169
The Undertaker's Daughter (1915), 184n
The Unfaithful Wife (1915), 337
Union Features, 242–4, 342
Universal, 111, 127, 294, 297, 322
Universal Ike, Jr. and the Vampire (1914), 297
Universal Ike Makes a Monkey of Himself (1914), 240
Universal Weekly, *154*, 261, 283, 294
The Untamable Whiskers (1904), 128
An Unwelcome Visitor [stereo view], 80
Upham, Charles, 149
"uplift movement," 103
The Upper Berth [story], 32
The Up-to-Date Spiritualism (1903), 176
Up-to-Date Surgery (1902), 313
Uranie [story], 311
Urban-Eclipse, 153
Ure, Andrew, 49
Uricchio, William, 368
Uriella, the Demon of the Night [ballet], 127, 203
The Usurer (1913), 298
Ute Indian Snake Dance (1903), 260

The Vacant Lot [story], 30
The Vampire [painting], 204–6, 295, 326
The Vampire [poem], 204–6
The Vampire (1910), 297, *297*
The Vampire (1912), 297
The Vampire (1913), 297, *298*
The Vampire (1915), 308n
The Vampire; or, Detective Brand's Greatest Case [story], 31
vampire bat, 203–4
"vampire dance," 204–6
vampires, 31, 42–3, 202–8
The Vampire's Trail (1914), 297
vampirism, 295–8, 299–300, 308n
The Vampyre [play], 42, 57n
The Vampyre, A Tale [story], 25
The Vampyre; or, The Bride of the Isles [play], 12, 41, 42–3
Vanishing Lady (1897), 116n
Vanishing Lady (1898), 116n
Variety
    audience reactions, 386
    Entombed Alive (1909), 349
    executions, 227
    ghosts, 164, 179
    The Human Soul (1914), 316
    "Jekyll-Hyde" character, 309
    Life Without Soul (1915), 328
    lighting effects, 206
    Lola (1914), 324
    The Moonstone (1909), 340
    The Moonstone (1915), 271
    Mortmain (1915), 315
    The Professor's Great Discovery (1908), 335n
    The Raven (1915), 356
    Rose O' Salem-Town (1910), 156
    The Witch's Cavern (1909), 154
variety shows, 46, 73
vaudeville, 46, 289, 372, 377
    Bud's Inferno, 138
    The Jack O'Lantern, 50
    Too Much Trilby, 53
Vedder, Elihu, 67
Velle, Gaston, 115n
Vendetta (1914), *221*, 222
Vengeance (1913), 349
The Vengeance of Egypt (1912), 198, *199*, 337, 380
ventriloquism, 24

INDEX 419

Verdi, Giuseppe, 349
Vermont Gazette, 189
Verne, Jules, 312
Verne, Margaret, 169
Vestiges of the Natural History of Creation [book], 235
Vetere, Lisa M., 149
Victor, 283, 316
Viele, Herman Knickerbocker, 51
Views and Film Index
    age and gender, 375
    audience reactions, 374
    censorship, 384
    The Ghost Holiday (1907), 165
    The Ghost Story (1907), 163, *163*
    The Haunted Hotel (1907), 170
    Legend of a Ghost (1908), 206
    The Legend of Sleepy Hollow (1908), 344
    music, 377
    posters, 380
    realism, 376
    The Red Spectre (1908), 192–3
    The Spectre (1908), 181n
    A Spiritualist Meeting (1906), 176
    trick pictures, 95
The Village Scare (1909), 245
The Village Witch (1906), 156
The Virginia Mummy [farce], 195, 196
Vision of Salome (1908), 377, 379
Visit to a Spiritualist (1900), 176, 185n
A Visit to the Spiritualist (1899), 176, 372
Vitagraph
    The Cavalier's Dream (1898), 129
    A Curious Dream (1907), 22, 337
    The Dust of Egypt (1915), 207
    The Egyptian Mummy (1914), 198
    Entombed Alive (1909), 349
    exhibition, 370
    The Gambler and the Devil (1908), 203
    The Ghost (1914), 173–4
    The Ghost Story (1907), 163
    The Haunted Hotel (1907), 169–70
    Liquid Electricity: or, The Inventor's Galvanic Fluid (1907), 313
    [*The*] *Mesmerist and Country Couple* (1899), 290–1
    Miss Jekyll and Madame Hyde (1915), 318
    Mortmain (1915), 315, 390
    "mysterious," 101
    publicity, 390
    scientist as adviser, 330
    The Skeleton (1910), 191
    The Tiger (1913), 219–20
    Too Much Champagne (1908), 131
    And the Villain Still Pursued Her (1906), 314
    A Visit to the Spiritualist (1899), 176
    The Witch, The (1908), 156
    The Wrath of Osaka (1913), 273
"vital fluid," 286, 288
Vitascope, 94, 292, 369–70, 391n
Vitascope Concert Company, 370
The Vivisectionist (1915), 314–15, *314*
Volcanic Eruption of Mt. Pelee at St. Pierre (1902), 218, 230n
Von Tilzer, Harry, 290
voodoo, 258–9, 264–6
Voodoo, or a Lucky Charm [musical comedy], 51
Voodoo Tales as Told among the Negroes of the Southwest [stories], 264
Voodoo Vengeance (1913), 264, *264*

The Wages of Sin (1908), 222, 386
Waggner, George, 243
Wagner, the Wehr-Wolf [story], 200
Wallack's Theatre, New York, 39, 43, 44
Walpole, Horace, 22
Walter, Leslie, 63

Walthall, Henry B., 352–3, 356, 388
Wandering Ghosts [story], 32, 69
Ward, Montgomery, 76
Warner, H. B., 54–5, 179
Warner, Lyman, 238
Warner's Features, 174, 293–4
Was She a Vampire? (1915), 308n
Was She Justified? (1911), 338
Washington Post, 53, 216, 225, 237, 246, 367, 384
The Watermelon Patch (1905), 263
Watkins, Harry, 44
Watts, Mary S., 6
The Wax Lady (1913), 187
waxwork exhibitions, 38
Wegener, Paul, 140
Weinstock, Jeffrey Andrew, 24
"weird," 9, 107
    ghosts, 171
    "Hindoo," 269
    mummies, 195
    night photography, 111
    The Phantom Violin (1914), 341–2
    play, 126
    plays, 51
    skeletons, 189
    trick pictures, 101–2
    The Woman in White, 339
"weird art," hypnotism, 289
Weird Fancies (1907), 97
The Weird Nemesis (1915), 292
Weisenburg, Theodore H., 282
Welle, John P., 137
Wells, H. G., 309, 312, 316–17
    The Invisible Man, 316–17
    The Island of Dr. Moreau, 312
    The Time Machine, 309
Wentersdorf, Karl P., 150
Were-Wolf, A Bohemian Gipsy Ballad, The [poem], 200
The Werewolf [story], 200
The Werewolf (1913), 201
Werewolf [poem], 200
werewolves, 199–202, 207–8, 213n
Werewolves [monograph], 200
West, Benjamin, 40, 41, 66
West, Nancy M., 78
Whale, James, 13–14, 243
Wharton, Edith, 30
    Afterward, 30
    The Eyes, 30
    The Lady's Maid's Bell, 30
What Hypnotism Can Do (1899), 290
What Is Man? [essay], 236
Wheeler, Dora, 67
When Ghost Meets Ghost (1913), 165, 386
When Soul Meets Soul (1913), 198
When Soul Meets Soul (1914), 198
When Spirits Walk (1913), 173
When the Mummy Cried for Help (1915), 196, *197*
When the Spirits Moved (1915), 177
White, H. C., 79
White, John, 49
White, John B., 40
White, Pearl, 196, 256
The White Captive of the Sioux (1910), 262
The White Medicine Man (1911), 261
"white slave" films, 269, 388
The White Wolf of the Hartz Mountains [story], 200
The White Wolf (1914), 201
Whitman Features, 341
Whitney, Claire, 339, 389–90
Who Killed George Lambert? (1913), 221
Who Killed Olga Carew? (1913), 349
Who Said Chicken? (1901), 263

Wid's Film and Film Folk, 110, 298, 356
Wieland, or The Transformation [story], 24
Wiers-Jenssen, H., 152
Wiggins, Robert A., 21–2
Wilde, Oscar, 357
Wilkins, Mary E., 30, 151–2
William and Mary College, Virginia, 38
William Wilson [story], 28, 140, 326, 347
Williams, Brown & Earle, 187, 324
Williams, Earle, 285
Williams, James, 148–9
Williams, Kathlyn, 154
Wilson, Eric G., 285
Wilson, Francis, 54, *54*
Wiltermood, Frank M., 316
The Wise Witch of Fairyland (1912), 154
The Witch [play], 152, 156
The Witch (1906), 152–3
The Witch (1907), 162n
The Witch (1908), 156
The Witch (1909), 153–4, 386
The Witch (1913), 158, *158*
The Witch Girl (1914), 154, *154*, 388
The Witch in Sky [lantern slides], 73
The Witch Kiss (1907), 153
The Witch of Carabosse (1910), 153
The Witch of Prague [illustrations], 68
The Witch of Salem (1913), 158
The Witch of Salem (1914), *157*
The Witch of the Everglades (1911), 154, 276n
The Witch of the Range (1911), 154
witchcraft, 152–9, 345
  immigrants and, 148
  and mesmerism, 281
Witchcraft Illustrated [book], 149
Witchcraft; or, The Martyrs of Salem [play], 151
witches, 13, 147–62, 343–4
Witches' Flight [painting], 65
Witches' Spectacles (1910), 153
witch-hunts, 125–6, 155–8
The Witch's Ballad (1910), 155
The Witch's Cave (1906), 153
The Witch's Cavern (1909), 154
Witch's Dance [song], 379
The Witch's Donkey (1909), 153

The Witch's Revenge (1903), 152
The Witch's Secret (1908), 153
"wizard," 310, 312
"Wizard of Makeup," 389
The Wolf Man (1915), 213n
The Wolf Man (1941), 243
Wolfe, S. J., 194
The Woman in Black (1914), 136
The Woman in White [story], 339
The Woman in White (1912), 339
The Woman of Mystery (1914), *113*, 270–1
women audiences, 373, 385, 390
Women Hanging Huns [engravings], 69
Won through a Medium (1911), 178
Wonder of Wonders! Or, the Wonderful Appearance of an Angel, Devil and Ghost, The [story], 66–7
"wonder shows," 45–6
The Wonderful Electro Magnet (1909), 322
A Wonderful Remedy (1909), 242
The Wonders of the Invisible World [book], 3
Wood, Amy Louise, 226
Woods, Frank E., 322
Wood's Museum, 259
Workers Leaving the Lumière Factory in Lyon (1895), 96
The Works of Edgar Allan Poe [illustrations], 67
World Film Corporation, 323–4
Wormwood (1915), 221
The Wrath of Osaka (1913), 273
Wreck of the Schooner "Richmond" (1897), 191

X-rays, 86

Yale University, 38
"yellow peril," 266
"yellowface," 256
you-are-what-you-eat, 212–13n
Young, Clara Kimball, 298
Young, James, 324
Young Goodman Brown [story], 29, 150, 259

Zamecnik, John Stepan, 379
Zecca, Ferdinand, 224, 383
Zola, Émile, 338
Zudora (1914), 86, *86*, 110, 167, 322
Zuma, the Gypsy (1913), 111

EU representative:
Easy Access System Europe
Mustamäe tee 50, 10621 Tallinn, Estonia
Gpsr.requests@easproject.com